Practical Algorithms for 3D Computer Graphics

R. Stuart Ferguson
The Queen's University of Belfast

A K Peters
Natick, Massachusetts

Editorial, Sales, and Customer Service Office

A K Peters, Ltd.
63 South Avenue
Natick, MA 01760
www.akpeters.com

The cover images were created using algorithms described in the book and implemented in
the OpenFX software package. The Celtic cross and underwater animation were made by my
former students Kate Devlin and Colin Murray respectively.

Library of Congress Cataloging-in-Publication Data

Ferguson, R. Stuart (Robin Stuart), 1953-
    Practical algorithms for 3D computer graphics / R. Stuart Ferguson.
      p. cm.
    Includes index.
    ISBN 1-56881-154-3
      1. Computer graphics. 2. Computer animation. 3. Computer algorithms. 4.
    Three-dimensional display systems. I. Title.

    T385 .F455 2001
    006.6'9–dc21   2001021583

Printed in the United States of America
05 04 03 02 01   10 9 8 7 6 5 4 3 2 1

Contents

Preface

Taken as a whole, the topics covered in this book will enable you to create a complete suite of programs for three-dimensional computer animation, modeling, and image synthesis. It is about practical algorithms for each stage in the creative process. The text takes you from the construction of polygonal models of objectss (real or imaginary), through rigid-body animation into hierarchical character animation, and finally down the rendering pipeline for the synthesis of realistic images of the models you build.

The content of the book arises from a postgraduate course on computer graphics that I have given for many years and the experience of working on two comprehensive 3D animation and modeling application programs (*Envisage 3D* and *SoftFX*) for the personal computer in the 1990s. In that time the capabilities of both the hardware and software for creating computer graphics have increased almost unimaginably.

Until the appearance (in the 1980s) of the personal computer, experiments with 3D graphics were limited to the lucky few who had access to some very expensive equipment. Even then, the images produced were, well, *somewhat rudimentary*. Some of the first 3D graphics emerged from the Computer Aided Design (CAD) industry. Even on the newly emerging super-minicomputers the most one could hope to see appearing from the plotter was a *wireframe* drawing or, if you were very lucky, a slightly more solid look, achieved by a very slow *hidden line* algorithm. It wasn't until the work of Jim Blinn with his animated simulations of NASA's Voyager space probe that it began to dawn on the viewer that computers had the potential to generate moving pictures to rival real photographs!

All this seems a world away from the images that we almost take for granted today. Now it is almost impossible to tell a computer-generated picture apart from a photograph. Very often the only visual clue is that it would be impossible to get such a shot with a real camera. Perhaps the most amazing fact is that these stunning images are produced not on a $10m supercomputer, but on the machine sitting in the corner of most people's living rooms, the humble $1000 personal computer a piece of hardware that is mostly used for typing letters or playing games. Perhaps surprisingly, it is the games and multimedia PC businesses that forced 1980s supercomputer processing power onto everyone's laptop.

So, what does it take to turn the domestic typewriter or Internet terminal into a *graphics workstation?* It's the software of course, and all graphics software relies on basic mathematics and fairly simple algorithms.

Therefore: *It is the primary purpose of this book to present the key algorithms that lie at the heart of all 3D computer graphics software packages.*

I hope to be able to introduce these algorithms in such a way that they can readily be put into practice. I will try to describe them in a way that doesn't limit their application to any one particular family of computers. I will attempt to cover a spectrum of useful algorithms, from the simple act of transforming between coordinate systems to the sophisticated "Boolean" operation, Inverse Kinematics and beautiful surface textures. Where possible the algorithms are accompanied by practically useful computer codes. I hope that, by concentrating on algorithms, most of the content of the book will not be overtaken too rapidly by events such as the release of a new version of a particular operating system.

A Quick Look at the Contents of the Book

The book is divided into three parts: the first, *Basic Principles*, covers the key concepts of 3D computer graphics.

After a brief introduction in Chapter 1, the focus moves to the fundamental mathematical ideas (Chapter 2) that lie at the heart of all the other algorithms discussed in the book. Personally, I find it very satisfying that in just a few pages we can set out *all the mathematics* you need to produce beautiful photorealistic pictures.

A computer-generated image of a 3D universe requires that the objects which inhabit it are described using numbers and stored in some form of structured database. Chapter 3 discusses the pros and cons of 3D data organization and describes several algorithms that are useful in manipulating faceted models of the universe's inhabitants.

Chapters 4 and 5 cover the topic of rendering and take a step by step approach to the design of algorithms, from the fastest scanline Z buffer procedure to the high quality ray-traced approach. I have tried to include those little things that generally get overlooked in the grand theoretical texts but are of practical importance, for example, how to optimize your 3D database for ray tracing.

A very active area in computer graphics software development today is animation, character animation in particular. Chapter 6 outlines the basic principles of animation techniques and discusses some ideas for character animation and other effects that can be expressed procedurally rather than having to *do it by hand.* The principles of *Inverse Kinematics* are introduced and presented in a way specific to computer animation.

The second part of the book is intended for the professional 'plugin' or game engine developer and provides (hopefully) a rich collection of algorithms covering such diverse topics as polygonal modeling procedures (Chapter 7), pseudo 3D video transition effects (Chapter 8) and procedural textures for use with a photorealistic Z buffer or ray tracing renderer (Chapter 9).

The final part of the book is devoted to example programs produced with widely-available 3D graphics libraries. I have concentrated on examples for Microsoft's Windows operating system primarily executing on PC platforms using the Intel microprocessor. I have chosen to explore two graphics libraries because their Application Programming Interfaces (APIs) are so different. One has wide acceptance and the other growing popularity. OpenGL has an established history and is now available for all versions of Windows. In 1996 Microsoft introduced a system called Direct3D that has growing popularity, particularly among 3D game developers. Chapters 10 and 11 exemplify the use of these APIs by showing the step by step development of programs that draw (*in real time*) views of 3D objects such as those produced by 3DS Max, SoftImage etc. Chapter 12 shows you how to develop a Windows program that bypasses all the bottlenecks imposed by the system when you want to play animated image sequences (movies) so that they occupy the full screen and run at maximum speed.

Target Readership

I hope that this book will be useful for anyone embarking on a graphics research program, starting work on a new 3D computer game, beginning a career in an industry associated with computer graphics, or just wanting a reference to a range of useful algorithms.

I would also hope that the algorithms presented in Part II might prove useful for more experienced professional software developers, typically any of you who wish to write *plugin* modules for any 3D application program or games engine commercially available today.

Assumed Knowledge

I make the assumption that the reader is familiar with the concepts of the *Vector* and has a basic knowledge of *Coordinate Geometry*. Some experience of using 3D graphics application software would also be an advantage, at least enough to know the significance of the terms *vertex*, *triangular facet/polygon* and *pixel*. For the programming sections, a knowledge of the **C** programming language would be a decided advantage and to make full use of the *Windows* examples it would help if the reader has used *Visual C++* or the Windows Software Development Kit.

Acknowledgments

Many individuals have given me much valued encouragement, ideas, feedback and other assistance in preparing the book. Others have inspired a more general interest in this fascinating and engrossing subject; to all of you, thanks.

I would like to single out the following for special mention:

Tomas Möller for his expert opinion on the draft manuscript, this really helped in getting the book together. My close colleagues Dan Sprevak and Quamer and Mary Hossain who took time out of their busy schedules to review the manuscript and make some excellent suggestions and very helpful comments. It was with the encouragement of Ron Praver that I started the book project at all.

Alice and Klaus Peters and their staff at A K Peters, especially my production editor Sarah Gillis, without whom, this book would never have seen the light of day.

Mark Sprevak, who helped me develop my first 3D programs. Paul Hermon, Brian McCullough, Doug Kelly, Jeremy Pyles, Glenn Lewis, all of whom helped me focus on 3D as a professional activity rather than just an academic curiosity. Eric Graham, who first demonstrated to me that it was technically possible to do fantastic 3D in a microprocessor, with his wonderful Amiga programs. My former students Anand and Anil Madhavapeddy, who taught me a few things.

And finally, to all my friends at the Queen's University of Belfast: Uncle Q, The Caretaker, Yvonne, Dodi, Brian2, MT, Joanne, Paula, G4, Sean, Bert and The Laird, who helped me keep a sense of humor while getting the book together — you make working in the Ashby just such fun.

Again, everyone, many thanks.

Stuart Ferguson
May 2001

Part I
Basic Principles

CHAPTER **I**

Introduction

Computer graphics can arguably be defined as the process of creating pictures using a computer. Such a definition embraces a broad spectrum of applications including such things as painting and drawing programs; even an advanced word processor, e.g., Microsoft Word [1], could be said to fall into the category of a graphics program.

Three-dimensional (3D) computer graphics, the main topic covered in this book, began as a separate discipline in the early 1980s, where those few fortunate individuals who had access to computing hardware costing tens or hundreds of thousands of dollars began to experiment with the wondrous science of producing, through mathematics alone, pictures that in many cases could not be distinguished from a photograph. The "Voyager" animations of Jim Blinn for NASA were perhaps the first really well-publicized use of computer graphics. The title from a television program of the period sums up perfectly the subject of Computer Graphics; it was: *Painting by Numbers*.

We can think of four main applications for 3D computer graphics: Computer Aided Design, Scientific Visualization, and the ever growing entertainment businesses (Cinema or TV animation) and Computer Games.

There is some overlap between these categories. At the level of the mathematical theory on which graphics algorithms are based they are exactly the same. At the program level however, it is usually possible to identify an application as belonging to one of four categories.

1. In a Computer Aided Design (CAD) application the most important feature is to be able to use the graphics to present accurate and detailed plans that have the potential to be used for further engineering or architectural work.

2. Scientific visualization is the process of using graphics to illustrate experimental or theoretical data with the aim of bringing into focus trends, anomalies, or special features that might otherwise go unnoticed if they were

presented in simple tabular form or by lists of numbers. In this category one might include medical imaging, interpreting physical phenomena, and presentations of weather or economic forecasts.

3. Computer Animation for the entertainment industry is itself a broad subject with two distinct divisions which at the moment are still mutually exclusive. The first desire is to produce realistic pictures or sequences of pictures that would be very difficult, impossible, or too expensive to obtain by conventional means. The movie, TV, and advertising industries have adopted this use of 3D computer animation with great enthusiasm and, therefore, perhaps it is they who have provided the main driving force behind the rapid improvements in realism that can be achieved with 3D computer graphics. For computer animation it is the visual appeal of the images on screen or page that is of prime importance. The fact that geometric details might not be quite correct or that the laws of physics be violated is pretty inconsequential.

4. In the case of computer game development *fast and furious* is the watch word, with as many twists and turns as can be accomplished in real time. The quality of images produced from games-rendering engines improves daily and the ingenuity of the games programmers ensures that this is a very active area of computer graphics research and development.

Essentially, this book is targeted at those who work on applications under the broad heading of computer animation, rendering, and 3D modeling. If you are interested in scientific visualization, the book by Schroeder, Martin, and Lorensen [5] is an extensive resource. Many of their algorithms complement those described here (in Chapter 7) and they provide readily adaptable code. Development of application programs for computer aided design is now an industry in itself. Unigraphics Inc. has developed an advanced modeling *kernel* for its Solid Edge and Parasolid [2] packages. The term *kernel* is used to refer to a key set of algorithms for *solid modeling* with complex shapes. These packages tend to have their key use in the mechanical, chemical, and aeronautical industries and therefore they are somewhat outside the scope of this book. Our discussions will be limited to modeling with primitive planar shapes. The essentials of computer aided geometric design are well covered in Farin [3] and information on solid modeling for CAD/CAM can be found in Mortenson [4]. For computer game developers the key element is the ability to render large numbers of polygons in real time. The book on real-time rendering by Möller and Haines [6] describes the most important algorithms and provides links to a wealth of research material.

1.1 A Note on Mathematics for 3D Computer Graphics

Geometry is the foundation on which computer graphics and specifically 3D computer graphics is built. A familiarity with the basic concepts of geometry and what I can only express as *a "feel" for three dimensions* will make the understanding of existing, and creation of new 3D algorithms much more straightforward.

In this book only two assumptions are made about the reader's mathematical prowess: firstly that you have an appreciation of the Cartesian frame of reference which is used to map three-dimensional space and, secondly, that you know the rules for manipulating vectors and matrices. For any reader who wishes to *brush up* on their vector geometry a general introduction can be found in [8]. It will be comforting to know that if you have a knowledge of the *vector* and the *matrix* there is nothing in this book that you cannot readily appreciate. In fact the production of most photorealistic images is fundamentally determined by the intersection of straight lines and primitive shapes.

1.2 Getting Up to Speed

This book is not a general introduction to the subject of computer graphics or even to 3D computer graphics. If you want to acquire background knowledge of hardware, software packages, or the current state of what is now a huge industry there are many excellent sources of information available. The following short list covers items that I personally have found very useful in my work:

- For a general introduction to the subject, examples of what is possible with current hardware/software technology, and information on the very latest ideas and achievements, I recommend reading some back issues of one of the monthly magazines specializing in computer graphics. Computer Graphics World [9], is generally regarded as the industry's trade journal and there are a number of others. There are also many web sites specializing in one or more aspects of computer graphics, almost too many to mention individually. For example the Game Developer magazine provides code associated with their articles [10]. A list of other useful links can be found on the web site associated with this book.

- Watt [11] provides a good introduction to the main concepts of 3D computer graphics and a comprehensive (but a bit dated) reference on all aspects of computer graphics is that of Foley, Van Dam, Feiner, and Hughes [12]. The book by Watt and Watt [13] is useful for filling in specific details on rendering and animation. For the mathematically inclined a rigorous evaluation on a very broad range of computer graphics algorithms can be found in Eberly's book [14].

- For the real nitty gritty of **C** programming, it is impossible to better the original work by Kernighan and Ritchie [15] and for **C++** that by Stroustrup [16].

- While the bookshelves in every bookstore creak under the weight of tombs describing the Visual C++ compiler, its integrated development environment and the Microsoft Foundation Classes, the book by Stanfield [17] provides all the details one needs and gives a multitude of useful tips. It is ideal for enhancing the examples presented here in Chapters 10, 11, and 12.

- Very little background, save for the mathematics, is assumed when presenting the modeling and image processing algorithms in Part II. If you cannot find the algorithm you are looking for in the chapters forming Part II then try looking into the five volumes of the Graphics Gems series [18]. Some Gems of particular use for game developers can be found in Deloura's volume [19]. O'Rourke's book on Computational Geometry [20] provides a useful alternative view of some of the modeling algorithms discussed in Chapter 7.

- For background and to complement the procedural textures described in Chapter 9, the book of Ebert et al. [21] is ideal. It goes on to explore the use of fractals in computer graphics and demonstrate the techniques of volume shading and hypertextures with which realistic images of hair and fur can be created.

I have tried to keep this list short with only one reference for a specific topic. This is done, not because there are no other texts worthy of consultation, but simply because one might have too much of a good thing. The web site associated with this book has an up-to-date set of links to useful online resources.

1.3   Using the Accompanying Software

The software that accompanies this book is primarily associated with Parts II and III of the book.

The code that accompanies the examples described in Part III is supplied in a number of subdirectories; they represent a series of *snapshots* of the state of the Visual C++ projects taken at key stages in development. It should be relatively straightforward to load, compile, and experiment with these projects if you are using Visual C++. The Direct X examples can be used with any version ≥ 3. They use the *Retained Mode* which is now regarded as complete.

The code associated with the algorithms described in Parts I and II is included. It is a good idea to examine this code at the same time as the description of the algorithms in the book since reading commented code can enhance the explanation of the procedure. In many cases the implementation of the algorithms require the use of specific data structures, to represent a vertex for example, and thus some modifications will most likely be necessary to interface them to other programs. The *primary* purpose of the code linked to the algorithms of Parts I and II is to illustrate the *fine detail* of the procedures, details that generally get omitted from the macroscopic presentation of an algorithm. For example, the *Capping* procedure presented in Section 7.1 requires a number of *fiddle factors* (more scientifically one might call them tolerances) which arise because of the limit to the accuracy with which a computer can perform numerical calculations.

1.4 Where Do You Want to Go Tomorrow?

I hope that this book will kindle your interest in creating your own algorithms in all the diverse areas of 3D computer graphics that we are going to explore. One of the best ways today to accomplish this is by writing *plugins* for one of the many 3D applications available commercially. To do this you will need an SDK, *a Software Developers Kit*; one of the most comprehensive SDKs is that accompanying Kinetics 3D Studio Max [7] package. Although the interface provided by Max's SDK is extensive and quite challenging to understand, it allows virtually any procedure one might imagine to be added to that package. It is well documented and based on state-of-the-art C++ object-orientated programming principles. The Visualization toolkit [5] is another excellent framework within which to develop algorithms, especially for 3D modeling.

References

[1] Microsoft Word, Microsoft Corporation, Redmond WA.

[2] Unigraphics Solutions Inc., *http://ugsolutions.com*

[3] G. Farin, D. Hansford. The Essentials of CAGD. A K Peters, Natick MA, 2000.

[4] M. E. Mortenson, *Mathematics for Computer Graphics Applications: An Introduction to the Mathematics and Geometry of CAD/CAM, Geometric Modeling, Scientific Visualization.* Industrial Pr, 1999.

[5] W. Schroder, K. Martin, B. Lorensen, *The Visualization Toolkit and Object-Orientated Approach to 3D Graphics.* Prentice Hall PTR, Englewood Cliffs NJ, 1996.

[6] T. Möller and E. Haines, *Real-Time Rendering*. A K Peters, Natick MA, 1999.

[7] *3D Studio Max Software Developers Kit*. Autodesk Inc. Sausilito CA, 1996 *http://www.ktx.com*.

[8] J. H Kindle, *Plane and Solid Geometry, Schaum's Outline Series*. McGraw-Hill, New York, 1950.

[9] *Computer Graphics World*, published by PenWell Press, Nashua NH, *http://www.cgw.com*.

[10] *Game Developer Magazine, http://www.gdmag.com/*

[11] A. Watt, *3D Computer Graphics*. Longman Higher Education, Essex, UK,1999.

[12] J. Foley, A. Van Dam, S. Feiner, J. Hughes, *Computer Graphics: Principles and Practice, Second Edition*. Addison-Wesley, Reading MA, 1990.

[13] A. Watt, M. Watt, *Advanced Animation and Rendering Techniques*. Addison-Wesley, Reading MA, 1992.

[14] D. H. Eberly, 3D Game Engine Design. Morgan Kaufmann, San Francisco CA, 2000.

[15] B. W. Kernighan, D. M. Ritchie, *The C Programming Language*. Prentice-Hall, Englewood Cliffs NJ, 1978.

[16] B. Stroustrup, *The C++ Programming Language*. Addison-Wesley, Reading MA, 1991.

[17] S. Stanfield, *Visual C++ 4 How-To, The Definitive MFC Problem Solver.* Waite Group Press, Corte Madra CA, 1996.

[18] A. S. Glassner, *Graphics Gems* (Volumes I to V), Academic Press, Cambridge MA, 1990–1995.

[19] M. DeLoura (Editor), *Game Programming Gems*, Charles River Media, Hingham MA, 2000.

[20] J. O'Rourke, *Computational Geometry in C*. Cambridge University Press, Cambridge UK, 1993.

[21] D. S. Ebert, F. K. Musgrave, D. Peachey, K. Perlin, S. Worley, *Texturing and Modeling a Procedural Approach*. Academic Press, Cambridge MA, 1994.

CHAPTER 2

Basic Theory and Mathematical Results

This chapter describes the essential mathematical concepts that form the basis for most 3D computer graphics theory. It also establishes the notation and conventions that will be used throughout the book. There are many texts that cover 3D computer graphics in great detail, and if you are unfamiliar with the details considered in this chapter consult one or more of the following: [1], [2], [3]. For books that cover the mathematical theory in more detail you might consult [4], [5], or [6].

If you wish you can skip directly to Chapter 4 where the main topics of the book begin with details of algorithms for the rendering pipeline. Refer to the appropriate sections in this chapter here when required.

2.1 Coordinate Systems

A coordinate system provides a numerical frame of reference for the 3D universe in which we will develop our ideas and algorithms. Two coordinate systems are particularly useful to us: the ubiquitous Cartesian (x, y, z) rectilinear system and the spherical polar (r, θ, ϕ) or angular system. Cartesian coordinates are the most commonly used, but angular coordinates are particularly helpful when it comes to directing 3D animations where it is not only important to say where something is located but also in which direction it is looking or moving.

2.1.1 Cartesians

Figure 2.1 illustrates the Cartesian system. Any point P is uniquely specified by a triple of numbers (a, b, c). Mutually perpendicular coordinate axes are conventionally labeled x, y, and z. For the point P the numbers a, b, and c can be thought of as distances we need to move in order to travel from the origin to the

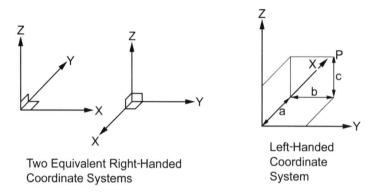

Two Equivalent Right-Handed
Coordinate Systems

Left-Handed
Coordinate
System

Figure 2.1.   Right- and left-handed coordinate systems with the z-axis vertical.

point P. (Move a units along the x-axis then b units parallel to the y-axis and finally c units parallel to the z-axis).

In the Cartesian system the axes can be orientated in either a *left* or *right-handed* sense. A right-handed convention is consistent with the vector cross product and all algorithms and formulae used in this book assume a right-handed convention.

2.1.2 Spherical Polars

Figure 2.2 shows the conventional spherical polar coordinate system in relation to the Cartesian axes. r is a measure of the distance from the origin to a point in space. The angles θ and ϕ are taken relative to the z- and x-axes respectively. Unlike the Cartesian x, y and z values, which all take the same units, spherical polar coordinates use both distance and angle measures. Importantly, there are some points in space that do not have a unique one-to-one relationship with an (r, θ, ϕ) coordinate value. For example points lying on the positive z-axis can have any value of ϕ; $(100, 0, 0)$ and $(100, 0, \pi)$ both represent the same point.

Also, the range of values which (r, θ, ϕ) can take is limited. The radial distance r is such that it is always positive $0 \leq r < \infty$; θ lies in the range $0 \leq \theta \leq \pi$ and ϕ takes values $0 \leq \phi < 2\pi$. There is no unique way to specify a range for ϕ; one could equally well choose $-\pi \leq \phi < \pi$, but to avoid confusion it is best to adhere rigidly to one interval.

It is quite straightforward to change from one coordinate system to the other. When the point P in Figure 2.2 is expressed as (r, θ, ϕ) the Cartesian coordinates (x, y, z) are given by the trigonometric expressions:

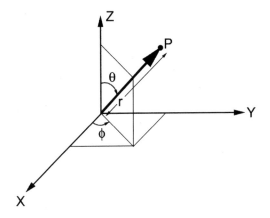

Figure 2.2.   The spherical polar coordinate system.

$$x = r \sin \theta \cos \phi$$
$$y = r \sin \theta \sin \phi$$
$$z = r \cos \theta$$

Conversion from Cartesian to spherical coordinates is a little more tricky, requiring an algorithm that tests for the special cases where P lies very close to the z-axis. A suitable implementation is presented in Figure 2.3.

The parameter ϵ is necessary because no computer can calculate with total accuracy. What value is chosen depends on the relative size of the largest and

```
if (x² + y²) < ε  {
  r = z
  θ = 0
  φ = 0
}
else {
  r = √(x² + y² + z²)
  θ = arcsin(√(x² + y²)/r)
  φ = ATAN2(y, x) + π
}
```

Figure 2.3.   Algorithm for conversion from Cartesian to spherical coordinates.

smallest measurements. For example a 3D animation of atomic and molecular processes would have a very different value of ϵ from one illustrating planetary dynamics.

In general a satisfactory result will be obtained when ϵ is chosen to be about 0.0001% of the smallest unit in use.

The function $ATAN2(y, x)$ is provided in the libraries of many computer languages. It returns a value in the range $(-\pi, \pi)$ which is the angle made with the x-axis by a line from $(0, 0)$ to (x, y). In the first quadrant this is equivalent to $\arctan(y/x)$, which is of course not defined at $\pi/2$.

2.2   Vectors

The vector, the key to all 3D work, is a triple of real numbers (in most computer languages these are usually called floating point numbers) and is noted in a **bold** typeface, e.g., **P** or **p**. When handwritten (and in the Figures of this book) vectors are noted with an underscore; e.g., $\underline{P}$.

Care must be taken to differentiate between two types of vector; see Figure 2.4.

- Position Vector

  A position vector runs from the origin of coordinates $(0, 0, 0)$ to a point (x, y, z) and its length gives the distance of the point from the origin. Its components are given by (x, y, z). The essential concept to understand about a position vector is that it is anchored to specific coordinates (points in space). The set of points or *vertices* that are used to describe the *shape* of all models in 3D graphics can be thought of as position vectors.

  Thus a point with coordinates (x, y, z) can also be identified as the end point of a position vector **p**. We shall often refer to a point as (x, y, z) or **p**.

- Direction Vector

  A direction vector differs from a position vector in that it is **not** anchored to specific coordinates. Frequently, direction vectors are used in a form where they have unit length; in this case they are said to be *normalized*. The most common application of a direction vector in 3D computer graphics is to specify the orientation of a surface or ray direction. For this we use a direction vector at right angles (*normal*) and pointing away from the surface. Such *normal* vectors are the key to calculating lighting and surface shading effects.

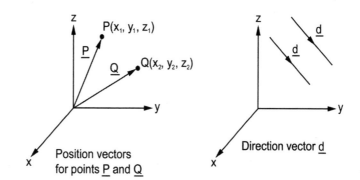

Figure 2.4.   Position and direction vectors.

2.3 The Line

There are two useful ways to express the equation of a line in vector form. For a line passing through a point $\mathbf{P_0}$ and having a direction $\hat{\mathbf{d}}$, then any point $\mathbf{p}$ which lies on the line is given by:

$$\mathbf{p} = \mathbf{P_0} + \mu\hat{\mathbf{d}}$$

$\mathbf{P_0}$ is a position vector and $\hat{\mathbf{d}}$ is a unit length (*normalized*) direction vector.

Alternatively any point $\mathbf{p}$ on a line passing through two points $\mathbf{P_0}$ and $\mathbf{P_1}$ is given by:

$$\mathbf{p} = \mathbf{P_0} + \mu(\mathbf{P_1} - \mathbf{P_0})$$

The parameter μ takes values in the range $-\infty < \mu < \infty$. Note that when $\mu = 0$ then $\mathbf{p} = \mathbf{P_0}$.

On a line passing through two points, $\mathbf{p} = \mathbf{P_0}$ when $\mu = 0$ and $\mathbf{p} = \mathbf{P_1}$ when $\mu = 1.0$.

Using two points to express an equation for the line is useful when we need to consider a finite segment of a line. (There are many examples where we need to use segments of lines, such as calculating the point of intersection between a line segment and a plane.)

Thus if we need to consider a line segment we can assign $\mathbf{P_0}$ and $\mathbf{P_1}$ to the segment end points with the consequence that any point on the line $\mathbf{p}$ will only be part of the segment if its value for μ in the equation above lies in the interval $[0, 1]$.

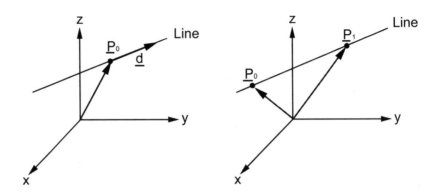

Figure 2.5.   Specifying a line.

2.4   The Plane

A plane is completely specified by giving a point on the plane $\mathbf{P_0}$, and the direction $\hat{\mathbf{n}}$ perpendicular to the plane.

To write an equation to represent the plane we can use the fact that the vector $(\mathbf{p} - \mathbf{P_0})$ which lies in the plane must be at right angles to the normal to the plane, thus:

$$(\mathbf{p} - \mathbf{P_0}) \cdot \hat{\mathbf{n}} = \mathbf{0}$$

Alternatively a plane could be specified by taking three points $\mathbf{P_2}$, $\mathbf{P_1}$ and $\mathbf{P_0}$ lying in the plane. Provided they are not co-linear it is valid to write the equation

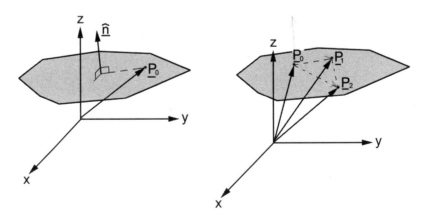

Figure 2.6.   Specifying a plane.

of the plane as:

$$(\mathbf{p} - \mathbf{P_0}) \cdot \frac{(\mathbf{P_2} - \mathbf{P_0}) \times (\mathbf{P_1} - \mathbf{P_0})}{|(\mathbf{P_2} - \mathbf{P_0}) \times (\mathbf{P_1} - \mathbf{P_0})|} = 0$$

Figure 2.6 illustrates these two specifications for a plane. It should be noted that these equations apply to planes that extend to infinity in all directions. We shall see later that the intersection of a line with a *bounded* plane plays a very important role in rendering and modeling algorithms.

2.5 Intersection of a Line and a Plane

The intersection of a line and a plane is a point $\mathbf{p_i}$ that satisfies the equation of the line and the equation of the plane simultaneously. For the line $\mathbf{p} = \mathbf{P_1} + \mu\hat{\mathbf{d}}$ and the plane $(\mathbf{p} - \mathbf{P_p}) \cdot \hat{\mathbf{n}} = 0$ the point of intersection $\mathbf{p}_I$ is given by:

$$
\begin{aligned}
&\text{if } |\hat{\mathbf{d}} \cdot \hat{\mathbf{n}}| < \epsilon \ \{ \text{ no intersection} \} \\
&\text{else } \{ \\
&\qquad \mu = \frac{(\mathbf{P_p} - \mathbf{P_1}) \cdot \hat{\mathbf{n}}}{\hat{\mathbf{d}} \cdot \hat{\mathbf{n}}} \\
&\qquad \mathbf{p}_I = \mathbf{P_1} + \mu\hat{\mathbf{d}} \\
&\}
\end{aligned}
$$

Note that we must first test to see whether the line and plane actually intersect. The parameter ϵ allows for the numerical accuracy of computer calculations and, since $\hat{\mathbf{d}}$ and $\hat{\mathbf{n}}$ are of unit length, ϵ should be of the order of the machine arithmetic precision.

2.5.1 Intersection of a Line Segment with a Plane

Given a line segment joining $\mathbf{P_0}$ to $\mathbf{P_1}$ and a plane $(\mathbf{p} - \mathbf{P_p}) \cdot \hat{\mathbf{n}} = 0$, the algorithm of Figure 2.7 determines whether the plane and line intersect. Note that this does not actually calculate the point of intersection. It is a good idea to separate the calculation of an intersection point by first testing whether there will be one before going on to determine the point. This is especially useful when we need to consider clipping, see Section 4.8.

The parameters ϵ_0 and ϵ_1 are again chosen as non-zero values because of the numerical accuracy of floating point calculations.

$$\mathbf{a} = \mathbf{P}_0 - \mathbf{P}_p$$
$$\mathbf{b} = \mathbf{P}_1 - \mathbf{P}_p$$
$$d_a = \mathbf{a} \cdot \mathbf{n}$$
$$d_b = \mathbf{b} \cdot \mathbf{n}$$

if $|d_a| \leq \epsilon_0$ and $|d_b| \leq \epsilon_0$ {
    both $\mathbf{P}_0$ and $\mathbf{P}_1$ lie in the plane
}
else {
    $d_{ab} = d_a d_b$
    if $d_{ab} < \epsilon_1$ {
        The line crosses the plane
    }
    else {
        The line does not cross the plane
    }
}

Figure 2.7.   Algorithm to determine if the line joining two points crosses a plane.

2.6   Closest Distance of a Point from a Line

Consider the line L passing through the points $\mathbf{P}_1$ and $\mathbf{P}_2$ as shown in Figure 2.8. To find the closest distance, l, of the point $\mathbf{p}$ from L we recognize that the projection of the vector $\mathbf{p} - \mathbf{P}_1$ onto $\mathbf{P}_L$ allows us to find the point, $\mathbf{q}$, on L which is closest to $\mathbf{p}$. Thus, the closest distance is given by the steps:

Let $\mathbf{d} = (\mathbf{P}_2 - \mathbf{P}_1)$

then $\mu = \dfrac{(\mathbf{p} - \mathbf{P}_1) \cdot \mathbf{d}}{\mathbf{d} \cdot \mathbf{d}}$

and $\mathbf{q} = \mathbf{P}_1 + \mu \mathbf{d}$

thus $l = |\mathbf{p} - \mathbf{q}|$

When $\mu < 0$ or $\mu > 1.0$ { $\mathbf{p}$ is closer to the line outside of
the segment $\mathbf{P}_1, \mathbf{P}_2$ }

As illustrated in Figure 2.8 it is only when $0 < \mu < 1$ that the perpendicular from $\mathbf{p}$ to the line meets the position vector $\mathbf{d}$; i.e., between the points $\mathbf{P}_1$, $\mathbf{P}_2$.

This algorithm is useful for a 3D application program where it is necessary to interactively pick a line by pointing to it on a CRT display with a user input device such as a mouse.

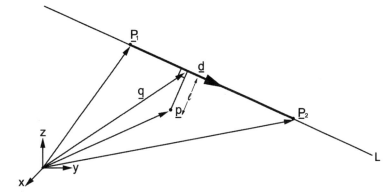

Figure 2.8.   Closest distance of a point from a line segment.

2.7 Closest Distance of Approach between Two Lines

In three-dimensional space two arbitrary lines rarely intersect. However it is useful to be able to find the closest distance of approach between them. In the geometry shown in Figure 2.9 the segment AA' (vector **b**) joins the points of closest approach between the lines:

$$\mathbf{p} = \mathbf{P}_1 + \lambda\hat{\mathbf{r}}$$
$$\mathbf{p} = \mathbf{P}_2 + \mu\hat{\mathbf{d}}$$

At the points of closest approach **b** is perpendicular to both lines and therefore:

$$\mathbf{b} \cdot \hat{\mathbf{d}} = 0 \ and \ \mathbf{b} \cdot \hat{\mathbf{r}} = 0$$

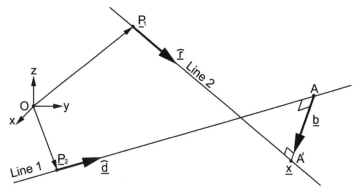

Figure 2.9.   Closest distance of approach between two lines.

To determine the length of $\mathbf{b}$ consider the alternative ways of specifying the point $\mathbf{x}$; i.e., following alternative paths from O to $\mathbf{x}$:

$$\mathbf{x} = \mathbf{P}_1 + \lambda \hat{\mathbf{r}}$$
$$\mathbf{x} = \mathbf{P}_2 + \mu \hat{\mathbf{d}} + \mathbf{b}$$

Thus:

$$\mu \hat{\mathbf{d}} - \mathbf{b} = \lambda \hat{\mathbf{r}} + (\mathbf{P}_1 - \mathbf{P}_2) \tag{2.1}$$

Once λ and μ are determined the length of $\mathbf{b}$ is readily found:

$$l = \left| \mathbf{P}_1 + \lambda \hat{\mathbf{r}} - (\mathbf{P}_2 + \mu \hat{\mathbf{d}}) \right| \tag{2.2}$$

Taking the dot product of Equation 2.1 with $\hat{\mathbf{r}}$ will eliminate $\mathbf{b}$ and give an expression for λ:

$$\lambda = \mu (\hat{\mathbf{d}} \cdot \hat{\mathbf{r}}) - (\mathbf{P}_1 - \mathbf{P}_2) \cdot \hat{\mathbf{r}} \tag{2.3}$$

The dot product of Equation 2.1 with $\hat{\mathbf{d}}$ eliminates $\mathbf{b}$ and substituting λ using Equation 2.3 gives:

$$\mu = \frac{((\mathbf{P}_1 - \mathbf{P}_2) \cdot \hat{\mathbf{d}}) - ((\mathbf{P}_1 - \mathbf{P}_2) \cdot \hat{\mathbf{r}})(\hat{\mathbf{d}} \cdot \hat{\mathbf{r}})}{1 - (\hat{\mathbf{d}} \cdot \hat{\mathbf{r}})^2} \tag{2.4}$$

With μ known Equation 2.3 gives λ and then the distance of closest approach follows from Equation 2.2.

Note: if the lines are parallel $\left| (\hat{\mathbf{d}} \cdot \hat{\mathbf{r}}) \right| < \epsilon$ (where ϵ is the machine tolerance of zero, approx 1×10^{-6} for single precision calculations) and the algorithm is terminated before it reaches Equation 2.4

2.8   Reflection in a Plane

In many rendering algorithms there is a requirement to calculate a reflected direction given an incident direction and a plane of reflection. The vectors we need to consider in this calculation are of the *direction* type and assumed to be of unit length.

If the incident vector is $\hat{\mathbf{d}}_{in}$, the reflection vector is $\hat{\mathbf{d}}_{out}$, and the surface normal is $\mathbf{n}$, we can calculate the reflected vector by recognizing that because $\hat{\mathbf{d}}_{out}$ and $\hat{\mathbf{d}}_{in}$ are normalized (the argument would work equally well provided $\mathbf{d}_{out}$ and $\mathbf{d}_{in}$ are the same length) then vector $(\hat{\mathbf{d}}_{out} - \hat{\mathbf{d}}_{in})$ is co-linear with $\hat{\mathbf{n}}$ (Figure 2.10); therefore:

$$\hat{\mathbf{d}}_{out} - \hat{\mathbf{d}}_{in} = \alpha \hat{\mathbf{n}} \tag{2.5}$$

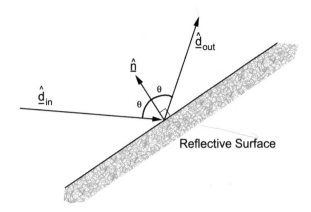

Figure 2.10.   Incident and reflection vector.

where α is a scalar factor. As the incident and reflected angles are equal

$$\hat{\mathbf{d}}_{out} \cdot \hat{\mathbf{n}} = -\hat{\mathbf{d}}_{in} \cdot \hat{\mathbf{n}} \qquad (2.6)$$

Taking the dot product of both sides of Equation 2.5 with $\mathbf{n}$, substituting in Equation 2.6 and using the fact that $\mathbf{n}$ is normalized we obtain for the reflected direction:

$$\hat{\mathbf{d}}_{out} = \hat{\mathbf{d}}_{in} - 2(\hat{\mathbf{d}}_{in} \cdot \hat{\mathbf{n}})\hat{\mathbf{n}}$$

2.9   Refraction at a Plane

Photorealistic renderers are required to be able to simulate transparent surfaces where rays of light are refracted as they pass through the boundary between materials of different refractive index. Figure 2.11 shows a refractive surface with an incident vector $\hat{\mathbf{d}}_i$, surface normal $\hat{\mathbf{n}}$, and refracted vector $\hat{\mathbf{d}}_r$. All three vectors are of the direction type.

The physical model of refraction is expressed in Snell's law which states:

$$\frac{n_r}{n_i} = \frac{\sin\theta_i}{\sin\theta_r}$$

where n_i and n_r are transmission constants for the media in which the incident and refracted light rays travel. Snell's law can also be written in vector form:

$$n_i(\hat{\mathbf{d}}_i \times \hat{\mathbf{n}}) = n_r(\hat{\mathbf{d}}_r \times \hat{\mathbf{n}})$$

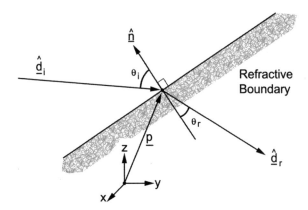

Figure 2.11.   Tracing a refracted ray. Note that the incident, refracted, and surface normal directions
                    all lie in a plane.

Since $\hat{\mathbf{d}}_i$, $\hat{\mathbf{d}}_r$, and $\hat{\mathbf{n}}$ all lie in a plane, $\hat{\mathbf{d}}_r$ can be expressed as a linear combination
of $\hat{\mathbf{d}}_i$ and $\hat{\mathbf{n}}$:

$$\hat{\mathbf{d}}_r = \alpha \hat{\mathbf{d}}_i + \beta \hat{\mathbf{n}} \tag{2.7}$$

Taking the vector product of both sides of Equation 2.7 with $\hat{\mathbf{n}}$ and substituting it
for the right hand side of the vector form of Snell's law gives a value for β which
is:

$$\beta = \frac{n_i}{n_r}$$

The dot product of both sides of Equation 2.7 produce a quadratic in α:

$$\hat{\mathbf{d}}_r \cdot \hat{\mathbf{d}}_r = 1 = \alpha^2 + 2\alpha\beta(\hat{\mathbf{n}} \cdot \hat{\mathbf{d}}_i) + \beta^2$$

This equation has only one physically meaningful solution. The appropriate root is
determined by considering an incident ray perpendicular to the surface. Once this
is done the meaningful value of α is substituted into Equation 2.7 and rearranged
to give a two-step calculation for the refracted direction:

$$r = (\hat{\mathbf{n}} \cdot \hat{\mathbf{d}}_i)^2 + \left(\frac{n_r}{n_i}\right)^2 - 1$$

$$\hat{\mathbf{d}}_r = \frac{n_i}{n_r}\left((\sqrt{r} - \hat{\mathbf{n}} \cdot \hat{\mathbf{d}}_i)\hat{\mathbf{n}} + \hat{\mathbf{d}}_i\right)$$

Note that if the term r is negative, reflection (Section 2.8) rather than refraction
occurs. RayTracingNews [7] contains an article on faster refraction computation.

2.10 Intersection of a Line with Primitive Shapes

Many 3D algorithms *(rendering and modeling)* require the calculation of the point of intersection between a line and a fundamental shape called a *primitive*. We have already dealt with the calculation of the intersection between a line and a plane. If the plane is bounded we get a primitive shape called a *planar polygon*. Most 3D rendering and modeling application programs use polygons that have either three sides (triangles) or four sides (quadrilaterals). Triangular polygons are by far the most common because it is always possible to reduce an n-sided polygon to a set of triangles. Most of the modeling algorithms in this book will refer to triangular polygons. An algorithm to reduce an n-sided polygon to a set of triangular polygons is given in Chapter 7.

Other important primitive shapes are the planar disc and the volume solids: the sphere and cylinder. There are more complex shapes that can still be termed primitive though they are used much less frequently. It is possible to set up analytic expressions for shapes made by lofting a curve along an axis or by sweeping a curve round an axis; see [26] for examples. There are a large number of other primitive shapes such as Bézier, spline and NURBS patches, and subdivision surfaces to mention a few.

In this section we will examine the most important intersection in the context of software that uses planar polygons as the basic unit for modeling objects. Appendix A provides a number of useful tests for the intersection between a line and non-planar primitives.

2.10.1 Intersection of a Line with a Triangular Polygon

This calculation is used time and time again in modeling algorithms (Booleans, capping, and normal calculations) and in rendering algorithms (image and texture mapping and in ray tracing). The importance of determining whether an intersection occurs in the interior of the polygon, near one of its vertices, or at one of its edges, or indeed just squeaks by outside, cannot be overemphasized.

This section gives an algorithm that can be used to determine whether a line intersects a triangular polygon. It also classifies the point of intersection as being internal, at a point close to one of the vertices, or within some small distance from an edge.

The geometry of the problem is shown in Figure 2.12. The point $\mathbf{P}_i$ gives the intersection between a line and a plane. The plane is defined by the points $\mathbf{P}_0$, $\mathbf{P}_1$, and $\mathbf{P}_2$, as described in Section 2.5. They also identity the vertices of the triangular polygon. Vectors $\mathbf{u}$ and $\mathbf{v}$ are along two of the edges of the triangle under consideration. Provided $\mathbf{u}$ and $\mathbf{v}$ are **not** co-linear the vector $\mathbf{w}$:

$$\mathbf{w} = \mathbf{P}_i - \mathbf{P}_0$$

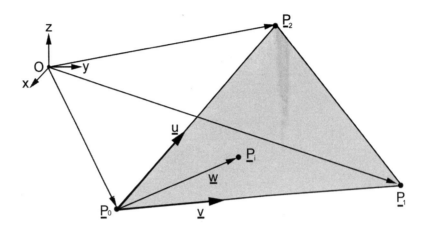

Figure 2.12.   Intersection of line and triangular polygon.

lies in the plane and can be expressed as a linear combination of $\mathbf{u}$ and $\mathbf{v}$:

$$\mathbf{w} = \alpha\mathbf{u} + \beta\mathbf{v} \tag{2.8}$$

Once α and β have been calculated a set of tests will reveal whether $\mathbf{P}_i$ lies inside or outside the triangular polygon with vertices at $\mathbf{P}_0$, $\mathbf{P}_1$, and $\mathbf{P}_2$.

Algorithm overview:

1. To Find $\mathbf{P}_i$ we use the method described in Section 2.5.

2. To calculate α and β take the dot product of Equation 2.8 with $\mathbf{u}$ and $\mathbf{v}$ respectively. After a little algebra the results can be expressed as:

$$\alpha = \frac{(\mathbf{w} \cdot \mathbf{u})(\mathbf{v} \cdot \mathbf{v}) - (\mathbf{w} \cdot \mathbf{v})(\mathbf{u} \cdot \mathbf{v})}{(\mathbf{u} \cdot \mathbf{u})(\mathbf{v} \cdot \mathbf{v}) - (\mathbf{u} \cdot \mathbf{v})^2}$$

$$\beta = \frac{(\mathbf{w} \cdot \mathbf{v})(\mathbf{u} \cdot \mathbf{u}) - (\mathbf{w} \cdot \mathbf{u})(\mathbf{u} \cdot \mathbf{v})}{(\mathbf{u} \cdot \mathbf{u})(\mathbf{v} \cdot \mathbf{v}) - (\mathbf{u} \cdot \mathbf{v})^2}$$

Since both expressions have the same denominator it need only be calculated once. Products such as $(\mathbf{w} \cdot \mathbf{v})$ occur more than once and therefore assigning these to temporary variables will speed up the calculation. It is very worthwhile to optimize the speed of this calculation because it lies at the core of many *time critical* steps in a rendering algorithm, particularly image and texture mapping functions. **C++** code for this important function is available with the book.

The pre-calculation of $(\mathbf{u} \cdot \mathbf{u})(\mathbf{v} \cdot \mathbf{v}) - (\mathbf{u} \cdot \mathbf{v})^2$ is important, because should it turn out to be too close to zero we can not obtain values for α or β. This problem occurs when one of the sides of the triangle is of zero length. In practice a triangle where this happens can be ignored because if one of its sides has zero length, it has zero area and will therefore not be visible in a rendered image.

3. Return hit code as follows:

if $\alpha < -0.001$ or $\alpha > 1.001$ or $\beta < -0.001$ or $\beta > 1.001$ miss polygon
if $(\alpha + \beta) > 1.001$ miss polygon beyond edge $\mathbf{P}_1 \rightarrow \mathbf{P}_2$
if $\alpha \geq 0.0005$ and $\alpha \leq 0.9995$
         and $\beta \geq 0.0005$ and $\beta \leq 0.9995$
         and $\alpha\beta \leq 0.9995$ inside polygon
else if $\alpha < 0.0005$ { *along edge* $\mathbf{P}_0 \rightarrow \mathbf{P}_1$
     if $\beta < 0.0005$ at vertex $\mathbf{P}_0$
     else if $\beta > 0.9995$ at vertex $\mathbf{P}_1$
     else On edge $\mathbf{P}_0 \rightarrow \mathbf{P}_1$ not near vertex
}
else if $\beta < 0.0005$ { *along edge* $\mathbf{P}_0 \rightarrow \mathbf{P}_2$
     if $\alpha < 0.0005$ at vertex $\mathbf{P}_0$
     else if $\alpha > 0.9995$ at vertex $\mathbf{P}_2$
     else On edge $\mathbf{P}_0 \rightarrow \mathbf{P}_2$ not near vertex
}
else if $(\alpha + \beta) > 0.9995$ on edge $\mathbf{P}_1 \rightarrow \mathbf{P}_2$
else miss polygon

Note that the parameters -0.001, etc., are not dependent on the absolute size of the triangle because α and β are numbers in the range $[0, 1]$.

Alternative algorithms for ray/triangle intersection are presented by Badouel [8] and Möller [9].

2.11 Transformations

Transformations have two purposes in 3D graphics: *to modify the position vector of a vertex* and *to change the orientation of a direction vector.* It is useful to express a transformation in the form of a matrix. In the previous sections we discussed vectors; a vector itself is just a special case of a matrix. If you are unfamiliar with matrices, vectors, or linear algebra in general it might be useful to consult one of the following: [10], [11], or [12].

The vectors we have used so far apply to the 3D universe and thus have three components (x, y, z). In matrix form they also have three elements and are written in a single column:

$$\begin{bmatrix} x \\ y \\ z \end{bmatrix}$$

This matrix is said to have three rows and one column, a 3×1 matrix. Matrices can have any number of rows and columns; for example, a 4×4 matrix might be represented by:

$$\begin{bmatrix} a_{00} & a_{01} & a_{02} & a_{03} \\ a_{10} & a_{11} & a_{12} & a_{13} \\ a_{20} & a_{21} & a_{22} & a_{23} \\ a_{30} & a_{31} & a_{32} & a_{33} \end{bmatrix}$$

It turns out that all the transformations appropriate for computer graphics work, moving, rotating, scaling, etc., can be represented by a matrix of size 4×4. Matrices are mathematical objects and have their own algebra just as real numbers do. You can add, multiply, and invert a matrix.

Several different notations are used to represent a matrix. Throughout this text we will use the [ ] bracket notation. When we discussed vectors we used a bold type to represent a vector as a single entity. When we want to represent a matrix as an individual entity we will use the notation of a capital letter in square brackets, e.g., $[P]$. Since a 3D vector and a 3×1 matrix represent the same thing we will use the symbols **P** and $[P]$ interchangeably.

If a transformation is represented by a matrix $[T]$ a point **p** is transformed to a new point **p**' by matrix multiplication according to the rule.

$$[p'] = [T][p]$$

The order in which the matrices are multiplied is important: $[T][p]$ is different from $[p][T]$; indeed, one of these may **not** even be defined.

There are two important points which are particularly relevant when using matrix transformations in 3D graphics applications:

1. How to multiply matrices of different sizes.

2. The importance of the order in which matrices are multiplied.

The second point will be dealt with in Section 2.11.4. As for the first point, to multiply two matrices the number of columns in the first must equal the number of rows in the second. For example a matrix of size 3×3 and 3×1 may be multiplied giving a matrix of size 3×1. However a 4×4 and a 3×1 matrix cannot be multiplied. This poses a small problem for us because vectors are represented by 3×1 matrices and transformations are represented as 4×4 matrices.

The problem is solved by introducing a new system of coordinates called *homogeneous coordinates* in which each vector is expressed with four components; the first three are the familiar (x, y, z) coordinates and the fourth is usually set to '1' so that now a vector appears as a 4×1 matrix. A transformation applied to a vector in *homogeneous* coordinate form results in another *homogeneous* coordinate vector. For all the work in this book the fourth component of vectors will be set to unity and thus they can be transformed by matrices. We will also use transformations that leave the fourth component unchanged. Thus the vector **p** with components (p_0, p_1, p_2) is expressed in homogeneous coordinates as:

$$\mathbf{p} = \begin{bmatrix} p_0 \\ p_1 \\ p_2 \\ 1 \end{bmatrix}$$

Note that many texts use the fourth component for certain transformations and the OpenGL library (used in Chapter 10) also offers facilities to use a non-unity value.

The transformation of **p** into **p'** by the matrix $[T]$ can be written as:

$$\begin{bmatrix} p_0' \\ p_1' \\ p_2' \\ 1 \end{bmatrix} = \begin{bmatrix} t_{00} & t_{01} & t_{02} & t_{03} \\ t_{10} & t_{11} & t_{12} & t_{13} \\ t_{20} & t_{21} & t_{22} & t_{23} \\ t_{30} & t_{31} & t_{32} & t_{33} \end{bmatrix} \begin{bmatrix} p_0 \\ p_1 \\ p_2 \\ 1 \end{bmatrix}$$

2.11.1   Translation

The transformation:

$$[T_t] = \begin{bmatrix} 1 & 0 & 0 & dx \\ 0 & 1 & 0 & dy \\ 0 & 0 & 1 & dz \\ 0 & 0 & 0 & 1 \end{bmatrix}$$

moves the point with coordinates (x, y, z) to the point with coordinates $(x + dx, y + dy, z + dz)$

The translated point $[p'] = [T_t][p]$ or:

$$\begin{bmatrix} 1 & 0 & 0 & dx \\ 0 & 1 & 0 & dy \\ 0 & 0 & 1 & dz \\ 0 & 0 & 0 & 1 \end{bmatrix} \begin{bmatrix} x \\ y \\ z \\ 1 \end{bmatrix} = \begin{bmatrix} x + dx \\ y + dy \\ z + dz \\ 1 \end{bmatrix}$$

2.11.2 Scaling

The transformation matrix:

$$[T_s] = \begin{bmatrix} s_x & 0 & 0 & 0 \\ 0 & s_y & 0 & 0 \\ 0 & 0 & s_z & 0 \\ 0 & 0 & 0 & 1 \end{bmatrix}$$

Scales expand or contract a position vector $\mathbf{p}$ with components (x, y, z) by the factors s_x along the x-axis, s_y along the y-axis and s_z along the z-axis. The scaled vector of $\mathbf{p}'$ is $[p'] = [T_s][p]$.

2.11.3 Rotation

A rotation is specified by an axis of rotation and the angle of the rotation. It is a fairly simple trigonometric calculation to obtain a transformation matrix for a rotation about one of the coordinate axes. When the rotation is to be performed around an arbitary vector based at a given point, the transformation matrix must be assembled from a combination of rotations about the Cartesian coordinate axes and possibly a translation.

Rotate about the z-axis

To rotate around the z-axis by an angle θ, the transformation matrix is:

$$[T_z(\theta)] = \begin{bmatrix} cos\theta & -sin\theta & 0 & 0 \\ sin\theta & cos\theta & 0 & 0 \\ 0 & 0 & 1 & 0 \\ 0 & 0 & 0 & 1 \end{bmatrix} \tag{2.9}$$

We can see how the rotational transformations are obtained by considering a positive (counterclockwise) rotation of a point $\mathbf{P}$ by θ-round the z-axis (which points out of the page). Before rotation $\mathbf{P}$ lies at a distance l from the origin and at an angle ϕ to the x-axis; see Figure 2.14. The (x, y)-coordinate of $\mathbf{P}$ is $(l \cos \phi, l \sin \phi)$. After rotation by θ, $\mathbf{P}$ is moved to $\mathbf{P}'$ and its coordinates are $(l \cos(\phi + \theta), l \sin(\phi + \theta))$. Expanding the trigonometric sum gives expressions for the coordinates of $\mathbf{P}'$:

$$\begin{aligned} P_x' &= l \cos \phi \cos \theta - l \sin \phi \sin \theta \\ P_y' &= l \cos \phi \sin \theta + l \sin \phi \cos \theta \end{aligned}$$

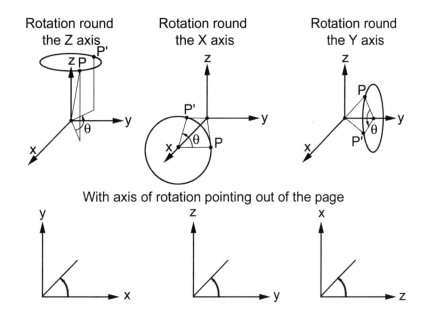

Figure 2.13.   Rotations, counterclockwise looking along the axis of rotation, towards the origin.

Since $l \cos \phi$ is the x-coordinate of $\mathbf{P}$ and $l \sin \phi$ is the y-coordinate of $\mathbf{P}$ the coordinates of $\mathbf{P}'$ becomes:

$$
\begin{aligned}
P_x' &= P_x \cos \theta - P_y \sin \theta \\
P_y' &= P_x \sin \theta + P_y \cos \theta
\end{aligned}
$$

Writing this in matrix form we have:

$$
\begin{bmatrix} P_x' \\ P_y' \end{bmatrix} = \begin{bmatrix} \cos \theta & -\sin \theta \\ \sin \theta & \cos \theta \end{bmatrix} \begin{bmatrix} P_x \\ P_y \end{bmatrix}
$$

There is no change in the z component of $\mathbf{P}$ and thus this result can be expanded into the familiar 4×4 matrix form by simply inserting the appropriate terms to give:

$$
\begin{bmatrix} P_x' \\ P_y' \\ P_z' \\ 1 \end{bmatrix} = \begin{bmatrix} \cos \theta & -\sin \theta & 0 & 0 \\ \sin \theta & \cos \theta & 0 & 0 \\ 0 & 0 & 1 & 0 \\ 0 & 0 & 0 & 1 \end{bmatrix} \begin{bmatrix} P_x \\ P_y \\ P_z \\ 1 \end{bmatrix}
$$

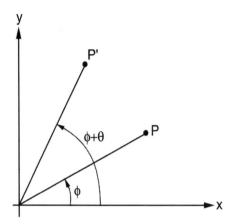

Figure 2.14.   Rotation of point $\mathbf{P}$ by an angle θ around the z-axis.

Rotation about the y-axis

To rotate around the y-axis by an angle θ, the transformation matrix is:

$$[T_y(\theta)] = \begin{bmatrix} cos\theta & 0 & sin\theta & 0 \\ 0 & 1 & 0 & 0 \\ -sin\theta & 0 & cos\theta & 0 \\ 0 & 0 & 0 & 1 \end{bmatrix}$$

Rotation about the x-axis

To rotate around the x-axis by an angle θ, the transformation matrix is:

$$[T_x(\theta)] = \begin{bmatrix} 1 & 0 & 0 & 0 \\ 0 & cos\theta & -sin\theta & 0 \\ 0 & sin\theta & cos\theta & 0 \\ 0 & 0 & 0 & 1 \end{bmatrix}$$

Note that as illustrated in Figure 2.13, θ is positive if the rotation takes place in a clockwise sense when looking from the origin along the axis of rotation. This is consistent with a right-handed coordinate system.

2.11.4   Combining Transformations

Section 2.11 introduced the key concept of a transformation applied to a position vector. In many cases we are interested in what happens when several operations are applied in sequence to a model or to one of its points (*vertices*). For example: *move the point* **P** *10 units forward, rotate it 20 degrees round the z-axis and shift it 15 units along the x-axis.* Each transformation is represented by a single 4×4 matrix and the compound transformation is constructed as a sequence of single transformations as follows:

$$
\begin{aligned}
[p'] &= [T_1][p] \\
[p''] &= [T_2][p'] \\
[p'''] &= [T_3][p'']
\end{aligned}
$$

where $[p']$ and $[p'']$ are intermediate position vectors and $[p''']$ is the end vector after the application of the three transformations. The above sequence can be combined into:

$$[p'''] = [T_3][T_2][T_1][p]$$

The product of the transformations $[T_3][T_2][T_1]$ gives a single matrix $[T]$. Combining transformations in this way has a wonderful efficiency; if a large model has 50,000 vertices and we need to apply 10 transformations, by combining the transformations into a single matrix, 450,000 matrix multiplications can be avoided.

It is important to remember that the result of applying a sequence of transformations depends on the order in which they are applied. $[T_3][T_2][T_1]$ is **not** the same compound transformation as $[T_2][T_3][T_1]$. Figure 2.15 shows the effect of applying the transformations in a different order.

There is one subtle point about transformations that ought to be stressed. The parameters of a transformation (angle of rotation, etc.) are all relative to a **global** frame of reference. It is sometimes useful to think in terms of a local frame of reference that is itself transformed relative to a global frame and this idea will be explored when we discuss key frame and character animation. However it is important to bear in mind that when a final scene is assembled for rendering, all coordinates must be specified in the same frame of reference.

2.11.5 Rotation about an Arbitrary Axis

The transformation corresponding to rotation of an angle α around an arbitrary vector (for example, that shown between the two points $\mathbf{P}_0$ and $\mathbf{P}_1$ in Figure 2.16) cannot readily be written in a form similar to the rotation matrices about the coordinate axes.

The desired transformation matrix is obtained by combining a sequence of basic translation and rotation matrices. (Once a single 4×4 matrix has been obtained representing the composite transformations it can be used in the same way as any other transformation matrix.)

The following outlines an algorithm to construct a transformation matrix to generate a rotation by an angle α around a vector in the direction $\mathbf{P}_1 - \mathbf{P}_0$:

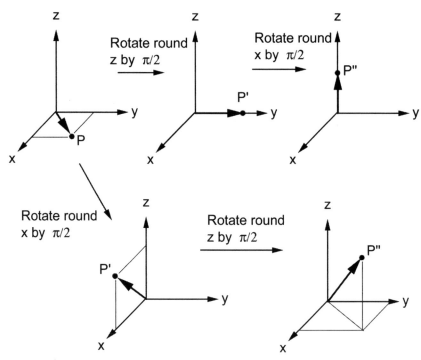

Figure 2.15.   Effect of transformations applied in a different order.

1. Translate P_0 to the origin of coordinates.

2. Align rotation axis $P_1 - P_0$ with the x-axis.

3. Rotate by angle α around x-axis.

4. Make inverse transformation to undo the rotations of step two.

5. Translate origin of coordinates back to P_0 to undo the translation of step one.

The full algorithm is given in Figure 2.17. Möller and Haines [13] give a more robust method of rotating around any axis.

2.11.6 Viewing Transformation

Before rendering any view of a 3D scene (see Chapter 4) one has to decide from where to view/photograph the scene and in which direction to look (point the camera). This is like setting up a camera to take a picture. Once the camera

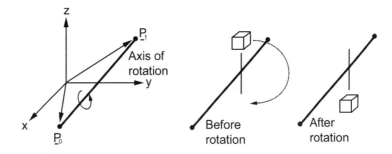

Figure 2.16.   Rotation around an arbitrary vector.

Let $\mathbf{d} = \mathbf{P}_1 - \mathbf{P}_0$
$[T_1] =$ a translation by $-\mathbf{P}_0$
$d_{xy} = d_x^2 + d_y^2$
if $d_{xy} < \epsilon$ { *rotation axis is in the* $\mathbf{z}$ *direction*
        if $d_z > 0$ make $[T_2]$ a rotation about z by α
        else $[T_2] =$ a rotation about z by $-\alpha$
        $[T_3] =$ a translation by $\mathbf{P}_0$
        return the product $[T_3][T_2][T_1]$
}
$d_{xy} = \sqrt{d_{xy}}$
if $d_x = 0$ and $d_y > 0$ $\phi = \pi/2$
else if $d_x = 0$ and $d_y < 0$ $\phi = -\pi/2$
else $\phi = ATAN2(d_y, d_x)$
$\theta = ATAN2(d_z, d_{xy})$
$[T_2] =$ a rotation about z by $-\phi$
$[T_3] =$ a rotation about y by $-\theta$
$[T_4] =$ a rotation about x by α
$[T_5] =$ a rotation about y by θ
$[T_6] =$ a rotation about z by ϕ
$[T_7] =$ a translation by $\mathbf{P}_0$
Multiply the transformation matrices to give the final result
$[T] = [T_7][T_6][T_5][T_4][T_3][T_2][T_1]$

Figure 2.17.   Algorithm for rotation around an arbitrary axis. d_x, d_y, and d_z are the components of vector $\mathbf{d}$.

is set we just click the shutter. The camera projects the image as seen in the viewfinder onto the photographic film and the image is rendered. This is a two stage process. The projection stage will be discussed in Section 2.11.7, and we will now consider how to set a viewpoint and direction of view.

In mathematical terms we need to construct a suitable transformation that will allow us to choose a viewpoint (place to set up the camera) and direction of view (direction in which to point the camera). Once we have this *view transformation* it can be combined with any other transformations that need to be applied to the scene or to objects in the scene.

We have already seen how to construct transformation matrices that move or rotate points in a scene. In the same way that basic transformation matrices were combined in Section 2.11.5 to create an arbitrary rotation, we can build a single matrix, $[T_o]$, that will transform all the points (vertices) in a scene in such a way that the projection of an image becomes a simple standard process. To do this we arrange that the camera is fixed at the center of the universe $(0,0,0)$ and locked off to point in the direction $(1,0,0)$, along the x-axis.

There is nothing special about the direction $(1,0,0)$; we could equally well have chosen to fix the camera to look in the direction $(0,1,0)$, the y-axis, or even $(0,0,1)$, the z-axis. Since we have chosen to let z represent the **up** direction and it is not a good idea to look directly up, $(0,0,1)$ would be a poor choice for viewing. (Note: The OpenGL and Direct3D software libraries for 3D graphics have their z-axis parallel to the viewing direction.)

Once $[T_o]$ has been determined it is applied to all objects in the scene. If necessary $[T_o]$ can be combined with other transformation matrices to give a single composite transformation $[T]$.

A viewing transformation depends on:

1. Position of the view point (camera location): a vector $\mathbf{p}_o$, Figure 2.18.

2. The direction in which we wish to look, north, south, east, or west. This is measured by an angle ϕ which is relative to the **x**-axis and lies in the xy plane. ϕ is positive to the right of the **x**-axis when looking along **x** from the view point.

3. The amount by which we look up or down. The angle θ measures this amount relative to the xy plane and is positive when looking down. Note that when determining a viewing transformation the effect of looking up or down comes into play after the direction of view has been accounted for, and therefore it is equivalent to a rotation around the **y**-axis.

4. The degree to which our head is tilted to the left or right. This is measured by the angle α. To be consistent with the right-handed frame of reference and sense of rotation α is positive when the camera tilts to the right as it looks from $\mathbf{p}_o$ along the **x**-axis.

A viewing transformation appears to operate in reverse to ordinary transformations. For example, if you tilt your head to the left, the world appears to tilt to the right. Note carefully that the angle θ is positive if we are looking down, and negative if we looking up. If you prefer, you can think of ϕ as the **heading**, θ as the **pitch**, and α as the degree of **banking**. The viewing transformations are also combined in the reverse order with respect to the order in which a transformation is assembled for objects placed in a scene; in that case the rotation around **x** is applied first and the translation by $\mathbf{p}_o$ is applied last.

Given the parameters $\mathbf{p}_o$, ϕ, θ, and α (illustrated in Figure 2.18), the transformation $[T_o]$ is constructed by the following algorithm:

Place observer at $(0, 0, 0)$ with the transformation:
$[T_1] =$ a translation by $-\mathbf{p}_o$
Rotate the direction of observation into the xz plane with:
$[T_2] =$ a rotation about z by $-\phi$
Align the direction of observation to the **x**-axis with:
$[T_3] =$ a rotation about y by $-\theta$
Straighten the camera up with transformation:
$[T_4] =$ a rotation about x by $-\alpha$
Multiply the individual transformation matrices to give
one composite matrix representing the viewing transformation:
$[T_0] = [T_4][T_3][T_2][T_1]$

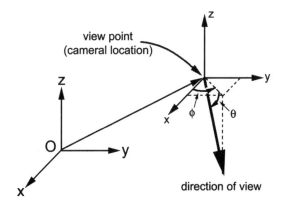

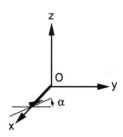

After alignment to the x axis
the direction of view is still
tilted by angle α to the right.

Figure 2.18.   Viewpoint and direction of view.

2.11.7 Projection

We saw in Section 2.11.6 that after setting up a camera to record an image the view must be projected onto film or electronic sensing device. In the conventional camera this is done with a lens arrangement or simply a *pinhole*. One could also imagine holding a sheet of glass in front of the viewer and then have them trace on it what they see as they look through it. What is drawn on the glass **is** what we would like the computer to produce: a 2D picture of the scene, even showing the right way up as in Figure 2.19.

It is straightforward to formulate expressions needed to perform this (non-linear) transformation. A little thought must be given to dealing with cases where parts of the scene go behind the viewer or are partly in and partly out of the field

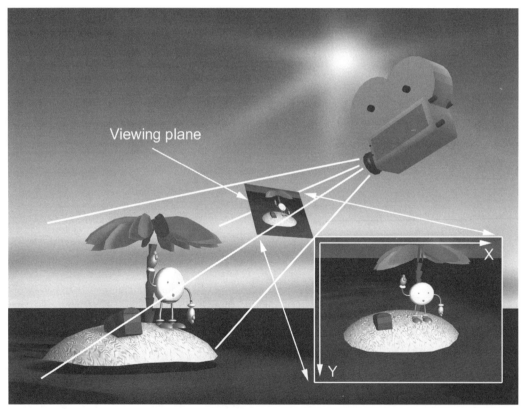

Figure 2.19.   Project the scene onto the viewing plane. The resulting 2D image is then recorded or displayed.

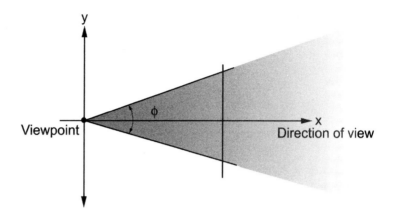

y

Viewpoint ϕ → x Direction of view

Figure 2.20. The field of view ϕ governs how much of the scene is visible to a camera located at the viewpoint. Narrowing the field of view is equivalent to using a zoom lens.

of view, (discussed in Section 4.8). The field of view (illustrated in Figure 2.20) governs how much of the scene you see; it can be changed. In photography, tele-photo and fish-eye lenses have different fields of view. For example the common $50mm$ lens has a field of view of $45.9°$. Because of its shape as a truncated pyramid with a regular base the volume enclosed by the field of view is known as a *frustum*.

One thing we can do with a projective transformation is to adjust the *aspect ratio*. The *aspect ratio* is the ratio of height to width of the rendered image. For television work it is $4 : 3$ and $16 : 9$ for basic cine film. The aspect ratio is related to the vertical and horizontal resolution of the recorded image. Get this relationship wrong and your spheres will look egg shaped.

Before formulating expressions to represent the projection we need to define the coordinate system in use for the projection plane. It has become almost universal (however not in the OpenGL library discussed in Chapter 10) to represent the computer display as a pair of integers in the range $0 \to (X_{max}-1)$ horizontally and $0 \to (Y_{max}-1)$ vertically. The coordinate origin $(0,0)$ is in the top left corner; see Figure 2.19.

The distance of the projection plane from the viewpoint can be chosen ar-bitrarily; setting it to one unit simplifies the calculations. Thus if the plane of projection is located at $(1,0,0)$ and orientated parallel to the yz plane (i.e., the viewer is looking along the x-axis), then the screen coordinates (X_s, Y_s) for the projection of a point (x, y, z) are given by:

$$X_s = \frac{X_{max}}{2} - \frac{y}{x}s_x \tag{2.10}$$

$$Y_s = \frac{Y_{max}}{2} - \frac{z}{x}s_y \tag{2.11}$$

The parameters s_x and s_y are scale values to allow for different aspect ratios and fields of view. This effectively lets us change the *zoom* settings for the camera. Obviously, X_s and Y_s must satisfy $0 \le X_s < X_{max}$ and $0 \le Y_s < Y_{max}$.

If f_f (measured in *mm*) is the focal length of the desired camera lens and the aspect ratio is $A_x : A_y$ then:

$$s_x = \frac{X_{max}}{2}\frac{f_f}{21.22}A_x$$

$$s_y = \frac{Y_{max}}{2}\frac{f_f}{21.22}A_y$$

The numerical factor 21.22 is a constant to allow us to specify f_f in standard *mm* units. For a camera lens of focal length f_f, the field of view θ can be expressed as:

$$\theta \simeq 2ATAN2(21.22, f_f)$$

Any point (x, y, z) for which $x < 1$ will not be transformed correctly by Equations 2.10 and 2.11 and steps must be made to eliminate them before the projection is applied. This process is called *clipping*. How the clipping is done depends on whether a wireframe or shaded solid is to be rendered and is discussed in Section 4.8.

It is possible to express the perspective transformation as a 4×4 matrix. However the matrix cannot be combined with other matrices (such as the viewing transformation in Section 2.11.6) and applied to all points in a single step, because the matrix include one of the co-ordinates of the point being transformed.

2.12 Parametric Curves

In two dimensions a curve is generally expressed as a function in the form $y = f(x)$. Unfortunately this can be a cumbersome representation to work with. It is fine for curves like the one shown in Figure 2.21(a) but when the curve is closed or loops, like the one in Figure 2.21(b), then a parametric representation is better.

The difficulties of expressing a curve in the form $y = f(x)$ can be illustrated by considering the equation of a circle: $y = \pm\sqrt{x^2 - r^2}$. The problem here is that to draw a curve with a $\pm$ in its equation requires special-purpose handling.

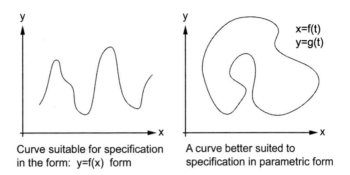

Curve suitable for specification
in the form: y=f(x) form

A curve better suited to
specification in parametric form

Figure 2.21.   2D curves.

A better alternative is to obtain separate functions for x and y in terms of a single parameter θ:

$$x = r \cos \theta \qquad (2.12)$$
$$y = r \sin \theta \qquad (2.13)$$

where θ is an angle in the range $[0, 2\pi)$. Equations 2.12 and 2.13 are well behaved: given a θ each returns one value only. This is ideal for plotting because it wouldn't matter if the curve twisted, turned, or looped.

Actually, since angles are measured in radians, and radians are a measure of the arc length of a unit circle, θ could also be thought of as a *length along the curve*.

The idea of the parameter having a physical meaning like *length* is a very useful one for curves in both two and three dimensions. We shall use it in Section 6.2.2 when studying the animation of objects following paths. An alternative and equally useful parameter is *time*.

Equations 2.12 and 2.13 are specific to a 2D circular curve; for work in three dimensions a set of parametric functions that apply to a general curve can be written in the form:

$$x = u(\tau) \qquad (2.14)$$
$$y = v(\tau) \qquad (2.15)$$
$$z = w(\tau) \qquad (2.16)$$

Here τ is the parameter. Any curve (we shall call it a path) in 3D space, be it a straight line, a Bézier curve, a cubic spline or even a curve constructed from pieces of other curves can be specified by three functions. Figure 2.22 illustrates a typical three-dimensional parametric curve.

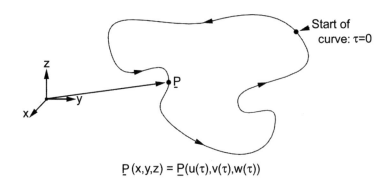

$$\underline{P}(x,y,z) = \underline{P}(u(\tau),v(\tau),w(\tau))$$

Figure 2.22.   A 3D parametric curve.

2.13   Interpolation

Suppose we have a set of data containing n $(n > 1)$ pairs of values (x_0, y_0), (x_1, y_1), (x_2, y_2), ... (x_i, y_y), ... (x_{n-1}, y_{n-1}). These can be plotted on a two-dimensional diagram as shown in Figure 2.23.   Joining the points (x_i, y_i) together in the order, $0 \to 1 \to 2 \to$ ... $\to i \to$ ... $\to n - 1$ will create a path through the points. The path will have a beginning and an end as illustrated in Figure 2.24. To draw the path we had to use **interpolation**; that is, *we had to assume what the path looks like as it goes* **through** *the data points.* For the

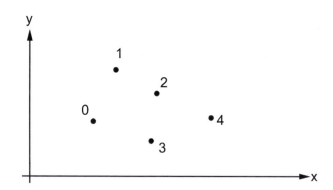

Figure 2.23.   Data points for interpolation.

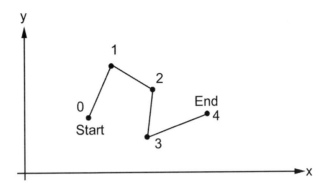

Figure 2.24.   Joining up the data points to make a path.

path of Figure 2.24, with all its *kinks* we might be forgiven for thinking that our assumption on how it behaves between the points is a poor one, because the path shown in Figure 2.25, which also passes through the data points, looks smoother, and for many application it is therefore a better path.

Since we know nothing more about the path other than the points it passes through, the *"which is better"* argument is unresolvable. The paths shown in Figures 2.24 and 2.25 are only two out of an infinite number of possible paths, all of which pass through the points (x_0, y_0) etc.

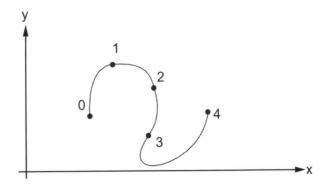

Figure 2.25.   Smoothly joining up the data points.

The path shown in Figure 2.24 was drawn by using the following simple procedure to join up the points:

1. Take the points two at a time and obtain the equation of a straight line passing through them in parametric form. For example, for points 0 and 1,

$$x = x_0 + \mu(x_1 - x_0)$$
$$y = y_0 + \mu(y_1 - y_0)$$

2. For each line use its equations to obtain (select values of μs in the range $(0, 1)$) x and y values corresponding to points lying on the line. Plot the points on the diagram. When enough of them have been plotted the line will look continuous.

This procedure of finding extra points on the line joining consecutive data points is called *linear* interpolation. To draw a smoother path through the same set of data another type of interpolation is required.

Interpolation procedures that use curves rather than straight lines to plot the path between data points use more than two consecutive points. For example, by taking groups of three points at a time it is possible to specify a quadratic curve for the path between the data points. This is illustrated in Figure 2.26 where three quadratic curves make up the path through seven points. Unfortunately there are *kinks* (discontinuous first derivatives) at the points where the curves join. The path looks smooth near point 1 but at point 2 there is a kink. To eliminate the kinks we could consider using four points at a time, but then the kinks would appear at every fourth point. So why not build an $(n-1)$th order curve to go through all the n data points in the path? The reason we cannot consider more than about four or

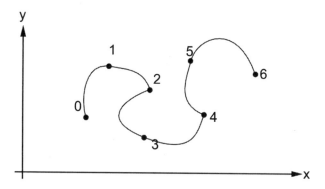

Figure 2.26.   Quadratic interpolation using points $(0 - 1 - 2)$ and then $(2 - 3 - 4)$, etc.

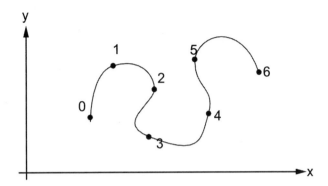

Figure 2.27.   Blending cubic curves to make a smooth path.

five points as a group is because the calculation becomes *ill-conditioned*. There are ways round the *ill-conditioning* problem but even when that is solved a very *wiggly* path will be produced that looks totally unrealistic. A better approach is to group three or four points together and blend them so that the kinks disappear. For example, a good blend is achieved with the curves making up the path shown in Figure 2.27.

The path of Figure 2.27 was obtained by *blending* pieces of cubic curves. A cubic curve was constructed to pass through points $0 - 1 - 2 - 3$ but it was only used to draw that part of the path between points $0 - 2$. Another cubic was designed to pass through points $1 - 2 - 3 - 4$ but this time it was used to draw (by interpolation from the cubic) the piece of the path between points $2 - 3$.

There are more elaborate ways to blend curves together and much analysis has been done on the topic; a detailed discussion of such issues can be found in [14].

An alternative but effectively similar strategy to that of blending pieces of curves together over a range of points is to insist that, at all data points, the slope or gradient of the curve is the same on both sides of the point. This will eliminate *kinks* such as those that are so obvious in Figure 2.26.

2.13.1   Linear Interpolation

Given two points with position vectors $\mathbf{P_0}$ and $\mathbf{P_1}$ any point lying on a straight line between them satisfies:

$$\mathbf{p} = \mathbf{P_0} + \mu(\mathbf{P_1} - \mathbf{P_0})$$

Choosing μ such that $0 \leq \mu \leq 1$ returns a linearly interpolated point. When $\mu = \frac{1}{2}$ then $\mathbf{p} = \mathbf{P_{\frac{1}{2}}}$ will lie midway between $\mathbf{P_0}$ and $\mathbf{P_1}$.

In terms of the (x, y, z) coordinates of $\mathbf{p}$, three interpolating equations can be written as

$$
\begin{aligned}
x &= x_0 + \mu(x_1 - x_0) \\
y &= y_0 + \mu(y_1 - y_0) \\
z &= z_0 + \mu(z_1 - z_0)
\end{aligned}
$$

(x_0, y_0, z_0) are the coordinates of $\mathbf{P}_0$ and (x_1, y_1, z_1) is $\mathbf{P}_1$.

2.13.2   Quadratic Interpolation

Quadratic interpolation fits a quadratic to three points $\mathbf{P}_0$, $\mathbf{P}_1$, and $\mathbf{P}_2$ to be taken together. The equation

$$
\mathbf{p} = (2(\mathbf{P}_2 - \mathbf{P}_0) - 4(\mathbf{P}_1 - \mathbf{P}_0))\mu^2 - ((\mathbf{P}_2 - \mathbf{P}_0) - 4(\mathbf{P}_1 - \mathbf{P}_0))\mu + \mathbf{P}_0
$$

gives the point $\mathbf{p}$ as μ varies between 0 and 1. When $\mu = \frac{1}{2}$ the point is $\mathbf{p} = \mathbf{P}_1$ and $\mathbf{p} = \mathbf{P}_2$ is reached when $\mu = 1$.

Note that in this case μ is **not** the length of the curve.

2.14   Bézier Curves

In the preceding discussion on interpolation it was assumed that to describe a path by a number of component curves they all pass through points from which their shape was derived. This doesn't have to be the case. It is true however that, for computer graphics work, it is likely that our interest is in paths and curves that *do* pass through all their *control* points. Nevertheless there is one important exception, the Bézier curve.

Curves of this form are named after Pierre Bézier who worked for the French company Renault and first used them in the design of automobiles. Today perhaps their most common usage is to provide a mathematical descriptions of typefaces and scalable character fonts for the printing industry. The text you are reading was printed by instructing a printer to fill in the outline of each character that has been described by a closed path made up from straight line and Bézier curve segments. Postscript and TrueType fonts that are used by virtually every personal computer to display and print text are specific variants of this method of describing character and other shapes. Figure 2.28 shows a basic Bézier curve constructed from four points. It is readily seen that the curve itself only passes through the first and last point. Bézier curves can have as many *control* points as desired but only the first and last will lie on the curve. For all Bézier curves the direction of the curve as it leaves the first point is towards the second (off curve) point.

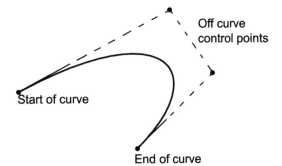

Figure 2.28.   Basic Bézier curve with two control points on and two control points off the curve.

The direction in which the curve approached the last point is from the penultimate one; see Figure 2.31. Many books and journal articles refer to the control points of Bézier and spline curves as *knots*. Figure 2.29 shows a Bézier curve with n knots (control points).

As the number of knots in a Bézier curve increase, the properties that make it so useful become diluted; the curve just gets lazy and meanders from start to finish paying little heed to the intervening knots. The most useful Bézier curve turns out to be the simplest 4-knot curve. These 4-knot curves can be readily joined together to make the most complex shapes. Figure 2.30 shows a path with four Bézier segments. Using Bézier segments has the advantage that while it is not too difficult to avoid *kinks* in the path, on the occasions when *kinks* are desirable they can be easily incorporated.

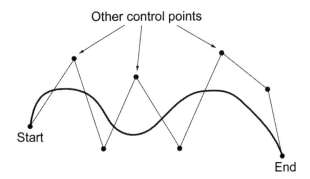

Figure 2.29.   Bézier curve with two control points (knots) on the curve and $n-2$ other knots (control points).

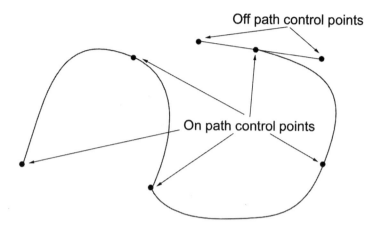

Figure 2.30.   Path made from several 4-knot Bézier curves.

There are several algorithms for drawing Bézier curves; one suitable for any number (n) of knots is the de Casteljau recursive procedure [15]. De Castlejau's algorithm is relatively short but because it is recursive its calculation can be quite slow, especially when n is large.

In the case of Adobe's Postscript language [16], font and other curved shapes are described by a set of 4-knot Bézier curves and straight line segments. A 4-knot Bézier curve is specified by a cubic polynomial in parametric form. Figure 2.31 illustrates the effect on the Bézier of moving the knots to different positions. By linking 4-knot Bézier curves together, the most complicated calligraphic shapes can be made, as illustrated in Figure 2.32.

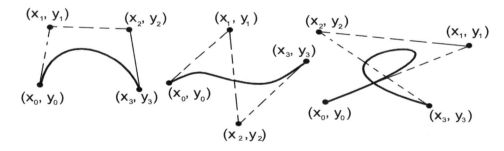

Figure 2.31.   2D Bézier curves showing the effect of different placement of the *intermediate* points (the knots).

Figure 2.32. Calligraphic shape (the letters CG) made from many 4-knot Bézier curves.

For the four knots, (x_0, y_0), (x_1, y_1), (x_2, y_2), and (x_3, y_3) a point (x, y) on the Bézier can be interpolated using:

$$x(t) = a_x t^3 + b_x t^2 + c_x t + x_0 \qquad (2.17)$$
$$y(t) = a_y t^3 + b_y t^2 + c_y t + y_0 \qquad (2.18)$$

where t is the parameter and

$$x_1 = x_0 + \frac{c_x}{3} \qquad (2.19)$$
$$x_2 = x_1 + \frac{c_x + b_x}{3} \qquad (2.20)$$
$$x_3 = x_0 + a_x + b_x + c_x \qquad (2.21)$$

Usually the (x_0, y_0), (x_1, y_1), etc., are known; a_x, b_x, and c_x can be calculated by rearranging Equations 2.19, 2.20, and 2.21 to give:

$$c_x = 3(x_1 - x_0)$$
$$b_x = 3(x_2 - 2x_1 + x_0)$$
$$a_x = x_3 + 3(x_1 - x_2) - x_0$$

Similar expression for a_y, b_y, etc. can be obtained.

Equations 2.17 and 2.18 are readily extended to give a description of a 4-knot curve in three dimensions. The knots are specified by position vectors and the interpolated points can be obtained by varying the parameter t.

2.15   Cubic Splines

Spline is a term that owes its origins to the flexible strip of wood draftsmen used to draw curves. Weights would hold the spline in place at the points on the drawing through which the curve must pass. Tracing along the wooden strips produced a smooth and pleasing curve. An examination of the properties of the spline suggests a suitable mathematical model, for it is a cubic function. Splines come in many flavors: B-spline, recursive B-spline, β-splines, and cubic splines.

The spline, like the Bézier curve, can be used to describe a smooth path given a set of data points. Unlike the Bézier curve, a spline passes through all the data points. Splines are constructed by fitting a cubic curve to pass through two adjacent points with additional conditions on the gradient of the curve at the points.

We touch on two aspects of spline curves; Bartels et al. [17] present a useful general study of spline theory for both curves and surfaces introducing the highly-useful non-uniform rational B-spline (NURBS) that has proved its utility in CAD applications.

The Graphics Gem (Peterson [18]) is particularly worth looking at if you need to implement a practical scheme using NURBS in a modeling or rendering program.

A cubic spline is written in the form:

$$\mathbf{p}(\tau) = \mathbf{K}_3\tau^3 + \mathbf{K}_2\tau^2 + \mathbf{K}_1\tau + \mathbf{K}_0 \qquad (2.22)$$

or equivalently (to speed up its calculation):

$$\mathbf{p}(\tau) = (((\mathbf{K}_3\tau + \mathbf{K}_2)\tau + \mathbf{K}_1)\tau + \mathbf{K}_0)$$

The unknown vector constants $\mathbf{K}_0$, $\mathbf{K}_1$, $\mathbf{K}_2$, and $\mathbf{K}_3$ have to be determined, as their components are independent of each other. τ is a parameter having values in the interval $[0, 1]$ such that when $\tau = 0$, $\mathbf{p}(0) = \mathbf{P}_i$ and when $\tau = 1$, $\mathbf{p}(1) = \mathbf{P}_{i+1}$

To determine the unknown vector constants we impose four conditions on Equation 2.22:

1. The spline passes through the point $\mathbf{P}_i$ at the start of the curve.

2. The spline passes through the point $\mathbf{P}_{i+1}$ at the end of the curve.

3. The derivative $\mathbf{P}'_i$ of the spline at $\mathbf{P}_i$ is given.

4. The derivative $\mathbf{P}'_{i+1}$ of the spline at $\mathbf{P}_{i+1}$ is given.

These apply to each of the components of $\mathbf{p}$; i.e., for its x component we need to consider the values: x_i , x_{i+1}, x'_i , x'_{i+1}. Differentiating Equation 2.22 with respect to τ gives:

$$\mathbf{p}'(\tau) = 3\mathbf{K}_3\tau^2 + 2\mathbf{K}_2\tau + \mathbf{K}_1 \qquad (2.23)$$

Substituting for x_i and x_{i+1} in Equation 2.22 with $\tau = 0$ and $\tau = 1$ respectively and then with x_i' and x_{i+1}' in Equation 2.23 while $\tau = 0$ and $\tau = 1$ gives four simultaneous equation for the x component of the $\mathbf{K}$s. Written in matrix form these are:

$$
\begin{bmatrix}
0 & 0 & 0 & 1 \\
1 & 1 & 1 & 1 \\
0 & 0 & 1 & 0 \\
3 & 2 & 1 & 0
\end{bmatrix}
\begin{bmatrix}
K_{3_x} \\
K_{2_x} \\
K_{1_x} \\
K_{0_x}
\end{bmatrix}
=
\begin{bmatrix}
x_i \\
x_{i+1} \\
x_i' \\
x_{i+1}'
\end{bmatrix}
$$

On solution the following expressions are obtained:

$$
\begin{aligned}
K_{3_x} &= 2x_i - 2x_{i+1} + x_i' + x_{i+1}' \\
K_{2_x} &= -3x_i + 3x_{i+1} - 2x_i' - x_{i+1}' \\
K_{1_x} &= x_i' \\
K_{0_x} &= x_{i+1}'
\end{aligned}
$$

If $\mathbf{P}_i$ and $\mathbf{P}_{i+1}$ are part of a set of points making up a path, such as, ... $\mathbf{P}_{i-1}$, $\mathbf{P}_i$, $\mathbf{P}_{i+1}$, $\mathbf{P}_{i+2}$ ..., the $\mathbf{K}$s are obtained using the value of p at $\mathbf{P}_{i-1}$, $\mathbf{P}_i$, $\mathbf{P}_{i+1}$, and $\mathbf{P}_{i+2}$ as follows:

$$
K_{3_x} = -\frac{1}{2}x_{i-1} + \frac{3}{2}x_i - \frac{3}{2}x_{i+1} + \frac{1}{2}x_{i+2} \tag{2.24}
$$

$$
K_{2_x} = x_{i-1} - \frac{5}{2}x_i + 2x_{i+1} - \frac{1}{2}x_{i+2} \tag{2.25}
$$

$$
K_{1_x} = -\frac{1}{2}x_{i-1} + \frac{3}{2}x_{i+1} \tag{2.26}
$$

$$
K_{0_x} = x_i \tag{2.27}
$$

Similar expressions may be written for K_{3_y} and K_{3_z} etc., and thus the constant vectors $\mathbf{K_i}$ become:

$$
\mathbf{K_i} =
\begin{bmatrix}
K_{i_x} \\
K_{i_y} \\
K_{i_z}
\end{bmatrix}
$$

for $i = 0, 1, 2, 3$.

In summary, the calculations we used to obtain the $\mathbf{K_i}$ vectors are *local*. That is, they only depend on coordinates of the two knots between which the cubic is used for interpolation and the two other nearest neighbor knots. Therefore, when we draw pieces of a path with many knots, segments can be drawn independently. There is no need to take a global view of the whole path in order to draw just a little piece of it.

A couple of notes on splines:

- Extending this type of spline for use in three dimensions is relatively easy. A parameter τ replaces the variable x, and there are two additional polynomials, one in each of the other coordinates.

- Usually τ takes integer values at the knots; i.e., $-1, 0, 1, 2$ In this case there is no relationship between the parameter τ and the distance between the points.

2.16   A Spline in One Dimension

An alternative view of the calculation of the spline constants arises by considering **all** the knots of the spline together in a single step. A set of cubic curves, one for each pair of knots, is still obtained but the blending is done implicitly and the overall curve is smooth and well behaved. "Well behaved" means that if one of the knots is moved the curve will change shape only in the vicinity of the knot. Far away, the shape of the curve will not be affected. Contrast this with another interpolation method, Lagrange polynomial interpolation, for example. If a Lagrange polynomial is fitted to the data, a change in one knot will show a ripple effect throughout the curve. Some examples of this effect are shown in Figure 2.33, where spline and Lagrangian interpolating functions are compared.

To study the idea of a global spline curve we shall examine a 2D set of n points, (x_i, y_i), where the data is ordered so that $x_0 < x_1 < x_2 < \ ... < x_{n-2} < x_{n-1}$, Figure 2.34 illustrates the setup.

For the ith interval, between the points (x_i, y_i) and (x_{i+1}, y_{i+1}), the form of the cubic is:

$$y = a_i(x - x_i)^3 + b_i(x - x_i)^2 + c_i(x - x_i) + d_i \qquad (2.28)$$

This curve must be satisfied by both (x_i, y_i) and (x_{i+1}, y_{i+1}). Blending is achieved by assuming that at (x_i, y_i), the slope and curvature are the same as in the previous interval, between points (x_{i-1}, y_{i-1}) and (x_i, y_i). Slope and curvature are given by first and second derivatives respectively.

Letting $h_i = (x_{i+1} - x_i)$ and S_i represent the second derivative at the point (x_i, y_i), an equation in which the S_i's are unknown may be written for a general point i,

$$h_{i-1}S_{i-1} + 2(h_{i-1} + h_iS_i + h_i)S_{i+1} = 6\left(\frac{y_{i+1} - y_i}{h_i} - \frac{y_i - y_{i-1}}{h_{i-1}}\right) \qquad (2.29)$$

Equation 2.29 is obtained by differentiating Equation 2.28 twice rearranging and making use of the assumptions about slope and curvature at point i.

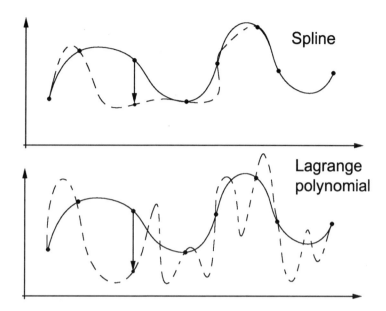

Figure 2.33. Effect of displacing control knot on the shape of spline and Lagrange polynomials.

Since Equation 2.29 applies at the points on the spline (except the first and last) a set of $n-2$ simultaneous equations may be written for the n values of S_i; that is, an equation for each of the internal points 1, 2, ... $(n-2)$.

A set of $n-2$ equations in n unknowns does not have a unique solution and so two additional equations, for S_0 and S_{n-1}, are obtained by specifying some pertinent end conditions. Possible end conditions are:

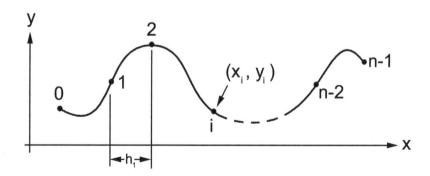

Figure 2.34. A 2D spline curve passing through n data points.

1. The end cubics approach linearity, $S_0 = S_{n-1} = 0$, the so called natural boundary conditions.

2. The end cubics approach parabolas. $S_0 = S_1$ and $S_{n-1} = S_{n-2}$.

3. S_0 is a linear extrapolation from S_1 and S_2 and S_{n-1} is a linear extrapolation from S_{n-3} and S_{n-2}.

Using the natural boundary conditions a set of $n-2$ linear equations in $n-2$ unknowns (the S_i) are established. In matrix form, these are written as $[H][S] = [Y]$ where:

$$[H] = \begin{bmatrix} 2(h_0 + h_1) & h_1 & 0 & 0 & .. & 0 \\ h_1 & 2(h_1 + h_2) & h_2 & 0 & .. & 0 \\ 0 & h_2 & 2(h_2 + h_3) & h_3 & & \\ .. & .. & .. & .. & .. & .. \\ 0 & .. & 0 & h_{n-4} & 2(h_{n-4} + h_{n-3}) & h_{n-3} \\ 0 & .. & 0 & 0 & h_{n-3} & 2(h_{n-3} + h_{n-2}) \end{bmatrix}$$

$$[S] = \begin{bmatrix} S_1 \\ S_2 \\ S_3 \\ .. \\ .. \\ S_{n-2} \end{bmatrix}$$

$$[Y] = 6 \begin{bmatrix} \left(\dfrac{y_2 - y_1}{h_1} - \dfrac{y_1 - y_0}{h_0} \right) \\ \left(\dfrac{y_3 - y_2}{h_2} - \dfrac{y_2 - y_1}{h_1} \right) \\ \left(\dfrac{y_4 - y_3}{h_3} - \dfrac{y_3 - y_2}{h_2} \right) \\ .. \\ .. \\ \left(\dfrac{y_{n-1} - y_{n-2}}{h_{n-2}} - \dfrac{y_{n-2} - y_{n-3}}{h_{n-3}} \right) \end{bmatrix}$$

The matrix $[H]$ is very sparse (it has many zero elements), and *tridiagonal*. Linear equations with this structure are amenable to very rapid solution by using an algorithm such as the one presented in Section A.2.2.

Once the S_i have been found the constants a_i, b_i, c_i, and d_i in Equation 2.28 are obtained from:

$$a_i = \frac{S_{i+1} - S_i}{6 h_i}$$

$$b_i = \frac{S_i}{2}$$

$$c_i = \frac{y_{i+1} - y_i}{h_i} - \frac{2h_i S_i + h_i S_{i+1}}{6}$$

$$d_i = y_i$$

After that, the cubic polynomial Equation 2.28 is used to yield values for y given x in the interval between (x_i, y_i) and (x_{i+1}, y_{i+1}).

2.17 Angular Interpolation—Quaternions

Implicit in the previous discussion on interpolation was the use of the Cartesian coordinate system. This is ideal for interpolating position vectors. On the other hand there are many scenarios where it will be required to interpolate direction vectors.

Consider the following:

> *You are standing on the top of a hill with a camera on a motorized tripod looking North, and you wish to set the camera so that it pans round to face East taking pictures every* $10°$.

This is a job for angular interpolation: first direction $0°$, last direction $90°$ and 8 intermediate steps. In this case linear interpolation of the angle is the natural way to obtain the directions to use for the intermediate shots. As we shall see when we consider computer animation, a combination of interpolated positions and interpolated angles is a very efficient method of directing the action.

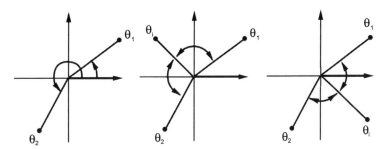

Two possible interpolation angles

Figure 2.35. In this example of angular interpolation there are two possible values for an angle bisecting the angles θ_1 and θ_2.

Angles are cyclic of period 2π; therefore the angle α is the same angle as $\alpha + 2\pi$, $\alpha + 4\pi$, ... $\alpha + 2n\pi$. This makes interpolation a little tricky. As shown in Figure 2.35 there are two possible solutions to the problem of finding the angle θ_i that lies halfway between the two angles θ_1 and θ_2.

This problem of interpolation gets more complex when three dimensions are involved. Firstly, to be able to specify an arbitrary orientation three angles are needed. Section 2.11.6 introduced three measures that describe the orientation of a camera observing a collection of objects: *heading*, *pitch* and *roll (bank)*. Three angles specifying an orientation are known as *Euler* angles. However, there are 12 possible conventions for describing Euler angles, making their specification rather confusing. We will choose the convention for orientation illustrated in Figure 2.36. Thus, in three dimensions, interpolation between two orientations reduces to the problem of obtaining the triple (ϕ, θ, α) given two or more sets of angles $(\phi_0, \theta_0, \alpha_0)$, $(\phi_1, \theta_1, \alpha_1)$, etc.

Unfortunately, orientations specified with Euler angles (ϕ, θ, α) can not be interpolated in the same way that positions are interpolated because of the periodic way in which angles are defined. This poses something of a problem; however, an excellent solution has been waiting in the wings since 1843 when Hamilton [19] developed the mathematics of the quaternion as part of his attempt to find a generalization of the complex number. The significance of the quaternion for computer graphics was first recognized by Shoemake [20] and since then, he and others have explored the topic in detail [21], [22].

For the work in this book it is unnecessary to explore the details of the quaternion in depth. We are interested in using quaternions to help us achieve angular interpolation between given orientations and this requires that we can interpolate between quaternions and switch back and forward between equivalent representations of orientation; i.e., Euler angles, quaternions, and rotation matrices.

2.17.1   The Quaternion

A quaternion q is an ordered pair $(w, \mathbf{v})$ of a scalar and a 3D vector $\mathbf{v}$ with components (x, y, z). Like vectors, a *unit length* or normalized quaternion must satisfy:

$$w^2 + x^2 + y^2 + z^2 = 1$$

Quaternions have their own algebra with rules for addition and multiplication. Addition is straightforward: add the scalar components and the vector components. Multiplication is more interesting. Given two quaternions q_1 and q_2, the product is the quaternion:

$$q_1 q_2 = (w, \mathbf{v}) = (w_1 w_2 - \mathbf{v_1} \cdot \mathbf{v_2}, w_1 \mathbf{v_2} + w_2 \mathbf{v_1} + \mathbf{v_1} \times \mathbf{v_2})$$

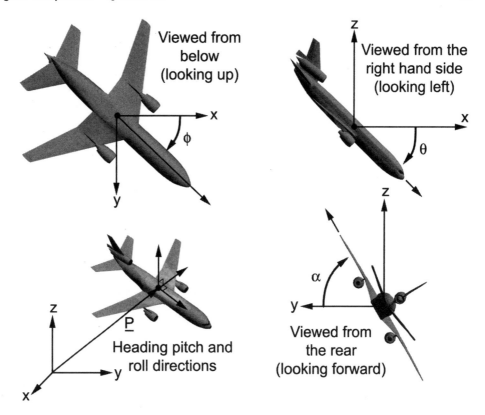

Figure 2.36.   One set of Euler angles (ϕ, θ, ϕ) used to specify orientation. In each of the views the third axis is directed into the page. Each angle is specified by a radian measure relative to a base axis and is considered to be positive when the orientation is clockwise, if observed from the coordinate origin while looking in the direction of the base axis. For computer animation work it is appropriate to think of an object as having a *rest* orientation, say directed along the x-axis without any tilt (roll or bank). To pivot the object into some other orientation a series of rotations are applied until it has taken up the orientation specified by the Euler angles (ϕ, θ, α) relative to the reference direction.

A conjugate quaternion to q is defined as $\bar{q} = (w, -\mathbf{v})$. Thus, the magnitude of q is:

$$q\bar{q} = |q|^2 = w^2 + |\mathbf{v}|^2$$

Note that if q is of unit magnitude its inverse q^{-1} equals its conjugate, $q^{-1} = \bar{q}$ and $q\bar{q} = 1$

2.17.2   Quaternions and Rotations

We have seen in Section 2.11.3 that the action of rotating a vector $\mathbf{r}$ from one orientation to another may be expressed in terms of the application of a transformation matrix $[R]$ which transforms $\mathbf{r}$ to $\mathbf{r}' = [R]\mathbf{r}$ which has a new orientation. The matrix $[R]$ is independent of $\mathbf{r}$ and will perform the same (**relative**) rotation on any other vector.

One can write $[R]$ in terms of the Euler angles, i.e., as a function $[R(\phi, \theta, \alpha)]$; however, the same rotation is achieved by specifying $[R]$ in terms of a unit vector $\hat{\mathbf{n}}$ and a single angle γ. That is, $\mathbf{r}$ is transformed into $\mathbf{r}'$ by rotating it round $\hat{\mathbf{n}}$ through γ. The angle γ is positive when the rotation takes place in a clockwise direction when viewed along $\hat{\mathbf{n}}$ from its base. The two equivalent rotations may be written as:

$$\begin{aligned} \mathbf{r}' &= [R(\phi, \theta, \alpha)]\mathbf{r} \\ \mathbf{r}' &= [R'(\gamma, \hat{\mathbf{n}})]\mathbf{r} \end{aligned}$$

At first sight it might seem difficult to appreciate that the same transformation can be achieved by specifying a single rotation round one axis as opposed to three rotations round three orthogonal axes. It is also quite difficult to imagine how $(\gamma, \hat{\mathbf{n}})$ might be calculated given the more naturally intuitive and easier-to-specify Euler angles (ϕ, θ, α). However, there is a need for methods to switch from one representation to another.

> *In a number of important situations it is necessary to use the $(\gamma, \hat{\mathbf{n}})$ representation. For example the Virtual Reality Modeling Language (VRML) [23] uses the $(\gamma, \hat{\mathbf{n}})$ specification to define the orientation adopted by an object in a virtual world.*

Watt and Watt [24] derive an expression that gives some insight into the significance of the $(\gamma, \hat{\mathbf{n}})$ specification of a rotational transform by determining $[R]\mathbf{r}$ in terms of $(\gamma, \hat{\mathbf{n}})$:

$$\mathbf{r}' = [R]\mathbf{r} = \cos\gamma\,\mathbf{r} + (1 - \cos\gamma)(\hat{\mathbf{n}} \cdot \mathbf{r})\hat{\mathbf{n}} + (\sin\gamma)\hat{\mathbf{n}} \times \mathbf{r} \qquad (2.30)$$

This expression is the vital link between rotational transformations and the use of quaternions to represent them. To see this consider two quaternions:

1. $p = (0, \mathbf{r})$, a quaternion formed by setting its scalar part to zero and its vector part to $\mathbf{r}$ (the vector we wish to transform) and

2. $q = (w, \mathbf{v})$, an arbitrary quaternion with unit magnitude: $q\bar{q} = qq^{-1} = 1$

The product qpq^{-1} gives the quaternion:

$$qpq^{-1} = (0, (w^2 - (\mathbf{v} \cdot \mathbf{v})\mathbf{r} + 2(\mathbf{v} \cdot \mathbf{r})\mathbf{v} + 2w(\mathbf{v} \times \mathbf{r}))) \qquad (2.31)$$

Since q is an arbitrary quaternion of unit magnitude there is no loss of generality by expressing it in the form:

$$q = \left(\cos\left(\frac{\gamma}{2}\right), \sin\left(\frac{\gamma}{2}\right)\hat{\mathbf{n}}\right) \tag{2.32}$$

by substituting $\cos\left(\frac{\gamma}{2}\right)$ for w and $\sin\left(\frac{\gamma}{2}\right)\hat{\mathbf{n}}$ for $\mathbf{v}$ in Equation 2.31. The vector part of qpq^{-1} is identical, term for term, with the rotation expressed by Equation 2.30. Therefore if we express a rotation in the form $[R(\gamma, \hat{\mathbf{n}})]$, its action on a vector $\mathbf{r}$ is equivalent to operating the following four steps:

1. Promote the vector $\mathbf{r}$ to the quaternion $p = (0, \mathbf{r})$

2. Express $[R(\gamma, \hat{\mathbf{n}})]$ as the quaternion $q = (\cos\frac{\gamma}{2}, \sin\frac{\gamma}{2}\hat{\mathbf{n}})$

3. Evaluate the quaternion product $p' = qpq^{-1}$, and finally

4. Extract the transformed vector $\mathbf{r}'$ from the vector component of $p' = (0, \mathbf{r}')$. (Note that the scalar component of operations such as these will always be zero.)

This isn't the end of our story of quaternions because, just as rotational transformations in matrix form may be combined into a single matrix, rotations in quaternion form may be combined into a single quaternion by multiplying their individual quaternion representations together. For example consider rotations $[R_1]$ and $[R_2]$ represented by quaternions q_1 and q_2 respectively. Applying them in turn to $p' = q_1 p q_1^{-1}$ and $p'' = q_2 p' q_2^{-1}$ gives:

$$
\begin{aligned}
p'' &= q_2 p' q_2^{-1} \\
p'' &= q_2 (q_1 p q_1^{-1}) q_2^{-1} \\
p'' &= (q_2 q_1) p (q_1^{-1} q_2^{-1}) \text{ and finally} \\
p'' &= q_c p q_c^{-1}
\end{aligned}
$$

Here $q_c = q_2 q_1$ and as quaternions satisfy $(q_2 q_1)^{-1} = q_1^{-1} q_2^{-1}$, we can write $(q_1^{-1} q_2^{-1}) = (q_2 q_1)^{-1}$.

2.17.3 Converting Euler Angles to Quaternion

From the Euler angles (ϕ, θ, α) shown in Figure 2.36, a quaternion that *encapsulates the same information* is constructed by writing quaternions for rotation ϕ about the $\mathbf{z}$, θ about the $\mathbf{y}$ and α about the $\mathbf{x}$-axes:

$$q_{\mathbf{x}} = \left[\cos\frac{\alpha}{2}, \sin\frac{\alpha}{2}, 0, 0\right]$$

$$q_{\mathbf{y}} = \left[\cos\frac{\theta}{2}, 0, \sin\frac{\theta}{2}, 0\right]$$

$$q_{\mathbf{z}} = \left[\cos\frac{\phi}{2}, 0, 0, \sin\frac{\phi}{2}\right]$$

and then multiplying them together as $q = q_{\mathbf{z}}q_{\mathbf{y}}q_{\mathbf{x}}$. The components of q are:

$$w = \cos\frac{\alpha}{2}\cos\frac{\theta}{2}\cos\frac{\phi}{2} + \sin\frac{\alpha}{2}\sin\frac{\theta}{2}\sin\frac{\phi}{2}$$

$$x = \sin\frac{\alpha}{2}\cos\frac{\theta}{2}\cos\frac{\phi}{2} - \cos\frac{\alpha}{2}\sin\frac{\theta}{2}\sin\frac{\phi}{2}$$

$$y = \cos\frac{\alpha}{2}\sin\frac{\theta}{2}\cos\frac{\phi}{2} + \sin\frac{\alpha}{2}\cos\frac{\theta}{2}\sin\frac{\phi}{2}$$

$$z = \cos\frac{\alpha}{2}\cos\frac{\theta}{2}\sin\frac{\phi}{2} - \sin\frac{\alpha}{2}\sin\frac{\theta}{2}\cos\frac{\phi}{2}$$

2.17.4   Converting a Quaternion to a Matrix

In Section 2.11.3 it was shown that a rotational transformation in matrix form could be applied to a position vector to pivot it into a new orientation $[p'] = [T_\theta][p]$. A quaternion contains rotational information but it cannot be directly applied to a position vector in the same way that a matrix can. Therefore it is useful to have a method of expressing the rotational information in the quaternion directly as a matrix which in turn can be used to rotate position vectors.

For a normalized quaternion $[w, x, y, z]$ the corresponding 4×4 matrix is:

$$\begin{bmatrix} 1 - 2y^2 - 2z^2 & 2xy + 2wz & 2xz - 2wy & 0 \\ 2xy - 2wz & 1 - 2x^2 - 2z^2 & 2yz + 2wx & 0 \\ 2xz + 2wy & 2yz - 2wx & 1 - 2x^2 - 2y^2 & 0 \\ 0 & 0 & 0 & 1 \end{bmatrix}$$

It is important to note that a 4×4 matrix can encapsulate positional transformations as well as rotational ones. A unit quaternion only describes pure rotations. So, when quaternions are combined the complex rotation they represent is with respect to axes passing through the coordinate origin $(0, 0, 0)$.

2.17.5   Converting a Matrix to a Quaternion

If the rotational matrix is given by:

$$[M] = \begin{bmatrix} a_{00} & a_{01} & a_{02} & 0 \\ a_{10} & a_{11} & a_{12} & 0 \\ a_{20} & a_{21} & a_{22} & 0 \\ 0 & 0 & 0 & 1 \end{bmatrix}$$

and the quaternion q by:

$$q = [w, x, y, z]$$

Shoemake's [20] algorithm of Figure 2.37 obtains q given $[M]$.

2.17.6 Converting a Quaternion to Euler Angles

To convert the quaternion to the equivalent Euler angles, first convert the quaternion to an equivalent matrix, and then use the matrix to Euler angle conversion algorithm. Sadly matrix to Euler angle conversion is unavoidably ill-defined because the calculations involve inverse trigonometric functions. To achieve this conversion use the algorithm shown in Figure 2.38 which converts the matrix $[M]$ with elements a_{ij} to Euler angles (ϕ, θ, α).

The angles (ϕ, θ, ϕ) lie in the interval $[-\pi, \pi]$ but they can be biased to $[0, 2\pi]$ or some other suitable range if required.

2.17.7 Interpolating Quaternions

The advantage of using quaternions in 3D computer graphics work that is that interpolation between two orientations $(\phi_0, \theta_0, \alpha_0)$ and $(\phi_1, \theta_1, \alpha_1)$ when expressed in their quaternion form is easily done. To illustrate the advantage of quaternions we recall that *linear* interpolation between two position vectors gives a straight line and in Cartesian geometry a straight line is the shortest path between two points. A similarly simple interpolation for quaternions is desirable. Therefore for quaternions the question arises: what is equivalent to a straight line?

A clue to the answer comes from the concept of latitude and longitude. Latitude and longitude are angular directions from the center of the earth to a point on its surface whose position is desired. Thus a pair of values *(lat, long)* represent a point on the earth's surface. To go from one place to another by the shortest route one follows a *Great Circle*, illustrated in Figure 2.39. The great circle is the line of intersection between a sphere and a plane that passes through the center of the sphere. Intercontinental flight paths for aircraft follow great circles; for example, the flight path between London and Tokyo passes close to the North Pole. We can therefore say that just as the shortest distance between two points in a Cartesian frame of reference is by a straight line, the shortest distance between two *(latitude,longitude)* coordinates is along a *path* following a great circle. The *(latitude,longitude)* coordinates at intermediate points on the *great circle* are determined by interpolation, in this case by *spherical interpolation*.

Quaternions are used for this interpolation. We think of the end points of the path being specified by quaternions q_0 and q_1. From these a quaternion q_i is interpolated for any point on the Great Circle joining q_0 to q_1. Conversion of q_i back to *(latitude, longitude)* allows the path to be plotted. In terms of angular

$$w = \tfrac{1}{4}(1 + a_{00} + a_{11} + a_{22})$$

```
if w > ε {
```

$$w = \sqrt{w}$$

$$w_4 = \frac{1}{4w}$$

$$x = w_4(a_{12} - a_{21})$$
$$y = w_4(a_{20} - a_{02})$$
$$z = w_4(a_{01} - a_{10})$$

```
}
else {
```

$$w = 0$$
$$x = -\tfrac{1}{2}(a_{11} + a_{22})$$

```
    if x > ε {
```

$$x = \sqrt{x}$$

$$x_2 = \frac{1}{2x}$$

$$y = x_2 a_{01}$$
$$z = x_2 a_{02}$$

```
    }
    else {
```

$$x = 0$$
$$y = \tfrac{1}{2}(1 - a_{22})$$

```
        if y > ε {
```

$$y = \sqrt{y}$$
$$z = \frac{a_{12}}{2y}$$

```
        }
        else {
```

$$y = 0$$
$$z = 1$$

```
        }
    }
}
```

Figure 2.37.   An algorithm for the conversion of rotational transformation matrix $[M]$ with coefficients $a_{i,j}$ to quaternion q with coefficients (w, x, y, z). The parameter ϵ is the machine precision of zero. A reasonable choice would be 10^{-6} for floating point calculations. Note: Only elements of $[M]$ that contribute to rotation are considered in the algorithm.

$$\sin \theta = -a_{02}$$
$$\cos \theta = \sqrt{1 - \sin^2 \theta}$$
if $| \cos \theta | < \epsilon$ {

 It is not possible to distinguish heading
 from pitch and the convention that
 ϕ is 0 is assumed, thus:

$$\sin \alpha = -a_{21}$$
$$\cos \alpha = a_{11}$$
$$\sin \phi = 0$$
$$\cos \phi = 1$$
}
else {

$$\sin \alpha = \frac{a_{12}}{\cos \theta}$$
$$\cos \alpha = \frac{a_{22}}{\cos \theta}$$
$$\sin \phi = \frac{a_{01}}{\cos \theta}$$
$$\cos \phi = \frac{a_{00}}{\cos \theta}$$
}
$$\alpha = ATAN2(\sin \alpha, \cos \alpha)$$
$$\theta = ATAN2(\sin \theta, \cos \theta)$$
$$\phi = ATAN2(\sin \phi, \cos \phi)$$

Figure 2.38. Conversion from rotational transformation matrix to the equivalent Euler angles of rotation.

interpolation we may think of latitude and longitude as simply two of the Euler angles. When extended to the full set (ϕ, θ, α) a smooth interpolation along the equivalent of a Great Circle is the result.

Using the concept of moving along a Great Circle as a guide to angular interpolation a *Spherical Interpolation function*, *slerp()* may be derived. The form of this function that works for interpolating between quaternions $q_0 = [w_0, x_0, y_0, z_0]$ and $q_1 = [w_1, x_1, y_1, z_1]$ is given in [20] as:

$$slerp(\mu, q_0, q_1) = \frac{\sin(1 - \mu)\theta}{\sin \theta} q_0 + \frac{\sin \mu \theta}{\sin \theta} q_1$$

Where μ, the interpolation parameter, takes values in the range $[0, 1]$. The angle θ is obtained from $\cos \theta = q_0 \cdot q_1 = w_0 w_1 + x_0 x_1 + y_0 y_1 + z_0 z_1$. The following

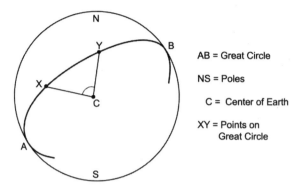

N

Y

B

X

C

S

A

AB = Great Circle

NS = Poles

C = Center of Earth

XY = Points on
        Great Circle

Figure 2.39.   A Great Circle gives a path of shortest distance between two points on the surface of a
sphere. The arc between points X and Y is the shortest path.

algorithmic implementation of the $slerp()$ function for the interpolated quaternion
$q_i = [w_i, x_i, y_i, z_i]$ avoids the problem of division by zero when θ is close to zero.

$$\sigma = w_0w_1 + x_0x_1 + y_0y_1 + z_0z_1$$
if $\sigma > 1$ then normalize q_0 and q_1 by
    dividing the components of q_0 and q_1 by σ
$$\theta = \cos^{-1}(\sigma)$$
if $|\theta| < \epsilon$ {
$$\beta_0 = 1 - \mu$$
$$\beta_1 = \mu$$
}
else {
$$\beta_0 = \frac{\sin(1 - \mu)\theta}{\sin\theta}$$
$$\beta_1 = \frac{\sin\mu\theta}{\sin\theta}$$
}
$$w_i = \beta_0 w_0 + \beta_1 w_1$$
$$x_i = \beta_0 z_0 + \beta_1 x_1$$
$$y_i = \beta_0 y_0 + \beta_1 y_1$$
$$z_i = \beta_0 z_0 + \beta_1 z_1$$

References

[1] P. Burger and D. Gillies, *Interactive Computer Graphics.* Addison-Wesley, Reading MA, 1989.

[2] A. Watt, *Fundamentals of Three-Dimensional Computer Graphics.* Addision-Wesley, Reading, MA, 1990.

[3] V. B. Anand, *Computer Graphics and Geometric Modeling for Engineers.* John Wiley and Sons, NY, 1993.

[4] J. D. Foley, A. Van Dam, *Fundamentals of Interactive Computer Graphics.* Addison-Wesley, Reading MA, 1982.

[5] D. F. Rogers and J. A. Adams, *Mathematical Elements for Computer Graphics, Second Edition.* McGraw-Hill, New York, 1990.

[6] J. D. Foley, A. Van Dam, S. K. Feiner and J. F. Hughes, *Computer Graphics — Principles and Practice.* Addison-Wesley, Reading MA, 1989.

[7] Ray Tracing News web site *www.raytracingnews.org.*

[8] D. Badouel, An Efficient Ray-Polygon Intersection in *Graphics Gems I* Academic Press, Cambridge MA, 1990.

[9] Möller and Trumbore, *Journal of Graphics Tools* www.acm.org/jgt.

[10] S. Lipschutz, *Linear Algebra.* Schaum's Outline Series, McGraw-Hill, New York.

[11] F. Ayres, *Matrices.* Schaum's Outline Series. McGraw-Hill, New York.

[12] R. H. Crowell and R. E. Williamson, *Calculus of Vector Functions.* Prentice-Hall, Englewood Cliffs NJ. 1962.

[13] T. Möller and E. Haines, *Real-Time Rendering.* A K Peters, Natick MA, 1999, page 41.

[14] P. Burger and D. Gillies, *Interactive Computer Graphics.* Addison-Wesley, Reading MA, 1989, Chapter 6.

[15] P. Burger and D. Gillies, *Interactive Computer Graphics.* Addison-Wesley, Reading MA, 1989, Section 6.2 pages 243-245.

[16] Adobe Systems Inc. *Postscript Language Reference Manual.* Addison-Wesley, Reading, MA. 1990.

[17] R. H. Bartles, J. C. Beatty, B. A. Barsky, *An Introduction to Splines for use in Computer Graphics and Geometric Modeling.* Morgan Kaufmann, Los Altos CA, 1987.

[18] J. W. Peterson, *Tessellation of NURB Surfaces.* in *Graphics Gems IV*, Academic Press, San Diego CA, 1994.

[19] W. R. Hamilton, *On quaternions: Or on a new system of imaginaries in algebra.* Philosophical Magazine, Vol. 25, 1844, pages 10-14.

[20] K. Shoemake, *Animating Rotation with Quaternion Curves.* SIGGRAPH 85 Conference Proc. pages 245–54, Association of Computing Machinery, July 1985.

[21] K. Shoemake, *Quaternion Calculus and Fast Animation.* Siggraph Course Notes, Vol. 10, 1985.

[22] M. Mac an Airchinnigh *Quaternions for Rotation*, Proc. First Irish Computer Graphics Workshop, Trinity College Dublin, Nov. 1992.

[23] J. Hartman and J. Wernecke, *The VRML 2.0 Handbook: Building Moving Worlds on the Web.* Addison-Wesley, Reading, MA, 1996.

[24] A. Watt and M. Watt, *Advanced Animation and Rendering Techniques: Theory and Practice.* Addison-Wesley, Reading MA, 1992 page 359.

[25] B. A. Wichman and I. D. Hill, *An Efficient and Portable Pseudo-Random Number Generator.* Applied Statistics, Vol 32, No 2, 188–190, 1992.

[26] P. Burger and D. Gillies, *Interactive Computer Graphics.* Addison-Wesley, Reading MA, 1989, Section 5.7.2 page 287.

[27] T. R. McCalla, *Introduction to Numerical Methods and FORTRAN Programming.* John Wiley and Sons, NY, 1967.

CHAPTER **3**

Data Structures for 3D Graphics

The visual appearance of 3D models representing all kinds of objects is dictated by the properties of their surfaces, with color being the most important. Often the surface of a model is constructed by building it up from a series of primitive shapes. A polygon with three sides (*a triangle*) is the simplest form of primitive shape. In Chapter 2 other simple primitives like the sphere were discussed. Today in CAD application programs more complex surface shapes referred to as *patches* have proved popular. These include Bézier and NURBS (Non-Uniform Rational B-Spline) patches which have curved edges and continuously varying internal curvature. A model can usually be accurately represented by combining a few of these more sophisticated surface shapes. Whether using primitive polygons or curved patches to describe a model there are advantages and disadvantages. The simplest polygon is fast to render and easy to manipulate, the more complex patches usually give a better approximation to the original object, especially if it has many curved parts. Occasionally, it is a matter of personal preference which sort of patch to use. For example, a cube is modeled just as effectively with triangular polygons as it is with Bézier patches. Figure 3.1 shows the famous Utah Teapot in Polygonal and Bézier patch form.

Whatever type of patch is used to describe the surface of a 3D model it must be *located* in space, which means attaching it to three or more *vertices* or points somewhere in 3D space. With appropriate transformations applied to the vertex coordinates a visualization (more commonly called a rendering) can be produced on the computer monitor or other output device.

The minimal description of a 3D model requires a list of surface patches and a list of vertex coordinates. Each entry in the surface patch list must identify the vertices to which it is connected and have some way of allowing its surface to take on the appearance of wood, marble, glass, chrome, etc. Indeed, one of the most popular ways to provide a comprehensive set of surface attributes is for each surface patch to store an index into a table of *materials*. The material provides a

Figure 3.1.   Polygonal and Bézier patch surface representations.

color and many other properties. With careful choice of parameter an extremely realistic look to the model can be achieved.

Despite the fact that real-time shading can now be done routinely on basic personal computers it can still be useful to use a wireframe display when designing interactive 3D animations or complex models. Shaded rendering is done in a subsequent step to whatever degree of realism is required, a process that can take minutes or even hours.

A wireframe model is a set of straight lines that join vertices together. The edges of each polygonal surface constitute the members of this set. Sometimes it can be useful to maintain a separate list of edges rather than to have to generate it from the polygons each time a drawing of the wireframe is made. This policy has the advantage of a faster display and, since edges are not normally rendered, they can be used to link various parts of a model together for editing purposes.

There are three alternative schemes for storing the geometric description of a model:

1. For the n vertices of each surface polygon store n integers. Each integer identifies an entry in the vertex list. For each entry in the vertex list store the coordinates (x, y, z) of a position vector. Most 3D programs store (x, y, z) as single precision floating point numbers, but a few use `long` integers. If polygon edges are needed then they can be obtained by pairing consecutive vertices.

2. For each surface polygon that is connected to n vertices store n integers. Each integer identifies an entry in the vertex list. For each entry in the vertex list store a position vector giving its (x, y, z)-coordinates. If required a separate list for the m edges can be included. It holds two integers for each edge that index entries in the vertex list.

3. For each surface polygon with k edges store k integers identifying the entry in an edge list. An edge list identifies connections between vertices.

Normally edges are part of the boundaries of polygons but it is possible to have edges in a model that have no connection with its polygonal surfaces. These will show up in a wireframe drawing of the model but will not be visible in either a hidden line or shaded rendering. For each edge, store two integers to index entries in the vertex list corresponding to the vertices at the end of the edge. For each entry in the vertex list store a position vector giving its (x, y, z)-coordinates.

These organizations are summarized in Figure 3.2.

To complete the requirements for a useful data structure we add a material index for each polygon and *texture coordinates* to every vertex. *Texture coordinates* allow a two-dimensional frame of reference to cover the surface of a model, rather like the way latitude and longitude are a two-dimensional coordinate system used to reference any point on the surface of the earth (a 3D spheroid).

In addition to this information it is a good idea to add a few temporary variables to the structure for use by modeling and rendering algorithms. For example, some of the algorithms described in Chapter 7 require additional members in the data structures for vertices, edges, and faces.

3.1   Structure Addressing Conventions

The pseudo-code algorithms given here refer to members of data structures. For example, the vertex data structure contains a position vector and texture coordinates. So, if the members of the vertex data structure are:

p	position vector of vertex
ν, μ	surface texture coordinates

and $Vert$ is defined as an array of vertex structures, then the position vector for array element i can be referenced by

$$Vert(i).\mathbf{p}$$

To address a member of a structure the **C**-like method of using a '.' is employed.

Since **p** is a vector it is represented in the computer as an array of three floating point numbers and as a result the three coordinate components can be addressed individually by:

$$Vert(i).\mathbf{p}(j)$$

For example, to extract the μ texture coordinate for vertex 6 into a temporary variable one would write $x = Vert(5).\mu$.

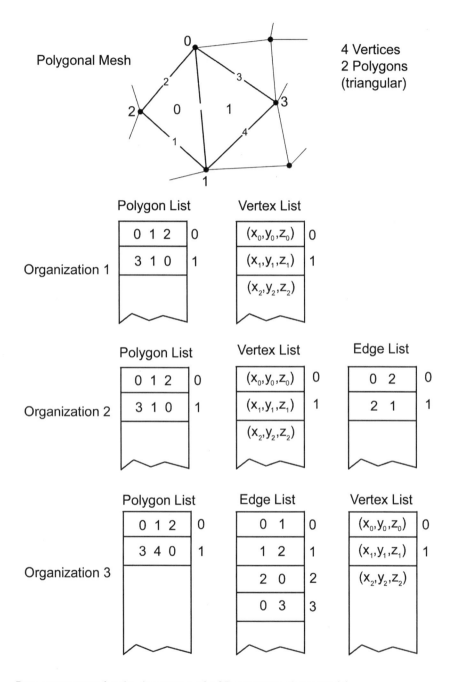

3.2 Linked Lists or Arrays of Structures?

In the first data organization scheme (illustrated in Figure 3.2) two lists of data describe a 3D model. The question remains: how should these lists be organized efficiently? There are two useful ways to do this:

1. A doubly-linked list of structures

   A doubly-linked list as illustrated in Figures 3.3 and 3.4 is preferable when the data structure is to be modified frequently, for example in a 3D CAD design package. In this setup it is very easy to remove or insert an item. Unfortunately the method requires additional memory for the list pointers. Also, because memory allocation/deallocation procedures can be quite slow when tens of thousands of small memory blocks are needed, performance may be noticeably degraded.

2. An array of structures

   An array of structures is good for rapid indexing, as in rendering algorithms. However, adding and particularly deleting entries, can be very slow.

   For both methods it is assumed that dynamic memory allocation is available with procedures to perform the following functions:

   (a) Allocate a block of memory of size n bytes.

   (b) Reallocate a block of memory to a new size of m bytes.
       Notes:

       i. *The reallocated memory might not be returned at the same location in the address space.*

       ii. *If $m > n$ then the first n bytes of reallocated memory will maintain the integrity of the original data.*

       iii. *If $m < n$ then the first m bytes will remain unchanged*

   (c) Release the block of memory previously allocated so that it can be used again.

In common with all computer applications, the careful use of these functions is required for a robust graphics program. Choosing the best method of data organization clearly depends on the application. So, if your application is primarily used for design and modeling, a doubly linked list should be favored; if you want to render models with tens of thousands of polygons as quickly as possible, then a single array of structure is preferable.

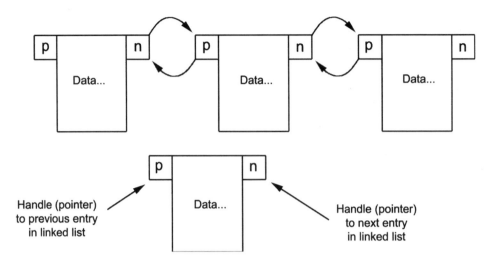

Figure 3.3.   A doubly-linked list before adding an extra item.

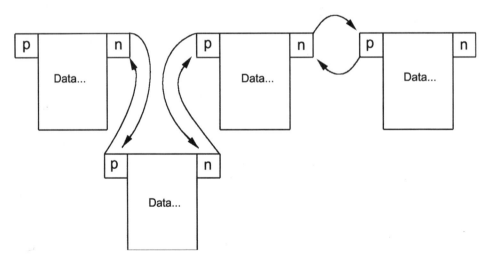

Figure 3.4.   A doubly-linked list after insertion of a new item.

3.3   Algorithms for Editing Arrays of Structures

When structures are to be accessed consecutively, using *arrays of data structures* usually give optimal performance. (Access by pointer indexation in the **C** language, for example.) When such a data organization is chosen, editing functions are needed and so a quick procedure must be developed to allow items to be inserted and or removed from the list.

For 3D data, the order in which polygons and vertices appear in a list is usually unimportant. Therefore, when items are added to a list, they can simply be tagged on to the end. Of course, the memory has to be dynamically extended to accommodate the extra items. To delete items from the list is more complex and if not done efficiently can be unacceptably time consuming. This section presents a very efficient algorithm for the removal of one or more items from anywhere in a list of vertex or polygon data structures.

Figure 3.5 illustrates a representation of the list of polygon structures; those to be deleted are marked with a *. Each structure will be composed of perhaps 16 - 32 bytes. The last entry n could be removed simply by reallocating the memory space to hold $n - 1$ polygons, but to eliminate polygon 2 the data for polygons 3 to n must be shifted to lower memory before the memory is reallocated. However this shifting operation is very slow and it gets slower if there are other entries to be removed later. Note that the vertex and polygon lists are *dependent*, because each polygon list entry points to an entry in the vertex list; therefore, if the vertex list is modified, even if the polygon list is not, the polygon vertex identifiers will need to be updated, a process termed *re-vectoring*.

A very fast scheme can be developed by using the fact that the order of items in the list is unimportant. In this case all that has to be done is to copy the last entry in the list into the place held by the item to be deleted. The list may then be shortened by one entry. If several items are deleted the reduction in the size of the list is done in one step. In the example shown in Figure 3.5, copy item $n - 1$ to item 2 (remember item n is also to be deleted).

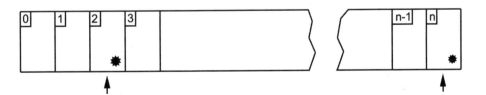

Figure 3.5.   Array of *polygon structures* numbered 1 to n.

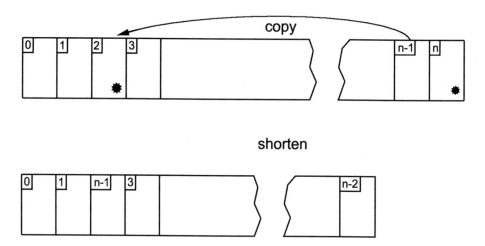

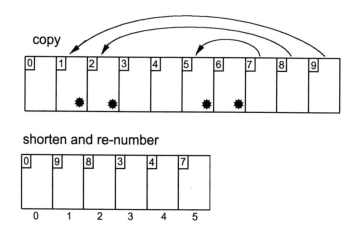

Figure 3.6.   Deleting two items from the list of structures.

The whole of the structure can be copied with one call to a fast *memory copy* function, usually available as part of any system API (*Application Programming Interface*). The algorithm works through the list and when it finds an entry to be deleted it copies an entry from the end of the list and shortens the list by one. See the examples illustrated in Figures 3.6 and 3.7. When all the entries have been processed one call to the reallocation function tidies up the memory.

Figure 3.7.   Deleting multiple items from the list.

```
set i = 0, k = 0 and newN = Npolys
repeat while i < Npolys {
    if Poly(k) flagged for deletion {
        if i < Npolys − 1 {
            copy size of Poly structure (bytes)
                from Poly(newN − 1) to Poly(k)
        }
        newN = newN − 1
    }
    else k = k + 1
    i = i + 1
}
Npolys = newN
```

Figure 3.8.   Outline of an algorithm to remove unwanted entries from a list of $Npoly$ $Poly$ structures. The unwanted entries will be *flagged* in some convenient manner.

The algorithm for removing unwanted entries from a list of $Poly$ structures with $Npolys$ entries is summarized in Figure 3.8. Note that by not indexing k when the structure is to be deleted we get the chance to immediately delete the one replacing it if it too is flagged for deletion.

This algorithm can be applied to the polygon and vertex lists in exactly the same way. However, as mentioned above, any change to the vertex list will invalidate entries in the polygon and edge lists that point to items in the vertex list. For example, if a polygon is attached to vertices $100, 101, 102$ in the vertex list but vertex 2 is removed from the list, then vertices indexed as $100, 102$, or 103 may have moved to a different place in the vertex list. So, if we don't fix up the polygon data a memory violation will probably occur, at the very least the model will be a mess.

The fix is easily done by employing a dummy index variable in the vertex structure. As the algorithm steps through the vertex list copying down from the end to over-write the entries to be erased, it writes into the dummy index of the copied entry *the location where the copy has moved to.* At the end of the pass, but before the vertex list is resized, the polygon list is scanned again so that each reference to an entry in the vertex list is tested. If the reference points to one of the vertices that have been moved, then it is replaced by the new location (stored in the dummy index) that was determined in the first pass. Memory reallocation completes the algorithm. This algorithm is shown in detail in Figure 3.9.

Such a scheme is very efficient and uses as few operations as possible when removing items from a 3D data structure which has been stored in a contiguous memory block.

Erase items from the Polygon list but don't
release the recovered memory yet

set $i = 0, k = 0, j = 0$ and $newN = Nverts$
repeat while $i < Nverts$ {
    if $Vert(k)$ flagged for deletion {
        if $i < Nverts - 1$ {
            copy size of $Vert$ structure (bytes)
            from $Vert(newN - 1)$ to $Vert(k)$
            $Vert(newN - 1).x = j$ (extra index in $Vert$ structure)
        }
        $newN = newN - 1$
    }
    else {
        $k = k + 1$
        $j = j + 1$
    }
    $i = i + 1$
}
$Nvert = newN$

Now process the dependent $Poly$ data structure to fix it up

set $i = 0$
repeat while $i < Npolys$ {
    set $j = 0$
    repeat while $j < NvertPerPoly$ {
        if $Poly(i).V_{id}(j) \geq Nvert$ {
            $Poly(i).V_{id}(j) = Vert(Poly(i).V_{id}(j)).x$
        }
        $j = j + 1$
    }
    $i = i + 1$
}

Tidy up the memory allocation for $Poly$ and $Vert$ structures

Figure 3.9.   Details of the algorithm to remove unwanted entries from a polygonal database when the database uses a contiguous list rather than a doubly linked list to record the polygons and vertices.

3.4 Making an Edge List from a List of Polygonal Faces

When producing a wireframe drawing of a model or converting between the data formats of alternative 3D CAD and animation packages it is important to be able to build a list of *edges* from a list of *polygons*.

It is straightforward to make a list of edges by creating one edge for each polygon side, but most polygons will share edges. The task of removing multiple entries from the edge list becomes excessively time consuming as the number of polygons increase. In the case of n polygons approximately $3n^2$ tests need to be performed to make sure that the same edge is not recorded more than once in the edge list. When dealing with more than a few hundred polygons it is essential to find a more efficient procedure.

The following gives the outline of an algorithm that deals with the issue more efficiently:

- For each vertex i in the model set up a list to hold the identity of other vertices in the model attached to vertex i by an edge. Initially these lists will be empty.

- Take each polygon in the model in turn and with every edge of the polygon consider the vertices at both ends of the edge.

- Label the vertices j and k. For vertex j look at j's list of adjacent vertices. If it is empty or does not contain vertex k then add k to j's list. For vertex k look at its list of adjacent vertices and if it is empty or does not contain vertex j then add j to k's list.

- When all the polygons have been examined consider each vertex in turn. Call the current one i. For vertex i create an edge between vertex i and all the vertices in i's list of attached vertices. For an example see Figure 3.10.

Vertex	Vertex attached to...		Edges
0	0	1,2,3	0 - 1
1	1	1,4,6,9	0 - 2
2	2	...	0 - 3
3	3		1 - 4
.	.		1 - 6
.	.		1 - 9
n	n	7,11,19	

Figure 3.10. Building an edge list from a polygon list.

$\mathbf{p}$	position vector of vertex
ν, μ	surface texture coordinates
x	temporary integer index
n	number of adjacent vertices
V_{adj}	list of adjacent vertices

Figure 3.11.   Entries in the vertex data structure.

The advantage of this procedure comes from the fact that the number of comparison tests will be very many fewer than would be required by the simplistic approach of checking all polygons against all polygons.

To accommodate the adjacency list it is necessary to augment the vertex data structure with two items, n and V_{adj} as shown in Figure 3.11. V_{adj} is a dynamically sized array of vertex identifiers.

Pseudo-code for the algorithm outlined on page 73 is given in Figures 3.12 and 3.13. Part 1 of the algorithm calls to a subroutine which inserts vertices in the adjacency list and extends it if necessary.

Part 1 Recording

set $i = 0$ and repeat while $i < Npolys$ {
    InsertInVertexList($Poly(i).V_{id}(0), Poly(i).V_{id}(1)$)
    InsertInVertexList($Poly(i).V_{id}(1), Poly(i).V_{id}(2)$)
    InsertInVertexList($Poly(i).V_{id}(2), Poly(i).V_{id}(0)$)
    $i = i + 1$
}

Part 2 Building Edges

set $i = 0$ and repeat while $i < Nvert$ {
    if $Vert(i).n > 0$ {
        set $j = 0$ and repeat while $j < Vert(i).n$ {
            Create edge between vertices i and $Nvert(i).V_{adj}(j)$
            $j = j + 1$
        }
    }
    $i = i + 1$
}

Figure 3.12.   Part one of the algorithm to make an edge list from a list of connected polygonal facets.

Subroutine InsertInVertexList(V_1, V_2)
V_1 and V_2 are indexes into the vertex list

if $Vert(V_1).n > 0$ {
    set $i = 0$ and repeat while $i < Vert(V_1).n$ {
        if $Vert(V_1).V_{adj}(i) = V_2$ then already present so return
        $i = i + 1$
    }
}
if $Vert(V_2).n > 0$ {
    set $i = 0$ and repeat while $i < Vert(V_2).n$ {
        if $Vert(V_2).V_{adj}(i) = V_1$ then already present so return
        $i = i + 1$
    }
}
Extend the list $Vert(V_1).V_{adj}$ by 1
$Vert(V_1).V_{adj}(Vert(V_1).n) = V_2$
$Vert(V_1).n = Vert(V_1).n + 1$

Figure 3.13.   Part two of the algorithm to make an edge list from a list of connected polygonal facets. In part two the subroutine checks to see if an edge already has an entry in the edge list.

In the subroutine (part 2) the adjacency lists for vertices V_1 and V_2 are checked. If an entry is already present in the list the subroutine returns immediately.

3.5   Hierarchical Models

Partitioning a polygonal model into sub-units that are linked in a parent-child-grandchild relationship is useful. For example hierarchical linkages are very significant in character animation. An easily implemented and practically useful scheme is one that is analogous to the familiar filestore structure of computer systems; i.e., a root directory with files and subdirectories which themselves contain files and subdirectories and so on to whatever depth you like.

A doubly linked list of *hierarchy* entries is the best way to organize this data. In addition to *previous* and *next* pointers each entry will have a pointer to its *parent*; see Figure 3.14. Other data can easily be appended to the structure as necessary. When using the structure for character animation or to reference parts of a big model, the entries can be given symbolic names, an example of which is shown in Figure 3.14.

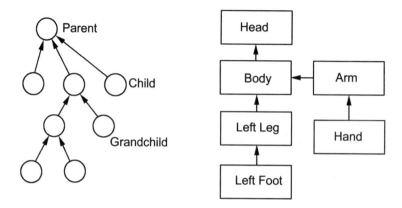

Figure 3.14.   A hierarchical data structure for editing and character animation.

To complete a hierarchical description every polygon or vertex in the model is identified with one of the hierarchical names, a similar concept to the one in which files on a computer disk are identified by the folders in which they are stored.

In a connected network of vertices and facets it is probably more useful to associate vertices, rather than polygons, with one of the hierarchical names. To implement this association the vertex data structure shown in Figure 3.11 must be extended with the entry h_{id} where, for a vertex h_{id}, identifies which hierarchical name the vertex is associated with. The new structure is shown Figure 3.15. A basic version of a structure that specifies a polygonal surface patch is illustrated in Figure 3.16.

Note: The hierarchical names do not record any information about which vertices are assigned to them. Thus if it becomes necessary to modify the vertex lists (by adding or deleting, for example) there is no need to update the hierarchy. However, the converse is **not** true. If a name in the hierarchy is removed, then all the vertices must be checked for any reference to the deleted hierarchical name and that reference removed.

$\mathbf{p}$	position vector of vertex
ν, μ	surface texture coordinates
x	temporary integer index
n	number of adjacent vertices
V_{adj}	list of adjacent vertices
h_{id}	pointer to hierarchical element vertex is assigned to

Figure 3.15.   Vertex data structure with hierarchical identifier.

V_{id}	list of vertex ids to which polygon is attached
$id_{material}$	pointer to material in materials list
n	normal to surface plane

Figure 3.16.   Typical surface patch data structure.

3.6   Finding Adjacent Polygons

Some of the algorithms to be discussed in later chapters require that every polygon (in a mesh model) knows the identity of its neighboring polygons. A neighboring polygon is one that shares an edge. For the example in Figure 3.17, polygons 1 and 2 share an edge as do polygons 2 and 3.

Algorithms that need this information include:

- Delaunay triangulation.

- Subdivision of surfaces.

- Algorithm to make surface normal orientations consistent.

Like the procedure for finding edges given a set of polygons (section 3.4) finding adjacent polygons can be a prohibitively lengthy task if an exhaustive comparison is used.

The algorithm below describes a procedure that will be significantly faster than an exhaustive comparison; it is known to work with many thousands of triangular polygons. In principle this procedure is quite similar to the *edge-generating* algorithm of Section 3.4. However, before it can be used, the vertex

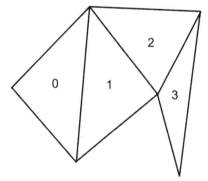

Polygon	Adjacent To		
0	-1	-1	1
1	0	2	-1
2	1	-1	3
3	2	-1	-1

Figure 3.17.   Identity of adjacent triangular polygons.

$\mathbf{p}$	position vector of vertex
ν, μ	surface texture coordinates
x	temporary integer index
n_V	number of adjacent vertices
V_{adj}	list of adjacent vertices
h_{id}	pointer to hierarchical element to assign vertex to
n_F	number of adjacent polygons
F_{adj}	list of adjacent polygons

V_{id}	list of vertex ids to which polygon is attached
$id_{material}$	pointer to material in materials list
$A_{id}(3)$	list of the ids of polygons with a common side
$\mathbf{n}$	normal to surface plane

Figure 3.18.   Vertex and polygon data structures to accommodate calculation and storage of polygon adjacency information.

data structure must be enhanced by adding a counter for the number of adjacent polygons and a list to identify them. Also, the polygon data structure needs a list in which to store the identity of the adjacent facets.

In the case of a triangular polygon the adjacent facet identifier list will be required to hold up to a maximum of three integers. When polygons have one or more edges that are not adjacent to other polygons, this can be flagged by storing a -1 as the identity of the neighboring polygon. The augmented data structures are illustrated in Figure 3.18.

The detailed pseudo-code implementation of the algorithm is presented in Figures 3.19 and 3.20. However, before presenting the algorithm in detail the following gives a simple overview:

1. For each vertex create a list to hold the identity of polygons which are attached to it. Initially all the lists will be empty.

2. Work through all the triangular polygons, j, and consider each of its vertices in turn. For each vertex (call it k) of j, add j to k's polygon adjacency list F_{adj}. (For each vertex this builds up a list of which polygon is attached to which vertex).

3. Again work through all the polygons. Call the current one j, and then taking each side in turn, identify the two vertices to which it is attached. Call them i_1 and i_2. For vertices i_1 and i_2, look through each one's list of attached polygons and see if any have an edge between i_1 and i_2 (remembering

to exclude the current polygon j). If they have, then this is the polygon adjacent to polygon j along the side between vertices i_1 and i_2. This can be done by checking all polygons adjacent to i_1 against all polygons adjacent to i_2 and, if they have a polygon in common, it can only be polygon j or another one with vertices i_1 and i_2 in common, which is the one adjacent to polygon j.

Part1: Build polygon adjacency list for each vertex

set $i = 0$ and repeat while $i < Npolys$ {
    set $j = 0$ and repeat while $j < 3$ {
        $id = Poly(i).V_{id}$
        $n = Vert(id).n_F$
        extend the list $Vert(id).F_{adj}$ to $n + 1$ spaces
        $Vert(id).F_{Adj}(n) = i$
        $Vert(id).n_F = n + 1$
        $j = j + 1$
    }
    $i = i + 1$
}

Figure 3.19.   Part I of the algorithm to make a list of polygons attached to each vertex from a facet/vertex 3D database.

3.7 Finding Polygons Adjacent to Edges

Some of the algorithms to be discussed in later chapters require that every edge knows the identity of its neighboring polygons. For most closed surfaces approximated by a network of polygons an edge will have at most two neighboring polygons.

The algorithm itself is very similar to that for finding polygons adjacent to polygons (Section 3.6). An example code for both algorithms is given below:

```
//
// Function to build adjacency lists for triangulated data structures
//

//   The data types (EDGE and FACET) will need to be modified
//   to fit whatever framework you are using.

typedef struct tagEDGE {
  long Vid[2];      // identity of vertices to which the edge is attached
```

Part2: Build polygon adjacency list for each polygon
i_1 and i_2 are vertex id's for polygon edges

```
set i = 0 and repeat while i < Npolys {
    set l = 0 and repeat while l < 3 {
        /* check all polygons adjacent to i1 and i2 */
        /* to see if any of them have an adjacent polygon */
        /* in common (it must not be of course be i) */
        Poly(i).A_id(l) = -1 /* record -1 if nothing adjacent */
        if l = 0 {
            i1 = Poly(i).V_id(0)
            i2 = Poly(i).V_id(1)
        }
        else if l = 1 {
            i1 = Poly(i).V_id(1)
            i2 = Poly(i).V_id(2)
        }
        else if l = 2 {
            i1 = Poly(i).V_id(2)
            i2 = Poly(i).V_id(0)
        }
        if Vert(i1).nF > 0 and Vert(i2).nF > 0 {
            set j = 0 and repeat while j < Vert(i1).nF {
                t = Vert(i1).F_adj(j)
                set k=0 and repeat while k < Vert(i2).nF {
                    u = Vert(i2).F_adj(k)
                    /* u and v are polygons adjacent to i1
                    and i2 if they are the same then the edge
                    between i1 and i2 is a boundary of polygons
                    t and u. it is either i or the desired polygon */
                    if u = t and u ≠ i {
                        Poly(i).A_id(l) = u
                        jump to label /* no need to continue */
                    }
                    k = k + 1
                }
                j = j + 1
            }
        }
        label
        l = l + 1
    }
    i = i + 1
}
```

Figure 3.20.   Part 2 of the algorithm to make a list of adjacent polygons from a facet/vertex 3D database.

```
    long Fid[2];      // list to identify the facets on either side of edge    *
    //
    // add other members as required
} EDGE;

typedef struct tagFACET {
  long Vid[3];      // identity of vertices to which facet is attached
  long Fid[3];      // list to identify facets with an edge in common        *
  long Eid[3];      // list of the identity of edges surrounding the facet    *
  //
  // add other members as required
} FACET;

// The items labeled * above are filled in by the algorithm. If there are
// no adjacent items -1 is recorded. Identifiers are integers >= 0

////////// The following data type is used internally by the function
////////// to record temporary information

typedef struct tagTEMPV {
  long *Fadj;      // list of facets adjacent to this vertex
  long nF;         // number of facets adjacent to this vertex
  long *Eadj;      // list of edges adjacent to this vertex
  long nE;         // number of edges adjacent to this vertex
} TEMPV;

////////// The following are standard functions and definitions that
////////// are usually provided as part of a compilers library.
////////// Substitute then with the ones you wish to use.

#define NULL 0
extern void *malloc(long X);       // allocate X bytes, return pointer to it.
// update memory block pointed to by P so that it has X bytes.
extern void *realloc(void *P, long X);
extern void free(void *P);         // release memory block pointed to by P

// Function to fill out the adjacency information in the EDGE and FACET
// structures. Algorithms for Delaunay triangulation and Boolean Modelling
// will require to call upon it.

void MakeAdjacencyData(    // Parameters
  long  nVertex,           // Number of vertices
  long  nEdges,            // Number of edges
  EDGE  *EdgeList,         // List of edge structures
  long  nFacets,           // Number of facets
  FACET *FacetList)        // List of facet structures
{
  TEMPV *vlist=NULL;
  long i,j,k,l,n,i0,i1,t,u,*list;
  //
```

```
// Initialize the temporary data structure
//
if((vlist=(TEMPV *)malloc(nVertex*sizeof(TEMPV))) == NULL)return;
for(i=0;i<nVertex;i++)
{
  vlist[i].nF=0;
  vlist[i].nE=0;
  vlist[i].Fadj=NULL;
  vlist[i].Eadj=NULL;
}
//
// Make the list of facets adjacent to each vertex.
//
for(i=0;i<nFacets;i++)
{
  for(j=0;j<3;j++)  // for all vertices round facet
  {
    k=FacetList[i].Vid[j]; // vertices of facet i
    list=vlist[k].Fadj;
    n=vlist[k].nF;
    // extend the list
    if(list == NULL)
    {
      if((list=(long *)malloc(sizeof(long))) == NULL)return;
    }
    else
    {
      if((list=(long *)realloc(list,(n+1)*sizeof(long))) == NULL)return;
    }
    //
    // add the identity of facet i to list for vertex  k
    //
    list[n]=i;
    vlist[k].Fadj=list;
    vlist[k].nF=n+1;
  }
}
//
// Make the list of edges adjacent to each vertex.
//
for(i=0;i<nEdges;i++)
{
  for(j=0;j<2;j++)
  {
    k=EdgeList[i].Vid[j];
    list=vlist[k].Eadj;
    n=vlist[k].nE;
    if(list == NULL)
    {
      if((list=(long *)malloc(sizeof(long))) == NULL)return;
```

```
      }
      else {
        if((list=(long *)realloc(list,(n+1)*sizeof(long))) == NULL)return;
      }
      list[n]=i;
      vlist[k].Eadj=list;
      vlist[k].nE=n+1;
  }
}
//
// Now build the list of facets adjacent to each facet
//
for(i=0;i<nFacets;i++)
{
  for(l=0;l<3;l++)    // for each edge of facet i
  {
    FacetList[i].Fid[l] = -1;  // default that no facet is adjacent
    if(l == 0)
    {
      i0=FacetList[i].Vid[0];  i1=FacetList[i].Vid[1];
    }
    else if(l == 1)
    {
      i0=FacetList[i].Vid[1];  i1=FacetList[i].Vid[2];
    }
    else if(l == 2)
    {
      i0=FacetList[i].Vid[2];  i1=FacetList[i].Vid[0];
    }
    if(vlist[i0].nF > 0 && vlist[i1].nF > 0) // some facets attached
    {
      //
      // check all possible combinations
      //
      for(j=0;j<vlist[i0].nF;j++)
      {
        t=vlist[i0].Fadj[j];
        for(k=0;k<vlist[i1].nF;k++)
        {
          u=vlist[i1].Fadj[k];
          if(u == t && u != i) // this is the one  vertices i1 and i2 common
          {
            FacetList[i].Fid[l]=u;  // record facet identity
            goto JUMP_POINT1;
          }
        }
      }
    }
    JUMP_POINT1:;
  }
```

```
  }
  //
  // Now build the list of facets adjacent to each edge - it's basically
  // the same as above
  //
  for(i=0;i<nEdges;i++)
  {
    i0=EdgeList[i].Vid[0];
    i1=EdgeList[i].Vid[1];
    n=0; // count number of adjacent facets found for edge  i
    EdgeList[i].Fid[0] = -1;  // default no faces adjacent
    EdgeList[i].Fid[1] = -1;
    if(vlist[i0].nF > 0 && vlist[i1].nF) // some possibilities
    {
      for(j=0;j<vlist[i0].nF;j++)
      {
        t=vlist[i0].Fadj[j];
        for(k=0;k<vlist[i1].nF;k++)
        {
          u=vlist[i1].Fadj[k];
          if(u == t)  // two faces with a common edge between vertices i0 i1
          {
            EdgeList[i].Fid[n]=u;  // record facet identity
            n++;
            if(n == 2)goto JUMP_POINT2;  // two adjacent facets found
          }
        }
      }
      JUMP_POINT2:;
    }
  }
  //
  // Build the list of edges that surround a facet - there will always
  // be three for a triangular facet. The argument is very similar to
  // that used to determine adjacent Facets
  //
  for(i=0;i<nFacets;i++)
  {
    for(l=0;l<3;l++) // for each edge of facet  i
    {
      if(l == 0)
      {
        i0=FacetList[i].Vid[0];  i1=FacetList[i].Vid[1];
      }
      else if(l == 1)
      {
        i0=FacetList[i].Vid[1];  i1=FacetList[i].Vid[2];
      }
      else if(l == 2)
      {
```

```
      i0=FacetList[i].Vid[2];  i1=FacetList[i].Vid[0];
    }
    FacetList[i].Eid[1] = -1; // default - this should never be needed
    if(vlist[i0].nE > 0 && vlist[i1].nE > 0)
    {
      for(j=0;j < vlist[i0].nE;j++)
      {
        t=vlist[i0].Eadj[j];
        for(k=0;k < vlist[i1].nE;k++)
        {
          u=vlist[i1].Eadj[k];
          if(t == u) // only one edge can have i0 and i1 in common
          {
            FacetList[i].Eid[1]=t;
            goto JUMP_POINT3; // no need to look any further
          }
        }
      }
    }
    JUMP_POINT3:;
  }
}
//
// release the temporary resources
//
for(i=0;i<nVertex;i++)
{
  if(vlist[i].Fadj != NULL)free(vlist[i].Fadj);
  if(vlist[i].Eadj != NULL)free(vlist[i].Eadj);
}
free(vlist);
//
// All done
//
return;
}
```

3.8   A Data Structure for Image Processing

An image is made up from pixels; each pixel is a sample of the color in a
small rectangular area of the image. The color of a pixel is usually recorded
as three values, one for each of the primary colors red, green, and blue (RGB).
A combination of primary colors is usually sufficient to give the illusion that a
full rainbow color spectrum is reproducible on a computer monitor. To record
an excellent approximation to a **full** spectrum the standard method is to allocate
one byte for each of the red, green, and blue (RGB) components. This topic is
discussed in detail in Chapter 8.

CHAPTER 4

Fast Realistic Rendering

In the context of computer graphics, rendering is the process of artificially generating a picture of *something* from a numerical data set or other form of specification. This usually involves billions of calculations as the picture is synthesized. Continuing advances in computer technology are allowing pictures to be produced more and more rapidly. Some systems can deliver an image in only a few milliseconds. However the quest for more and more lifelike pictures requires calculating processes of rapidly increasing complexity. Consequently, no matter how quickly developments in processor technology deliver increased performance, there are always grumblings of discontent among the artists and designers who use computer graphics in their work.

From the point of view of describing algorithms for the rendering task there is a point where a quantum leap in the time it takes to render a picture (an image) occurs. Thus it is useful to classify rendering algorithms in two groups: those that are very fast and those that are not. At one end of the fast rendering spectrum are the *Real-Time Rendering* engines. *Engine* is a term with its origin in the computer games industry where rendering a standard TV or video sized image usually takes a few milliseconds. A comprehensive introduction to *Real-time* rendering may be found in Möller and Haines [1]. At the other end of the fast rendering spectrum the images produced have a very realistic quality but may take a few seconds to produce. Slow rendering (the subject of Chapter 5) requires minutes or possibly hours to paint a single picture; however, in many cases the result is so good that it is impossible to tell a computer-generated image from a photograph of the real thing.

3D graphics are becoming more and more commonly used and certain standards are gaining widespread acceptance. Probably the best known fast rendering system is Silicon Graphics' OpenGL library [3] [4] and, now that Microsoft has licensed it for use with their Windows operating systems, powerful 3D graphics libraries are available to all programmers. If you want to experiment with OpenGL programming in a Windows environment, then Walnum's [5] book is a good place to start.

Input Model Description

16376 Polygons 10040 Vertices

Polygon List

Polygon	Vertex ID	Material
1	3 1 2	1
2	2 3 4	1
3	...	
16376	16374 16375 3	10

VertexList

Vertex	Coordinates
1	0.0 5.1 7.1
2	0.0 5.3 7.2
...	
10040	1.8 7.5 6.6

Rendered
Output

Figure 4.1.   An example of the input to and output from a renderer.

4.1   The Basic Rendering Algorithm

The basic rendering procedure takes a list of polygons and vertices and produces a picture of the object they represent. The picture (or *image*) is recorded as an array (sometimes referred to as a *raster*), of a large number of little regions of the picture called *pixels* (shortened "picture element"). The raster is organized into rows and each row holds a number of pixels.

Each pixel in the array holds a number, to give value to the color or intensity at the equivalent location in the image. Because the number of pixels in a raster is finite (the pixel value represents a small area, not a single point) there will always be some inaccuracy when they are used to display the image they represent. The quality of an image is primarily related to the accuracy with which the pixel color value is recorded and to the number of pixels in the raster. A raster is regarded as a 2D array with a height and a width. For example a broadcast quality NTSC television screen is represented by a raster of 720×480 pixels (horizontal $\times$ vertical resolution). The equivalent PAL television system raster is 752×576 pixels in size.

All TVs and computer monitors use the three primary colors (Red, Green, and Blue) model to represent shades of color. At least seven bits will be required for each primary in order to represent all the $\approx 350,000$ different shades of color that the human eye can distinguish. Since computers like to work in *byte* sized chunks each pixel is most commonly represented by three bytes: one byte each for the Red, Green, and Blue primary colors (the so-called 24 bit system). Rendering processes producing output for film or HDTV will require a much higher raster resolution ($\approx 3000 \times 2000$) while output destined for multimedia clips or games will be satisfied by somewhat smaller rasters (although some games are making use of resolutions in excess of $\approx 1024 \times 768$).

It is worth mentioning here the space required to store these pixelated images; for example, one single TV frame requires ≈ 1Mb to hold its raster. Given that a TV displays 30 frames a second, it would require ≈ 1.7Gb to record digitally one minutes' worth of computer-generated images. These figures are large and it is a testament to the science of image compression and custom integrated circuit design that hardware is available (for even the humble personal computer) to make the production of totally computer-generated movies a very real prospect. *One day soon people will be doing this kind of thing in their own front parlor.*

Even though there are many algorithms that can be classified as rendering procedures they are probably variations on the general theme set out in the following short list of sequential steps (often called *the graphics pipeline* [2]):

1. Load the data describing objects in the scene into memory (RAM).

2. Use translation, scaling, and rotational transformations to move each object into their appointed position.

3. Apply the viewing transformation. After this step keep a record of the 3D coordinates of each vertex in the scene.

4. Apply the projection transformation to find equivalent coordinates in the viewing plane for all vertices in the scene. Store these 2D projected screen coordinates along with the data recorded in step 3. Store all coordinate data in floating point form.

   Note: *The number of instructions the computer must perform in each of the preceding steps is primarily proportional to the number of vertices in the scene.*

5. For each pixel in the output raster calculate what is visible and record this information.

   The number of instructions the computer must perform in this last step will depend on the rendering algorithm but, more importantly, *it will be proportional to the number of pixels in the raster. However on some hardware the number of times a pixel is overwritten can also make a significant contribution to the execution time.* Therefore, for something even as simple as a cube (8 vertices and 6 polygons) you might still be drawing it into a raster with $500,000$ pixels. Any optimization that can be done in this last step will be immensely rewarding.

   It is usual to retain the pixel information in the computer's fast memory until the whole raster has been filled. This block of data is called a **framebuffer**. Once rendering is complete the contents of the framebuffer can be transferred to a mass storage device or copied to the screen. The framebuffer is also an ideal environment in which to carry out additional image processing.

All the renderers we will discuss perform steps 1-4 above and it is only in step 5 that significant differences occur. Procedures for the execution of step 5 form the bulk of the topics to be discussed in this chapter. As we go along we shall see that most of the calculations that a renderer must perform have already been covered in Chapter 2.

4.2   Wireframe Drawing

The simplest way to visualize the numerical model for an object is to draw it in wireframe. A wireframe drawing involves relatively few calculations to render it. The action of step 5 in the rendering algorithm is simply to work through all the polygons that describe the model and, taking each side in turn:

1. Check to see if it has been drawn already.

2. If not identify the vertices it is connected to.

3. Retrieve the screen coordinates determined in step 4 of the rendering algorithm.

4. Draw a line connecting these two points in the frame buffer.

If a list of edges in the model is available so much the better since there is no need to check whether or not the edge has been drawn before.

For a wireframe drawing, such as that shown in Figure 4.2, to be recorded in the framebuffer or drawn on a raster display, a procedure for rendering lines is required. Both framebuffer and display are composed of pixels and to draw a line from a to b the pixels through which the line passes must be given an appropriate value to represent the color of the line.

The line drawing procedure should be fast and as simple as possible to implement. Perhaps the most commonly used procedure yet established is in Bresenham [6] and we will consider this now for the case of a raster equivalent to a 2D array of integer coordinates in the range $(0 \rightarrow X_{max})$ and $(0 \rightarrow Y_{max})$. The algorithm works incrementally from a starting point (x_1, y_1), and the first step is to identify in which one of eight octants the direction of the end point lies. These octants are identified in Figure 4.3. How the algorithm proceeds depends on which octant contains the end point of the line in question. A faster procedure reported by Wyvill [7] could be considered if there are a huge number of

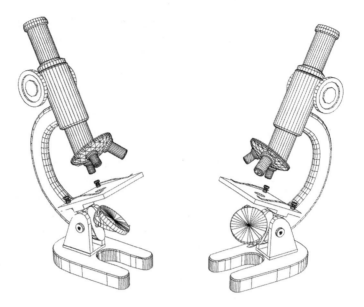

Figure 4.2.   A wireframe drawing.

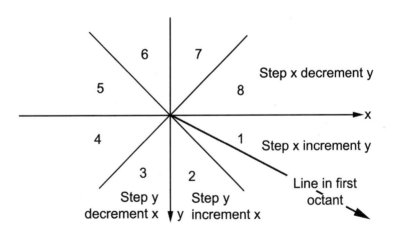

Figure 4.3.   The Cartesian octants. Note that the positive y-coordinate is downwards. When drawing lines the center of the octants is taken to lie at the same place as the first point on the line. The illustrated line lies in the first octant.

lines to be drawn, but since most *line* rendering is done by some library API and, for any 3D application the amount of time spent drawing lines is insignificant, Bresenham's procedure is sufficient for most purposes.

In the case of a line lying in the first octant, say between points (x_1, y_1) and (x_2, y_2), it is drawn by stepping one horizontal pixel at a time from x_1 to x_2 and at each step making the decision whether or not to step ± 1 pixel in the y direction. Since the gradient or slope of the line is $\Delta = \dfrac{y_2 - y_1}{x_2 - x_1}$ each horizontal increment will contribute a y displacement of Δ. Of course increments in y must be in integer steps (one pixel at a time) and since $\Delta \ll 1$ is a common occurrence it is usual to accumulate an error term δ that adds small changes at each step, i.e., $\delta = \delta + \Delta$. When $\delta = 1$ the current y-coordinate is incremented by 1 while δ is reset to zero. The cycle continues until x_2 is reached.

This basic procedure can be optimized by reformulating the equations so that the calculation is done with integer arithmetic alone and by making comparisons with zero rather than unity. The enhanced procedure goes by the name of *the integer differential line generator* and an algorithm for it is presented in Figure 4.4.

For lines in the first octant $y_{inc} = 1$ in the algorithm of Figure 4.4. To draw a line in the second octant where $x_{inc} = 1$, the roles of x and y are reversed in Figure 4.4; initially $\delta = -\Delta y/2$, and the x-coordinate is incremented and δ is reduced by Δy at each step.

For a general line between any two points the drawing algorithm starts by making appropriate choices for x_{inc} and y_{inc}. If necessary $x_1 \leftrightarrow x_2$ or $y_1 \leftrightarrow y_2$

$$\Delta x = x_2 - x_1$$
$$\Delta y = y_2 - y_1$$
$$\delta = -\Delta x/2$$
set $x = x_1$ and $y = y_1$
draw pixel at (x, y) with color c
while $x < x_2$ do {
    $\delta = \delta + \Delta y$
    if $\delta \geq 0$ {
        $y = y + y_{inc}$
        $\delta = \delta - \Delta x$
    }
    $x = x + 1$
    draw pixel at (x, y) with color c
}

Figure 4.4.   The basic integer differential line generator algorithm.

$$\Delta x = x_2 - x_1$$
$$\Delta y = y_2 - y_1$$
if $|\Delta x| > |\Delta y|$ {
    if $\Delta x < 0$ {
        swap $x_2 \leftrightarrow x_1$
        swap $y_2 \leftrightarrow y_1$
    }
    if $y_2 > y_1$ then $y_{inc} = 1$
    else $y_{inc} = -1$
    Call the first octant algorithm
}
else {
    if $\Delta y < 0$ {
        swap $x_2 \leftrightarrow x_1$
        swap $y_2 \leftrightarrow y_1$
    }
    if $x_2 > x_1$ then $x_{inc} = 1$
    else $x_{inc} = -1$
    Call the second octant algorithm
}

Figure 4.5.   Algorithm for the drawing of an arbitrarily directed straight line in a raster display.

are swapped, and in the final step a call is made to first or second octant line drawing procedures. This algorithm is presented in Figure 4.5.

As a final thought on wireframe drawing it is worth making the following brief comment: in drawing the wireframe on the projection plane it is assumed that straight edges in 3D space project to give straight edges on the 2D projection plane—fortunately this assumption is true.

4.3   Hidden Surface Drawing

A hidden surface drawing procedure is the next logical step in the quest for realistic, but synthetically generated, pictures of objects. In contrast to a wireframe drawing in which all the edges of polygons making up the model are drawn, the hidden surface procedure attempts to color in the drawing so that joins between polygons and indeed polygons that are out of sight (hidden by others) are not shown. For example if you look at a solid cube you will be able to see at most

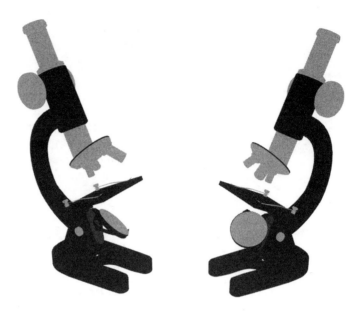

Figure 4.6.   A hidden surface drawing.

three of its six facets at any one time, or from any one viewpoint. Unlike a
wireframe drawing, where a list of edges is sufficient to complete the drawing, a
list of polygons must be used to render a hidden surface picture.

To construct a hidden surface view, each polygon edge is projected onto the
viewing plane, then, instead of just drawing the projected edges, pixels lying
inside the boundary formed by the projected edges of a polygon are given an
appropriate color.

Sadly, if all we did was work through the list of polygons sequentially and fill
in appropriate pixels it is certain that the drawing would be a mess. At the very
least we would see parts of the model that should have remained hidden. It is the
purpose of Sections 4.4, 4.5, and 4.6 to describe algorithms that will make sure
that those parts of a model which should be obscured from view never get drawn.

Before considering the hidden surface algorithm it is worth pausing to consider
the implications of the statement:

> *Pixels lying inside the boundary formed by the projected edges of a*
> *polygon are given an appropriate color.*

Finding which pixels lie inside a polygon is itself not always a trivial task especially when the polygon is non-convex. A convex polygon is one in which **any**
point in the interior can be joined to **any** vertex on the boundary by a line that

does not cross any edge of the polygon. Because there are so many pixels in a raster and in most cases such a high number of polygons are to be filled, any procedure to implement the filling task must be very efficient. We will look at three potential algorithms in Section 4.3.1. An even more important task than filling pixels within a specified outline is the calculation of the appropriate color with which to fill those pixels. Determining the color value for any pixel in the output raster is the **most** significant task any rendering algorithm has to perform. It governs the shading, texturing (e.g., wood, marble, or decals), and quality of the final image.

Figure 4.7. Examples of non-convex polygons. Any polygon that has a hole in it is always non-convex.

4.3.1 Filling Polygons

Three potential algorithms that fill a closed polygonal region specified by a set of coordinates at the vertices of the boundary $(x_0, y_0) \to (x_1, y_1) \to (x_2, y_2)... \to (x_{n-2}, y_{n-2}) \to (x_{n-1}, y_{n-1}) \to (x_0, y_0)$, are:

1. Recursive Seed Fill

    This is the simplest of all the methods but it is also the slowest. A pixel that lies inside the region to be filled is taken as a *seed*, set to record the chosen color. Then the seed's nearest neighbors are found and with each in turn this procedure is executed recursively. The process continues until the boundary is reached.

2. Ordered Seed Fill

This is a method that many *paint* packages use to color in regions of a drawing. The procedure works by first choosing a seed pixel inside the region to be filled. Each pixel on that row in the raster, to the left and right of the seed, is filled, pixel by pixel, until a boundary is encountered. While scanning that row a series of extra seeds are placed on the rows above and below subject to certain conditions. After all the pixels in the row have been filled any additional seeds placed on other rows are processed in exactly the same manner. This algorithm is also recursive but it has the advantage that the number of recursive calls is dramatically reduced. A full explanation of this and the Recursive Seed Fill can be found in Burger [8].

3. Scanline Fill

The polygon is filled by stroking across each row in the raster and coloring any pixels on that row if they lie within the polygon (see Figure 4.9).

This is the most useful filling procedure for a 3D polygon rendering algorithm because it works very efficiently for simple convex shapes. The drawing stage in a large number of rendering algorithms is commonly performed with triangles, because a triangle is the simplest polygon and is also planar. All triangles are convex. Quadrilaterals are easily divided into two triangles and higher order polygons are rare. In any case it is always possible to divide up polygons with more than three sides into two or more triangular facets.

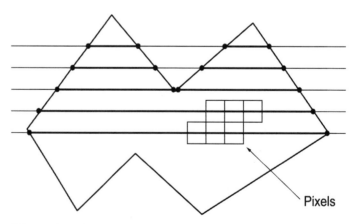

Figure 4.8.   Scanline fill by stroking the rows of the output raster.

An algorithm to scanline fill a triangular polygon

Let the three vertices projected onto the view plane have coordinates (x_0, y_0), (x_1, y_1), and (x_2, y_2) and let c be the color to assign to the pixel. For the geometry illustrated in Figure 4.9 the following six-step procedure will fill pixels with color c that occur within the triangle $(x_0, y_0) \rightarrow (x_1, y_1) \rightarrow (x_2, y_2)$:

1. Find minimum and maximum y-coordinates of the polygon's vertices:

$$y_{min} = \min(y_0, y_1, y_2)$$

   and

$$y_{max} = \max(y_0, y_1, y_2)$$

2. Find the largest integer i_0, such that $i_0 \le y_{min}$, and the smallest integer i_1, such that $i_1 \ge y_{max}$. *Note that this step requires mixing* real *and* integer *arithmetic and therefore care must be exercised in coding these statements.* After this step we know that horizontal scanline i, such that $i_0 \le i \le i_1$, will cross the polygon somewhere.

3. For all scanlines $i_0 \le i \le i_1$ repeat the following steps.

4. Consider each of the lines $0, 1,$ and 2 in Figure 4.9 in turn; if a line crosses the scanline between the vertices at either end of the segment find the x-coordinate of the intersection with i. If any of the lines are horizontal assume there is no intersection. There will be either two or three such values; three

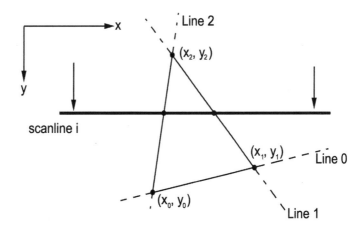

Figure 4.9.   Scanline filling a triangular polygon.

if $y_1 < i$ and $y_2 < i$ then no intersection
if $y_1 > i$ and $y_2 > i$ then no intersection
$\Delta y = y_2 - y_1$
if $|\Delta y| < \frac{1}{2}$ then line horizontal $\Rightarrow$ no intersection
$\Delta x = x_2 - x_1$
$$d = \frac{(i - y_1)\Delta x}{\Delta y}$$
$x_{int} = x_1 + d$

Figure 4.10.   Determining the intersection between raster scanline i and the side joining points (x_1, y_1) to (x_2, y_2).

values may occur because one of the vertices of the triangle may lie on scanline i. To obtain the x-coordinate of the intersection between scanline i and the side joining (x_1, y_1) to (x_2, y_2), a simple 2D line intersection calculation is all that is required. The algorithm given in Figure 4.10 takes advantage of the fact that the scanline is horizontal, and the first thing it does is to check and see if the scanline crosses the triangle at all. (This step will be performed many times, proportional to both the number of polygons and the resolution of the framebuffer so the tests are ordered with the least common one performed first.)

5. Find the minimum and maximum x-coordinates, x_{min} and x_{max} of the intersection.

6. Step, j, across the row of pixels from x_{min} to x_{max} setting pixel (j, i) to color c at each step. Use the nearest integer values of x_{min} and x_{max}.

4.4 The Painter's Algorithm

This is the simplest of all the hidden surface rendering techniques. It does not deliver true hidden surface behavior because it cannot resolve polygons which intersect each other or overlap in certain ways. Some shapes that are not amenable to rendering with the painter's algorithm are illustrated in Figure 4.12. It does give very good results if there are a large number of similarly sized polygons in a scene because the small inaccuracies are less noticeable.

The painter's procedure relies on the simple observation that if you paint on a surface, you paint *over* anything that had previously been there, hiding it. Therefore if the list of polygons can be arranged so that those polygons nearest

Sort the list of polygons so that it is ordered by
distance from the viewpoint with the polygon furthest
away at the start of the list.

Repeat the following for all polygons in the ordered list{
        Draw projected polygon into the framebuffer
        using the procedure described in Section 4.3.1.
}

Figure 4.11.   An outline of the painter's rendering algorithm.

the viewer occur at the end of the list you can just paint every polygon into the framebuffer and the nearest ones will over-write those further away. Once all the polygons have been drawn the result is a hidden surface view. This simple idea can be summarized in the steps given in Figure 4.11, which constitutes a possible procedure for step 5 in the basic rendering algorithm of Section 4.1.

As noted above there are occasions where this simple procedure fails. The reason it fails is that in the depth sorting step we have to assume that each polygon is represented by only **one** depth. Polygons however are not just points lying at one value of depth. They cover large portions of the projection plane with different areas on the polygon visible in different pixels. Consequently the depth of the polygon in each of the pixels that it covers will not necessarily be the same. We really need to look at depth on a pixel by pixel basis not on a polygon by polygon basis. Therefore, if it were possible to depth sort for *every* pixel covered by a polygon we would have a true hidden surface procedure; a method that accomplishes this is discussed in Section 4.5.

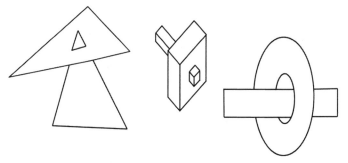

Figure 4.12.   Polygon arrangements that confuse the painter's algorithm.

4.4.1   Sorting

The painter's algorithm needs to sort a list of items using a specific criterion (depth from observer). There are many good algorithms that perform the sorting required by the painter's algorithm. One that is in common use is the standard Quicksort another is the basic shell sort.

4.5   The Z Buffer Hidden Surface Algorithm

In the comment at the end of Section 4.4 the observation was made that the painter's algorithm was inadequate because depth sorting was done on a per polygon basis rather than at every pixel in the raster or framebuffer. Because of the very large number of pixels making up the raster it is quite impractical to carry out a depth sort among every polygon for every pixel. *This is one of the drawbacks of a simple ray tracing algorithm.* However an alternative procedure that accomplishes the same task is available: *the Z buffer algorithm.*

Look at Figure 4.13; it shows a polygon and its projection onto the viewing plane where an array of pixels is illustrated. Imagine adding a matching array of similar dimension that is capable of recording a real number for each pixel; this is the Z buffer. The main action of the algorithm is to record in the Z buffer at address (i, j) the *distance* from V the viewpoint, to P the point where a line through V and pixel (i, j) intersects polygon k. This action is repeated for all pixels inside the projection of polygon k.

When it comes to drawing another polygon, say l, it too will paint into a set of pixels, some of which may overlap those previously filled with data from polygon k. It is now that the Z buffer comes into play. Before information for polygon l is written to the pixel at location (i, j), the Z buffer is checked to see whether polygon l appears to be in front of polygon k. If l is in front of k then the data from l is placed in the frame buffer and the Z buffer depth at location (i, j) is updated to take account of l's depth.

The algorithm is known as the "Z buffer algorithm," because the first programs to use it arranged their frame of reference with the viewpoint at the origin and the direction of view aligned along the z-axis. In these programs the distance to any point on the polygon from the view point was simply the point's z-coordinate. (OpenGL and Direct3D use this direction for their direction of view.) The Z buffer algorithm is summarized in Figure 4.14.

There are some important details regarding the Z buffer procedure:
Following the convention established in Section 2.11.6 the viewpoint V occurs at $(0, 0, 0)$ and the direction of view is along the x-axis. It is therefore the x component of the point P that is inserted into the Z buffer.

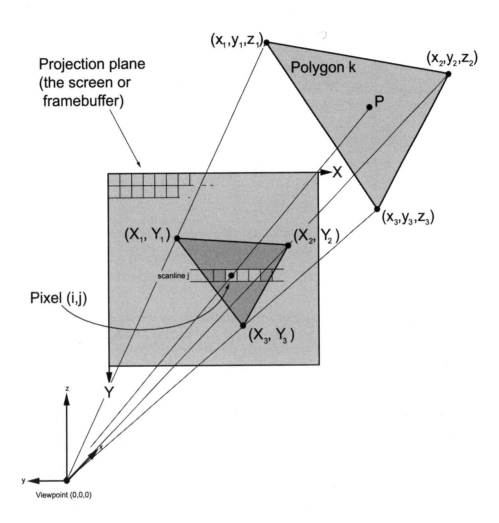

Figure 4.13.   Projecting back from the viewpoint through pixel (i,j) leads to a point in the interior of polygon k.

Fill the depth buffer at $Z(i,j)$ with a *far away* depth.
i.e. Set $Z(i,j) = \infty$ for all i,j.

Repeat for all polygons k {
    For polygon k find pixels (i,j) covered by it. Fill
    these with the color of polygon k. Use the procedure
    outlined in section 4.3.1.

    With each pixel (i,j) covered by k repeat {
        Calculate the Depth (Δ) of P from V (see Figure 4.13)
        If $\Delta < Z(i,j)$ {
            Set pixel (i,j) to color of polygon k
            Update the depth buffer $Z(i,j) = \Delta$
        }
    }
}

Figure 4.14.   The basic ideas of the Z buffer rendering algorithm.

Note that the x-coordinate of P is not quite the same thing as the distance between V and P. However, so long as one is consistent this not important and using the x-coordinate requires much less computation than the actual Euclidean distance.

To find P, and hence its x-coordinate, we call on the ideas of Section 2.5 for the intersection of line and plane. The plane in this case is the polygonal facet k with surface normal $\mathbf{n}$. To find a point in the plane we can choose any of the vertices of polygon k, say $\mathbf{P_0}$. It is usual to pre-calculate the normals and record them as part of the data structure associated with every polygon as suggested in Chapter 3.

For the equation of the line we know that it originates at $(0,0,0)$ and that it passes through a pixel in the raster given by Equations 2.10 and 2.11 in Section 2.11.7. Rearranging these equations and arbitrarily choosing a value of $x = 1$ gives the direction vector $\mathbf{d}$, (with components d_x, d_y, d_z):

$$\mathbf{d} = \begin{bmatrix} 1 \\ \left(\dfrac{\frac{X_{max}}{2} - X_s}{s_x} \right) \\ \left(\dfrac{\frac{Y_{max}}{2} - Y_s}{s_y} \right) \end{bmatrix}$$

Following the analysis of Section 2.5, the point of intersection is given by $\mathbf{P} = \mu\mathbf{d}$ where:

$$\mu = \frac{\mathbf{P_0 \cdot n}}{\mathbf{n \cdot d}}$$

Since the x component of $\mathbf{d}$ is unity, the x component of $\mathbf{P}$ is μ and in the frame of reference that we are using this is the value that is written into the Z buffer for pixel (i, j).

Using general expressions to determine the Z depth is not an efficient way to do the calculation. It is possible to take advantage of some of the special circumstances under which the depth is determined:

1. The constant $(\mathbf{P_0 \cdot n})$ is dependent only on the polygon. It could therefore be calculated at the same time as the polygon's normal is determined and stored along with the normal in the data structure allocated to every polygon: say we call it c_k.

2. Filling pixels one scanline after another implies that those parts of the expression for Z which are independent of horizontal coordinate need only be calculated once per scanline. This will save many arithmetic operations since most pixels on each scanline will need to have a Z depth determined. The z component of $\mathbf{d}$ is constant across the scanline and therefore if we let $d_2 = n_z d_z$, the calculation of Z at pixel (i, j) simplifies to:

$$Z = \frac{c_k}{n_x + n_y d_y + d_2}$$

One division, one multiplication, and two additions—quite a significant saving over the direct use of the general expressions.

Comments:

1. Since the Z buffer works on a per pixel basis it solves all the problems of the painter's algorithm and, *up to the resolution of a pixel*, gives a perfect hidden surface visualization.

2. Spending time determining the color to write into framebuffer or display on a monitor only to have it be replaced later when a polygon is found lying closer to the viewpoint is **very** unsatisfactory. It may have taken quite a bit of effort to calculate that color, shading, texturing, etc. Here is what might be regarded as an important clue to fast rendering:

   First calculate what you **can** *see, then calculate what you* **do** *see.*

   Instead of calculating a pixel's color and then storing that in the framebuffer, store the identity of the polygon that can be seen at that pixel. *(Imagine you are standing at the viewpoint and are looking at the scene through a wire grid held at the projection plane. Through each square you will see a polygon in the scene).* Once the Z buffer algorithm has run its course go through the *identity* buffer, extract the identity of which polygon is visible in the pixel and calculate the appropriate color value, then write that color into the framebuffer. This way the expensive calculations are not wasted and there may be an advantage when one needs to apply anti-aliasing techniques as described in Section 4.9. Perhaps a little more memory will be needed but it is certainly worth the expense. When memory resource is scarce the next algorithm is an ideal alternative.

4.6   The Scanline Z Buffer Algorithm

This version of the Z buffer algorithm was preferred in practice because it did not need to maintain a full-screen Z buffer and so would work in the much smaller memory of an early PC. In most respects it involves the same calculations as the full Z buffer procedure, but with a buffer size that is only required to store one row of pixels, called a scanline, at a time. For example, to generate an image at a resolution of 1024×768 requires a full Z and frame buffer of some $786,000$ elements (5.25Mb); using a scanline Z procedure one can get away with a storage requirement for $1,024$ elements (16kb).

Now of course if the Z buffer is only one row high, it must be applied to each row in the raster (with respect to the example above, 768 times). This means that every polygon has to be checked every time a raster row is processed. In theory this should be much slower than using a full Z buffer but in practice this is not usually the case. To see why just remember that to build up the depth information in the Z buffer each polygon has to be scanline filled over a number of rows anyway. In fact if there is a polygon that nearly fills the whole raster then there is almost exactly the same work to do in both full Z and scanline Z procedures. With a careful organization of the algorithm, rendering speed can approach that of the full Z buffer, especially when the *slow* step of *rendering* the pixel (to record *what you do see*) is taken into account.

A typical implementation of the scanline Z algorithm is given in Figure 4.15.

The very low memory requirement of the scanline Z buffer algorithm has the added advantage that if you want to simulate transparent or semi-transparent surfaces then two or more scanline buffers can be easily accommodated. Separate scanline buffers are used for the *opaque* and *transparent* surfaces visible in pixel (i, j). A comparison of the *depth* between buffers will tell us whether transparent parts of the surface lie in front of the opaque parts or vice versa. Maintaining two scanline buffers for transparent surfaces allows two overlapping transparent sur-

```
repeat for all scanlines, j, in the raster {
    repeat for all pixels i on scanline, 0 ≤ i < Xmax
        Z(i) = ∞ /* set the scanline Z buffer to a far away depth */
        Id(i) = −1 /* set the polygon ID buffer to indicate
                        no polygon visible */
    }
    repeat for all polygons, k, such that 0 ≤ k < Npoly {
        if polygon k does not span scanline j {
            skip on to next polygon
        }
        find first, i₁, and last, i₂, pixels covered
        by polygon k on scanline j, use the procedure
        of section 4.3.1.
        repeat with each i such that i₁ ≤ i ≤ i₂ {
            calculate the depth, Δ, of P (see Figure 4.13)
            if Δ < Z(i) {
                Id(i) = k /* record ID of polygon k for pixel i,j */
                Z(i) = Δ /* update the depth buffer */
            }
        }
    }
    repeat for all i, on scanline j, such that 0 ≤ i < Xmax {
        if Id(i) ≥ 0 set pixel (i,j) to color of polygon Id(i)
    }
}
```

Figure 4.15.   The scanline Z rendering algorithm.

faces to be rendered correctly. After about four *transparency* buffers are employed synthetic images of glass objects can look pretty good.

A trick very often used to draw complex shapes (e.g., trees in an architectural fly by), is to paint them on transparent quadrilateral polygons and then render the scene: see Section 4.14.1 on transparency mapping.

4.7 Hidden Line Drawing

A hidden line drawing looks quite similar to a wireframe drawing except that the drawing has a look of some *solidity* about it. We achieve this by not drawing edges which are hidden behind polygons lying closer to the viewpoint; we might

Figure 4.16.   A hidden line drawing from a set of triangular polygons.

call this a kind of *hybrid* hidden line - hidden surface procedure. Hidden line drawings are very useful in CAD applications because it allows engineers to see something of the structure of their design as well as its appearance.

There are two procedures that can be used to generate an accurate hidden line drawing such as that shown in Figure 4.16, and of course there are approximate procedures that are fast but can be confused by all but the simplest shapes. Quite a reasonable hidden line drawing of convex shapes can be achieved if a culling process to remove faces that cannot be seen is performed before all the edges of the remaining polygons are drawn as a wireframe. The two procedures we will consider are:

1. A spin-off from the hidden surface Z buffer procedure.

2. Drawing the edges in the scene where they are not obscured by any polygons (the visible edges procedure).

4.7.1   The Hidden Surface Spin-off

This algorithm is summarized in the short algorithm of Figure 4.17.

Working from a Z buffer procedure has the big advantage that it accurately represents edges in a hidden line drawing which occur because polygons might intersect. These are edges that can't exist as entries in any polygon and/or edge

Use either the scanline or full Z buffer procedure to record
at each pixel the identity of which polygon is visible.

Work though the raster in the order shown in Figure 4.18
and check for a change of recorded value both above
and to the left of the current pixel, pixels $i - 1, j$ and $i, j - 1$

If a difference is detected place a *foreground* color value in the
framebuffer otherwise place a background color.

Figure 4.17.   Rendering a hidden surface image as a "spin off" from the basic Z buffer procedure.

list describing the scene. For example a drawing of a cylinder poking through a
cube (Figure 4.19) will have edges that are not part of any polygon in either the
cube or the cylinder.

An interesting effect can be achieved with a hidden line drawing based on
hidden surface procedures. It arises because adjacent polygonal faces with normal
vectors pointing in the same direction are planar, and in most situations little
benefit is gained by drawing the common edge between adjacent co-planar faces;
indeed a picture in which these are omitted can have a much cleaner look. (The
drawing in Figure 4.16 had a few such edges removed.) However edges between
adjacent polygons should not be omitted if the polygons have different colors even
if they are co-planar. This idea can be pushed to the limit by relaxing the planarity
condition, $\mathbf{n}_1 \cdot \mathbf{n}_2 = 1$, say to $\mathbf{n}_1 \cdot \mathbf{n}_2 > \theta$ with $\theta \approx \frac{1}{2}$. Doing this will lead to
cartoon-like drawings like that in Figure 4.20.

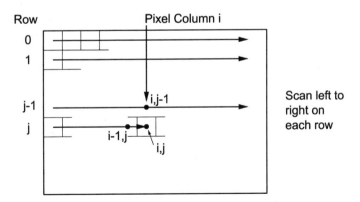

Figure 4.18.   Working through a raster to produce a hidden line drawing.

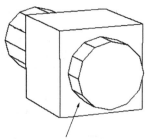

Edges are introduced where cylinder and cube
intersect. They are not in the polygon database.

Figure 4.19.   A hidden surface drawing showing edges that must be drawn but are not part of the
specification of the models in the drawing.

Figure 4.20.   A hidden line drawing with edges drawn only if they are adjacent to the background, a
different model or another polygon such that i) the color is different or ii) the angle
between them is $> 60°$.

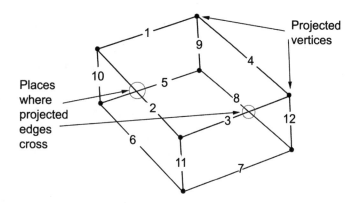

Figure 4.21.   Wireframe cube labeling edges and crossovers.

4.7.2   A Visible Edge Hidden Line Algorithm

Look at Figure 4.21 which shows a wireframe drawing of a cube (with the top removed so that we can see inside it). It has six polygons and twelve edges; the edges labeled $1, 2, 3, 4, 6, 7, 10, 11, 12$ will be fully visible in a hidden line drawing. Edge 9 will be partially visible. To decide whether edge i is visible it has to be tested against each of the polygons to see whether it lies behind any of them. However it is not sufficient to treat edge visibility as simply either *visible* or *not visible* for the whole edge because a case can arise where part of an edge will be visible and part will be obscured. So, before the visibility test can be made the edges must be broken up into appropriate segments.

To see how we can do this look again at Figure 4.21, but this time think of it purely as a 2D drawing. Anywhere that the lines cross is a potential site for one of the edges to change from being visible to hidden. These crossing points are the only places where the visibility status of an edge can change. Dividing the lines at these crossing points gives us the segments we need to test for visibility against the polygons in the model. For example, edge 11 will be composed of two segments because it is crossed by edge 5. After the edges have been divided into segments the segments can be tested to see if they are obscured by any polygons. If a segment is not obscured then it is drawn.

Most of the geometric calculations for this algorithm have been covered in Chapter 2 and thus only the logical steps in the algorithm are summarized in Figure 4.22. As discussed previously this approach to hidden line drawing does not allow for edges that are introduced by the intersection of polygons. However because the output is a list of line segments the drawing can be made on an output device in any resolution; i.e., it is not subject to the aliasing effect (see Section 4.9)

In the 2D projection plane find the intersections of all
projected edges with all the other projected edges. For each
edge make a list of the segments it is divided into. (Including
the coordinates at the ends of the segments.)

With each line segment make the following tests to see if
that segment is visible, if it is then *draw it*.

Repeat for every projected edge i {
    Repeat for every segment j of edge i {

        Project back from the ends of segment j to the
        polygon of which edge i is a boundary. This gives
        a *depth* that can be associated with the line segment.
        Call these points p_1 and p_2 and let their x
        coordinates be x_1 and x_2, which we will use as the depths.

        Repeat tests 1-3 below for every polygon k {
            Test 1:
            In projection: test if segment j of edge i is
            inside polygon k. If it is not then move on to the
            next polygon.
            Test 2:
            If x_1 and x_2 are both greater than the maximum x
            coordinate of vertices of polygon k then segment i
            is obscured so jump on to next segment.
            Test 3:
            Find the points q_1 and q_2 on polygon k
            where the lines from the viewpoint through p_1
            and p_2 intersect it.
            If the x coordinate of $q_1 < x_1$ and the x
            coordinate of $q_2 < x_2$ then segment i is
            obscured so jump on to the next segment.
        }
        If this point is reached then segment j
        of edge i is not obscured so draw it.
    }
}

Figure 4.22.   The visual edges algorithm.

that the hidden surface algorithms suffer from. Therefore, it is not necessary to render the picture again in order to work at a higher resolution. This form of output is ideal for recording in the device-independent encapsulated postscript format. Another useful alternative procedure for the production of hidden line drawings was developed by Janssen [9].

4.8   Culling and Clipping

For the final two steps (4 and 5) of the basic rendering algorithm to work correctly, it is imperative that the vertices of all facets have an x-coordinate $x > 0$ (i.e., in front of the viewpoint) and that the projected coordinates (X, Y) are such that $0 \leq X < X_{max}$ and $0 \leq Y < Y_{max}$. In all the topics we have discussed before, this has been implicitly assumed. However these conditions are not always satisfied in practice; indeed in some common uses of 3D graphics, e.g., *Walkthroughs*, these conditions will be met by only a very few of the vertices in the scene.

In order to reduce the number of calculations and remove artifacts that can occur when the conditions given above are violated it is necessary to perform culling and clipping. For our work the term "culling" will apply to the action of discarding **complete** polygons, i.e., those polygons with all their vertices outside the field of view, or in the case of a wireframe drawing, the vertices at both ends of an edge. "Clipping" will refer to the action of modifying those polygons (or edges) that are partially in and partially out of the field of view. Culling should always be performed first because it is likely to give you the biggest performance gain.

4.8.1   Culling

For 3D graphics there are three important types of cull:

1. Remove polygons behind the viewpoint.

   If the x-coordinate of *all* vertices for polygon k are such that $x \leq 1$ then cull polygon k. Note that this is equivalent to removing any polygons that lie behind the projection plane.

2. Remove polygons projected to lie outside the raster.

   If the projected coordinates (X, Y) for **all** the vertices of polygon k are such that $X < 0$ or $X \geq X_{max}$ or $Y < 0$ or $Y \geq Y_{max}$ then cull polygon k.

3. Cull any *backfaces*.

   A *backface* is any polygon that faces away from the viewpoint. It is called a backface because if the model were solid then any polygons facing away from the viewer would be obscured from view by polygons closer to the viewer.

In order to say whether a polygon faces towards or away from an observer a convention must be established. The most appropriate convention to apply is one based on the surface normal vector. Every polygon (which is essentially a bounded plane) has a surface normal vector as defined in Section 2.4. Since it is possible for a surface normal to point in two opposite directions it is usual to assume that it is directed so that, in a general sense, it points away from the inside of an object. Figure 4.23 shows a cube with the normal vectors illustrated.

If the dot product of the normal vector with a vector from the viewpoint to a point on the polygon is negative the polygon is said to be a *frontface*; if the dot product is positive the polygon is a *backface*.

Comments:

- There are a number of alternative ways to organize culling. One can use a bounding volume for groups of polygons and organize them in a hierarchical way with one bounding volume, multiple bounding volumes, yet more bounding volumes, etc. Two other culling techniques, view frustum cull and occlusion culling, are proving popular in game engines but their discussion is outside the scope of this chapter. For more information on these culling techniques consult Möller and Haines [1].

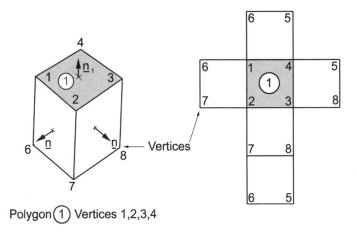

Polygon ① Vertices 1,2,3,4

Figure 4.23.   Surface normal vectors for a cube and a plan of the vertices showing a consistent ordering of the vertices round each polygonal face. For example, $n_1 = (P_2 - P_1) \times (P_3 - P_1)$.

- Since the normal to a plane can be determined from the position vectors of three points in that plane, a consistent ordering of the vertices around a polygon should be observed whenever possible. Figure 4.23 includes a plan of a cube with vertex orderings consistent with the outward facing normals.

- A cube has a definite inside and outside; it is solid. Some shapes, particularly if in one dimension they are very thin with respect to the other two, might be represented by a single layer of polygons, for example a model of a CD (compact disk) could be made from a *fan* of triangles. A model made in this way has no sense of inside and outside. In such cases it is necessary to think of each polygon as double sided and therefore dispense with a backface cull altogether.

4.8.2 Clipping

We need to consider clipping in both two and three dimensions. 2D clipping is important so that memory access violations do not occur in the screen buffer. The algorithm due to Sutherland and Cohen [10] has achieved almost universal usage as the most pertinent procedure for drawing lines in a 2D pixelated raster. Another procedure by Devai [12] has been demonstrated to perform faster when the implementation is in a high level language. In any case the clipping of lines amounts to a series of tests which eliminate the most common cases:

1. Both points inside, or

2. The line does not span the visible area.

The tests are followed by a step to calculate one or two points on the line where it crosses the boundary of the visible area.

In a 3D rendering algorithm, the 2D tests are applied after each polygon has been projected onto the viewing plane. There is no need for intersection calculations since all drawing occurs on one scanline at a time. Thus, the following modifications to the Z buffer algorithm will accomplish 2D clipping:

1. Begin by adding the instructions given in Figure 4.24 to the loop that is processing the polygons; a flag is used to indicate whether the polygon should be culled or not.

2. Conclude by inserting the instructions given in Figure 4.25 in the procedure to scanline fill the projected polygon.

In a general Z buffer algorithm any 3D clipping should be done before the polygons are projected onto the viewing plane. Clipping is usually done against a set of planes that bound a volume. Polygons (or parts of polygons) that lie inside

```
While repeating for all polygons k add the following:

{
    Set flag
    repeat for all vertices i of polygon k {
        /* let (X, Y) be projected coordinates of vertex i */
        if X ≥ 0 and X < Xmax {
            clear the flag
            jump to next polygon
        }
        if Y ≥ 0 and Y < Ymax {
            clear the flag
            jump to next polygon
        }
    }
    if the flag is set cull the polygon
}
```

Figure 4.24.   Amendments to the Z buffer algorithm to cull polygons which lie outside the field of view.

```
/* Check scanline, i, to see if it is inside the raster. */
if i < 0 or i ≥ Ymax skip to next scanline

/* On scanline i polygon k spans pixels x1 to x2./*
/* Before setting pixel values apply limits to x1 and x2. */

x1 = max(0, x1)
x2 = max(0, x2)
x1 = min((Xmax − 1), x1)
x2 = min((Xmax − 1), x2)
```

Figure 4.25.   Amendments to the Z buffer algorithm to clip polygons partially lying outside the field of view.

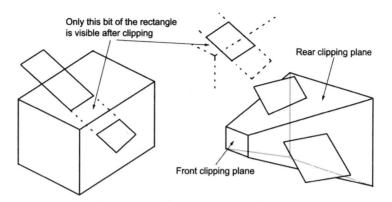

Only this bit of the rectangle
is visible after clipping

Rear clipping plane

Front clipping plane

Figure 4.26.   Cubic and truncated pyramidal clipping volumes penetrated by a rectangular polygon. Only that portion of the rectangle which lies inside the clipping volume would appear in the rendered image.

the volume are retained for rendering. A cubic volume is the simplest to create but since the field of view establishes a pyramidal shaped volume, this is commonly used as the clipping volume. This frustum is arranged so that its sides correspond to the edges of the field of view. The top and bottom of the frustum form the so-called front and back clipping planes. The front clipping plane is used to prevent polygons from extending to the wrong side of the projection plane. The front and back clipping planes are at right angles to the direction of view (see Figure 4.26). For the purposes of a Z buffer rendering algorithm, it is essential to use the front clipping plane; a back clipping plane is required because the Z buffer has finite resolution, an important point if the Z buffer is implemented in hardware using 16 or 24 bits per pixel. Other necessary clipping can be accomplished in the 2D projection plane. For multiple clipping planes it is sufficient to apply them one at a time in succession; for example, clip with the back plane, then the front plane, then the side plane, etc. An interesting application of the use of clipping planes is to produce animated cutaway views; for example, by moving the clipping plane through a model the inside can be revealed gradually.

Clipping a triangular polygon with a clipping plane

To see how 3D clipping is achieved we consider the following: Figure 4.27 it shows a triangular polygon ABC which is to be clipped at the plane PP' (seen end on). Clipping is accomplished by splitting triangle ABC into two pieces: BDE and $ACED$. The pieces are then either removed from, or added to, the polygon database as necessary. For example, when PP' is the back clipping

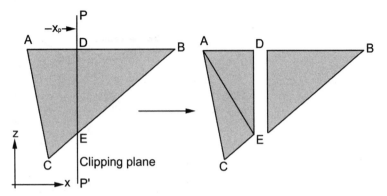

Figure 4.27.   Clipping a triangular polygon, ABC, with a yz plane at PP', at $(x_p, 0, 0)$. Clipping divides
                    ABC into two pieces. If the polygons are to remain triangular the piece $ADEC$ must
                    be divided in two.

plane triangles ADE and AEC are added to the database, while triangle BDC is removed. Points D and E are determined by finding the intersection between the lines joining vertices of the polygon and the clipping plane. The calculation is straightforward (Section 2.5 considered a general case) but, since the clipping plane is at right angles to the x-axis and because clipping to such a plane is commonly used, it is worth writing expressions specifically for these particular circumstances. Therefore the intersection point, $\mathbf{p}$, between a line joining points $\mathbf{P}_1$ and $\mathbf{P}_2$ and the yz plane at x_p is given by:

$$p_x = x_p$$
$$p_y = P_{1y} + \frac{(x_p - P_{1x})}{(P_{2x} - P_{1x})}(P_{2y} - P_{1y})$$
$$p_z = P_{1z} + \frac{(x_p - P_{1x})}{(P_{2x} - P_{1x})}(P_{2z} - P_{1z})$$

Once the coordinates of the points D and E are known the algorithm to clip the triangular polygon ABC is complete and is given in Figure 4.28.

4.9 Anti-Aliasing

Aliasing is a term arising from the theory of sampled signals. The manifestation of aliasing depends on how the signal is interpreted (audio, video, etc.), but in all cases aliasing effects are regarded as undesirable and at least some effort should be

There are three possible cases to consider as illustrated
in Figure 4.29.

```
if edges AB and BC cross PP' {
    calculate point D on edge AB
    calculate point E on edge BC
    Re-label the triangle ABC to have vertices DBE
    Add new triangles ADC and DEC to database
}
else if edges AB and CA cross PP' {
    calculate point D on edge AB
    calculate point E on edge CA
    Re-label the triangle ABC to have vertices ADE
    Add new triangles DBE and BCE to database
}
else if edges BC and CA cross PP' {
    calculate point D on edge CA
    calculate point E on edge BC
    Re-label the triangle ABC to have vertices CDE
    Add new triangles DAE and ABE to database
}
```

This procedure has ensured that there will be an edge actually in
the clipping plane. Polygons will lie on one side or the other.
No polygons will span the clipping plane.
Despite this it is useful to keep a record of all polygons
because another clipping plane might be added later.
A flag can be used to indicate which triangle lies inside the
appropriate clipping volume.

Figure 4.28.   Algorithm to clip the triangular polygons ABC with a plane PP' (seen in cross section)
as illustrated in Figure 4.27.

devoted to minimizing their interference. Anti-aliasing refers to the steps taken to
minimize the deleterious effects of aliasing. For our purposes the only significant
problem with aliasing is due to the fact that the output device or framebuffer is
of finite resolution. In computer graphics work the artifacts of aliasing are often
referred to as the *jaggies* because the finite dimensions of the raster causes a
straight line drawn at an angle across it to take on the appearance of a *staircase*
rather than a straight line. Aliasing artifacts are also a significant problem in
rendering image maps and textures, as discussed in Sections 4.13 and 8.5.2.

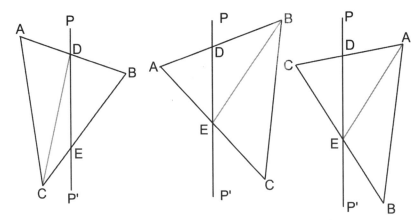

Figure 4.29.   Possible configurations for clipping a triangular polygon. Note that in Figure 4.28 there is a consistent counterclockwise ordering of the vertices for all the polygons created. This is vital for a consistent sense of inside and outside to be maintained. Although the second and third configurations look the same they are in fact different because the clipping plane crossed edges AB and AC in the second but edges BC and AC in the third.

The obvious way to reduce the aliasing effect is to increase the resolution of the raster or framebuffer. An alternative approach is to use the range of color or brightness provided by the display to smooth out the obvious aliasing artifacts. Figure 4.30 illustrates this alternative technique; on the left it shows a couple of characters from a text font that have been rendered into a pixelated raster. By fading the edges with lighter shades of gray (shown on the right) the curves look smoother and angled straight lines look less jagged. At the bottom of Figure 4.30 the effect of the same technique on a straight line is also illustrated. To consider

Figure 4.30.   Anti-aliasing by fading the brightness in pixels near the edge of lines and shapes.

anti-aliasing further it is useful to investigate procedures to anti-alias the drawing of points, lines, and pictures.

4.9.1 Anti-Aliasing Points

In the context of 3D graphics the most common need to draw points in the frame-buffer or on a screen is as the result of a particle model of some sort; for example, rain, snow, fireworks, etc.

After projection a point $\mathbf{p}$ will have coordinates (X, Y) which are scaled to lie within the dimensions of the raster, but X and Y will be floating point numbers and to record a color value it is necessary to fill the best-guess pixel at some integer coordinate (X_i, Y_j). Unfortunately simply rounding X or Y to the nearest integer will result in aliasing artifacts. The effect will be especially noticeable in a sequence of images where the particles will appear to jitter and move about in fits and starts.

A point can be successfully anti-aliased by spreading out its color value over not only the nearest integer pixel but also into those adjacent to it in the raster. For example, if the projected point is at raster coordinates $(1.3, 3)$ and has a brightness value of 0.7 (on a $[0, 1]$ scale), pixel $(1, 3)$ will be assigned a brightness of 0.7 and pixel $(2, 3)$ a brightness of 0.4. This *blending* will give the point the appearance of being located to the left side of pixel $(1, 3)$. Using the notation given in Figure 4.31 the instructions in Figure 4.32 will draw, with anti-aliasing, a point P with brightness c.

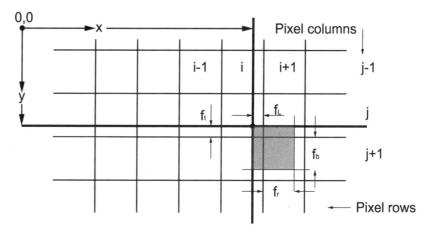

Figure 4.31.   When a point P is projected to the view plane, its coordinates (X, Y) will not always be dead center in pixel (i, j). Blending the brightness of P into adjacent pixels $(i, j+1)$, $(i+1, j)$, and $(i+1, j+1)$ will help to lessen the effect of the display raster (or framebuffer) being composed of discrete elements.

```
/* The projected point is (X, Y) (float data types) */
/* Function frac(x) returns the fractional part of x */
/* Each pixel is one unit square */

i = X /* rounded down to integer */
j = Y
fl = 1 − frac(X)
fr = frac(X + 1)
ft = 1 − frac(Y)
fb = frac(Y + 1)
set pixel (i, j) to value c × ft × fl
set pixel (i + 1, j) to value c × ft × fr
set pixel (i, j + 1) to value c × fb × fl
set pixel (i + 1, j + 1) to value c × fb × fr
```

Figure 4.32. Using the notation given in Figure 4.31 this algorithm will draw, with anti-aliasing, a point P with brightness c.

4.9.2 Anti-Aliasing Lines

To minimize the aliasing effect when drawing lines in a pixelated raster, blend the brightness in the pixels of adjacent rows and columns (see Figure 4.30). This can be accomplished by modifying the Bresenham line drawing algorithm to that given in Figure 4.33.

4.9.3 Anti-Aliasing Pictures

The simplest way to anti-alias synthesized images is to *super-sample*. That is, divide each pixel into a number of sub-pixels, render each of them as if they were individual pixels, and then average the results. For example, divide each pixel into four subpixels. An alternative way of doing this is to render into a raster that is twice as wide and twice as high and then average over adjacent groups of four pixels. For example, rendering to a raster of 1280×960 and averaging pixels (i, j), $(i + 1, j)$, $(i, j + 1)$, and $(i + 1, j + 1)$ will give the same result as rendering to a raster of 640×480 with each pixel divided into four. This box filtering is quick and easy to apply but in theory the best results are obtained from a $\frac{\sin x}{x}$ filter function.

Because a supersample of n requires $(n - 1)$ additional pixel values to be determined the rendering process slows down as anti-aliasing is applied. For example, if it takes one minute to render a frame of TV resolution without anti-aliasing, it will take about nine minutes to anti-alias it on a 3×3 supersample.

$$\Delta x = x_2 - x_1$$
$$\Delta y = y_2 - y_1$$
$$\delta = -\Delta x / 2$$
set $x = x_1$ and $y = y_1$
draw pixel at (x, y) with color c
while $x < x_2$ do {
$\qquad \delta = \delta + \Delta y$
$\qquad$ if $\delta \geq 0$ {
$\qquad\qquad y = y + y_{inc}$
$\qquad\qquad \delta = \delta - \Delta x$
$\qquad$ }
$\qquad x = x + 1$

$\qquad$ /* modified section */
$\qquad$ draw pixel at (x, y) with color $c(1 - \dfrac{\delta}{\Delta x})$
$\qquad$ draw pixel at $(x, y + 1)$ with color $c\dfrac{\delta}{\Delta x}$
$\qquad$ /* end modification */

}

Figure 4.33.   A modified Bresenham's algorithm for rendering anti-aliased lines.

Sadly, for a good enough quality TV sized image it **is** necessary to use at least a 3×3 supersample.

There are a couple of tricks that can be employed to accelerate the anti-aliasing process, and both of them rely on the fact that the most noticeable aliasing artifacts occur near edges where color or brightness changes occur.

Techniques to accelerate super-sampled anti-aliasing

1. Once the first supersample has been obtained for pixel (i, j) the remaining samples are only rendered if the color differs from that for pixels $(i - 1, j)$ or $(i, j - 1)$ by more than a certain threshold.

2. Use the fact that relatively few calculations are required to determine the identity of the polygon visible in each of the supersamples for pixel (i, j). If the same polygon appears in each supersample then there is no need to perform the more time consuming work of determining a color value for all the supersamples. Simply do it once and record that as the value

for pixel (i,j). If different polygons appear in each supersample the we must get color values for those that are different and average the results for pixel (i,j).

Using either of these techniques can lead to significantly reduced rendering times without much loss in picture quality. Plates 1, 2, and 3 illustrate an image recorded at a resolution of 640×480 with no anti-aliasing, anti-aliasing on a 3×3 super-sample, and the same 3×3 super-sample with acceleration. The relative timings were 1.0, 3.6, and 2.0 respectively. The fact that the ratio between the first two is much less than $9:1$ is a consequence of the image having a large area of the background color.

4.10   Lighting

Plate 4 illustrates a simple scene rendered with a hidden surface algorithm. Only those triangular polygons that should be visible *are* visible but there is definitely still something not very realistic about the image: it certainly doesn't look like a photograph. Plate 5 shows the same scene after the simplest possible lighting model has been included in the renderer; the level of realism is certainly improved.

It is without doubt the way in which light interacts with surfaces of a 3D model that is the most significant effect that we can simulate to provide visual realism. A hidden surface procedure may determine *what you can see* but it is mainly the interaction with light that determines *what you do see*.

To simulate *lighting* effects it stands to reason that at least the location and color of one or more lights must be known. In addition to this we need to classify the light as being one of the three types illustrated in Figure 4.34; i.e.,

1. A point light source that illuminates in all directions.

2. A directional or parallel light source. In this case the light comes from a specific direction which is the same at all points in the scene. (The illumination from the sun is an example of this type of illumination.)

3. A spotlight illumination that is limited to a small region of the scene. The beam of the spotlight is normally assumed to have a graduated edge so that the illumination is a maximum inside a cone of half angle θ_1 and falls to zero intensity inside another cone of half angle θ_2, naturally $\theta_2 > \theta_1$.

For a lot of scenes the type 1 source gives the best approximation to the lighting conditions. In simulated outdoor scenes the sun is so far away that its illumination is simulated as a directional light source with all rays arriving at the scene in a parallel direction.

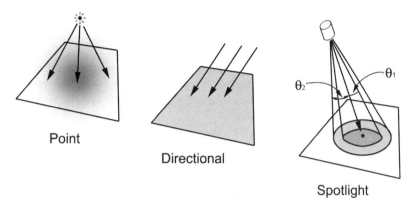

Point

Directional

Spotlight

Figure 4.34.   Three types of light source.

Before proceeding we should consider the format for recording a value for the surface color and illumination: call it c. In computer graphics programs a model to describe color must be employed; a detailed description of various color models may be found in [14]. The simplest color model that fulfills all the requirements is one with three components, one for each of the primary colors Red, Green, and Blue, the so-called RGB values. Any color the eye can perceive can be expressed in terms of an RGB triple. Thus c is recorded as c_R, c_G, c_B which are usually stored as unsigned eight bit integers giving a range for each of 256 discrete values. For preliminary calculation it is more usual to assume that c_R, c_G, and c_B are recorded as floating point numbers in the range $[0, 1]$. We will also assume that any light or surface color is also given as an RGB triple in the same range.

There are other models to describe color; HSV (Hue, Saturation Value) and CMYK (Cyan, Magenta, Yellow, blacK) are alternatives that have advantages in certain situations. It is possible to convert back and forward between any of these models if necessary.

To determine the color that is recorded in a pixel the effect of lights need to be combined with the surface properties of the polygon visible in that pixel. The simplest way to do this is to break up the mathematical model for light-surface interaction into a number of terms, each one of which represents a specific physical phenomenon.

In the following expressions s_R, s_G, s_B represents the color of the surface, and l_R, l_G, l_B the color of the light. I_a, I_c, I_d, and I_s are the four contributions to the lighting model and we will discuss them shortly. Using this terminology the color c calculated for the pixel in question may be expressed as:

$$c_R \quad = \quad I_a s_R + I_c (I_s + I_d s_R) l_R \tag{4.1}$$

$$c_G = I_a s_G + I_c(I_s + I_d s_G)l_G \qquad (4.2)$$
$$c_B = I_a s_B + I_c(I_s + I_d s_B)l_B \qquad (4.3)$$

Writing the expressions in this form with s_R, etc., as separate terms facilitates the calculation because the surface color may be determined independently of the remainder of the terms in the lighting model; indeed it might possibly be calculated in a separate module.

To obtain expressions for the four components in our illumination model (I_a, I_c, I_d, and I_s) we must consider the spatial relationship between the lights, the camera, and the action, illustrated in Figure 4.35. In the expressions below we will assume that $\mathbf{p}$ is the point to be illuminated on the visible polygon which has a surface normal $\hat{\mathbf{n}}$ at $\mathbf{p}$. We will now proceed to consider models for the components:

1. *Ambient reflection (I_a)*

   When there are no lights in a scene the picture will be blank. Including a small fraction of the surface color, s_R, etc., helps to simulate the effect of light reflected from the world around the scene. Without it pictures of objects would look like they had been taken in outer space. An image rendered with an ambient light factor of unity is equivalent to a hidden surface drawing such as that which produced the *flat* look shown in the picture of Plate 4. The component of a lighting model due to ambient reflection is designated as I_a and it is always constant: i.e., $I_a = k$.

2. *Diffuse reflection (I_d)*

   Diffuse lighting is the most significant component of an illumination model. The term *reflection* is used here because it is light reflected from surfaces

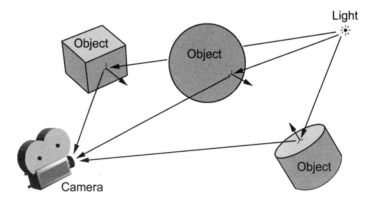

Figure 4.35.   Lights, camera, action. Reflected light finds its way to the observer.

which enters the camera. To model the effect we assume that a polygon is most brightly illuminated when the incident light strikes the surface at right angles. The illumination falls to zero when the direction of the beam of light is parallel to the surface. This behavior is known as the Lambert cosine law and is illustrated in Figure 4.36. The diffuse illumination component I_d for a point light source located at $\mathbf{P}_l$ is thus given by:

$$I_d = \frac{\mathbf{P}_l - \mathbf{p}}{|\mathbf{P}_l - \mathbf{p}|} \cdot \hat{\mathbf{n}}$$

In the case of a directional light source with incident direction $\hat{\mathbf{d}}$ the diffuse component becomes:

$$I_d = -\hat{\mathbf{d}} \cdot \hat{\mathbf{n}}$$

For a spotlight located at $\mathbf{P}_l$, pointing in direction $\hat{\mathbf{d}}$ and having light cone angles θ_1 and θ_2:

$$I_d = \begin{cases} \dfrac{\mathbf{P}_l - \mathbf{p}}{|\mathbf{P}_l - \mathbf{p}|} \cdot \hat{\mathbf{n}} & \text{if } \theta < \theta_1 \\[2ex] \left(\dfrac{\mathbf{P}_l - \mathbf{p}}{|\mathbf{P}_l - \mathbf{p}|} \cdot \hat{\mathbf{n}} \right) \left(1 - \dfrac{(\theta - \theta_1)}{(\theta_2 - \theta_1)} \right) & \text{if } \theta_1 \leq \theta \leq \theta_2 \\[2ex] 0 & \text{if } \theta_2 < \theta \end{cases}$$

where $\cos \theta = \hat{\mathbf{d}} \cdot (\mathbf{p} - \mathbf{P}_l)$.

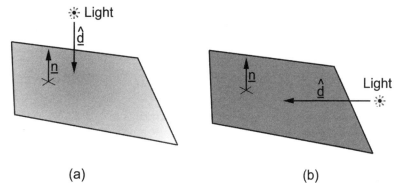

(a)   (b)

Figure 4.36.   Diffuse illumination. (a) The brightest illumination occurs when the incident light direction is at right angles to the surface. (b) The illumination tends to zero as the direction of the incident light becomes parallel to the surface.

3. *Specular reflection (I_s)*

   It is the specular component of the light reflected from a surface that makes it look shiny. In practice the effect of specular reflection is to add a *highlight* to parts of a model that have been designated as shiny. The specular highlight takes the color of the light and not that of the surface on which it is visible. To set up a model for specular reflection we need to consider in a little more detail something of its origin.

   A perfect mirror reflects all rays of light perfectly and the angle of reflection is equal to the angle of incidence. However shiny surfaces that are not perfect mirrors introduce small random fluctuations in the direction of the reflected rays. These random fluctuations in the direction of the reflected rays of light tend to be small, so that they all lie within a cone-shaped volume that has its apex at the point of reflection and its axis lying in the direction that a ray would take if the surface was a perfect mirror (see Figure 4.37).

   In the lighting model the specular illumination component I_s is normally modeled with the empirical expression suggested by Phong [13]:

   $$I_s = \cos^m \phi$$

   in which ϕ is the angle between the reflection vector and the vector leading from the viewpoint at $\mathbf{P}_v$ to $\mathbf{p}$ on the surface. To determine ϕ from the known geometry shown in Figure 4.37 it is necessary to use a few intermediate steps.

   First calculate the vector $\mathbf{b}$ which bisects the vectors between $\mathbf{p}$ and the viewpoint and between $\mathbf{p}$ and $\mathbf{P}_l$. The vector $\mathbf{b}$ takes an angle β between these vectors. From that the angle α is easily determined because $\cos\alpha = \hat{\mathbf{b}} \cdot \hat{\mathbf{n}}$ (the surface normal $\hat{\mathbf{n}}$ is known) while $\mathbf{b}$ is given by:

   $$\mathbf{b} = \frac{\mathbf{p} - \mathbf{P}_l}{|\mathbf{p} - \mathbf{P}_l|} - \frac{\mathbf{p} - \mathbf{P}_v}{|\mathbf{p} - \mathbf{P}_v|}$$

   $$\hat{\mathbf{b}} = \frac{\mathbf{b}}{|\mathbf{b}|}$$

   In Figure 4.37 we note that:

   $$\beta = \phi + \theta - \alpha$$

   and that:

   $$\beta = \theta + \alpha$$

   Eliminating β and canceling θ gives:

   $$\alpha = \frac{\phi}{2}$$

In terms of the known geometry I_s therefore becomes:

$$I_s = \cos^m \phi \text{ or:}$$
$$I_s = (2\cos^2 \frac{\alpha}{2} - 1)^m \text{ or:}$$
$$I_s = (2(\hat{\mathbf{b}} \cdot \hat{\mathbf{n}})^2 - 1)^m$$

The cosine power, m, is the parameter which governs the *shininess* of a surface. Very shiny surface have a high m, typical values lie in the range 10 to 99.

If accelerated hardware or fast processors are not available, the presence of a power function in the calculation of specular reflection can be quite slow. In this situation it is a good idea to establish a two-dimensional lookup table with a few values of m and the dot product $(\mathbf{b} \cdot \mathbf{n})$. The table can be quite small because the visual appearance of specular highlights does not change too rapidly, perhaps 16 values of m and 1000 values covering the interval $[0, 1]$ in which the dot product $\mathbf{b} \cdot \mathbf{n}$ lies. Setting aside a 64k block of memory to store the table will be a very good investment when the time saved in rendering is taken into account. When very fast processors or accelerated hardware is available the memory access time can often exceed the time for a power calculation, and in this case it is better to do the calculation.

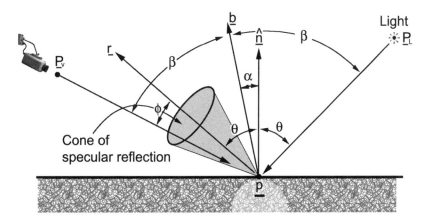

Figure 4.37.   Specular reflection.

4. *Depth cueing (I_c)*
   Like any electromagnetic radiation light is attenuated as it travels away from
   its source. The reflected light (mainly diffuse) arriving at the viewpoint has
   traveled from the light source to the object where it was reflected on to the
   observer. In theory the light intensity should be attenuated with distance
   from its source using an inverse square law, but in practice a linear fall-off
   looks much more realistic. Quite often depth cueing can be omitted entirely
   from the model with only mildly noticeable effect. A linear model is usually
   written in the form:

$$I_c = \frac{1}{d_o + d}$$

   where d_o is a constant and d is the distance of **p** from the viewpoint.
   Assuming that the viewpoint is at $(0,0,0)$ and the observer is looking along
   the x-axis, a good assumption is to let $d = p_x$, the x-coordinate of **p**.

   If depth cueing is to be used it is also a good idea to perform an *exposure*
   test by examining all the polygons and scaling the light intensities so that
   the maximum is always unity. If this is not done then it can require quite
   a lot of trial and error testing to generate a picture that is neither under- or
   over-exposed.

Once each component of the illumination model in equation 4.1 is known a
general expression for the effect of lighting a surface in the scene at some point
p with n lights becomes:

$$c_R = I_a s_R + I_c \sum_{i=0}^{n-1} (I_s(i) + I_d(i)s_R)l_R(i)$$

$$c_G = I_a s_G + I_c \sum_{i=0}^{n-1} (I_s(i) + I_d(i)s_G)l_G(i)$$

$$c_B = I_a s_B + I_c \sum_{i=0}^{n-1} (I_s(i) + I_d(i)s_B)l_B(i)$$

I_d and I_s depend on the position of light i and on which type of light it is:
spotlight, etc. If $n > 1$ each term in the lighting model must be limited so that it
falls in the range $[0, 1]$, otherwise an overexposed picture will be produced.

4.11 Shading

Figure 4.38 shows two pictures of the same faceted model of a sphere. The one
on the right looks smooth (apart from the silhouetted edges which we will discuss
later); it is the way a sphere should look. The one on the left looks like just

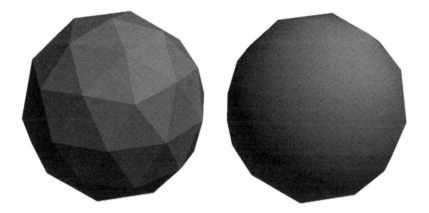

Figure 4.38.   Shading of two similar polygon models of a sphere.

what it is, a collection of triangular polygons. Although the outline of neither is perfectly circular it is the appearance of the interior that first grabs the attention. This example highlights the main drawback of the representation of an object with a model made up from polygonal facets. To model a sphere so that it looks smooth by increasing the number, or equivalently decreasing the size, of the facets is quite impractical; 10,000s would be required just for a simple sphere. However both the spheres shown in Figure 4.38 contain the same number of facets and yet one manages to look smooth. How?

The answer is the use of a trick that fools the eye by smoothly varying the shading within the polygonal facets. The point has already been made that if you look at the outlines of both spheres you will see that they are made from straight segments. In the case of the smooth-looking sphere it is because the discontinuities in shading between adjacent facets have been eliminated that it looks smooth. To the eye a discontinuity in shading is much more noticeable than a small angular change between two edges.

So how is the smooth shading achieved? There are two useful possibilities; one, the Phong approach, gives a more realistic look than the other, the Gouraud approach. Unfortunately Phong's shading model achieves its realism at the expense of a greater number of calculations, so we will look at them both. Combining shading with lighting makes another major contribution to obtaining a realistic picture of an object from its numerical model as illustrated in Figure 4.39, which shows the effect on the test image of adding a shading procedure to the renderer.

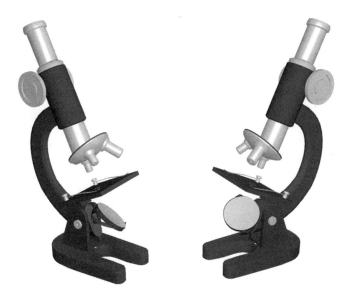

Figure 4.39.   After lighting and Phong shading have been added to a hidden surface rendering, the image
                  starts to look much more realistic.

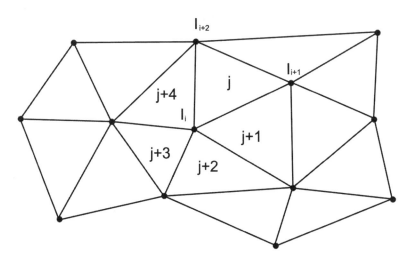

Figure 4.40.   Averaging light intensities in polygons j to $j + 4$ adjacent to vertex i will provide an
                  appropriate intensity, I_i, at vertex i. Similarly light intensities I_{i+1} and I_{i+2} are determined
                  from the light falling on polygons adjacent to those vertices.

4.11.1 Gouraud Shading

To simulate smooth shading across a polygon the Gouraud approach is a two-step process:

1. Calculate the intensity of the light at each vertex of the model.

2. Use a bi-linear interpolation to obtain the intensity at any point within a polygon from the intensity at the vertices of the polygon.

To calculate the light intensity at vertex i, as shown in Figure 4.40, it is necessary to take account of all the polygons attached to vertex i. Section 4.10 showed how the intensity of the light falling on a point within a polygon can be calculated. We then average the intensity of the light falling on polygons attached to vertex i. For example, in Figure 4.40 polygons j, $j+1$, $j+2$, $j+3$, and $j+4$ will contribute to the average shading at vertex i. Thus to calculate light intensities at n vertices with m polygons recorded in a list, $Poly(k)$, (remember that polygons store the ID of the vertices they are attached to, as seen in Figure 3.18), use the short algorithm of Figure 4.41.

To interpolate the intensity I_p at the point **p**, as shown in Figure 4.42, there are two alternatives:

1. Work directly in three dimensions from the known intensities I_0, I_1, I_2, and the vertices at $\mathbf{P}_0$, etc., which have coordinates (x_0, y_0, z_0), (x_1, y_1, z_1), and (x_2, y_2, z_2) respectively. Use the procedure described in Section 2.10.1 to obtain α and β and then interpolate bi-linearly to obtain I_p:

$$I_p = I_0 + (I_2 - I_1)\alpha + (I_1 - I_0)\beta$$

```
for all vertices i < n {
    set vertex intensities I_i = 0
}
for all polygons k < m {
    set running average intensity I_l = 0
    for vertices i of polygon k {
        calculate light intensity at vertex
        l = Poly(k).V_id(i) and update
        running average intensity I_l
        make sure that 0 ≤ I_l ≤ 1
    }
}
```

Figure 4.41.   The Gouraud shading procedure.

Finding I_p directly in three dimensions is slow. It would be better if we could do the calculation after the polygon's vertices have been projected onto the viewing plane. We can indeed do this because shading is the last step in the rendering algorithm and all the necessary 3D calculations have already been carried out. This leads to our second alternative.

2. Use the 2D coordinates after projection of the polygon's vertices to the viewing plane; i.e., to points (X_0, Y_0), (X_1, Y_1), and (X_2, Y_2). Further, because the rendering procedure will normally be filling pixels sequentially across a scanline, a few additional arithmetic operations can be saved by calculating an increment in intensity I which is added to the value obtained for the previous pixel on the scanline.

For a triangular polygon, k, which spans scanline j (see Figure 4.42) starting at pixel i, the intensity $I_{i,j}$ can be obtained from the following formulae:

$$\Delta = (Y_2 - Y_0)(X_1 - X_0) - (X_2 - X_0)(Y_1 - Y_0)$$

$$\alpha = \frac{(Y_2 - Y_0)(i - X_0) - (X_2 - X_0)(j - Y_0)}{\Delta}$$

$$\beta = \frac{(j - Y_0)(X_1 - X_0) - (i - X_0)(Y_1 - Y_0)}{\Delta}$$

$$I_{i,j} = \alpha(I_1 - I_0) + \beta(I_2 - I_0)$$

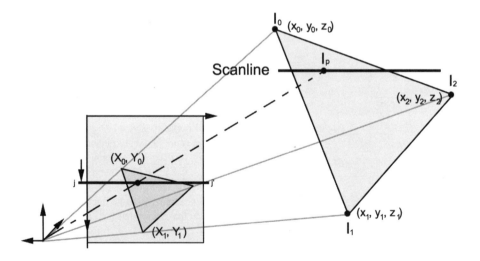

Figure 4.42.   To calculate the light intensity at an internal point of a triangular polygon, interpolate from the intensity at the polygon's vertices.

The intensity in adjacent pixels $I_{i+1,j}$, etc., is determined by calculating an increment δI from:

$$\delta I \quad = \quad \frac{(Y_1 - Y_2)I_0 + (Y_2 - Y_0)I_1 + (Y_0 - Y_1)I_2}{\Delta}$$

Then for all the remaining pixels on scanline j covered by polygon k the intensity is given by:

$$I_{i+1,j} \quad = \quad I_{i,j} + \delta I$$

4.11.2 Phong Shading

The Gouraud shading procedure works well for the diffuse reflection component of a lighting model, but it does not give a good result when specular reflection is taken into account. Specular highlights occupy quite a small proportion of a visible surface and the direction of the normal at precisely the visible point must be known so that the specular reflection can be determined. Thus Phong's approach was to interpolate the surface normal over a polygon rather than interpolate the light intensity. In the other aspects the procedure is similar to the Gouraud shading algorithm.

Gouraud's algorithm still has its uses because Phong's [13] approach requires much more work. The additional calculations include vector instead of scalar interpolation and a time consuming square root calculation to normalize the resultant normal before it can be used in the lighting equations. However most of the additional calculation occurs because the diffuse lighting scalar product must be evaluated for every pixel covered by the projection of the polygon and not just its vertices.

Phong shading is done in the following two stages:

1. Calculate a normal vector for each vertex of the model.

2. Use two-dimensional interpolation to determine the normal at any point within a polygon from the normals at the vertices of the polygon.

In stage 1 an analogous procedure to the first step of the Gouraud algorithm is used. In this case however averaging takes place with normal vectors instead of illumination intensities. Figure 4.43 shows a cross section through a coarse (six-sided) approximation of a cylinder. In (a) the facet normals are illustrated, (b) shows the vertex normals obtained by averaging normals from facets connected to a particular vertex, and in (c) the effect of interpolation on normal vectors is shown. A smoothly varying surface normal will interact with the incoming light beam to give smoothly varying shading which will also work correctly with the model for specular highlights.

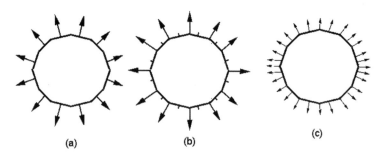

Figure 4.43.   In Phong smoothing the surface normals are averaged at the vertices and then the vertex
normals are interpolated over the flat facets to give an illusion of a continuously varying
curvature.

In stage 2 expressions very similar to those that occur in the Gouraud model
are derived. For a triangular polygon k that spans scanline j at the leftmost pixel
i, the normal vector $\hat{\mathbf{n}}_{i,j}$ is given by:

$$\Delta = (Y_2 - Y_0)(X_1 - X_0) - (X_2 - X_0)(Y_1 - Y_0)$$

$$\alpha = \frac{(Y_2 - Y_0)(i - X_0) - (X_2 - X_0)(j - Y_0)}{\Delta}$$

$$\beta = \frac{(j - Y_0)(X_1 - X_0) - (i - X_0)(Y_1 - Y_0)}{\Delta}$$

$$\begin{bmatrix} n_x \\ n_y \\ n_z \end{bmatrix}_{i,j} = \begin{bmatrix} \alpha(n_{1x} - n_{0x}) + \beta(n_{2x} - n_{0x}) \\ \alpha(n_{1y} - n_{0y}) + \beta(n_{2y} - n_{0y}) \\ \alpha(n_{1z} - n_{0z}) + \beta(n_{2z} - n_{0z}) \end{bmatrix}$$

$$\hat{\mathbf{n}}_{i,j} = \frac{\mathbf{n}_{i,j}}{|\mathbf{n}_{i,j}|}$$

For the remaining pixels on scanline j, i.e., pixels $i+1$, $i+2$, etc., the normals
$(\mathbf{n}_{i+1,j}, \mathbf{n}_{i+2,j})$ are determined by calculating an incremental vector $\delta\mathbf{n}$ given by:

$$\begin{bmatrix} \delta n_x \\ \delta n_y \\ \delta n_z \end{bmatrix} = \frac{1}{\Delta} \begin{bmatrix} (Y_1 - Y_2)n_{0x} + (Y_2 - Y_0)n_{1x} + (Y_0 - Y_1)n_{2x} \\ (Y_1 - Y_2)n_{0y} + (Y_2 - Y_0)n_{1y} + (Y_0 - Y_1)n_{2y} \\ (Y_1 - Y_2)n_{0z} + (Y_2 - Y_0)n_{1z} + (Y_0 - Y_1)n_{2z} \end{bmatrix}$$

Normals in the remaining pixels on scanline j covered by polygon k are thus
determined sequentially from:

$$\mathbf{n}_{i+1,j} = \mathbf{n}_{i,j} + \delta\mathbf{n}$$

$$\hat{\mathbf{n}}_{i+1,j} = \frac{\mathbf{n}_{i+1,j}}{|\mathbf{n}_{i+1,j}|}$$

Remember: the normal $\hat{\mathbf{n}}_{i,j}$ found by interpolation in the two-dimensional projection plane is still the three-dimensional normal vector at $\mathbf{p}$ on polygon k (which is the point visible in pixel (i, j)).

Before we finish discussing Phong shading there is one very important point that requires a little more thought. Look at Figure 4.44: in (a) we see a rendered half cylinder approximated by six rectangular facets on the curved side and one rectangular facet on the flat (cut) side; in (b) a plan of the section at plane XX' shows the facet normals. Now imagine what happens as stage 1 of Phong's procedure is applied. In (c) the averaged vertex normals are shown and (d) gives the interpolated normals. Even at the points labeled A and B the normal vector varies smoothly including round the sharp corner. This is **not** quite the desired result because the corner will be smoothed out and the distinct edge will just merge into the smooth shading. At points A and B the corners should really be retained. To achieve this make the following modification to the algorithm at stage 1:

- Do not update the running average for the vertex normal unless the angle $\alpha < \dfrac{\pi}{2}$ or the user overrides the decision. (α is illustrated in Figure 4.44).

Figure 4.44(e) shows the effect after this correction is applied. On a practical level to achieve this correction the vertex normals must be stored as part of the polygon data structures (see Chapter 3) because a discontinuity between the normals of adjacent polygons cannot be represented if a single vector is stored for each vertex. Thus the data structure associated with each polygon in a model, from Figure 3.18, requires to be updated to that shown in Figure 4.45.

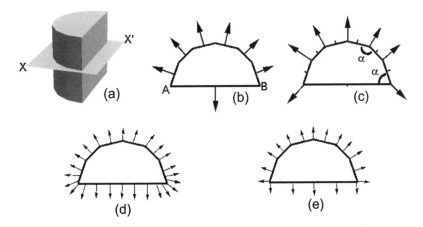

Figure 4.44.   A cross section through a cylinder that has been cut in half along its axis.

V_{id}	list of vertex identifiers to which polygon is attached
$id_{material}$	pointer to material in materials list
$A_{id}(3)$	list of the id's of polygons with a common side
n	normal to surface plane
$\mathbf{e}_{id}$	list of Phong vertex normals

Figure 4.45.   Vertex and polygon data structures with vertex normals $\mathbf{e}_{id}$.

4.12   Pseudo Shadows

Shadows are perhaps the most important consequence of lighting that an observer uses when looking at photographs to assess the relative positions of objects. For example, Figure 4.46 shows a simple scene with a twisted ribbon that is located somewhere above a flat plane extending to infinity in all directions, *what we might call a ground plane*. If you were asked: "how close to the ground is the ribbon?", how would you decide from this 2D picture? From the image on the left it's hard to tell, but add the shadow as shown on the right and you can easily tell that the ribbon is located well above the ground. You can also work out the relative position of the light. Unfortunately the calculations that allow perfect shadows to be determined are among the most time consuming a renderer can be called upon to execute. Techniques such as "Ray Tracing" need to be used to determine perfect shadows. This will be considered separately in Chapter 5. However, shadows are so important that much faster, but *approximate*, methods have been developed to render shadows. It is these *pseudo* shadow techniques that will be discussed in

Figure 4.46.   Adding shadows to a computer generated image gives the viewer some very powerful visual clues as to the relative position of objects in a scene.

this section. The shadow shown in Figure 4.46 was generated with just such a technique.

We will consider two approaches to pseudo shadowing which cover most eventualities; they are planar shadows and shadow maps.

4.12.1 Planar Shadows

If the surface on which the shadow falls is flat, then it is straightforward to find the shadow cast by a polygon. Once found the shadow is projected to the viewing plane where a buffer analogous to the Z buffer is used to hold a *shadow mask*. Because shadows are either on or off, a one byte per pixel mask can accommodate up to eight different planar shadowed surfaces.

The contents of the shadow mask must be determined in a step that precedes step 5 in the basic rendering algorithms (Section 4.1). In the final rendering step, as the Z or scanline buffers are being filled at pixel i, j, the following test is added:

> If the point $\mathbf{p}$ on polygon k is visible in pixel i, j and polygon k is part of one of the planes that has a shadow on it then the shadow buffer at coordinate i, j is checked to see if polygon k is in shadow or not. If it is then the color of pixel i, j is dimmed.

Figure 4.12 illustrates the geometry used to produce a shadow mask for the shadow cast on a plane (normal $\hat{\mathbf{n}}$ position $\mathbf{P}_p$) by a triangular polygon (vertices $\mathbf{P}_0$, $\mathbf{P}_1$, and $\mathbf{P}_2$) lit from a point light source at $\mathbf{P}_l$.

In the shadow buffer the shadow cast by a triangular polygon is always triangular too. If we let (X_0, Y_0), (X_1, Y_1), and (X_2, Y_2) be the coordinates in the shadow buffer equivalent to vertices $\mathbf{P}_0$, etc., we can use a scanline filling procedure to set all the appropriate flags in the shadow buffer. To calculate the coordinates (X_0, Y_0) in the shadow buffer equivalent to vertex $\mathbf{P}_0$ in the polygon casting the shadow, first obtain the intersection point of the line passing through $\mathbf{P}_l$ and $\mathbf{P}_0$ and the plane $(\mathbf{p} - \mathbf{P}_p) \cdot \hat{\mathbf{n}} = 0$, then project that point to (X_0, Y_0) with the same scale factor and aspect ratio used in step 4 of the basic rendering algorithm. Those calculations are detailed in Sections 2.5 and 2.11.7.

Planar shadows have sharply defined edges and are essentially perfect, which sometimes is an advantage but at other times may lead to less realistic results. The amount of memory required to hold the shadow buffer is not particularly excessive and depends on the resolution of the output raster. The disadvantage of planar shadows is that they cannot simulate realistic shadows falling on curved or non-planar surfaces. Shadow mapped lights which we will consider next do give pretty good-looking shadows across any shape of surface.

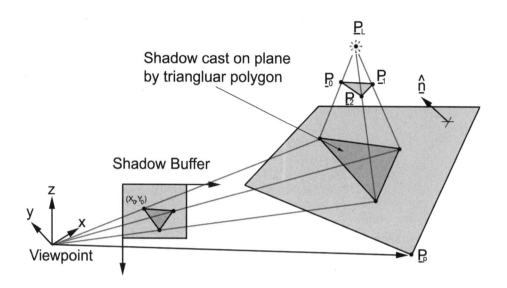

Figure 4.47.   Filling the shadow mask with the shadow cast on a flat plane by a triangular polygon.

4.12.2   Shadow Maps

Figure 4.48 shows a viewpoint (with associated projection plane) and spotlight directed towards the point **p** in the scene. The viewpoint is located at the origin of coordinates and the spotlight is at $\mathbf{P}_L$. Imagine now a viewpoint at the position of the light source $\mathbf{P}_L$ which is looking in the direction of the spotlight, towards the target at **p**. For a field of view that just encloses the spotlight's cone, a projection plane capable of showing everything visible from the light's point of view can be defined. We can use a Z depth buffer associated with this imaginary projection plane to help us render a shadow due to the spotlight. This technique requires us to *pre-render* a view of the scene for each spotlight and fill its *shadow* Z buffer, or what we will call its *shadow map*, as in the standard Z buffer algorithm.

During rendering of the scene when it comes time to determine if a point **p** lies in shadow or not, we imagine a line from **p** to $\mathbf{P}_L$; it must pass through one of the cells in the shadow map associated with the imaginary viewpoint at $\mathbf{P}_L$. That cell records the distance of the nearest point in the scene from the imaginary camera (and spotlight), say d_{min}.

Here then is our test to see if **P** lies in shadow: if the distance from **P** to $\mathbf{P}_L$ is greater that d_{min} then point **P** lies in shadow.

This procedure works because the spotlight shines on a limited area, and so its cone of illumination is bounded and therefore the pseudo camera's field of view

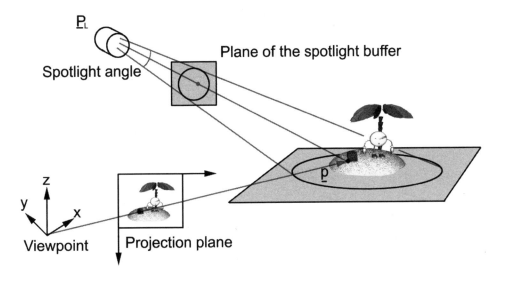

Figure 4.48.   A scene with spotlight illumination.

can be set to include all parts of the scene illuminated by the spotlight. Because the light's shadow map is of finite resolution the outline of the shadow will be subject to aliasing effects. The more memory allocated to hold the shadow map or the narrower the angle of the spotlight cone, the less noticeable the aliasing will be. To reduce the visual impact of the aliasing at the edges of the shadow a degree of blurring can be introduced by averaging shadow values over a number of adjacent cells. This will cause the shadow to have a soft (blurry) edge, but that is sometimes more realistic than the harsh crisp shadows produced by the shadow plane approximation.

To implement this technique the instructions in Figure 4.49 are inserted in the rendering algorithm after the viewing transformation has been performed. Note that the viewing transformation has been applied to the lights too.

For the scene illustrated in Figure 4.48 where the spotlight direction is given by the vector $\mathbf{d} = \mathbf{p} - \mathbf{P}_L$, a heading of:

$$\phi = ATAN2(d_y, d_x)$$

and pitch:

$$\theta = ATAN2(d_z, \sqrt{d_x^2 + d_y^2})$$

are used. Transformation $[T]$ is the product $[T] = [T_3][T_2][T_1]$ where

Repeat for all spotlights {
    Build a viewing transformation, $[T]$ for an imaginary
    camera located at the position of the spotlight.
    Apply $[T]$ to vertices in scene.
    Repeat for all polygons k {
        Project vertices of polygon k onto the *shadow buffer*
        plane and fill each entry with the depth to visible surface.
    }
}

Figure 4.49.   Procedure to fill the shadow map associated with a spotlight.

$$[T_1] \;=\; \text{a translation by } -\mathbf{P}_L$$
$$[T_2] \;=\; \text{a rotation round } z\text{axis (up) by} - \phi$$
$$[T_3] \;=\; \text{a rotation round} y \text{ axis by } - \theta$$

The projection is scaled so that the spotlight's outer cone (half angle θ_2) just fits inside the field of view. Thus, for a shadow buffer resolution of $n \times n$ and vertex coordinates (x', y', z'), after pre-multiplication by $[T]$, the shadow buffer coordinates (X, Y) are obtained from

$$d \;=\; \frac{n}{2 \tan \theta_2} \tag{4.4}$$

$$X \;=\; \frac{n}{2} - d\frac{y'}{x'} \tag{4.5}$$

$$Y \;=\; \frac{n}{2} - d\frac{z'}{x'} \tag{4.6}$$

The shadow map technique is completed by adding the following actions to the final rendering step after the surface color, shading, and lighting at $\mathbf{p}$ have been determined; repeat for all spotlights:

1. Apply transformation $[T]$ to $\mathbf{p}$ to give position (x', y', z'), in the frame of reference where the spotlight is at origin.

2. Apply the projection equations (4.4,4.5,4.6) to give (X, Y) and its nearest integer indices (X_i, Y_i).

3. Extract the shadow distance from the shadow map, $d_{min} = Z(X_i, Y_i)$.

4. If $x' > d_{min}$ then $\mathbf{p}$ is in shadow with respect to the spotlight.

Comment:

> While the above procedure works well in most cases it can be subject
> to some unpleasant Moiré patterning. This is due to the fact that each
> cell in the shadow map equates to quite a big area in the scene and
> within which there might be a significant depth variation, especially
> when the resolution of the buffer is low. As a result of this when the
> time comes to compare the depth of point **p** with values in the buffer
> then sometimes it will appear to be in and sometimes it will appear
> to be out of shadow. It is very important to set near and far planes
> as close to each other as possible as this gives better precision in the
> shadow map and therefore yields better results.
>
> A simple procedure (Woo [22]) can eliminate the visual disturbance.
> To apply it, a second (temporary) copy of the light shadow map is
> needed. In this second copy record the depth of the second closest
> polygon from the light, and when the full shadow is rendered simply
> average the depth between the two and use this as the shadow depth.
> In the case when there is only one surface (the second buffer holds
> infinity) then it cannot cast shadows on anything so ignore it. Af-
> ter each spotlight buffer has been checked the memory used for the
> temporary shadow map can be released. One final point: the shadow
> map only needs to be rebuilt in a non-static scene.

4.13 Surface Texturing

Even the best images synthesized from a polygonal model still lack the detail and richness of real surfaces. Imperfections due to wear and tear, regular color varia-tions, or natural material properties are very difficult to represent with polygons. Something as simple as text painted onto surfaces or detailed colored patterns would require polygon meshes to have prohibitively large numbers of facets and vertices. Two complimentary techniques, *image mapping* and *procedural textur-ing*, allow for realistic detail to be added to the images of polygonal or patched models without increasing the number of polygons.

Image mapping is probably the first choice of the 3D computer artist or CAD engineer when faced with the need to enhance a plain mesh model; it can make even the simplest model look tremendously lifelike and is the easiest and most adaptable way to add fine detail. The most popular real time rendering libraries use image mapping extensively (see Chapters 10 and 11). The theory of image mapping is discussed in Section 4.14.

Procedural or algorithmic textures provide some of the most beautiful surfaces seen in computer generated images. They have the advantage over the image mapping approach in that they can be rendered in any resolution and therefore do not exhibit the problems that an image map can suffer from when it is rendered in close-up. They do sometimes however show aliasing effects; see Apodaca [15].

The aliasing effect from which mapped images suffer is due to the fact that they must be recorded on an array of finite size, and thus their pixelated nature becomes all too apparent in close-up snapshots. Procedural textures have the additional advantages that they don't require the large amount of memory that may be required to record an image, nor is the problem that arises when an essentially flat (2D) image is mapped on to space filling solids evident. In Section 4.10, Equations 4.1, 4.2, and 4.3 described how the surface color S, at a point $\mathbf{p}$, is combined with the lighting conditions to produce a color value to represent what is seen at $\mathbf{p}$. The surface color S with its three components s_R, s_G, s_B can encapsulate not just a plain color but perhaps a blend or some other elaborate combination of shades. However, no matter how complex the procedure used to calculate S, the only variables on which it may depend are the position of $\mathbf{p}$, coordinates (x, y, z), or the 2D texture coordinates (X, Y) first introduced in Chapter 3; they are also commonly referred to as the u and v coordinates. This can be expressed formally as:

$$S = f(x, y, z, X, Y) \qquad\qquad (4.7)$$

It is unusual for $f(x, y, z, X, Y)$ to depend on x, y, z at the same time as it depends on X, Y, and therefore the term *volume texture* tends to be used for cases where $f()$ is independent of X or Y. Most volume textures tend to be generated from a fixed set of rules, and they are therefore called "procedural textures". When $f()$ is independent of x, y, or z the texture is called a surface texture and all image mapping methods fall into this category.

In addition to providing a way to alter the surface color S at $\mathbf{p}$, a texturing procedure might also modulate the direction of the surface normal or modify the transparency of the surface. In fact with a combination of these techniques and some ability to simulate reflections it can become difficult to distinguish a rendered image of the model from a photograph of the real thing; for example, see Figure 4.50.

Procedural textures can be used equally easily with functions of the form $f(x, y, z)$ (volume) or $f(X, Y)$ (surface); Figure 4.51 shows an example of a procedural texture applied to the same object in volume and surface modes. They are excellent for simulating naturally occurring surfaces such as wood, marble, granite, clouds, tree bark, veins, etc.; the list is almost endless. Chapter 9 details some algorithms to simulate a significant variety of surfaces.

We can establish two general types of procedural texture:

1. Those that use regular geometric patterns.

2. Those that use random patterns.

Figure 4.50.   Is this a photograph of the real thing or just a collection of numbers?

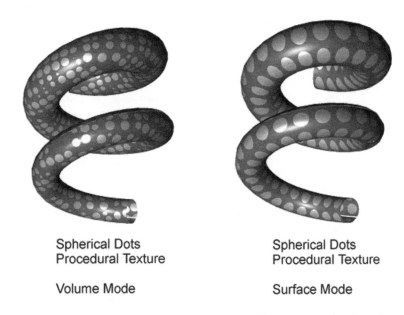

Spherical Dots   Spherical Dots
Procedural Texture   Procedural Texture

Volume Mode   Surface Mode

Figure 4.51.   Procedural texture in volume and surface modes. Note the way the dots cling to the
                  surface when texture coordinates are applied to the surface of the shape and how the
                  shape appears to be carved out of a block of *colored spheres* when volume coordinates
                  are used.

In many cases an enhanced appearance is achieved by combining the two types; the pattern of irregular paving slabs is one such example. Discolored and weathered bricks is another. Indeed this work has been extended to the concept of volume textures with the possibility of creating realistic clouds, smoke, coral, hair, and fur.

4.13.1   Basic Geometric Procedural Textures

Figure 4.52 presents an algorithm for generating a very simple geometric texture; i.e., a 3D system of bricks and mortar. Other simple textures that fall into this category include checks, dots, triangular shapes, stars, hexagonal patterns, and even a digital readout such as might appear on a clock.

The algorithm given in Figure 4.52 illustrates a compact interface between the texturing function and its host renderer. An input of a position, a small set of parameters, and an output of color value are sufficient to control all procedural functions. In fact we could standardize the parameter list so that the same function can be used by scanline, Z buffer, or ray tracing renderers interchangeably. Texturing functions are ideal candidates for implementation as run time definable libraries as, for example, DLLs under the Windows operating system.

4.13.2   Basic Random Procedural Textures

Simply generating random numbers does not lead to the creation of very interesting textures. What is required is a random function which is spatially correlated, that is, the surface attributes at two different locations are similar if the points are close together, but if the points are far apart then calculated surface attributes will be quite independent of one another.

A random number generator with just these properties was originally proposed by Perlin [16] in what turned out to be a seminal paper on the topic. Textures based on Perlin's ideas call upon one basic function: the noise generator. Given a position, $\mathbf{p}$, the noise generator returns a scalar value in the range $[0, 1]$; we will write it as $u = sNoise(\mathbf{p})$. This function has the essential property quoted above and, of equal importance for application in rendering, *if called with the same value of* $\mathbf{p}$ *it returns the same noise; although it has random properties they are quite repeatable.*

From $sNoise(\mathbf{p})$ three other useful functions are easily derived:

1. A noise generator that returns a vector given a position, $\mathbf{v} = vNoise(\mathbf{p})$.

2. A function called Turbulence, that is similar to the noise function but is smooth in some places while varying rapidly in others, something like the effect achieved when two colors of paint are stirred together. $u = sTurb(\mathbf{p})$ generates a scalar turbulence value.

3. $\mathbf{v} = vTurb(\mathbf{p})$ returns a vector-valued turbulence.

These *noise* functions have statistical properties (translational and rotational invariance) that make them particularly useful for 3D graphics work.

The turbulence functions are examples of a *fractal* or $1/f$ noise. They can be easily calculated by adding basic Perlin noises. *The idea is that the noise signal is built up by adding a number of components, with the amplitude of each component inversely proportional to its frequency.* Thus low frequency components have large amplitude but high frequency components have small amplitude.

```
/* the input to the algorithm is a position coordinate
(x, y, z), the mortar % thickness tm and the colors for brick and mortar.
The output is a color triple sR, sG, sB
and a function Floor(a) is called to return the nearest
lower integer to a. In the C language Floor would be
implemented as follows */
#define Floor(a) ((a) < 0.0? ((long)(a)-1L:(long)(a))
```

if integer part of z is divisible by 2 {
$\qquad x = x + \frac{1}{2}$
$\qquad y = y + \frac{1}{2}$
}
$x = x - Floor(x)$
$y = y - Floor(y)$
$z = z - Floor(z)$

```
/* a collection of if's divide the brick from the mortar */
```

if $z > 1 - t_m$ or $y > 1 - t_m$ or
$\qquad (y > \frac{1}{2} - t_m$ and $y < \frac{1}{2})$ or
$\qquad (y < \frac{1}{2}$ and $((x > \frac{1}{2} - t_m$ and $x < \frac{1}{2})$ or $x > 1 - t_m))$ or
$\qquad (y > \frac{1}{2}$ and $((x > \frac{1}{3} - t_m$ and
$\qquad\qquad x < \frac{1}{3})$ or $(x > \frac{7}{10}$ and $x < \frac{7}{10} + t_m)))$ {
$\qquad$ return the mortar color
}
else {
$\qquad$ return the brick color
}

Figure 4.52. An algorithm that creates a brick and mortar procedural texture. For a given point **p** which has coordinates (x, y, z) it determines whether **p** is inside the brick or the mortar.

Comment: the fractal noise function can also be useful for building models of natural shapes; e.g., trees and mountain landscapes.

There are many ways to implement the Perlin noise function; see Ward [17] for example. Another excellent Perlin implementation is available in the POV-Ray program [18].

One of the shortest and fastest ways to write a Perlin noise generator is to establish a 3D array of random numbers and then to interpolate linearly from that to obtain a noise value for a specific point **p**.

Perhaps the most versatile noise texture is that called Bozo (see Chapter 9 for examples); with appropriate scaling and level setting it can represent many natural phenomena such as clouds and solar corona. An algorithm for the Bozo texture is given in Figure 4.53.

For some practical hints on implementing procedural textures you might consult Worley's notes [19] and the work of the other contributors to the same SIG-GRAPH course or their later book [20].

```
/* The input to the algorithm is a position coordinate
(x, y, z), two threshold values t₁ and t₂, three color triples
c₁R, c₁G, c₁B, c₁R, c₁G, c₁B and c₁R, c₁G, c₁B
and a turbulence parameter τ which give the texture its
swirly look.
The output is a color triple sR, sG, sB
The Bozo texture is a threshold of the noise function. At each threshold
a color change occurs. */

if τ ≠ 0 {
    v = vTurb(p)
    p = p + τv
}
n = sNoise(p)
if n < t₁ {
    assign color s = c₁ (R,G and B)
}
else if n < t₂ {
    assign color s = c₂ (R,G and B)
}
else {
    assign color s = c₃ (R,G and B)
}
```

Figure 4.53.   An algorithm to creates a Bozo procedural texture. It calls upon the Perlin noise functions and returns a color setting at a point P with coordinates (x, y, z).

No rough texture

Rough texture added
to cylindrical surface

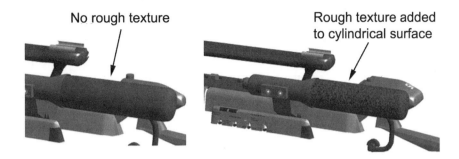

Figure 4.54.   A procedural texture that uses the $vNoise()$ function to *bend* the surface normal. The illustrated component is part of the model shown in Figure 4.50.

Procedural textures, especially the noise-based ones, give beautiful, richly detailed, and realistic-looking effects when the vector noise function is used to perturb the direction of the surface normal at P. Doing this has the effect of giving a rough, bumpy, or pitted appearance to the surface because of the way the Phong lighting model interacts with the surface normal. Figure 4.54 illustrates a procedural texture that modulates the surface normal to give a rough surface. The noise function can also be called upon to alter the transparency or reflectivity of the surface at P. When all of these effects are combined some of the most visually stunning computer-generated images emerge, even from shapes described with only a few hundred polygons.

Before ending this section it is worth pointing out that in step 2 of the rendering algorithm, models are moved or rotated to place them at appropriate positions in the scene. If any surface of that model is covered with a volume texture then the position argument to the noise function should be specified with respect to a frame of reference attached to the model and **not** some global frame. If a global frame of reference for the argument to the noise function were used, then an animation of a moving model will give the disturbing appearance that the model is moving through a kind of three-dimensional *sea* of the texture.

4.14   Image Mapping

An image map performs a very similar task to that of a 2D procedural texture: it adds detail to surfaces without the need for a very large number of small polygons. In contrast to a procedural texture, image maps provide the model designer much greater control over the appearance of the texture; in essence, any image may be used as the source for the image map. (2D art work or scanned photographs are common sources.) This is particularly useful in product design applications where text, manufacturers logos, or *labels* can be added to a 3D model of their product.

Figure 4.50 illustrated a model in which 32 small image maps were used to enhance the sense of realism. In this section we will consider how these 2D pictures are attached to a polygonal 3D model. Figure 4.57 shows a simple rectangular polygon mapped with a small picture applied in several useful ways, and we shall consider these later.

The expressions needed to determine the color s at a point $\mathbf{p}$ within a triangular polygon due to the application of an image map are analogous to those we obtained when considering a procedural texture applied in surface mode. If the vertices of a triangular polygon are $\mathbf{P}_0$, $\mathbf{P}_1$, and $\mathbf{P}_2$ then s, the color to be substituted into the lighting model, is determined by executing the following steps:

1. Use the coordinates of the vertices of the surface polygon relative to $\mathbf{p}$ to determine parameters α and β, where:

$$(\mathbf{p} - \mathbf{P}_0) = \alpha(\mathbf{P}_1 - \mathbf{P}_0) + \beta(\mathbf{P}_2 - \mathbf{P}_0)$$

Section 2.10.1 explains the necessary analysis.

2. Given texture coordinates of (X_0, Y_0), (X_1, Y_1), and (X_2, Y_2) at $\mathbf{P}_0$, $\mathbf{P}_1$, and $\mathbf{P}_2$ respectively, a texture coordinate for the point $\mathbf{p}$, say (X, Y), is determined by:

$$\begin{aligned} X &= X_0 + \alpha(X_1 - X_0) + \beta(X_2 - X_0) & (4.8) \\ Y &= Y_0 + \alpha(Y_1 - Y_0) + \beta(Y_2 - Y_0) & (4.9) \end{aligned}$$

3. From (X, Y) an index (i, j) into an array of pixels $A_{n,m}$ which record an image of resolution $n \times m$ is determined as follows:

$$\begin{aligned} i &= \text{nearest integer to } (nX) \\ j &= \text{nearest integer to } (mY) \end{aligned}$$

4. Copy the pixel color from $A_{i,j}$ to s. How the information in A is stored and addressed is a matter of personal choice as is whether the image is true color (16.7 million colors), hicolor (65536 colors), or paletted (one byte used to address a palette of 256 colors).

Figure 4.55 illustrates the mapping process.

There are two important issues that arise in step 3 above. Firstly to obtain a valid address in A both i and j must satisfy simultaneously $0 \leq i < n$ and $0 \leq j < m$ or, equivalently, by scaling to a unit square: $0 \leq X < 1$ and $0 \leq Y < 1$. Thus the question arises as to how to interpret texture coordinates that fall outside the range $[0, 1]$. There are three possibilities, all of which prove useful; they are:

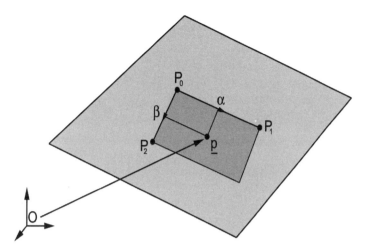

Figure 4.55. Mapping an image into a rectangle with texture coordinates of $(0,0)$ at $\mathbf{P}_0$, $(1,0)$ at $\mathbf{P}_1$ and $(0,1)$ at $\mathbf{P}_2$ respectively. At the point p an appropriate pixel color is determined from the image using the steps given in the text.

1. Do not proceed with the mapping process for any point with texture coordinates that fall outside the range $[0,1]$; just apply a constant color.

2. Use a modulus function to *tile* the image over the surface so that it is repeated as many times as necessary to cover the whole surface.

3. Tile the image over the surface, but choose a group of four copies of the image to generate blocks that themselves repeat without any seams: i.e., a mosaic pattern. To generate a mosaic pattern the α and β values in Equations 4.8 and 4.9 are modified to α_m and β_m (a procedure described in the algorithm of Figure 4.56).

These three methods of applying an image map to a polygon's surface are illustrated in Figure 4.57.

The second issue is the rather discontinuous way of rounding the floating point texture coordinates (X, Y) to the integer address (i, j) ($i = \text{truncate}(x)$ and $j = \text{truncate}(y)$) used to pick the color from the image. A better approach is to use a bilinear or higher order interpolation to obtain s which takes into account not only the color in pixel (i, j) but also the color in the pixels adjacent to it. Thus, if the texture coordinates at $\mathbf{p}$ are (X, Y), we obtain s by using color values from $A_{i-1,j}$, $A_{i+1,j}$, $A_{i,j-1}$, and $A_{i,j+1}$ in addition to the color from $A_{i,j}$. This procedure is given in Figure 4.58.

/* the Floor function is given in Figure 4.52 */

$$\alpha_m = (\text{float})Floor(\alpha)$$
$$\beta_m = (\text{float})Floor(\beta)$$
$$b_x = ((\text{truncate } \alpha_m)(\text{bitwise AND}) 1)$$
$$b_y = ((\text{truncate } \beta_m)(\text{bitwise AND}) 1)$$
$$\alpha_m = \alpha - \alpha_m$$
$$\beta_m = \beta - \beta_m$$
if $b_x \neq 0$ {
    if $b_y \neq 0$ {
        $\alpha_m = 1 - \alpha_m$
        $\beta_m = 1 - \beta_m$
    }
    else {
        $\alpha_m = 1 - \alpha_m$
    }
}
else if $b_y \neq 0$ {
    $\beta_m = 1 - \beta_m$
}

Figure 4.56.   Generating a mosaic repeat pattern for seamless image mapping.

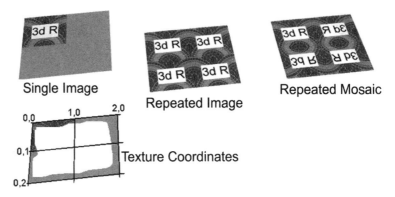

Figure 4.57.   Different ways of interpreting mapping coordinates over a flat surface. (a) No mapping outside unit rectangle. (b) Tiling by repeatedly copying the image map. (c) Mosaic tiling. In this case the image map is carefully arranged so that no discontinuous edges are visible when the map is tiled.

$$\delta X = X - \text{float}(i)$$
$$\delta Y = Y - \text{float}(j)$$
$$\text{if } \delta X > \tfrac{1}{2} \ \{$$
$$\quad \delta X = \delta X - \tfrac{1}{2}$$
$$\quad \text{if } \delta Y > \tfrac{1}{2} \ \{$$
$$\quad\quad \delta Y = \delta Y - \tfrac{1}{2}$$
$$\quad\quad s = A_{i,j}(A_{i+i,j} - A_{i,j})\delta X + (A_{i,j-1} - A_{i,j})\delta Y$$
$$\quad \}$$
$$\quad \text{else } \{$$
$$\quad\quad \delta Y = \tfrac{1}{2} - \delta Y$$
$$\quad\quad s = A_{i,j}(A_{i+i,j} - A_{i,j})\delta X + (A_{i,j+1} - A_{i,j})\delta Y$$
$$\quad \}$$
$$\}$$
$$\text{else } \{$$
$$\quad \delta X = \tfrac{1}{2} - \delta X$$
$$\quad \text{if } \delta Y > \tfrac{1}{2} \ \{$$
$$\quad\quad \delta Y = \delta Y - \tfrac{1}{2}$$
$$\quad\quad s = A_{i,j}(A_{i-i,j} - A_{i,j})\delta X + (A_{i,j-1} - A_{i,j})\delta Y$$
$$\quad \}$$
$$\quad \text{else } \{$$
$$\quad\quad \delta Y = \tfrac{1}{2} - \delta Y$$
$$\quad\quad s = A_{i,j}(A_{i-i,j} - A_{i,j})\delta X + (A_{i,j+1} - A_{i,j})\delta Y$$
$$\quad \}$$
$$\}$$

Figure 4.58.   Bilinear interpolation to calculate a color value, s, at texture coordinate (X,Y) from an image with color recorded in the pixel array A which has dimension $n \times m$.

Note: bilinear interpolation give good results when the image map is being magnified, but in cases were the image is being reduced in size, as the object being mapped moves away from the camera, for example the use of a mipmap (see Möller [11]) gives a better approximation.

In this section we have **not** discussed how the vertices were assigned texture coordinates. This topic is covered in Chapter 7, Section 7.10.

4.14.1 Transparency Mapping

Transparency mapping follows the same steps as basic image mapping to deliver a color value s for use at a point $\mathbf{p}$ on polygon k. However instead of using s directly as a surface color, it is used to control a mixture between the color settings for

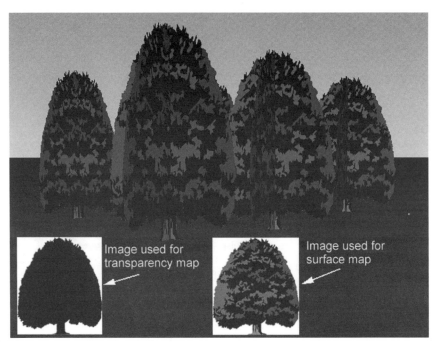

Figure 4.59.   An image of a model with just 11 rectangular polygons (some obscured). Ten of them have both a standard image map and a transparency map applied. The polygon representing the ground is made rough by applying a *bumpy* procedural texture.

polygon k and a color derived from the next surface recorded in the transparency buffer. (Remember that the Z buffer algorithm can be modified to hold several layers, so that if any of them were transparent the underlying surface would show through.) Note that when mixing the proportion of s due to the underlying surface **no** lighting effects are applied. That is: when you look through a window from inside a room it is not the light in the room that governs the brightness of the world outside. Figure 4.59 illustrates the use of a combination of two maps applied to a simple quadrilateral polygon. Incidentally, painting trees on glass is a very useful trick for decorating animated tours of architectural fantasies!

4.14.2 Bump Mapping

This technique, introduced by Blinn [21], uses the color from an image map to modulate the direction of the surface normal vector. Again there is a similarity with those procedural textures that cause the surface normal vectors to tilt away from the direction determined by the Phong shading model. For example, this technique can be used to produce the appearance of embossed text. Many animators use a sequence of bump maps to give the illusion of waves on the surface of a lake or the sea although such surfaces are probably more realistically simulated by the *noise* type procedural texture of Perlin [16].

To implement a bump map it is the change (gradient or derivative) of the image from one pixel to another which determines the *displacement vector* added to the surface normal of polygon k at point $\mathbf{p}$. Most of the analysis we need in order to calculate the perturbing vector $\boldsymbol{\Delta}\mathbf{n}$, has been covered already. Bump mapping usually uses the same texture coordinates as are used for basic image mapping; in fact, it is essential to do so in cases where an image and bump map are part of the same material. For example, a brick surface can look very good with a bump map used to simulate the effect of differential weathering on brick and mortar.

To determine $\boldsymbol{\Delta}\mathbf{n}$ we need to find incremental vectors parallel to two of the sides of polygon k, call them $\boldsymbol{\Delta}\mathbf{n}_1$ and $\boldsymbol{\Delta}\mathbf{n}_2$. Do this by first finding texture coordinates at points close to $\mathbf{p}$ (at $\mathbf{p}$ the texture coordinates are (X, Y) given by Equations 4.8 and 4.9). The easiest way to do this is to make small increments, say δ_α and δ_β, in α and β and use Equations 4.8 and 4.9 to obtain texture coordinates (X_r, Y_r) and (X_b, Y_b).

Before using the texture coordinates to obtain 'bump' values from the map it is necessary to ensure that the distance *in texture space* between (X, Y) and (X_r, Y_r) and between (X, Y) and (X_b, Y_b) is small. To achieve this write:

$$\Delta_t = \sqrt{(X_r - X)^2 + (Y_r - Y)^2}$$
$$X_r = X + \delta \frac{(X_r - X)}{\Delta_t}$$
$$Y_r = Y + \delta \frac{(Y_r - Y)}{\Delta_t}$$

and do the same thing to (X_b, Y_b). These equations include an additional scaling factor δ that will be discussed shortly. The next step is to obtain values from the *bump* image at texture coordinates (X, Y), (X_r, Y_r), and (X_b, Y_b). Using the bilinear interpolation algorithm given in Figure 4.58, three *bump* values s_0, s_1, and s_2 are obtained. It only remains to construct $\boldsymbol{\Delta}\mathbf{n}$ and add it to the normal, $\hat{\mathbf{n}}$, for polygon k. Thus:

$$\mathbf{d}_1 = (\mathbf{P}_1 - \mathbf{P}_0)$$
$$\mathbf{d}_2 = (\mathbf{P}_2 - \mathbf{P}_0)$$
$$\boldsymbol{\Delta}\mathbf{n}_1 = (s_1 - s_0)\left(\frac{\mathbf{d}_1}{|\mathbf{d}_1|}\right)$$
$$\boldsymbol{\Delta}\mathbf{n}_2 = (s_2 - s_0)\left(\frac{\mathbf{d}_2}{|\mathbf{d}_2|}\right)$$

$$\mathbf{n} = \mathbf{n} + h(\mathbf{\Delta n_1} + \mathbf{\Delta n_2})$$
$$\mathbf{\hat{n}} = \mathbf{n}/|\mathbf{n}|$$

h is a parameter that facilitates control of the apparent height of the bumps. Its range should be $[0, 1]$.

The choice of δ, δ_α, and δ_β are critical to determining how well the algorithm performs.

In the case of δ it is unlikely that the change in a texture coordinate across a polygon will exceed a value of about 1 or 2. Therefore a $\delta = 0.01$ will work well in most cases, although a little experimentation is well worthwhile. The increments δ_α and δ_β should also be small and values of ≈ 0.05 seem appropriate; again a little experimentation may pay dividends.

4.14.3   Reflection Mapping

True reflections can only be simulated with ray tracing or other time-consuming techniques, but for quite a lot of uses a *reflection map* can visually satisfy all the requirements. Surfaces made from gold, silver, chrome, and even the shiny paint work on a new automobile can all be realistically simulated with a skillfully created reflection map, a technique introduced by Blinn and Newell [23].

An outline of a reflection map algorithm is:

1. With the knowledge that polygon k, at point $\mathbf{p}$, is visible in pixel (i, j), determine the reflection direction $\mathbf{d}$ of a line from the viewpoint to $\mathbf{p}$. (Use the procedure given in Section 2.8.)

2. Because step 3 of the basic rendering algorithm transformed the scene so that the observer is based at the origin $(0, 0, 0)$ and is looking in direction $(1, 0, 0)$, the reflected direction $\mathbf{d}$ must be transformed with the inverse of the rotational part of the viewing transformation. The necessary inverse transformation can be calculated at the same time as the viewing transformation.

   Note: the inverse transformation must not include any translational component because $\mathbf{d}$ is a direction vector.

3. Get the Euler angles that define the direction of $\mathbf{d}$; these are the heading ϕ which lies in the range $[-\pi, \pi]$ and pitch θ which lies in the range $[\frac{-\pi}{2}, \frac{\pi}{2}]$. Scale the range of ϕ to cover the width, X_{max}, of the reflection image. Scale the range of θ to cover the height, Y_{max}, of the reflection image.

$$X = \frac{(\pi + \phi)}{2\pi} X_{max}$$
$$Y = \frac{(\frac{\pi}{2} - \theta)}{\pi} Y_{max}$$

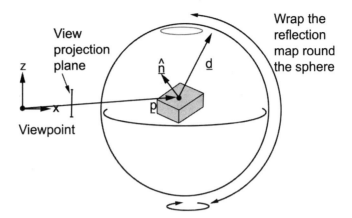

Figure 4.60.   A reflection map can be thought of a as an image painted on the inside of a hollow sphere with the reflective model placed at its center.

4. Use the bilinear interpolation algorithm of Figure 4.58 to obtain a color value s from the image in the vicinity of (X, Y).

5. Mix s with the other sources contributing to the color seen at pixel (i, j).

You can think of the reflection mapping process as one where the reflected surface is located at the center of a hollow sphere with the image map painted on its inside. Figure 4.60 illustrates the relationship of object to reflection map. Another reflection mapping procedure that gives good results is the cubic environment (Greene [24]).

When procedural textures, pseudo shadows, and reflection maps are added to the Phong shaded rendering of Figure 4.39 a highly realistic looking image (for example, Figure 4.61) can be generated without having to pay the very heavy time penalty that ray traced rendering procedures impose.

4.15   Tricks and Tips

The *key* to fast rendering is smart algorithms, but efficient programming can also help. Here are a few tricks and tips to speed up the code.

1. Try not to calculate the same things more than once, particularly if it is a time consuming calculation. After calculation store it in a temporary variable. For example normalizing a vector is slow because it requires a square root.

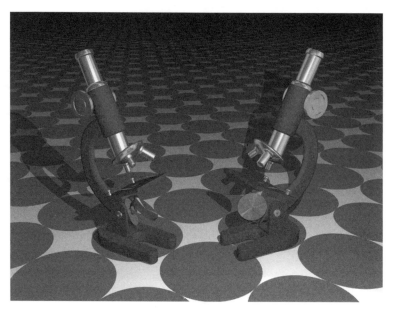

Figure 4.61.   Final image of models first shown in Figure 4.6 now using a pseudo shadow, procedural texture, and reflection map.

2. When rendering, always calculate as much as possible on a per polygon basis before proceeding to the rendering pass. A big scene may have 200,000 polygons; a medium sized anti-aliased image might have the equivalent of 9,000,000 pixels!

3. When testing several things that will result in a calculation being avoided, make the most common test first. See Section 4.6.

4. Arrange nested loops so that complex calculations are as high in the nest as possible and therefore done as infrequently as possible.

5. Sometimes it is more efficient to repeat code than to call a function. For example, in **C** or **C++** programs use macros to add, subtract, copy, and take dot and cross products of vectors.

6. Where possible use look-up tables; the Perlin noise functions are an excellent case in point. Another candidate is the replacement of the power function in the calculation of specular reflection.

References

[1] T. Möller and E. Haines, *Real-Time Rendering.* A K Peters, Natick MA, 1999.

[2] J. Blinn, *Jim Blinn's Corner: A Trip Down the Graphics Pipeline.* Morgan Kayfmann, San Fransisco CA, 1996.

[3] OpenGL Architecture Review Board, *OpenGL Reference Manual.* Addison-Wesley, Reading MA, 1992.

[4] J. Neider, T. Davis and M. Woo, *OpenGL Programming Guide.* Addison-Wesley, Reading MA, 1993.

[5] C. Walnum, *3-D Graphics Programming with OpenGL.* Que Corp. Indianapolis IN, 1995.

[6] J. E. Bresenham, *Algorithm for computer control of a digital plotter.* IBM Syst. J. Vol. 4(1), 1965, pages 35–30.

[7] B. Wyvill, *Symmetric Double Step Line Algorithm.* in Graphics Gems, Academic Press, Boston, 1990, pages 101–106.

[8] P. Burger and D. Gillies, *Interactive Computer Graphics.* Addison-Wesley, Reading MA, 1989, Section 3.3.2 pages 88–94.

[9] T. L. Janssen, *A Simple Efficient Hidden Line Algorithm.* Computers and Structures, Vol. 17 No. 4, 1983, pages 563–571

[10] E. Angel, *Computer Graphics.* Addison-Wesley, Reading MA, 1990, page 477.

[11] T. Möller and E. Haines *Real-Time Rendering.* A K Peters, Natick MA, 1999, page 41.

[12] F. Devai, *Revisting the Problem of Clipping Line Segments.* Proc. 2nd Irish Computer Graphics Workshop, University of Ulster, Oct. 1994.

[13] B. T. Phong, *Illumination for Computer Generated Pictures* CACM 18(6) 1975.

[14] A. Watt, *3D Computer Graphics.* Longman Higher Education, Essex, UK, 1999.

[15] A. A. Apodaca and L. Gritz, *Advanced Renderman : Creating Cgi for Motion Pictures (Computer Graphics and Geometric Modeling).* Morgan Kaufmann, San Francisco CA, 1999.

[16] K. Perlin, *An Image Synthesizer.* Computer Graphics, Vol. 19, No. 3, July 1985.

[17] G. Ward, *A Recursive Implementation of the Perlin Noise Function.* In Graphics Gems II, Academic Press, Boston, 1991, page 396.

[18] POV-Ray Software archive at www.povray.org.

[19] S. Worley. et al., Siggraph 2000 Course Notes.

[20] D. S. Ebert et. al., *Texturing and Modeling a Procedural Approach.* Acadameic Press, Cambridge MA, 1994.

[21] J. Blinn, *Simulation of wrinkled surfaces.* Computer Graphics 12, page 286, 1978.

[22] A. Woo, *The Shadow Depth Map Revisited.* In Graphics Gems III, Academic Press, Boston, 1991, page 338.

[23] J. Blinn and M. E. Newell, *Texture and reflection in computer generated images*, Communications of the ACM, 19(10), page 542, 1976.

[24] N. Greene, *Environment mapping and other applications of world projections*, IEEE Computer Graphics and applications, 6(11), page 21, 1986.

CHAPTER 5

Ray-Traced Realistic Rendering

When images produced using the rendering techniques described in Chapter 4 just are not giving you the realism you require, probably the first technique that comes to mind to improve things is *ray tracing*. There are other techniques for generating high quality synthetic images but they will not be discussed here. Ray tracing may be slow but it does give superb, almost photographic quality images and better algorithms are being developed all the time, so that under certain conditions it is even possible to achieve real-time ray tracing. There are many texts that describe the theory of ray tracing in detail; Watt [1] covers all the basics and in Glassner [2] the story is continued. Shirley [3] specializes in realistic ray tracing. A full description of a complete package is given in [5], and there are also quite a few good publicly available freeware and shareware ray-tracing programs with code that can be retrieved from many FTP sites around the globe. One of the best is POV-Ray [4], and it is well worth investigating codes such as these if you want to experiment.

The idea on which ray tracing is based seems almost too simple to be true. If you could *follow the paths taken by particles of light (photons) on their journey from source through the scene (as they are scattered back and forth between objects) and on until they are either captured by the camera or head off to infinity,* then you would be simulating exactly the physical mechanism that enables us to see and take photographs.

In practice this is a hopeless task because of the huge number of photons emitted by a light source and the fact that all but a minute fraction of them will ever be scattered into the camera. Therefore, ray tracing does it in *reverse*. It sends *feelers or rays* from the camera out into the scene. If the feeler rays find anything they work back towards the sources of illumination and give us a path for the photons to follow from source to photographic plate. Sometimes these feeler rays may encounter reflective surfaces, and when that happens they follow a new path and continue their journey. There are lots of other things that can happen to feeler rays. Sometimes they may divide, with each sub-ray following separate paths. The way in which the ray-tracing algorithm handles such situations, and the sophistication of the mathematical models it uses for light/surface interaction, governs the quality of the images produced.

So, we can get away with following a few rays of light, but what about the next question: how few? Our digital camera records its image at a finite number of pixels in a raster and, since each pixel holds one value, we need send only one feeler ray per pixel—well almost. In Section 4.9 we saw that pixelated displays suffer from aliasing. Ray-traced images are no exception and thus they require some anti-aliasing. Dispatching more than one ray per pixel and averaging the result is equivalent to the technique of supersampling.

5.1   The Standard Ray-Tracing Algorithm

The standard algorithm for ray tracing follows the first three steps of the basic rendering procedure described in Section 4.1.

1. Load the data describing objects in the scene to memory.

2. Move each model into its appointed position.

3. Apply the viewing transformation. (Not all ray-tracing applications use this step.)

After step 3 instead of projecting the polygons from the scene onto the viewing plane, a ray tracer calculates the direction of a feeler ray, $\hat{\mathbf{d}}$, from $(0,0,0)$ so that it passes through the point in the projection plane equivalent to pixel (i,j) of the display raster (which is of size X_{max} by Y_{max}). For a projection plane located at $(1,0,0)$ we can obtain the same field of view for the ray tracer as we get from the Z buffer renderer by using Equations 2.10 and 2.11 to calculate $\hat{\mathbf{d}}$ as follows:

$$\begin{bmatrix} d_x \\ d_y \\ d_z \end{bmatrix} = \begin{bmatrix} 1 \\ \left(\frac{\frac{X_{max}}{2} - \text{float}(i) + \frac{1}{2}}{s_x} \right) \\ \left(\frac{\frac{Y_{max}}{2} - \text{float}(j) + \frac{1}{2}}{s_y} \right) \end{bmatrix}$$

$$\hat{\mathbf{d}} = \mathbf{d}/|\mathbf{d}|$$

The fraction $(\frac{1}{2})$ is included so that the feeler ray passes through the center of the pixel. To jitter the feeler ray for anti-aliasing purposes a different offset in the range $[0,1]$ would be used.

When using ray tracing to render a scene it is inappropriate to cull or clip any model or model facet because rays can bounce back and strike models lying behind the camera or out of the field of view.

In the visualization step the *feeler ray* (origin $(0,0,0)$ direction $\hat{\mathbf{d}}$) is followed (traced) out into the scene until it intersects a polygon. Once the point of inter-section, $\mathbf{p}$, is located the surface properties can be determined and the pixel set to the appropriate color value, a process illustrated in Figure 5.1. If on first hit the ray isn't totally absorbed we can continue to trace its path until it reaches a final destination or is so attenuated that there is nothing to see. It is usual to do this recursively so that the same code is used to trace all rays, not just those originating from the viewpoint. Each time the ray hits a surface a calculation is made of the illumination using the methods described in Sections 4.10 and 4.11.2.

While the spotlight shadow effect (described in Section 4.12.2) with its soft edges is sometimes used by a ray tracer, the normal procedure to trace shadows is by checking the path from the visible point $\mathbf{p}$ to each light source. If any facet in a model in the scene intersects this path then $\mathbf{p}$ is deemed to be in shadow.

So the full basic ray-tracing algorithm can be summarized in the two parts presented in Figures 5.2 and 5.3 respectively.

Note the recursive use of the $DoRay()$ function in the algorithm of Figure 5.3. In the practical implementation of any recursive function care is often taken to ensure that the function doesn't become stuck in an infinite loop. In $DoRay()$ this might happen if a ray hits a reflective surface, which bounces it to another reflective surface, which reflects it back to the first so that it continues to bounce

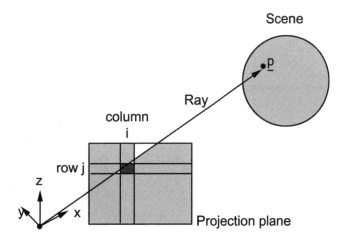

Figure 5.1.   Tracing a ray from the viewpoint out through pixel (i, j) until it hits an object in the scene.

Load model descriptions and move them into position.
Apply viewing transformation.
Repeat for all rows, j, in the raster {
    Repeat for all columns, i, in the raster {
        Initialize color value, s, (RGB components)
        For pixel (i,j) calculate ray direction $\hat{\mathbf{d}}$
        Set ray origin, $\mathbf{p}$, to $(0,0,0)$
        Call recursive function to return s for pixel (i,j)
        $DoRay(\mathbf{p}, \hat{\mathbf{d}}, s)$
        Copy s into the pixel array at address (i,j)
    }
}

Figure 5.2.   Ray tracing–part 1: Set up the geometry (view direction, etc.), launch a feeler ray for every pixel, and store the color it returns.

back and forward forever unless the mirrors are less than perfect. In practice the recursion must be terminated at some preset depth. For most scenes after three or four reflections the ray can be assumed to have left the scene.

All the calculations and procedures needed for the steps in the basic ray-tracing algorithm have already been studied in Chapters 2 and 4. Sophisticated extensions to the basic algorithm tend to be directed at simulating surface properties, color patterns, transparency lighting, and inter-object reflections. By using more and more rays a better approximation to ambient lighting conditions and the penumbra of shadows can be included. The red, green, and blue primary color model is only an approximation to the continuous spectrum of illumination from natural light and other color models need to be employed in order to develop more sophisticated physical models of the way light interacts with surfaces. The dispersion of light through a prism is one example. Recent developments [6] in procedural textures can deliver realistic models of smoke plumes, steam, cloud, hair, and fur. However it is the realistic shadows and true reflections that are the **most** significant reasons to call on the use of a ray tracer.

The basic algorithm in Figures 5.2 and 5.3 involves an almost impossibly large number of calculations when it is applied to rendering realistic models with more than a few hundred primitive shapes. Note the term *primitive shape* could include spheres, torii, swept or lofted analytic curves, and even more complex structures built by Boolean operations on basic primitives. Nevertheless your main observation probably was the *hours* it took the computer to trace even an image of moderate resolution. What is worse is that the rendering time increases as the number of models in the scene increases; thus, if you need to render a scene with

function $DoRay(\mathbf{p}, \hat{\mathbf{d}}, s)$ {
    Find the identity of the polygon, k, that intersects the ray $\mathbf{p} + \mu\hat{\mathbf{d}}$
    at $\mathbf{p}_i$ and is closest to $\mathbf{p}$.

    Calculate surface color s_s for polygon k at $\mathbf{p}_i$ $\hat{\mathbf{d}}_t$
    /* use procedural texture or image map if required */

    If the material properties of k indicate that it is partially
    reflective or transparent then cast extra rays.

    If reflective get reflective direction $\hat{\mathbf{d}}_r$
    $DoRay(\mathbf{p}_i, \hat{\mathbf{d}}_r, s_r)$

    If transparent get transparent direction $\hat{\mathbf{d}}_t$
    $DoRay(\mathbf{p}_i, \hat{\mathbf{d}}_t, s_t)$

    Get surface normal, $\hat{n}_i$ at $\mathbf{p}_i$, use Phong's interpolation
    and any procedural or bump mapping if necessary.

    From $\mathbf{p}_i$ send feeler ray to each light source.
    Test every polygon in model to see if feeler ray intersects it.
    If it does then the surface is in shadow from that light source.

    Combine s_s with s_r and s_t and apply lighting to give
    the final s value that is returned.

}

Figure 5.3. Ray tracing–part 2: The key recursive function, $DoRay(\mathbf{p}, \hat{\mathbf{d}}, s)$ that does the key work of a ray-tracing algorithm. For a given ray, origin $\mathbf{p}$, direction $\hat{\mathbf{d}}$, determine the color, s, of the surface seen.

models made up from thousands of polygonal facets, a basic ray-tracing renderer is virtually useless.

So the main question is: why is ray tracing so much slower? The answer lies in the first two lines of the algorithm given in Figure 5.3. *For each pixel: test every polygon and find the one closest to the origin of the ray.* This is potentially an enormous number of operations; if the raster is of size $n \times m$ and the scene is described with k polygons, $\approx n \times m \times k \times r$ (r is the average recursion depth) testing and swapping operations must be performed. For example, to synthesize an image of size 640×480 using a 2×2 anti-aliasing supersample with a scene with $20,000$ polygons (e.g., the model shown in Figure 4.50) requires ≈ 24 billion tests. With each test taking many processor cycles, you could be waiting a very long time for the image to materialize.

The remainder of this chapter is devoted to techniques that can be used to speed up the ray-tracing algorithm. Given favorable circumstances it is possible to produce ray-traced images with thousands of polygons in a fraction of the time that it would take using the basic algorithm and perhaps only five or ten times slower than a Z buffer procedure.

5.2 Optimization

A huge step in optimizing the ray-tracing algorithm would result if we could reduce the number of pixels through which we need to trace rays. So consider this: *in Section 5.1 the ray-tracing algorithm was designed so that it used the same viewpoint, view direction, and field of view as the basic Z buffer renderer.* As a consequence both rendering algorithms will see the same polygons in the same pixels. For the most part the same equations and algorithms are used to determine illumination, Phong shading, procedural texturing, and image mapping. Thus we can use a Z buffer algorithm to render the scene and trace additional rays to track reflections, refractions, ambient lighting, or for shadow determination.

5.2.1 Hybrid Tracing

Just adding a Z buffer to the ray-tracing procedure *alone* will result in a huge saving in execution time, especially if shadow determination is not required. Without shadows perhaps as few as $1 - 5\%$ of the image pixels will need to be traced. If shadows are required one of the pseudo techniques described in Section 4.12 could still be included as an option in a ray-tracing renderer.

Another factor that adds to the advantage of a hybrid algorithm is that the shape of most models is such that often (particularly in animated sequences) there can be a substantial proportion of pixels showing the background color. Making a Z buffer rendering first will identify which pixels are showing background and as a result don't need to be traced at all. Thus, combining Z buffer and ray-tracing renderers produces a **Hybrid tracer** which can be summarized as:

> Use the Z or scanline buffer to determine the identity of which polygon is visible in each pixel. Store the identity in a list.
>
> Jump into the ray-tracing procedure using the identity of the polygons from the list as the surface of first hit.
>
> Continue with the standard ray-tracing procedure from there.

Comment: *for a hybrid tracer it is probably better to use a scanline Z buffer procedure; it saves on memory because the additional buffer which records the identity of the visible polygon has to accommodate only one row of pixels at a time.*

Switching to hybrid tracing is particularly useful in saving execution for those scenes with a significant amount of background showing. However if a model should, after projection, cover the whole raster and every visible point on it requires having its shadow status determined, then other optimization techniques will need to be developed as well.

In essence, what all ray-tracing optimization techniques try to do is minimize the number of intersection tests a ray needs to make. This includes secondary rays and shadow feelers. There are two approaches that have received much investigation:

1. Bounding volumes

2. Spatial subdivision

We will look at both of these, but, in the case where models are constructed from a large number of convex planar polygons, spatial subdivision will probably be the easiest method to implement, so we will consider that technique in much greater detail. Both optimization methods work by creating some form of hierarchical subdivision prior to tracing any rays. When it comes to following a ray it is hoped that the use of the hierarchical data will obviate the need for a large number of intersection tests.

5.2.2 Bounding Volumes

Bounding volumes, sometimes called extents, are a simple primitive shape, sphere or cube, for example, that encloses the whole model. When a ray is traced the first *hit* test is against a very few of these bounding volumes and only when an intersection occurs is it necessary to test the ray against individual surface pieces; Figure 5.4 illustrates the idea.

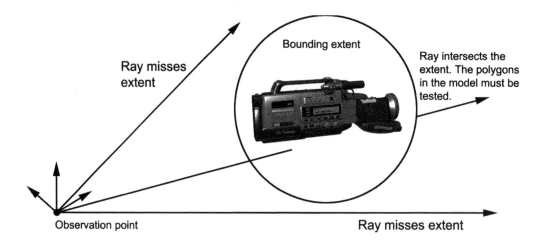

Ray misses extent

Bounding extent

Ray intersects the extent. The polygons in the model must be tested.

Observation point   **Ray misses extent**

Figure 5.4.   A ray need only be tested against surface polygons if it also intersects a bounding extent.

Within a bounding volume it is possible to create nested bounding volumes that gradually break the scene up into smaller and smaller regions with fewer and fewer polygons in each. Figure 5.5 illustrates nested spherical extents and their hierarchical relationship. Should a ray not intersect an extent at one level in the hierarchy then there is no need to test any extent (or polygon bounded by that extent) if it is a descendant of that level.

So the idea of extents is simple in theory but unfortunately it is more difficult to apply it in practice. Look again at the situation in Figure 5.4; how would you proceed to generate descendant extents for that model after the first and most obvious? It *is* necessary to do so because unless the number of polygon tests can

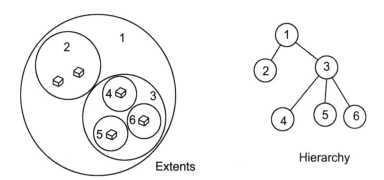

Extents   Hierarchy

Figure 5.5.   Nested bounding volumes and their hierarchical relationship.

be limited to a few hundred per extent we will still have an interminable wait for the image to develop.

Many experiments have been conducted on the use of unusual bounding volumes (see Arvo and Kirk [7], Figure 6) but in most cases very good optimization seems only to be obtained when the shape of the models are known and appropriate extents can be designed. For general work a spatial subdivision is probably a better bet. Möller and Haines [8] discuss bounding volumes and their application in rendering speed optimization.

5.2.3   Spatial Subdivision

The idea here is again to break up space into a number of small boxes so that there are as few polygons in each little box as possible. In many ways this is a very similar idea to that of the bounding extent except that no attempt is made to optimize the *fit* of the extent around the whole or parts of a model. In addition, the regularity of the subdivision means that it is easy to trace rays from one box to another as they pass through the scene.

For explanatory purposes in this section, and because it is easier to illustrate the spatial subdivision procedure in two dimensions, most of the diagrams used to illustrate the process are 2D. We should however remember that in reality the process is taking place in three dimensions.

To begin, consider the scene shown in Figure 5.6. On the left it illustrates five objects and on the right a spatial subdivision which arranges for each little rectangle to contain at most one object. The subdivision was produced successively with vertical and horizontal cuts so that at any stage rectangles are only divided if they contain more than one object. From Figure 5.6 note the following:

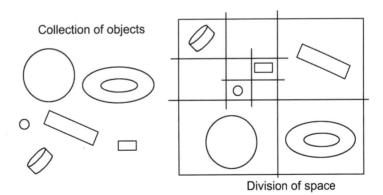

Figure 5.6.   Subdividing a 2D space into small rectangles so that at most one object is contained in each.

1. The subdivision is hierarchical. It continues until each rectangle holds only one object or until you reach a maximum user-defined depth.

2. The size of the rectangles are not uniform: some are large, some are small. The size is chosen so that the objective of *"one object in each subdivision"* is achieved with the fewest number of subdivisions. One way to do this is to recursively choose a dividing line at each step that places half the objects to the right and half to the left of it.

3. The example shows discrete *separated* objects.

All this looks great in theory until we come to consider a model made from a connected network of polygonal facets; then we have a bit of a dilemma! Figure 5.7 shows a small network of connected polygonal facets. No matter how hard we try, (how many times we subdivide), there is **no** way that we can separate each polygon so that a rectangle in the subdivision contains only one polygon, because the polygons are connected. The very best we could probably do is associate polygons $1, 2, 3, 4, 5, 6$ with rectangle k and polygons $2, 3, 4, 5, 7, 8$ with rectangle l. We are going to have to accept that in practice a "one polygon to one subdivision" goal is unattainable. There are two possible solutions: any polygon that spans a subdivision is split. For example, triangle 2 in Figure 5.7 could be split into three smaller triangles, with one piece in rectangle "l" and two pieces in rectangle "k" (Figure 5.8). This approach will increase the number of triangles in the model and increase the complexity of the code, since image mapping coordinates, etc., will need to be recalculated. An alternative solution is to accept that in some

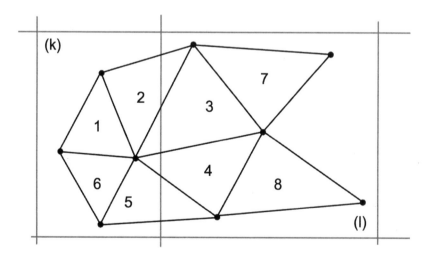

Figure 5.7.   Part of a model made from a connected network of polygonal facets.

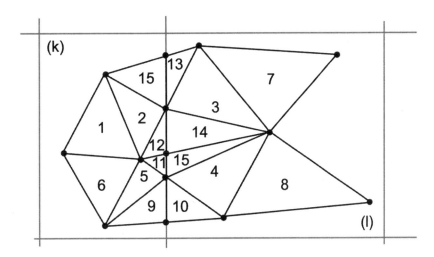

Figure 5.8.   Split any polygon that spans a plane of subdivision.

cases the maximum limit of number of polygons per subdivision may be exceeded and design the subdivision algorithm carefully, so that it recognizes when further division is pointless.

To develop an algorithm for spatial subdivision we begin with the principles illustrated in Figure 5.6. Thus the procedure starts with a big region that encloses all polygons: in two dimensions a rectangle, in three dimensions a box. After that, split the region into four (two dimensions) or eight (three dimensions). Continue recursively splitting each subdivision until all of them satisfy the terminating condition.

In 3D this algorithm is called octree decomposition, because it divides a volume into subunits eight at a time.

5.2.4 Octree Decomposition

Before developing the algorithm further let us be clear as to the inputs that are available and what outputs we require.

The inputs are a list of polygons and a list of vertices typically recorded using one of the alternative data structures described in Chapter 3. The output we need is a hierarchical representation of the octree decomposition and for each small box, at the ends of the branches of the octree, a list of the polygons which, at least partially, lie inside it. With this information rays can be traced as they travel through the scene moving from one box in the octree to another. Figure 5.9 shows a cubic region of space and how that might be divided up into cubic volumes.

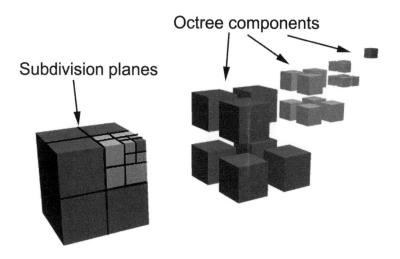

Octree components

Subdivision planes

Figure 5.9.	The first few subdivisions of a spatial octree decomposition.

That particular subdivision would occur as a result of most of the polygons being located in one corner at the top of the cube.

The algorithm to build an octree will be based on a recursive function that calls itself eight times, once for each branch of the octree. The recursive function will consist of a number of short steps. The data structure that we shall use for each node in the octree is listed in Figure 5.10.

The first stage in the octree-building algorithm shown in Figure 5.11 launches the recursive function. After that, recursive subdivision proceeds until the full octree has been established; the steps executed within the recursive function are given in Figure 5.12.

x_{min}, x_{max} y_{min}, y_{max} z_{min}, z_{max}	Dimensions of the box associated with octree node k.
n $Poly(i)$	Number of polygons falling inside box for node k. List of identities of the n polygons falling inside the box associated with node k.
$Child(i)$ $Parent$	List of 8 pointers to *child* nodes of node k. Pointer to parent node of node k.

Figure 5.10.	Data recorded at each node, k, in the octree.

Create the first, *root*, node in the octree.

Determine a bounding box that encloses all the polygons in the model. It might be useful to include a small *guard* region so that nothing is missed when it comes to tracing rays.

Assign all polygons in the model to the root node's polygon list.

Assign the child and parent pointers to indicate that this node has no descendants or parent.

Start the recursive procedure by subdividing the *root* node.

Call function $Xtend(Root)$

Figure 5.11.   The first step in decomposing the octree creates a root node and launches the recursive subdivision.

Before illustrating the octree decomposition process with an example, a little more detail needs to be given for some of the steps carried out by the recursive function of Figure 5.12. Consider the following after looking at Figure 5.12:

Step 1

The procedure can be terminated if:

1. The number of polygons attached to node O is less than a preset threshold.

2. The size of the box is smaller than a preset minimum.

3. The octree depth has exceeded a preset limit.

Step 2

There are a number of criteria that could be used. A coordinate average in each of x, y, and z at the centroid of the polygons is a logical choice.

Step 3

A fairly quick test is needed here. The centroid of each polygon is a possible candidate point with which to test for inclusion in one of the subdivided volumes.

Step 1:
> Check the terminating conditions to see if node O should be
> further subdivided or not. If not then exit the function.

Step 2:
> Using the location of all n polygons assigned to node O find
> suitable planes parallel to the x, y, and z axes which
> divide the box associated with node O into 8 smaller boxes.

Step 3:
> Check to see that the division has accomplished something!
> i.e. each subdivided box will contain $< n$ polygons.
> If not then exit the function.

Step 4:
> Create 8 child nodes for node O and then
> repeat the following for each: $0 \le i < 8$. {
>
>> Step 4a:
>>> Indicate that node i has no descendants, no associated polygons
>>> and that it is descended from node O.
>>
>> Step 4b:
>>> Assign bounding limits using a combination of the planes
>>> determined in step 2.
>>
>> Step 4c:
>>> For all the polygons k, assigned to node O check to see
>>> if they intersect the box associated with child i.
>>> If there is an intersection then add k to the polygon
>>> list $Poly(n_c) = k$ and increment n_c, the counter
>>> for the number of polygons assigned to child i.
>
> }

Step 5:
> Clear the list of polygons associated with node O. All
> polygons will now have been reassigned to one or more of
> node O's descendants.

Step 6:
> Extend the octree by calling function $Xtend()$ for
> each of node O's descendants in turn.

Figure 5.12.   Function $Xtend(O)$ which uses recursion to subdivide the volume associated with node O.

Step 4c

This is the most significant step in the algorithm and will require a test that is capable of determining if any part of a polygon falls within one of the subdivisions. The test can be performed in a sequence of increasingly complex checks with the simplest and most clear cut performed first. The following checks rely on the fact that the box has 12 edges and thus for triangular polygons there will be an intersection if either: one of the 12 sides of the box intersect the triangle, or one of the three sides of the triangle intersect one of the six sides of the box.

Thus the checks to apply for polygon k against the volume associated with node i are:

1. If the maximum x-coordinate of every vertex of polygon k is less than the minimum x-coordinate of the sides of the box for node i, then the polygon **does not** overlap the box. The same criteria is applied to the y- and z-coordinates.

2. If the minimum x-coordinate of every vertex of polygon k is greater than the maximum x-coordinate of the sides of the box for node i, then the polygon and box **do not** overlap. The same applies to the y- and z-coordinates.

3. Having performed these simple checks to eliminate candidate overlaps there is another quick check that will detect certain overlaps: if any of polygon k's vertices lies inside the box for node i then the box and polygon **do** overlap.

   The following two checks are relatively slow to apply.

4. Each edge of polygon k is tested against each side of the box. This is a two-part check: first determine that the edge crosses the plane containing the side and then check whether the intersection point lies within the bounds of the rectangular side.

   Since the box's sides are conveniently parallel to the reference axes, the general geometry for line/plane intersection described in Section 2.5 can be considerably simplified. For example, if the side lies in the xy plane at z-coordinate z_0, and it is bounded between $[X_{min} - X_{max}]$ and $[Y_{min} - Y_{max}]$, then an edge from $\mathbf{p}_0$ to $\mathbf{p}_1$ may be checked by the following procedure:

   ---

   if $p_{1z} - p_{0z} < \epsilon$ {
       return *no intersection* /* line does not cross plane */
   }
   Let $\mu = \dfrac{z_0 - p_{0z}}{p_{1z} - p_{0z}}$
   and $\alpha = p_{0x} + \mu(p_{1x} - p_{0x})$

Then if $\alpha \leq X_{min}$ or $\alpha \geq X_{max}$ {
    return *no intersection* /* crosses plane outside box */
}
Let $\beta = p_{0y} + \mu(p_{1y} - p_{0y})$
if $\beta \leq Y_{min}$ or $\beta \geq Y_{max}$ {
    return *no intersection* /* crosses plane outside box */
}
return *intersection*

5. The 12 edges are checked against the polygon using the line triangle intersection algorithm described in Section 2.10.1

Even though the above steps have been described for triangular polygons there
is no reason why the procedure could not be applied to any convex planar polygon.

5.2.5 A Simple Octree Decomposition Example

Let's examine an example of the construction of an octree from the six connected
triangular polygons shown in Figure 5.13(a). Figures 5.13 and 5.14 illustrate
the progressive subdivision and growth of the octree. For ease of illustration the
example is restricted to two dimensions.

Figure 5.13(b) shows the box associated with the octree's root node and the
identity of the polygons assigned to the root, at this stage all of them. In 5.13(c)
the dividing planes at XX' and YY' are shown as added. Using these planes,

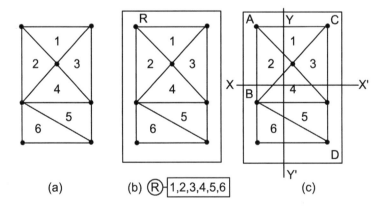

(a)   (b) (R)⎯1,2,3,4,5,6   (c)

Figure 5.13.   Building a very simple octree for six connected triangles. (a) The system. (b) The root
node, its associated box, and octree polygon assignments. (c) Add the dividing lines.

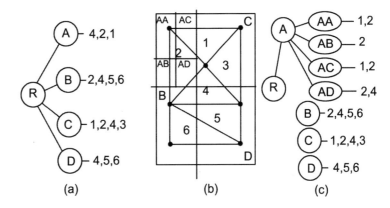

Figure 5.14.   Continuing the example from Figure 5.13. (a) Octree data after first division. (b) Add the division for node (A). Assume boxes C, D, and E have attained their target limit for division so that they are not divided again. (c) The octree data and polygon assignments after division of box A.

polygons are assigned to the nodes of the octree as illustrated in Figure 5.14(a). Dividing the area for node A into AA, AB, AC, and AD as shown in 5.14(b) produces the assignments given in 5.14(c). After this stage we will assume that further subdivision is unnecessary.

The most important thing to note here is that sometimes a polygon may be assigned to more than one node of the octree. There is no getting away from this unless the polygons are split, i.e., clipped, at the sides of the box so that each fragment (itself a polygon) may be assigned to only one node. However this will not improve the efficiency of the procedure. It is just as easy to trace a ray if the lists of polygons assigned to a node contain multiple occurrences as it is when the polygons are broken into pieces. (The work involved in testing ray/polygon intersection is independent of the position, orientation or extent of either).

One final comment: *the depth of the octree never need grow too deep; a depth of 20 can accommodate a range of feature sizes as large as* 1 *to* 10^6.

5.2.6   Tracing Rays through an Octree

Once a subdivision of space containing the scene is obtained the basic ray-tracing algorithm can proceed. However it must be modified so that as a ray is traced through the scene, it moves in increments. Each increment takes the ray from one subdivided volume into the next one along its path, i.e., into one of those that are adjacent to the current location of the ray. At each incremental step the following actions are carried out:

1. Identify the octree node i, which is the node associated with the volume of space where the ray is currently located.

2. Test the ray for intersection with any polygons in the list held at node i and record the identity id of the polygon which is closest to the origin of the ray. Also note the point of intersection **p** between polygon id and the ray.

3. Using polygon id's material and the point **p** calculate appropriate surface texture and lighting. If necessary dispatch additional rays to determine reflections, shadows, etc.

To determine which node in the octree we should use for i in the above, we have to descend through the tree starting at its root and taking branches according to the rule that **p** lies within the box associated with that branch and its node. When we can descend *no* further down the tree, this is node i.

As a simple example consider the case illustrated in Figure 5.15 with the equivalent octree given in Figure 5.16. We will assume that the ray originates at **p**; thus, the first set of polygons we need to test for intersection are those that intersect the rectangle in which **p** lies. To determine this we start at the root, R, of the octree (Figure 5.16) and perform a simple **if then else** test to see whether **p** lies in the rectangle associated with R; it does. Next, the same test is applied to all immediate descendent nodes, those labeled A, B, C, and D. The test shows that **p** does not lie in A but that it does lie in B. Since B has no descendants, we have reached the end of the search and can proceed to test for intersection with any polygon in the list attached to the data structure for octree node B.

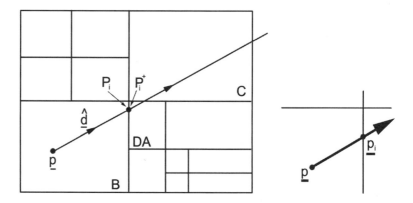

Figure 5.15.   Tracing a ray originating at p through a subdivided space. (A 2D representation of the division).

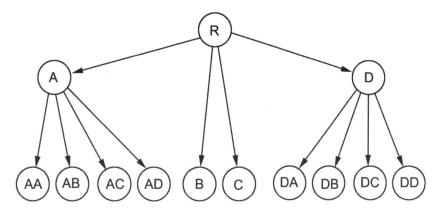

Figure 5.16.   The hierarchical octree corresponding to the spatial subdivision shown in Figure 5.15. (Again this is a 2D representation of an octree.)

If there are no intersections at this stage we need to track the ray into an adjacent box: for this example, the rectangle labeled DA in Figure 5.15. This we can do in three steps:

1. Project the ray in direction $\hat{\mathbf{d}}$ to find the spot on the sides of the box associated with node B, where the ray leaves box B; call it the point $\mathbf{p}_i$.

2. Project the ray forward by a *small amount* to get another point; call it $\mathbf{p}_i^+$ given by:

$$\mathbf{p}_i^+ = \mathbf{p}_i + \Delta\hat{\mathbf{d}}$$

3. Work down through the octree to find the node whose boundaries are such that $\mathbf{p}_i^+$ lies in its associated box.

Once a new octree node has been identified the process is repeated using $\mathbf{p}_i^+$ as the starting point for the next increment of the ray.

Notes:

1. The small increment Δ used to extend the ray into the next box should be chosen carefully. A magnitude somewhat less than the smallest dimension of the smallest box in the octree will be satisfactory because then there is no chance of $\mathbf{p}_i^+$ falling in a non-neighboring box. In addition Δ must be greater than zero, so that even glancing rays get into the neighboring box.

2. The time penalty incurred by tracking rays in this way is not as great as it may seem because finding which branch of the octree holds $\mathbf{p}_i^+$ involves checking relatively few levels of the tree with quite simple comparison tests.

3. The same tracking procedure can be used equally well for rays that originate as a result of a reflection or refraction and for feeler rays checking for shadows.

5.2.7 Following Reflected Rays

The procedure set out in Section 2.8 deals with reflection by generating a secondary ray with its origin at the point where the primary ray intersects the reflective surface. Like all other rays the secondary ray is passed to the basic tracing function $DoRay()$ (Figure 5.3). The value $DoRay()$ returns is mixed with lighting and texture values as usual.

5.2.8 Following Refracted Rays

Using the procedure set out in Section 2.9, a secondary ray is generated with its origin at the point where the primary ray intersects the transparent surface. Like all other rays the secondary ray is passed to the basic tracing function $DoRay()$ (Figure 5.3). The color value $DoRay()$ returns is mixed with lighting and texture values as usual.

5.2.9 Tracing Shadows

A feeler ray from the point **p** where the shadow status is to be tested is tracked through the octree subdivision toward each light in the same way as any other ray. If in each subdivision a polygon intersects the ray, then **p** is deemed to be in shadow, and consequently there is no need to follow the ray any further.

5.3   Multi-Threading and Parallel Processing

Multi-threading can be regarded as a form of parallel processing. It has most recently found favor with Microsoft's 32bit operating systems. UNIX based workstations and other so-called mainframe computers have always offered concurrent processing, i.e., two or more tasks apparently doing work at the same time. It is mentioned here for two reasons:

1. In theory ray tracing is the **ideal** application for implementation in a parallel processor because each ray is to all intents and purposes independent of all the others.

2. Computers based on an architecture designed around Intel Pentium family CPUs are now available with two or more processors.

Thus, in systems which provide hardware to take advantage of concurrent tasks, it makes sense to design a ray-tracing algorithm which farms out the tracing of individual rays to different *threads* of execution. However, there is **no** advantage and perhaps even a significant penalty to be incurred if a multi-threaded algorithm is executed by a system with just one processor.

Threaded algorithms must conform to the following standard:

1. Have a separate function which when called carries out all calculations and can be used re-enterently.

2. Variables needed for temporary use within a thread must **not** be placed in memory locations that are available to concurrently executing threads. In practice this means storing all intermediate data on a stack.

3. So-called global variables (accessible to all threads) are usable for *read only* or *write only* access, but not read and write unless some kind of lock is applied when working with these data.

In the case of a ray-tracing application program, the geometry of a scene may be recorded in global memory. This description is read and used simultaneously by different threads to trace a ray and calculate a pixel color value, which is placed in another globally accessible matrix, the output raster, at an address unique to each thread.

From a practical point of view perhaps the most significant design decision for a multi-processor rendering algorithm is the strategy for dispatching tasks to the host processors. Do we use a separate thread for each pixel, scanline, or something else? Since we have already stated that it is very undesirable to create more threads than processors the best idea is to divide the output raster into as many regions as there are processors in the hardware and direct each processor to render all the pixels in its region. This has a *little* drawback because part of the image might need very little processing, say background only, while another might be showing a complex model with multiple reflective surfaces.

A good practical compromise is to use what one might call *interlaced scan-lines*. For example in a dual processor environment, processor A renders rows 1, 3, 5, 6, etc., while processor B renders rows 2, 4, 6, 8, etc., The advantages of this approach are firstly, that in any image there will be high correlation between the content of adjacent rows so calculation times will be very similar for all processors. Secondly, the overheads of spawning threads will not be too great, as might happen if every pixel's calculation dispatched a new thread.

References

[1] A. Watt, *Fundamentals of Three-Dimensional Computer Graphics.* Addison-Wesley, Reading MA, 1989, Chapters 7 and 8.

[2] A. S. Glassner, *An Overview of Ray Tracing.* In *An Introduction to Ray Tracing*, Edited by A. S. Glassner. Academic Press, London, 1989.

[3] P. Shirley, *Realistic Ray Tracing.* A K Peters, Natick MA, 2000.

[4] POV-Ray Software archive at www.povray.org.

[5] C. Lindley, *Practical Ray Tracing in C.* John Wiley and Sons, New York, 1993.

[6] K. Perlin and E. M. Hoffert, *Hypertexture.* Computer Graphics, Vol. 23, July 1989, pages 253–262.

[7] J. Arvo and D. Kirk, *A Survey of Ray Tracing Acceleration Techniques.* In *An Introduction to Ray Tracing*, Edited by A. S. Glassner. Academic Press, London, 1989.

[8] T. Möller and E. Haines *Real-Time Rendering.* A K Peters, Natick MA, 1999, page 194.

CHAPTER 6

Computer Animation

This chapter starts with an introduction to the most commonly used approach to 3D computer animation: i.e., *keyframe in-betweening (tweening)*. It shows how this is used for the animation of rigid body behavior and illustrates possibilities for the extension of the keyframe approach to cover the more complex topic of character animation. Following the discussion on character animation we will proceed with an explanation of a technique often used for character animation, namely Inverse Kinematics or IK for short. IK has applications in non-character animation but it is probably its association with articulated models (i.e., characters) that animators would find it most useful. Finally there is a discussion and a few examples of aspects of the simulation of realistic motion that arise from some basic physical laws.

6.1   Keyframes—Tweening

The idea of the keyframe is well known to *paper and pencil* animators. It is a "description" of a scene at one instant of time, a key instant. Between key instants it is assumed that nothing "startling" happens. It is the role of the *key* animators to draw the *key* scenes which are used by a team of others to draw a series of scenes filling in the gaps between the keys so that jumps and discontinuities do not appear; this is called *"tweening"* (derived from the rather long and unpronounceable word inbe*tweening*.)

To convince an observer that the animation is smooth and flicker-free, a number of pictures must be flashed quickly before them. Cine film presents 24 pictures per second and television either 25 or 30 per second depending on the system in use. A 30-minute animated feature will require upwards of 54000 images. Each of these pictures, whether for TV or the movies, is known as a frame.

The task of *tweening* is a fairly monotonous repetitive one and thus is ideally suited to some form of automation with a computer. A half-hour animated movie may only need a couple of thousand keyframes, about 4% of the total length. Some predefined and commonly used actions described by library "scripts" might cut the work of the animators even further. For example, engineering designers commonly need to visualize their design rotating in front of the camera; a script or template for rotation about some specified location at a fixed distance from the camera will cut the work of the animator even further.

Thus in computer animation the basic idea is:

> *Set up a description of a scene (place models, lights, and cameras in three dimensions) for each keyframe. Then use the computer to calculate descriptions of the scene for each frame in between the key frames and render appropriate images.*

Most (if not all) computer animation application programs give their users the task of describing the state of the action in keyframes and then do their best to describe what happens in the snapshots taken during the remaining frames. This is invariably done by interpolating, between the description of at least two but possibly three or four keyframes.

Applications programs offer quite a lot of diversity in the power they provide to their users and in how they implement the interpolation, but most of them offer the following features:

1. As many models as required can be included in a scene and each can be independently instructed how to behave. A viewpoint emulates the behavior of a Camera and can take a specific field of view and other lens properties.

2. Each model is associated with a number of keyframes which specify different features of the actions they might undertake. Probably the most important is to specify where in the scene a model is located. The animator specifies which frame is a keyframe and assigns a location the model is to occupy in the scene corresponding to that frame.

3. The animator is allowed some control of parameters governing the interpolation algorithm used in determining the position of a model at the time of the non-keyframe snapshots.

4. Many other actions of a model in an animation can also be described in terms of a keyframe, with parameter values determined by interpolation. To supplement the specification of position, all application programs give the animator the option to specify an orientation (or *attitude*) for the model in a keyframe. Typically, with the three angles heading, pitch, and roll, the angles will be interpolated during the "tween" frames.

5. The option for hierarchical behavior, for example, a formation air display, can be animated by describing the motion of the leading aircraft with the others instructed to *follow* it. Hierarchical motion allows quite complex action to be produced with ease. An aerobatic display by a helicopter is a good example of hierarchical motion. The fuselage follows the display path, and the main and tail rotor blades all follow the fuselage while at the same time rotating in appropriate planes which themselves tilt as the machine rolls, dives, and loops the loop.

In the remaining sections of this chapter we will investigate some details of the theory underlying these features.

6.2   Animating Rigid Motion

Rigid object are things like motor vehicles, airplanes, buildings, or even people who do not move their arms or legs about. All *fly-by* and *walk-through* type animations fall into this category. Rigid motion is the simplest type of animation because each model is considered as an immutable entity and the animator only has to specify parameters for its position and orientation.

We saw in Section 6.1 that an animation is built up frame by frame with the position and orientation being either specified (because it is a key frame) or interpolated from at least two key frames. In three dimensions a point in space is specified by a position vector, $\mathbf{p} = (x, y, z)$. To specify an *orientation* three parameters are required. There are a number of possibilities but the scheme illustrated in Figure 2.36 where values of heading, pitch, and roll (ϕ, θ, α) are given is a fairly intuitive and easy to work with description of a model's orientation. Once the six numbers $(x, y, z, \phi, \theta, \alpha)$ have been determined for each model a transformation matrix is calculated and inserted into the standard rendering pipeline, which then proceeds to paint a picture for that frame. All the other frames are rendered in the same way.

In an animation it is not only the models in view that exhibit action; some of the most important uses for computer graphics arise because the camera (the view point) can move, pivot, and tumble. However it doesn't matter whether it is a model built from vertices and polygonal facets, or a light or viewpoint; the behavior of every element associated with a snapshot is uniquely specified by the set of six numbers $(x, y, z, \phi, \theta, \alpha)$. Chapter 2, Section 2.11.6 describes how to calculate terms in the *view* matrix, given an $(x, y, z, \phi, \theta, \alpha)$ for the camera.

Taking all this into account we can write a modified form of the basic rendering algorithm first introduced in Section 4.1 that serves as quite a comprehensive template for any animation algorithm:

1. Load the description of the action of the animation. The action is described by a list of keyframes for each participating element; an element is either a model, a light, or camera. Each keyframe will record the position and orientation of an element for a specific frame. For every model participating in the animation, load its vertex, edge, and facet data.

2. Repeat all the remaining steps for every frame i in the animation.

3. Determine the parameters $(x, y, z, \phi, \theta, \alpha)$ for the camera in frame i by interpolation from the record of its keyframes. Build the associated viewing transformation matrix $[T_c]$ by following the steps given in Section 2.11.6.

4. Repeat the following for every model k in the animation:

   (a) Determine the parameters $(x, y, z, \phi, \theta, \alpha)$ for model k at frame i by interpolation from the record of these at two or more of the model's keyframes.

   (b) Build a transformation matrix, say $[T_k]$, which will be applied to the vertices of model k so that, in effect, the vertex coordinates of **all** models participating in the animation will be based on the same *global* frame of reference. $[T_k]$ is obtained by the combination of transformations for orientation and position. The orientation transformation is obtained with sequential rotations about the x-, y-, and z-axes by angles α, θ, and ϕ respectively. Moving the model to its position (x, y, z) is given by a translation through $\mathbf{p}_o = [x, y, z]^T$. Thus $[T_k]$ is given by:

   $$
   \begin{array}{l}
   [T_p] = \text{a translation by } \mathbf{p}_o \\
   [R_x(\alpha)] = \text{a rotation about } x \text{ by } \alpha \\
   [R_y(\theta)] = \text{a rotation about } y \text{ by } \theta \\
   [R_z(\phi)] = \text{a rotation about } z \text{ by } \phi \\
   [T_k] = [T_p][R_z(\phi)][R_y(\theta)][R_x(\alpha)]
   \end{array}
   $$

   Note that the rotational transformations are applied before the model is moved into position.

   (c) Combine $[T_k]$ with $[T_c]$ to give a single transformation for application to the vertices of model k.

   $$[T_{ck}] = [T_c][T_k]$$

   (d) Apply $[T_{ck}]$ to the vertices of model k. Note that because each frame will probably require a model to alter its location it is essential to hold a copy of the original vertex positions and apply $[T_{ck}]$ to that.

The final two steps below are taken from the basic rendering algorithm of Section 4.1.

5. Apply the projection transformation to all vertices.

6. For each pixel in the output raster determine what is visible and record this information.

Note:

In practice, animation software will probably not have one long list of vertices and facets. There will be several lists, one for each model in the animation. However, because all vertex coordinates are known relative to the same axes (thanks to the application of the $[T_{ck}]$) no further processing is required.

6.2.1 Position Tweening

To find the position of any object (camera, light, or model) in an animation during a non-keyframe frame, say i where there are n keyframes such that $0 \leq i < n$, an interpolation of one form or another is performed. The simplest way to do this is by linearly interpolating from the position in two keyframes.

Using the notation of Section 2.13.1, let $\mathbf{P}_0$ be the position associated with keyframe l, which is chosen so that $l < i$ and there is no other k such that $k < i$ and $k > l$. Then find $\mathbf{P}_1$, which is the position associated with keyframe m chosen so that $m > i$ and there is no other k such that $k > i$ and $k < m$. If we let parameter μ be given by:

$$\mu = \frac{i - l}{m - l}$$

then during frame i the position of the object is given by:

$$\mathbf{p} = \mathbf{P}_0 + \mu(\mathbf{P}_1 - \mathbf{P}_0)$$

For an animation with several keyframes, linear interpolation will direct the object to move from the positions plotted at the keyframes as illustrated in Figure 6.1.

There are two things to note about the movement shown in the example of Figure 6.1:

1. The path taken by the object has abrupt changes of direction at a keyframe. In some situations this might be desirable behavior but most of the time we would expect a simulation of realistic behavior to make the object follow a smooth curve which passes through the points associated with the keyframes.

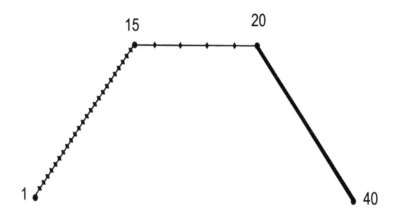

Figure 6.1.   Using linear interpolation to plot the movement of an object at, and between, keyframes.
The keyframes are plotted with a • and labeled with the frame when they occur.

2. Unless the ratio of distance between keyframes to time interval between keys
is approximately constant in adjacent sections of the path, the object will
appear to move erratically and make abrupt changes of speed at keyframes.
In the example depicted by Figure 6.1 it takes approximately four times as
long to cover the distance between keyframes 20 and 40 as it does to cover
twice the distance between keyframes 15 and 20.

Avoiding erratic behavior requires some skill on the part of the animator in
choosing when to make a keyframe and where the associated position should be.
As an alternative it is possible to specify a path which is to be followed during a
specific time interval (say between frames f_l and f_m) and instruct the computer
to calculate where a model or camera is during the snapshot at frame i.

Higher order interpolation, e.g., with a quadratic polynomial (Section 2.13.2)
or a cubic spline (Section 2.15), will remove the abrupt changes of direction during
keyframes. It is important to appreciate that for spline interpolation the movement
of any element in an animation must be specified by at least four keyframes.
Splines have the big advantage that they will be well behaved; they can have
their flexibility adjusted by user-specified parameters so that even for the same
control points (at the keyframes) a wide variety of paths are possible. Figure 6.2
illustrates the effect of increasing and decreasing the "tension" in a spline.

To obtain the position $\mathbf{p}$ of camera or model during frame i, using a cubic
spline requires the position of four keyframes, $\mathbf{P}_{-1}$ in frame a, $\mathbf{P}_0$ in frame b,
$\mathbf{P}_1$ in frame c, and $\mathbf{P}_2$ in frame d. These must be chosen so that $a < b < c < d$
and $b < i < c$. This situation is illustrated in Figure 6.3.

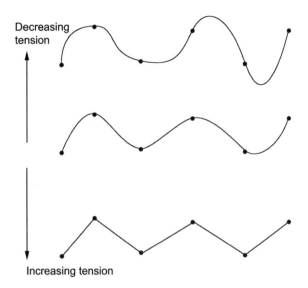

Figure 6.2.   Changes in the flexibility (or tension) of a spline allow it to represent many paths through the same control points.

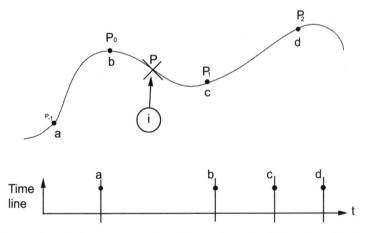

Figure 6.3.   Building a spline for interpolation of position in frame i. Below the spline the figure depicts a "timeline" diagram illustrating the time (in frames) of the occurrence of position keyframes. Most animation software packages give some form of graphical presentation of such information.

Equation 2.22, repeated as Equation 6.1 below, provides an expression for the determination of any point $\mathbf{p}$ on the spline in terms of a parameter τ.

$$\mathbf{p}(\tau) = \mathbf{K}_3\tau^3 + \mathbf{K}_2\tau^2 + \mathbf{K}_1\tau + \mathbf{K}_0 \qquad (6.1)$$

The constants $\mathbf{K}_0$, etc., are determined from $\mathbf{P}_{-1}$, $\mathbf{P}_0$, $\mathbf{P}_1$, and $\mathbf{P}_2$ as given by Equations 2.24, 2.25, 2.26, and 2.27.

To make use of the spline it only remains to relate parameter τ to frame i for which $\mathbf{p}$ is required. Before writing an expression let us consider the following:

1. When $\tau = 0$, Equation 6.1 gives $\mathbf{p} = \mathbf{P}_0$, which occurs when $i = b$.

2. If $\tau = 1$ then $\mathbf{p} = \mathbf{P}_1$, which occurs when $i = c$.

The first relationship between τ and *time* that one might consider is a linear one, effectively parameterizing the spline by time with:

$$\tau = \frac{i - b}{c - b}$$

Although this approach is acceptable it can give rise to a problem when the spline is highly curved. To see this look at Figure 6.4; it shows part of a spline curve with four keyframes and three "tween" frames in the interval between the keys.

The curve has a sharp loop between frames 14 and 18. The position of each tween frame is plotted with a cross and corresponds to τ values of 0.25, 0.5, and 0.75. It is evident that the τ values are 0.25 units apart but (*and this is the problem*) in the highly curved segment the distance between the points on the curve corresponding to successive frames is not uniform.

This effect is even more evident on the insert graph of *time vs. distance along curve* which shows significant discontinuities near keyframes 14 and 18. Discontinuities such as these are very noticeable to the observer. An object following this spline will appear to slow down near keyframes and speed up in the middle of segments. Such disturbing behavior may be minimized by reducing the curvature of segments but this requires that the number of keyframes be increased, and even then it will not be eliminated.

The reason that tween frames aren't uniformly distributed along the path is that the relation between τ and time is not a simple linear one. To achieve a uniform velocity between key frames (or as uniform as possible given the number of tween frames) we need to parameterize the spline not by time but by *arc length*.

The arc length is the length of the segment between two keyframes. For example, in the case of the segment between frames 14 and 18 of Figure 6.4, if we let L be the length of the segment then we need to find τ's which give $\mathbf{p}$'s at distances along the curve of $L/4$, $L/2$, and $3L/4$ from the point $\mathbf{P}_0$.

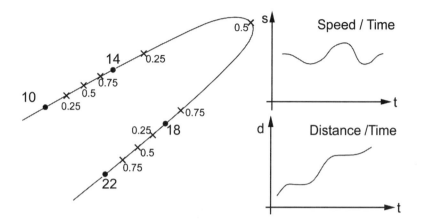

Figure 6.4.   Non-uniform distribution of spline-interpolated positions for tween frames. The insert graph illustrates the relationship between distance along the curve and time (i.e., which frame).

The phrase "along the curve" is of key importance. The length of a curve is determined by working out the distance traveled on the curve from $\mathbf{P}_0$, to $\mathbf{P}_1$. If we represent the segment between $\mathbf{P}_0$ and $\mathbf{P}_1$ by the curve C then:

$$L = \int_C \mathbf{ds}$$

This is known as a "*line integral*" and for our purposes it to be evaluated numerically as an approximate sum with n steps. The larger n is the more accurate approximation to L. A value for n of between $20 \sim 50$ is usually good enough for most animation calculations. Remembering that any point on the curve is given by Equation 2.22, an algorithm to determine L based on the simple trapezoidal numerical integration method is presented in Figure 6.5.

This algorithm allows us to calculate L, but suppose we were to stop adding while $j < n$, we would get a distance somewhat short of L, say d. With some trial and error we could choose to stop (say when $j = n'$) so that d (the cumulative distance along C) equals $L/4$. Suppose we let $\tau = \dfrac{n'}{n}$ and substitute this in Equation 6.1, then a point $\mathbf{p}$ (on C) will be obtained which is at a distance $L/4$ from $\mathbf{P}_0$.

By defining $\tau = \dfrac{n'}{n}$ the algorithm effectively provides a functional relationship $d = f(\tau)$ but to parameterize by arc length we need to know τ given d, i.e.,

For the spline segment determine the constant vectors
$\mathbf{K}_0$, $\mathbf{K}_1$, $\mathbf{K}_2$ and $\mathbf{K}_3$

Define the function $\mathbf{p}(\tau) = (((\mathbf{K}_3\tau + \mathbf{K}_2)\tau + \mathbf{K}_1)\tau + \mathbf{K}_0)$

Set n to the number of intervals in the summation,
a value between 20 and 30 should be accurate enough in
context of computer animation.

Set length $L = 0$
Set step counter $j = 0$
Repeat the following while $j < n$ {
    Calculate the incremental vector using the
    function $\mathbf{p}(\tau)$ as follows:
    Let $\tau_0 = \dfrac{j}{n}$ and $\tau_1 = \dfrac{(j+1)}{n}$
    $\Delta\mathbf{p} = \mathbf{p}(\tau_1) - \mathbf{p}(\tau_0)$

    Increment L by the length of $\Delta\mathbf{p}$
    $L = L + |\Delta\mathbf{p}|$
    $j = j + 1$
}

Figure 6.5.   Calculating the length of a segment of a cubic spline.

$\tau = f^{-1}(d)$. This cannot be written directly; it can only be obtained by the systematic equivalent of trial and error, i.e., *iteration*.

There are many iterative procedures we could use to find a τ that satisfies $f(\tau) = d$. Since we know that $\tau = 0 \Rightarrow d = 0$ and $\tau = 1 \Rightarrow d = L$, the easiest to implement and most reliable procedure is the simple bisection method [1]. Bisection may not be the most rapidly convergent procedure for finding the root of a non-linear equation, but when we know that there is only one possible τ and that it lies in the interval $[0, 1]$ the Bisection method is guaranteed to find the answer. *There is no point in a practical animation program issuing an error message "root not found".*

A bisection algorithm to determine the position $\mathbf{p}$ during keyframe i by interpolation from a spline passing through points $\mathbf{P}_{-1}$, etc., subject to the same end conditions is given in Figure 6.6.

Figures 6.3 and 6.4 illustrated that part of the curve between the central two points of a cubic spline fit through four points lying on the curve. A spline path must start and end somewhere, and when interpolating in the first or last segment

Use the algorithm given in Figure 6.5 to define
the function $\mathbf{p}(\tau)$, calculate the length of the
segment L, and evaluate the vector constants $\mathbf{K}_j$, $0 \leq j \leq 3$

Calculate the distance along the spline from point $\mathbf{P}_0$
to the point where the object should be in frame i
(assuming uniform speed).
$$d = \left(\frac{i - b}{c - b} \right) L$$

Call the function $\tau_d = Bisect(d)$ to determine by iteration
the parameter for substitution in Equation 6.1 to give
the location on the spline during frame i.
$$\mathbf{p} = (((\mathbf{K}_3 \tau_d + \mathbf{K}_2)\tau_d + \mathbf{K}_1)\tau_d + \mathbf{K}_0)$$

// Function $Bisect(d)$

$Bisect(d)$ returns a τ in the interval $[0, 1]$
which when substituted in $\mathbf{P}(\tau)$ will return a point at a
distance d from $\mathbf{P}_0$.
Set upper and lower bounds for the interval in which τ_d lies
$\tau_1 = 0$ and $\tau_2 = 1.0$
LOOP:
    Test whether the interval in which τ_d lies is small enough
    so that the iteration can be terminated: $\epsilon < 10^{-3}$
    if $\tau_2 - \tau_1 < \epsilon$ jump on to DONE:

    Call the function given in Figure 6.7 to calculate the distance
    along the spline up to the point determined by $\tau_d = \frac{1}{2}(\tau_1 + tau_2)$
    $d_m = SegLength(\tau_d)$

    if $d_m < d$ {
        Reduce the interval size by lowering the upper bound
        Set $\tau_2 = \tau_d$
    }
    else {
        Reduce the interval size by raising the lower bound
        Set $\tau_1 = \tau_d$
    }
    jump back to LOOP: to repeat iteration

DONE:
return the value of τ_d which is accurate to within
ϵ of the exact value of τ corresponding to d

Figure 6.6. An algorithm to determine the position $\mathbf{p}$ of an object during keyframe i when it follows a path described by a spline. The spline is given by the four points $\mathbf{P}_{-1}$ at frame a, $\mathbf{P}_0$ at frame b, $\mathbf{P}_1$ at frame c, and $\mathbf{P}_2$ at frame d. Keyframes must satisfy the condition $a < b < c < d$ and frame c and d must be chosen so that $b < i < c$.

Function $SegLength(\tau_d)$

Use the constants $\mathbf{K}_0$, etc., and function $\mathbf{p}(\tau)$
determined in the algorithm of Figure 6.5

Set n to the number of intervals in the summation;
a value between 20 and 30 should be accurate enough.

Set length $d = 0$ and parameter $\tau = 0$.
Calculate the increment in parameter $\Delta\tau$
$$\Delta\tau = \frac{\tau_d}{n}$$
Repeat the following while $\tau < \tau_d$ {
    Calculate the incremental vector using the function $\mathbf{p}(\tau)$
    $$\Delta\mathbf{p} = \mathbf{p}(\tau + \Delta\tau) - \mathbf{p}(\tau)$$

    Increment d by the length of $\Delta\mathbf{p}$
    $$d = d + |\Delta\mathbf{p}|$$

    Increment parameter
    $$\tau = \tau + \Delta\tau$$
}
Return the calculated distance d

Figure 6.7.   Determining the length of the part of the spline segment up to the point where the parameter $\tau = \tau_d$. This function is similar to the function given in Figure 6.5.

then the algorithm must be modified. For the example in Figure 6.8 tween frames 2 through 9 and 21 through 59 fall into this category.

There are a number of possible approaches which can be applied to determine a position near the beginning or end of a spline path. One that works well is to introduce fictitious control points $\mathbf{P}'_{-1}$ and $\mathbf{P}'_2$ given by:

$$\mathbf{P}'_{-1} = \mathbf{P}_0 - (\mathbf{P}_1 - \mathbf{P}_0) \text{ At the start of spline.}$$
$$\mathbf{P}'_2 = \mathbf{P}_1 + (\mathbf{P}_1 - \mathbf{P}_{-1}) \text{ At the end of spline.}$$

Finally in this section it is worth stressing the following two points:

1. We have assumed that interpolation is done on groups of four keyframes at a time. For example, animating the motion over the 400 frames depicted in Figure 6.9 involves interpolation with the following groups of points:

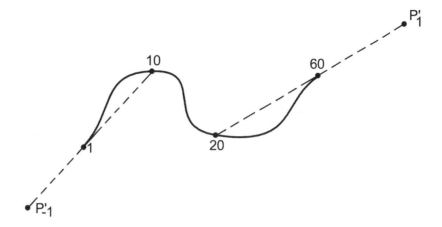

Figure 6.8.   Interpolating over the first and last segments of a cubic spline.

Tween Frames	Use Key Frames
2 to 9	1, 10 and 60 (with fictitious point)
11 to 59	1, 10, 60 and 100
61 to 99	10, 60, 100 and 200
101 to 199	60, 100, 200 and 300
201 to 299	100, 200, 300 and 400
301 to 400	200, 300 and 400 (with fictitious point)

2. There is no guarantee that the motion in different segments will take place at the same velocity, but at least within a segment it will be constant.

6.2.2   Motion along 3D Paths

In Section 6.2.1 it was observed that it is quite difficult for an animator to describe a complex 3D movement by placing the object executing that motion in appropriate locations at key times. Even when the path followed by the object is interpolated from a spline curve, the motion may still appear jerky because the ratio of distance between key locations to their time interval may vary from interval to interval.

Probably the simplest way to avoid such difficulties is to dispense with the hard and fast rule that during a keyframe the object has to be located exactly at the location recorded for that keyframe. This can be achieved by defining a path along which the object is to move during a preset interval. The shape of the path is described by as many *control points* as may be needed to push it through given

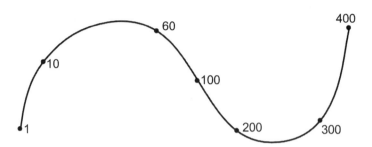

Figure 6.9.   Figure 6.9.   An example of position interpolation for a 400-frame animation with seven keyframes.

locations. A model following a path will thus embark on its journey at a specific frame and arrive at its destination again at a specified time, but how it behaves during its travels is determined by the computer.

To find the location of a model during the interval, a calculation similar to that for a spline segment must be performed (see Section 6.2.1). However, for a path the summation applies to the full length of the spline. In cases where the path is composed of several segments from different cubic splines the summation switches from spline to spline as it works out the length. For example, the path shown in Figure 6.10 contains seven control points; determining its length involves repeating the summation algorithm of Figure 6.5 six times using cubic splines passing through the points:

Path segment	Control points
A	(-1) 1 2 3
B	1 2 3 4
C	2 3 4 5
D	3 4 5 6
E	4 5 6 7
F	5 6 7 (8)

Points (-1) and (8) are fictitious points which influence the way in which the path approaches the points at its start and finish.

Finding where on the path any element may be during frame i uses a procedure similar to that for basic tweening as set out in Figure 6.6. The only significant difference is that a path may be composed of several different spline segments and the one to be used must first be identified before the bisection algorithm is applied. Once an appropriate τ has been obtained, Equation 6.1 yields the location $\mathbf{p}$ of any object following the path.

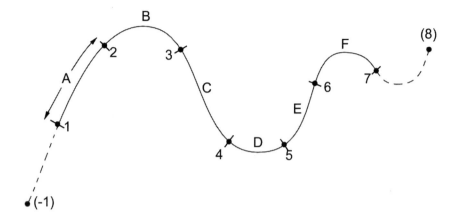

Figure 6.10.   A path through seven control points.

If we assume that the length of the path L is known and each control point records its distance from the start of the curve, determining on which segment **p** lies is simply a matter of comparing the distance d (from the start of the curve to **p**) with the distance of the control points from the start of the path. When two are found which bracket d then they are the ones we need. Thus the distance d is given by:

$$d = \left(\frac{i - s}{f - s} \right) L$$

where s identifies the frame in which the object is at the start of the path and f is the frame where it reaches the end.

6.2.3   Orientation Tweening

An overall transformation that places a model in the scene includes components of translation and rotation. In this section we turn our attention to how to obtain the rotation to apply in a tween frame, given known rotations (or *attitudes*) in adjacent keyframes. The transformation matrix that represents the combined translation and rotation $[T]$ may be written as the product:

$$[T] = [T_p][T_a]$$

where $[T_p]$ expresses the translational component and $[T_a]$ expresses the rotational component. Writing the matrices in this order is equivalent to applying the rotation *before* the translation. While it is possible to use the reverse order, applying the rotation first means that we can interpolate orientations independently from positions.

Determining the orientation taken by model or camera in a tween frame therefore requires the interpolation of angles. However, angles *cannot* be interpolated in the same way that position coordinates are. Section 2.17 discussed this problem and introduced the quaternion as a mathematical entity with properties that are ideally suited to the specific problem of orientation tweening. It is how $[T_a]$ is obtained during tween frame k (say $[T_a]_k$) that is the subject of this section.

We have seen already that it is *not* possible to interpolate angles (ϕ, θ, α) for frame k given angles in adjacent keyframes l and m by saying:

$$\alpha_k = \alpha_m \left(\frac{k - l}{m - l} \right) + \alpha_l$$

Therefore $[T_a]_k$ cannot be determined by composing individual rotations:

$$[T_a]_k = [R_z(\alpha_k)][R_y(\theta_k)][R_x(\alpha_k)]$$

Neither is it possible to obtain $[T_a]_k$ during frame k by interpolating directly with matrices expressing the orientation at keyframes l and m, (see Section 2.17).

During the keyframes l and m, the matrices $[T_a]_l$ and $[T_a]_m$ are determined from the known values of $(\phi_l, \theta_l, \alpha_l)$ and $(\phi_m, \theta_m, \alpha_m)$ respectively. It may not be possible to interpolate matrices but it is possible to interpolate a quaternion associated with a rotation matrix. This was discussed in Section 2.17.7 where the *slerp()* function was introduced. Section 2.17 showed how the same orientation could be expressed in terms of Euler angles (ϕ, θ, α), a quaternion $[w, x, y, z]$, or a matrix T which pivots the object into that orientation. Algorithms were given for conversion from any representation into any other.

The quaternion provides a solution to our angular interpolation problem, and its use can be summarized in the following three steps:

1. Given an orientation expressed in Euler angles at two keyframes, l and m, calculate equivalent quaternions q_l and q_m, using the algorithm given in Section 2.17.3.

2. Interpolate a quaternion q_k that expresses the orientation in frame k using:

$$\mu = \frac{k - l}{m - l}$$

$$\rho = \cos^{-1} q_l \cdot q_l$$

$$q_k = \frac{\sin(1 - \mu)\rho}{\sin \rho} q_l + \frac{\sin \mu \rho}{\sin \rho} q_m$$

See Section 2.17.7 for details.

3. Use the expressions from Section 2.17.4 to obtain $[T_a]_k$ given the quaternion q_k.

And there we have it: $[T_a]_k$ so obtained is a matrix representing the orientation adopted in frame k so that the orientation of any model changes smoothly during the interval between keyframes l and m.

In practice it is not essential to record orientation explicitly with Euler angles. Most practical animation software sets up the direction in which a model is pointing interactively. In this case the keyframe could record an orientation as a matrix or possibly even as a quaternion directly; there is no need to use Euler angles. The visual feedback from a refreshed display of the object is usually sufficient for the animator to decide that the orientation they require has been adopted.

6.2.4 Hierarchical Animation

Hierarchical animation occurs when *the action of one element is specified relative to the action of another element.* The simplest example of a hierarchical animation is for one model to follow another. Using recursive calls, very little programming effort is required to allow an animation program to support hierarchical behavior. The only noteworthy event from a programming point of view is that an infinite recursion must be prevented. Infinite recursion will occur if, for example, an element ends up following itself.

There are an almost infinite variety of ways in which hierarchical links can be established involving not only the relative positions of elements but also their orientation. For example it is usually easier for an animator to tell the camera to keep "looking at" some target which can then be instructed to move or follow a model. The result is that the model will always remain in the center of the field of view.

Here is a list of a few potentially useful hierarchical links:

1. One item follows another.

2. One item follows another at a fixed distance from the first.

3. One item follows another with the *artificial condition* that any of the x-, y-, or z-coordinates do not participate in the hierarchical link.

4. One item remains orientated so that its x-axis always points at a fixed location or at another item.

5. One item rotates round an axis, without the need for orientation tweening, while it moves about.

6. One item's orientation mimics that of another item.

6.3   Character Animation

The computer has proved a very effective tool in generating animated sequences. It has been particularly effective when the observer/camera is moving, for example, in *fly-by* or *walk-through* animations. The basic algorithm of Section 6.2 showed how several models may be placed in a global scene and individually directed how to behave. This approach works very well provided the model is rigid; in this context rigid means that its behavior is specified by setting only a few parameters.

Sadly, characters, both human and animal, usually behave in a far-from-rigid way, and, in order to make animations that include characters, a way must be found to allow them to behave as realistically as possible. The motion of characters is very complex but one can think of them as having a "global" behavior similar to that of a rigid object; they move about from place to place, for example. They also have superimposed on their general motion an internal (local) behavior that arises from internal flexibility. If we insisted on animating every last detail of a character's local behavior then it would quickly become quite impossible to achieve anything. Some form of compromise will have to be accepted. In many ways this is a similar problem to that in modeling the fine detail of a surface; polygonal patches can not be made small enough to represent perfectly every detail, and other techniques such as image mapping and procedural textures are required.

In animation it is possible that some types of action might be initiated algorithmically so that the animator does not have to move every vertex in a model by hand at a few keyframes. Some physical actions such as the flexible behavior of fabric, plastic deformation, flapping in the wind, twisting and bending, etc., can be simulated directly from the laws of physics. Section 6.5 discusses a few examples of this approach to animation.

Perhaps some of the more autonomous behavior of a character might be simulated from a set of rules or repetitive patterns of action. Character animation is still a very active area of research in computer graphics and therefore there is at present no correct answer to the question: what is the *best* method to adopt? So, what is the best way to proceed? Obviously a stiff *wooden* performance is unacceptable and the simulation of every muscular twinge is currently impractical; the goal then is to achieve as good a result as practically possible with the equipment at our disposal and within the resources available for software development, i.e., *time*. We saw in Section 6.2.4 and Figure 6.11 that an internal action can be given to a character by constructing it from many components which behave in a hierarchical way.

A large number of animal species have their movements primarily controlled by some form of *skeleton* that is in essence hierarchical; for example, a finger is attached to a hand which is connected to a lower arm, etc. The skeleton imposes constraints on how an animal behaves (it cannot suddenly double the length of its

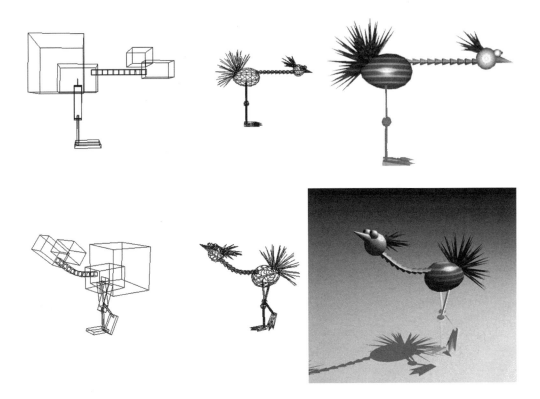

Figure 6.11.   An example of the use of hierarchical links in animation. The figure illustrated has 20 separate models (boxes bounding the models, wireframe and hidden surface drawings are shown). The models are linked hierarchically. Each model has been instructed to follow another at a point offset relative to the coordinate system of the one it is following; they have then been aligned individually. Taken together, various arrangements of the models lead to the appearance of a single entity. Tweening the orientation between linked models at given key instances (keyframes) will produce an animation with the composite object moving smoothly from one pose to another.

legs, for example). For animation purposes the idea of a skeleton is very useful. In traditional clay animation a rigid wire *skeleton* is embedded in the clay and this allows the animator to manipulate the model in a realistic way. (The Oscar-winning Wallace and Gromit are excellent examples of clay characters with a wireframe skeleton.) We can use a skeleton in computer animation too; it fulfills two functions:

1. It provides a rigid framework which can be pivoted, twisted, and rotated. Vertices and polygons are assigned to follow a specific *bone* in the skeleton and thus the model will appear to take up various poses, just as does the clay model.

2. The hierarchical nature of the skeleton allows for natural behavior; for example, pivoting the upper arm about the shoulder in a model of a human figure will cause the lower arm and hand to execute the same pivot without the animator having to do it explicitly.

Consider the example shown in Figure 6.12, where the model is pictured on the left; in the center is its skeleton shown as a thick black line and on the right is a diagrammatic representation of the hierarchical links in the skeleton. Using the skeleton, the animator has the option to pivot parts of the model about the end points (nodes) of any of its bones. Taking the model in Figure 6.12 as an example, a rotation of the front right upper leg around the hip joint moves the whole front right leg (see Figure 6.13(a)). If this is followed by rotations of the lower leg and foot the pose illustrated in Figure 6.13(b) results.

Using a skeleton in the context of well-designed interactive software which lets the animator see what is happening from multiple viewpoints, the key elements

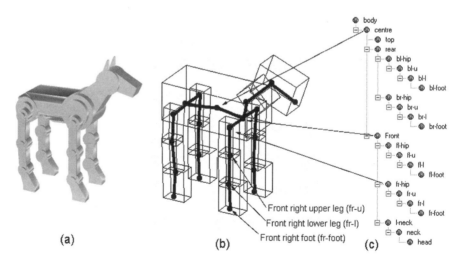

Figure 6.12.   A model with its skeleton. In (a) the model is shown; (b) shows the skeleton (the thick lines). A pivot point is shown at the end of each *bone*. The thin lines represent boxes that contain all the parts of the model attached to each bone. In (c) a hierarchical representation of all the *bones* and how they are connected is illustrated.

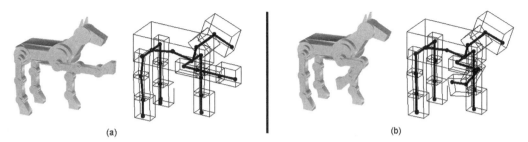

(a)   (b)

Figure 6.13.   Pivoting the leg of the model shown in Figure 6.12 into two poses.

of character animation can be achieved despite the fact that control is restricted to a *mouse* and the display is only on a flat screen. In the next four subsections we will look at one possible way to describe the skeleton, record its pose, and interpolate between two *keyframe* poses.

6.3.1 Specifying Character Poses

Any skeleton has what we can term a *rest* pose, which is simply the form in which it was created, before any manipulation is applied. The skeleton illustrated in Figure 6.12 is in a rest pose. With the knowledge of hierarchical *connectivity* in a skeleton, a position vector giving the location of the end (the node or the joint) of each bone uniquely specifies the skeleton's rest position. To behave like the wireframe of a clay animation figure any other pose adopted by the skeleton should satisfy the criteria:

1. Be obtained with a rotational transformation about an axis located at one of the nodes of the skeleton.

2. If a transformation is deemed to apply to a specific bone, say i, then it must also be applied to the descendent (child) bones as well.

For example, consider the simple skeleton illustrated in Figure 6.14. It shows four bones; bones 2 and 3 are children to bone 1, and bone 4 is child to bone 3. Each bone is given a coordinate frame of reference (e.g., (x_3, y_3, z_3) for bone 3). (For the purpose of this example the skeleton will be assumed to lie in the plane of the page.) $\mathbf{P}_0$ is a node with no associated bone; it acts as the base of the skeleton and is referred to as the **Root**.

Suppose that we wish to move bone 3; the only option is to pivot it around a direction vector passing through node 1 (to which bone 3 is attached). We saw in Chapter 2 Sections 2.11, 2.11.4, and 2.11.5 how to specify a rotational transformation as a 4×4 matrix, and to combine rotations round different axes to

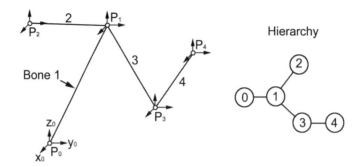

Figure 6.14.   Specifying a rest pose of a skeleton with four bones 1 – 4. In addition to the positions $\mathbf{P}_i$ of the nodes at the end of the bone, a local frame of reference $(\mathbf{x}_i, \mathbf{y}_i, \mathbf{z}_i)$ is attached to each node. On the right a hierarchical diagram of the skeleton is shown. $\mathbf{P}_0$ is a **Root** node which has no bone attached and acts as the base of the skeleton.

give a single matrix $[M]$ that encodes information for any sequence of rotations performed at a point. This matrix takes the form:

$$[M] = \begin{bmatrix} a_{00} & a_{01} & a_{02} & 0 \\ a_{10} & a_{11} & a_{12} & 0 \\ a_{20} & a_{21} & a_{22} & 0 \\ 0 & 0 & 0 & 1 \end{bmatrix} \tag{6.2}$$

The last row and column contain zeros because there are no translation components when manipulating a skeleton, and *all rotations are relative to a coordinate system with its origin at the point around which the skeleton is pivoted.*

Once $[M]$ has been calculated, its application to $\mathbf{P}_3$ and $\mathbf{P}_4$ will move them to appropriate locations for the new pose. The example pose in Figure 6.15 was obtained by a rotation of π around axis y_2. There are a few important observations that emerge from this simple example:

1. Node 4 is affected by the transformation because it is descended from node 3.

2. Nodes 0, 1, and 2 are *unaffected* and remain at locations $\mathbf{p}_0$, $\mathbf{p}_1$, and $\mathbf{p}_2$. Importantly the node about which the rotation is made is **not** disturbed in any way.

3. The coordinate frames of reference attached to nodes 3 and 4 are also transformed; they become $(\mathbf{x}'_3, \mathbf{y}'_3, \mathbf{z}'_3)$ and $(\mathbf{x}'_4, \mathbf{y}'_4, \mathbf{z}'_4)$.

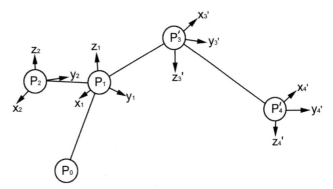

Figure 6.15.   Specifying a pose for the skeleton in Figure 6.14 by a rotation of bone 3 and its descendants
                    around the node at the end of bone 1.

4. Although node 4 (at $\mathbf{p}_4$) is moved, its position is unchanged in the local frame of reference attached to node 3.

5. When $[M]$ is applied to nodes 3 and 4 it is assumed that their coordinates are expressed in a frame of reference with origin at $\mathbf{P}_1$.

It is possible to apply additional rotational transformations until any desired pose is achieved for a specific keyframe in the animation. To attain the pose depicted in Figure 6.13(b) several successive transformations from the rest position of Figure 6.12 were necessary.

Note that even if the positions of the nodes in two poses are identical it does **not** mean that the poses are identical. Figure 6.16 shows four bones (four nodes) co-positional with the nodes in the pose of Figure 6.15; a close inspection reveals that the local frames of reference are very different. The skeletons look the same because they have cylindrical symmetry, but a network of polygons and vertices attached to the bones would not necessarily exhibit this property and therefore the model might look quite different. (The pose depicted in Figure 6.16 was obtained in two steps, a rotation around $\mathbf{x}_1$ followed by rotation around $\mathbf{x}_2'$.)

6.3.2   Interpolating Character Poses

Character animation using a skeleton is similar in principle to rigid body animation. Given a pose for keyframes l and m we need to determine how the skeleton is posed for some frame $k : l < k < m$.

In the last section we saw that it might take several operations to manipulate the skeleton into the desired pose. In interpolating how the skeleton changes between the two poses it does not necessarily follow that operations used to position the

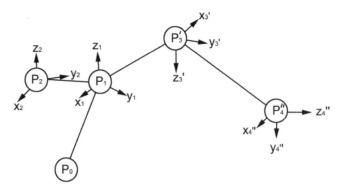

Figure 6.16.   Co-positional nodes do not imply that two poses are identical. The nodes in this pose of
                the skeleton from Figure 6.14 are at the same location as the nodes in the pose shown in
                Figure 6.15, but the local frames of reference do not take the same orientation.

skeleton should be mimicked. We would like the character to *flow* from one pose
to another with the *minimum of fuss*. To achieve this we will need to think of
interpolating the angular change between linked bones, i.e., between a child and
its parent bone.

      To see how this will work look at the example in Figure 6.17, where two
poses of a very simple skeleton are shown in plan view. In pose (a) the second

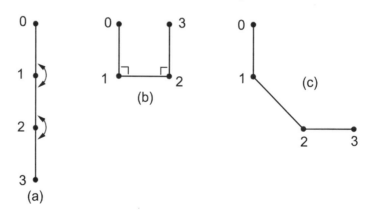

Figure 6.17.   (a) and (b) show two poses of a simple skeleton with three bones. (The circles represent
                the nodes at the end of the bones). (c) shows an interpolated pose midway between (a)
                and (b).

and third bones are orientated π apart from their respective parents. In (b) they are $\dfrac{\pi}{2}$ apart. Interpolation should proceed smoothly as the skeleton moves from pose (a) to pose (b). This is accomplished by changing the angles between bones 1 and 2 and between bones 2 and 3 simultaneously, in both cases from π to $\dfrac{\pi}{2}$. Interpolating in this way leads to the pose depicted in (c) half way through the move.

Note how the angular changes are always *relative* (child to parent) so that a rotation of a child is expressed in the frame of reference of the parent. The parent bone and its frame of reference may themselves be pivoting, and this in turn adds an additional rotation to any children which accentuates the children's global movement. Simultaneous angular changes in two bones often leads to a realistic motion. The act of raising an arm will involve pivoting the whole arm around the shoulder while simultaneously bending it at the elbow.

If we extrapolate the 2D concept depicted in Figure 6.17 into a 3D one, we will have a pretty good method of simulating "animal" behavior, with the animator required to provide only a few key poses. Indeed it is quite possible to imagine building up a library of poses from which the animator can choose the appropriate ones for the computer to link together over a specified time interval.

Thus, we return to the question of how to interpolate the difference in the angles between child to parent of the same two bones in two poses. Angular interpolation has been discussed in Chapter 2, Section 2.17 and in Section 6.2.3, where the quaternion was introduced as the mathematical entity of choice for angular interpolation. In character animation we have the little complication of determining just what are the appropriate quaternions for interpolation; this will be considered in the next section.

6.3.3 Interpolating One Bone Relative to Its Parent

Figure 6.18 shows two bones that form part of a simple skeleton that we will use in this section. The skeleton is in its *rest* position. For each bone their associated nodes i and $i+1$ and local frames of reference given by basis vectors $(\mathbf{u}_i, \mathbf{v}_i, \mathbf{w}_i)$ and $(\mathbf{u}_{i+1}, \mathbf{v}_{i+1}, \mathbf{w}_{i+1})$ are illustrated. The local basis vectors are labeled $\mathbf{u}, \mathbf{v}$, and $\mathbf{w}$ so that they are not confused with the global $\mathbf{x}, \mathbf{y}, \mathbf{z}$ coordinate system.

Suppose now that a number of rotations of node $i+1$ around the axes at node i are made so that node $i+1$ takes up the position and orientation depicted in Figure 6.19. The rotational transformation which moves node $i+1$ between the two orientations in Figures 6.18 and 6.19 can be expressed as a single matrix $[M]$ of the form given by Equation 6.2. The elements a_{00}, etc., of $[M]$ may be calculated from the local basis vectors in the two orientations, $(\mathbf{u}_{i+1}, \mathbf{v}_{i+1}, \mathbf{w}_{i+1})$ and $(\mathbf{u}'_{i+1}, \mathbf{v}'_{i+1}, \mathbf{w}'_{i+1})$.

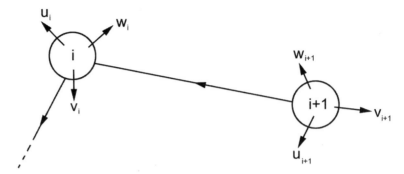

Figure 6.18.   Part of skeleton at *rest*. Two bones are shown with their nodes (i and $i + 1$) and local
                coordinate systems.

Another way to think about matrix $[M]$ is that when it is applied to node $i+1$
at $\mathbf{P}_{i+1}$ in Figure 6.18, it will move node $i + 1$ to the new position at $\mathbf{P}'_{i+1}$ as
shown in Figure 6.19. Remember, this assumes that the position of node i is used
as the origin while executing the rotation.

We can now propose that given $[M]$ (which pivots node $i + 1$ from $\mathbf{P}_{i+1}$ to
$\mathbf{P}'_{i+1}$) the following three-step algorithm will return a matrix $[M_k]$ which pivots
node $i + 1$ partway along an arc through $\mathbf{P}_{i+1}$ and $\mathbf{P}'_{i+1}$. How far along the arc
$[M_k]$ takes $\mathbf{P}_{i+1}$ depends on the parameter:

$$\tau = \frac{k - f}{l - f} : f \leq k < l$$

where f and l are the frames in which the movement begins and ends respectively.

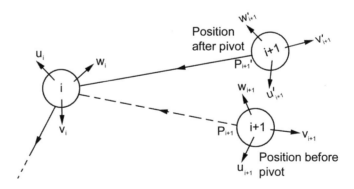

Figure 6.19.   A combination of rotational movements of node $i + 1$ around node i produces another
                pose of the part of the skeleton given in Figure 6.18.

The algorithm:

1. Convert the matrix $[M]$ to an equivalent quaternion q_m. (An algorithm for this appears in Section 2.17.5.)

2. Use the *slerp* function (From Section 2.17.7) to obtain a quaternion:

$$q_k = slerp(\tau, q_i, q_m)$$

q_k is a quaternion that holds the same information that in $[M]$ will pivot $\mathbf{P}_{i+1}$ into its position during frame k.

q_i is the unit quaternion. It is used here because $\mathbf{P}_{i+1}$ is the rest position for node $i + 1$.

3. Convert q_k to the equivalent rotational transformation matrix $[M_k]$ which when applied to $\mathbf{P}_{i+1}$ will pivot it round $\mathbf{P}_i$ into position (for frame k) on the arc joining $\mathbf{P}_{i+1}$ to $\mathbf{P}'_{i+1}$.

6.3.4 Hierarchical Interpolation

The previous section demonstrated how angular interpolation is used to animate a child node pivoting around its parent's axes. In a skeleton there is likely to be a long chain of *parent to child* linkages and any parent bone is thus also likely to execute some rotation around its own parent. In this scenario we have a situation in which the frame of reference for the orientation of a child relative to its parent is a moving one. This greatly complicates the issue, and it is the purpose of this section to develop a strategy for hierarchical interpolation which minimizes the complexity.

The main difficulty with a moving frame of reference can be illustrated by looking back to the example in Figure 6.17, which is reproduced in Figure 6.20 with additional vectors depicting the local frames of reference at the nodes on the end of the bones.

Consider what happens to node 3 and its frame of reference as the skeleton changes from the pose on the left to the pose on the right of Figure 6.20. In absolute terms the vectors $\mathbf{u}_3$ and $\mathbf{v}_3$ undergo a complete reversal; i.e., $\mathbf{u}'_3 = -\mathbf{u}_3$ and $\mathbf{v}'_3 = -\mathbf{v_3}$. Interpolating between these two sets of directions is not possible because node 3 could *swing* either clockwise or counterclockwise, since the result would be the same. It is only by considering the relative change between node 3 to its parent (node 2) that it becomes obvious that node 3 must rotate in an counterclockwise sense by $\frac{\pi}{2}$ round the vector $\mathbf{w}_2$.

From this example we can see that the orientation of a child relative to its parent's frame of reference must be taken into account when performing interpolation. There are two ways in which this might be done:

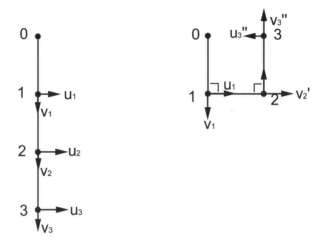

Figure 6.20.   A simple skeleton in two poses with local frames of reference given by vectors **u**, **v**, and **w**. All the **w** vectors are at right angles to both **u** and **v**, and therefore they point into the page and thus are not visible in the diagram.

1. Use the frames of reference of child and parent to calculate rotational transformations that relate:

   (a) The child's frame of reference to the parents in the first pose, say $[T_1]$.

   (b) The child's frame of reference to the parents in the second pose, say $[T_2]$.

   Interpolation proceeds as described in Section 6.3.3 between quaternions representing the matrices $[I]$ and $[T_2][T_1]^{-1}$.

2. Specify every pose in terms of the rest pose. Thus if:

   (a) $[T_1]$ is a transformation matrix that rotates node $i + 1$ round its parent so as to adopt the first pose and

   (b) $[T_2]$ is a transformation matrix that rotates node $i + 1$ round its parent so as to adopt the second pose.

   then interpolation proceeds as described in Section 6.3.3 between quaternions representing the matrices $[I]$ and $[T_2][T_1]^{-1}$. If $[M_k]$ is the matrix equivalent to the interpolated quaternion then the product $[T_1][M_k]$ is the matrix that pivots node $i + 1$ (and all its descendants).

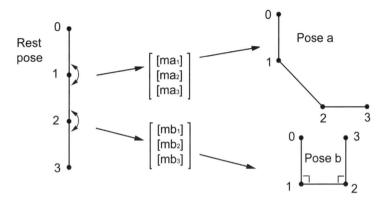

Figure 6.21. Specifying a specific pose with a series of rotational transformations based on the skeleton's rest position.

In either of the above approaches we will have a collection of transformation matrices (one for each node) that describe their *local* behavior, i.e., relative to their parent only. To render the model based on the pose of a skeleton, the skeleton itself and the vertices attached to each bone must be moved into position.

If we use the second approach as an example then the poses (a) and (b) shown in Figure 6.21 are recoded in the sequence of transformations $[M_a]_1$, $[M_a]_2$, $[M_a]_3$ and $[M_b]_1$, $[M_b]_2$, $[M_b]_3$ respectively. (An interpolated pose would be determined by the sequence $[M_k]_1$, $[M_k]_2$, $[M_k]_3$.) To bend the skeleton into poses (a) and (b) the sequence of operations illustrated in Figure 6.22 and outlined below is performed:

1. Start with skeleton at rest.

2. Multiply on the left and right the matrix $[M_a]_1$ by translations $[T(-\mathbf{P}_1)]$ and $[T(\mathbf{P}_1)]$ respectively so that its rotation is centered on skeleton node 1 at $\mathbf{P}_1$:
$$[M'_a]_1 = [T(\mathbf{P}_1)][M_a]_1[T(-\mathbf{P}_1)]$$

   Apply transformation $[M'_a]_1$ to skeleton nodes 2 and 3 and all vertices attached to bones 2 and 3.

   This is depicted in Figure 6.22(a); note that skeleton nodes $\mathbf{P}_2$ and $\mathbf{P}_3$ have moved to $\mathbf{P}'_2$ and $\mathbf{P}'_3$.

3. Modify matrix $[M_a]_2$ so that its rotation is centered on skeleton node 2 at $\mathbf{P}'_2$ by pre- and post-multiplying by translations $[T(-\mathbf{P}'_2)]$ and $[T(\mathbf{P}'_2)]$ respectively:
$$[M'_a]_2 = [T(\mathbf{P}'_2)][M_a]_2[T(-\mathbf{P}'_2)]$$

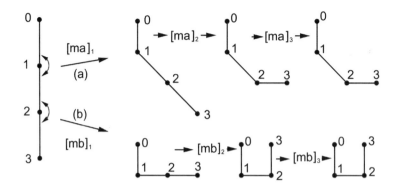

Figure 6.22. Applying the transformations down the chain. Attaining pose (a) from Figure 6.21 is depicted at the top and pose (b) at the bottom. (This example is discussed in the text.)

Apply transformation $[M'_a]_2$ to skeleton node 3 and all vertices attached to bone 3.

This is depicted in Figure 6.22(b); note that skeleton node $\mathbf{P}'_3$ has moved to $\mathbf{P}''_3$.

4. Modify matrix $[M_a]_3$ so that its rotation is centered on skeleton node 3 at $\mathbf{P}''_3$ by pre- and post-multiplying by translations $[T(-\mathbf{P}''_3)]$ and $[T(\mathbf{P}''_3)]$ respectively:

$$[M'_a]_3 = [T(\mathbf{P}_1)][M_a]_2[T(-\mathbf{P}''_2)]$$

Apply transformation $[M'_a]_3$ to all vertices attached to bone 3.

This is depicted in Figure 6.22(c). Note that skeleton node $\mathbf{P}''_3$ has not moved; only the local frame of reference at node 3 and any vertices attached to the last bone in the hierarchy will be affected.

It must be stressed that it is only the final result of these successive transformations that is rendered or displayed.

6.3.5 The Quest for More Realistic Character Animation

A rigid skeleton with polygons and vertices attached to a specific bone is ideal for *robots* like the model depicted in Figure 6.12. It also works pretty well for human figures but, in reality, the surface of an animal might well have a detailed texture (e.g., hair or fur) and this will tend to move flexibly as muscles expand and contract and skin stretches and bends.

To simulate these effects a polygonated mesh covering the surface of an object is still quite applicable provided it is fine enough and a procedure is provided to the animator that enables specification of appropriate behavior without having to move every vertex in the model by hand.

One approach that is used in a few commercial animation packages is to use a "field" which behaves in a way that is analogous to the effect a magnetic or electric field has on charged or magnetic materials. The effect of the field is proportional to the distance from its source, and two or more sources can be called into play to provide a combined effect. In the context of a polygon/vertex/skeleton computer model the vertices attached to the bone of a skeleton can have their position perturbed by a force proportional to their distance from adjacent bones or other structures (muscles) which themselves might be attached to one or two adjoining bones in the skeleton.

Another approach to attaining realistic behavior with the minimum of amount of work on the part of the animator is to use *goal-directed motion*. Using this approach the animator does not have to manipulate every bone in the structure to set up a particular pose. For example, to make a figure walk, all the animator has to do is drag the feet into position and the rest of the body will follow. Perhaps this is a little bit of an oversimplification but it serves to illustrate the intention of goal-directed animation. At the center of goal-directed animation lies the technique of *Inverse Kinematics*, which we will discuss in Section 6.4. What we have been investigating thus far is basically called *Forward Kinematics*.

6.4   Inverse Kinematics

Inverse Kinematics (IK) is popular as a technique employed by animators to reduce their workload in setting up complex actions, particularly those involving hierarchical motion. Just as *tweening* helps in making it much quicker to compile animations of many frames by getting the computer to fill in the gaps between keyframes, IK helps by reducing the number of adjustments an animator has to make to set up a keyframe. Animating characters with all the complexity of posing the figure springs immediately to mind as a good example, but other actions can also benefit from the application of an IK engine. The term *IK engine* is often used to describe a "black box" mathematical function which applies an IK solution to a specific hierarchically linked set of models according to IK theory. For example, a moving chain or any folding structure can be animated much more quickly with the help of IK. Animators also use IK to describe complex motions such as a figure riding a bicycle. The figure's feet are told to follow the pedals and its hands the handlebars. All the animator has to do is set up the motion of the bicycle itself and the character will follow it.

A good discussion of the basics of IK, the pros and cons of forward versus inverse kinematics [3], and IK applied to skeletons is provided by Watt and Watt [2]. They also introduce the theory but leave out some of the detail. In this section we will look in a detailed way at how IK calculations are set up and solved. We will adopt a different approach to that of Watt and Watt but we will obtain the same results.

Perhaps we should begin by stating that IK calculations are *not* trivial. They involve solving non-linear systems of equations in which there are always more unknowns than equations. Thus the system is either poorly constrained or not constrained at all. As we proceed to look at IK we will see how these problems are solved, and a few demonstrator applications are provided to allow you to see the effect of IK in practice.

A 3D computer animation use of IK is obviously going to require a 3D IK engine. However it is much simpler to understand a 2D IK engine and therefore this is where we will begin. The solution of the 3D IK problem follows exactly the same procedure as that used in 2D. It is only in setting up the problem that differences occur; thus we will use a 2D example to present a method of solution.

6.4.1   The IK Problem

Most of the work on which the concept of IK is based originated in the field of robotics, robotics in the sense of the machines used in automation and manufacturing processes. The articulated linkages that form the arms and hands of machines designed to fulfill a manipulation role must be able to reach any point within a working region, and the hand at the end of the robot's arm must also be able to adopt any orientation.

For a robot used as a surrogate human on a production line an important feature of its design is that the hand can approach the working materials at the correct angle. To do this there must be enough linkages from the place where the robot is anchored to its hand and each link must have sufficient degrees of freedom. If the robot can put its hand in the correct place then the next question is: how does it get there? It may be starting from a rest position or the place where it has just finished a previous task. From the operator's point of view it would be very helpful if one only had to move the hand, not adjust every link from base to hand. However the hand must be at the end of the articulated linkage, and it is the relative orientation of the links that dictate where the hand is.

Thus, given the relative orientation of articulated linkages, say Θ (which represents the angles that establish how each link is orientated; e.g., by the set: $\theta_1, \theta_2, \dots \theta_n$), the location of the end of the articulation $\mathbf{X}$ is given by some function:

$$\mathbf{X} = f(\Theta) \tag{6.3}$$

This is called **forward kinematics** because the links are set by the operator who gives values to elements of Θ.

However in the ideal operating environment the robot's operator would like to set $\mathbf{X}$; thus the problem is: given $\mathbf{X}$ can we find a suitable Θ? Posed in this way it is an **inverse** kinematic problem. To solve it we must find the inverse of the function $f()$ so that we can write Equation 6.3 as:

$$\Theta = f^{-1}(\mathbf{X}) \tag{6.4}$$

Thus we can summarize in a single statement the IK problem:

How, given the design of an articulation and a desired position for the last linkage, do we obtain $f^{-1}()$ and hence from it the configuration of all the links?

It must be stressed that it may not be possible for the articulation to reach the desired position $\mathbf{X}$ and hence we call it a *goal*.

Since $\mathbf{X}$ and Θ are both vectors we might hope to be able to write Equation 6.3 in matrix form:

$$[X] = [A][\Theta] \tag{6.5}$$

and solve it by calculating the inverse of A and hence Θ from the set of linear equations:

$$[\Theta] = [A]^{-1}[X]$$

Unfortunately $f()$ is in most cases a non-linear function and thus it is not possible to express Equation 6.3 in the form given by Equation 6.5. To solve the problem we must use an iteration technique, which is essentially the same as that used for finding the solution of a set of simultaneous non-linear equation; McCalla [4] describes the usual procedure. The procedure essentially linearizes Equation 6.3 by expressing it in differential form:

$$\Delta\mathbf{X} = f'(\Theta)\Delta\Theta \tag{6.6}$$

and then incrementally stepping towards the solution. Since $f()$ is a multi-variable function $f'()$ is the Jacobian matrix of partial derivatives given by:

$$J(\Theta) = \begin{bmatrix} \dfrac{\partial X_1}{\partial\theta_1} & \dfrac{\partial X_1}{\partial\theta_2} & \cdots & \dfrac{\partial X_1}{\partial\theta_p} \\ \dfrac{\partial X_2}{\partial\theta_1} & \dfrac{\partial X_2}{\partial\theta_2} & \cdots & \dfrac{\partial X_2}{\partial\theta_n} \\ \cdots & \cdots & \cdots & \cdots \\ \dfrac{\partial X_m}{\partial\theta_1} & \dfrac{\partial X_m}{\partial\theta_2} & \cdots & \dfrac{\partial X_m}{\partial\theta_n} \end{bmatrix}$$

By calculating an inverse for J Equation 6.6 may be written:

$$\Delta\Theta = J^{-1}\Delta\mathbf{X}$$

J is of course dependent on Θ so an initial guess must be made for the values θ_1, θ_2, .. θ_3. In the case of the IK problem the initial guess is simply the current configuration. After the first step we proceed to find a new Θ by iterating:

$$\Theta_{n+1} = \Theta_n + \Delta\Theta$$

where n is a count of the number of iterations and at each step J^{-1} is recalculated from the current Θ_n.

Iteration will be discussed in detail when we come to consider the procedure for 2D IK in Section 6.4.2, when we will also address some outstanding issues such as how an inverse of a **non-square** Jacobian matrix is obtained and how we iterate towards the desired goal.

6.4.2   Solving the IK Problem in Two Dimensions

We will look at an example of a three-link articulation. Restricted to two dimensions it moves only in the plane of the page. When equations have been obtained for this specific case we will see how they may be extended to a system with n links. The links are fixed at one end, which we will designate as the origin $(0,0)$. The other end, at point (x, y), is moved towards a goal point, which it may or may not reach. Where it gets to is what we hope a solution to the IK problem will reveal.

A solution of Equation 6.4 gives us the orientation of each link in the chain and from that we can find out how close to the goal the end point actually gets. Figure 6.23 illustrates several possible configurations for a three-link articulation and Figure 6.24 presents the notation used to specify and solve the three-link IK problem.

Figure 6.24 shows us that if we know the values of $\mathbf{P}_1$ (anchor point), l_1, l_2, l_3, (lengths of the links) and θ_1, θ_2, and θ_3 (the relative orientation between one link and the next) then the current position of every joint in the link is fully specified (including the end point $\mathbf{P}_4$).

Since $\mathbf{P}_1$, l_1, l_2, and l_3 are constant and independent of the orientation of the linkage, it is only the θ_i that are the unknowns in our IK function, Equation 6.4. For our specific example:

$$\mathbf{P}_4 = \mathbf{f}(\theta_1, \theta_2, \theta_3)$$

Note carefully how θ_i is specified as an angle measured counterclockwise from the direction in which link $(i - 1)$ is pointing to the direction in which link i is

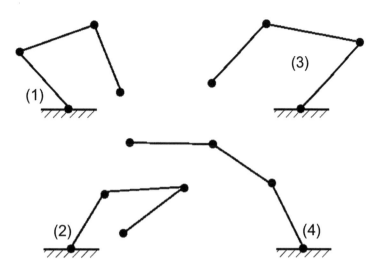

Figure 6.23.   Several possible orientations for a three-link 2D articulated figure. In configurations 1
and 2 the articulation reaches to the same end point. We may therefore surmise that
simply specifying the location of an end point does not guarantee a unique configuration
for the links.

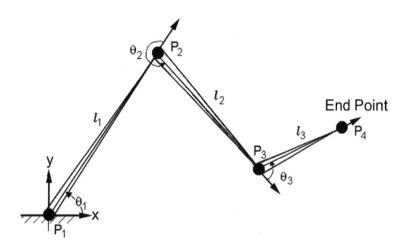

Figure 6.24.   Specifying the three-link articulation. The first link is anchored at (0,0) and lies at an angle
of θ_1 to the x-axis. The lengths of the links are l_1, l_2, and l_3 and link 2 makes an angle
of θ_2 from link 1. The end point $\mathbf{P}_4$ lies at coordinate (x, y).

pointing. The first link angle θ_1 is referenced to the x-axis. Using this information we can write an expression for the (x, y) coordinate of $\mathbf{P}_4$:

$$\begin{bmatrix} x \\ y \end{bmatrix} = \begin{bmatrix} l_1 \cos(\theta_1) + l_2 \cos(\theta_1 + \theta_2) + l_3 \cos(\theta_1 + \theta_2 + \theta_3) \\ l_1 \sin(\theta_1) + l_2 \sin(\theta_1 + \theta_2) + l_3 \sin(\theta_1 + \theta_2 + \theta_3) \end{bmatrix} \qquad (6.7)$$

Equation 6.7 shows that $f(\theta_1, \theta_2, \theta_3)$ is as we suspected a non-linear function. Therefore we will need to solve the IK problem by linearizing Equation 6.7 and iterating toward the desired goal position of $\mathbf{P}_4$. The first step in this procedure is to obtain the Jacobian and, for the 2D IK problem of three links, this is the 2×3 matrix:

$$J = \begin{bmatrix} \dfrac{\partial x}{\partial \theta_1} & \dfrac{\partial x}{\partial \theta_2} & \dfrac{\partial x}{\partial \theta_3} \\ \dfrac{\partial y}{\partial \theta_1} & \dfrac{\partial y}{\partial \theta_2} & \dfrac{\partial y}{\partial \theta_3} \end{bmatrix}$$

The terms $\frac{\partial}{\partial \theta_i}$ are obtained by differentiating Equation 6.7 to give:

$$J = \begin{bmatrix} J_{11} & J_{12} & J_{13} \\ J_{21} & J_{22} & J_{23} \end{bmatrix} \qquad (6.8)$$

where:

$$\begin{aligned} J_{11} &= -l_1 \sin(\theta_1) - l_2 \sin(\theta_1 + \theta_2) - l_3 \sin(\theta_1 + \theta_2 + \theta_3) \\ J_{12} &= -l_2 \sin(\theta_1 + \theta_2) - l_3 \sin(\theta_1 + \theta_2 + \theta_3) \\ J_{13} &= -l_3 \sin(\theta_1 + \theta_2 + \theta_3) \\ J_{21} &= l_1 \cos(\theta_1) + l_2 \cos(\theta_1 + \theta_2) + l_3 \cos(\theta_1 + \theta_2 + \theta_3) \\ J_{22} &= l_2 \cos(\theta_1 + \theta_2) + l_3 \cos(\theta_1 + \theta_2 + \theta_3) \\ J_{23} &= l_3 \cos(\theta_1 + \theta_2 + \theta_3) \end{aligned}$$

With J calculated we are nearly ready to go through the iteration process that moves $\mathbf{P}_4$ towards its goal. An algorithm for this will be based on the equations:

$$\begin{aligned} \mathbf{\Theta}_{n+1} &= \mathbf{\Theta}_n + J(\mathbf{\Theta}_n)^{-1} \mathbf{\Delta X} \\ \mathbf{X}_{n+1} &= f(\mathbf{\Theta}_{n+1}) \end{aligned}$$

Before we can do this we must investigate how J^{-1} is obtained from J.

The generalized inverse

The definition of the inverse of a matrix A is a matrix A^{-1}, such that if $|A| \neq 0$ then A and A^{-1} satisfies:

$$AA^{-1} = A^{-1}A = I$$

This definition of the inverse only applies to square matrices. In the case of any matrix A it is possible to define a generalized inverse A^- which satisfies:

$$AA^-A = A \qquad (6.9)$$

If A is square and $|A| \neq 0$ then $A^- = A^{-1}$. Post-multiplying both sides of Equation 6.9 by the transpose of A gives us:

$$AA^-(AA^T) = AA^T$$

AA^T is a square matrix and therefore if $|AA^T| \neq 0$ we can find its *conventional* inverse $(AA^T)^{-1}$ and write:

$$
\begin{aligned}
AA^-(AA^T)(AA^T)^{-1} &= AA^T(AA^T)^{-1} \text{ or} \\
AA^- &= AA^T(AA^T)^{-1}
\end{aligned}
$$

The implication here is that for any (not necessarily square) matrix if we need its inverse we may use its (generalized) inverse A^- given by:

$$A^- = A^T(AA^T)^{-1} \qquad (6.10)$$

This is exactly the expression that we need in order to invert the $n \times m$ Jacobian matrix.

For more information on generalized inverses and their properties and limitations consult [5]. Specifically the two points most important for IK are the existence of an inverse for AA^T and the fact that normally we have more unknowns than equations (i.e., $m > n$). The practical implication of $m > n$ is that the articulation can attain its goal in more than one configuration.

Iterating towards the goal

Having found a way to invert J we develop an algorithm to iterate from one configuration towards the goal. A suitable algorithm is given in Figure 6.25.

Step 4 of the algorithm given in Figure 6.25 provides the mechanism to test for convergence of the IK solution procedure. It is based on ensuring that the norm of the vector $\mathbf{\Delta X} - J(\mathbf{\Theta})\mathbf{\Delta\Theta}$ is smaller than a specified threshold:

$$\|\mathbf{\Delta X} - J(\mathbf{\Theta})\mathbf{\Delta\Theta}\| < \epsilon$$

If we substitute for $\mathbf{\Delta\Theta}$ and call J^- the generalized inverse of J then in matrix form:

$$\|(I - JJ^-)\mathbf{\Delta X}\| < \epsilon$$

We use this criterion to determine a $\mathbf{\Delta X}$ that satisfies the condition on the norm. We also use this to determine whether the iteration can proceed or if we must accept that the goal cannot be reached. A simple test on the magnitude of $\mathbf{\Delta X}$ will suffice: when it is less than a given threshold then either the goal has been reached or it is so small that the end will never get there.

Start with the linkage configuration defined by the set of angles:
$\theta_1, \theta_2, \theta_3, ...\theta_n$ (which we will write as $\boldsymbol{\Theta}$),
and end point located at $\mathbf{P}$, i.e., at coordinate (x, y).
Apply the steps below to move the end point towards its goal
at $\mathbf{P}_g$ (i.e., at :(x_g, y_g)).

Step 1:
Calculate the incremental step $\boldsymbol{\Delta X} = \mathbf{P}_g - \mathbf{P}$

Step 2:
Calculate $J(\theta_1, \theta_2, \theta_3, ...\theta_n)$
(use the current values of θ_1, etc.)

Step 3:
Find the inverse of J which we will call J^-
$J^- = J^T (JJ^T)^{-1}$
(if J is a $2 \times n$ matrix J^- is a $n \times 2$ matrix)

Step 4:
Test for a valid convergence of the iteration:
if $\|(I - JJ^-)\boldsymbol{\Delta X}\| > \epsilon$ the step towards the
goal (the $\boldsymbol{\Delta X}$) is too large, so set $\boldsymbol{\Delta X} = \dfrac{\boldsymbol{\Delta X}}{2}$
and repeat step 4 until the norm is less than ϵ.
If the inequality cannot be satisfied after a certain number
of steps then it is likely that the goal cannot be reached and
the IK calculations should be terminated
(This step is discussed in more detail in the text)

Step 5:
Calculate updated values for the parameters θ_1, etc.
$\boldsymbol{\Theta} = \boldsymbol{\Theta} + J^- \boldsymbol{\Delta X}$
$\boldsymbol{\Theta}$ is the vector of angles for each link $[\theta_1, \theta_2, ...]^T$

Step 6:
Calculate the new state of the articulation from θ_1, θ_2, etc.
Check the end point $\mathbf{P}_4$ to see if is close enough to the goal.
It is likely that $\boldsymbol{\Delta X}$ will have been reduced by Step 4
and thus the end point will be somewhat short of the goal.
In this case *go back and repeat the procedure from Step 1.*
Otherwise we have succeeded in moving $\mathbf{P}_4$ to the goal point $\mathbf{P}_g$

Figure 6.25.   Iterative algorithm for solving the IK problem to determine the orientation of an articulated linkage in terms of a number of parameters θ_i given the goal of moving the end of the articulation from its current position $\mathbf{X}$ towards $\mathbf{X}_{goal}$.

Equations for a general 2D articulated linkage

At the beginning of this section we said that it was easy to extend the problem from one involving three links to one which can take any number, say n links. In essence we use the same algorithm but the expressions for (x, y) and the Jacobian terms $\dfrac{\partial x}{\partial \theta_i}$ become:

$$x = \sum_{i=1}^{n} l_i \cos(\sum_{j=i}^{i} \theta_j)$$

$$y = \sum_{i=1}^{n} l_i \sin(\sum_{j=i}^{i} \theta_j)$$

$$\frac{\partial x}{\partial \theta_k} = -\sum_{i=k}^{n} l_i \sin(\sum_{j=1}^{i} \theta_j)$$

$$\frac{\partial y}{\partial \theta_k} = \sum_{i=k}^{n} l_i \cos(\sum_{j=1}^{i} \theta_j)$$

$$k = 1 \to n$$

6.4.3 Solving the IK Problem in Three Dimensions

All the steps in the solution procedure for the 2D IK problem presented in the algorithm of Figure 6.25 are equally applicable to the 3D IK problem. The calculation of generalized inverse, iteration towards a goal for the end of the articulation, and termination criteria are all the same.

Where the 2D and 3D IK problems differ is in the specification of the orientation of the links, the determination of Jacobian, and the equations that tell us how to calculate the location of the joints between links.

Although the change from 2D to 3D involves an increase of only one dimension, the complexity of the calculations increases to such an extent that we cannot normally determine the Jacobian by differentiation of analytic expressions. In this section we will take an "Engineering Approach" to obtain the information we need. Watt and Watt [6] give a rigorous analysis but basically obtain the same result although they express it in a different form. No matter what way the analysis proceeds we recognize that a greater number of variables will be needed to specify the state of a 3D articulation. You will remember that one angle per link is sufficient for a 2D articulation, since in that case each link had only one degree of freedom, i.e., rotation. In a 3D system with three degrees of freedom for each link we must choose to use three parameters for each link. It turns out that

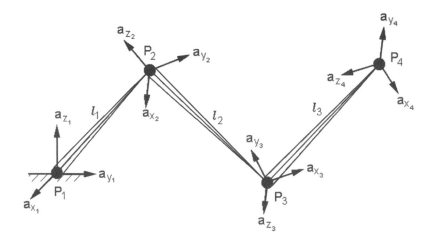

Figure 6.26.   A 3D articulated linkage. It has an orthogonal frame of reference given by the basis vectors $(\hat{a}_x, \hat{a}_y, \hat{a}_z)$ attached to the joint at the end of each link. Any structure associated with a link is regarded as fixed relative to the frame of reference for that link. As the linkages move and pivot to reach towards a new goal the local frames of reference twist and turn and their bases move. The first link is attached to a fixed base at $\mathbf{P}_1$.

indeed three parameters per link is sufficient, and the three Euler angles which are sometimes used to define the orientation of objects in the scene being rendered by a computer animation program is one possibility.

For our explanation we will start by considering the three-link articulation depicted in Figure 6.26.

Just as in the 2D IK problem we will obtain a differential formulation relating small changes in the orientation of the links to changes in the location of the end point. Later we will extend this to accommodate changes in the orientation of the local frame of reference at the end of the linkage. Thus as for the 2D case we will write an equation relating a small change in end point to a change in parameters for each linkage:

$$\mathbf{\Delta X} = J(\mathbf{\Theta})\mathbf{\Delta\Theta} \qquad (6.11)$$

In this case $\mathbf{X}$ is a 3D vector and $\mathbf{\Delta\Theta}$ measures, in some as-yet-to-be-defined sense, the orientation of each link. The inverse of Equation 6.11 will provide the information on how to arrange the linkage so that its end point moves towards its goal.

As far as the iterative steps for the 3D algorithm are concerned they mirror exactly the 2D algorithm; it is only the dimensions of the vectors and matrices that change.

With a solution procedure for the 3D IK problem based on Equation 6.11 in place, we need only consider how the 3D Jacobian is obtained and in what form $\Delta\Theta$ must be expressed. Unfortunately the one thing we cannot do is write an analytic expression for $\mathbf{X}$ given Θ and obtain J by analytic differentiation. An alternative method will have to be found. It is here that we use a so-called "engineering approach" to determine J. Hopefully the assumptions we make regarding how a rotation propagates through a linkage and how it affects the end points will be fairly obvious, but if you insist on a rigorous proof then one can be found in [6].

Our goal is to write an expression that relates a small change in the orientation of each link to a small change in position of the final link; this is J. Two assumptions are made during this calculation and they are justifiable because only *infinitesimal* changes in link orientation are being considered. These assumptions are:

1. In rotational transformations the trigonometric functions $\sin\theta \mapsto \theta$ and $\cos\theta \mapsto 1$.

2. The order in which rotational transformation are applied does not affect the outcome of a rotation.

With these assumptions in mind we proceed by considering the effect of small orientational changes at each link of the structure shown in Figure 6.26. These rotations are made by rotating all links lying further away from the base of the linkage by $\Delta\theta$ around some axis $\hat{\mathbf{n}}$. In Section 2.17.2 it was stated that any rotation can be expressed as a single angle of rotation and an axis for that rotation. Equation 2.30 reproduced below as Equation 6.12 expresses the equivalence of a rotational transformation, acting on an arbitrary vector $\mathbf{r}$, as a matrix R or a vector equation for rotation by angle θ around the direction vector $\hat{\mathbf{n}}$ on:

$$\mathbf{r}' = R\mathbf{r} = \cos\theta\,\mathbf{r} + (1 - \cos\theta)(\hat{\mathbf{n}} \cdot \mathbf{r})\hat{\mathbf{n}} + \sin\theta(\hat{\mathbf{n}} \times \mathbf{r}) \qquad (6.12)$$

In the limit where rotation is by a very small angle, Equation 6.12 may be written as:

$$\mathbf{r}' = R\mathbf{r} = \mathbf{r} + \Delta\theta(\hat{\mathbf{n}} \times \mathbf{r}) \qquad (6.13)$$

The incremental change in the position of $\mathbf{r}$ given by:

$$\Delta\mathbf{r} = \Delta\theta(\hat{\mathbf{n}} \times \mathbf{r}) \qquad (6.14)$$

We are now in a position to consider the effect on the end of an articulation of incremental rotations at each link. Figure 6.28(a) shows the effect on a three-link structure of a rotation of $\Delta\theta_1$ around the vector $\hat{\mathbf{n}}_1$ based at point $\mathbf{P}_1$. From

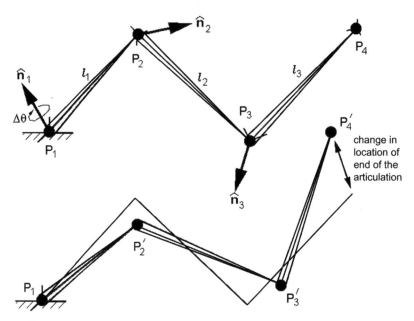

change in
location of
end of the
articulation

Figure 6.27.   The articulated linkage from Figure 6.26 before and after a small rotation is applied to
each link. The rotation may be specified by giving an angle $\Delta\theta$ and an axis $\hat{n}$ around which
the rotation is made.

Equation 6.14 we can calculate that the change in position of $\mathbf{P}_4$ by this single
rotation is:

$$(\mathbf{\Delta P}_4)_1 = (\Delta\theta_1\hat{\mathbf{n}}_1) \times (\mathbf{P}_4 - \mathbf{P}_1)$$

Figure 6.28(b) shows the effect of subsequently rotating the linkage by $\Delta\theta_2$
around $\hat{\mathbf{n}}_2$ which is based at the point $\mathbf{P}_2$. Again Equation 6.14 lets us write an
expression for the change in $\mathbf{P}_4$ due to that rotation:

$$(\mathbf{\Delta P}_4)_2 = (\Delta\theta_2\hat{\mathbf{n}}_2) \times (\mathbf{P}_4 - \mathbf{P}_2)$$

We can see that a rotation around a vector based at $\mathbf{P}_3$ will also have an effect
on the position of $\mathbf{P}_4$, and that the accumulated change in the position of $\mathbf{P}_4$ is
the sum of the effects of rotations around the vectors based at points 1 to 3; that
is:

$$\mathbf{\Delta P}_4 = \Delta\theta_1\hat{\mathbf{n}}_1 \times (\mathbf{P}_4 - \mathbf{P}_1) + \Delta\theta_2\hat{\mathbf{n}}_2 \times (\mathbf{P}_4 - \mathbf{P}_2) + \Delta\theta_3\hat{\mathbf{n}}_3 \times (\mathbf{P}_4 - \mathbf{P}_3) \quad (6.15)$$

Equation 6.15 gives a linear relationship between the change in position at the end
of an articulation and a rotation applied to each link. We have almost achieved
our goal of obtaining the Jacobian matrix.

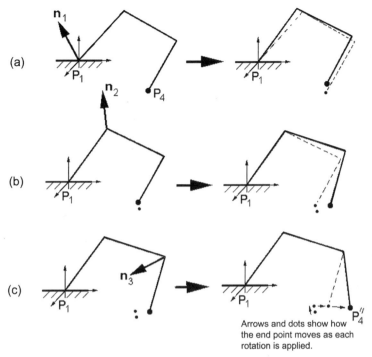

Figure 6.28. Accumulating the small rotations occurring at each link of a three-link articulation leads to an accumulated change in the position of the end point of the linkage P_4. In (a) the linkage is slightly repositioned by a small rotation round $\hat{n}_1$. For (b) and (c) the small rotations only apply to links lying between the point of rotation and the end of the articulation at P_4.

Before making the final step little further exploration of the result of an incremental rotation defined in Equations 6.13 and 6.14 is necessary. One reason for this is that we have not explained how the vectors $\hat{n}_i$ are obtained. We shall now see how these are in fact not needed explicitly because we can work directly from the frames of reference (the $\hat{a}_{xi}$, $\hat{a}_{yi}$, and $\hat{a}_{zi}$ basis vectors depicted in Figure 6.26) attached to the end of every link.

Using the components of $\hat{n}$, r, and Δr we can express Equation 6.14 as a matrix:

$$
\begin{bmatrix} \Delta r_x \\ \Delta r_y \\ \Delta r_z \end{bmatrix} = \begin{bmatrix} 0 & -n_z \Delta\theta & n_y \Delta\theta \\ n_z \Delta\theta & 0 & -n_x \Delta\theta \\ -n_y \Delta\theta & n_x \Delta\theta & 0 \end{bmatrix} \begin{bmatrix} r_x \\ r_y \\ r_z \end{bmatrix} \tag{6.16}
$$

In Section 2.11.3 matrices were given which would rotate a vector by a specified angle around either the x-, y-, or z-coordinate axis. If rotations around all three axes are performed on a vector $\mathbf{r}$ we can write a matrix expression for the change in $\mathbf{r}$:

$$\Delta\mathbf{r} = (R_x(\Delta\theta_x)R_y(\Delta\theta_y)R_z(\Delta\theta_z) - I)\mathbf{r} \qquad (6.17)$$

$R_x(\Delta\theta_x)$ represents a rotation of $\Delta\theta_x$ radians around the x-axis. I is the identity matrix.

For pure rotations R is a 3×3 matrix and, if as stated in our prerequisite assumptions $cos\theta \mapsto 1$ and $\sin\theta \mapsto \theta$, then the rotation matrices for axial rotation by angles $\Delta\theta_x$, etc., become for x, y, and z respectively:

$$\begin{bmatrix} 1 & 0 & 0 \\ 0 & 1 & -\Delta\theta_x \\ 0 & \Delta\theta_x & 1 \end{bmatrix} \begin{bmatrix} 1 & 0 & \Delta\theta_y \\ 0 & 1 & 0 \\ -\Delta\theta_y & 0 & 1 \end{bmatrix} \begin{bmatrix} 1 & -\Delta\theta_z & 0 \\ \Delta\theta_z & 1 & 0 \\ 0 & 0 & 1 \end{bmatrix}$$

Using the assumption that the order of multiplication is unimportant for small angle rotations and neglecting second order product terms like $\Delta\theta_x\Delta\theta_y$, Equation 6.17 becomes:

$$\begin{bmatrix} \Delta r_x \\ \Delta r_y \\ \Delta r_z \end{bmatrix} = \begin{bmatrix} 0 & -\Delta\theta_z & \Delta\theta_y \\ \Delta\theta_z & 0 & -\Delta\theta_x \\ -\Delta\theta_y & \Delta\theta_x & 0 \end{bmatrix} \begin{bmatrix} r_x \\ r_y \\ r_z \end{bmatrix} \qquad (6.18)$$

Note the similarity between Equations 6.18 and 6.16; if terms such as $\Delta\theta_x$ are identified with terms such as $\Delta\theta n_x$ there is a one to one correspondence. Thus we can say that in the case of incremental rotations:

A small rotation of θ around a single axis $\hat{\mathbf{n}}$ can be accomplished equivalently by performing three small rotations around three basis vectors.

Returning now to Equation 6.15 and the term associated with link i:

$$\Delta\theta_i\hat{\mathbf{n}}_i \times (\mathbf{P}_4 - \mathbf{P}_i)$$

For the specific three-link example in Equation 6.15 i satisfies $1 \leq i < 4$, and we may express $\hat{\mathbf{n}}_i$ in terms of the known basis vectors for frame i as:

$$\Delta\theta_i(\alpha\hat{\mathbf{a}_{xi}} + \beta\hat{\mathbf{a}_{yi}} + \gamma\hat{\mathbf{a}_{zi}}) \times (\mathbf{P}_4 - \mathbf{P}_i)$$

where α, β and γ are constants. Now, writing $\alpha\Delta\theta_i$ as $\Delta\theta_{xi}$, $\beta\Delta\theta_i$ as $\Delta\theta_{yi}$, and $\gamma\Delta\theta_i$ as $\Delta\theta_{xi}$ we may express $\Delta\theta_i\hat{\mathbf{n}}_i \times (\mathbf{P}_4 - \mathbf{P}_i)$ as:

$$\Delta\theta_{xi}\hat{\mathbf{a}_{xi}} \times (\mathbf{P}_4 - \mathbf{P}_i) + \Delta\theta_{xi}\hat{\mathbf{a}_{yi}} \times (\mathbf{P}_4 - \mathbf{P}_i) + \Delta\theta_{xi}\hat{\mathbf{a}_{zi}} \times (\mathbf{P}_4 - \mathbf{P}_i)$$

Substituting this expression into Equation 6.15 for $i = 1$, $i = 2$, and $i = 3$ gives a set of unknowns, the $\Delta\theta_{xi}$, etc. There is a simple linear relationship between them and their contribution to $\Delta \mathbf{P}_4$ which when written in matrix form gives the Jacobian that we have been seeking.

$$[\Delta \mathbf{P}_4] = \begin{bmatrix} \mathbf{J}_{x1} & \mathbf{J}_{y1} & \mathbf{J}_{z1} & \mathbf{J}_{x2} & \mathbf{J}_{y2} & \mathbf{J}_{z2} & \mathbf{J}_{x3} & \mathbf{J}_{y3} & \mathbf{J}_{z3} \end{bmatrix} \begin{bmatrix} \Delta \theta_{x1} \\ \Delta \theta_{y1} \\ \Delta \theta_{z1} \\ \Delta \theta_{x2} \\ \Delta \theta_{y2} \\ \Delta \theta_{z2} \\ \Delta \theta_{x3} \\ \Delta \theta_{y3} \\ \Delta \theta_{z3} \end{bmatrix}$$
$$(6.19)$$

where:

$$
\begin{aligned}
\mathbf{J}_{x1} &= \hat{\mathbf{a}}_{x1} \times (\mathbf{P}_4 - \mathbf{P}_1) \\
\mathbf{J}_{y1} &= \hat{\mathbf{a}}_{y1} \times (\mathbf{P}_4 - \mathbf{P}_1) \\
\mathbf{J}_{z1} &= \hat{\mathbf{a}}_{z1} \times (\mathbf{P}_4 - \mathbf{P}_1) \\
\mathbf{J}_{x2} &= \hat{\mathbf{a}}_{x2} \times (\mathbf{P}_4 - \mathbf{P}_2) \\
\mathbf{J}_{y2} &= \hat{\mathbf{a}}_{y2} \times (\mathbf{P}_4 - \mathbf{P}_2) \\
\mathbf{J}_{z2} &= \hat{\mathbf{a}}_{z2} \times (\mathbf{P}_4 - \mathbf{P}_2) \\
\mathbf{J}_{x3} &= \hat{\mathbf{a}}_{x3} \times (\mathbf{P}_4 - \mathbf{P}_3) \\
\mathbf{J}_{y3} &= \hat{\mathbf{a}}_{y3} \times (\mathbf{P}_4 - \mathbf{P}_3) \\
\mathbf{J}_{z3} &= \hat{\mathbf{a}}_{z3} \times (\mathbf{P}_4 - \mathbf{P}_3)
\end{aligned}
$$

From Equation 6.19 it is relatively straightforward to see how a Jacobian matrix can be obtained for an articulation with any number of links. Since $\Delta \mathbf{P}_4$ is a vector, the dimension of the Jacobian for an n-link articulation is $3 \times 3n$ with the three terms associated to link i given by:

$$\begin{bmatrix} \cdots & \hat{\mathbf{a}}_{xi} \times (\mathbf{P}_{n+1} - \mathbf{P}_i) & \hat{\mathbf{a}}_{yi} \times (\mathbf{P}_{n+1} - \mathbf{P}_i) & \hat{\mathbf{a}}_{zi} \times (\mathbf{P}_{n+1} - \mathbf{P}_i) & \cdots \end{bmatrix}$$

Having found a way of calculating the Jacobian for the 3D IK problem we can summarize the procedure used to apply IK in the manipulation of a 3D articulated linkage such as that illustrated in Figure 6.26. The steps are:

1. A linkage (e.g., the one shown in Figure 6.26) is established in its initial configuration. The location of the end points of all links are known and the frames of reference associated with each link are defined. A goal point for the end of the link to move towards is given.

2. From the coordinates of end points of each link and the reference frames axes a Jacobian matrix is calculated and its inverse is used to determine small angles of rotation to apply to the structure.

3. The linkage is pivoted by carrying out rotation by these angles around the basis vectors. This establishes new coordinates for the end points of the linkage; it also changes the direction of the basis vectors.

4. If the end point has not reached its goal the previous two steps are repeated until either the end point does reach its goal or it is not possible for it to move any closer to the goal. The procedure given in Figure 6.25 details the iterative process because it applies equally well to both 2D and 3D IK problems.

Setting a goal for the orientation at the end of the chain

If you look back at Figure 6.26 you will see that at the end of the chain (the point $\mathbf{P}_4$) there is a reference frame whose basis vectors are $(\hat{\mathbf{a}}_{x4}, \hat{\mathbf{a}}_{y4}, \hat{\mathbf{a}}_{z4})$. Nothing has been said about how they move as $\mathbf{P}_4$ is dragged towards its goal. If no prescription is placed on the base vectors at $\mathbf{P}_4$, they will pivot in the same way that the other base vectors pivot when the articulation is rotated in the incremental steps which take $\mathbf{P}_4$ towards its goal.

To obtain an expression for the change in direction of these base vectors consider the effect of the incremental changes in Equation 6.15 for the example in Figure 6.27. There:

1. A rotation around $\hat{\mathbf{n}}_1$ based at $\mathbf{P}_1$ pivots base vectors at $\mathbf{P}_2$, $\mathbf{P}_3$, and $\mathbf{P}_4$.

2. A rotation around $\hat{\mathbf{n}}_2$ based at $\mathbf{P}_2$ pivots base vectors at $\mathbf{P}_3$ and $\mathbf{P}_4$.

3. The rotation experienced by a base vector at $\mathbf{P}_4$ is subject to the accumulated rotations at all the other joints in the linkage.

To obtain an expression for the effect of accumulated rotations we consider again Equation 6.13, but this time write it in the form of a small rotation around vector $\hat{\mathbf{n}}_1$:

$$\mathbf{r}' = \mathbf{r} + (\Delta\theta_1 \hat{\mathbf{n}}_1 \times \mathbf{r}) \tag{6.20}$$

A subsequent rotation of $\mathbf{r}'$ around $\hat{\mathbf{n}}_2$ can be expressed in the same terms:

$$\mathbf{r}'' = \mathbf{r}' + (\Delta\theta_2 \hat{\mathbf{n}}_2 \times \mathbf{r}') \tag{6.21}$$

Substituting for $\mathbf{r}'$ from Equation 6.20 in Equation 6.21, we obtain an expression for the accumulation of two rotations on $\mathbf{r}$:

$$\mathbf{r}'' = \mathbf{r} + (\Delta\theta_2 \hat{\mathbf{n}}_2 + \Delta\theta_1 \hat{\mathbf{n}}_1) \times \mathbf{r} + (\Delta\theta_2 \Delta\theta_1)(\hat{\mathbf{n}}_2 \times (\hat{\mathbf{n}}_1 \times \mathbf{r}))$$

For very small rotations second order terms may be neglected giving:

$$\mathbf{r}'' = \mathbf{r} + (\Delta\theta_2 \hat{\mathbf{n}}_2 + \Delta\theta_1 \hat{\mathbf{n}}_1) \times \mathbf{r}$$

Comparing this with Equation 6.20 it is evident that the accumulation of two rotations may be expressed as a single rotation around one axis:

$$\Delta\theta\hat{\mathbf{n}} = (\Delta\theta_2\hat{\mathbf{n}}_2 + \Delta\theta_1\hat{\mathbf{n}}_1)$$

Extending the argument by induction results in an expression for the change in $\mathbf{r}$ due to n small rotations:

$$\Delta\mathbf{r} = (\sum_{i=1}^{n}\Delta\theta_i\hat{\mathbf{n}}_i) \times \mathbf{r} \tag{6.22}$$

Applying the above results shows that the accumulated rotation at the end of a three-link articulation is equivalent to a single rotation given by:

$$\Delta\theta_4\hat{\mathbf{n}}_4 = \Delta\theta_3\hat{\mathbf{n}}_3 + \Delta\theta_2\hat{\mathbf{n}}_2 + \Delta\theta_1\hat{\mathbf{n}}_1 \tag{6.23}$$

The $\hat{\mathbf{n}}_i$ vectors in Equation 6.23 can be expanded in an analogous way to that used in the derivation of Equation 6.15. When this is done Equation 6.23 becomes:

$$\Delta\theta_4\hat{\mathbf{n}}_4 = \sum_{i=1}^{i=3}(\Delta\theta_{xi}\hat{\mathbf{a}}_{xi} + \Delta\theta_{xi}\hat{\mathbf{a}}_{yi} + \Delta\theta_{xi}\hat{\mathbf{a}}_{zi}) \tag{6.24}$$

Since this involves the same incremental rotations to those of Equation 6.19 it is appropriate to augment the Jacobian given in Equation 6.24 and solve the position and orientation problems together. Thus Equation 6.19 becomes:

$$\begin{bmatrix} \Delta\mathbf{P}_4 \\ \Delta\theta_4\hat{\mathbf{n}}_4 \end{bmatrix} = \begin{bmatrix} \mathbf{J}_{x1} & \mathbf{J}_{y1} & \mathbf{J}_{z1} & \mathbf{J}_{x2} & \mathbf{J}_{y2} & \mathbf{J}_{z2} & \mathbf{J}_{x3} & \mathbf{J}_{y3} & \mathbf{J}_{z3} \\ \hat{\mathbf{a}}_{x1} & \hat{\mathbf{a}}_{y1} & \hat{\mathbf{a}}_{z1} & \hat{\mathbf{a}}_{x2} & \hat{\mathbf{a}}_{y2} & \hat{\mathbf{a}}_{z2} & \hat{\mathbf{a}}_{x3} & \hat{\mathbf{a}}_{y3} & \hat{\mathbf{a}}_{z3} \end{bmatrix} \begin{bmatrix} \Delta\theta_{x1} \\ \Delta\theta_{y1} \\ \Delta\theta_{z1} \\ \Delta\theta_{x2} \\ \Delta\theta_{y2} \\ \Delta\theta_{z2} \\ \Delta\theta_{x3} \\ \Delta\theta_{y3} \\ \Delta\theta_{z3} \end{bmatrix} \tag{6.25}$$

($\mathbf{J}_{x1}$ etc. are unchanged from Equation 6.19).

By using the solution of Equation 6.25 in the iterative algorithm of Figure 6.25, we have a comprehensive IK solution for a 3D articulated linkage in which it is possible to specify a goal for both the position and the orientation (of the reference frame) at the end point.

An alternative view of the basis vectors

Throughout this section we have described articulation in terms of a set of position vectors for the end point of each link in the articulation (the $\mathbf{P}_i$) and a set of basis vectors (the $\hat{\mathbf{a}}_x, \hat{\mathbf{a}}_y, \hat{\mathbf{a}}_z$) located there. However one can take an alternative view of how these positions and bases might be determined. Such an alternative view is sometimes useful because of the way in which most computer animation programs describe the hierarchical linking of models in an articulation.

For example, one might want to animate with IK the raising of a "chain" from a heap lying on the ground until it becomes fully extended, as shown in Figure 6.29. The chain in this example is made up from a number of "links" and since all the links look the same it is only necessary to build a vertex/polygon model for one of them. The vertices in the model are specified relative to the frame of reference used for construction, usually the global frame. To build the multi-link chain the individual model is copied and then rotated and/or translated as necessary to assemble the chain.

What we will show in this section is that it is possible to obtain all the necessary terms for the calculation of the Jacobian in Equations 6.19 or 6.25 from the same series of transformation matrices used to position copies of a model in some hierarchical combination, such as the chain example.

To see how this is done, consider the illustrations in Figure 6.30. They depict a series of actions which start from a point $\mathbf{P}_1$ located at the origin of the global frame of reference and proceed as follows:

1. A rotation (say around the vector $\hat{\mathbf{n}}_1$) is applied to $\mathbf{P}_1$ and also to a copy of the original basis axes ($\hat{\mathbf{x}}, \hat{\mathbf{y}}, \hat{\mathbf{z}}$). The rotation is followed by a translation that takes $\mathbf{P}$ and the rotated basis frame to $\mathbf{P}'_1$. The composite transformation

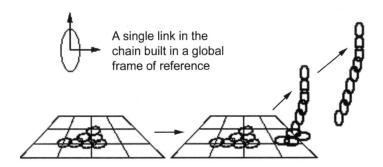

A single link in the chain built in a global frame of reference

Figure 6.29.   IK is used to animate the raising of a chain from a pile of links on the floor until it dangles from a hook.

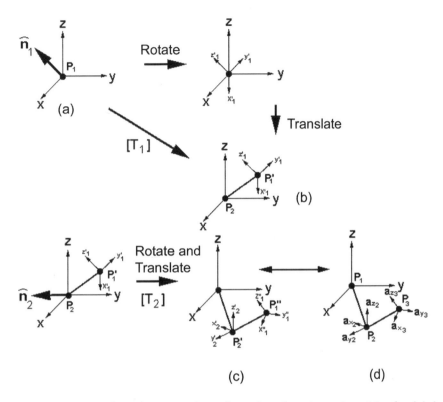

Figure 6.30. Assembling an articulation by repeated transformation of a point at the origin of a global frame of reference and a copy of the global frame's basis vectors. The illustrations are discussed in the text.

$[T_1]$ is a 4×4 matrix:

$$
\begin{bmatrix}
r_{11} & r_{12} & r_{13} & t_x \\
r_{21} & r_{22} & r_{23} & t_y \\
r_{31} & r_{32} & r_{33} & t_z \\
0 & 0 & 0 & 1
\end{bmatrix}
$$

The elements r_{ij} represent the rotation and the t_i the translation.

If we imagine a link existing between $\mathbf{P}'_1$ and $\mathbf{P}_1$ the illustration labeled (b) resembles closely a 3D articulated structure with one link. It has an end point at $\mathbf{P}'_1$ and a set of basis vectors which are no longer coincident with the global frame even through they were derived from it. For the moment we will label these $\hat{\mathbf{x}}'_1$, $\hat{\mathbf{y}}'_1$, and $\hat{\mathbf{z}}'_1$.

2. Suppose we now repeat the process (i.e., apply a transformation T_2 to effect a rotation around the vector $\hat{n}_2$ followed by a translation), P'_1 will move to P''_1 and the copy of the original base axes will reorient themselves as illustrated in (c). A point P_2 at the origin in (b) will move to P'_2.

Now it doesn't take too much imagination to recognize the emergence of a linkage suitable for the application of IK. A comparison between illustration (c) and Figure 6.26 will show us that illustration (c) is equivalent to a two-link articulated system. A two-link system using the notation of Figure 6.26 and mirroring illustration (c) is given in (d) and this illustrates the one to one correspondence. Figure 6.31 gives a table listing the items which correspond.

3. With a correspondence established between the points and bases used in the derivation of J and the application of a transformation to a point at the origin and global coordinate frame we can proceed to obtain P_i and $\hat{a}_{xi}$, etc., directly from the transformation matrices $[T_1]$ and $[T_2]$.

Point P_1 is at the origin and is just $(0,0,0)$, point P_2 is given by applying $[T_2]$ to $(0,0,0)$, point P_3 is given by applying the composite transformation $[T_{21}] = [T_2][T_1]$ to $(0,0,0)$.

A similar argument applies to the basis vectors; for example, $\hat{a}_{y_3}$ is obtained by applying $[T_{21}]$ to the vector $(0,1,0)$.

Immediately we can see that these simple multiplications have the effect of extracting elements of rows or columns from the appropriate transformation

Illustration (c)	Illustration (d)
Origin	P_1
P'_2	P_2
P''_1	P_3
Global x	$\hat{a}_{x1}$
Global y	$\hat{a}_{y1}$
Global z	$\hat{a}_{z1}$
x'_2	$\hat{a}_{x2}$
y'_2	$\hat{a}_{y2}$
z'_2	$\hat{a}_{z2}$
x''_1	$\hat{a}_{x3}$
y''_1	$\hat{a}_{y3}$
z''_1	$\hat{a}_{z3}$

Figure 6.31.   Table giving correspondence between points and axes in illustrations (c) and (d) of Figure 6.30.

matrix. Thus the matrix which establishes link i is effectively:

$$
\begin{bmatrix}
(a_x)_x & (a_x)_y & (a_x)_z & P_x \\
(a_y)_x & (a_y)_y & (a_y)_z & P_y \\
(a_z)_x & (a_z)_y & (a_z)_z & P_z \\
0 & 0 & 0 & 1
\end{bmatrix}
$$

where $(a_x)_x$ is the x component of the $\hat{\mathbf{a}}_x$ basis vector for link i and $\mathbf{P}_i = (P_x, P_y, P_z)$.

Finally it is worth just reiterating that these values are extracted from the transformations that built the linkage by moving a copy of the model from its reference frame into position along the chain. So for the point at the end of an n-link system, its location and base axes orientation are read from the composite transformation: $[T] = [T_n][T_{n-1}]...[T_2][T_1]$

6.5 Physical Animation

This section presents a few examples of an approach to animation where the action is not specified in a set of keyframes; rather, models follow paths, twist, turn, deform, or accelerate using the same physical laws that govern the dynamics of objects in the real world. Before looking at the examples it is worth considering how such physical process are used in the context of 3D graphics. There are two main aspects to consider:

1. How is the effect of a physical process applied to the model?

2. How is the effect determined given that the animator wants to retain some degree of control over the action but not to the extent of violating the physical laws the effect is trying to simulate?

Let's look at each of these aspects in a little more detail:

How is the effect applied?

Since a physical effect usually either moves or distorts the model in some way, it should affect the coordinates of the vertices that give the model its form. There are two points in the basic animation algorithm where it is possible to consider introducing the effect of a physical process. Vertices can be displaced either before or after the model is moved into position.

For example, the side to side flapping motion of a swimming fish simulated by a lateral wave should be applied to a model of a fish before the fish is directed to swim in circles. In this case the effect acts in the *local* coordinate frame of the

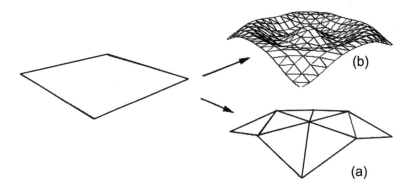

Figure 6.32.   Simulating a radial wave by displacing vertices in a mesh. In (a) the wave is represented by an array of nine vertices, while in (b) there are 225 vertices. When flat (on the left) both meshes have the same appearance, while it is only the finer mesh that gives a good representation of the wave effect when it is applied.

model. Alternatively an object falling under gravity might be tumbling as it falls; tumbling is simulated by angular interpolation. In this case the effect of gravity must act in the *global* frame of reference; otherwise, the object might at times appear to fall upwards.

There is another important issue to consider when using an effect that moves individual vertices in a model: the number and location of its vertices. This is important because there is little point applying a distortion to a model if the vertices are located so far apart that the detail created by the effect is missed. For example, one way to simulate the animation of a wave is to take a planar mesh and apply a time-dependent displacement to the vertices in it. Since a flat plane can be represented with a mesh of very few vertices the wave will appear very *rough* unless some redundant vertices are build into to original flat plane. This example is illustrated in Figure 6.32.

How is the effect controlled?

Let's consider the example of an effect that simulates the action of gravity on an object so that it falls to the floor and bounces a couple of times before coming to rest.

In a keyframe system the animator might direct that the whole action is to occur over a period of 100 frames and that the object is to bounce twice. Unless the distance from release point to the floor and coefficient of restitution (bounciness) fit the equation of motion under gravity the object will not behave as directed and at the end of the 100-frame period it might be left hanging in mid-air.

The question then is do we let the physics overrule the animator? The answer is equivocal. For the example cited it is possible to achieve a compromise that lets the animator have control over the duration and number of bounces while still giving the appearance of realistic behavior by "*massaging*" the value used for g, the acceleration of gravity.

6.5.1 Standardization

An important practical concern when you need to implement a large variety of effects is that they should act through some sort of a common interface.

For physically based effects implemented in the **C** or **C++** languages, one approach uses a table of pointers to functions. Each function in the table implements one effect and they all use the same parameters.

The first function parameter defines a range of frames $[f_s, f_f]$ over which the effect acts, and from this calculate a parameter $\tau : 0 \leq \tau < 1$ determined by:

$$\tau = \frac{currentframe - f_s}{f_f - f_s + 1}$$

Written in this form the effect can be implemented in a way that is independent of the number of integer frames in the interval during which it is to occur. The other essential parameters are the number of vertices and access to the list of vertices in the model being affected.

All functions will behave in a standard way such that when $\tau = 0$ the vertex data will be modified to reflect the initial state of the effect, and when $\tau = 1$ the final state is put into effect. The function would be called during two of the steps in the basic animation algorithm:

1. Before the model is moved into position (in the coordinate frame of reference used for design and specification of the model). In this frame of reference the point $(0, 0, 0)$ is the so-called *hold point*.

2. After the model has been moved into position but before the viewing transformation is applied (in the global coordinate frame of reference).

Now we turn to consider three examples of animation effects arising from some simple physical laws.

6.5.2 Falling and Bouncing

On earth objects fall because they are subject to the constant gravitational force and, if dropped, their velocity increases linearly until they hit a solid surface at which point they may rebound. In this section we will develop a model that conforms to the constraints discussed in the previous section. Our model will allow the animator to specify parameters that correspond to useful control variables. In this case the control variables of choice are:

1. The height to fall, d_0.

2. The number of bounces to be performed, n_b.

3. The coefficient of restitution, μ.

The coefficient of restitution is a measure of how elastic the bounce is; it is defined as:

$$\mu = \frac{\text{velocity after impact}}{\text{velocity before impact}}$$

To satisfy our standardization criteria the fall must be completed when the parameter $\tau = 1$.

Figure 6.33 illustrates graphically how a dropped object behaves by plotting a curve of its height above the ground against time since dropped.

In our computer simulation we have two options as to how we apply the effect to a model built around a network of vertices. The first idea that comes to mind is to treat the model as a single entity and then use the distance from the model's center to the rebound plane for d_0. Every vertex in the model is moved by the same amount and as a result the whole model behaves as a rigid entity. An alternative idea (and perhaps a more interesting one) treats each vertex individually so that d is the distance of a vertex to the rebound plane. This can give the illusion of a *floppy* or *flexible* model.

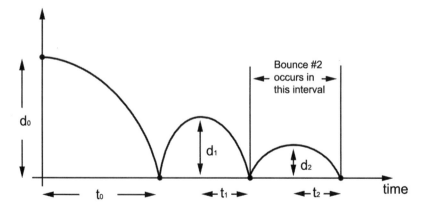

Figure 6.33.   Graph of position against time for an object falling and making several bounces.

The algorithm that we will use must be based on the standard equations for motion under constant acceleration but, in order to satisfy the constraints above, we will have to determine an artificial acceleration. In other words g, the acceleration due to gravity, will not be $9.8ms^{-2}$. From a visual point of view this will not be a problem because the acceleration of an object will still look quite realistic. To obtain a suitable value of g we recognize that the time to first impact t_0 is related to the distance fallen d_0, by:

$$d = \frac{gt_0^2}{2}$$

Thus if t_0 is known g can be found.

Determining t_0 involves calculating the time intervals $t_1, t_2, ..\ t_{nb-1}$ (illustrated in Figure 6.33) and, using the fact that the overall time is scaled to unity, thus we have:

$$t_0 + 2(t_1 + t_2 + t_{nb-1}) = 1$$

The relationship between t_i and t_{i+1} is known because $t_{i+1} = \mu t_i$ and thus g may be determined from:

$$
\begin{aligned}
t_0 &= \frac{1.0}{1.0 + 2(\mu + \mu^2 + ...\mu^{nb-1})} \\
g &= \frac{2d_0}{t_0^2}
\end{aligned}
$$

The height of any rebound d_i is given by $d_i = \mu^i d_0$ and the position at any instant of time (τ) is calculated with the usual expression $d = v_i\tau + \frac{1}{2}g\tau^2$, where v_i is the initial velocity for bounce i in which τ will satisfy:

$$t_0 + 2(t_1 + ... + t_i) \leq \tau < t_0 + 2(t_1 + ... + t_i + t_{i+1})$$

6.5.3 Projectiles

The behavior of a projectile forms the basis for the simulation of explosions, fireworks, etc. The same equations governing the behavior of an object falling under gravity also apply to a projectile. This time however the projectile is fired with an initial velocity in the direction $\mathbf{d}$ of magnitude $V = |\mathbf{d}|$ (see Figure 6.36).

Under the influence of gravitational acceleration g and assuming that the projectile is fired from the point $(0, 0, 0)$, parametric equations for the motion are written as:

$$
\begin{aligned}
r &= V\cos\alpha t \\
z &= -\frac{1}{2}gt^2 + V\sin\alpha t
\end{aligned}
$$

Gravity is assumed to act in the negative z direction and r is a radial coordinate along the direction in which the projectile will fly.

From the point of view of describing the action in the context of practical animation software the initial velocity V and projection angle α are probably less desirable *user*-controlled parameters than say the point where the projectile is to hit the ground or where it is to reach maximum height. If either of these are specified then the equations can be rearranged so that not only appropriate V and α are determined internally but the direction in which the projectile is launched is also uniquely specified.

6.5.4 Explosions

To simulate an object exploding a combination of dynamic motion applied to individual polygons in the model and some sort of post-process to add a glow or smoke clouds can result in very realistic images. Probably the four most significant elements are:

1. Each polygon from which a model is constructed is treated as a projectile and fired off with a high initial velocity in a direction away from the center of the explosion.

2. A bright *flash* of light centered on the site of the explosion is expanded radially away from its origin over a short time interval.

3. A large number of *particles* (pixels of bright color) are projected away from the center of explosion, their color faded to black after a few frames.

4. Drawing a waxing and waning bright halo around and within the polygons as they fly off; this simulates burning and fire.

The last three effects in this list do not involve polygons or vertices in the model and are created by processing the image after it has been rendered and stored in a framebuffer. This process is discussed in Chapter 8. Figures 6.34 and 6.35 illustrate a variety of explosions simulated by combining one or more of these elements.

Ballistic projectiles

To simulate the first element in the list above involves treating each polygonal facet in a model as if it were a projectile with the center of the polygon acting as its center of mass. We can imagine several scenarios:

1. The projectiles are influenced by gravity, falling back to a *ground* plane. Some polygons will be projected downwards and consequently hit the ground at high velocity; they may bounce back up.

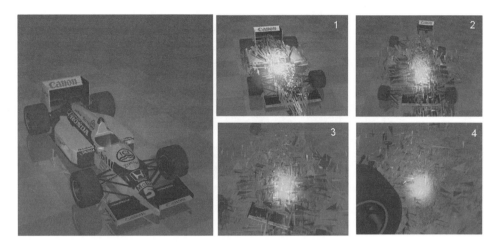

Figure 6.34.   Simulating an explosion by breaking the model up into its component polygons and ballistically firing them off from the center of the explosion. A few of the larger components are retained as single entities and a *bright* flare is painted over the image at the seat of the explosion.

2. Polygons might not be affected (noticeably) by gravity, e.g., some fireworks which simply burst away radially from the center of explosion and gradually fade away.

3. Polygons which are not simply point projectiles will be subjected to rotational forces causing them to tumble randomly.

4. Because explosion is a time-dependent process, polygons further away from the origin of the explosion will be projected at later times. This simulates the action of a shockwave traveling through the model.

One of the most difficult things to achieve with simulations of this type is to provide meaningful control to the animator. For the simulation it is probably desirable that the explosion occurs over a fixed-time interval, say unit time. A function executing the effect moves the polygons into appropriate positions according to some parameter τ $(0 \leq \tau \leq 1)$ derived from the frame being rendered. Other possible control parameters might include *how big* the effect is to look (this can be achieved by specifying the maximum displacement a polygon is to achieve or in the case of gravitational influence the maximum height reached by the projected polygons).

Let us consider the example of an explosion occurring at a point $\mathbf{P}_e$ somewhere inside an object built from n polygonal facets, the centers of which are located

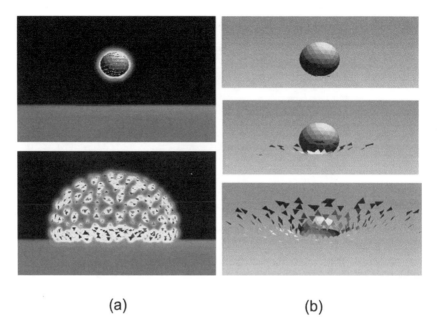

(a)   (b)

Figure 6.35.   Simulating explosions. The sphere is broken up into its polygonal components and they
                      are projected away from the point of the blast. In (a) the effect is enhanced by an image
                      processor which uses an alpha channel (see Chapter 8) to draw a *fire-like* glow round the
                      model. The glow increases in intensity and size as the explosion progresses. In (b) the
                      polygons are blasted out after a delay which is proportional to their distance from the
                      seat of the explosion; this simulates a *shock* front.

at $\mathbf{P}_i : 0 \leq i < (n-1)$. The direction in which polygon i is projected is
therefore $\mathbf{d} = \mathbf{P}_i - \mathbf{P}_e$. Assuming that gravitation forces are significant and that
the animator has specified that the explosion must rise to a maximum height of
Δz above the model's position and then fall to a ground plane at $z = 0$, the
equations of projectile motion allow us to obtain a value for g (acceleration due
to gravity) that will have all the polygons on the ground at the latest when $\tau = 1$.
The geometry of projectile motion is illustrated in Figure 6.36.

The longest time of flight will occur when polygon k (the one with maximum
z-coordinate) is thrust vertically. Thus from the equations for parabolic motion:

$$r = V\cos\alpha t$$
$$z = -\frac{1}{2}gt^2 + V\sin\alpha t$$

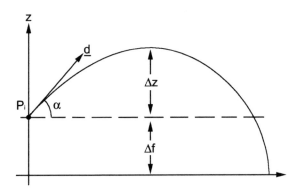

Figure 6.36.   The trajectory of a projectile released from point $\mathbf{P}_i$ in direction d.

we can see that the time it takes a projectile to reach its apex is:

$$\frac{V \sin \alpha}{g}$$

As expected, this will be a maximum when $\alpha = \frac{\pi}{2}$. At the apex of its motion a projectile fired vertically will have zero velocity and the time it takes for it fall back to ground, a distance $\Delta z + \Delta f$ ($\Delta f = \mathbf{P}_{i_z}$ the height of polygon i above ground), is given by:

$$t_{fall} = \sqrt{\frac{2(\Delta z + \Delta f)}{g}}$$

The time it takes a projectile to reach the highest point is determined from the usual equations:

$$\Delta z = \frac{V \sin \alpha}{2g}$$

$$t_{up} = \frac{V^2 \sin^2 \alpha}{g}$$

giving:

$$t_{up} = \sqrt{\frac{2\Delta z}{g}}$$

By assuming that the total flight time is normalized to unity the acceleration g must be:

$$g = (\sqrt{2\Delta z} + \sqrt{2(\Delta z + \Delta f)})^2$$

and the initial velocity V is:
$$V = \sqrt{2g\Delta z}$$

Using V and g, the location of all the exploding polygons at any τ is given by substituting for t in the equations of parabolic motion. Each polygon will have a different α depending on its position relative to the center of explosion.

Polygons reaching the ground before $\tau = 1$ will need to be prevented from falling further.

References

[1] C. F. Gerald, *Applied Numerical Analysis*. Addison-Wesley, Reading MA, 1978.

[2] A. Watt, M. Watt, *Advanced Animation and Rendering Techniques*. Addison-Wesley, Reading MA, 1992. Section 16.2, page 371.

[3] A. Watt, M. Watt, *Advanced Animation and Rendering Techniques*. Addison-Wesley, Reading MA, 1992. Section 16.4.5, page 382.

[4] T.R. McCalla, *Introduction to Numerical Methods and FORTRAN Programming*. John Wiley and Sons, NY, 1967.

[5] T. Boullion and P. Odell, *Generalized Inverse Matrices*. John Wiley and Sons, New York, 1971.

[6] A. Watt, M. Watt, *Advanced Animation and Rendering Techniques*. Addison-Wesley, Reading MA, 1992. Section 16.4.2, page 375.

Part II
Practical Algorithms:
Modeling, Video Processing and
Procedural Textures

CHAPTER **7**

Modeling with Polygonal Datasets

In creating models of objects for use in computer animation and visualization programs, the most popular and versatile approach is to build them from a large number of very simple primitive planar polygons. Highly successful application programs like 3D Studio Max, Lightwave 3D, and Truespace all use this approach. It would be quite impractical to build polygonated models by entering lists of facets and numerical data for the coordinates of their vertices. In all *useful* programs the computer provides many pre-built collections of flat triangular or rectangular polygons to represent primitive shapes such as cylinders, spheres, and torii. It is rarely sufficient to limit the modeling process to a simple combination of primitive shapes, and therefore application programs must provide a wide variety of algorithmic procedures to help the user combine and manipulate the basic shapes as well as creating other more complex ones.

It is within this context that we may state: the primary goal of a modeling algorithm is to construct medium to high-complexity shapes automatically from basic planar polygons. For example the helical tube illustrated in Figure 4.51 and the ribbon in Figure 4.46 were both constructed algorithmically by creating and combining many triangular polygons.

Any algorithm which builds models by combining polygonal shapes (triangles or quadrilaterals) must do so within a framework imposed by the way the specification of the model is recorded. Chapter 3 investigated a number of commonly used recording strategies and data structures to hold the specification of the model. Those components of a model's specification that are essential for the procedures described in this chapter are the vertex, the edge, and the (planar polygonal) facet. Since any planar polygonal facet can be reduced to a set of triangular facets (by the first algorithm to be discussed) all the remaining algorithms we will consider use triangular polygons.

The algorithms described in this chapter are straightforward. Some are short, some are basically just statements of common sense, but a few are quite long.

However even the longest can be broken down into a number of sections which themselves may be further subdivided. All of them will be written as a sequence of logical steps that are readily translated into whatever computer language happens to be currently in favor. Most call upon the geometric mathematics discussed in Chapter 2.

In order to keep the length of each algorithm as short as possible it is appropriate to define a few procedures that perform basic tasks. The most fundamental of these create new elements in the description of a model, a vertex, an edge, or a facet. These procedures which we can name as:

$newV(x, y, z)$ Create a new vertex at coordinates (x, y, z).
$newE(v_0, v_1)$ Create a new edge joining vertices v_0 and v_1.
$newF(v_0, v_1, v_2)$ Create a new facet with v_0, v_1, and v_2 as its vertices.

belong to a group that manage data structures of the type described in Chapter 3. Each function returns an index for the new item in the array of items. In an alternative implementation the same functions might instead return a pointer to a new item at the end of a linked list. We will assume that in practice these procedures handle any internal failure, possibly as a result of shortage of storage space. In the same class of function, procedures to remove one or more object of each type from the database will be needed. A neat way to do this is to use a flag in the data structure for each element which, if set, will cause that element to be deleted during the execution of a *deleting* procedure (for that type of element); this is discussed in Section 3.3 and Figure 3.6.

$deleteV()$ Remove all flagged vertex objects from the description database.
$deleteE()$ Remove all flagged edge objects from the description database.
$deleteF()$ Remove all flagged facet objects from the description database.

Other *helper* procedures will be called upon to make lists; for example, make a list holding the identity of a group of vertices connected together, or make a path among a list of connected edges as illustrated in Figure 7.1.

7.1   Triangulating Polygons

This is one of the longer algorithms to be considered in this chapter, but it plays a key role in a number of others too. It is used not only to reduce an n-sided polygon to a combination of triangular polygons but also to add facets that cover or *cap* the inside of a curve recorded as a set of edges. Capping is a vital step in building 3D models of text characters, such as those shown in Figure 2.32. TrueType or postscript font systems describe their characters as a set of outlines.

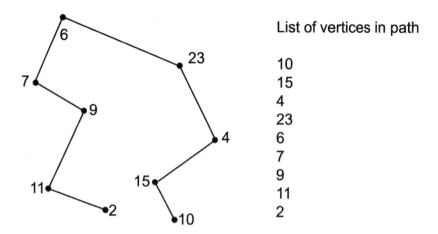

List of vertices in path

10
15
4
23
6
7
9
11
2

Figure 7.1.   The action of a *helper* function $GetPath(s_{id})$ to build a list (shown on the right) which sequentially identifies each vertex starting at s_{id} and connected by edges forming a path. The procedure will stop when the path can go no further or a loop back to the start occurs.

For a 3D model of a text character to be of any use, the interior of the characters must be filled with facets so that they can be colored, textured, and interact with the lighting. Incidentally, reducing an n-sided polygon to a set of triangles, to all intents and purposes, requires the same algorithm as one that caps a closed path of n line segments. So we really only need to consider one algorithm.

One final comment in the preamble to this section: an enormous simplification can be made in cases were the polygon to be triangulated is convex. However. a significant complication is introduced if the polygon has a hole in it, so much so that a discussion about capping of polygons with holes is postponed until Section 7.2.

7.1.1   The Case of Convex Polygons

Let's look at the simple case first: Section 4.3 gave a definition of a convex polygon, called say P, the implication of which is that a triangulation may be simply obtained by adding a vertex V anywhere inside the polygon, edges joining V to all vertices of P, and facets between V and two adjacent vertices of P. This forms a structure known as a *triangle fan*, one of which is illustrated in Figure 7.2. The algorithm given in Figure 7.3 creates a triangle fan.

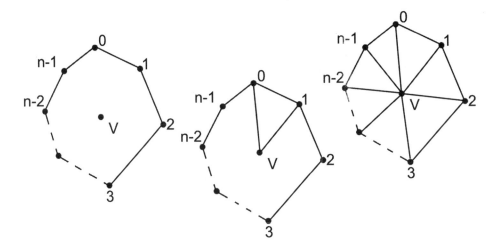

Figure 7.2.   Triangulating a convex n-sided polygon. One additional vertex V is created; edges and facets are added linking V to the original n vertices.

Find a point (x_c, y_c, z_c) that lies inside the polygon.
(Possibly, a point halfway between vertices 0 and $\dfrac{n}{2}$)
Add a vertex: $newV(x_c, y_c, z_c)$
(This is vertex number n.)

Repeat for $0 \leq i < n$ {
        Add edge between vertices n and i: $newE(n, i)$
}

Repeat for $0 \leq i < n - 1$ {
        Add facet: $newF(n, i, (i + 1))$
}
Add facet (linking back to the start): $newF(n, (n - 1), 0)$

Figure 7.3.   Algorithm to replace an $n > 2$-sided convex polygon with n triangular facets. The vertices are labeled $0, 1, 2, \ldots (n - 1)$.

7.1.2 Non-Convex Polygons

When it comes to filling non-convex (concave) polygons the approach described in Section 7.1.1 will not work. Figure 7.4 illustrates the problem. Some of the new edges fall outside the polygon and some of the new facets overlap each other. A strategy must be devised that does not let new edges or facets fall outside the original boundary of the polygon. It does not really matter whether additional vertices are added or not.

Before developing an algorithm for a capping procedure that applies to non-convex polygons consider the following tentative procedure for capping the eight-sided polygon shown in Figure 7.5. Start with the eight-sided polygon, then: (a) add an edge between vertices $0 - 2$, making a facet with vertices $0 - 1 - 2$; (b) add another edge, $2 - 4$, again making a facet between vertices $2 - 3 - 4$. Similarly add edges $4 - 6$ and $6 - 0$ (c) Returning to vertex 0 completes the first pass through the algorithm; the original eight-sided polygon has been partially capped, but a hole is left in the center.

Suppose we now consider the edges joining vertices $0 - 2 - 4 - 6 - 0$ as a four-sided polygon. To cap this, all we would have to do is go back and repeat the process. Joining vertices $0 - 4$ adds a facet with vertices $0 - 2 - 4$. This leaves a single three sided polygon $0 - 4 - 6$ which can be immediately turned into a facet to complete the capping procedure as shown in Figure 7.5(d).

With a little refinement this simple idea can be automated to give an algorithm that will cap (triangulate) any nearly planar, (convex or concave) outline (polygon boundary) provided that there are no holes in it. The "little" refinement mentioned is necessary because it is not always possible to join vertices like $0 - 2$ without that edge lying *outside* the polygon. However because the boundary of the polygon

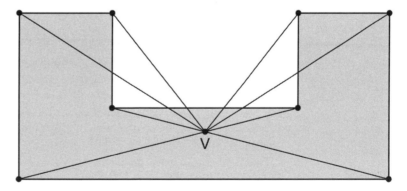

Figure 7.4.   A concave polygon cannot be triangulated by simply joining its vertices to an extra vertex placed somewhere inside. In fact there is **no** point inside that would be satisfactory.

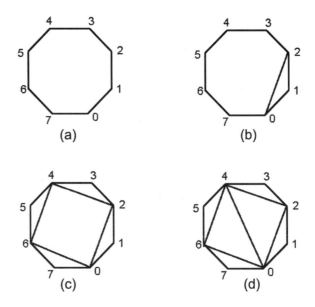

Figure 7.5.   Steps in a possible capping procedure for a convex eight-sided polygon.

is closed there must exist some place where it is possible to make a connection between some vertices i and $i + 2$ and thus reduce the number of sides in the polygon by one. Consequently after at most $n-2$ repetitions of the above procedure the polygon will be capped.

From this tentative set of instructions it is now possible to write a general algorithm that follows the ideas set out in the example of Figure 7.5. However it is not easy to write specific logical instructions that are equivalent to some rather vague statements. For example, to comply with the wishes of the instruction "... *this reduces the number of sides by one; repeat the procedure with the remaining sides ...*", some way of logically recognizing that an edge has been removed from the polygon must be found. Probably the best approach to resolve this specific issue is to design and use temporary data structures. The temporary structures will be used only during the execution of a particular algorithm; when it finishes, resources allocated temporarily will be released.

The advantage of using temporary structures is that the primary vertex, edge, and facet structures that record the description of a model don't have to change to facilitate specific needs of the procedure.

A suitable format for recording the temporary information is a list of n structures, $List(i)$. Each structure ($List(i)$) will correspond to one of the vertex/edge pairs that constitute the border of the outline to be capped and it will record the following information:

V_{id}	A *pointer to* (identifier for) the vertex associated with this item.
L_l	An index into the list indicating the previous vertex that has not yet been eliminated.
L_n	An index into the list indicating the next vertex that has not yet been eliminated.
f_f	A flag to indicate whether this item needs no further consideration.
$\mathbf{p}$	The position vector recording the location of the vertex V_{id}.
$\hat{\mathbf{n}}$	The normal to the edge associated with this item.

The n items in $List(i)$ will be ordered sequentially round the border of the polygon, a border which must form a closed loop. The edge associated with item i in the list joins the vertex for item i to the vertex for item $i + 1$. The edge associated with item $n - 1$ joins the vertex for item $n - 1$ to the vertex for item 0. For the example illustrated by Figure 7.5, the initial state of the list is shown in Figure 7.6.

The purpose of the entries L_l and L_n are to allow the algorithm to skip over those edges that have been eliminated as the reduction continues. The members $\hat{\mathbf{n}}_i$ and $\mathbf{p}_i$ are important in determining whether it is possible to join vertex i with vertex $i + 2$ (i.e., determining whether the candidate edge lies inside the border). The normal to the plane in which the polygon lies, $\hat{\mathbf{n}}$, is also necessary for this determination.

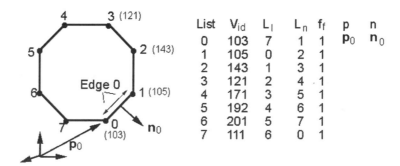

Figure 7.6. The contents of the temporary vertex/edge list before the first step of the example given in Figure 7.5. The numbers shown in brackets beside the list indices are vertex identifies; for example, the first vertex in the list is vertex number 103.

At first sight it would appear that it should be obvious whether an edge joining vertices i and $i + 2$ lies inside or outside a closed polygon (see Figure 7.5), but there are two problems:

1. In three dimensions what does it mean to say: inside of a polygon? The answer is: there is no meaning, unless we assume that the curve is planar and the concept of inside and outside is applied in the 2D sense to the plane in which the polygon lies.

2. Even in two dimensions how does one algorithmically tell if a point lies inside or outside a curve? A human observer seems to find this a simple thing to do provided the curve is not too convoluted.

To test whether an edge joining vertices i and $i + 2$ lies inside the boundary or not, it is sufficient to test whether the midpoint, given by:

$$\mathbf{p}_m = \frac{1}{2}(List(i).\mathbf{p} + List(i + 2).\mathbf{p})$$

lies inside the boundary. A test should be made to see if this new edge intersects other edges in the boundary. The latter requirement need only be satisfied by edges not adjacent to either vertices i or $i + 2$. Edges adjacent to vertices i and $i + 2$ cannot possibly intersect an edge joining vertices i and $i + 2$.

Thus: referred to a 2D plane containing a closed curve C, the test of whether a point P lies inside C is a three-step process:

1. From P draw a line in any direction until it is far away from C. (Say out to a circle which is large enough so that it encloses all of C and contains P.)

2. Move along the line from P counting the number of times C crosses the line.

3. If the count is an odd number, then P is inside C; otherwise, P is outside the curve.

this is called the *Jordan Curve Theorem* [8]. Figure 7.7 illustrates some examples of the use of this test. This simple procedure works because: to go from being inside to being outside C (or vice versa), C must be crossed. To go from inside to outside and back to inside, or outside to inside to outside, C has to be crossed an even number of times.

It is important to keep in mind that in all the algorithms described in this chapter curves are represented by a finite number of straight line segments. Thus to test how many times the line L, from P, crosses C we have to only to check L against each segment of C. There is no need to worry about going far enough

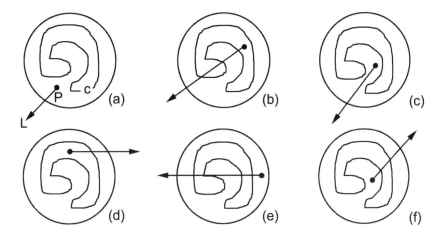

Figure 7.7.   Some examples of testing whether the point P lies inside the curve C. (a) Zero crossings - outside. (b) Three crossings - inside. (c) Zero crossings outside. (d) One crossing inside. (e) Four crossings outside. (f) Two crossings outside.

along L because we are essentially checking every point on C. Since L can in theory be any line at all it is appropriate to choose something simple, say a line at right angles to the edge for which $\mathbf{p}_m$ is the midpoint.

Unfortunately, the accuracy of computer calculations can cause even this simple test to go wrong. To see this look at the example in Figure 7.8(a). Does the test line cross C within edge i or edge $i + 1$? The answer is critically important because if the calculation shows that it crosses both, then the test will deliver an erroneous result. The only way to ensure a correct answer is to be very careful in determining intersections that occur near the ends of the edges that make up C. For example, one might say that if L intersects edge i within a very small distance of the end joined to edge $i + 1$, the test for intersection with edge $i + 1$ would not be done. This would work for cases like Figure 7.8(a) but in 7.8(b), *alas*, another mistake would occur.

To avoid all these problems the following action can be taken: if the intersection between L and C is near the end of edge i don't check edge $i + 1$, instead check to see if vertices V_i and V_{i+2} are on the same side of L. If they are then L does not cross C; otherwise it does. One final complication: if a piece of C is parallel to L ignore it, e.g., as in Figure 7.8(c), but don't forget that the vertex comparison now applies to V_i and V_{i+3}.

In the discussion above it was assumed that containment was tested for in two dimensions. The capping algorithm requires that the polygon be planar but not necessarily lying in the (x, y) plane, i.e., that all the vertices lie in some plane,

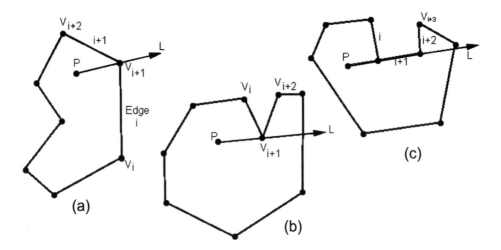

Figure 7.8.   The tricky question: does line L cross C in segment i or segment $i + i$ or not at all?

such that it is possible to determine a single $\hat{n}$ for the plane of the polygon. The plane may however be orientated in any direction. Therefore, all the calculations for containment, etc., must be performed in the plane of the polygon. One could imagine finding an inverse transform that brings $\hat{n}$ in line with, say, the z-axis, apply it to the vertices around the polygon and make the edge-crossing tests in the xy plane. The alternative is to make the edges take on a 3D character by placing small rectangular planes parallel to $\hat{n}$ and lying along each edge of the polygon, what might be described as *fencing* it in (Figure 7.9). It doesn't really matter how the test is done; both approaches are subject to the same problems of accuracy and the result they deliver is the same.

Once allowance is made for these complications we can set out an algorithm for capping any closed polygon C, given that it is recorded as n straight edges in an array of structures $List(i)$. The algorithm is presented in Figure 7.10.

Revisiting the inside outside question

Associated with the decision as to whether an edge falls inside or outside the bounding outline are two problems that warrant additional comment. They are illustrated in Figure 7.11.

1. In the case of the polygon illustrated in Figure 7.11(a) an edge e, joining vertices i and $i + 2$, lies along the border of the polygon C; if inserted it would create a triangle with zero area. To prevent the need to ask the question whether the mid-point of e is inside or outside C (which is not an

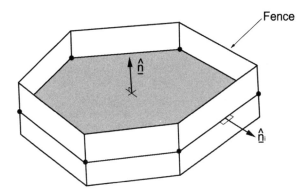

Figure 7.9. Fencing in a polygon prior to testing whether or not an edge lies inside a polygon's boundary or net.

easy question to answer), a preemptive test for co-linearity between lines joining vertices i to $i+1$ and i to $i+2$ should be performed. This can be done by creating vectors for the direction of these lines and testing that the dot product $> (1 - \epsilon)$, where ϵ is of the order of magnitude of the precision of the calculation.

2. In the situation illustrated in Figure 7.11(b), the midpoint of the edge joining vertices i and $i+2$, $\mathbf{p}_m$, is inside C, but other edges of C intersect it. In this case vertex i should not be joined to vertex $i+2$. To prevent edges being falsely labeled as internal an additional test should be performed to check whether any edge in C crosses the proposed edge (the one between vertices i and $i+2$). In making this test all the edges in C should be checked except those linked to vertices i and $i+2$, i.e., the edges $i-1$, i, $i+1$, and $i+2$.

Notes:

1. For a polygon that is planar, any three vertices which are not co-linear can be used to determine the normal $\hat{\mathbf{n}}$ of the plane in which the polygon lies.

2. No matter how careful one is in making the calculation there will always be the potential for the algorithm to make a mistake. So in any practical implementation care should be taken to build in an escape mechanism.

O'Rourke [1] and Berg [2] offer a rich source of algorithms for computational geometry problems like capping.

For the n edges making up C build the array holding
$List(i)$, the temporary data discussed in the text.

Set the current index indicator $i = 0$.
Set the number of edges remaining to be eliminated: $m = n$.

Repeat the following while $m > 3$ {
    Get the next two entries in the list.
    $j = List(i).L_n$ and $k = List(j).L_n$
    Test whether an edge joining vertices $List(i).V_{id}$ and $List(k).V_{id}$
    lies inside the polygon.
    If it does then {
        Add an edge: $newE(List(i).V_{id}, List(k).V_{id})$
        Add a facet: $newF(List(i).V_{id}, List(j).V_{id}, List(k).V_{id})$
        Flag list entry j as begin invalid: $List(j).f_f = 0$
        Switch it out of the list: $List(i).L_n = k$ and $List(k).L_l = i$
        Reduce the number of valid entries in the list: $m = m - 1$
        Update the normal $List(i).\hat{n}$ to take account of
        the fact that edge i replaces edges i and j and therefore
        joins vertices $List(i).V_{id}$ and $List(k).V_{id}$.
        Move on to the next edge. Set $i = k$
    }
    Otherwise {
        Move on to the next edge to try again. Set $i = j$
    }
}
Make a facet with the remaining three valid edges.
(with the vertices for those entries for which $List().f_f = 1$)

Figure 7.10.   An algorithm to cap a planar polygon. It can also be used to cap a single closed piecewise
linear curve, one that does not loop or consist of several pieces.

7.2   Triangulating Polygons with Holes

The algorithm developed in Section 7.1 was restricted to capping an area enclosed by a single curve. It would very useful if it were possible to extend it
to automatically cope with more elaborate situations. Three typical examples are
depicted in Figure 7.12. The first labeled (a) shows three simple closed curves;
a fairly straightforward extension of the basic procedure could cope with this. In
diagram (b), a closed outline is shown containing three holes. This is a much
more difficult case to cap satisfactorily and a procedure to accomplish this is the

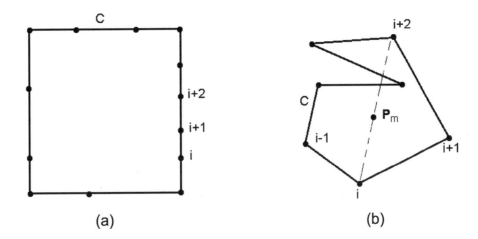

Figure 7.11.   Additional tests will need to be added to the procedure for determining whether a point lies inside an polygon. In (a) an edge joining vertices i with $i+2$ would form a triangle with zero area. In (b) the edge joining vertices i with $i+2$ is partially outside the polygon.

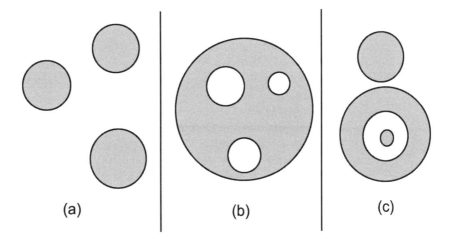

Figure 7.12.   Some examples of more elaborate shapes that commonly arise and need to be capped. The shaded areas are the parts of the figures that should be covered with triangular polygons.

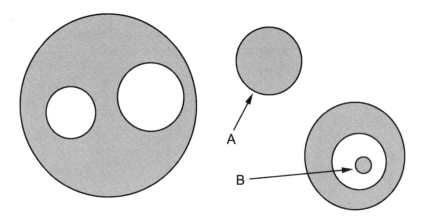

Figure 7.13.   Example of a complex outline to be capped. The shaded area represents the interior. Curves labeled A and B are referred to in the text.

subject we will turn to now. Illustration (c) shows another potentially troublesome situation with three separate pieces to be capped, one of which lies inside the hole in another. In fact it turns out that once an algorithm capable of capping separate pieces which have holes is developed, any of the examples in Figure 7.12 can be capped successfully.

Most of the steps described in Section 7.1 can be used again here by carefully pre-processing the set of outlines to be capped. Consider the example in Figure 7.13, where the shaded area represents the interior of the outlines that are to be capped. The example shows two separate shapes, labeled A and B, which if they could be treated separately would be directly amenable to capping with the algorithm of Section 7.1. Note that piece B lies inside a hole, and that the holes themselves could be described as an outline associated with the boundary of the shape that contains the hole.

Using these ideas as a guide we can write down three preprocessing steps that will prepare almost any combination of shapes for capping with the algorithm we have just discussed:

1. Make a list of all separate pieces in the outline; call these C_i. Check that each piece forms a closed curve. Checks could also be done to make sure that the curve does not cross itself or bifurcate, but these are probably less necessary. Record the information about each piece in an array, say $List(i)$, of the data structures described in Section 7.1.

2. After step 1 each piece in the outline will either be the outline of a hole or the outline of part of the shape. Determine into which category all the

pieces fall. Deciding whether a curve C_i is the outline of a hole or the outline of a shape or, indeed, the outline of a shape lying within a hole is essentially the same as determining whether a point P (any point on C_i) lies inside a curve.

3. If the piece C_k is the outline of a hole determine which of the curves C_i is holed by C_k. Then amalgamate curves C_k with C_i and any other holes inside C_i to form a single curve. Order the structures in the list $List(i)$ so that a continuous path occurs round the augmented outline.

After preprocessing each separate piece of the outline can be passed to the algorithm given in Figure 7.10 for capping.

Taking the outlines shown in Figure 7.13 as an example, the preprocessing steps will reduce seven discrete pieces to the four outlines shown in Figure 7.14. The pieces labeled A and B in Figure 7.13 become the outlines labeled 2 and 4. The holes lying inside outline 1 have been joined to it, a consistent direction has been assigned to the outline, and at the joins a small *gap* has been inserted to emphasize the fact that there are **no** holes. The small gap does not really exist but it is essential to include it in the position vectors that are part of the $List(i)$ structures. This is so that the *inside/outside* test does not get confused by coincident edge segments.

Well, that's the theory; we should now consider the preprocessing steps in a little more detail.

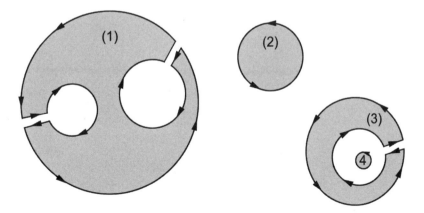

Figure 7.14.   Preprocessing the example in Figure 7.13 to eliminate holes and preparing for capping each piece of the outline by using the algorithm of Figure 7.10.

Listing the pieces of the outline

The simplest way to do this is to define an array of $List()$ structures; let's call it $ListOfLists()$. Each entry records the following:

$List(i)$	Array of $List$ structures. The $List$ structure is defined in Section 7.1.
n	The number of $List$ structures in this piece of the outline.
f_i	Identity of closest enclosing piece if this is the outline of a hole.
f_d	A flag to indicate whether this piece has been processed.
$\hat{\mathbf{n}}$	A normal vector for the plane in which this piece lies.

Determining the status of a piece of the outline

This procedure follows closely the arguments used to determine whether a point lies inside or outside a closed polygon. For this situation the test does not have to be quite so rigorous because we can assume that the pieces of the outline don't overlap. The test can take the coordinates of the vertex at the start of the first edge in each piece (i.e., $ListOfLists(i).List(0).\mathbf{p}$) as the point to determine whether or not it lies inside the other outlines (i.e., those which are $\neq i$).

  If the point $ListOfLists(i).List(0).\mathbf{p}$ lies inside an odd number of pieces, then it is the boundary of a hole and the identity of the piece $\neq i$ closest to it is recorded in the variable $ListOfLists(i).f_i$.

Joining holes to make a single outline to be capped

Each hole H should be joined to the piece of the outline B surrounding it by linking the vertices V_h and V_b in each that are closest together. These vertices are found by comparing distances between every pair and choosing the smallest, provided the following conditions are satisfied:

1. An edge joining V_h to V_b does not cross H.

2. An edge joining V_h to V_b does not cross B.

3. An edge joining V_h to V_b does not cross any other hole inside B.

Once a valid V_h and V_b have been found, a new outline B' that combines B and H is constructed by building a replacement for the $ListOfLists()$ entries holding curves H and B. The combined list will contain two additional edges in the outline. These link V_b to V_h as the path goes from B to H and V_h to V_b as the path rejoins B.

After that, as hinted above, the vertices at the ends of the two additional edges are *pulled back* by a small displacement to prevent numerical problems in the capping stage. The distance to pull back can be a small fraction of the length of the edges. This perturbs some of the $ListOfLists(i).List(j).\mathbf{p}$ vectors but, because they are copies of vertex positions, the vertices themselves will not be moved.

Completing the jigsaw

A **C** language code for this algorithm is included with the book. It takes as input an array of n of the $ListOfLists$ data structures described above and uses the functions $newE$ and $newF$ to create the edges and facets that complete a triangulation of the outlines described by the $List$ members of each structure in the $ListOfLists$ array.

The code uses the approach of bounding the outline with a series of planes parallel to the normal $\hat{\mathbf{n}}$ as illustrated Figure 7.9. This means that the calculations to determine whether or not a piece of the outline is part of a hole, or if an edge joining two vertices lies inside or outside, must find the intersection between a line L and a bounded plane P where:

L is a *feeler ray* designed to detect the number of times it crosses a boundary. It starts at the point to be tested for containment, $\mathbf{p}_m$, which is usually the midpoint of an edge between two vertices. L is directed at right angles to the edge and to $\hat{\mathbf{n}}$. P (the piece of the *fence*) is a plane perpendicular to the plane in which the curves lie. For any edge i it is given by the equation: $(\mathbf{p} - List(i).\mathbf{p}) \cdot List(i).\hat{\mathbf{n}} = 0$.

The piece of the *fence* along edge i is bounded by two lines parallel to $\hat{\mathbf{n}}$ (perpendicular to the plane of the curve) and passing through $List(i).\mathbf{p}$ and $List(i+1).\mathbf{p}$ respectively. The geometry is pictured in Figure 7.15.

The test is divided into two parts:

1. Find $\mathbf{p}_i$, the point of intersection between L and P,

2. Establish whether $\mathbf{p}_i$ lies between the vertices i and $i+1$. Specifically in this case we know that $\mathbf{p}_i$ will lie on the line through the points $\mathbf{p}_a = List(i).\mathbf{p}$ and $\mathbf{p}_b = List(i+1).\mathbf{p}$; therefore, a parameter μ may be determined from:

$$(\mathbf{p}_i - \mathbf{p}_a) = \mu(\mathbf{p}_b - \mathbf{p}_a) \qquad (7.1)$$

If $0 \leq \mu \leq 1$ then C is crossed by L in C's edge segment between vertices i and $i+1$. Note that in Equation 7.1 any one

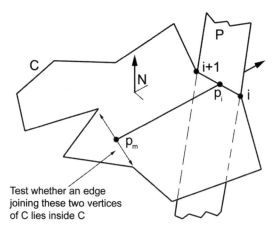

Figure 7.15.   Part of the test for containment of a point $\mathbf{p}_m$ inside a piecewise linear curve C. The test line L is checked for intersection with a piece P of the *fence* bounding the curve.

of the components of the vectors could be used to determine μ. To prevent division by zero, we choose the component of $(\mathbf{p}_i - \mathbf{p}_a)$ with the largest magnitude. To determine $\mathbf{p}_i$ use the expressions given in Section 2.5.

When all the above steps are combined the algorithm is complete. The results of its action when presented with an outline containing multiple nested shapes and holes is shown in Figure 7.16.

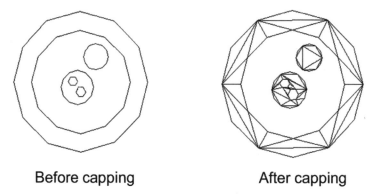

Before capping   After capping

Figure 7.16.   Triangulating the shape shown on the left gives the result on the right. The shape contains nested holes.

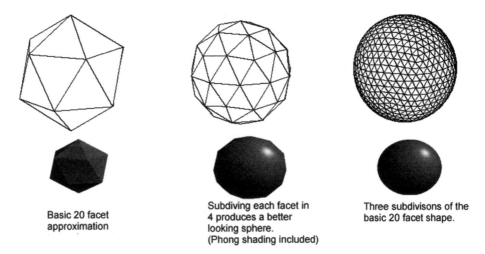

Basic 20 facet
approximation

Subdiving each facet in
4 produces a better
looking sphere.
(Phong shading included)

Three subdivisons of the
basic 20 facet shape.

Figure 7.17.   Approximating a sphere by repeated subdivision of the facets of which it is composed.

7.3   Subdividing Polygonal Facets

The major reason to subdivide a polygon is to provide additional mesh elements so that finer detail in a model may be included. For example, a sphere might be represented by 20 carefully arranged triangular polygons. However such an approximation is very coarse, and if rendered from a nearby viewpoint it would be hard to convince any observer that it actually represented a sphere. Dividing each edge of the 20 polygons will produce an approximation to the sphere with 80 triangular facets. After moving the additional vertices at the midpoint of the edges to the surface of a sphere a much better, *but still faceted*, approximation is produced. Subdividing these 80 facets in the same way and repeating the operation once more produces an excellent approximation to a sphere which, after rendering, is hard to distinguish from a mathematically perfect CSG sphere.

> *CSG (Constructive Solid Geometry) is a method of building models from the functional description of a number of simple primitives. A CSG sphere is represented by its mathematical equation and thus will appear perfectly spherical when rendered at all resolutions and from all viewpoints.*

The example of constructing better and better approximations to a sphere by repeated subdivision of a faceted model is illustrated in Figure 7.17.

Interior subdivision places a vertex at the center of each triangular facet and thus divides it into three. The important thing to note is that no edges in the model are divided. Thus in this form of subdivision, changes made to one facet have no effect on facets sharing a common edge. Interior subdivision is illustrated in Figure 7.18.

Internally subdividing a triangular polygon is straightforward since (as illustrated in Figure 7.18) there are no consequential effects in adjacent facets. It is simply a matter of modifying the data structure for the facet being subdivided (to re-vector its vertex entries). Two additional facets with appropriate vertex data are created and, if an edge list is required, then three new entries go into that too.

A subdivision that involves the insertion of a vertex at the midpoint of the edges of a facet is more difficult to accomplish, since we want to avoid creating a polygon with more than three vertices. The case shown in Figure 7.19(b) illustrates one aspect of the problem; for the facet labeled B there are three possible outcomes:

1. Only the edge common with facet A is divided.

2. All its edges are divided.

3. It is not divided but is modified to become a quadrilateral with four vertices.

The last outcome is undesirable because if the vertex labeled 3 is moved, then the quadrilateral facet B will no longer be planar and it is possible to open up a gap in the previously closed network of facets. The first two outcomes will ensure that the subdivisions of B are triangular and planar, but the second case has knock on implications for any facets attached to B along the edges not common to A.

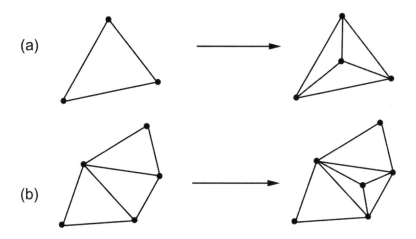

Figure 7.18.   (a) Subdividing the interior of a triangular facet. In (b) it may be seen that a subdivision in one facet does not affect the vertex network of other facets. Compare this to the subdivision shown in Figure 7.19.

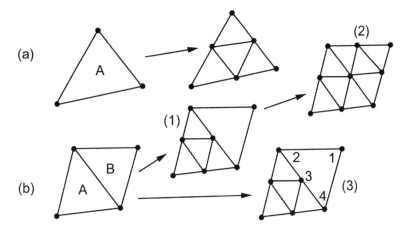

Figure 7.19.   Subdividing a facet: (a) Vertices are added along the midpoints of the edges of the facet. This necessarily affects adjacent facets if a triangulated polygonal network is to be maintained. Part (b) shows the effect of subdividing a facet on its neighbors; either the facet labeled B is subdivided or it becomes a quadrilateral, which may not be planar. The cases labeled (1), (2), and (3) are the outcomes discussed in the text.

Before the algorithm can be declared complete there is another practical problem that needs to be addressed. To see what this is, see Figure 7.20(a), which shows a connected network of eight triangular facets, each one of which is to be subdivided. They have to be processed in order, but subdividing facet 0 also affects facets 1, 3, and 4. It would not be a good idea to modify facets 1, 3, and 4 as illustrated in (b), because when it comes time to subdivide them it would then not be possible to obtain the optimal subdivision shown in (c). Yet another minor annoyance is that every facet must know the identity of its neighbors (e.g., facet 0 is a neighbor of facets 1, 3, and 4). If this information is not available then

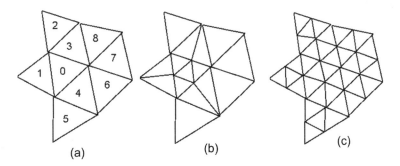

Figure 7.20.   The *knock-on* effect of subdividing one facet at a time.

every facet will have to be tested against every other facet to see if they share a common edge, or equivalently, have two vertices in common.

The algorithm given in Figure 7.21 builds a subdivision by using an auxiliary list to record the identity of vertices which divide the edges of the facets. This list is called on to provide vertex information as new facets are added, three for each original facet. The algorithm assumes that a list of facets adjacent to edges has been prepared using the procedure given in Section 3.7.

7.4   Lofting

The name lofting is given to the procedure that takes a set of closed curves lying in parallel planes and joins them up to form a surface. For example, the curves shown on the left of Figure 7.23 can be automatically linked with edges and facets to form the solid surface shown on the right. The curves are recorded as a list of vertex-edge pairs. (This data structure was introduced in the discussion on capping in section 7.1.)

The core part of the algorithm involves linking two adjacent curves with edges and facets. The whole set of curves is then linked by considering pairs of curves in turn. For example, in Figure 7.23 the *loft* was produced by linking curves 1 and 2, then curves 2 and 3, then curves 3 and 4, followed by curves 4 and 5, and finally curves 5 and 6.

For any two planar closed curves with n and m vertex/edge pairs respectively it is essential that the *join* is made with triangular facets and that vertices near each other are connected together. In other words: vertices from one side of the first curve must not be connected to the far side of the second. It would also be desirable to make the connections so that the triangular facets are as near equilateral as possible. For some curves it is almost impossible to automatically decide what form the join should take. Even *by eye* it can sometimes be none too easy either. Figure 7.24 illustrates how the simple act of displacing two curves can lead to very different arrangements of edges and facets in a join.

Given the above caveats the following procedure will loft a set of k planar curves recorded in an array of lists identifying the vertex/edge pairs that make up each closed curve. For example, the two curves depicted in Figure 7.24 are composed of 11 and 20 vertex/edge pairs in the upper and lower curves respectively.

The algorithm consisting of eight main steps is:

1. Pick the curves in pairs: 0 and 1, 1, and 2 etc., and repeat the following steps to join them. We will think of these curves as paths with a starting point that may or may not be the first vertex/edge in the list. The paths will be labeled P_n and P_m with n elements (vertex/edge pairs) in P_n and m in P_m.

Establish a temporary list, $List(j)$, to record for each facet the identity
of the vertices that may be inserted in the three sides of a facet.
Each entry in the list will record up to three items.
1) The ID of vertex inserted between $Poly(i).Vid(0)$ and $Poly(i).Vid(1)$
2) The ID of vertex inserted between $Poly(i).Vid(1)$ and $Poly(i).Vid(2)$
3) The ID of vertex inserted between $Poly(i).Vid(2)$ and $Poly(i).Vid(0)$

Use the algorithm of Section 3.7 to find the
identity of the facets adjacent to the edges in the network.

Repeat the following for all edges i in the network {
  Create a vertex, say V_n, at the midpoint of edge i
  Create an edge between V_n and $Edge(i).Vid(1)$
  Modify edge i so that it now connects vertices
  $Edge(i).Vid(1)$ and V_n
  if $Edge(i).Fid(0) \geq 0$ {
    If edge i joins vertex $Poly(Edge(i).Fid(0)).Vid(0)$ to
    vertex $Poly(Edge(i).Fid(0)).Vid(0)$, record V_n in the first
    item in the temporary list for facet $Edge(i).Fid(0)$.
    If it does not try the other two sides.
  }
  Do the same thing for facet $Edge(i).Fid(1)$
}

Repeat the following for all facets j in the network {
  [Note that at this stage the list $List(j)$ will have a
  [vertex identity for all three items in each element because
  [every side of all facets will have been subdivided.
  [Note also that it is very important that a consistent ordering
  [of vertices for new facets is maintained so that the surface
  [normal vectors will point in the outward direction for all facets.
  Add three facets between the vertices below:
  Facet 1) $List(j).V_{01}$, $List(j).V_{12}$, $List(j).V_{20}$
  Facet 2) $List(j).V_{01}$, $Poly(j).Vid(1)$, $List(j).V_{12}$
  Facet 3) $List(j).V_{12}$, $Poly(j).Vid(2)$, $List(j).V_{20}$
  And three edges between the vertices below:
  Edge 1) $List(j).V_{01}$, $List(j).V_{12}$
  Edge 2) $List(j).V_{12}$, $List(j).V_{20}$
  Edge 3) $List(j).V_{20}$, $List(j).V_{01}$
  [These are illustrated in Figure 7.22
  Modify facet j and so that it is attached to vertices
  $Poly(j).Vid(0)$, $List(j).V_{01}$ and $List(j).V_{20}$.
}

Figure 7.21. The key steps in an algorithm to subdivide a network of connected triangular facets. $Edge(i)$ is a list of structures that defines the edges; $Edge(i).Fid(j) : j = 0, 1$ are the identities of the facets adjacent to edge i, $Edge(i).Vid(j) : j = 0, 1$ are the identities of the vertices to which edge i is connected. $Poly(i)$ is a list of structures that describe each facet in the network.

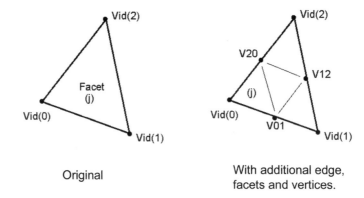

Original

With additional edge,
facets and vertices.

Figure 7.22.   Labeling of vertices for the subdivision algorithm given in Figure 7.21.

2. Find the elements in P_n and P_m that are closest together and label these f_n and f_m.

3. Re-make the lists for P_n and P_m so that f_n and f_m are the first elements in each list. This is the step that requires the curves to be closed. (It is possible to modify this algorithm to loft a set of open curves by arranging the elements in the list so that the first ones are f_n and f_m).

4. The procedure requires that P_n has fewer elements than P_m so, if $m > n$, swap the curves.

This completes the preparation, but before we can build the join, which involves simultaneously moving along the paths stitching together elements that are "close", we must decide in which directions to move.

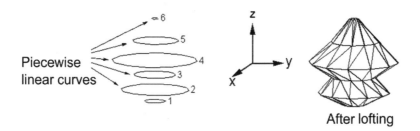

After lofting

Figure 7.23.   Lofting involves joining a set of closed curves to form a solid surface. In this example the curves lie in xy planes and are displaced from one another in the z direction.

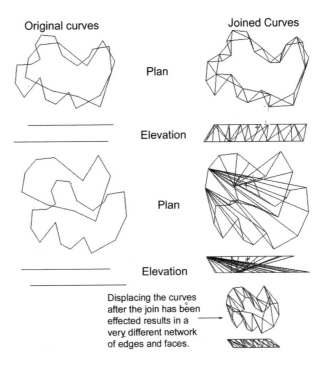

Original curves

Joined Curves

Plan

Elevation

Plan

Elevation

Displacing the curves
after the join has been
effected results in a
very different network
of edges and faces.

Figure 7.24. The effect on the join between two curves when one is displaced from the other before the join is executed. The curves are shown in plan and elevation view.

5. To decide in which direction to move compare the distance l_x between the second vertices in P_n and P_m with the distance l_y between the second vertex in P_n and the last vertex in P_m. If $l_x > l_y$ then the curves are oriented the wrong way around and one of them must be reversed; reverse P_m. This is illustrated in Figure 7.25.

Getting the curves the right way around allows us to follow both curves in ascending vertex order and basically join them up, vertices 1 to 1, 2 to 2, etc. Because P_m may have more vertices than P_n, a protocol will have to be adopted to allow the extra ones to *join in*. These actions occur in the next two steps.

6. For every element i, in P_n, find the element j in P_m so that vertex j is closest to the vertex for i. Element j must be chosen so that **no** vertex further along P_m is already connected to any vertex in P_n. (This is very important.) While this step is proceeding record in the data structure for

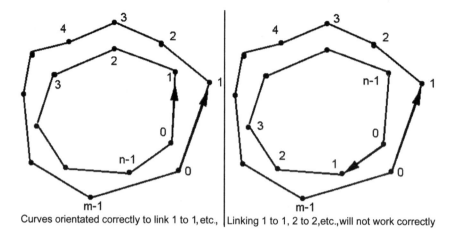

Curves orientated correctly to link 1 to 1, etc., | Linking 1 to 1, 2 to 2,etc.,will not work correctly

Figure 7.25.   If curves are not orientated appropriately then the join will not work.

the elements of P_n the identity of the element in P_m to which each one is attached.

After this step every vertex in P_n will be connected to a vertex in P_m. There may be some vertices in P_m not connected and triangular facets need to be created, but we have achieved a framework that has a reasonable geometry and no overlapping edges. Figure 7.26 illustrates an example of the state of the join after this step.

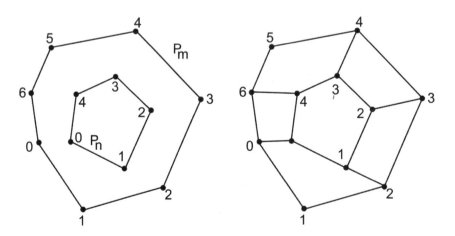

Figure 7.26.   An example of joining two curves before and after the execution of step 6 in the algorithm.

7. Make a second pass along path P_n to join in the unconnected vertices of P_m and build the facets. For each element i in P_n do the following:

   (a) Set an index, i_0, to the identity of the element in P_m to which the vertex i is attached. If i is not at the end of P_n set another index, i_1, to the element in P_m to which vertex $i + 1$ in P_n is attached. If i is at the end of P_n set i_1 to some value $> m$.

   (b) If $i_1 = i_0$ then vertices i and $i + 1$ in P_n are attached to the same vertex in P_m and it is only necessary to add one facet, as illustrated in Figure 7.27(a).

   (c) If $i_1 = i_0 + 1$ then two facets are required as shown in Figure 7.27(b).

   (d) if $i_1 > i_0 + 1$ then a variable number of facets and edges need to link i and $i + 1$ in P_n to j in P_m such that $i_0 + 1 \leq j < i_1$. There are a number of arrangement that can accomplish this. In the example shown in Figure 7.28, the vertices in P_m are joined to vertex i until one of them gets closer to vertex $i + 1$, after that they are linked to vertex $i + 1$.

8. The final step is to add the facets where the ends of P_n and P_m link back to the start.

This procedure will work in the vast majority of cases, but it may run into problems where one oriented curve has a very large number of points while the one next to it has only a few.

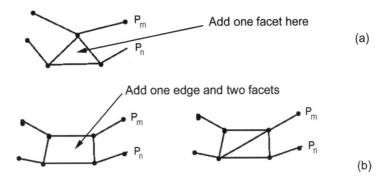

Figure 7.27. Inserting one or two facets to make up the join. (a) Adding one facet. (b) Adding two facets requires an edge too.

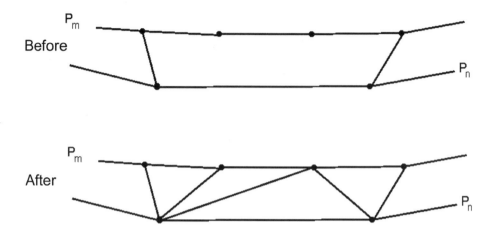

Figure 7.28.   Linking a longer gap in P_m to two adjacent vertices in P_n.

7.5   Surfaces of Revolution

A surface of revolution is the formal way to describe the shape produced in a workshop with a lathe. It has an axis around which some curve is rotated to build a network of vertices and facets. The curve could be expressed analytically or it could be a piecewise linear approximation to a smooth curve. An analytic description is often used in Constructive Solid Geometry applications but in the context of the polygon faceted description of surfaces used in this chapter it is appropriate to use a piecewise linear description of the curve.

A typical example of a model built with a single surface of revolution is the torus illustrated in Figure 7.29

Typically the axis of revolution will be parallel to one of the Cartesian axes. Other parameters required are:

1. The angle through which the revolution occurs. A positive angle will result in a counterclockwise direction of rotation. A full revolution of 360° will produce a closed surface; in this case the direction of rotation is irrelevant.

2. Because the surface is to be approximated by a finite number of polygonal pieces, the number of steps (*sections*) in the rotation must be specified. For a 360° rotation more steps will result in a better approximation to a smooth surface of revolution. (The example of Figure 7.29 used a section placed every 15°, which is about the minimum acceptable).

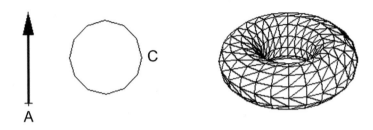

Figure 7.29.   The surface of revolution on the right was produced by revolving the curve C around the axis A, shown on the left.

Producing a surface of revolution is one of the most fundamental actions in constructing 3D models, because some of the most commonly used primitive shapes are surfaces of revolution. The sphere, ellipse and torus may all be constructed by revolving the appropriate curve.

An algorithm that builds a 3D surface of revolution will need to construct a network of connected facets and edges from vertices placed at the position of the sections. The algorithm proceeds one section at a time and, if the revolution is for a full 360°, a final step will add facets to connect the last section back to the first. Care will also be needed to account for the revolution of a curve which is closed, such as that in Figure 7.29, because in those cases the last vertex in the piecewise representation is assumed to be connected to the first.

Starting with a curve (in the form of a set of vertices and edges) for the outline of one half of the final shape, each section is added by the following actions:

1. Copy the original curve (its vertices and edges).

2. Rotate the copied vertices into position; the copied edges will automatically follow.

3. Build edges and facets to link the new curve onto the old one as illustrated in Figure 7.30.

The code for a function to implement this algorithm is included with the book. The input takes the following: an ordered list of n vertex identifiers $List(i)$ describing the curve, a flag f_{loop} indicating if the curve is closed; a vector $\mathbf{p}$ which is a point on the axis of rotation; $\hat{\mathbf{d}}$, the direction of the axis of rotation; n_s, the number of steps in the revolution, and finally θ, the counterclockwise angle of revolution. It is important that the algorithm creates facets with a consistent ordering so that all the facet-normal vectors point outwards. Of course if a full revolution is not completed, then there will be a viewpoint from which the rear of the facets will be visible.

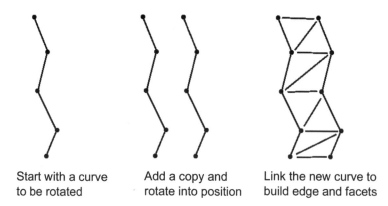

Start with a curve   Add a copy and   Link the new curve to
to be rotated   rotate into position   build edge and facets

Figure 7.30.   Link on the next section as part of the process of building a surface of revolution.

7.6   Beveling

Beveling (alternatively called filleting) removes sharp corners from objects. As such it therefore plays an important role in many CAD application programs. In 3D graphics beveled edges are commonly used to enhance the appearance of models of text strings.

Adding a bevel to a model built from triangular polygons is difficult because it involves cutting and modifying polygons; it is much easier to build the bevel into the model as it is constructed. This is the way the model of the *letters* shown in Figure 7.31 was constructed.

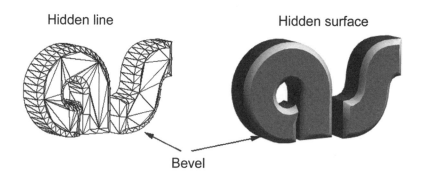

Hidden line   Hidden surface

Bevel

Figure 7.31.   Models for the letters A *and* S showing a bevel on the front face.

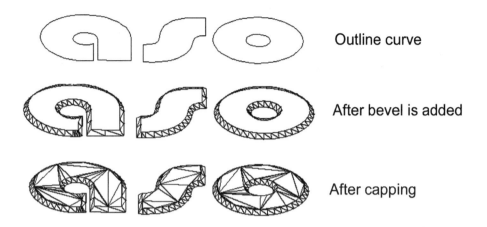

Outline curve

After bevel is added

After capping

Figure 7.32.   Beveling an outline.

The generation of a beveled shape can begin with a set of closed curves using a modified version of the triangulation algorithm described in Section 7.1. Once the curve has been beveled it can be capped with the triangulation algorithm to produce a closed shape; see Figure 7.32 for an example.

To create a bevel from a series of closed outlines there are two issues to be addressed:

1. To which side of the curve is the bevel formed? This is tied in with the idea of a curve with a hole in it, because the bevel around a hole should slant in the opposite direction to the bevel around the outside of the curve. The curves shown in Figure 7.32 contain both a series of outside outlines and a hole; you should be able to see how the bevel is made accordingly.

2. How does the bevel behave as it goes around a bend? This will depend on whether:

    (a) The bevel is to appear on the inside of the bend as you go around (shorter path).

    (b) The bevel is to appear on the outside of the bend as you go around (longer path).

These cases are shown in Figure 7.33 (a and b). Since all the curves used in this chapter are built from straight edges (piecewise linear) the problem of how to arrange the facets in the bevel is accentuated when the curve goes around a bend that is greater than about 270°. The question therefore is: how to build the bevel?

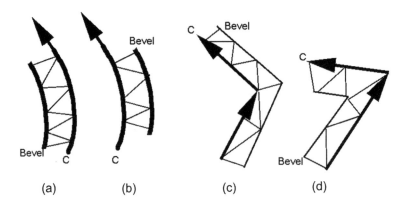

Figure 7.33.   Beveling a curve that goes around a bend. (a) The bevel is on the inside of the curve C.
                    (b) The bevel is on the outside of C. (c) On the outside of a hairpin bend. (d) On the
                    inside of a hairpin bend.

A first guess for a procedure might be: add one edge lying parallel to each
edge in the original curves, offset it by the depth of the bevel, and link it to
the main curve with edges and facets. However, this won't work for curves
with hairpin bends, Figure 7.33 (c and d), because the repositioned edges
overlap or leave a gap as shown in Figure 7.34. Even though this first idea
may not work immediately it is a good starting point for a better procedure,
because an edge can be inserted to fill any gap and edges that would overlap
can be shortened. This approach leads to satisfactory-looking bevels; see
Figure 7.35.

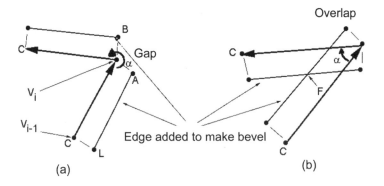

Figure 7.34.   Beveling a hairpin bend either leaves a gap or causes an overlap.

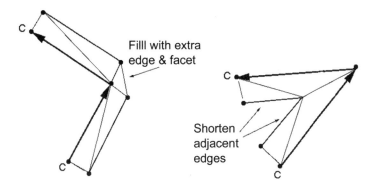

Figure 7.35.   Beveling a hairpin bend with the gap filled in and overlapping edges shortened.

A reasonable algorithm that produces such a bevel around a set of outline curves requires the following three steps:

1. Given a list of closed curves (closed curves are needed so that the bevel can be placed to the *inside*), determine whether each curve represents the outline of a hole or an outside edge.

2. For each vertex/edge pair V_i, determine a normal to the edge, $\hat{\mathbf{n}}_i$. Choose $\hat{\mathbf{n}}_i$ so that it lies in the plane of the curve and points in the direction in which the bevel is to be made. In addition, for each V_i obtain the average of the normals to the curve at V_i and its neighbor V_{i-1}; call this $\hat{\mathbf{v}}_i$. Use $\hat{\mathbf{v}}_i$ to obtain the necessary extension or shortening for the edges in the bevel.

3. Travel around each curve and consider in turn the individual vertex/edge pairs V_i making up the curve. With each V_i, (we assume that the bevel has been constructed up to V_{i-1}), check the angle α between V_i and V_{i-1} (on the side where the bevel is to be built) and do the following:

   If $\alpha > 270°$ (Figure 7.34(a)), add a vertex in the bevel beside V_i (labeled A), and link it with an edge to the *last* vertex in the bevel (labeled L beside V_{i-1}). Add another vertex B, again beside V_i (but offset in a direction perpendicular to the edge V_i). Join B to A with an edge and add appropriate facets. The vertex B becomes the *last* vertex in the bevel.

   If $\alpha < 270°$, determine the position of the point labeled F in Figure 7.34(b). Add a vertex at F, join it to the *last* vertex, and add other edges and facets as appropriate to build the bevel. The case shown in Figure 7.34(b) has an α for which the edge of the bevel is shorter than the edge parallel to it in the curve C. This will be true for cases were $\alpha < 180°$. If $180° < \alpha < 270°$ the edge in the bevel will be longer than the one it is parallel to in the curve C.

Figure 7.35 illustrates the result of applying this procedure to the curve fragments of Figure 7.34.

There is one irritating complication when beveling part of a curve like that shown in Figure 7.34(b). What happens if the edge segments are shorter than the depth of the bevel? In such cases the location of the point F (Figure 7.34(b)) determined from two consecutive edges would cause an overlap as shown in Figure 7.36(a). To avoid this a test should be inserted before creating a vertex at F to see if an overlap is going to occur. If the result of the test is positive then F should not be created, and the algorithm will just skip forward to consider the next edge.

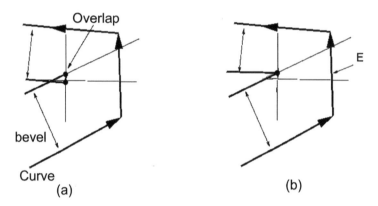

Figure 7.36.   Resolving the problem that can occur if the curvature is too great to accommodate the required bevel depth. In (a) the edges in the bevel overlap. By preventing the creation of a vertex and edge associated with edge E in the original curve, the overlap is avoided (b).

7.7 Orienting Surface Normals

Sometimes the order in which the vertices to which a polygon is attached are not listed in a consistent order. That is, if you look at a plan of a network of facets, some facets have their vertices listed in a clockwise sense and some have their vertices listed in a counterclockwise sense. An example is illustrated in Figure 7.37. If this happens a renderer cannot determine if the front or back of

Plate 1.   Image rendered at resolution of 640 x 480 without anti-aliasing.

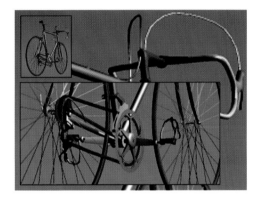

Plate 2.   Image rendered at resolution of 640 x 480 with anti-aliasing with a 3 x 3 supersample.

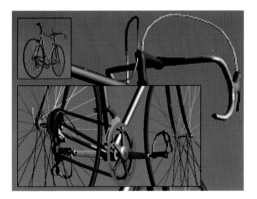

Plate 3.   Image rendered at resolution of 640 x 480 with accelerated anti-aliasing with a 3 x 3 supersample.

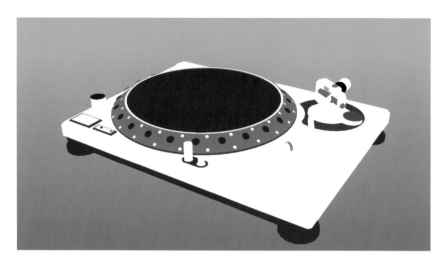

Plate 4. Scene rendered with hidden surfaces removed.

Plate 5. Scene rendered with hidden surfaces removed and a basic lighting effect included in the rendering algorithm.

Plate 6.   Lens flare giving the appearance of the use of a star filter.

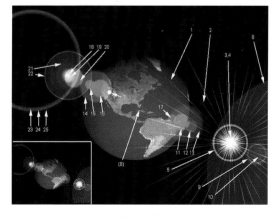

Plate 7.   Lens flare with inter lens reflections.

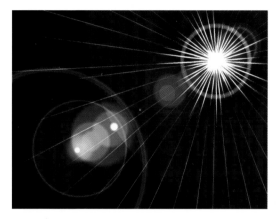

Plate 8.   The elements which go to make up a lens flare effect. (This is a reproduction of Figure 8.12.)

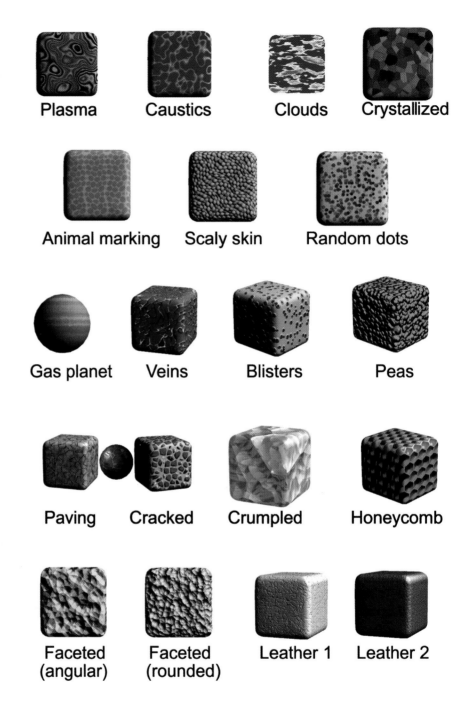

Plasma Caustics Clouds Crystallized

Animal marking Scaly skin Random dots

Gas planet Veins Blisters Peas

Paving Cracked Crumpled Honeycomb

Faceted (angular) Faceted (rounded) Leather 1 Leather 2

Plate 9. Some of the procedural textures discussed in Chapter 9.

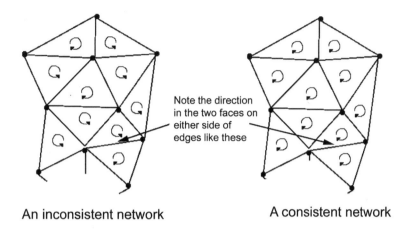

Note the direction in the two faces on either side of edges like these

An inconsistent network   A consistent network

Figure 7.37. The order in which the vertices bordering a polygon are recorded can produce a consistent or an inconsistent network. A consistent network is one in which the surface normals (formed by a vector cross product between two non-co-linear edges) of connected polygons are directed towards the same side of the network.

a polygonal is the one facing the camera. Thus it is not possible to perform a backface cull (Section 4.8.1), because this might lead to holes appearing in the model. Consequently all facets have to be rendered, slowing the rendering procedure. A further complication of inconsistent orientation in surface patches is that it is very difficult to calculate appropriate normal vectors and, as a consequence, unpleasant artifacts can appear when the Phong or Gouraud shading procedures are used to simulate curved surfaces.

This section presents a procedure that will orientate a network of connected triangular facets by making the order in which the vertices of any facet are recorded consistently counterclockwise when looking at the facets from the "*outside*" of the model. Although some models do not have a definite inside or outside (a flat sheet of facets, for example), one side can be arbitrarily designated the outside. Models that consist of several pieces can be orientated simply by treating each piece as a separate network.

For the purposes of this algorithm a facet is part of a network only if it is connected to other facets along at least one of its edges. Facets that meet only at a vertex are considered as separate networks.

The algorithm, which is recursive, can be summarized in the following five steps:

1. Add an integer identifier s_{id} to the data structure describing each polygon. This will be used to identify separate pieces in the model.

2. Flag every polygon as being unidentified; i.e., set $s_{id} = -1$.

3. For every polygon work out the identity of the polygons adjacent to it; i.e., those that have a common edge will have two of their vertices the same as the polygon being checked. A suitable procedure is given in Section 3.6.

4. For each polygon k, check if it is unidentified. If it is, then call the recursive function $IdentifyConnected(LastOneSet, SetThisOne)$ to assign it and all facets connected to it. The function also makes all connected facets adopt the same counterclockwise vertex ordering scheme.

   The function will be called with the identity of the polygon to be checked (the parameter $SetThisOne$), and the identity of the last one that has been checked (parameter $LastOneSet$). Since $0 \leq k$ we can use -1 as the starting value for $LastOneSet$. The initial call then takes the form $IdentifyConnected(-1, k)$. A counter c is initialized $c = 0$ which will count the number of discrete pieces in the model. On execution $IdentifyConnected()$ performs the following functions:

   (a) For polygon $SetThisOne$ check if its flag $s_{id} \geq 0$; if it is then return from the functions, because facet $SetThisOne$ has already been set. This test stops further recursion.

   (b) If $LastOneSet \geq 0$, make the orientation of polygon $SetThisOne$ the same as $LastOneSet$ by swapping two vertices in the vertex list if necessary. However if $LastOneSet < 0$ then increment the count c because *as yet* there are no adjacent facets.

   (c) Assign the flag $s_{id} = c$ for polygon $SetThisOne$.

   (d) Call $IdentifyConnected()$ once for the polygons adjacent to polygon $SetThisOne$, with of course the $LastOneSet$ parameter now specifying the polygon identified by $SetThisOne$.

5. With each individual piece, i.e., all those facets having the same values of s_{id}, do the following:

   (a) Find a bounding box.

   (b) Choose an arbitrary point P outside the bounding box. (If rendering is taking place the best choice for P is the viewpoint.)

   (c) Find the polygon closest to P, say k. If k's normal is directed so that the back of k is visible from P, reverse all the normal vectors and vertex orderings of polygons identified with the same s_{id} as k.

7.8 Delaunay Triangulation

Sometimes an arbitrary collection of points are encountered without any details as what happens between them. Perhaps they represent samples from a scientific experiment, for example. To be able to visualize them (by rendering) they must be connected together by a network of polygons. This specific problem occurs frequently in engineering design and analysis. If the number of points is large, then doing it by hand, say in an interactive design application, is out of the question and an automated procedure must be sought.

For any set of more than three points building a network of triangular polygons is always possible. Grouping more than three points to form the basic polygonal unit has the advantage that fewer polygons will need to be rendered. However there are many drawbacks, not the least of which is the complexity of the procedure to determine the polygonization.

Invariably the triangulated mesh used in a mathematical analysis requires that it should be as regular as possible; that is, the triangles should be approximately *equiangular*, (or to put it another way: no long thin triangles). This requirement is exactly the one we strive to attain in producing models for 3D visualization because it makes the writing of a good quality renderer so much easier. All the numerical pitfalls that occur because of long thin facets are avoided when the triangles are nearly equiangular. A method that guarantees to deliver a locally equiangular arrangement of edges and facets has been devised; it goes by the name of *Delaunay triangulation*.

The Delaunay triangulation technique is particularly helpful in visualizing functions of two variables: $z = f(x, y)$, especially when the sample points (x, y) are arranged randomly. A very good example of this is a Geographic Information System (GIS) which records topographic data. The height z is sampled at a set of (x, y)-coordinates. A triangulation based on the (x, y)-coordinates, with the z-coordinate derived from the height value at each point, gives a 3D surface that can be sent to a standard renderer to produce informative images such as that illustrated in Figure 7.38. The locations of the data points for the scene in Figure 7.38 and mesh created by Delaunay triangulation are shown in Figure 7.39. A GIS therefore does not need to record any edge or facet information.

Many other scientific and engineering disciplines find this approach to visualizing information very useful, and it is one use for 3D graphics. Another reason for us to consider the Delaunay procedure for triangulating a set of points is that it forms an important step in the construction of faceted models using the technique of Boolean operations to be discussed in Section 7.9.

The algorithm presented in this section will follow the approach of Sloan [4] with the exception that we will allow the plane in which the triangulation is built to lie in any orientation rather than a horizontal xy plane. An arbitrary plane of triangulation is essential for the Boolean procedure of Section 7.9. Delaunay

Figure 7.38.   Making a Delaunay triangulation from a collection of geographic data allows a 3D renderer
                to produce a visualization of the landscape that the data represents. An animation of
                the *fly-by* type is readily generated over a model of a landscape from earth or some
                other world.

triangulations are produced on a flat plane; the third dimension is irrelevant because a surface cannot be assigned to an arbitrary collection of points in three
dimensions.

The essence of the Delaunay triangulation algorithm is relatively straightforward. The basic premise is:

> *Take one point from the data set at a time and insert it into a*
> *pre-existing triangulation, making any necessary adjustments to the*
> *edge/facet information so that all the facets remain as equiangular*
> *as possible.*

The process is started by making a dummy facet big enough to enclose all the
points. After completing the Delaunay triangulation the vertices of this *enclosing* triangle are removed and consequently, any edges or facets attached to them
disappear too. The basic idea of the algorithm is illustrated in Figure 7.40.

The basic steps are:

1. Add a triangular facet in the same plane in which the points lie; make it
   large enough so that all points are inside it. Thus the initial triangulation
   contains just a single triangle. Call this the **supertriangle**.

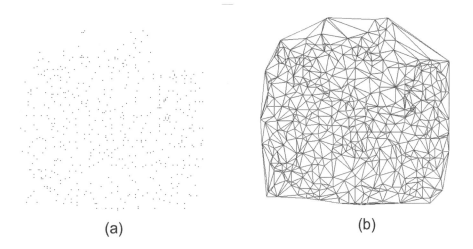

Figure 7.39.   The data points and mesh from which the image in Figure 7.38 was generated. (a) The
                location of the sample points. (b) The mesh generated by Delaunay triangulation.

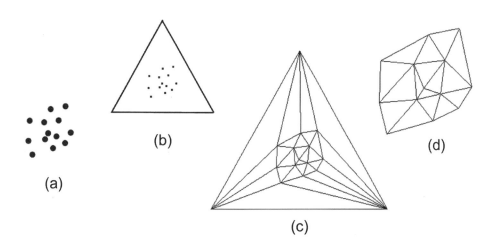

Figure 7.40.   The triangulation of a set of points. (a) The points, (b) enclosed by a supertriangle,
                (c) triangulated, and (d) with the supertriangle removed (enlarged view).

2. With each point P in the list of points to be inserted, do the following:

   (a) Find an existing triangle that encloses P, say triangle k.

   (b) Form three new triangles by connecting P to the vertices of k. The net gain of triangles is two and three new edges are created.

   (c) The new triangulation is updated so that the properties of a Delaunay triangulation again apply to the whole network of edges and facets. *This is the main step in the algorithm and it will be discussed below.*

3. Once all the points have been inserted in the triangulation, the vertices that form the supertriangle are removed. Any edge or facet attached to one of these supertriangle vertices must also be removed. Figure 7.40 illustrates the outcome after the main steps in the algorithm.

In step 3 above it was stated: *after a point P is inserted in the triangulation, the triangulation is updated so that the properties of a Delaunay network are re-established.* This is accomplished by the following three steps:

1. All the triangles that have a common edge with one of the three triangles adjacent to P are placed on a last-in, first-out stack. The facets labeled X, Y, and Z in Figure 7.41 are adjacent to P, and the facets A, B, and C are opposite to P.

2. If the stack is empty this phase of the algorithm is complete. Otherwise, a triangle is popped off the stack and a test made to see if the edge common to it and its neighbor with P as a vertex should be switched, e.g., pairs A and X, B and Y, etc. (See Figure 7.41.) This test effectively decides whether the internal angles of the triangles X and A in Figure 7.42 are closer to being equiangular in configuration (a) or configuration (b).

   If a swap from configuration (a) to configuration (b) is made then two triangles replace two triangles so no new edges or facets are created. However the action of making such a swap will have implications for the other triangles adjacent to that labeled A in Figure 7.42(a), and this must be accounted for in the next step.

3. If a swap is made any triangles that become opposite P are **pushed** onto the stack; there will be at most two, those labeled U and V in the example of Figure 7.42.

   Execution then loops back to step 2 to continue processing the (possibly extended) stack.

Finally, to complete the description of the algorithm we must discuss the test that determines whether to swap the **common edge**. In two dimensions this

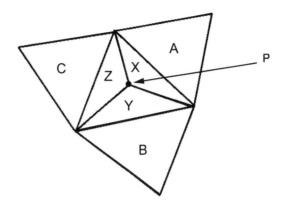

Figure 7.41.   The triangles A, B, and C, respectively, share a common edge with the three triangles X, Y, and Z which have P as one of their vertices. A, B, and C are said to be *opposite* P.

is equivalent to deciding whether P lies inside the circumcircle of the triangle opposite P. If it does the edge is swapped; if it does not then no change is necessary (Figure 7.43).

The point P (in Figure 7.44) lies on the circumcircle of the triangle V_1, V_2, V_3 if $\alpha + \beta = \pi$. It lies inside the circumcircle if $\alpha + \beta > \pi$ and outside if $\alpha + \beta < \pi$. To calculate α and β directly would involve inverse trigonometric

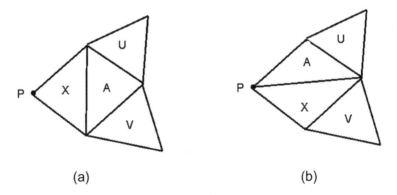

(a)   (b)

Figure 7.42.   Should the edge common to triangles A and X shown in (a) be swapped to give the configuration shown in (b)? If configuration (b) is adopted then the triangles labeled U and V will need to be reconsidered because they will now be *opposite* P, and we need to check whether their common edge needs to be swapped.

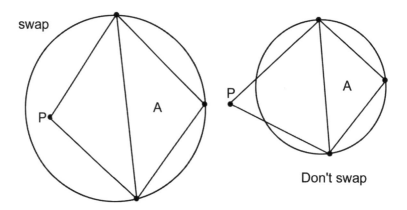

Figure 7.43.   Swap the common edge if P lies inside the circumcircle of the triangle, A, opposite P.

functions (which are always undesirable), but since $\alpha + \beta < 2\pi$ the point P will lie inside the circumcircle if $\sin(\alpha + \beta) < 0$. Using this formulation avoids the inverse trigonometric function, but there are some numerical difficulties due to round-off errors when $\alpha + \beta \approx \pi$; however the four-step algorithm Cline and Renka [5] can solve such problems. We can extend their 2D procedure to apply to any plane where the points P, V_1, etc., in Figure 7.44 are given by position vectors $\mathbf{v}_1$, $\mathbf{v}_2$, $\mathbf{v}_3$, and $\mathbf{p}$. This algorithm is presented in Figure 7.45.

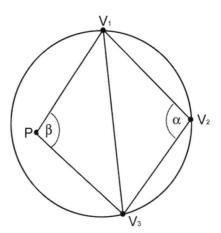

Figure 7.44.   The geometry used to test whether P lies inside the circumcircle of the triangle V_1 - V_2 - V_3.

Start by calculating the vectors below:

$$\hat{\mathbf{v}}_{13} = \frac{\mathbf{v}_1 - \mathbf{v}_3}{|\mathbf{v}_1 - \mathbf{v}_3|}$$

$$\hat{\mathbf{v}}_{23} = \frac{\mathbf{v}_2 - \mathbf{v}_3}{|\mathbf{v}_2 - \mathbf{v}_3|}$$

$$\hat{\mathbf{v}}_{1p} = \frac{\mathbf{v}_1 - \mathbf{p}}{|\mathbf{v}_1 - \mathbf{p}|}$$

$$\hat{\mathbf{v}}_{2p} = \frac{\mathbf{v}_2 - \mathbf{p}}{|\mathbf{v}_2 - \mathbf{p}|}$$

Then make the scalar products:

$\cos \alpha = \hat{\mathbf{v}}_{13} \cdot \hat{\mathbf{v}}_{23}$

$\cos \beta = \hat{\mathbf{v}}_{1p} \cdot \hat{\mathbf{v}}_{2p}$

Now apply the test:

if $\cos \alpha \geq 0$ and $\cos \beta \geq 0$ Do **not** swap.

else if $\cos \alpha < 0$ and $\cos \beta < 0$ **Do** swap.

else {

    Calculate:

    $\sin \alpha = |\hat{\mathbf{v}}_{13} \times \hat{\mathbf{v}}_{23}|$

    $\sin \beta = |\hat{\mathbf{v}}_{2p} \times \hat{\mathbf{v}}_{1p}|$

    Then: if $\sin \alpha \cos \beta + \sin \beta \cos \alpha < 0$ **Do** swap.

    else Do **not** swap.

}

Figure 7.45.   Algorithm to test whether the edge of the triangle between $\mathbf{v}_1$ and $\mathbf{v}_2$ should be swapped to join $\mathbf{p}$ to $\mathbf{v}_3$; see Figure 7.44.

In the coding of the Delaunay algorithm that accompanies the book the following points should be noted:

1. For this implementation the plane in which the points to be triangulated lie may be selected to be parallel to the xy, yz, or zx planes.

2. The supertriangle, which may be specified arbitrarily, is chosen by first finding the rectangle enclosing all the points in the plane. Let the center of this rectangle be (x_c, y_c) and d its longest dimension. An equilateral triangle with the circle, radius d, center (x_c, y_c), inscribed inside it will also enclose all the points. The vertices of the supertriangle are therefore located at $(x_c, y_c + 2d)$, $(x_c - \sqrt{3}d, y_c - d)$, and $(x_c + \sqrt{3}d, y_c - d)$.

3. In order to swap an edge, the data structure representing the facets needs to keep a record of which facets are adjacent to which facets, and which edge is adjacent to which facet. When an edge is swapped it is not only vital to update the adjacency information in the facets directly affected but

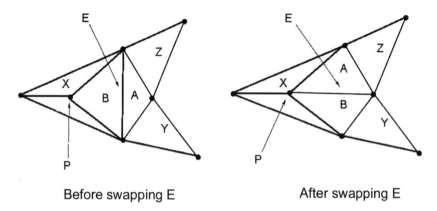

Before swapping E   After swapping E

Figure 7.46.   Swapping the edge E will alter which triangles are adjacent to which other triangles not
only in those directly affected, labeled A and B, but also those labeled X and Y. However
triangle Z is *not* affected because it remains adjacent to A irrespective of the orientation
of edge E.

also to update the information in those adjacent to the modified facets both
before and after the swap. For example, swapping the edge E shown in
Figure 7.46 will affect the adjacency information not only in the triangles
labeled A and B but also in triangles X and Y. The triangle Z is not
affected because it remains adjacent to A.

4. Care must be taken when swapping edges so that the order in which the
   vertex data is recorded remains consistent; we don't want some of the normal
   vectors pointing to one side of the plane and the remainder pointing to the
   other.

5. The code for this algorithm will generate a mesh from 10,000 points in a
   few seconds on a standard personal computer.

7.9 Boolean Modeling

Boolean modeling is the name given to a procedure for building models from a
combination of primitive shapes or indeed from other models. The name is taken
from the algebra of mathematical logic devised by George Boole in 1847, because
its operations provide a very useful analogy to describe the way in which shapes
may be combined.

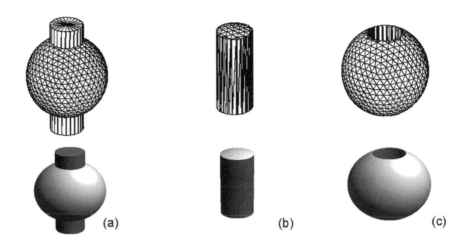

Figure 7.47. (a) *OR-ing* a sphere and cylinder, expressed in Boolean algebra $S+C$. (b) *AND-ing* a sphere and cylinder; in Boolean notation: $S \cdot C$. (c) The result of the Boolean expression $S\bar{C}$, we can think of this as *subtracting a cylinder from a sphere*. Notice that the cylinder, which is not visible, appears to cut a hole in the sphere.

The simplest way to combine two models is to add them together. This can be represented by a Boolean operation called **or**, which is written using the $+$ symbol. For example, if we let the symbol A represent an eight-sided polygonal cube, then a model made from two cubes can be described symbolically as $A+TA$ (where T represents a translation). If you need a model of a cylinder C with a sphere S sitting on top of it you can build a model for C and a model for S and then **or** them together; the result is $C+S$.

Suppose however you want a model where C pokes through S something like the illustration of Figure 7.47(a). It would be quite difficult to design by hand a mesh of facets to cover such a surface. However since this shape is just another manifestation of $S+C$, if there were an automatic way to go from the meshes for S and C to one for $S+C$, a very useful modeling procedure would result.

Incidentally, to generate an image of the combination $S+C$ with a hidden surface renderer there is no need to work out a mesh for $S+C$. The two components can be used in their original form, and the renderer will avoid drawing those parts of the facets of C that lie inside S because they are obscured by S.

If $S+C$ was the only Boolean combination then (from a 3D modeling point of view) there would be no advantage in using it. However $S+C$ is not the only possibility that *Boolean algebra* allows. The other relevant Boolean operations are:

- **not**, written as $\bar{A}$. It's *not* possible to show a picture of $\bar{S}$ or $\bar{C}$ because such a solid fills the whole universe **except** that small volume occupied by S or C. You might argue that **not** is *not* a very useful operation; on its own that's true but when it is used in conjunction with the next operation the true power of "Booleans" as a 3D modeling tool is evident.

- **and**, written as $S \cdot C$ or simply SC. Again **and** is an unfortunate name. The symbols $+$, and . are much more revealing as to the actual effect of operations, if you liken them to the *add* and *multiply* operations of basic algebra. SC (S AND C) is a solid that occupies the space where S and C overlap; an example is illustrated in Figure 7.47(b).

The real power of a Boolean operation as a modeling idiom is that it allows shapes like that shown in Figure 7.47(c) to be produced from simple primitives, S and C in that example. We can think of the shape in Figure 7.47(c) as being the result of the removal of that part of S where S and C overlap. One might call it a **subtractive** operation but strictly speaking it is $S\bar{C}$, that part of the universe occupied by the sphere and **not** by the cylinder. This *subtractive* operation is exceptionally useful; a number of very important constructional methods are based on the principles of *drilling a hole* or *cutting a bit off*.

In theory it should be possible to build a model of any shape by emulating some combination of Boolean operations on a very small subset of primitive shapes. Indeed this topic is so important it is given the name *Constructive Solid Geometry*. Most CAD applications use some CSG. A number of ray-tracing programs are based on the CSG concept, because it can reduce the number of elements that need to be rendered in any one scene while not restricting the models to a few textured spheres or cubes.

In the context of a model made with polygonal facets it is more difficult to use the Boolean concept because:

1. The models are not based on a relatively small number of primitive shapes but on a large number of flat planar pieces. Therefore there are many more possible configurations that need to be considered and this can take a long time.

2. CSG objects always have a very well-defined sense of inside and outside, faceted models do not necessarily have that sense. Suppose we build a faceted model for a sphere but decide to remove a few facets from one side of it. How could we then use this *open* sphere in Boolean operations?

3. Whereas a CSG representation of say a sphere and a cylinder will produce an intersection that is smooth, if we try the same thing with faceted models the line of intersection will be a jagged edge. This is especially noticeable

when the faceted approximation is a coarse one. There is nothing much can be done about this except increase the resolution of the mesh.

4. The facets that result from a *Boolean cutting* operation tend to be poorly shaped; long thin facets often occur and these tend not to render very well and preclude much additional processing.

5. The algebra of the intersections of bounded planes in three dimensions is very sensitive to the round-off errors that occur in computer calculations.

Despite these difficulties the fact is that some shapes are so much more easily made by *subtraction* and, indeed, some are virtually impossible to make in any other way (think about how you might produce a 3D mesh to represent a Swiss cheese). It is therefore essential to devise an algorithm that can provide Boolean-like functionality to as good an approximation as possible.

Such an algorithm is presented in this section. The algorithm takes care to produce a triangulation that minimizes the number of small and thin facets and to avoid (where possible) the problems due to round-off errors. The algorithm is quite long, but it is possible to break it up into a number of sections that can be considered separately and a relatively simple overview of the strategy it uses can also be given. The procedure is based on a presentation at ICGW 95 [6] and owes some of its heritage to the ideas of [7].

Before presenting the strategy of the procedure there are a few points that are worth considering:

1. For a computer graphics application we do not need to consider an operation equivalent to Boolean addition. Indeed because a polygonated model might not have a definite inside, *subtraction* is also meaningless in some cases. A better way to think of the process is of a model being cut into pieces, some of which will be discarded to leave the appropriate shape (Figure 7.48).

2. With a model made from a collection of triangular facets we must know which facets are doing the cutting and which are being cut. This can be accomplished by making a list of facets that fall into these two groups; we will call these lists:

   (a) The Work list

   (b) The Tool list

   For the example shown in Figure 7.48, the facets that make up the sphere S are placed in the Work list while those in the cylinder C belong to the Tool list.

3. Breaks in the model occur where the facets from these two lists intersect each other and both sets need to be divided. We can achieve this by first

breaking the facets in the Work list along the line of intersection with the facets in the Tool list. When that has been done the lists may be swapped and the algorithm repeated.

4. The intersection occurs along one or more piecewise linear sections which form a path across the surface. Each linear segment occurs as the result of the intersection of two planes. Some of these paths might form closed loops. For example, the *line of intersection* between cylinder and sphere in Figure 7.48 will consist of two circles on the sphere and two circles on the cylinder.

5. The $S\bar{C}$ operation depicted in Figure 7.48 results in both S and C being completely cut into three pieces each. However, any Boolean modeling procedure that is based on a network of planar polygons must be able to cope with the possibility that some shapes may not be completely dissected. For example, an intersection between two triangular facets might not split either or might split just one of them (Figure 7.49).

Taking these observations into account we can propose a possible algorithm to cut two sets of facets along their line(s) of their intersection as follows:

1. With all facets in the model make two lists: 1) the Work list and 2) the Tool list.

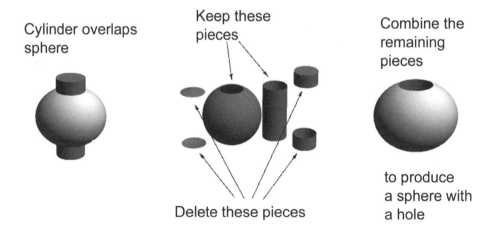

Cylinder overlaps sphere

Keep these pieces

Combine the remaining pieces

Delete these pieces

to produce a sphere with a hole

Figure 7.48.   The intersection of the faceted models for a sphere S and a cylinder C cuts them into three pieces each. By discarding unwanted pieces a model of the Boolean subtraction $S\bar{C}$ is obtained.

2. Find the line of intersection through the facets of the Work list due to intersection with the facets in the Tool list. Since all the facets are planar the line of intersection will consist of a finite number of straight line segments.

3. Build the line of intersection into the facets of the Work list.

4. Split the facets in the Work list along the line of intersection.

5. Swap the facets in the Tool and Work list and repeat the previous three steps.

Steps 2, 3, and 4 above cover the main actions of the algorithm. However, adding a series of edges into a network of facets is very difficult, and so it is preferable to carry out the actions of creating and inserting (steps 2 and 3) at the same time. Thus the line intersection is built into the facets from the Work list at the same time as it is determined.

If we are able to implement these ideas we will have an acceptable procedure for creating separated pieces that are the best approximation to Boolean products one can obtain from a network of polygonal facets. The next sections will expand on the detail of the two main steps, 2 and 3.

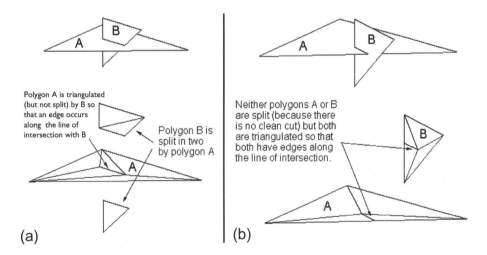

(a)   (b)

Figure 7.49.   An intersection between two triangular polygons. In (a) the polygon labeled B is split in two by polygon A. In (b) neither polygon is split.

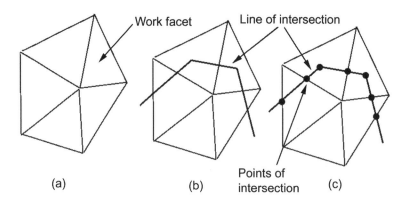

Figure 7.50.   (a) A plan view of some facets in the Work list. (b) Adding the *edge on* view of facets in the Tool list shows the *line of intersection*. (c) The line of intersection will pass through the points of intersection between edges of facets in the Tool list and facets in the Work list and vice versa. There are **no** other places where it can change direction.

7.9.1   Determining and Incorporating the Line of Intersection

The first main action of the algorithm is to determine the line of intersection between facets in the Tool and Work lists and to make sure that this is built into the network of Work facets. To see how this works consider the small network shown in plan view in Figure 7.50. In (b) the line of intersection is shown and for ease of illustration, we will assume that facets in the Work list lie in the plane of the page and facets in the Tool list lie perpendicular to it. Hence they appear as a line in the diagram. Note that the intersection line appears as a number of straight line segments.

Consider now how the line of intersection is determined: it is made up from a number of line segments. So finding the points where these segments begin and end determines the line of intersection. Thus the algorithm is based on the idea that:

> *The segments that go to make up the line of intersection have their end points at the locations where either an edge of a facet in the Work list intersects a facet in the Tool list or where an edge of a facet in the Tool list intersects a facet in the Work list.*

Once we know where these points are everything else follows fairly readily. We proceed in two phases:

- Phase 1: For every edge of a facet in the **Tool** list find its point(s) of intersection with a facet in the **Work** list.

- Phase 2: For every edge of a facet in the **Work** list find its point(s) of intersection with a facet in the **Tool** list.

Figure 7.50(c) highlights where these points are for that particular example.

Now consider another question: how is the line of intersection built into the triangular polygon network, given that we know the points through which it must pass? And the answer:

> The line of intersection **emerges** *automatically if we insist that as vertices are inserted at the points where edges meet facets, the network is constantly updated to make sure that all the facets in it remain triangular.*

Figure 7.51 illustrates the progress of these phases of the algorithm for the example of Figure 7.50 and shows how the line of intersection becomes evident with edges along it.

All of this looks quite straightforward and for the example shown it is. Unfortunately however both phases can be plagued by the creation of too many edges and facets. To see how this might occur consider again the example shown in Figure 7.51. After Phase 1 is complete in diagram (c), six new edges are associated with facets in the Work list; there are four additional facets too. These edges must themselves be used during Phase 2 to check for intersection with the Tool facets. In the example of Figure 7.51 they don't intersect any of the tool facets, but that's just the case in this particular example.

There is another problem that is manifest in Phase 1 itself. Look at the example in Figure 7.52. The Work list consists of one facet only and all the facets in the Tool list intersect it. Inserting the points of intersection in the order 1, 2, 3, 4 gives configuration (d) at the end of Phase 1. Phase 2 completes the triangulation but at the price of the inclusion of another point P as shown in (e).

Configuration (e) is unsatisfactory because the extra point P is unnecessary; configuration (f) is much more acceptable but to achieve it the edge labeled E had to be flipped so that it joined points 3 and 4. Fortunately we have already discussed an algorithm that does just this (Delaunay triangulation) in Section 7.8. To apply the Delaunay procedure to Phase 1 of this stage in the Boolean algorithm we consider each facet in the Work list separately. Every facet in the Work list is considered as a Delaunay supertriangle and is used to produce a *best* triangulation with any intersection points that fall inside it. After all the intersection points are inserted however the supertriangle is not deleted. Figure 7.53 illustrates the result of performing two Delaunay triangulations in two work facets A and B.

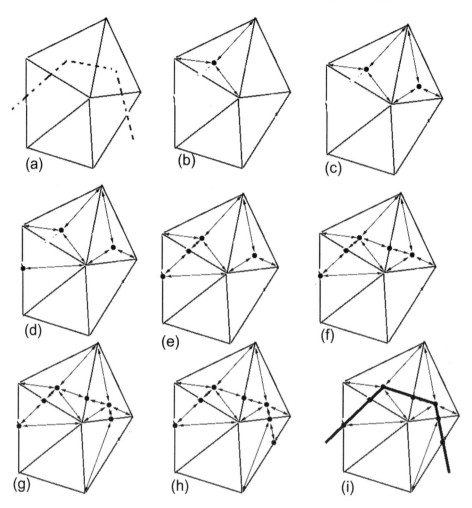

Figure 7.51.   Inserting the points of intersection between the edges of facets in the Work and Tool
                lists one at a time into the network of Work facets produces edges lying along the line of
                intersection. (a) The initial network; the line of intersection is shown dotted. (b) and (c)
                insert the two points where the edge of the facets in the Tool list intersect facets in the
                Work list. In (d), (e), (f), (g), and (h) five points are inserted where the edges of facets in
                the Work list intersect facets in the Tool list. By the time all points have been inserted (h),
                edges along the full length of the intersection have been created. Diagram (i) highlights
                the resultant line of intersection along these edges.

Thus the algorithm for Phase 1 is summarized as follows:

Repeat the following with all the edges i of the facets in the Tool list {
    Repeat the following with all the facets j in the Work list {
        if edge i intersects facet j at point P {
           Add P into a Delaunay triangulation with
           facet j as the original supertriangle.
        }
    }
}

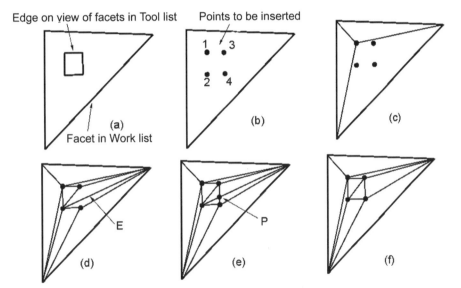

Figure 7.52.   In (a) a the single facet is cut by facets in the Tool list (shown edge on, this is equivalent to the line of intersection too). This gives rise to four intersection points as shown in (b) and labeled in the order in which they are to be inserted. After the first point is inserted the Work facet is shown divided in three (c). When Phase I is completed the triangulation (d) is the result. After checking **all** the edges in the work facet for intersection with facets in the Tool list, the final triangulation with edges along the full length of the intersection; line is produced (e). However, if the edge E in (d) had been "flipped" the triangulation (f) would have been produced. None of the edges in (f) intersect any of the Tool facets and the full length of the line of intersection is completely covered without the need for the extra point P.

Edge on view of facets in the Tool list

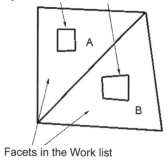

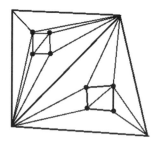

Facets in the Work list

Build Delaunay triangulation
in both triangles A and B

Figure 7.53.   Delaunay triangulations are built (independently) in facets A and B, which are the entries
in the Work list at the start of the algorithm.

There are a couple of observations that we will need to consider carefully
when implementing the algorithm for Phase 1:

1. If it turns out that a point to be inserted just happens to hit an edge e of
the growing Delaunay triangulation it must be left out. We do this because
in Phase 2 the intersection of e with a facet in the Tool list will create a
point at the same place, and if it were inserted in Phase 1 it would create
an infinitesimally thin facet which might not be removed by the Delaunay
procedure.

2. We must also be careful to use not only edges from Tool facets that cross
Work facets but also edges where the vertex at one end actually lies in the
plane of the Work facet.

These two observations are made because they are significantly influenced
by round-off error in calculations. *Numerical problems caused by the limited
accuracy to which computers calculate implies that there are always going to be
a few configurations of Work and Tool facets that result in a Boolean operation
failing.*

Now consider the actions of Phase 2:

> *Take each edge of the facets in the Work list (including the edges
> and facets added in Phase 1), find their point of intersection with
> the facets in the Tool list, and build these points into the network of
> Work facets.*

We cannot use a Delaunay procedure in this phase because the intersections
are occurring at the edge, of a facet rather than in its interior. This will effect

facets on both sides of the edge and they will have to be divided so that both remain triangular. We will also have to be careful because, when an edge is created in Phase 2, it has the potential to intersect other facets in the Tool list, indeed possibly one that has already been checked.

It turns out that by a careful rearrangement, somewhat analogous to the Delaunay *triangle flipping* procedure, it is possible to ensure that edges created in Phase 2 will not intersect any facet. They will either:

1. Stop short of a facet, or

2. Lie in the plane of a Tool facet and thus be part of the line of intersection.

In Phase 2 the edges associated with facets in the Work list are processed twice. In the first pass those edges arising from facets in the Work list as it stands after Phase 1 are tested. If an intersection occurs, a vertex is added at the point of intersection and the facets on both sides of the edges are split. Note that the four facets and two edges created by the split are considered to be in the Work list but they play no role in the first pass. This process is illustrated in Figure 7.54.

In the first pass any edges that lie in the plane of a Tool facet are marked because they contribute a segment to the line of intersection. The second pass uses an iterative procedure to rearrange the edges added in the first pass, and it terminates when no edges of a Work facet cross any of the Tool facets.

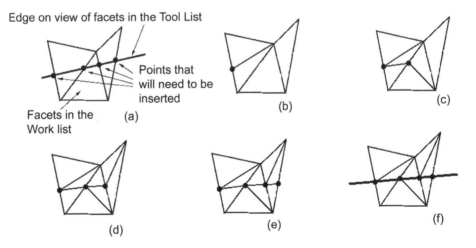

Figure 7.54.   The first part of Phase 2 finds the point of intersection between Tool facets and the edges of Work facets. If an intersection occurs then the edge is divided in two and the facets on both sides are split.

Edge on view of facets in the Tool list

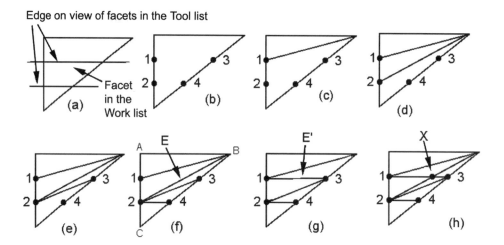

Figure 7.55.   This example is discussed in the text.

To see what the iterative procedure does, consider the example shown in Figure 7.55. In (a) a single facet is held in the Work list and the facets in the Tool list form two separate pieces. In this example no edge of any facets in the Tool list intersects a facet in the Work list and therefore the only points of intersection arising in Phase 2 are at the four points indicated in (b). The points are to be inserted in the order 1, 2, 3, 4. The triangulations shown in (c), (d), (e), and (f) illustrate the network as each point is built in.

On comparing triangulation (f) (Figure 7.55) with the view (a) it can be seen that the edge joining points $(2-4)$ lies in the plane of one of the Tool facets and is therefore part of the line of intersection. Of the other internal edges created in Phase 2 it is only the edge E, joining point 2 to vertex B (B is a vertex of the original triangle), which still intersects a facet in the Tool list. All the other edges do not cross a facet in the Tool list. For the next step the edge labeled E will either have to be split, as in diagram (h), or flipped, as in diagram (g), so that E' joins vertices $(1-3)$. Triangulation (h) with its extra vertex X is obviously less desirable than triangulation (g), and it is the job of the iterative procedure to seek out edges like E and flip them.

Unfortunately, simply looking for internal edges created in the first part of Phase 2 which intersect a Tool facet and then flipping them is not satisfactory in some cases. The example shown in Figure 7.56 illustrates the problem. Both edges, e_1 and e_2, intersect a facet in the Tool list. However if edge e_1 is flipped the resulting triangulation will have overlapping facets and this is **most** undesirable.

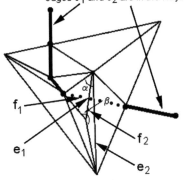

These sections of the line of intersection are completed. They should be joined but edges e_1 and e_2 are in the way.

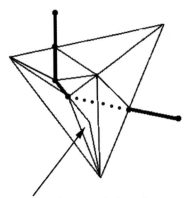

Flipping edge e_1 results in two faces overlapping here which has unsatisfactory consequences.

Figure 7.56.   A configuration in which the edges e_1 and e_2 intersect a facet in the Tool list. Flipping e_1 will result, at best, in a triangulation with overlapping facets or, at worst, will cause subsequent steps to get stuck in an infinite loop!

The reason that facets overlap is that after flipping, the edge e_1 no longer lies inside the quadrilateral formed by facets f_1 and f_2. In fact a flip will result in overlapping facets if either of the angles α or β are $\geq \pi$. Thus we must not allow edges such as e_1 to be flipped if $\alpha \geq \pi$ or $\beta \geq \pi$.

Of course it is unacceptable to leave e_1 so that it crosses a Tool facet. Fortunately the edge e_2 can be flipped and when that is done it becomes possible to also flip edge e_1. As a result, an appropriate triangulation is created with edges along all parts of the line of intersection. This is illustrated in Figure 7.57.

Because an algorithmic procedure can only consider edges in the order in which they are stored and can not *know* which edge to flip first, it must *iterate*. All candidate edges are tested for intersection with a Tool facet; if they intersect but can't be flipped, a flag is raised and the process continues trying to flip the remainder. After all the edges have been tested and if the flag is raised the tests are repeated (iterated) until no edges intersect a Tool facet. This process relies on the fact that if an edge to be flipped does not currently satisfy the interior angle constraint, then flipping another edge will cause conditions to change making it possible to achieve the required flip (in a subsequent interation). Fortunately this will always happen because of the way in which the original configuration was derived.

Taking all these features into account Phase 2 of this part of the algorithm is summarized in Figure 7.58.

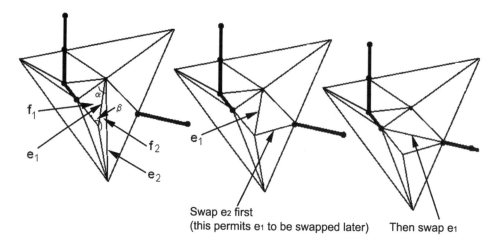

Swap e₂ first
(this permits e₁ to be swapped later)   Then swap e₁

Figure 7.57.   Flipping edge e_2 first allows edge e_1 to be flipped without creating an overlap and produces a triangulation with edges covering the line of intersection.

7.9.2   Splitting Facets along the Line of Intersection

Having built the line of intersection into the facets in the Work list, it only remains to split them along it. Of course the network of Work facets will not be split unless segments of the line of intersection form a complete cut, either by forming loops or crossing from one outside edge to another. This is illustrated in Figure 7.59

This stage of the algorithm is quite straightforward because the procedure of Section 7.9.1 has already marked which edges in the model are part of the line of intersection. With this knowledge the following steps will cut the facets in the Work list along the line(s) of intersection if they split the network:

1. Set a counter l (initially to $l = -1$). This will be used to count the number of pieces and identify to which piece each facet belongs. Label all facets in the work list as unidentified. This can be done by assigning a member of the facet data structure $Facet(i).l = l$.

2. Repeat steps (a) and (b) below until all Work facets are identified. (This procedure is very similar to the "Orienting" algorithm of Section 7.7).

   (a) Increment l and pick an unidentified facet, say k; we could choose it to be the first one for which $Facet(k).l = -1$. Assign $Facet(k).l = l$.

   (b) Find the neighboring facets to facet k; this information is recorded in the $Fid(j)$ member variables for the facet data structure. Let $n = Facet(k).Fid(j)$ with $0 \leq j < 3$ in turn. If the edge common to

First pass of Phase 2

Repeat the following for each Tool facet i {
    Repeat the following for each edge j of the Work facets {
        if edge j lies in the plane of facet i {
            Mark edge j as a boundary edge
        }
        else if edge j intersects facet i {
            Split j in two at the point of intersection and divide
            the two facets that lie on either side of j
        }
    }
}

Second pass of Phase 2

Repeat the following for each Tool facet i {
LOOP: This is the loop back to point of the iteration.
    Set iteration flag: $f = 0$
    Repeat the following for each edge j of the Work facets {
        Skip any edge that was not added during the first
        part of Phase 2
        Skip any edge that is part of the line of intersection.
        (Both these type of edges must be left in place because
        they are important in defining the outline shape of
        the model.)
        if edge j lies in the plane of facet i {
            Mark edge j as a boundary edge
        }
        else if edge j intersects facet i {
            if edge j cannot be flipped raise the flag: $f = 1$
            else {
                Flip edge j so that it becomes *the other*
                diagonal of the quadrilateral formed by the two
                facets on either side of edge j.
                If (after flipping) edge j lies in the plane of facet i
                mark it as part of the line of intersection.
            }
        }
    }
    if $f = 1$ (flag raised) jump back to LOOP
}

Figure 7.58.   The procedure for Phase 2 of the first part of the *Boolean cutting algorithm*.

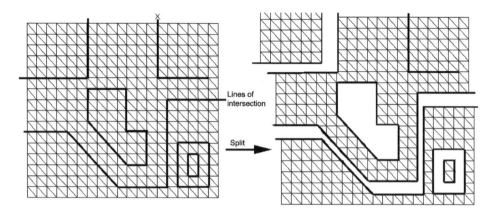

Figure 7.59.   Lines of intersection that split a network of facets. Note that the part of the line of
                 intersection labeled X does not cause a split.

facets n and k (given by $Facet(k).Eid(j)$) is **not** part of the line of
intersection, then n is in the same piece as k and we repeat (recursively)
this step in facet n and in n's neighboring facets until progress is
blocked either by the line of intersection or the edge of the model.

Note that Eid and Fid can be determined by the algorithm given in
Section 3.6 and that they are also kept up to date by the Delaunay
algorithm, as it flips edges and facets around.

3. Once all facets have been identified as belonging to one of the l pieces,
   repeat step (a) below for each $i : 0 \leq i < l$

   (a) Make a copy of all the facets with $Facet(k).l = i$.

       When copying facet k remember that the vertices it is attached to and
       the edges which bound it must also be copied. Care will be needed to
       make sure that no edge or vertex is copied twice, for example, from
       adjacent facets with a common edge.

4. Remove from the database all the facets, edges, and vertices recorded in the
   Work list. *Note:* it may be easier to make copies of all the relevant bits and
   remove the originals rather than to try and copy the structure along the line
   of intersection.

Figure 7.60 illustrates the identification of facets up to a boundary or line of
intersection. Note that if the edge of intersection does not completely split the
network of facets then they will be identified as part of the same piece; this is
desirable.

The code for this algorithm is included with the book.

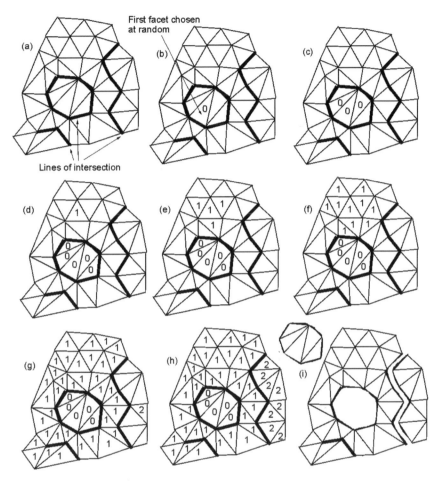

Figure 7.60.   Identifying the pieces to be split up. (a) The edges that form the line of intersection are highlighted. (b) Choose any facet at random and label this as part of the first piece. (c) Label the facets adjacent to the first one chosen unless that facet is on the other side of the outline. (d) Finish labeling all facets adjacent to those identified with a 0; remember a boundary may not be crossed. When there are no facets adjacent to 0 remaining, choose another at random and label this 1. (e) Label with a 1 the facets adjacent to the facet labeled 1 in (d). (f) Label with a 1 the facets adjacent to the facets labeled 1 in (e). (g) Finish labeling all possible facets adjacent to those facets labeled 1 in (f). Pick another at random and label this 2. (h) Label all possible facets adjacent to the one labeled 2 in (f). Since there are no unidentified facets left the identification is complete. (i) Copy all the facets labeled 1, 2, and 3 as separate pieces and delete the originals. This gives us the three pieces formed by the cutting operation.

7.10   Texture Coordinates

In Section 4.14 the use of texture coordinates was discussed. It was not stated there how texture coordinates are generated. It was stated that images were applied to a 2D *texture* coordinate system (X, Y), commonly referred to as (u, v) coordinates, and that a single copy of the image occupied the region in which the coordinates satisfied $0 \leq X < 1.0$, $0 \leq Y < 1.0$.

One obvious way to assign texture coordinates is by hand; the example in Figure 7.61 shows two triangular facets with texture coordinates and a rendered picture with the image shown mapped across the facets.

Manual assignment is however only satisfactory if a very few facets are involved. An automatic procedure that assigns mapping coordinates according to some more usable scheme is essential if we are to apply maps to models with many facets and non-planar geometry. It turns out that three basic formats provide map coverage for almost all situations:

1. Planar mapping

2. Cylindrical mapping

3. Spherical mapping

These are illustrated in Figure 7.62.

Planar mapping is the most appropriate method of application when the surface to be covered is approximately flat. Cylindrical and spherical mapping are most appropriate when the surfaces to be painted are approximately cylindrical or spherical. Since it is impossible to achieve an undistorted mapping from a plane to a cylinder or plane to a sphere, it is obvious that at least these three types of

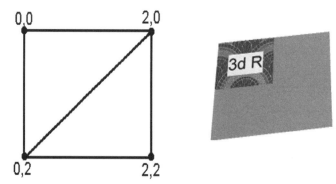

Figure 7.61.   The result of assigning texture coordinates to the vertices of two triangular facets.

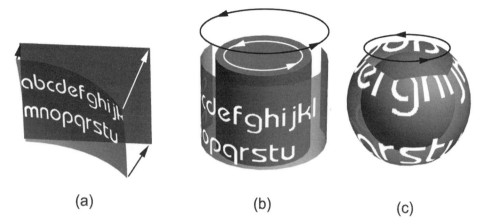

(a)   (b)   (c)

Figure 7.62.   Projected image texture mapping. (a) A planar map. (b) A cylindrical map. (c) A spheri-
                    cal map.

mapping must be available. Most potential uses for an image map are covered by
one of these three cases.

From a usability point of view each of these mapping methods requires only
a few parameters for their specification. Texture coordinates for each vertex are
readily calculated from one of these mapping methods.

7.10.1 Planar Mapping

Figure 7.63(a) illustrated the mapping relationship. A network of triangular facets
is shown overlapped by a rectangle R, which is assumed to bound the image being
mapped. The question then is: what are the mapping coordinates of any vertex V
in the network of facets?

The case shown in Figure 7.19(a) doesn't tell the whole story because the
facets are located in three dimensions and, while ideally they should be planar
so that the map is not distorted, they don't have to be. Neither do they have
to lie in the plane of R, and therefore to obtain mapping coordinates for V we
must assume that the mapping coordinates are determined by a projection in three
dimensions from R to V; this is illustrated in Figure 7.63(b).

The procedure for determining mapping coordinates at V is as follows: a
straight line through V, given by position vector $\mathbf{P}_v$, is constructed in the direction
of the normal to the plane of R, i.e., parallel to the normal to R (say $\hat{\mathbf{n}}$). It intersects
the plane in which R lies at the point $\mathbf{P}_i$. Since $\mathbf{P}_i$ is in the plane of R it can be
expressed as a linear combination of the two vectors along the sides of R. Thus
if R is defined by the three points $\mathbf{P}_0$, $\mathbf{P}_\alpha$, and $\mathbf{P}_\beta$, the vectors along the edges

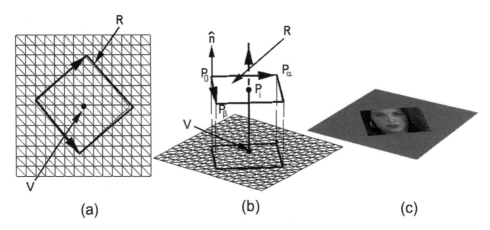

(a)   (b)   (c)

Figure 7.63.   (a) A rectangle bounding the image to be mapped is shown overlapping a network of
                facets. (b) A 3D view of the same situation that shows how the mapping rectangle R is
                projected on to the surface at right angles to R. (c) Rendering the facets after assignment
                with mapping coordinates.

are $\mathbf{P}_\beta - \mathbf{P}_0$ and $\mathbf{P}_\alpha - \mathbf{P}_0$. The algorithm from Section 2.10.1 will allow us to
find an α and β which satisfy:

$$\mathbf{P}_i = \mathbf{P}_0 + \alpha(\mathbf{P}_\alpha - \mathbf{P}_0) + \beta(\mathbf{P}_\beta - \mathbf{P}_0)$$

$\mathbf{P}_i$ is obtained by calculating the intersection point in the plane of R, $(\mathbf{p}-\mathbf{P}_0)\cdot\hat{\mathbf{n}} = 0$, and the line $\mathbf{p} = \mathbf{P}_v + \alpha\hat{\mathbf{n}}$. (See Section 2.5)

    The mapping coordinates of V follow by assuming that at $\mathbf{P}_0$ the mapping
coordinates are $(0,0)$, at $\mathbf{P}_\alpha$ they are $(1,0)$, and at $\mathbf{P}_\beta$ they are $(0,1)$ and therefore,
at V, the (X_v, Y_v) are simply:

$$\begin{aligned} X_v &= \alpha \\ Y_v &= \beta \end{aligned}$$

    If this procedure to assign texture coordinates to all vertices is followed, an
image will be painted on the facets so that it lies inside the projection of R in a
perpendicular direction to the plane in which R lies. The top left corner of the
image will occur at $\mathbf{P}_0$, the top right corner of the image at $\mathbf{P}_\alpha$, and the bottom
left corner of the image at $\mathbf{P}_\beta$.

    Note that the planar mapping described here uses three points to define the
location of the map, and therefore, the opposite sides are always parallel even
though the angle between $\mathbf{P}_\alpha$ and $\mathbf{P}_\beta$ does not have to be $90°$.

It would be possible to define a map using four points, one at each corner of the rectangle, but it is considerably more complex to determine the mapping coordinates from such a map because the opposite sides would not necessarily be parallel. Haines [8] gives expressions (without derivation) for a *convex quadrilateral* mapping that could form the basis of the necessary procedure.

7.10.2 Cylindrical Mapping

In cylindrical mapping one imagines that the picture is wrapped around a cylinder enclosing the surface to be textured (Figure 7.62(b)). The texture coordinates are assigned to a vertex V by finding the point on the cylinder where a line from the axis of the cylindrical map passing through V (at $\mathbf{P}_v$) intersects the cylindrical surface at $\mathbf{P}_i$. This is illustrated in Figure 7.64. Since $\mathbf{P}_i$ lies on the cylinder its position in a frame of reference associated with the cylinder can be specified as a fraction of the distance between the top and bottom of the cylinder d and a fraction of a full rotation round the cylinder θ. The angle of rotation is specified relative to a line where the left hand edge of the image is stuck to the cylinder.

To define a cylindrical map the radius of the cylinder used to define the map is not important. We can assume $r = 1$, but the following must be specified:

- The axis of the cylinder. The best way to do this is with a point on the axis at the top of the cylinder $\mathbf{P}_1$ and a point at the bottom of the cylinder $\mathbf{P}_2$. We will assume that the Y mapping coordinate is zero at the top of the cylinder and unity at the bottom.

- The location of the left-hand edge of the map on the curved surface of the cylinder. An easy way to do this is by specifying some point $\mathbf{P}_L$ which may be any point that is **not** on the axis of the cylinder.

  The left-hand edge is a line running parallel to the axis of the cylinder through a point unit distance from the cylinder's axis in the direction of $\mathbf{P}_L$.

- The angle of rotation ϕ, from the left-hand edge of the map around the cylindrical axis which is to be equivalent to one copy of the image. This is the location where the X mapping coordinate is unity. When $\phi = 2\pi$ it takes one copy of the map to go all the way around the cylinder. If $\phi = \frac{\pi}{4}$ the map occupies one-eighth of the cylinder, or to put it another way, it takes eight copies to paint all around it.

This geometry is illustrated in Figure 7.64.

In view of the discussion above the assignment of mapping coordinates at any vertex is made using the following procedure:

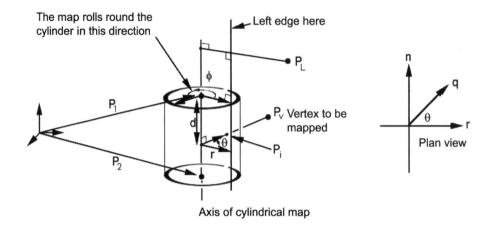

Figure 7.64.   Cylindrical mapping.

Given that ϕ is the angle around the cylinder equivalent to an X mapping coordinate of unity, and the distance between the top and bottom of the cylinder is assumed to cover one unit of the Y mapping coordinate, vertex V will be assigned texture coordinates according to:

$$X_v = \frac{\theta}{\phi}$$
$$Y_v = d$$

d and θ are illustrated in Figure 7.64. They may be calculated in terms of $\mathbf{P}_1$, $\mathbf{P}_2$, and $\mathbf{P}_L$ using the algorithm given in Figure 7.65; here $\mathbf{P}_v$ is the position vector for vertex V.

7.10.3   Spherical Mapping

A spherical mapping can be described in a very similar way to a cylindrical mapping except that the central axis serves only to define the position of the North or South poles of the sphere. One can imagine the image being *squeezed* onto the sphere as illustrated in Figure 7.62.

To map the image to the sphere we use the angular components (ϕ, θ) of spherical polar coordinates (defined in Section 2.1.2), where θ and ϕ satisfy $0 \leq \theta < \pi$ and $-\pi < \phi \leq \pi$. The parameters θ and ϕ will need to be equated to mapping coordinates (X, Y) in the range $0 \leq Y < 1$ and $0 \leq X < 1$. For any

First find d:

Let $\mathbf{y} = \mathbf{P}_2 - \mathbf{P}_1$ (the axis of the cylinder)
Thus d is the projection of $(\mathbf{P}_V - \mathbf{P}_1)$
onto the axis of the cylinder.

$$d = \frac{(\mathbf{P}_V - \mathbf{P}_1) \cdot \mathbf{y}}{\mathbf{y} \cdot \mathbf{y}}$$

Secondly find θ:

Let $\mathbf{x} = \mathbf{P}_L - \mathbf{P}_1$ (a direction towards the 'seam')
Let $\mathbf{q} = (\mathbf{P}_V - \mathbf{P}_1) - d\mathbf{y}$
($\mathbf{q}$ is the direction of $\mathbf{P}_V$ from the cylinder's axis)
Set $\hat{\mathbf{q}} = \dfrac{\mathbf{q}}{|\mathbf{q}|}$
We need a direction perpendicular to the cylinder's axis that is toward

the seam: Let $l = \dfrac{(\mathbf{P}_L - \mathbf{P}_1) \cdot \mathbf{y}}{\mathbf{y} \cdot \mathbf{y}}$
and $\mathbf{r} = (\mathbf{P}_L - \mathbf{P}_1) - l\mathbf{y}$
($\mathbf{r}$ is the direction of $\mathbf{P}_L$ from the cylinder's axis)
Set $\hat{\mathbf{r}} = \dfrac{\mathbf{r}}{|\mathbf{r}|}$
Then $\theta = \arccos(\hat{\mathbf{q}} \cdot \hat{\mathbf{r}})$

This only specifies θ in the range $0 \leq \theta < \pi$; we need to know
whether θ lies in quadrant 3 or 4. Determine this by
forming the vector $\hat{\mathbf{n}}$ which is perpendicular to the plane
in which $\mathbf{P}_1$, $\mathbf{P}_2$, and $\mathbf{P}_L$ lie.

$$\hat{\mathbf{n}} = \frac{\mathbf{x} \times \mathbf{y}}{|\mathbf{x} \times \mathbf{y}|}$$

if $\hat{\mathbf{q}} \cdot \hat{\mathbf{n}} < 0$ then $\theta = -\theta$

This algorithm gives θ in the range $-\pi < \theta \leq \pi$ other ranges
can be obtained by appropriate scaling.

Figure 7.65. Algorithm to determine the cylindrical mapping parameters d and θ for the geometry illustrated in Figure 7.64.

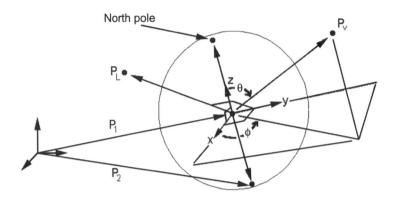

Figure 7.66.   Spherical mapping.

vertex V a ϕ and θ are obtained by drawing a line from V (with position vector $\mathbf{P}_v$) to a point at the center of the spherical map, (Figure 7.66), and calculating the point where this line intersects the unit sphere.

Once the point where this line intersects a unit sphere is known in terms of angle θ (from the North pole) and ϕ (longitude), the mapping coordinates for vertex V (X_v, Y_v) are given by:

$$Y_v = \frac{\theta}{\pi}$$

$$X_v = \begin{cases} \dfrac{\phi}{2\pi} & : 0 \le \phi \le \pi \\[2mm] \dfrac{2\pi + \phi}{2\pi} & : -\pi < \phi < 0 \end{cases}$$

This maps a picture with its top located at the North pole and its bottom at the South pole. Angles θ and ϕ are obtained by following an argument similar to the one used to derive the cylindrical mapping coordinates.

In the geometric specification illustrated in Figure 7.66 the center of the mapping sphere is at $\mathbf{P}_1$; we will assume that the South pole is located at $\mathbf{P}_2$ and that $\mathbf{P}_L$ is an arbitrary point not on the polar axis. In an analogous way to the way it was used for cylindrical mapping, $\mathbf{P}_L$ specifies where the "seam" of the map lies. Given this information the algorithm presented in Figure 7.67 will determine θ and ϕ.

First a right-handed frame of reference relative to the given spherical map must be established.

Let:
$$\mathbf{z} = \mathbf{P}_1 - \mathbf{P}_2$$
$$\mathbf{y} = \mathbf{z} \times (\mathbf{P}_L - \mathbf{P}_1)$$
$$\mathbf{x} = \mathbf{y} \times \mathbf{z}$$
normalize:
$$\hat{\mathbf{x}} = \frac{\mathbf{x}}{|\mathbf{x}|}$$
$$\hat{\mathbf{y}} = \frac{\mathbf{y}}{|\mathbf{y}|}$$
$$\hat{\mathbf{z}} = \frac{\mathbf{z}}{|\mathbf{z}|}$$

Now determine ϕ:

Let: $\mathbf{r} = \mathbf{P}_v - \mathbf{P}_1$
and : $\hat{\mathbf{r}} = \frac{\mathbf{r}}{|\mathbf{r}|}$
then: $\phi = ATAN2((\mathbf{r} \cdot \mathbf{x}), (\mathbf{r} \cdot \mathbf{y}))$

To determine θ use:

$$\theta = \arccos(\mathbf{r} \cdot \mathbf{z})$$

Figure 7.67.   Determining θ and ϕ relative to a specification of the spherical map for a vertex at $\mathbf{P}_v$.

7.11   Building Primitives

Most primitive shapes are readily constructed using one or more of the algorithms we have now considered.

In general it is therefore necessary to specify only a very small amount of structural information because the automatic procedures will do the bulk of the work. For example, we saw that a torus can be constructed by specifying a circle of edges and vertices followed by the generation of a surface of revolution.

The following list suggests how the most basic primitives might be constructed:

- **Cube**
  Start with a square four vertices, five edges, two facets, copy it, move the copy and loft the two outlines.

- **Pyramid**
  Start with a square, add the rest by hand, one vertex, four edges and four triangular facets.

- **Cone**
  Start with an angled line, two vertices, one edge. Construct a surface of revolution about an axis that passes through one of the vertices. If necessary, cap the base of the cone, which is a convex polygon.

- **Tube**
  Start with an line, two vertices, one edge. Construct a surface of revolution about an axis parallel to, but offset from, the line.

- **Cylinder**
  Build a tube as above then proceed to cap the top and bottom; both are convex polygons.

- **Sphere**
  Two possible methods:

  1. Start with a set of vertices and edges describing a semicircle. Then build a surface of revolution around an axis passing through both ends of the semicircle.

  2. Start with a very basic approximation to a sphere. Subdivide the edges and facets and move the additional vertices radially until they lie on a sphere. If necessary repeat this process until the faceted appearance is reduced to an acceptable degree.

- **Disk**
  Start with a set of vertices and edges describing a circle, then cap the circle.

- **Torus**
  Start with a set of vertices and edges describing a circle, construct a surface of revolution about an axis outside the circle.

References

[1] J. O'Rourke, *Computational Geometry in C*, Cambridge University Press, Cambridge UK, 1993.

[2] M. De Berg, *Computational Geometry: Algorithms and Applications*. Springer Verlag, New York, 2000.

[3] F. H. Jones and L. Martin, *The AutoCAD Database Book.* Ventana Press, Chapel Hill NC, 1989.

[4] S. W. Sloan, *A fast algorithm for constructing Delaunay triangulations in the plane.* Adv. Eng. Software, Vol 9, No. 1, 1987.

[5] A. K. Cline and R. L. Renka, *A storage efficient method for construction of a Thiessen triangulation.* Rocky Mountain Journal of Mathematics, Vol. 14, 1984, page 119.

[6] R. S. Ferguson, *Boolean Modelling in Polygonal Data Sets.* Proc. 2nd Irish Computer Graphics Workshop, University of Ulster, Oct. 1994.

[7] D. H. Laidlaw, W. B. Trumbore, J. F. Hughes, *Constructive Solid Geometry for Polyhedral Objects.* Computer Graphics, Vol. 20 No. 4, 1986.

[8] E. Haines, *Essential Ray Tracing Algorithms.* In *An Introduction to Ray Tracing*, Edited by A. S. Glassner. Academic Press, London, 1989.

CHAPTER **8**

Image and Video Processing

Image processing is the name given to any procedure that takes as its input a picture, manipulates it in some way, and creates another picture from it. It can range from the simple action of turning an image upside down to the application of sophisticated noise reduction algorithms such as those that enhance photographs from satellites, security cameras, and space probes.

Video processing can be thought of as an extension of image processing because a video signal is simply a collection of images. For most processes each video frame is processed one at a time in exactly the same way that a single image is. However, a few processes such as motion blur are simulated by considering a sequence of consecutive pictures. Another common video-processing action is to mix two or more video streams together; a simple wipe from one to the other is an example, as is a page turn effect.

In the context of 3D graphics, the output from a renderer is just an image, and therefore can be processed as such. However, a renderer has the potential to provide additional information. Indeed, quite a few 3D effects are more efficiently implemented as an image-processing stage executed after the rendering phase is complete. Particle models for explosions and fireworks are potential candidates for implementation in this way. An image processor working on the output of a 3D renderer has a decided advantage over one working on an image alone, because it can have access to the Z buffer and other information like the position of the observer, models in the scene, and the coordinate frame of reference used to describe the scene.

With the exception of those effects that use information recorded in a Z buffer all of the topics discussed in this chapter could be applied to any image or set of images, not just those generated by rendering a 3D scene.

A number of the algorithms given here are fairly simple to understand and therefore will be mainly illustrated with computer code using **C** and **C++** compatible constructs. The code for the processes discussed here is included with the book.

315

8.1   A Data Structure for Image Processing

An image is made up from pixels; each pixel is a sample of the color in a *small* rectangular area of the image. The color of a pixel is recorded as three values, one for each of the primary colors red, green, and blue (RGB). A combination of primary colors is sufficient to give the illusion that a full rainbow color spectrum is reproducible on a computer monitor. To record an excellent approximation to a **full** spectrum, the standard method is to allocate one byte for each of the red, green, and blue (RGB) components. Computers naturally work in powers of two, and it has proved very useful for image processing and 3D applications to allocate a fourth byte to each pixel for the support of an alpha channel (A).

An alpha channel is used to hold a compositing mask that covers part of an image. A 3D computer animation program typically uses an alpha channel to facilitate the overlay of computer-generated images onto video signals or background images from other sources. A specific example is the use of a live video signal as a background for a computer-generated model. If the model contains some "glass", the alpha channel allows the background to show through the glass with an appropriate level of attenuation. Figure 8.1 illustrates the use of an alpha channel to composit a computer-generated image onto a photograph.

As stated above, pixels in an image are conveniently represented by a four byte structure with members *R, G, B,* and *A*. An image with width w and height h is represented by a 2D array of such structures; we will represent this as $I(x, y)$. The array is usually recorded in an application as a one-dimensional block of memory ordered row-by-row; within a row pixels are stored left to right. Such

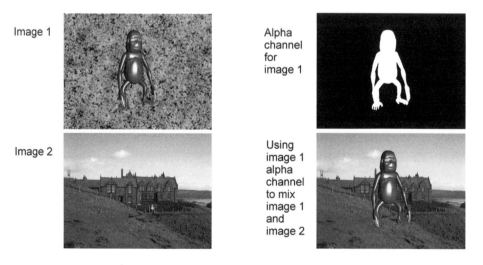

Figure 8.1.   Using an alpha channel to compose a computer-generated image with a photograph.

a storage scheme makes it easy for a program to process the whole image by indexing a pointer and to dynamically allocate memory so that images of differing resolution can be processed. A one-dimensional array fits naturally with the idea of an output raster and the scanline rendering algorithm.

In the **C** or **C++** languages a structure representing a pixel in the frame buffer may be defined as:

```
typedef unsigned char BYTE;

typedef tagPIXEL{
BYTE Red,
     Green,
     Blue,
     Alpha;
} PIXEL, *lpPIXEL;
```

Note that because the color and alpha entries are represented by unsigned eight bit quantities, they can only take values in the range $[0 - 255]$.

A framebuffer suitable to record an image n pixels wide and m lines high is established by:

```
lpPIXEL Image=(lpPIXEL)malloc(n*m*sizeof(PIXEL));
```

If the whole image is to be processed, each pixel can be accessed by pointer indexation. For example, to attenuate the brightness of an image by 50%, use the following code fragment:

```
lpPIXEL p=Image;

for(i=0;i<n*m;i++,p++)
{
  p->Red   /=2;
  p->Green /=2;
  p->Blue  /=2;
}
```

We might note that the above code fragment could equally well be written as:

```
for(i=0;i<n*m;i++)
{
  Image[i].Red   /=2;
  Image[i].Green /=2;
  Image[i].Blue  /=2;
}
```

where array addressing (with $[i]$) replaces the pointer indexation. Alternatively, it could even be written as:

```
for(i=0;i<n*m;i++)
{
   (Image+i)->Red   /=2;
   (Image+i)->Green /=2;
   (Image+i)->Blue  /=2;
}
```

Since these three methods of accessing the pixels in an image are equivalent, the description of the algorithms in this chapter will use whichever one of them allows the functions to be written in the most comprehensible form. The first method is usually translated by a compiler into the fastest possible code. The second method has the most in common with the way a mathematical expression of an algorithm is written.

Whenever a Z buffer (see Chapter 4) is available it records a floating-point number for each pixel. Entries in the Z buffer are accessed in the same way as entries in the framebuffer. For example, suppose we want to copy the contents of one framebuffer to another whenever the Z depth is greater than the specified value d. We might use the following function:

```
void CopyFrameBufferOnDepth(
        float d,                  // depth threshold
        int height,               // image height
        int width,                // image width
        lpPIXEL in_buffer,        // input buffer
        lpPIXEL out_buffer,       // output buffer
        float *Z_buffer)          // Z depth buffer
{
 long i;
 for(i=0;i<height*width;i++)
 {
   if(*Z_buffer++ > d)
   {
     out_buffer->Red   = in_buffer->Red;
     out_buffer->Green = in_buffer->Green;
     out_buffer->Blue  = in_buffer->Blue;
     out_buffer->Alpha = in_buffer->Alpha;
     //
     // an alternative is to use the memcpy function
     // memcpy(out_buffer,in_buffer,sizeof(PIXEL));
   }
   in_buffer++;
   out_buffer++;
 }
```

Many image-processing algorithms require access to a particular pixel at location (i, j) in the 2D array (w, h) of w columns and h rows which holds the image data. To address pixel (i, j) when the framebuffer is held in a dynamically allocated linear array, a calculation using either of the following methods is required:

```
.
//
// For example to extract the value of the Red component
// of pixel (i,j).
//
// Either use an array address
//
Red_pixel_i_j = Image_buffer[i+j*w].Red;
//
// Or calculate the pointer address
//
Red_pixel_i_j = (Image_buffer + i + (j*w))->Red;
.
```

8.2 Basic Functions for Drawing in a Framebuffer

Some image-processing functions draw simple geometric constructs into a framebuffer. The two most commonly used are those which render lines and points. To avoid the problems of aliasing that arise in all pixelated displays these functions should incorporate anti-aliasing techniques.

Two functions whose specifications are prototyped below are included with the code for the book. The functions require a parameter that points to the framebuffer in which the drawing is to occur and parameters to specify the color of the line or point as an RGB triple. The R, G, and B values are specified as a floating-point number in the range $[0, 1]$.

Basic framebuffer functions

1. `DrawAntiAliasedPoint( )`
   The algorithm for this function was described in Section 4.9.

   The parameters are as follows:

```
void DrawAntiAliasedPoint(
    float x,        // horizontal position of point to set
    float y,        // vertical position of point.  Row 0 is at top.
    float w,        // width and height of point.  w=1.0 => 1 screen
                    // pixel if w < 1.0 the brightness is attenuated to
```

```
                      // simulate smaller points
    int Brightness,// brightness [0 - 255] of the pixel to draw
    float Red,      // Red, Green, and Blue define the color of the pixel
    float Green,    // by giving the proportion of that primary color.
    float Blue,     // Each takes values in the range [0-1]
    long width,     // with of image stored in "buffer"
    long height,    // height of image stored in "buffer"

    lpPIXEL buffer // Pointer to the framebuffer to be drawn in.
    )
```

2. DrawAntiAliasedLine( )

   This function draws a line of width w; it uses the Bresenham algorithm
   described in Section 4.2 to draw the line by setting pixels. The pixels are
   set by calling *DrawAntiAliasedPoint()*. It is *not* optimized for speed because
   it is assumed that it is *not* being used in real-time systems; for most *off-line*
   image processing it will be fast enough.

   The parameters are as follows:

```
    void DrawAntiAliasedLine(
       long i1,       // horizontal position (column) of start of line
       long j1,       // vertical position (row) of start of line
       long i2,       // horizontal position (column) of end of line
       long j2,       // vertical position (row) of end of line
       float w,       // width and height of pixel. w=1.0 => 1 screen
                      // pixel if w < 1.0 the brightness is attenuated to
                      // simulate smaller Pixels
       int Brightness,// Brightness of the line
       float Red,      // Red, Green, and Blue define the color of the line
       float Green,    // by giving the proportion of that primary color.
       float Blue,     // Each takes values in the range [0-1]
       long width,     // with of image stored in "buffer"
       long height,    // height of image stored in "buffer"
       lpPIXEL buffer // Pointer to the framebuffer to be drawn in.
       )
```

   Note that these functions draw their shapes by blending them with the current
   contents of the framebuffer. Thus, for example, it is not possible to draw a *black*
   line because whatever the contents of the framebuffer, mixing zero intensity with
   them will leave the value unchanged.

   It's a simple *one-line* change to modify the functions so that they *overwrite*
   the contents of the framebuffer rather than blending them with the incoming line
   or point. For most of the processes discussed in this chapter, blending is essential
   to achieve the desired result.

8.3 Filtering Images

A very broad range of processes can be classified as one of applying a *filter* to an image. In these processes, one image is taken as the input, is passed through a function that considers each of its pixels, and generates a second image as output. The term filtering follows from the fact that to the computer an image is just a *digital signal* and therefore, like any other digital signal, it can be passed through a filter to alter its characteristics. Filtering digital signals is one aspect of signal processing, and digital signal processing in particular is a major focus for R&D in the electronics industry today. Like any other filter, a digital image filter modifies an image so that its spectral content is changed in some way. For example, in the context of image processing a *low-pass* filter which removes high-frequency components is equivalent to making the image appear *blurred*.

There is a wealth of theory on digital filtering and all of it is applicable to the filtering of signals representing images. However the practical application of a filter to an image is accomplished by a very simple algorithm which considers each pixel individually and calculates a new value based on a weighted combination of one or more pixels in the image according to the expression:

$$p_i = \sum_{\text{all pixels } j} w_j p_j$$

For most image filters it is usual for the weights w_j to be non-zero only in pixels adjacent to pixels i. This process called *convolution* is illustrated in Figure 8.2. The family of filters which follow the approach illustrated in Figure 8.2 have nine non-zero weights, at pixel i and its eight nearest neighbors. The array of weights used during a convolution process is commonly referred to as the *kernel*. The elements of the 3×3 array of weights govern the action of the filter. It is thus possible to write code for a general procedure to implement the convolution function and achieve the action of several different filters. Such a function which uses the data structures described in Section 8.1 is given below. In it there are a number of points to note:

1. The framebuffer uses a $0 - 255$ integer range with which to record the color intensities. Some of the filters have negative weights, and thus negative numbers can appear in the calculations. The `bias` parameter allows the *zero* level to be set anywhere in the range $0 - 255$.

2. The pixel value determined from some of the filters will exceed the $0 - 255$ integer range. In these cases the result can be clamped to 255 or scaled down. The parameter `scale` attenuates the weighted pixel average.

3. Linear arrays are used to record the 2D image and the convolution weights. Thus, when forming the convolution sum, an appropriate address calculation must be performed.

4. Care must be taken near the edges of the image because at those points there are no neighboring pixels on some sides. For example, a pixel on the left edge of the image has no neighbor to its left.

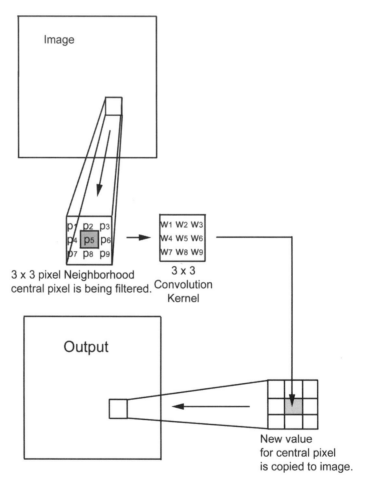

Image

p1	p2	p3
p4	p5	p6
p7	p8	p9

3 x 3 pixel Neighborhood
central pixel is being filtered.

W1	W2	W3
W4	W5	W6
W7	W8	W9

3 x 3
Convolution
Kernel

Output

New value
for central pixel
is copied to image.

Figure 8.2.   Convolution to implement an image filter. The value of pixel 5 becomes $p_5' = p_1 w_1 + p_2 w_2 + p_3 w_3 + p_4 w_4 + p_5 w_5 + p_6 w_6 + p_7 w_7 + p_8 w_8 + p_9 w_9$.

5. Although the majority of convolution filters have a 3×3 array of weights, the function can be used with an array of arbitrary dimension, say $m \times n$, but n and m must both be odd.

The convolution function

```
void Convolve(
 long Xres,      // Width of image
 long Yres,      // Height of image
 lpPIXEL Si,     // Pointer to location where image is recorded
 lpPIXEL So,     // Pointer to location for result
 float scale,    // Scale value to apply to result
 long bias,      // Bias added to all pixel values
 long filterX,   // Width of the filter matrix
 long filterY,   // Height of filter matrix
 float *filter)  // Pointer to filter matrix
{
 lpPIXEL S;
 long i,j,k,l,c,r;
 float ar,ag,ab,weight;
 //
 // To prevent addressing errors at or near the edges of the image
 // only work with pixels that are located at a distance of
 // >= half the width or height of the filter matrix from the
 // edge of the image.
 //
 r=filterY/2;
 c=filterX/2;
 for(i=r;i<Yres-r;i++)   // Do all valid rows in the image
 {
   for(j=c;j<Xres-c;j++) // Do all valid columns in the image
   {
     //
     // reset the accumulated weighted average for each color
     // of pixel (j,i)
     //
     ar=ag=ab=0.0;
     //
     // Apply the filter to pixel (j,i)
     //
     for(l=0;l<filterY;l++)for(k=0;k<filterX;k++)
     {
       //
       // Calculate the address in the linear input array
       //
       S=(Si+(Xres*(i+(l-r))+(j+(k-c))));
       //
       // Determine the weight for filter matrix element (k,l)
       //
```

```
weight = *(filter+filterX*l+k);
//
// Accumulate the weighted sum
//
ar+=(double)S->Red*weight;
ag+=(double)S->Green*weight;
ab+=(double)S->Blue*weight;
}
//
// Determine the address in the output array
//
S=(So+(Xres*i)+j);
//
// Write output values applying the "bias" and "scale". Note
// use of "max" and "min" functions to limit the output range
// to [0 - 255]. If not provided by the compiler "max" and "min"
// functions can be written as the following macros:
//#ifndef min
//#define min(a,b)  ( ((a) < (b)) ? (a) : (b) )
//#endif
//#ifndef max
//#define max(a,b)  ( ((a) > (b)) ? (a) : (b) )
//#endif
//
S->Red   = (unsigned char)max(0.0,(min(255.0,bias+ar*scale)));
S->Green = (unsigned char)max(0.0,(min(255.0,bias+ag*scale)));
S->Blue  = (unsigned char)max(0.0,(min(255.0,bias+ab*scale)));
}
}
}
```

Details of the analysis that provides values to use for the weights for each type of filter may be found in any one of a number of theoretical texts, for example, [2] or [3]. The following subsections discuss some specific examples.

8.3.1 Low-Pass Filters

By removing high-frequency components from an image, a low-pass filter increases the *blurriness* and can be useful when it is necessary to reduce the appearance of 'specs' of noise.

A 3×3 array of weights is sufficient to describe a low-pass filter. The array is passed to function Convolve, which then carries out the filtering process. There are three common settings for the value of the weights:

$$
\begin{array}{ccc}
\frac{1}{9} & \frac{1}{9} & \frac{1}{9} \\
\frac{1}{9} & \frac{1}{9} & \frac{1}{9} \\
\frac{1}{9} & \frac{1}{9} & \frac{1}{9}
\end{array}
\qquad
\begin{array}{ccc}
\frac{1}{10} & \frac{1}{10} & \frac{1}{10} \\
\frac{1}{10} & \frac{1}{5} & \frac{1}{10} \\
\frac{1}{10} & \frac{1}{10} & \frac{1}{10}
\end{array}
\qquad
\begin{array}{ccc}
\frac{1}{16} & \frac{1}{8} & \frac{1}{16} \\
\frac{1}{8} & \frac{1}{5} & \frac{1}{8} \\
\frac{1}{16} & \frac{1}{8} & \frac{1}{16}
\end{array}
$$

Figure 8.3.   Applying a low-pass filter to the image on the left gives the result shown on the right.

The different values of the weights cause slightly different contributions from neighboring pixels to be added to the central one. Note that when all the weights are added the sum is unity. This is important because it implies that there is **no** overall boosting of the brightness of the image and therefore no scaling is required.

Figure 8.3 shows the result of applying the first filter to an image of resolution 540×420.

8.3.2 High-Pass Filters

A high-pass filter is the opposite of a low-pass filter; it accentuates parts of an image that change rapidly and thus can give the illusion of clarifying or *sharpening* the picture. High-pass/low-pass filters are used in video recorders which have a "Soft/Sharp" control.

A 3×3 array of weights is sufficient to describe a high-pass filter. The array is passed to function Convolve, which then carries out the filtering process. The following sets of weight values are in common use:

$$
\begin{array}{ccc}
-1 & -1 & -1 \\
-1 & 9 & -1 \\
-1 & -1 & -1
\end{array}
\qquad
\begin{array}{ccc}
0 & -1 & 0 \\
-1 & 5 & -1 \\
0 & -1 & 0
\end{array}
\qquad
\begin{array}{ccc}
1 & -2 & 1 \\
-2 & 5 & -2 \\
1 & -2 & 1
\end{array}
$$

Note that some of the weights are negative and therefore the resulting image should be biased to the center of the $0 - 255$ range.

Figure 8.4.   Applying a high-pass filter to the image on the left gives the result shown on the right.

Figure 8.4 demonstrates the result of applying the first filter to an image of resolution 540×420.

8.3.3   Blurring

Again the convolution function can be used to blur an image. This time its effect is simply to replace the value of every pixel with the average of a square section of the image centered on that pixel. The bigger the area chosen, the more blurred the image becomes. A typical array of convolution weights is the 5×5 matrix:

$$
\begin{array}{ccccc}
1 & 1 & 1 & 1 & 1 \\
1 & 1 & 1 & 1 & 1 \\
1 & 1 & 1 & 1 & 1 \\
1 & 1 & 1 & 1 & 1 \\
1 & 1 & 1 & 1 & 1
\end{array}
$$

Note that the sum of all components is 25, and therefore a scale factor of $\frac{1}{25}$ must be used. Of course this could be accomplished by using an array of weights in which each entry is $\frac{1}{25}$. Figure 8.5 shows the effect of applying successively larger *blurring* areas to the original image. This simple blurring is really nothing more than a low-pass filter. However, if the weights are changed to emphasize regions of the convolution array, other filter shapes such as a Gaussian can be obtained; often these give better results.

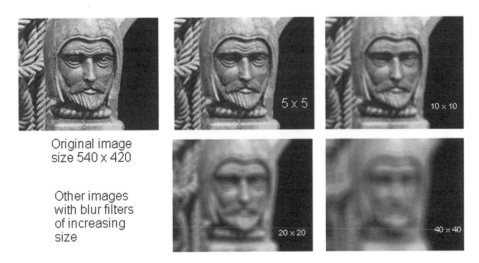

Original image
size 540 x 420

Other images
with blur filters
of increasing
size

Figure 8.5.   Blurring an image by averaging blocks of pixels centered on pixel (i, j). The "blurring" area is increased from 0 on the left to 40 $\times$ 40 at the bottom the right for an image of resolution 540 $\times$ 420.

8.3.4   Sharpening

It was stated above in Section 8.3.2 that a high-pass filter accentuated the fine detail in an image. To the eye this has the illusion of making the image look clearer and sharper.

A high-pass filter on its own is usually unsatisfactory, but if the output from such a filter is mixed with the original image, good results are obtained. For example, adding $\frac{1}{5}$ of the output from a high-Pass filter to $\frac{4}{5}$ of the original will give an image with a quite noticeable increase in *sharpness*. The following code fragment implements this:

```
.
.
.
{
//
// High-pass spatial filter convolution kernel
//
float filter[]={-1.0,-1.0,-1.0,  -1.0,9.0,-1.0,  -1.0,-1.0,-1.0};
//
// Implement the filter. Note the scaling factor of 1.0 and the
// bias of 128
//
Convolve(Xres,Yres,Si,So,1.00,128,3,3,filter);
//
```

Figure 8.6.   Giving the illusion of increased sharpness in an image by amplifying the high-frequency
                     components. The image on the right is a mixture of 80% original (left) and 20% high-pass
                     filter.

```
// mix in the high-frequency component. Note how the bias
// is removed before adding in the high-frequency component.
//
for(i=0;i<Yres;i++)for(j=0;j<Xres;j++)
{
  S=(So+(Xres*i)+j);
  s=(Si+(Xres*i)+j);
  S->Red   = (unsigned char)max(0.0,min(255.0,0.80*(double)s->Red +
  0.40*((double)S->Red - 128)));
  S->Green = (unsigned char)max(0.0,min(255.0,0.80*(double)s->Green +
  0.40*((double)S->Green - 128)));
  S->Blue  = (unsigned char)max(0.0,min(255.0,0.80*(double)s->Blue +
  0.40*((double)S->Blue - 128)));
}
}
.
.
```

The result of boosting the high-frequency components is illustrated in Figure 8.6.

8.3.5 Edge Detection

Edge detection is a significant topic in itself, because it has implications for pattern
recognition, robotic vision, and collision avoidance. From our point of view, the
most probable use of edge detection is in sharpening an image by mixing the
output of a high-pass filter with the original image in those areas where an edge
has been detected.

Figure 8.7.   Sobel's algorithm for edge detection. The threshold is set to detect significant edges.

There are several convolution kernels that can be used to detect specific types of edge, horizontal, vertical, diagonal, etc.; Lindley [1] gives examples of eight types.

Perhaps the best-known edge detection algorithm is Sobel's. It is non-linear and, in one of its forms, it can be coded quite simply and is therefore fast. Sobel's algorithm has the advantage that a threshold can be set which allows it to detect only *prominent* edges. It is also omni-directional; i.e., it does not favor horizontal or vertical lines. Figure 8.7 illustrates the detection of the most significant edges.

8.4   Effects Using the Z Buffer

A number of appealing visual effects that enhance the appearance of rendered images may be created in an 'postprocessing' stage, with access to the renderer's Z buffer.

8.4.1   Depth of Field

A photographer using a real camera usually tries to make sure that the scene in the viewfinder is in focus. For real cameras that have a finite aperture size it can prove difficult to ensure that all objects in the scene are in focus at the same time. When objects near to the camera are in focus, objects far away from the camera are out of focus, and vice-versa. With the perfect "pinhole" model for a camera used by a 3D rendering algorithm, all elements in a scene are always perfectly in focus. To simulate a real camera the finite diameter of its lens must be accounted for, and this is typically done by rendering and mixing slightly different views. It is only within a certain *depth of field*, centered at a fixed distance from the camera, that objects will appear to be in focus, elsewhere they will blurred and fuzzy. As objects move away from the center of the depth of field, their fuzziness will increase.

Having to render the same scene several times, or using multiple rays for each pixel in the case of a ray tracer, adds considerably to the time it takes to generate an image. If however, the values in the Z buffer are available, it is possible to set up a fairly good approximation to the *out of focus* effect by using a simple blurring filter in which the degree of blurring is proportional to the difference in Z distance between any point in the scene and the focal distance assigned to the camera.

Put another way, a blurring filter is applied to pixels in which the size of the filter's $(n \times n)$ matrix is made proportional to $|Z_i - d|$. Z_i is the depth recorded in the Z buffer for pixel i and d is the distance from the camera to a point that is to remain perfectly in focus. Typically, the filter kernel would increase from 1×1 when $Z_i = d$ to, say, 15×15 when $Z_i = 0$ or $Z_i = Z_{max}$.

In the case where the focal depth is d and Δd is the depth range within which the filter kernel reduces from a maximum n_{max} down to unity and back to n_{max}, the size of the $n \times n$ filter matrix is given by:

$$
n = \begin{cases}
n_{max} & : Z_i \geq d + \dfrac{\Delta d}{2} \\[2mm]
1 + \dfrac{2(n_{max} - 1)}{\Delta d}(Z_i - d) & : d \leq Z_i < d + \dfrac{\Delta d}{2} \\[2mm]
1 + \dfrac{2(n_{max} - 1)}{\Delta d}(d - Z_i) & : d - \dfrac{\Delta d}{2} < Z_i < d \\[2mm]
n_{max} & : Z_i \leq d - \dfrac{\Delta d}{2}
\end{cases}
$$

Here Z_i is the depth recorded in the Z buffer for pixel i. Figure 8.8 illustrates an image before and after application of this simulation of photographic depth of field.

8.4.2   Lens Flares

A lens flare is an artifact that appears in the lens of a camera when it is pointed in the direction of a source of light. Ideally it should never occur and, in the perfect world of computer graphics, it doesn't. However photographers sometimes use this effect for added atmosphere in their work, and as a result, many commercial graphics applications provide it as an option.

To simulate exactly the optical properties of lenses and how light interacts with the glass material to produce a *flare* would be an extremely complex process. It

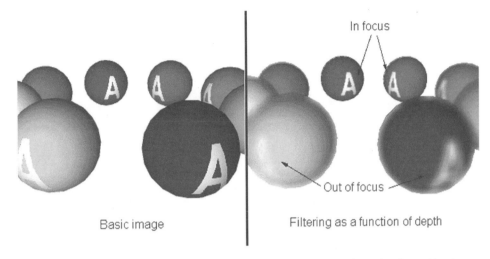

In focus

Out of focus

Basic image

Filtering as a function of depth

Figure 8.8.   Simulating the photographic depth of field. The image on the right shows blurring on objects close to the camera, while those at the back remain in focus.

would probably add far too much to the rendering times or not be realistic enough to be of practical value. A much simpler approach, one that actually gives the 3D programmer greater control, is to "*paint*" the lens flare into the framebuffer using simple drawing functions.

There are effectively three elements in a lens flare:

1. A glow, which may be multi-colored, disks, or rings or a combination of both.

2. A series of streaks leading away from the source of the flare, some random, some regular. Indeed photographers sometimes add *star* filters to the lens which enhances the effect; these produce fairly regular streaks.

3. In a multi-lens camera, inter-lens reflections occur that show up as rings and colored blotches in the image.

The most significant observation that makes it possible to *draw* a lens flare is that the first two effects are centered on the position in the picture where the source of the flare (usually a light, but also might be a bright reflection) is located. The third one lies along a line joining the location of the light to the center of the picture.

Figures 8.9, 8.11, and 8.10 illustrate the appearance of several types of lens flares. Given this basic idea it is possible to *draw* the flare to suit artistic taste.

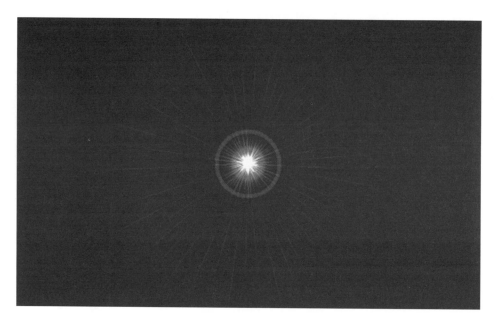

Figure 8.9.   Basic lens flare with halo centered on light.

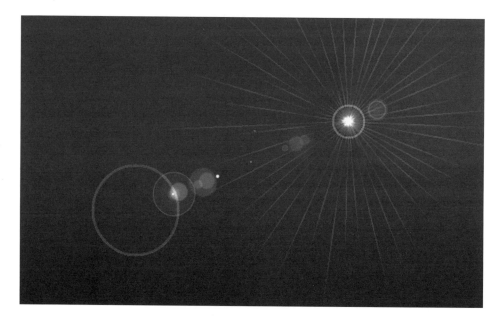

Figure 8.10.   Lens flare with inter-lens reflections.

Figure 8.11.   Lens flare when a star filter is in use on the camera lens.

In the context of 3D computer animation it is also desirable to make the flare interact with the scene in which the light sources occur. This can be accomplished by having the flare fade as the light approaches and eventually goes behind objects. The flare will disappear completely if the light is behind an object, although it might leave a "glow" round the object. The flare should also fade as the light moves out of the field of view. These actions, which fool the viewer into believing the light sources are *in the scene*, are accomplished by knowing the Z depth of the light source and having access to the Z buffer.

An example lens flare

Consider the flare shown in Figure 8.12 which is built up from 25 elements. Here a light source is located in the lower right quarter of the picture.

The 25 elements are used in three groups: (a) the halo around the light; (b) the fine spines radiating from the light; and (c) the inter-lens reflections spaced along a line passing through the center of the screen and the point where the light is visible.

To specify the position of the items in group (c) we define l as the distance from the center of the image at $\mathbf{P}_c$ to the position of the light at $\mathbf{P}_l$, and let:

$$\Delta \mathbf{L} = \frac{\mathbf{P}_l - \mathbf{P}_c}{|\mathbf{P}_l - \mathbf{P}_c|}$$

which is a unit vector that points from the center of the image toward the position of the light. The feature size of the items in group (c), all of which have circular symmetry, is specified as multiples of a basic radius r. Using this notation, the 25 components in the lens flare of Figure 8.12 are:

1. A set of 45 spines drawn as anti-aliased lines radiating from the light. Each spine increases in width towards its midpoint and then narrows and fades as the end is neared. The length of a spine is chosen randomly from a uniform distribution in a given interval. The direction (the angle of the spine) lies in the interval $[0 - 360°]$ with the addition of a small random perturbation.

2. Another three sets of 45 spines with lengths that are proportional to the length of the first set, in the ratios of $\frac{1}{5}$, $\frac{1}{10}$, and $\frac{1}{20}$.

   Where the two set of spines overlap, an irregular bright white region occurs.

3. A bright disk, radius $3r$, centered on the light which fades out linearly.

4. Another disk, radius $20r$, around the light but reddish in color and $\frac{1}{3}$ as bright.

5. A medium brightness red ring centered on the light with inner radius $20r$ and outer radius $23r$.

6. A bright dot at the center of the image of radius r.

7. A white disk with faded edge centered on the point $\mathbf{P}_c - 0.35l\Delta\mathbf{L}$ and radius $3r$.

8. A large brown faint disk centered at $\mathbf{P}_c + 1.8l\Delta\mathbf{L}$ and with radius $120r$. (Remember that the light is positioned at $\mathbf{P}_c + 1.0l\Delta\mathbf{L}$.)

9. A yellow disk at $\mathbf{P}_c + 1.3l\Delta\mathbf{L}$, radius r.

10. The center of the yellow disk above.

11. Faint blue disk at $\mathbf{P}_c + 0.5l\Delta\mathbf{L}$, inner radius $20r$, outer radius $25r$.

12. Second blue disk offset from the first away from the light.

13. Third blue disk offset from the first but toward the light.

14. Faint brown disk at $\mathbf{P}_c - 0.5l\Delta\mathbf{L}$, inner radius $18r$, outer radius $21r$.

15. Second brown disk offset from the first but further away from the light.

16. Third brown disk offset from the first but nearer to the light.

17. A single faint brown disk lying between the screen center and light, at $\mathbf{P}_c + 0.35l\Delta\mathbf{L}$, radius $5r$.

18. A fading blue disk at $\mathbf{P}_c - 0.8l\Delta\mathbf{L}$, and with radius $10r$.

19. A white spot offset from the blue disk.

20. A faded green disk offset from the fading blue disk.

21. A faint green disk at $\mathbf{P}_c - 0.8l\Delta\mathbf{L}$, radius $30r$.

22. An outline for the green disk.

23. The red section of a rainbow ring centered on $\mathbf{P}_c - 1.2l\Delta\mathbf{L}$.

24. The green section of the rainbow ring.

25. The blue section of the rainbow ring.

Code which draws a number of types of lens flares including that shown in Figure 8.12 is included with the book.

8.4.3 Motion Blur

When fast-moving objects are photographed they appear blurred, because they have moved during the short interval of time in which the camera shutter is open. Technically this is a failing in the system. Computer animation programs don't make such mistakes, but because we *expect* moving objects to look blurred in a photograph, when they don't (especially in movies) we feel they look *less realistic*.

To be precise, motion blur occurs as a result of a type of anti-aliasing called *temporal anti-aliasing*. In the context of computer animation it should be done by averaging the images from several pictures with each one rendered during the time interval between successive frames. (Spatial anti-aliasing, Section 4.9, is accomplished by the equivalent of averaging several images made from slightly different camera positions.)

Strictly speaking, to accurately simulate motion blur requires a modification to the basic algorithm for computer animation. However if that is not possible a reasonable approximation can be achieved by appropriate manipulation of the image in the framebuffer. This works particularly well if all the objects are moving in the same direction or the camera is panning across a scene. In such cases the

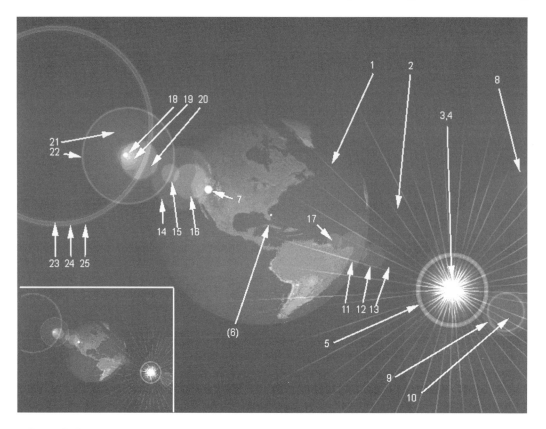

Figure 8.12.   Building a lens flare by blending 25 elements. These are labeled and discussed in the text. (This figure is reproduced in Color Plate 8.)

basic blurring kernel is modified to accommodate a *directional* bias. For example, the 5×5 kernels become:

$$
\begin{array}{ccccc}
0 & 0 & 0 & 0 & 0 \\
0 & 0 & 0 & 0 & 0 \\
1 & 1 & 1 & 1 & 1 \\
0 & 0 & 0 & 0 & 0 \\
0 & 0 & 0 & 0 & 0 \\
\end{array}
\qquad \text{or} \qquad
\begin{array}{ccccc}
0 & 0 & 0 & 0 & 1 \\
0 & 0 & 0 & 1 & 0 \\
0 & 0 & 1 & 0 & 0 \\
0 & 1 & 0 & 0 & 0 \\
1 & 0 & 0 & 0 & 0 \\
\end{array}
$$

Using these give the illusion of movement in horizontal and diagonal directions respectively. The illusion of vertical or horizontal motion can be further accentuated by adding a small random displacement to the rows or columns of pixels in the framebuffer. Figure 8.13 illustrates the illusion of rapid horizontal motion produced with this technique.

(a) (b)

Figure 8.13. Directional blurring to simulate motion: (a) original image and (b) distorted image.

8.4.4 Atmospheric Effects (Fog)

Fog is simulated by using the value from the Z buffer to determine the proportion of a *fog* color to be blended with the image recorded in the framebuffer. A fog effect is independent of the absolute properties of a scene and depends solely on the distance from the point of observation, i.e., the very values recorded in a Z buffer. To build a scene with a rolling fog, a volume texture will be required. Modern graphics hardware often includes the capability of rendering fog effects.

There are a number of possible models that simulate different fog conditions, such as a haze or mist. If Z_i is the depth of the point visible within pixel i, then three models for fog give rise to a fraction f:

1. Exponential (Haze):
$$f = e^{-density \cdot Z_i}$$

2. Double Exponential (Dense fog):
$$f = e^{-density \cdot Z_i^2}$$

3. Pseudo fog, gives greater control and simulates a fog curtain:
$$f = \frac{d_{end} - Z_i}{d_{end} - dstart}$$

The fraction f is used to mix values in the framebuffer with the fog color as follows:

```
Image[i].Red   = f*Image[i].Red   + (1.0 - f)*FogColor_Red;
Image[i].Green = f*Image[i].Green + (1.0 - f)*FogColor_Green;
Image[i].Blue  = f*Image[i].Blue  + (1.0 - f)*FogColor_Blue;
```

8.5   Video Effects

Video effects are image processes that modify a sequence of frames. The simplest video effect is to fade from one image or sequence of images into another. Sophisticated hardware devices are available that allow a huge variety of mixes and other special effects to be applied to a video signal in real time, i.e., 25-30 frames per second. These effects are all implemented on digital data streams using custom built processors which are directed by algorithms that would execute equally well on any processor (if not quite in real time).

It is the aim of this section to present some algorithms that can be used to perform a range of effects from simple cross-fading up to a non-linear *swirl* action that gives the illusion of an image being stirred round its center.

Each algorithm operates through a standard interface, which takes two pointers to framebuffers holding the input images and a parameter τ indicating the proportion of the effect to implement. It is usual to put the result into a separate output framebuffer of similar size. Some effects require a single input buffer; when more than two input streams are needed they can be accommodated by mixing them two at a time. The parameter τ is deemed to lie in the range $[0, 1]$ and therefore, if the effect is to occur between say frames a and b, the processing for frame $i : a \leq i < b$ will be determined using τ given by:

$$\tau = \frac{i - a}{a - b}$$

Using the structures and notation established in Section 8.1, we write a function prototype for each video effect as follows:

```
void VideoEffect_NAME(
      lpPIXEL input1,   // Pointer to the first input framebuffer
      lpPIXEL input2,   // Pointer to the second input framebuffer
      lpPIXEL output,   // Pointer to the output framebuffer
      long    Width,    // Width of image
      long    Height,   // Height of image
      float   tau);     // parameter to specify the progress of effect
```

Function `VideoEffect_NAME()` calculates each pixel (i, j) in the output buffer sequentially by obtaining an appropriate combination of pixels from the input buffers. It is this combination that makes one effect different from another. The annotated source code listings that accompany the book contain functions for the following actions.

8.5.1   Mixes, Wipes, and 2D Effects

The effects in this section are straightforward and can be followed from the source code listings that accompany the book. In the code and specifications below, I1 refers to the first video channel and I2 to the second.

1. `BasicMix()`
   The simplest effect possible. Mix images from I1 to I2 as the parameter changes from 0 to 1. The effect is illustrated in Figure 8.14.

2. `BasicLeftToRightWipe()`
   Image I2 appears from the left side of the screen as the parameter changes $0 \to 1$. The function is easily modified for right-to-left mix The effect is illustrated in Figure 8.15.

3. `LeftToRightWipeWithSoftEdge()`
   Image I2 appears from the left side of the screen as the parameter changes $0 \to 1$. The edge between the two images appears soft as the two images blend together over a small fraction of the width of the image.

4. `RightToLeftWipeWithSoftEdge()`
   Image I2 appears from the right side of the screen as the parameter changes $0 \to 1$. The edge between the two images appears soft as the two images blend together over a small fraction of the width of the image.

5. `HorizontalWipeTowardsCenterWithSoftEdge()`
   Image I2 appears from the left and right edges as the parameter changes $0 \to 1$. Edges between the two images appear soft since the two images blend together over a small fraction of the width of the image.

6. `HorizontalWipeAwayFromCenterWithSoftEdge()`
   Image I2 appears in the center of screen and moves towards the left and right edges as the parameter changes $0 \to 1$. Edges between the two images appear soft as the two images blend together over a small fraction of the width of the image. The effect is illustrated in Figure 8.16.

7. `BasicTopToBottomWipe()`
   Image I2 appears from the top of the screen as the parameter changes $0 \to 1$. The function is easily modified for BottomToTopWipe

8. `VerticalWipeTowardsCenterWithSoftEdge()`
   Image I2 appears from the top and bottom edges as the parameter changes $0 \to 1$. Edges between the two images appear soft as the two images blend together over a small fraction of the width of the image.

9. `VerticalWipeAwayFromCenterWithSoftEdge()`
   Image I2 appears in a horizontal band at the center of the image. It expands towards the top and bottom of framebuffer as the parameter changes $0 \to 1$. Edges between the two images appears soft as the two images blend together over a small fraction of the width of the image.

10. `BasicSquareWipeFromCenter( )`
   Image I2 emerges from the center of the screen.

11. `CircularWipeToCentre( )`
   Image I1 fades away towards the center of the screen leaving I2 behind. Edges between the two images appears soft as the two images blend together over a small fraction of the width of the image.

12. `CircularWipeFromCentre( )`
   Image I2 appears from the center of the screen in a soft-edged disk. The effect is illustrated in Figure 8.17.

13. `WipeWithRectangles( )`
   Wipe the image by exposing the second image in an increasing number of rectangles that spread in lines down from the top left corner.

14. `MirrorImage( )`
   Make the output the mirror image of input I1.

15. `UpsideDown( )`
   Turn the image in I1 upside down.

16. `SliceHorizontally( )`
   Slice the image from I1 into strips, sliding the strips apart to reveal the image from I2.

17. `RandomBlockMix( )`
   Mixes two images together by creating an increasing number of "squares" of I2 in I1 until eventually I2 replaces I1. The squares occur at random over the screen and can be any size from one pixel up. The effect is illustrated in Figure 8.18.

8.5.2   3D Transformations: Twists and Spins

In a 3D effect the image appears to be picked up off the screen, moved, twisted, or rotated, and then set back down onto the screen. To execute the process two components are required:

1. A transformation matrix $[T]$ which describes the twists and spins. A suitable $[T]$ can be obtained by a combination (Section 2.11.4) of the transformations given in Sections 2.11 and 2.11.5.

2. A mapping function which, when given a coordinate (i, j) in the output framebuffer, uses $[T]$ to map this to a pixel in the original image whose RGB value is recorded in the output framebuffer at (i, j).

Figure 8.14.   Basic fade between the two images shown on the left.

Figure 8.15.   Basic horizontal wipe between the two images shown on the left.

Figure 8.16.   Horizontal wipe from both sides of the image with a soft edge at the join.

Figure 8.17.   A circular wipe between the two images on the left with a soft edge as the fade progresses.

Figure 8.18.   Wipe image in a number of rectangles placed randomly over the image.

The theory that underlies these mapping functions is the same as that required for the planar image mapping discussed in Chapters 7 and 4. Section 4.14 gave a description on how mapping coordinates which cover a plane are used to determine an RGB value at a specific location. Section 7.10 described how mapping coordinates are assigned to a plane lying in an arbitrary orientation. For the specific case of the 3D video transitions under discussion in this section, these two stages in mapping can be combined into a single step without the need for a mesh or mapping coordinates.

To understand the action performed by the mapping function consider the setup shown in Figure 8.19. In (a), a representation of the input framebuffer is shown. The top left corner is designated as point $\mathbf{P}_p$, the top right corner as $\mathbf{P}_x$, and bottom left as $\mathbf{P}_y$. Vectors $\mathbf{\Delta x} = \mathbf{P}_x - \mathbf{P}_p$ and $\mathbf{\Delta y} = \mathbf{P}_y - \mathbf{P}_p$ lie along the top and left edges. Matrix $[T]$ is determined so that the points $\mathbf{P}_p$, etc., are moved to $\mathbf{P}'_p$, etc., as shown in (b). (For the specific case illustrated, the transformation is a combination of a rotation about an axis normal to the page and a translation).

Assuming that the input image is to appear inside the rectangle formed by the points $\mathbf{P}'_p$, $\mathbf{P}'_x$, and $\mathbf{P}'_y$, it is the job of the mapping function to:

1. Determine the transform $[T]$

2. Find its inverse $[T]^{-1}$

3. For each pixel (i, j) in the output buffer, use $[T]^{-1}$ to determine the corresponding pixel in the original image (i', j') and write its value into the

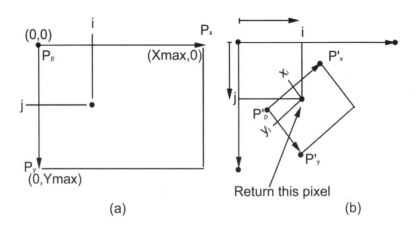

Figure 8.19.   Mapping pseudo-3D transformations.

output buffer. Since some of the pixels (i, j) lie outside the rectangle formed by $\mathbf{P}_p$, etc., they have no equivalent coordinate in the original image. In these cases the function returns with an error code.

Important note: mapping integer coordinates (i, j) with $[T]^{-1}$ to another set of integers is not satisfactory due to aliasing effects. In practice, coordinates (i, j) are promoted to real numbers (x, y) which are then mapped to real numbers (x', y'). It is unlikely that these will be exact integers. Therefore, rather than simply choosing the image value from the nearest integer coordinate (i', j'), we can use bilinear interpolation to a obtain a value from the pixels at (i', j') and its nearest neighbors; this should result in a decrease in the unpleasant effects of aliasing.

Code for a version of the mapping function that can be used with the 3D processes described in this section accompanies the book.

Codes to execute examples of 3D video mixes and wipes are included with the book. Each function establishes vectors that lie in the plane of the screen and then transforms them with a matrix corresponding to rotations, translations, and changes of scale. Once transformed the mapping function is used to determine what value is written into the output framebuffer. In the descriptions below, I1 refers to the first video channel and I2 to the second. The effects in this class are:

1. `BasicPictureInPicture( )`
   This effect creates a small scaled-down version of I1 inside the image I2. A small black border round I1 is added, and the effect progressively reduces the size of the rectangle over time.

Figure 8.20.   Rotating a picture around an axis perpendicular to the screen.

2. ZoomOutFromImage()
   This effect creates the illusion of the image receding away into the distance. The effect is generated by gradually scaling down the size of the image and moving it toward the center of the screen.

3. RotatePictureRoundZaxis()
   The image is rotated about an axis perpendicular to the screen. The effect is illustrated in Figure 8.20.

4. Tumble()
   The image is tumbled by simultaneously rotating it about several axes and optionally scaling it down so that it appears to fly off into the distance. The effect is illustrated in Figure 8.21.

Many other combinations are possible in this class of video effects; for example, rotating around an axis running down the left-hand side can appear to *partially turn the page* leaving space on the right to overlay and scroll text or other images.

8.5.3   Miscellaneous Effects

A few video effects that are neither mixes nor use a pseudo-3D transformation are also included with the book; they are:

1. FadeToMonochrome()
   Gradually remove the color from the input.

2. FadeToNegative()
   Gradually make a photographic negative from the input.

Figure 8.21.   Tumbling an image by rotating around several axes simultaneously.

3. QuantizeColor( )
   Fix the brightness and saturation of an image into certain bands. This function mimics the *colorizing* effect of digital video mixers. It also requires the use of the (H)ue, (S)aturation, and (V)alue (HSV) method of specifying a color. HSV is a more natural way to describe a color than can be achieved by choosing RGB values. The *Value* is analogous to the brightness of a color, e.g., bright red, dark red. The *Saturation* is a measure of how strong is the color; Red and Pink are both really a red color but Pink is less strongly red (the red being mixed with some white). The *Hue* is the parameter governing the color itself: Red, Green, Blue, etc. Hue is generally thought of as a vector, with the angle it makes to a base axis giving a value for a color measured in degrees. This is depicted in Figure 8.22.

4. RotateHue( )
   By incrementing the Hue, the illusion of color cycling an image can be simulated. For example, if a Red raster is given as I1, the output can be made to change color through yellow, green, blue, and purple and back to red over a time interval.

5. Pixelate( )
   Make the input image look like it is made up of large pixels. The color value for each large pixel is made by averaging all the actual pixels that lie within it. The effect is illustrated in Figure 8.23.

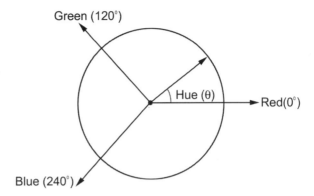

Figure 8.22.   Describing color with a Hue, a unit vector that points toward a unit circle with a continuous spectrum of color drawn round it.

6. RandomNoise( )

Make an output image that consists of nothing more than random noise. This effect is similar to the picture of a TV when no aerial is connected, or no transmitting station is selected.

7. ScrollImage( )

Scroll the image toward the right; parts of the image that disappear off the right edge reappear at the left-hand side. The effect is illustrated in Figure 8.24.

Figure 8.23.   A pixelated image.

Figure 8.24.   Scrolling the image. An image that matches along the left and right sides can use this effect to generate a scrolling background. Combine it with a left-right blur filter to enhance the motion.

8. RollImage( )

Roll the image down the display. Simulates a TV that has suffered a loss of vertical hold.

9. StirImage( )

Transform the image as if it were being stirred around the center of the screen. This is a similar effect to what would happen to a drawing on the surface of a viscous liquid as it is gently stirred round. The effect is illustrated in Figure 8.25.

8.5.4 Artistic Effects

Throughout this book we have looked at techniques which generate images of 3D models that try to approximate photographs of the object being modeled. However, in the real world, despite the fact that the science of photography has been around for more than 100 years artists continue to flourish. Portrait, landscape, and abstract pictures are as popular as ever; the interpretation by the artist adds an extra dimension that the perfect reproduction a photograph offers seems to sometimes miss. Artists will often use such features as brush strokes, *quantized colors*, canvas textures, etc., to add that personal touch. In this section we will look at the implementation of two such techniques, pointillization and crystallization. More details on these and other ideas, such as adding the illusion of brush strokes, can be found in [4]. Many examples of work embellished with these techniques

Figure 8.25.   Swirling an image around an axis at right angles to and running through the center of the image.

Figure 8.26.   A scanned photographic image.

Figure 8.27.   The picture from Figure 8.26 after processing with the crystallization filter.

can be found in the gallery of the *Computer Graphics World* magazine and its associated web site [5].

Figures 8.27 and 8.28 illustrate the action of two effects which are called filters, because they take an input image and process it point by point in much the same way as any other image-processing algorithm. In fact both crystallization and pointillization are manifestation, of the same algorithm with slightly changed parameters.

The idea behind both effects is to sample the original image at random locations (i, j) and replace the color values at all pixels inside a circle of fixed radius centered on (i, j) with the value at pixel (i, j). If two or more circles overlap, then an edge equidistant from their centers is found and it forms the boundary between the two regions. Where multiple circles overlap a series of irregular crystal grains begins to form. This process is illustrated in Figure 8.29.

Implementing this concept for an image stored in a framebuffer is quite straightforward if you imagine introducing a third dimension, perpendicular to the plane of the original image, and that the overlapping circles form the bases

Figure 8.28.   The picture from Figure 8.26 after processing with the pointillization filter.

of a set of cones rising out of the plane of the image. Viewed *from above* these cones overlap and the lines of intersection (which are *straight* lines) resemble the crystal edges we wish to obtain (see Figure 8.30).

The implementation of the effect is achieved using a Z buffer. For any pixel (i, j), we use the Z buffer to determine which cone is visible at coordinate (i, j) when looking from above, because at that point it is the cone that has attained the greatest height which will be visible. Figure 8.31 summarizes the steps necessary to determine which, of n possible cones, is the visible one.

If the number of cones is high then it might be appropriate to assign a Z buffer covering the whole image and work by looking at each cone in turn to see what pixels it covers, rather than looking at each pixel and seeing which cones cover it.

The difference between a pointillized and crystallized filter lies in the number of cones placed over the image. The radius of the base of the cone determines how large the crystals or points are. For the crystallization effect there must be enough cones to cover every pixel, and they must have sufficient overlap so that every cone is overlapped to some degree all around it. In the case of a pointillized

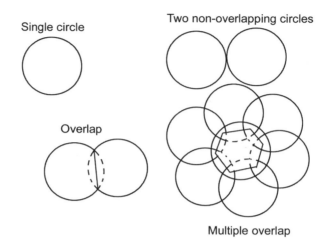

Figure 8.29.   Forming crystal boundaries by overlapping circles.

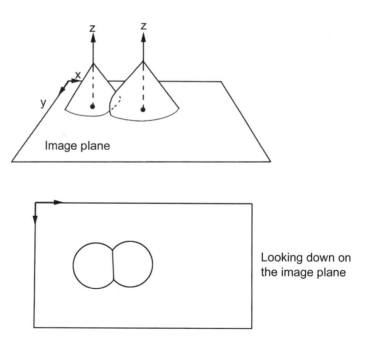

Figure 8.30.   Overlapping cones in 3D form the necessary 3D pattern when viewed from above.

Let the n cones base radius be r and the
maximum cone height also be r. Then for each
pixel (i, j) repeat the following algorithm:

Let each cone k have axis at pixel (x_k, y_k)

Set $z = 0$ and cone $id = -1$
repeat the following for $k = 0$ until $k = n$ {
    calculate d, the distance between pixel (i, j)
           and pixel (x_k, y_k)
    if $d < r$ then {
        if $r - d > z$ then {
            set $z = r - d$
            set cone $id = k$
        }
    }
}
if cone $id \geq 0$ then {
    pixel (i, j) is set to color value for
    cone id i.e. The color value at pixel (x_{id}, y_{id})
}

Figure 8.31.   Use a Z buffer to determine which one of n cones is visible at pixel coordinate (i, j).

appearance, some gaps should be left between cones so that the background color
is visible and some of the curved bases of the cones remain evident.

For both effects a large cone base radius will imply a large crystal size and
much less of a resemblance to the original picture. In the limit, a cone size of
less than one pixel for its base radius will show no filter effect at all. Pointillized
pictures usually benefit from adding a small random variation to the average color
used to fill each region covered by a cone. This results in a slight color variation
even within regions where samples taken at two different pixels have the same
values.

There are an almost infinite variety of other filters that could be built into this
framework; the only limitation is your imagination.

References

[1] C. A. Lindley, *Practical Image Processing in C.* John Wiley and Sons, New York, 1991, Page 369.

[2] G. A. Baxes, *Digital Image Processing, A Practical Primer.* Prentice Hall, Englewood Cliffs NJ, 1984.

[3] R. K. Castleman, *Digital Image Processing.* Prentice Hall, Englewood Cliffs NJ, 1979.

[4] P. Haeberli, *Paint By Numbers: Abstract Image Representations.* Computer Graphics, Vol. 24, No. 4, Aug. 1990.

[5] *Computer Graphics World,* published by PenWell Press, Nashua NH, *http://www.cgw.com.*

CHAPTER **9**

Algorithms for Procedural Textures

In Chapter 4 the basic idea of the procedural texture was introduced. In this chapter we will look at some examples that take advantage of those ideas to produce a collection of interesting surface textures. We will concentrate on what one might say follows the basic principles of mixing geometric and Perlin Noise patterns [1]. *It is important to realize that the procedural textures described in this chapter do not have any basis in physical or biological principles; they are essentially just "computer hacks" that look good and do the job.*

Perlin himself has greatly extended his original work, and others have developed the procedural texture so that now almost any surface appearance can be simulated. For example, Turk [2] and Watkin and Kass [3] have shown that *Reaction Diffusion* is a very successful technique for developing fascinating procedural textures, including many animal skin patterns (giraffe, zebra), coral, and weaved surfaces. Other useful sources of information are the notes that accompany Siggraph Courses [4] and the book by Ebert, et al. [5].

Ideally we would like to be able to have good procedural methods for other textures such as hair and fur, but unfortunately these do not work very well as simple shading functions for flat surfaces. This is primarily because these textures tend to have noticeable rough edges and, in a polygonated model, putting a large number of extra facets around the edges defeats the purpose of the procedural texture. Perlin and others [6] and [7] introduced the concept of the hypertexture which one could describe as a 3D equivalent of the procedural texture. Rather than applying a texture to a meshed surface, a volume of some sort is specified and calculations proceed to determine the opacity at points within that volume. To determine what is visible when looking at a hypertexture, the opacity must be calculated at a number of sample points along the viewing direction (or ray as it passes through the hypertexture volume). As a result hypertextures are extremely slow to compute, and therefore very careful thought is needed before embarking on their use. In this chapter we do not discuss hypertextures, but for more information the references [6] and [7] are a good place to look.

Consult the comments in the code that accompanies the book to obtain fine detail of the algorithms and their implementation. Each texture is represented by a separate function and could be used by any application program, provided that the standard interface described in Section 9.1 is modified to link with the program's internal data structures.

9.1   A Standard Interface

It is a good idea to arrange that procedural textures interface to their host renderer with a few standard parameters. All those rendering applications that offer their users the ability to write plugin textures communicate with their plugins through a standard interface. Some, e.g., Renderman [8], even go so far as to provide a whole C-like *texturing language*. All the code accompanying the examples of this chapter will interface to a client renderer through the following C language function and its parameter set:

```
BOOL TextureProcedure( // return FALSE if function fails, otherwise return TRUE
   VECTOR p,             // coordinate of surface point
   VECTOR n,             // surface normal at  "p"  (unit length)
   VECTOR P,             // position vector to origin of texture parallelepiped
   VECTOR U,             // normalized basis vectors of texture parallelepiped
   VECTOR V,
   VECTOR W,
   float  u,             // relation between "p" and texture parallelepiped
   float  v,             // i.e.,   p = P + uU + vV + wW
   float  w,
   MATRIX3 T,            // transform vector from (x,y,z) to (U,V,W) coordinate frame
   float *opacity,       // modify the opacity of the surface if required
   float *reflectivity,  // modify the reflectivity of the surface if required
   VECTOR color          // return the surface RGB color triple (0.0 - 1.0)
)
{
 .... Body of the texturing procedure
 ....
 return TRUE;
}
```

The function returns the Boolean value `FALSE` if the function fails for any reason; otherwise `TRUE` is returned. The function's parameters fall into five groups:

1. (Vectors: **p**, **n**)

   p is a position vector of the spot on the textured surface for which we wish to calculate the texture value, i.e., the surface color.

n is a unit direction vector normal to the surface being textured at **p**. Many textures redirect **n** away from its input direction. Some bend it in combination with a color variation, but a number of the most effective textures involve shifts in the direction of **n** alone.

2. (Vectors: **P**, **U**, **V**, **W** and scalars: u, v, w)
   These important parameters allow a texture to be applied in a way that is relative to a coordinate system that may move, be non-orthogonal, or differentially scaled. Perhaps this frame of reference follows an object in an animation, so that we don't get the unpleasant appearance of the object *moving through a sea of texture*! Many textures are repetitive; a regular checkerboard or wallpaper pattern, for example, is readily simulated with an appropriate use of u, v, and w. Section 9.1.2 discusses these parameters further.

3. (Matrix: $[T]$)
   A 3×3 transformation matrix that allows direction vectors (such as the surface normal **n**) which are specified in a global (x, y, z) frame of reference to be used in the $(\mathbf{U}, \mathbf{V}, \mathbf{W})$ frame. While it is possible to calculate $[T]$ in the body of a texture function from **U**, **V**, and **W**, it is much more efficient to do this only once, before rendering the image, rather than every time a pixel is rendered.

   If the components of **U**, etc., are (U_x, U_y, U_z), etc., then $[T]$ is given by:

   $$[T] = \begin{bmatrix} U_x & V_x & W_x \\ U_y & V_y & W_y \\ U_z & V_z & W_z \end{bmatrix}^{-1}$$

   In those cases where **U**, **V**, and **W** form an orthogonal basis, there is no need to calculate an inverse matrix because $[T]$ may be written immediately as:

   $$[T] = \begin{bmatrix} U_x & U_y & U_z \\ V_x & V_y & V_z \\ W_x & W_y & W_z \end{bmatrix}$$

4. (Scalars: *opacity and *reflectivity)
   If the client renderer is a ray tracer, then modifications to the opacity or reflectivity of the surface by a procedural texture might have interesting practical use. For example, a texture simulating "clouds" would have zero opacity in the *gaps* between the clouds, a rapid transition to a unit value at the edge, and unit opacity in the cloudy areas. Passing a pointer to these floating-point values allows the texture function to modify the value or just leave it alone (in C++ a `reference` could be used). Both parameters lie in the range $[0, 1]$.

5. (Vector: color) This is a floating-point triple (specified as a vector purely for convenience) that returns the Red, Green, and Blue (RGB) components of the texture color observed at **p**, each component is scaled into the range [0, 1]. When `TextureProcedure()` is called, this parameter should hold a basic underlying surface color that for certain textures (e.g., bumpy) will remain unchanged.

9.1.1 Noise Functions

Many textures make use of the Perlin noise generators which were introduced in Chapter 4 Section 4.13.2. Four fundamental functions were introduced there. In the algorithms described in this chapter and the code that accompanies them, single and vector valued *Noise* and *Turbulence* functions are specified by:

```
float fNoise(         // return a "Noise" value in the range [ 0.0 - 1.0]
            float x,  // Coordinates of the point at which the Noise value
            float y,  // is to be calculated.
            float z   //
            );

float fTurbulence(    // return a " 1/f Noise" value in the range [ 0.0 - 1.0]
            float x,  // Same as for fNoise function. Note that each
            float y,  // function will return the same number if called
            float z   // with the same "x y z" values.
               );

void  vNoise(          // return a normalized random vector with the
            VECTOR v, // returned vector
            float x,  // Coordinates of the point at which the vector
            float y,  // is to be calculated.
            float z   //
            );

void  vTurbulence(    // return a " 1/f" random vector
            VECTOR v, // returned vector
            float x,  // Same as for fNoise function.
            float y,  // ""
            float z   // ""
               );
```

Note that in this case the position coordinates x, y, z are specified as three separate values rather than as a VECTOR data type.

The implementations of `fNoise()`, etc., used in producing the textures illustrated in this chapter were taken from the POV Ray [18] program and modified to return single values in the range [0, 1] or vectors that are of unit length. There

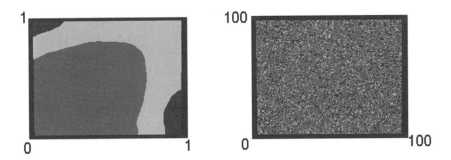

Figure 9.1.   (a) Noise texture at a resolution of one unit. (b) The same noise texture at a resolution of 100 units.

are many other codes that could be used to generate noise with the necessary statistical properties.

It is important to appreciate that these noises are adjusted so that they give a reasonable correlation between returned values when the input points are spaced one unit apart. That is, v1 (given by v1=fNoise(0.0,0.0.0)) will be fairly close to v2 (given by v2=fNoise(1.0,0.0.0)) whereas v3 (given by v3=fNoise(100.0,0.0.0)) will be virtually independent of v1. This point is illustrated in Figure 9.1 which shows a texture based on the same noise function viewed at two different scales.

9.1.2   A Reference Frame for Textures

The vector parameters $\mathbf{P}$, $\mathbf{U}$, $\mathbf{V}$, and $\mathbf{W}$, introduced in Section 9.1, are illustrated in Figure 9.2. They define a unit texture cell (or parallelepiped) that we regard as being a bounding volume inside which the essential features of the texture will be created. The basis vectors $\mathbf{U}$, $\mathbf{V}$, and $\mathbf{W}$ do not have to be orthogonal, and this allows skewed or sheared texture patterns to be readily simulated. The base vectors have an origin at $\mathbf{P}$, and if $\mathbf{U}$, $\mathbf{V}$, $\mathbf{W}$, and $\mathbf{P}$ are transformed in the same way as any object the texture is applied to, then the texture will look as if it is fixed to the object and not like some *field* through which the object is moving see (Figure 9.3).

Any point $\mathbf{p}$ on the surface of an object is specified relative to the texture cell by:

$$\mathbf{p} = \mathbf{P} + u\mathbf{U} + v\mathbf{V} + w\mathbf{W}$$

The coefficients u, v, and w are used as texture coordinates in calculating the surface shading. To make the texture appear larger or smaller or be distorted, they can be scaled before calling the texture function.

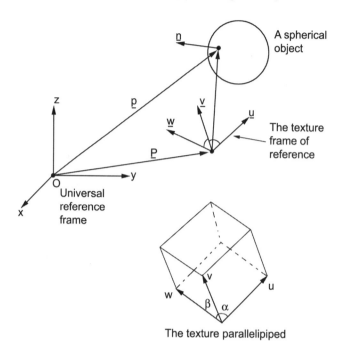

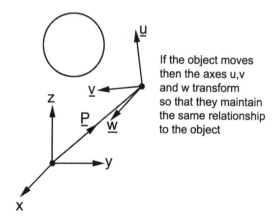

Figure 9.2.   A frame of reference in which to specify a volume texture.

Figure 9.3.   Transforming the texture cell keeps it in the same relative position to the object whose surface exhibits the texture.

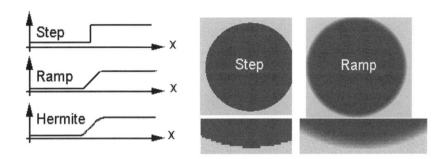

Figure 9.4.   Applying a ramp transition between the colored dot and the background removes the
                   unpleasant aliasing effects that are very noticeable when a step transition is used.

As we have seen, if $\mathbf{U}$, $\mathbf{V}$, and $\mathbf{W}$ form an orthogonal basis, then u, v, and w may be easily calculated. For a non-orthogonal basis, a set of three simultaneous equation must be solved every time u, v, and w are needed.

9.1.3   Color Blending

Textures that include color changes exhibit unpleasant aliasing effects when change is abrupt. On the other hand if the change is blended over a small distance the aliasing effect is much less noticeable. Several blending functions have been proposed, but a simple ramp is often acceptable although some texture developers recommend using hermite interpolation. Figure 9.4 illustrates alternative ramp shapes and the effect of a simple ramp on the edges of a large colored *dot*.

9.1.4   Repetitive Patterns

To repeat a texture pattern, the idea of the texture unit cell is a useful one. The unit cell depicted in Figure 9.2 can be tiled to fill space. Three of the sides of the cell lie in planes formed by pairs of the vectors $\mathbf{U}$, $\mathbf{V}$, and $\mathbf{W}$ with the others lying in parallel planes. Thus the texture cell is a parallelepiped with edges of unit length. Any point $\mathbf{p}$ with texture coordinates (u, v, w) may be tiled by first calculating:

$$u' = u - \mathrm{floor}(u)$$
$$v' = v - \mathrm{floor}(v)$$
$$w' = w - \mathrm{floor}(w)$$

where *floor(x)* returns the nearest lowest integer to x. The (u', v', w') are then substituted in the remainder of the texture calculation in place of (u, v, w).

This technique of modifying **p** through its (u, v, w) coordinates before calculating a texture can also be used to differentially scale the appearance of a texture. For example, the dots illustrated in Figure 9.4 can appear flattened along one or two of their axes if the values of u and v are prescaled by $\frac{1}{2}$. Figure 9.5 illustrates a repetitive array of elliptical dots produced using the following function:

```
#define EDGE 0.05        // give the spot a soft edge

BOOL TextureProcedure(
  VECTOR  p, VECTOR n,
  VECTOR  P,VECTOR U, VECTOR V, VECTOR W,
  float   u, float v, float w,
  MATRIX3 T,
  float   *opacity, float *reflectivity,
  VECTOR  color
)
{
 double r;
 VECTOR spot_color={1.0,0.0,0.0}; // Red spot
 double radius=0.25;              // Spot occupies half the unit cell

 u *= 0.8;                            // Apply differential scaling
 v *= 0.8;                            // for elliptical shapes

 u=(u-floor(u))-0.5;                  // Leave these lines out
 v=(v-floor(v))-0.5;                  // for a single dot at the
 w=(w-floor(w))-0.5;                  // center of the texture cell

 if((r=sqrt(u*u+v*v+w*w)) < radius)
 {
   color[0]=spot_color[0];       // Inside the spot copy the spot color
   color[1]=spot_color[1];       //
   color[2]=spot_color[2];       //
 }
 else if(r < radius+EDGE)             // blend the colors at the edge of
 {                                    // the spot to avoid aliasing.
   r= (r-radius)/EDGE;
   color[0] = color[0]*r + spot_color[0]*(1.0-r);
   color[1] = color[1]*r + spot_color[1]*(1.0-r);
   color[2] = color[2]*r + spot_color[2]*(1.0-r);
 }
 return TRUE;
}
```

Tiling a texture in this way makes it applicable for filling 3D space and not just covering a 2D surface. On those surfaces where mapping coordinates (Section 4.14) are available at **p**, they can be used to determine the value returned

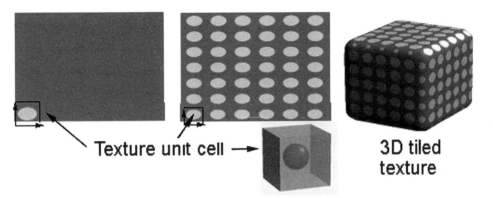

Texture unit cell ⟶   3D tiled texture

Figure 9.5.   Tiling a texture by repeating the unit texture cell shown on the left produces a *wallpaper* effect.

by a procedural texture; however, since there are only two mapping coordinates, we must choose to set the third to some arbitrary value, say zero.

As you have probably guessed, the example dot texture is generated by placing a colored *sphere* at the center of the texture cell and making the calculations in three dimensions. As a result the dots on the surface appear because the visible surfaces cut through the array of texture cells, the *voxels*.

9.2   Regular Dots

In the previous section we saw how to produce a repetitive pattern of dots by embedding a sphere in the basic texture cell. It would take only a small modification to place cubes or other patterns at the center of the cell. We can think of an analogy with the crystallographic arrangement of atoms in a solid. A dot at the center of the texture cell corresponds to a Body-Centered Cubic (BCC) structure. There are other crystallographic arrangements that produce regular patterns of dots; in fact, Hexagonal Close Packing (HCP) arrangement has proved to be very useful because quite a few of the textures to be described later are based on it.

On their own neither the HCP nor the Face-Centered Cubic (FCC) are particularly exciting, but they do raise an interesting and important issue:

> *Neither the FCC or HCP packaging arrangements can be tiled in a way so that all the spheres making up the basic repeat unit lie completely within the unit cell.*

This complicates the task of producing repetitive patterns, because when we need to determine what texture feature occurs at some coordinate (u, v, w) we must take account of adjacent texture cells so that the patterns match along their borders. If the patterns from neighboring cells don't match exactly, some dots in the pattern might look like they have been cut in half (a problem analogous to aligning the wallpaper pattern when hanging adjacent strips.)

9.2.1 FCC Dots

In an FCC pattern there is one spherical dot at the center of each face of the texture cell. Thus to determine the `color` at (u, v, w), six spherical intersection tests must be performed for each cell. In addition we must remember that each sphere is shared with an adjacent texture cell. To make sure that no discontinuity occurs, the dots on opposite faces of the texture cell need to be the same size and color.

This introduces another important point that we should remember as other textures are developed:

> We are determining the texture at one given point (either **p** or equivalently (u, v, w)) on each function call, **not** the texture of many points that satisfy some given property of the texture.

> For example, we cannot set the color of all points inside a dot in one call to the texturing function. This may seem like a trivial point but it is very significant in practice and for many textures, especially those based on random dots, it can significantly complicate the coding.

Figure 9.6 illustrates the relation of the FCC dots to the texture cell and pictures an example of the texture applied to a solid object. Details of the algorithm which consists of a simple test as to whether a point lies inside one of six spheres can be found by following the code that accompanies the book.

9.2.2 HCP Dots

In contrast to BCC and FCC dots, a Hexagonal Close Packed (HCP) arrangement of spheres forms the closest packing that it is possible to obtain. This pattern is of particular interest mainly because the hexagonal mesh, leopard, amphibian, honeycomb, and vein textures are derived from it.

Like the FCC dots we must be careful to remember that spheres from one cell will overlap into adjacent texture cells. In this case to obtain a repeatable texture cell, we will be required to use 22 spheres. Compare this to the single test required for a BCC dot pattern. Figure 9.7 visualizes the arrangement of the spheres in the unit HCP cell. Because of the regularity, any spheres that lie partly outside the texture cell exactly overlap spheres in adjacent cells, and thus, when working in adjacent cells, they are automatically considered. That is, a sphere on the right of cell i overlaps one from the left of cell $i + 1$.

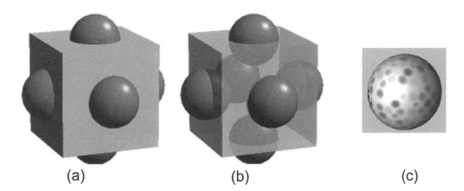

(a)   (b)   (c)

Figure 9.6.   The unit cell for an FCC dots texture and an example of its application to a solid object.
                   (a) Solid cell showing spheres protruding into adjacent cells. (b) Semi-transparent unit cell
                   showing the six spheres. (c) Soft edged dots applied to a sphere.

The HCP unit cell is not rectilinear; for a cell of unit width its length and height are both $\frac{\sqrt{3}}{2}$. Three layers of spheres are needed to fill the texture cell; the middle layer is an offset copy of layer one and the top layer is a repeat of the bottom one. This arrangement of spheres in the layers is depicted in Figure 9.8, where the dimensions are also presented. Note that this illustration depicts the case where the spheres just touch (as would be the case in a real HCP crystal). As we will see later, some very interesting textures arise when the sphere radii vary from this nominal value, a situation that is of course impossible in a real crystal. Seven spheres are needed for layers 1 and 3; eight spheres must be used in layer 2.

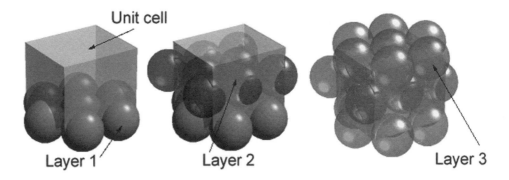

Figure 9.7.   Visualizing the spherical units that make up the HCP unit texture cell.

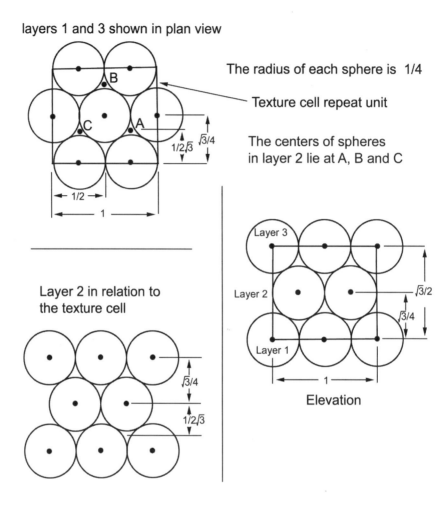

layers 1 and 3 shown in plan view

The radius of each sphere is 1/4

Texture cell repeat unit

The centers of spheres
in layer 2 lie at A, B and C

Layer 2 in relation to
the texture cell

Elevation

Figure 9.8.   Constructing the HCP unit cell from three layers of close-packed spheres. Each sphere is
of radius $\frac{1}{4}$ but the unit cell is not a precise cube.

In the HCP texture (as with those considered earlier) the actual pattern seen
on any given surface is that which appears as the surface cuts through an infinite
lattice of texture cells. This is depicted in Figure 9.9, where an angled plane is
shown cutting through a single texture cell.

The implementation of the algorithm for an HCP dot pattern follows closely
the same principles used in the FCC procedure. It basically tests to see if the

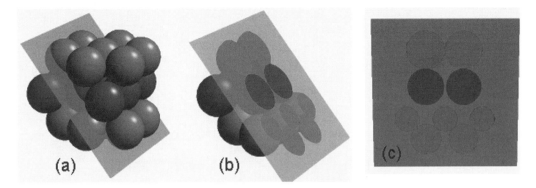

Figure 9.9.   (a) The texture cell with the planar surface cut through. (b) A cutaway view. (c) The pattern as it appears on the surface.

point **p** lies inside (or on the edge of, for soft edges) any of the 22 spheres in the unit cell. If the test proves positive, then the color or other surface attribute assigned to the dot is returned.

9.3   Regular Bumps

The BCC, FCC, or HCP dot pattern can be used to generate regular arrays of raised bumps or sunken dimples if the surface normal vector is pushed off the vertical at points lying inside the dots. For example, the bumps illustrated in Figure 9.10 were produced from a basic BCC dot pattern but, instead of changing the color of the surface inside the dot, the surface normal was perturbed in the way illustrated in the cross-sections. It is relatively straightforward to make bumps on a surface when the bumps are derived from a 2D function that covers the surface. However, more thought is necessary when the bumpy surface is to be derived from a texture that fills a 3D volume. In this case the surface bumps are formed at those locations where the surface intersects spheres in the texture cell. We must ensure that not only is the normal bent in the desired direction (bump or pimple) but also that the direction is consistent for adjacent points on the surface. For example, the bumps on the left, right, top, and bottom surfaces of the cubes in Figure 9.10 must all *bump* outward, irrespective of on which side they lie.

In Figure 9.11 a cross section is shown through the texture cell so that it also intersects one of the spheres inside it. The normal at any point **p** on the surface between points a and b is pushed away from the perpendicular in proportion

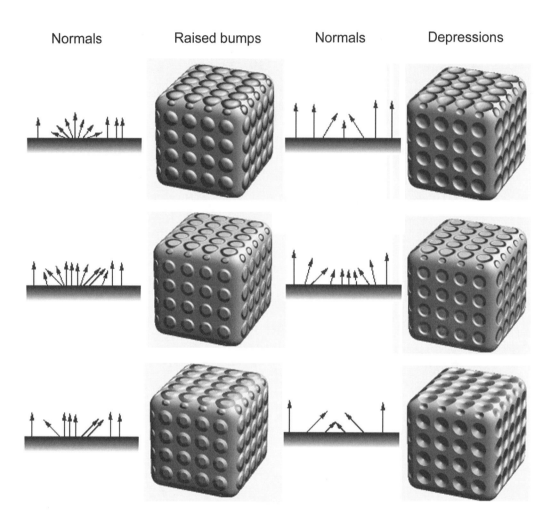

Figure 9.10.   Regular bumps and depressions formed by modulating the surface normal of a solid object. The amplitude and direction of the modulation at a point **p** is determined by its distance from a sphere placed at the center of a *texture cell*. The figure illustrates how the surface normal behaves in a cross section through one of the bumps. Bumps are show on the left and depressions on the right.

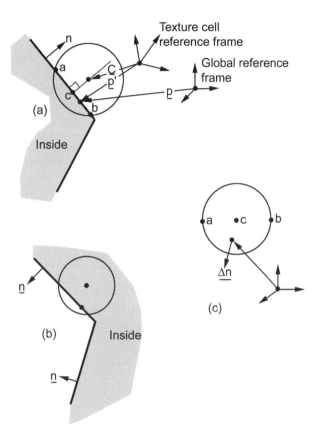

Figure 9.11.   A cross section through a surface intersecting one of the spheres in the texture cell.
(a) Case where the inside of the surface is on the left and (b) when it is on the right.
(c) Shows a plan view and again Δn is the direction in which n is bent at p.

to its distance from the center of the texture cell sphere at c. Working from a
specification of the geometry of the cell, a little vector algebra determines c. Once
c has been found, the direction in which to bend n is calculated; call this Δn.
The new normal vector (n_b after *bumping*) is given by:

$$n_b = n + \gamma \Delta n$$

where γ is the proportion of the bump to apply at p.

     Since the surface normal n is determined with respect to a global frame of
reference but the texturing algorithms require that all calculations are done in the

$(\mathbf{U}, \mathbf{V}, \mathbf{W})$ reference frame, we must transform $\mathbf{n}$ and $\mathbf{p}$ so that they can be used relative to the $(\mathbf{U}, \mathbf{V}, \mathbf{W})$ frame. The surface normal $\mathbf{n}$ in the $(\mathbf{U}, \mathbf{V}, \mathbf{W})$ frame of reference is obtained by applying:

$$\mathbf{n}' = [T]\mathbf{n}$$

To obtain an equivalent for $\mathbf{p}$, say $\mathbf{p}'$, we use the *known* texture coordinates (u, v, w) at $\mathbf{p}$, and by letting $\mathbf{p} = (u', v', w')$ with:

$$
\begin{aligned}
u' &= u - \text{floor}(u) \\
v' &= v - \text{floor}(v) \\
w' &= w - \text{floor}(w)
\end{aligned}
$$

account is taken of the fact that the texture cells repeat ad infinitum.

After transformation, $\mathbf{p}'$, like $\mathbf{n}'$, can be manipulated relative to the texture cell coordinate system. If calculation for the *bumped* surface normal proceeds with respect to the texture cell axes, then the repetition of the texture cell will occur automatically.

To determine the change in surface normal due to the *bumps*, we proceed as follows: let $r < 0.5$ be the radius of a sphere at the center of the texture cell, i.e., at $\mathbf{C} = (0.5, 0.5, 0.5)$. Find the point $\mathbf{p}'_c$ (at c in Figure 9.11a, c is the point on the surface closest to $\mathbf{C}$); using $\mathbf{p}' = (u', v', w')$, the position vector relative to the texture cell for the point p, we can write:

$$\mathbf{p}'_c = \mathbf{C} - ((\mathbf{p}' - \mathbf{C}) \cdot \mathbf{n}')\mathbf{n}'$$

and therefore the direction in which we must bend the surface normal, relative to the texture cell axes, is given by:

$$\Delta\mathbf{n}' = \frac{\mathbf{p}' - \mathbf{p}'_c}{|\mathbf{p}' - \mathbf{p}'_c|}$$

If $|\mathbf{C} - \mathbf{p}'| < r$ then the point of interest lies inside the sphere and the normal will be pushed in the direction of $\Delta\mathbf{n}'$ by an amount that depends on the proportion of the distance γ, at which p' lies between the points labeled a and c in Figure 9.11a. γ is given by:

$$\gamma = 1 - \frac{|\mathbf{p}' - \mathbf{p}'_c|}{\sqrt{r^2 - (|\mathbf{C} - \mathbf{p}'_c|)^2}}$$

$\gamma = 1$ when p is at c and $\gamma = 0$ when p is at either a or b.

The form of the rule used to mix $\Delta\mathbf{n}'$ with $\mathbf{n}$ determines the apparent shape of the bump, but before it is added to $\mathbf{n}$ it must be transformed back to a global frame of reference using:

$$\Delta\mathbf{n} = \Delta n'_u \mathbf{U} + \Delta n'_v \mathbf{V} + \Delta n'_w \mathbf{W}$$

9.3.1 Pimples

The raised bump (or pimple) textures illustrated on the left of Figure 9.10 were produced by adding $\mathbf{\Delta n}$ with $\mathbf{n}$ when $\gamma < 1$ according to the equation:

$$\mathbf{n} = \alpha \mathbf{n} + (1 - \alpha)\mathbf{\Delta n}$$

The parameter α is determined as follows for the three cases illustrated in the Figure with the rules:

1. Rounded pimples

$$\alpha = \sin \frac{\pi}{2}\gamma$$

2. Buttons

$$\alpha = \begin{cases} 1 & : \gamma < 0.5 \\ \frac{1}{2}\left(1 - \cos 4\pi\gamma\right) & : \gamma \geq 0.5 \end{cases}$$

3. Studs

$$\alpha = \begin{cases} 0.5 & : \gamma < 0.5 \\ 1 & : \gamma \geq 0.5 \end{cases}$$

9.3.2 Dimples

The depression (or dimple) textures illustrated on the right of Figure 9.10 were produced by adding $\mathbf{\Delta n}$ with $\mathbf{n}$ when $\gamma < 1$ using:

$$\mathbf{n} = \alpha \mathbf{n} - (1 - \alpha)\mathbf{\Delta n}$$

Again α is determined as follows for the three cases:

1. Rounded dimples, the same as for rounded pimples above: $\alpha = \sin \frac{\pi}{2}\gamma$

2. Flat dimples, the same as for buttons above:

$$\alpha = \begin{cases} 1 & : \gamma < 0.5 \\ \frac{1}{2}\left(1 - \cos 4\pi\gamma\right) & : \gamma \geq 0.5 \end{cases}$$

3. Conical pits

$$\alpha = 0.5$$

In all cases if $\gamma \geq 1$ no modulation is applied to $\mathbf{n}$.

9.3.3   A Hexagonal Mesh

Producing a hexagonal ridge pattern such as that illustrated in Figure 9.12 is relatively straightforward on a flat 2D plane. To construct an equivalent pattern that fills 3D space and at the same time satisfy the repetitive requirements of a procedural texture is a bit harder. One interesting method that leads to the 3D hexagonal honeycomb texture of Figure 9.12 and has potential as a technique for further development (e.g., the textures of Section 9.7) arises from the same ideas that produced the dimpled texture.

In essence the procedure is as follows: spheres used to produce the bumps of an HCP dimple pattern are expanded until they start to overlap. If the overlap is prevented, the rounded edges of the dimples flatten out so that hexagons start to appear. A **Z** buffer (which only needs one value) may be used to prevent spheres overlapping, in much the same way as it is used to produce the crystallization effect discussed in Section 8.5.4. This process is illustrated in Figure 9.13.

In the case of the unit texture cell illustrated in Figure 9.7, spheres of radius 0.25 give maximum space filling; i.e., they just touch. If the radius is increased to $\frac{\sqrt{3}}{2}$, perfect hexagonal shapes are the result. The algorithm presented in Figure 9.14 uses a **Z** buffer to determine inside which of the texture cell's 22 spheres (one sphere equates to one hexagon) any point p lies.

To produce the ridges along the edges of the hexagonal cells, we need to determine whether a point lies within a small distance from the edge of the cell, i.e., inside the ridge. We can do this by considering the value in the **Z** buffer. When p lies near the edges of the hexagon its **Z** buffer value (call it Z_p) will be

Figure 9.12.   A hexagonal ridge pattern produced by overlapping the HCP texture spheres.

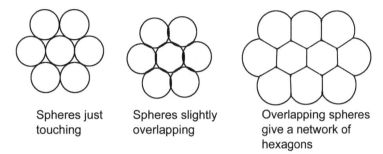

Spheres just   Spheres slightly   Overlapping spheres
touching   overlapping   give a network of
                                              hexagons

Figure 9.13.   A 3D hexagonal mesh produced by growing spheres.

of similar magnitude to the values in the **Z** buffers of adjacent spheres. Thus if the difference in value for two adject spheres is within some small tolerance, then p is said to be on the ridge between hexagons.

To bend the normal on the beveled sides of the hexagon, the change in normal direction is approximated with a vector $\mathbf{\Delta n}$ derived in a manner analogous to that used for the regular dimples. Strictly speaking this will not exhibit a crease at the point where two edges of the hexagon meet but this will hardly be noticed; the ridges in Figure 9.13 do not have such a crease.

9.4 Textures Derived from the Noise Functions

Apart from the basic *Bozo* texture (Section 4.13.2) and those simply derived from it by color blending and added turbulence (e.g., wood, marble, etc.) a number of interesting patterns can be produced by passing the output from Perlin's noise generators through a number of functions.

9.4.1 Contours

The contour pattern illustrated in Figure 9.15 is derived from the basic Bozo texture by passing it through a periodic function, in this case a sinusoid, and then thresholding the result as follows:

Given the point of interest as a (u, v, w) coordinate.

$n_{u,v,w} = \frac{1}{2}(1 + \sin(2\pi f_q \ \text{fNoise}(u, v, w))$
if $n_{u,v,w} > (1.0 - t)$ then {
    return the color of the contour
}
else return the background

Set the depth buffer $Z = 0$

Given point of intersection $\mathbf{p}$ check
each of the 22 spheres (i) to see if it lies inside;
i.e., is $(\delta_i = |\mathbf{p} - \mathbf{c}_i|) < r$?
If it does and $\delta_i > Z$ then {
     Set $Z = \delta_i$ and record the identity of sphere $i : id = i$
     (after all the spheres have been checked this
     reveals which sphere has its center closest to $\mathbf{p}$)
}

Set another depth buffer $Z_b = 0$

To determine how close to the edge of the hexagon $\mathbf{p}$ is,
work through all spheres (i) again.
if $i \neq id$ then {
     if $\delta_i > 0$ and $(r - \delta_i) > Z_b$ { then {
         Set $Z_b = (r - \delta_i)$
     }
}

if $|Z_b - Z| < a_1$ {
     $\mathbf{p}$ lies on the hexagonal ridge.
}
else if $|Z_b - Z| < a_2$ {
     $\mathbf{p}$ lies on beveled side.
}
else {
     $\mathbf{p}$ lies in the hexagonal depression.
}

Figure 9.14.   Algorithm to generate the basic elements of a hexagonal mesh pattern. a_1 and a_2 are parameters that determine the width of the ridges and their sloping sides.

The parameter t governs how thick the contours appear and f_q is a measure that can be most accurately described as a sort of *frequency* of the contours. Values of about 0.1 for t and 20 for f_q usually give good results, as illustrated in Figure 9.15.

9.4.2 Plasma

The texture illustrated in Figure 9.16 resembles the appearance of a brightly colored plasma field. It is produced by adding differently scaled noises and passing

Figure 9.15.   A contour pattern which, with some added turbulence and appropriate blend of color, could resemble a 3D wood grain pattern.

the result through a sinusoidal function to generate red, green, and blue color components with different frequencies and phases. If the phases and frequencies are the same for each color, a monochrome pattern will be observed.

Red, green, and blue (r, g, b) values of the plasma at coordinate (u, v, w) are determined by the following algorithm:

Given the point of interest as a (u, v, w) coordinate, the r, g, b color values are obtained as follows:

$n_1 = \text{fNoise}(u, v, w)$
$n_2 = \text{fNoise}(\frac{1}{2}u, \frac{1}{2}v, \frac{1}{2}w)$
$n_3 = \text{fNoise}(\frac{1}{4}u, \frac{1}{4}v, \frac{1}{4}w)$
$N = n_1 + n_2 + n_3$

$r = \frac{1}{2}(1 + \cos(2\pi f_r N + \phi_r))$

$g = \frac{1}{2}(1 + \cos(2\pi f_g N + \phi_g))$

$b = \frac{1}{2}(1 + \cos(2\pi f_b N + \phi_b))$

9.4.3   Underwater (Caustics)

The caustic pattern that appears on the bottom and sides of swimming pools and underwater surfaces can be simulated by another modification of the basic noise

Figure 9.16.   A texture that gives the illusion of a plasma field.

pattern with appropriate color mixing. In the underwater pattern the noise is passed to a function that *folds* high values down to lower values, and then scales and mixes the color of the caustic with a background shade. Two parameters govern the appearance of the caustics: the sharpness s controls the rapidity of color transitions; the coverage c gives an overall increase in the percentage of the surface area covered by the caustic. The algorithm used to produce the caustic pattern in Figure 9.17 and return an RGB triple on the interval $[0, 1]$ is:

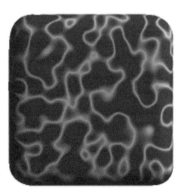

Figure 9.17.   A caustic pattern gives the appearance of the patterns of light that play on underwater surfaces. The features have a sharpness of 0 and a coverage of 0.8.

Given the point of interest as a (u, v, w) coordinate.

$n = \text{fNoise}(u, v, w)$
Use a triangular function on the noise value:
if $(n > 0.5) n = 2(1 - n)$
else $n = 2n$
Rescale the noise:
$n = 0.3 + 0.9n$
Mix the caustic color with the background:
if $(n > c)$ then {
$$n = \frac{n - c}{1.2 - c}$$
$n = n(1 + s)$
if $n > 1$ then $n = 1$
$r = nR_c + (1 - n)R_b$
$g = nG_c + (1 - n)G_b$
$b = nB_c + (1 - n)B_b$
}

9.4.4 Other Worlds

A simple combination of the basic noise and turbulence functions with differential scaling can give a very good approximation to the appearance of a gas planet, like Jupiter. It is especially effective when applied to a spherical object such as that depicted in Figure 9.18. The algorithm in Figure 9.19 (where n, β, f_f, and f_s are parameters that affect visual appearance) outlines the main steps in producing the textured surface of Figure 9.18.

Figure 9.18. Simulating the appearance of the banding in the atmosphere of a large gaseous planet by differentially scaling the basic noise function.

Given the point of interest as a (u, v, w) coordinate.

Note the differential scaling applied to the w coordinate.

$t = \text{fTurbulence}(20u, 20v, 10w)$
$w' = w + f_f t$
$s = \text{fNoise}(\frac{u}{1000}, \frac{v}{1000}, \beta w')$
$s' = s + n(\text{fNoise}(50u, 50v, 25w') - 0.5)$
Limit s' to lie in range $[0, 1]$
$s = 0.5 + (s' - 0.5) * f_s$
Finally blend the banding color with the background:
$r = sB_r + (1 - s)C_r$
$g = sB_g + (1 - s)C_g$
$b = sB_b + (1 - s)C_b$

Figure 9.19.   Procedure to create the texture illustrated in Figure 9.18. If $f_f > 0$ eddies and vortices appear in the atmosphere. If $b = 10$ then approximately 10 bands of gas lie in the unit cell. If $n > 0$ local perturbations in the atmospheric color appear. As $f_s \to 0$ the bands tend to fade. The input point is at coordinate (u, v, w) and the RGB triple r, g, b is the result of mixing the background color (B_r, B_g, B_b) with the band color (C_r, C_g, C_b).

9.4.5 Clouds

Another simple use of the noise function is to simulate a cloudy sky. Appropriate color mixing gives the clouds white edges and dark gray centers; wispy clouds can be produced by differential scaling, and the degree of shearing (a blustery day) is simulated by adding some turbulence. A point of interest is the way in which the

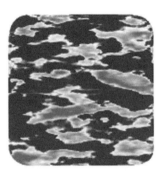

Figure 9.20.   A cloudy day.

Given the point of interest as a (u, v, w) coordinate.

Displace the sampling point (u, v, w) by obtaining a turbulence
vector $\mathbf{\Delta p}$ vTurbulence$(\mathbf{\Delta p}, u, v, w,)$
$u' = u + t\Delta p_u$
$v' = v + t\Delta p_v$
$w' = w + t\Delta p_w$
Sample the noise function at (u', v', w') and blend colors:
$n = \text{fNoise}(u', v', w')$
if $n < 0.5$ return the background color
else if $n < 0.6$ then {
    Blend to white from background B
    $f = 10(n - 0.5)$
    $r = r + f(1 - B_r)$
    $g = g + f(1 - B_g)$
    $b = b + f(1 - B_b)$
}
else {
    Blend to gray:
    $f = 1 - 5(n - 0.6)$
    $r = fr$
    $g = fg$
    $b = fb$
}

Figure 9.21. Procedure to create the texture illustrated in Figure 9.20. The parameter t governs the *wispiness* of the clouds.

turbulence is put into effect. Given a (u, v, w) coordinate at which a color is to be determined, the turbulence is added to the position $(u + \Delta_u, v + \Delta_v, w + \Delta_w)$ before it is passed to the position-dependent noise generator. This approach to modifying a texture, i.e., pre-modulating the position, is a useful one with utility for generating other interesting textures. Figure 9.20 illustrates the cloudy texture. The algorithm in Figure 9.21 outlines the main steps in producing the textured surface of Figure 9.20.

9.5 Regular Dots Perturbed by Noise

In the discussion of the cloud texture it was pointed out that perturbing the position coordinate before passing it to the noise function was a useful way of producing textures. In this section we look at three textures produced by perturbing the (u, v, w) coordinate before passing it to an HCP dot or bump generator.

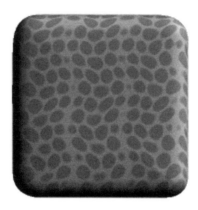

Figure 9.22.   An animal skin pattern.

9.5.1 Leopard

The pattern illustrated in Figure 9.22 was generated from a regular cell of HCP spheres by perturbing the position (u, v, w) with a number of sinusoids prior to testing for containment within one of the 22 HCP spheres. The algorithm in Figure 9.23 outlines the main steps in producing the textured surface of Figure 9.22.

Given the point of interest as a (u, v, w) coordinate.

Displace the sampling point (u, v, w)

$$u' = u + 0.11 \sin(\ \mathrm{fmod}(3u, 2\pi))$$
$$u'' = u' + 0.2 \sin(\ \mathrm{fmod}(0.1v, 2\pi))$$
$$v' = v + 0.15 \cos(\ \mathrm{fmod}(4u'', 2\pi))$$
$$v'' = v' + 0.2 \sin(\ \mathrm{fmod}(0.1w, 2\pi))$$
$$w' = w + 0.15 \cos(\ \mathrm{fmod}(5v'', 2\pi))$$
$$w'' = w' + 0.2 \sin(\ \mathrm{fmod}(0.1u'', 2\pi))$$

Check each of the 22 spheres of radius 0.25 in the HCP texture cell; if (u'', v'', w'') lies inside sphere i at a distance r from its center then mix from the background color to the texture's color.

Figure 9.23.   Procedure to create the texture illustrated in Figure 9.22. The $\mathrm{fmod}(a, b)$ function returns the remainder of $\frac{a}{b}$.

Figure 9.24.   A perturbed regular array of overlapping HCP bumps can resemble a scaly skin.

9.5.2   Reptile

If the regular bump pattern of Section 9.3 is changed to an HCP arrangement and the radius of each bump is increased and allowed to overlap, then a texture resembling a "scaly" skin is the result. Modulating the pattern with a combination of sinusoids adds to the realistic appearance which can be further enhanced by color blending near the edges of the bumps, as shown in Figure 9.24. The algorithm used to produce the texture is given in Figure 9.25.

Given the sampling point as the (u, v, w) coordinate.

Displace the sampling point: (u, v, w)

$u' = u + 0.16 \sin(\text{ fmod}(2w, 2\pi))$
$v' = v + 0.16 \cos(\text{ fmod}(3u, 2\pi))$
$w' = v + 0.16 \cos(\text{ fmod}(4v, 2\pi))$

Check each of the 22 spheres of radius 0.5 in the HCP texture cell, stopping when (u', v', w') lies inside one of them, say at a distance r from its center. Bend the surface normal in proportion to r.

If $r > 0.15$ blend from the background color to the texture color.

Figure 9.25.   Procedure to create the *scaly* texture illustrated in Figure 9.24.

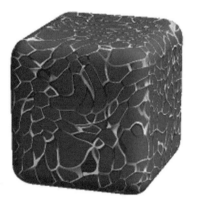

Figure 9.26.   This veined texture could be used to represent leaded glass when the surface is partially transparent.

9.5.3   Veins

The regular honeycomb pattern of Section 9.3.3 is readily transformed into the veined pattern of Figure 9.26 if the point of interest (u, v, w) is perturbed by a noise value before executing the algorithm of Figure 9.14. The beveled sides of the hexagonal ridges are organized so that they form a trough rather than a ridge.

The changes shown in the box below transforms the regular hexagonal mesh of Figure 9.12 into the veined surface of Figure 9.26:

To produce a veined texture proceed as follows:
Given the point of interest is the coordinate (u, v, w).

Get the random vector $\mathbf{d}$ from the noise function:
vNoise($\mathbf{d}, u, v, w$)
Disturb the input point:
$u = u + 0.7d_u$
$v = v + 0.7d_v$
$w = w + 0.7d_w$
Proceed with the honeycomb pattern.

Note:
$\mathbf{d} = (d_u, d_v, d_w)$ is a vector in the texture cell's frame of reference.

9.6 Random Dots and Crystals

One might think that producing random dots would be one of the easier textures to create; after all, one is just laying out a few spheres randomly in space and then determining whether a point $\mathbf{p}$ or (u, v, w) lies inside one of them. Unfortunately however, because the texture must extend throughout an infinite volume, we would need to make an infinite number of tests to see whether $\mathbf{p}$ lies inside one of the random dots or not. Clearly this is not a practical proposition and another method will have to be found.

Again one might think that considering the texture as a repetition of the unit cell would help because then we could confine our tests to a finite number of randomly placed dots inside the cell. Unfortunately there are two problems here, firstly: dots placed near the edge of the cell will overlap adjacent cells and, unless we organize things so that the arrangement of dots within the cell allows it to tile seamlessly, then a disjoint pattern will be visible. This is analogous to what happens when the adjacent strips of patterned wallpaper are not lined up correctly. Secondly, even when a wallpaper tiling is correctly set or if the dots are kept away from the edges of the cell, then the pattern will not appear random and areas near the edges of the unit cells will stand out visually. Thus, to create a random array of dots an approach is needed that can be used on a texture cell basis while still allowing the random placement of dots, at least to the tolerance of a visual inspection.

Consider a single dot of radius $r \leq 0.5$ placed randomly in a unit cell, say as that shown in Figure 9.27. Unless it is placed dead center it will overlap into adjacent cells. However, at most it will only intrude into the immediate neighbors. Therefore if we construct a random dot texture by placing one sphere somewhere in every unit cell, when the time comes to check whether a point at (u, v, w) lies

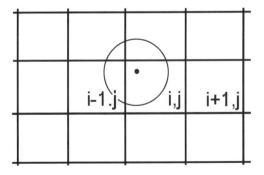

Figure 9.27.   A random dot in texture cell i, j will overlap into at most cell i, j's nearest neighbors. (In this 2D example, the dot in cell i, j could lie in at most nine cells.)

inside the sphere (which forms the dot) only the spheres from the cell in which (u, v, w) lies and its 26 immediate neighbors need be considered. Since one dot is put somewhere in each texture cell the pattern will be quite pleasing to the eye, because there will be no large gaps between dots nor will the dots tend to cluster. Each dot in the texture cell is readily drawn with different colors or radii to add to the effect.

There are two apparent difficulties in implementing the algorithm suggested in the previous paragraph; these are:

1. The first is that the random placement of dots must be done in a reproducible manner. To put it another way: if points (u, v, w) and (u', v', w') both lie in cell i, j, k, the set of spheres used throughout the algorithm (which will basically be the same as that discussed in Section 9.5) must be consistent. We must also remember that in practice points will not be passed to a texture-generating function in any particular order (this was one of the criteria under which Perlin's noise function was developed).

2. Our second difficulty is that, in considering points lying in texture cell i, j, k, we must consider the effect of cells $i - 1, j, k$, etc., and therefore we need to be able to reproduce the random placements of the dots in these cells as well.

The solution to both of these problems is straightforward in practice because the numbers that emerge from a pseudo-random number generator are a reproducible sequence based on some *seed* value. Therefore if a seed is derived from the identity (the i, j, k) of the cell under test, the random position of the sphere within it may be reproduced exactly. Two alternative ways to generate such a seed are:

1. Use fNoise(i, j, k)

2. Use i, j, k and a hashing function to generate a pointer to an entry in a table of random numbers.

The first way is easier to implement but the second is faster and can be used in cases were we need more than one dot per unit cell.

9.6.1 Random Dots

The random dots illustrated in Figure 9.28 are the results of the implementation of the method described above with an index into a table of 2000 random vectors obtained by the hashing functions:

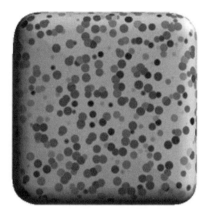

Figure 9.28.   Variably sized random colored dots.

```
#define IMOD(z,a) ((z) - ((z)/(a))*(a))
#define PATTERN(x,y,z)   ( ((z)+16384L)*64536L +  \
                           ((y)+16384L)*32768L +  \
                           ((x)+16384L))
 .
index=IMOD(PATTERN(i,j,k),1999);
 .
```

Once selected a random vector is used to place each sphere at some point in the texture cell. Random vectors from the same table are also used to vary the color and radius of the dot. Blending dot and background color near the dot edge helps to alleviate aliasing artifacts.

9.6.2   Crystals

By allowing the dot radius to increase until adjacent dots overlap, and then bringing into effect a **Z** buffer as used in Section 9.3.3, the dots will appear to lock together into a matrix of colored *crystals*. Figure 9.29 illustrates a basic one sphere per unit cell texture after crystallization with the color of each dot chosen at random.

9.6.3   Blisters

Blisters are another example of the extension of the random dots texture. In this case the surface normal inside the dots is perturbed in much the same way as was done for the case of the regular bumps. Blisters are flatter than bumps but

Figure 9.29.   Random colored crystals. (Basically a random dot texture but with a dot radius that exceeds the size of the unit cell.)

are readily produced by using a slightly different mix of normal and perturbing vectors. Points that lie near the center of the dots can be colored differently for added effect.

Figure 9.30.   Random blisters: Raised random dots.

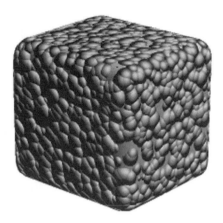

Figure 9.31.   Peas: rounded high-density blisters.

9.6.4   Peas

The pea texture is yet again another version of the blisters texture. A greater density of random bumps is produced by placing three spheres in each unit cell. No flattening of the bumps is used, but by changing the sphere radius, the surface can be covered to a lesser or greater extent; see Figure 9.31.

9.7   Sharply Edged Features

These textures are constructed by a combination of the ideas already derived.

9.7.1   Honeycombs

The honeycomb cube shown in Figure 9.32 uses the steps from the hexagonal mesh algorithm (Section 9.3.3) but without applying an inner limit to the extent of the beveled edge.

9.7.2   Paving Stones

The paving stone and fractured texture (Figure 9.33) are derived from the crystal texture (Section 9.6.2). By simply beveling the edges of the crystals, the cracks between the paving stones appear. Points near the crystal edges are identified

Figure 9.32.   Honeycomb: a hexagonal mesh.

using the same calculation that identified whether points were on the ridges of a regular hexagonal mesh. In the case of the cracked texture, very wide ridges were used.

A neat trick is to make the interior of the paving stones look dirty or weathered by mixing in a dark color modulated by $fNoise(u, v, w)$. Additionally, if each stone is given a slight color variation (a toned-down multi-colored crystal) the whole surface looks more natural.

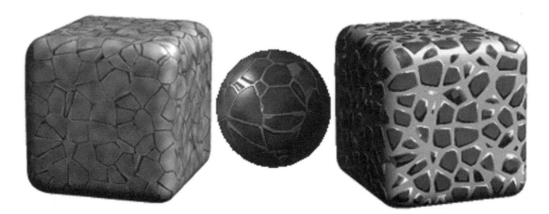

Figure 9.33.   Paving stones and chipped fragments.

9.8   Rough Surfaces

Rough surfaces fall into two categories:

1. Those with smooth changes to the direction of the surface normal, which are derived from combinations of vector noises.

2. Those with sharp changes to the surface normal direction vector. Often some smooth undulations are mixed with the more pronounced sharp features.

9.8.1   Basic Rough Surface

The basic rough surface is a straightforward mix of surface normal $\mathbf{n}$ and output from $vNoise(\mathbf{\Delta n}, u, v, w)$. Many different appearances are achieved by:

1. Scaling: calculate $\mathbf{\Delta n}$ from $vNoise(\mathbf{\Delta n}, su, sv, sw)$ after scaling the input coordinate (u, v, w) by s.

2. Amplification: vary the *bumpiness* through the parameter α and perturb $\mathbf{n}$ by:

$$\mathbf{n} = \mathbf{n} + \alpha \mathbf{\Delta n}$$

The bumpy cubes shown in Figure 9.34 represent examples of different s and α values.

An almost infinite variety of other *continuous* rough and bumpy surfaces can be achieved by adding $vNoise()$ and $vTurbulence()$ vectors in different proportions and at different scales. Experimentation is very often the best way of finding pleasing effects.

Figure 9.34.   Some examples of basic undulating textures.

The remaining three rough textures discussed in this section are primarily based on the algorithm for the *Pea* (Section 9.6.4), which is a discontinuous bumpy surface. Each adds a new component to $\mathbf{\Delta n}$, either a $vNoise()$ or a scaled version of the *Pea* itself with minor features superimposed on it.

9.8.2   Crusts

The crusted texture shown in Figure 9.35 is the result of the following modifications to the *Pea* texture algorithm:

1. Add a vector noise displacement to (u, v, w) before applying the *Pea* algorithm.

2. The radius of the *peas* are chosen from a random distribution in the range $[0.6 - 1.8]$ relative to the size of the unit texture cell.

3. A power law ($a' = a^2$) is applied to the fraction of $\mathbf{\Delta n}$ mixed with $\mathbf{n}$ by:

$$\mathbf{n} = a'\mathbf{n} + (1 - a')\mathbf{\Delta n}$$

4. A continuous noise at a magnified scale is added to the final result; this adds a little fine detail to the gnarled look of the crusted texture.

The overall appearance will change depending on the resolution at which the texture is rendered, as is evident from the examples illustrated in Figure 9.35.

Figure 9.35.   Crusted surfaces.

Figure 9.36.   A crumpled surface showing ridge features at decreasing scales.

9.8.3 Crumpled

A crumpled surface that can resemble *used aluminum foil* is an example of an angular texture and is produced by adding **inverted** *Pea* textures at smaller and smaller scales and with different amplitudes. Usually there is no need to go beyond about three overlapping textures. The illustration in Figure 9.36 was produced by perturbing (u, v, w) prior to computing the second and third components. Each component is calculated at a scale which is twice as small as the previous one and added in the proportions 1.0, 0.8, and 0.95.

9.8.4 Faceted

Crumpled surfaces exhibit features of a combination of basic rough surfaces with decreasing amplitudes and reducing scales. A faceted texture uses the same idea of summing effects at decreasing scales but without changing the amplitudes. Flat surfaces (which give the texture and appearance of some sort of naturally occurring mineral) are produced by quantizing $\Delta \mathbf{n}$ using integer arithmetic before mixing it with the surface normal.

The *Pea* texture in Section 9.6.4 forms the basis for this texture. This time the hemispherical peas are inverted so that they appear to be pushed into the surface. The normal vector is quantized as shown in the following **C/C++** code fragment. This example gives approximately 16 flat quadrilaterals per hemispherical depression:

Figure 9.37.   Two examples of a faceted surface with angular and rounded features.

```
.
// dn is the vector that bends the surface normal.
//
Normalize(dn);
dn[0]=0.5*(double)((int)(dn[0]*2.0));    // Quantize the 3 components
dn[1]=0.5*(double)((int)(dn[1]*2.0));    // components of "dn" using
dn[2]=0.5*(double)((int)(dn[2]*2.0));    // integer arithmetic.
Normalize(dn);
.
```

Faceted rectangular surfaces are illustrated in Figure 9.37; the sample on the right depicts an alternative version in which three unquantized faceted textures are mixed by offsetting their position and only making a slight change of scale. The following code fragment documents the offset and scale change at each of the three steps:

```
u += 20.0; v += 21.0; w += 22.0; // offset the (u,v,w) coordinate and scale
u *= 1.2;  v *= 1.2;  w *=1.2;    // it before adding the next 'inverted Peas'
```

9.9   Stucco Surfaces

Stucco textures are very useful in situations where rich surface detail is desirable but without it becoming the center of attention. All the stucco textures involve bending the surface normal to form ridges, troughs or raised plateau-like features. Figure 9.38 illustrates three typical variations. The curved edges of the features may themselves twist gently, twist tightly, or be very ragged indeed.

Plateau   Canyons   Ridges

Figure 9.38.   Stucco surfaces.

Stucco surface are simulated by thresholding the noise function:

$$n = fNoise(u, v, w)$$

For example, in the plateau effect illustrated in Figure 9.38, points on the surface where $n > 0.5$ are on the plateau and points where $0.55 < n < 0.6$ are on the slope. The ridge effect requires points satisfying $0.4 < n < 0.45$ to be on the upslope and points where $0.55 < n < 0.6$ to be on the downslope.

Determining the direction in which to bend the normal on the slopes requires the calculation of the gradient of $fNoise()$ at the point (u, v, w), i.e., $\mathbf{\Delta n} = -\nabla f_{u,v,w}$ or:

$$\mathbf{\Delta n} = -\left(\frac{\partial f}{\partial u}\hat{\mathbf{u}} + \frac{\partial f}{\partial v}\hat{\mathbf{v}} + \frac{\partial f}{\partial w}\hat{\mathbf{w}}\right)$$

In practical terms this means using finite differences to determine the partial differentials. Thus the change in surface normal $\mathbf{\Delta n} = (\Delta n_u, \Delta n_v, \Delta n_w)$ is given by:

$$\begin{aligned}
\Delta n_u &= -(fNoise(u + \delta, v, w) - fNoise(u - \delta, v, w)) \\
\Delta n_v &= -(fNoise(u, v + \delta, w) - fNoise(u, v - \delta, w)) \\
\Delta n_w &= -(fNoise(u, v, w + \delta) - fNoise(u, v, w - \delta))
\end{aligned}$$

δ is a small increment in the coordinates of magnitude about 0.01. This value is chosen because the texture cell is of unit size and we are only interested in features whose sizes are of the order of about 0.05 units on this scale.

The steepness of the slopes of the features are governed by a parameter α, which scales $\mathbf{\Delta n}$ before adding it to $\mathbf{n}$,

$$\mathbf{n} = \mathbf{n} + \alpha\mathbf{\Delta n}$$

Applying a turbulent perturbation to (u, v, w) before proceeding with the Stucco algorithm will give very ragged and irregular boundaries, and mixing the stucco surface with other bumpy textures also makes interesting surfaces.

9.10 Leather and Cauliflower

In this last section we will look at a couple of interesting combination textures. Leather is a natural material in common use and it would be nice to have a computer-generated texture that approximates it. There is no one *correct* leather pattern so we will look at two variations. The first is produced by mixing stucco textures, and the second is yet another variant of the ubiquitous *Pea*. In some circumstances the *Cauliflower* pattern, so called because it resembles the florets of that vegetable, could even be used as a leather texture. The leather textures are illustrated in Figure 9.39 and the cauliflower in Figure 9.40.

The stucco leather is composed with the sum of four Stucco (*Canyon*) textures (using thresholds of 0.48, 0.54, 0.60, and 0.66) preprocessed by perturbing (u, v, w) with a little turbulence, viz.:

```
vTurbulence(D, u, v, w);
u += D[0] * 0.4;
v += D[1] * 0.4;
w += D[2] * 0.4;
```

As each of the texture layers are added, they are scaled and offset by:

```
u += 30;   v += 40;   w += 50;     // offset
u *= 1.01; v *= 1.02; w *= 1.03;   // scale
```

Figure 9.39.   Leather: (a) A derivative of Stucco textures and (b) Truncated Peas.

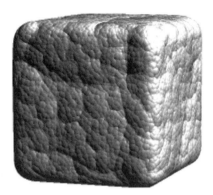

Figure 9.40.   A Cauliflower.

The only slight complication in this texture compared with a basic stucco is that special consideration must be given to those points where the canyons overlap; *a canyon within a canyon* must not be allowed to develop. One way to achieve this is by using a flag to indicate if point (u, v, w) is on the floor or side of a canyon; the floor takes precedence. After all four patterns have been processed, the flag is used to select the correct $\Delta\mathbf{n}$.

The second potential leather pattern follows the *Pea* algorithm until the slope α of the pea at (u, v, w) is determined. Then α is modified as follows:

1. Thresholded: (if $\alpha < 0.4$ do not bend $\mathbf{n}$)

2. Subjected to a functional transformation $\alpha = \alpha^{0.25}$

3. Perturbed by an attenuated standard noise vector $vNoise()$ at $\frac{1}{5}$ scale.

For the cauliflower surface the *Crumpled* algorithm is followed with the following exceptions:

1. The point (u, v, w) (input coordinate) is not perturbed after the addition to $\Delta\mathbf{n}$.

2. The "bumps" are inverted, so that they bump out.

3. The amplitude of $\Delta\mathbf{n}$ is not attenuated during the phase in which the *Pea* procedure is repeated three times.

4. The feature size is reduced much more rapidly: four times on each loop.

Please consult the annotated code listings that accompany the book for the fine details of the implementation of the algorithms discussed in this chapter.

References

[1] K. Perlin, *An Image Synthesizer.* Computer Graphics, Vol. 19, No. 3, July 1985.

[2] G. Turk, *Generating Textures on Arbitrary Surfaces Using Reaction-Diffusion.* Computer Graphics, Vol. 25, No. 4 July 1991

[3] A. Witkin and M. Kass, *Reaction-Diffusion Textures.* Computer Graphics, Vol. 25, No. 4 July 1991.

[4] S. Worley in *Course 8.* Siggraph 94 Course Notes.

[5] D. S. Ebert et. al., *Texturing and Modeling a Procedural Approach.* Academic Press, Cambridge MA, 1994.

[6] K. Perlin and E. M. Hoffert, *Hypertexture.* Computer Graphics, Vol. 23, pages 253–262, July 1989.

[7] J. T. Kajiya and T. L. Kay, *Rendering Fur With Three-Dimensional Textures.* Computer Graphics, Vol. 23, No. 3, July 1989.

[8] S. Upstill, *The RenderMan Companion.* Addison-Wesley, Reading MA, 1990.

Part III
Real-Time 3D Graphics for Windows

CHAPTER 10

3D Graphics with OpenGL

Since the introduction of true 32-bit versions of the Windows operating systems on the *humble personal computer* and the insatiable demand for more and more realistic computer games, attention is focusing on hardware acceleration of many stages in the rendering pipeline. To derive maximum benefit from hardware implementations of such things as geometric transformations, rasterization, and shading, application programmers are turning to the use of standard libraries for their application programming interface (API). For a number of years workstations have had access to the very successful OpenGL API designed by the graphics specialist system designer *Silicon Graphics Inc*.

For many years the PC family suffered as a platform for graphics applications because of the lack of a standard display mode. The Macintosh proved a much more popular platform despite the fact that the raw processing power of the IBM clones were always more cost effective. Today this has changed; Microsoft's Windows has imposed a de facto standard, and thus the 3D graphics API libraries have been *ported* to work on PCs and with the hardware acceleration in 3D video adapter cards from such manufacturers as Nvidia and ATI.

Sadly however it seems that the old lessons of compatibility problems have not been learned, and there are at least three APIs competing for the attention of application developers. The three that come to mind are OpenGL [1], Direct3D [2] and QuickDraw 3D [3]. OpenGL and Direct3D (a new component of Direct X) are supported as part of Windows and both will, as a consequence, probably continue to have the support of the graphics adapter manufacturers.

OpenGL has a long and successful track record, first appearing on PCs with the Windows NT Version 3.51 release. DirectX's first public appearance was in the August 96 release of the MSDN. Both these APIs provide quite a lot of functionality in common, but the way this functionality is achieved is quite different. In this chapter and the next, we take as an example the development of two programs that use OpenGL and Direct3D respectively to display 3D models recorded in the file format of the 3D Studio package.

An application developer targeting Windows has very little choice other than to write the application in C or C++ and, while there are still a few vendors offering C/C++ compilers, Microsoft's Visual C++ has become for all practical purposes the only development tool for 3D graphics application programs. This does not mean the application has to be developed in C++, but the Application and Class "Wizards" in Visual C++ make for rapid creation of an application using the MFC (Microsoft Foundation Classes).

Two approaches may be used to develop a Windows application in C/C++:

1. Follow a basic template program that calls directly to the Window's Application Programming Interface (API) functions as described in the Software Development Kit (SDK). Such a template will exhibit the core features of message loop, Window Class, and message handling function. The API functions are provided in a set of libraries that are implemented as *dynamic link libraries* (DLL's). Most of the DLLs that an application will use are components of the operating system itself. `SHELL32.DLL`, `GDI32.DLL` and `USER32.DLL` are examples of these components. The SDK also includes a large number of "header" files which define constants and provide prototypes for the myriad of API functions.

2. Use the Microsoft Foundation Class (MFC) library. It provides a framework for constructing programs by deriving classes from those that are part of the MFC. It includes suitable default processing so that an application program can have quite a sophisticated user interface with only minimal effort on the part of the programmer.

These approaches present code that looks very different to the programmer. An application based on calls to functions in the SDK libraries has an entry point in the conventional **C** language sense, the `WinMain()` function. Many books provide a concise introduction to programs written for Windows using this approach including the link between code modules, resources, and libraries. The `WinMain()` function performs the following three tasks:

1. Register a Windows class (not to be confused with a C++ class). Each Window class has an associated function that acts upon the messages dispatched to any window of that class. There is no practical limit to the number of windows for each class. One window is designated as the **main** window.

2. Create one or more visible windows of that class and go into a loop to check for and dispatch *messages* to the appropriate window function.

3. When a *quit* message is received by the program's main window, the loop is broken and the program exits.

In programs that use the MFC library, the main elements of a Windows application are hidden inside the library classes. The code for handling messages, registering *Windows classes*, and performing any other necessary task is automatically included. The programmer need only write *handler functions* for messages that are needed by the program, such as the press of a mouse button or in response to a menu command. These functions are members of C++ classes derived from the base MFC classes.

The MFC is based on the "Object Orientated" programming model as defined in the **C++** language. Each program is represented by an object, called an *Application Object*; this has a *Document* associated with it and one or more *views* of the document. It is up to the programmer to decide what information is recorded about the document and how that is processed. The MFC offers built-in classes to help process the document, for example, reading or writing it to disk files. It is also the responsibility of the application to draw into the view(s) window whatever aspect of the document it wishes to display. In the context of the MFC a document can be as diverse as a text file, a JPEG picture, or a 3D polygonal CAD model.

Perhaps the main advantage of the MFC is that it provides a number of detailed user interface objects, for example, dockable toolbars, tooltips, and status information with virtually no extra work on the part of the programmer. However *nothing is for free*; the documentation for the MFC is extensive and it takes quite a while to become familiar with the facilities offered by it. The complexity of the MFC has reached such a stage that it is more or less essential to use an integrated development environment such as that provided by Visual C++ to help you get a basic application up and running. The so-called Application and Class Wizards, which are nothing more than sophisticated code generating tools, make the construction of a Windows application relatively painless. For more information on the use of the MFC and Visual C++ programming in general, see [4] or [5].

The example code that accompanies Chapters 10 and 11 was produced using Visual C++. The OpenGL libraries first appeared with Windows 95 (OEM service release 2) and Windows NT Version 3.51 and therefore the codes can be used on machines running these or later versions of the operating system. The code is presented in the form of a number of "snapshots" (copies of all the files in the project directory and its subdirectories) taken at various stages in the development of the applications. This includes the Project, Makefile, and Class Wizard files.

10.1 The Example Application

Before we start writing any code let's look at the finished example and examine its functionality. This can be done by executing the file GL3D.EXE in directory GL3D. A few sample models (the files with filename extension .3DS) are provided

Figure 10.1.   The appearance of a basic Microsoft Foundation Class (MFC) application.

in the same directory. When the program starts it presents a conventional MFC style application interface, with Window/Menu/Toolbar/Statusbar (Figure 10.1). The status bar provides an immediate instruction as to what to do, and when the mouse pointer passes over a button in the toolbar or a menu is browsed, it gives an indication of the function of the command.

> *Note that you cannot execute GL3D.EXE from the command prompt in Windows 95 because a message "Bad Pixel Format" will appear. You must run it from the Run command on the Taskbar or possibly create a desktop shortcut.*

The development of the GL3D.EXE example will occur in a number of stages:

1. Build a standard MFC application.

2. Convert the **View** class window from a standard window to one with OpenGL capability.

3. Modify the **Document** class to read the 3D model from the .3DS file and build lists of vertex and facet data structures in memory. These lists will be used by functions to *draw* the model using OpenGL procedure calls [6].

4. Add a function that will draw a view of the model when requested by Windows. The use of an OpenGL Display List [7] will give the fastest response.

5. Accommodate user interaction such as moving the viewpoint and positioning the model so that it may be examined in close up. Customize the program: add a special mouse cursor, update the *About* dialog box, modified menu, toolbar, and messages.

6. Change the application to support the Multi-Document interface so that several models can be examined simultaneously.

There are a very large number of ways in which the application could be extended further; for example, support could be added to display the image maps which the 3DS format supports.

We will now examine the stages of development in greater detail. A copy of the state of the project after each stage is given in a set of directories GL3D_x where "x" is either 0, 1, 2, 3, 4, or 5.

10.1.1 A Basic MFC Application

In Visual C++ a basic MFC application is established by a few simple steps using what is called the Application Wizard (AppWizard). This is a tool that is part of the integrated development environment of Visual C++, and it helps a program designer to construct a basic application very quickly using question and answer dialogs. To create the application by hand would take somewhat longer, but the result should be the same. Any edition of Visual C++ Version 4 or above can be used to build the applications.

The project in directory G13D_0 was created with the following properties:

1. The project is given the name **GL3D**; this is entered into Visual C++'s AppWizard which bases the class names it creates on these four characters.

2. A single document application.

3. No database support is required.

4. No OLE support is needed.

5. The default file type associated with the application is set to be the "3DS" file type. The last Wizard dialog gives the opportunity to review the class names that will be used and change them if necessary. The GL3D_x examples use the class names CGL3DApp for the application, CMainFrame for the frame window, CGL3DDoc for the document, and CGL3DView for the OpenGL window. These classes will be discussed in detail below.

After the question and answer exchange with AppWizard is complete, all the code for a fully functioning windows application will be produced automatically.

Before compiling and executing this first stage in the development of our
example project, we need to remove the automatic registration of all .3DS files
so that they are not associated with the GL3D application. This is done by
removing one line of code from the InitInstance() function of the main
application class CGL3DApp.

```
    .
    .
    .
// Enable DDE Execute open
EnableShellOpen();

// Remove the next line to avoid registering 3DS files for the this app.
RegisterShellFileTypes(TRUE);  ////////////

// Parse command line for standard shell commands, DDE, file open
CCommandLineInfo cmdInfo;
    .
    .
    .
```

*All MFC applications are based on a single object of the application class; its
constructor fulfills the C++ startup functions (equivalent to* WinMain()*).
In GL3D the object is declared globally by the following:*

```
///////////////////////////////////////////////////////////////////////////
// The one and only CGL3DApp object

CGL3DApp theApp;
///////////////////////////////////////////////////////////////////////////
```

which is to be found near the start of the file GL3D.CPP.

CGL3DApp *is a class derived from the MFC class* **CWinApp**. *The* InitInstance()
*function mentioned above must be overridden in all applications, and it is
this function that is responsible for creating the Document and any associated
Views. In GL3D this is done by:*

```
    .
    .
CSingleDocTemplate* pDocTemplate;
//
// Make a document template
//
pDocTemplate = new CSingleDocTemplate(
   IDR_MAINFRAME,              // Identifier used for loading resources
```

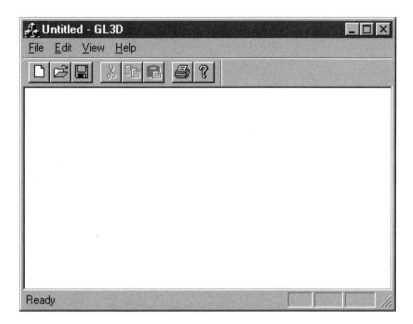

Figure 10.2.   The appearance of a basic framework application after creation with the Class Wizard.

```
                                        // associated with the application
        RUNTIME_CLASS(CGL3DDoc),    // Create a document of class CGL3DDoc
        RUNTIME_CLASS(CMainFrame),  // The main SDI frame window
        RUNTIME_CLASS(CGL3DView));  // Create a view (inside the frame) of
                                        // class CGL3DView
    AddDocTemplate(pDocTemplate);   // Call the function to make an MFC
                                        // application from the Template
    .
    .
    .
```

If you build and run the GL3D_0 application you will get the standard appearance illustrated in Figure 10.2.

10.1.2   Adding Support for OpenGL

Windows has a basic strategy that it uses for drawing with OpenGL functions into a window. A special structure (a *PixelFormat descriptor*) is used to describe some properties that the OpenGL window will have. The most useful property is the use of a double-buffered approach to rendering. Double buffering uses two drawing buffers (blocks of memory); one is visible while the OpenGL functions are drawing into the other. When drawing is complete the buffers are swapped to make the new drawing visible. Without double buffering the image would appear to flicker and on a slow computer the rendering of each facet would be quite noticeable.

The PixelFormat descriptor is used to create a special "Rendering Context" which is needed for drawing in the OpenGL window. A rendering context is used in an analogous way to the device context that is used in the conventional response to the WM_PAINT message.

Very few of the OpenGL functions are system dependent. Those with names beginning with the prefix **wgl**, e.g., wglCreateContext(...), are responsible for implementing Windows-specific requirements for OpenGL. The remainder, such as glEnable(...), glLoadIdentity(...), and gluPerspective(...), etc., are used for drawing, setting up view positions, and lighting. These functions begin with the prefix **gl** or **glu** (for the utility library).

To add support for OpenGL to our MFC application requires some modification to the code of the message handlers which are member functions of the **CGL3DView** class:

1. PreCreateWindow(...)

2. OnCreate(..)

3. OnDraw(..)

4. OnSize(...)

5. OnDestroy(...)

The *PreCreateWindow()* handler

OpenGL requires that the window to which it is attached has the WS_CLIPCHILDREN and WS_CLIPSIBLINGS styles; in the MFC this is done in the PreCreateWindow() function as follows:

```
BOOL CGL3DView::PreCreateWindow(CREATESTRUCT& cs)
{
    // OpenGL needs to have the following window class styles
    // added to the basic WS_CHILD etc. styles. This must be
    // done before the window and its associated OpenGL pixel
    // format and drawing contexts are created.
    //
    // Modify the CREATESTRUCT structure member "cs" ready for
    // creation of the OpenGL window.

        cs.style |= WS_CLIPCHILDREN | WS_CLIPSIBLINGS;
    //
```

```
                    // call the base class
                    //
                        return CView::PreCreateWindow(cs);
            }
```

The Application Wizard automatically creates rudimentary code fragments for
the PreCreateWindow() and OnDraw() handlers, but the other lines listed
above must be added manually or by using the Class Wizard.

The OnCreate(...) function

The OnCreate() function is called after the window associated with the
CGL3DView class has been created but before it is drawn. It is in this function that the pixel format is specified and rendering context created.

We can also use this function to establish a viewpoint, the viewing volume in
which the model will be drawn, and some lighting conditions:

```
int CGL3DView::OnCreate(LPCREATESTRUCT lpCreateStruct)
{
    //
    // Make sure the base class handler completes successfully
    //
    if (CView::OnCreate(lpCreateStruct) == -1)return -1;
    //
    // Add the OpenGL initiation code. This is in two parts;
    //
    // 1)A standard process for all Windows applications that
    //   use OpenGL.
    // 2)Lighting and Camera positions are established for this
    //   specific application.
    //////////////////////////////////////////////////////////////
    // First the standard setup:
    //
    // The desired format of pixels in the display
    //
    PIXELFORMATDESCRIPTOR pfd = {
    sizeof(PIXELFORMATDESCRIPTOR),    // size of this structure
      1,                             // version number
      PFD_DRAW_TO_WINDOW |           // supports drawing in a window
      PFD_SUPPORT_OPENGL |           // supports OpenGL
      PFD_DOUBLEBUFFER,              // double buffered OpenGL
      PFD_TYPE_RGBA,                 // RGB and Alpha type
      24,                            // 24-bit color depth
      0, 0, 0, 0, 0, 0,              // color bits ignored
      0,                             // no alpha buffer
      0,                             // shift bit ignored
```

```
    0,                              // no accumulation buffer
    0, 0, 0, 0,                     // accum bits ignored
    32,                             // 32-bit z-buffer
    0,                              // no stencil buffer
    0,                              // no auxiliary buffer
    PFD_MAIN_PLANE,                 // main layer
    0,                              // reserved
    0, 0, 0                         // layer masks ignored
  };
//
// Create a device context that will be associated with the
// OpenGL window. Although this will not be directly used
// after initialization it must not be deleted until the
// program terminates.
//
m_pDC = new CClientDC(this);
ASSERT(m_pDC != NULL);
//
// Get a pixel format that is as close a match as possible to
// the desired format.
//
int pixelformat = ::ChoosePixelFormat(m_pDC->GetSafeHdc(),&pfd);
if(pixelformat == 0)AfxMessageBox("Bad Format Choose");
//
// Apply this pixel format to the device context associated
// with the OpenGL window.
//
BOOL success=::SetPixelFormat(m_pDC->GetSafeHdc(),pixelformat,&pfd);
if(!success)AfxMessageBox("Bad Pixel Format");
//
// Get the pixel format that was set and the information about
// it, returned in the "pfd" pixelformatdescriptor.
//
int n = ::GetPixelFormat(m_pDC->GetSafeHdc());
//
// The :: indicates that these OpenGL specific function calls
// are global functions from a C language library. This application
// is written using C++ syntax
//
::DescribePixelFormat(m_pDC->GetSafeHdc(),n,sizeof(pfd),&pfd);
//
// Create a palette associated with the OpenGL window. It is
// not really necessary on display adapters that support Hi-color
// or True-color.
//
CreateRGBPalette();
//
// Create the Windows OpenGL rendering context that is used by
// OpenGL to render into the Device context associated with the
// window where the drawing will appear.
```

```
//
m_hRC=::wglCreateContext(m_pDC->GetSafeHdc());
//
// Make this context the current one for drawing.
//
::wglMakeCurrent(m_pDC->GetSafeHdc(),m_hRC);
//
//////////////////////////////////////////////////////////////////
//
// The remainder of this function completes the second part of
// the initialization.
//
// Build a viewport for a perspective view from (0,0,0)
// along the "Z" (depth) axis with a 45 degree field of
// view that fills the viewing window.
//
// Entering GL_PROJECTION mode implies that OpenGL commands
// apply to the Camera.
//
::glMatrixMode(GL_PROJECTION);
GetClientRect(&m_oldrect);
if(m_oldrect.bottom < 1)m_oldrect.bottom=1;
//
// The aspect ratio is a required parameter for the utility
// library function that establishes a perspective view. It is
// the ratio of the width to the height of the viewport (i.e.,
// the window).
//
GLfloat aspect = (GLfloat) m_oldrect.right /
                 (GLfloat)m_oldrect.bottom;
//
// Set the viewpoint to be at (0,0,0) looking along the -ve
// Z axis with a 45 degree field of view through a window of
// aspect ratio "aspect". OpenGL will draw any surfaces that
// lie between the front and back clipping plane and inside
// the pyramidal field of view as illustrated in the text below.
//
::gluPerspective(45.0f,aspect,m_near_plane,m_far_plane);
//
// Set the background color and that the surface material
// will be lit on both sides. Two-sided lighting will allow
// any models that have no definite inside or outside to be
// rendered correctly.
//
// Entering GL_MODELVIEW mode implies that OpenGL commands
// apply to any Vertices Facets etc. that describe the model
// being visualized.
//
::glMatrixMode( GL_MODELVIEW );
::glLoadIdentity();
```

```
::glClearDepth(1.0f);
::glEnable(GL_DEPTH_TEST);
::glClearColor(m_Red,m_Green,m_Blue,1.0f);
::glColorMaterial(GL_FRONT_AND_BACK,GL_AMBIENT_AND_DIFFUSE |
                                    GL_SPECULAR);
::glLightModeli(GL_LIGHT_MODEL_TWO_SIDE,GL_TRUE);
//
// Enable a "white" light positioned in front of the camera.
// The intensity of the light on a surface falls off the further
// it is from the light source. There are three components to
// illumination: ambient, diffuse, and specular; in OpenGL they
// can be specified independently.
//
GLfloat d[]={1.0f,1.0f,1.0f,1.0f};    // white diffuse light
GLfloat a[]={0.1f,0.1f,0.1f,1.0f};    // small ambient value
GLfloat s[]={1.0f,1.0f,1.0f,1.0f};    // white specular highlight
::glEnable(GL_LIGHT0);
::glLightfv(GL_LIGHT0,GL_DIFFUSE,d);
::glLightfv(GL_LIGHT0,GL_AMBIENT,a);
::glLightfv(GL_LIGHT0,GL_SPECULAR,s);
GLfloat p[]={0.0f,0.0f,1.0f,1.0f};
::glLightfv(GL_LIGHT0,GL_POSITION,p);
::glLightf(GL_LIGHT0,GL_LINEAR_ATTENUATION,0.05f);
::glLightf(GL_LIGHT0,GL_QUADRATIC_ATTENUATION,0.02f);
return 0;
}
```

Figure 10.3 shows the relationship between the field of view, aspect ratio, and clipping planes.

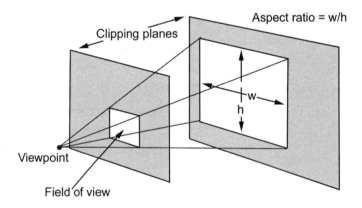

Figure 10.3.   The field of view and clipping planes for perspective drawing.

The *OnSize(...)* function

When the view window is resized its aspect ratio will probably change and, consequently, it is necessary to recalculate the settings for the viewpoint and establish a new *Projection* matrix.

```
void CGL3DView::OnSize(UINT nType, int cx, int cy)
{
    //
    // call the base class handler
    //
    CView::OnSize(nType, cx, cy);
    //
    // If the window is resized then the viewport has to be
    // rebuilt to accommodate the new size.
    //
    RECT rect;
    GetClientRect(&rect);
    ::glViewport(0, 0, rect.right, rect.bottom);
    m_oldrect.right = rect.right;
    m_oldrect.bottom = rect.bottom;
    //
    // Switch into Projection mode to set up a new viewing transformation
    //
    ::glMatrixMode(GL_PROJECTION);
    ::glLoadIdentity();
    if(m_oldrect.bottom < 1)m_oldrect.bottom=1;
    GLfloat aspect = (GLfloat) m_oldrect.right /
                     (GLfloat)m_oldrect.bottom;
    ::gluPerspective( 45.0f, aspect, m_near_plane, m_far_plane);
    //
    // Switch back to Modelview mode for any other drawing
    //
    ::glMatrixMode( GL_MODELVIEW );
    ::glLoadIdentity();
    RedrawWindow();
}
```

The *OnDestroy(...)* function

When the viewing window is closed, the device and resource contexts must be released. This is not so important in a single document MFC application because the window will only be destroyed when the application is terminated. However, in a multi-document MFC application, view windows are created and destroyed as each document is opened and closed and resources associated with a view window should be released, otherwise they will eventually become exhausted.

```
void CGL3DView::OnDestroy()
{
    CView::OnDestroy();
    //
    // Delete the OpenGL rendering and device contexts and if the
    // palette has been changed restore the old palette as well.
    //
    // Get the current rendering context  (This will need to be changed
    // for a MDI app.)
    //
    HGLRC hrc=::wglGetCurrentContext();
    //
    // Make NO context current
    //
    ::wglMakeCurrent(NULL,NULL);
    //
    // Delete the contexts
    //
    if(hrc != NULL)::wglDeleteContext(hrc);
    if(m_pOldPalette)m_pDC->SelectPalette(m_pOldPalette,FALSE);
    if(m_pDC != NULL)delete m_pDC;
}
```

The *OnDraw(...)* function

The OnDraw function is augmented so that it carries out the following tasks:

1. Clear the surface to be drawn on, both the picture itself (the back buffer) and the Z buffer.

2. Render into the back buffer.

   Note: *At this stage of application development* **no** *drawing has yet become visible.*

3. Flush the drawing pipeline.

4. And finally swap the front and back buffers so that the drawing in the back buffer becomes visible.

```
void CGL3DView::OnDraw(CDC* pDC)
{
        CGL3DDoc* pDoc = GetDocument();
        ASSERT_VALID(pDoc);
    //
    // clear the OpenGL window to the background color and
    // set the Z buffer to infinity.
    ::glClear(GL_COLOR_BUFFER_BIT | GL_DEPTH_BUFFER_BIT);
    //
```

```
// The drawing code will be added here ....
//
::glFinish();  // Finish the OpenGL drawing
//
// Flush the OpenGL drawing pipeline to make sure
// that all the drawing commands have been executed.
//
::glFlush();
//
// A double-buffered technique is used to prevent an
// unpleasant flicker. Two display buffers are used for drawing.
// At any one time only one is visible; the other is the one
// into which the drawing commands (above) draw.
// When an image is complete the buffers are swapped so that
// the new image becomes visible.
//
//
// Get a device context associated the OpenGL window
//
::HDC hDC = ::wglGetCurrentDC();
::SwapBuffers(hDC);
}
```

The view class *creator* function

This function sets default values for the member variables of the view class. The background color of the OpenGL window is one example.

```
CGL3DView::CGL3DView()
{
    //
    // Initialize the OpenGL member variables for the clipping
    // planes and a Gray color for the window background.
    //
    m_near_plane=1.0f;
    m_far_plane=800.0f;
    m_Red=0.5f;
    m_Green=0.5f;
    m_Blue=0.5f;
}
```

When a 3DS model is loaded it will be scaled so that it is centered at 4.0 units distance from the camera and scaled so that it just fits in the viewing frustum. The clipping planes are positioned so that the model is clipped by the near plane before it gets right on top of the camera. The far plane is set so that the model may be moved away from the camera.

10.1.3   Reading the 3DS Data File

With the view class' window **CGL3DView** modified to accommodate OpenGL
rendering, the next stage in the development of GL3D is to modify the document
class **CGL3DDoc** so that it extracts the vertex and facet information from a 3DS
file. The data will be recorded in an array of vertices and facet structures residing
in memory. The project files for this stage of development are given in directory
GL3D_2.

Data types for vertices, facets, and vectors need to be defined, and these take
the form:

```
typedef GLfloat vector[3];

typedef struct tagVERTEX {
  GLfloat p[3];                // position of the vertex
  GLfloat x,y;                 // surface mapping coordinates
} VERTEX;

typedef struct tagFACET {
  long V[3];                   // vertex identifier for triangular facet
  unsigned char color[3];      // color of facet
  unsigned char MapID;         // identify the image map
  BOOL Map;                    // facet is covered by image map
  BOOL Smooth;                 // facet is to have Gouraud shading applied
} FACET;
```

This structure information is placed in the **CGL3DDoc** class' header file
GL3DDOC.H and associated member variables are added to the class as follows:

```
class CGL3DDoc : public CDocument
{
//
// Add the following members and functions.
//
public:

// Member variables of appropriate data types

VERTEX   *m_MainVp;    // List of vertices in the model
FACET    *m_MainFp;    // List of facets in the model
long     m_Nvert,      // Number of vertices in the model
         m_Nface,      // Number of facets in the model
.
. Other class members and function prototypes go here
.
.
```

```
// Generated message map functions
protected:
        //{{AFX_MSG(CGL3DDoc)
        //}}AFX_MSG
        DECLARE_MESSAGE_MAP()
};
```

In addition to basic geometry, other data describing surface textures is included in the 3DS file. Of particular note are the surface textures, some of which will involve image mapping. Although we will not make use of any mapped textures in the OpenGL examples, they will be read from the file and recorded in data memory data structures.

Reading and parsing the 3DS file is accomplished by the function:

```
void Load3dsObject(char *FileName);
```

which is called from the OnOpenDocument(..) **CD3DDoc** class function.

```
BOOL CGL3DDoc::OnOpenDocument(LPCTSTR lpszPathName)
{
    //
    // This handler is added to open the 3DS document. Note
    // that the MFC serialize mechanism is not used in
    // this example.
    //
        if (!CDocument::OnOpenDocument(lpszPathName))
                return FALSE;
    //
    // Remove the old model if one exists.
    //
    FreeObject();
    //
    // Call the function to load the model from the 3DS data file
    // into Vertex/Facet arrays in memory.
    //
        Load3dsObject((char *)lpszPathName);
    //
    // At this stage of development the model is NOT displayed; a
    // simple MessageBox provides some information.
    //
    char txt[255];
    sprintf(txt,"Model data: %ld Vertices %ld Facets",Nvert,Nface);
    AfxMessageBox(txt);
    //
    return TRUE;
}
```

The `OnOpenDocument(..)` function makes use of another function, `FreeObject()`, which releases any memory resources used for vertex and facet data. The MFC serialization mechanism is unsuitable for reading the 3DS file and it is ignored. The final act of the open document handler is to report the number of facets and vertices read from the file.

The layout of the information in a 3DS file is based on a number of *chunks*. Each chunk is identified by a two-byte header identifying its contents and a long four-byte word giving its size. To see how this is used by the `Load3dsObject(...)`, examine the file `GL3DDOC.CPP` in directory `GL3D_2`.

Finally for this stage in product development, initial values for member variables of class **CGL3DDoc** are set in its constructor:

```
CGL3DDoc::CGL3DDoc()
{
    //
    // Initialize the variables - no vertices, no facets
    //
    m_MainVp=NULL;
    m_MainFp=NULL;
    m_Nvert=0;
    m_Nface=0;
}
```

10.1.4 Rendering the Model Using OpenGL

After the model data is loaded to memory and in a form that we can use for calling OpenGL drawing functions, the next stage (project GL3D_3) in development is to render the model. The memory data structures consist of an array of triangular facets, and therefore it is appropriate to use the following OpenGL drawing sequence:

```
//
::glBegin(GL_TRIANGLES);
//
// Draw the triangular facets by calling glVertex() three times for
// each facet in the model.
//
::glEnd();
//
```

To shade the facets in the model so that lighting effects work correctly, normal vectors to the surface at each vertex must be determined. Surface normal information is not recorded in the data file but it can be easily calculated. In those parts of the model that appear smooth, the normals of several facets must be averaged and for this reason it is appropriate to calculate surface normals prior to rendering the model.

The final and most important issue to consider is whether to place the drawing code in the **CGL3DView** or **CGL3DDoc** classes. We want our views to be drawn as quickly as possible and this may be achieved by using a Display List. A display list is a feature of OpenGL that allows a sequence of OpenGL commands to be partially processed and stored in a form that makes the execution of the drawing commands more rapid. It is a little analogous to the process of compilation of high level computer codes written in C, for example, into assembly language before they are executed. An OpenGL display list can be processed by other OpenGL commands to, for example, change the viewpoint of a scene. The Display List will be built from the model's facet and vertex data and will be viewpoint-independent. A specific view of the model can be generated by calling the Display List after executing commands to move, pivot the model, or change the position of the viewpoint. For this reason we will place the code to build the display list in the **CGL3DDoc** class and put in a few instructions to call it from the **OnDraw()** function of the **CGL3DView** class.

The following modifications to the **CGL3DDoc** class add an integer member variable to record the identity of the display list and some prototypes for functions which build it:

```
.
.
// GL3D_3 member
GLint listID;          // Identity of the OpenGL display list.
//
// GL3D_3 functions used to build a display list from the Vertex/Facet
//data structures.
//
BOOL same_color(unsigned char *color); // is the "color" the same as the
                                        // last time this function was called
BOOL Normalize(vector x);               // normalize the vector "x"
BOOL GetNormal(vector x, vector y, vector z,
            GLfloat *n);                // Given three vertices that lie in
                                        // a plane calculate the surface
                                        // normal.
GLfloat GetScaleValue(vector c);        // Calculate the center of the
                                        // model and a scaling factor to
                                        // force the model to fill the
                                        // viewing volume.
void MakeGLlist(void);                  // Make the OpenGL Display List.
.
.
```

Function `MakeGLlist()` builds the Display List. It is called from the `OnOpenDocument()` handler immediately after the file is read. `MakeGLlist()`'s

first task is to find the scaling factors which allow all models to fit inside a fixed
viewing volume. It then proceeds to build a list of normal vectors to the surface
at each vertex:

```
void CGL3DDoc::MakeGLlist(void)
{
 //
 // Make the OpenGL Display List
 //
 BOOL Mapped=FALSE;
 GLfloat scale;
 GLfloat x,y,z,n[3],color[4],
         glos_color[]={1.0f,1.0f,1.0f,1.0f},
         matt_color[]={0.0f,0.0f,0.0f,0.0f},
         shiny[]={120.0f},dot;
 FACET *fp;
 VERTEX *v,*v1,*v2,*v0;
 vector c,*nv;
 int i,j,Vi,V[3];
 if(Nface == 0)return;
 //
 // Calculate scaling values for this model
 //
 scale=(GLfloat)GetScaleValue(c);
 //
 // Reserve space for an array of vectors that will be
 // calculated for use by OpenGL to implement Gouraud shading.
 //
 if((nv=(vector *)Malloc(sizeof(vector)*Nvert)) == NULL)
 {
   return;
 }
 //
 // The vertices in the model must have a normal vector in order that
 // the OpenGL Gouraud algorithm can determine the correct shading
 // within the facets. This applies to Diffuse and Specular lighting
 // conditions.
 //
 // To determine the vertex normals each facet is tested and the normal
 // vector at each vertex of the facet is averaged with the normal
 // vector for the facet. This will force vertex normals to take on an
 // average of the surface normals of any facet that adjoins it.
 //
 for(i=0;i<Nvert;i++)
   nv[i][0]=nv[i][1]=nv[i][2]=0.0f;
 //
 // Go through the list of facets and with each of facet "i"'s vertices
 // average the normal.
 //
 fp=MainFp;
```

```
for(i=0;i<Nface;i++)
{
  V[0]=fp->V[0]; V[1]=fp->V[1]; V[2]=fp->V[2];
  v0=(MainVp+V[0]); v1=(MainVp+V[1]); v2=(MainVp+V[2]);
  //
  // If the facet is to be smoothed and its normal can be determined
  // proceed to average it with the normals to vertices "V[j]".
  //
  if(fp->Smooth && GetNormal(v0->p,v1->p,v2->p,n))
    {
    for(j=0;j<3;j++)
      {
      dot=Dot(nv[V[j]],n);
      //
      // These tests are used to ensure that adjacent facets have
      // consistent normals. 3DS always build models with consistent
      // normals but some other packages don't always do this.
      //
      if(fabs(dot) < 1.e-10)
        {
          //
          // In the cases where the vertex normal lies in the plane
          // of the facet we can't determine which is the front and
          // which is the back of the facet, so the vertex normal is
          // just assigned to the facets normal.
          //
          nv[V[j]][0]=n[0];
          nv[V[j]][1]=n[1];
          nv[V[j]][2]=n[2];
        }
      else if(dot >  0.5)
        {
          //
          // The facet faces forward so "ADD" in the facet normal to
          // the vertex normal.
          //
          VecSum(nv[V[j]],n,nv[V[j]]);
          Normalize(nv[V[j]]);
        }
      else if(dot < -0.5)
        {
          //
          // The facet faces forward so "SUBTRACT" in the facet normal to
          // the vertex normal.
          //
          VecSub(nv[V[j]],n,nv[V[j]]);
          Normalize(nv[V[j]]);
        }
      //
      // Any remaining cases are too ambiguous to use so they are
```

```
          // ignored.
      }
   }
   fp++;
}
```

At this point in the document class code the Display List is created. If a list already exists it is deleted and a new one opened:

```
if(listID > 0)
{
  ::glDeleteLists(listID,listID);
  listID=0;
}
//
// Start a new list, give it the identity "1"
//
color[3]=1.0f;
listID=1;
::glNewList(listID,GL_COMPILE);
```

With the display list open we draw the vertices and surface normals and give any commands to set facet color or material attribute as follows:

```
//
// Enable the OpenGL attributes to allow the surface to be
// colored and have a shiny "specular" material appearance.
//
::glEnable(GL_COLOR_MATERIAL);
//
// Begin the construction of the triangular facets
//
::glBegin(GL_TRIANGLES);
//
// Set the properties for specular reflection.
//
::glMaterialfv(GL_FRONT_AND_BACK,GL_SHININESS,shiny);
::glMaterialfv(GL_FRONT_AND_BACK,GL_SPECULAR,glos_color);
fp=MainFp;
for(i=0;i<Nface;i++,fp++)
{
  //
  // Process each triangular facet
  //
  v0=(MainVp+fp->V[0]);
  v1=(MainVp+fp->V[1]);
  v2=(MainVp+fp->V[2]);
  //
```

```
// Only give the OpenGL commands to change the surface color
// if it has changed; this speeds up the OpenGL drawing and
// reduces the size of the Display list.
//
 if(!same_color(fp->color))
 {
    color[0]=(GLfloat)fp->color[0]/255.0f;
    color[1]=(GLfloat)fp->color[1]/255.0f;
    color[2]=(GLfloat)fp->color[2]/255.0f;
    ::glColor4fv(color);
 }
 //
 // If a valid normal vector for the facet can be found then
 // add the facet to the display list. In OpenGL a triangular facet
 // is specified by drawing the three vertices at its corners.
 //
 if(GetNormal(v0->p,v1->p,v2->p,n))
 {
    for(j=0;j<3;j++)
    {
      //
      // Each vertex is moved so that the model appears in the
      // center of the display volume. It is also scaled so that
      // the whole model is visible in the display volume.
      //
      Vi=fp->V[j]; v=(MainVp+Vi);
      x=((GLfloat)(v->p[0]-c[0]))*scale;
      y=((GLfloat)(v->p[1]-c[1]))*scale;
      z=((GLfloat)(v->p[2]-c[2]))*scale;
      if(fp->Smooth)
      {
        //
        // If the facet is smooth (Gouraud shading) then the normal
        // vector from the vertex normals list is used (with
        // appropriate changes to take account of inside/outside
        // problems).
        //
        dot=Dot(nv[Vi],n);
        if(fabs(dot) < 0.5)
          ::glNormal3f(n[0],n[2],-n[1]);
        else if(dot  < 0.0)
          ::glNormal3f(-nv[Vi][0],-nv[Vi][2], nv[Vi][1]);
        else
          ::glNormal3f( nv[Vi][0], nv[Vi][2],-nv[Vi][1]);
      }
      else
      {
        //
        // If the facet is NOT smooth then use the facet normal
        // vector for each of the three vertices.
```

```
          //
            ::glNormal3f( n[0], n[2],-n[1]);
          }
          //
          // Draw the vertex. Note the  (x,z,-y) parameters and the
          // (n[0],n[2],-n[1]) parameters for the surface normal above.
          // This ordering is needed because OpenGL uses "Y" as the
          // up direction and 3DS uses "Z" as up, and OpenGL uses a left-
          // handed coordinate system while 3DS uses a right-handed one.
          //
            ::glVertex3f(x,z,-y);
        }
    }
}
//
// Terminate the creation of TRIANGULAR facets
//
::glEnd();
::glDisable(GL_COLOR_MATERIAL);
```

Now the Display List is complete; it only remains to close it, free any temporary memory assigned, and return:

```
::glEndList();
Free(nv);
}
```

The Display List encapsulates all the OpenGL commands to render the model without taking into account any specific point of view. To render a specific view the display list is packaged inside calls to OpenGL functions that specify an angle of rotation for the model and lighting conditions.

This code is added to CD3DView::OnDraw() as follows:

```
void CGL3DView::OnDraw(CDC* pDC)
{
        CGL3DDoc* pDoc = GetDocument();
        ASSERT_VALID(pDoc);
    //
    // Clear the OpenGL window to the background color and
    // set the Z buffer to infinity.
    //
        ::glClear(GL_COLOR_BUFFER_BIT | GL_DEPTH_BUFFER_BIT);
    //
    // Set the shading mode to Gouraud shading
    //
```

```
::glShadeModel(GL_SMOOTH);
//
// Move the model into view by translating it along the
// Z-axis away from the camera. The model is pivoted so
// that an oblique view will be drawn.
//
::glPushMatrix();                    // Record any transformations.
::glLoadIdentity();                  // Build the transformation
::glTranslatef(0.0f, 0.0f, -5.0f);  // to pivot the model so that one
::glRotatef(45.0f,1.0f,0.0f,0.0f);  // gets an oblique view.
::glRotatef(45.0f+180.0f,0.0f,1.0f,0.0f);
//
// If document has a valid display list draw it after
// enabling the lighting.
if(pDoc->listID > 0){
  ::glEnable(GL_LIGHTING);
  ::glCallList(pDoc->listID);
  ::glDisable(GL_LIGHTING);
}
::glPopMatrix();
//
::glFinish();  // Finish the OpenGL drawing
//
// Flush the OpenGL drawing pipeline to make sure
// that all the drawing commands have been executed.
//
::glFlush();
//
// A double-buffered technique is used to prevent an
// unpleasant flicker. Two display buffers are used for drawing.
// At any one time only one is visible; the other is the one
// into which the drawing commands (above) draw.
// When an image is complete the buffers are swapped so that
// the new image becomes visible.
//
::HDC hDC = ::wglGetCurrentDC();
::SwapBuffers(hDC);
}
```

The fourth stage of project development is now complete; on execution, the result is a fixed view of the model: for example, that shown in Figure 10.4.

10.1.5   Refining the Application

Stage five of the project development will make the following changes:

1. Add variables to specify how far the camera viewpoint is from the model, and record angles of rotation of the model around two orthogonal axes running through its center.

Figure 10.4.   The project after completion of four stages in development (project GL3D_3).

The following variables are added to the **CGL3DView** class defined in the
file gl3dview.H:

```
.
GLfloat m_up_angle,                    // Look from above/below
        m_round_angle;                 // Look from left/right/front/back
GLfloat m_distance;                    // Distance from the camera.
.
```

2. Add handler functions for mouse and mouse button action so that the program gives its user interactive control over the orientation of the model.

3. Add handlers for keyboard key press/releases so that if the "spacebar" is
   pressed, the model will be moved towards/away from the camera when we
   drag the mouse to the left or right.

4. Modify the drawing code to transform the model so that it takes the *attitude*
   given by m_up_angle and m_round_angle.

5. Change the default cursor for the View window to a hand shape. Add an
   OnSetCursor(..) handler to change the cursor to a SIZEALL stock
   cursor when a key is held down.

6. Remove unused toolbar buttons and menu items and perhaps redesign the
   application icon.

Item 6 is accomplished by using the Visual C++ resource editor to remove the unwanted items.

Item 5 requires the addition of a cursor in the resource file and a modification to the **CMainFrame::OnCreate()** function as follows:

```
//
// Add the following line at the start of CMainFrame::OnCreate( )
//
// The icon resource is given the identifier IDI_ICON1 and it is loaded
// by calling the "LoadIcon" function which is a member of "CWinApp" class.
//
::SetClassLong(m_hWnd,GCL_HICON,(LONG)AfxGetApp()->LoadIcon(IDI\_ICON1));
//
```

To change the mouse cursor to a "sizing" cursor when a key is held down, we must add a handler for the WM_SETCURSOR, WM_KEYDOWN, and WM_KEYUP messages. A variable, m_bKey, acts as a toggle switch to indicate whether a key is down or up. Handler functions for these messages are added by Visual C++'s Class Wizard. The result of these changes is evident in the following code:

```
void CGL3DView::OnKeyDown(UINT nChar, UINT nRepCnt, UINT nFlags)
{
        m_bKey=TRUE;
    SetCursor(AfxGetApp()->LoadStandardCursor(IDC_SIZEALL));
        CView::OnKeyDown(nChar, nRepCnt, nFlags);
}

void CGL3DView::OnKeyUp(UINT nChar, UINT nRepCnt, UINT nFlags)
{
        m_bKey=FALSE;
        SetCursor(AfxGetApp()->LoadCursor(IDC_HAND));
        CView::OnKeyUp(nChar, nRepCnt, nFlags);
}

BOOL CGL3DView::OnSetCursor(CWnd* pWnd, UINT nHitTest, UINT message)
{
        if(m_bKey){
          SetCursor(AfxGetApp()->LoadStandardCursor(IDC_SIZEALL));
          return FALSE;
        }
        else return CView::OnSetCursor(pWnd, nHitTest, message);
}
```

Detection of mouse movement and button activity is supported through message handlers for the View class. For our example we want to use the mouse to move and rotate the model (item 2); this is accomplished by the following

handlers. A few variables and flags need to be added to the **CGL3DView class**
as follows:

```
int m_mx,m_my;                  // Keep record of mouse location
CPoint m_LastPoint;             // in its last position.
BOOL m_bCaptured;               // Mouse movement captured by view
                                // window. All messages are passed
                                // to the handlers for the view.
BOOL m_bKey;                    // Moving model away/towards camera
                                // if TRUE, otherwise rotating model.
```

When the **OnMouseMove()** handler is called, the distance moved by the mouse
in the interval since the last call is determined and this is converted to appropriate
values for the variables m_up_angle and m_round_angle. To draw the new
view the client area is invalidated.

The mouse handler functions are:

```
void CGL3DView::OnLButtonDown(UINT nFlags, CPoint point)
{
    //
    // Capture the movement of the mouse so that all messages get
    // processed by this window's handlers.
    //
    m_bCaptured=TRUE;
    SetCapture();
    m_mx=point.x;
    m_my=point.y;
    m_LastPoint=point;
    //
    //  Call base class handler
    //
    CView::OnLButtonDown(nFlags, point);
}

void CGL3DView::OnLButtonUp(UINT nFlags, CPoint point)
{
    //
    //  Release the message capture
    //
    m_bCaptured=FALSE;
    ReleaseCapture();
    //
    CView::OnLButtonUp(nFlags, point);
}

void CGL3DView::OnMouseMove(UINT nFlags, CPoint point)
```

```
    {
        if(m_bCaptured)
        {
          //
          // Determine new angles for the orientation of the model
          // depending on how much the mouse has moved since the
          // last Mouse move message.
          //
          m_mx=point.x - m_mx;
          m_my=point.y - m_my;
          m_LastPoint.x=point.x - m_LastPoint.x;
          m_LastPoint.y=point.y - m_LastPoint.y;
          RECT rc;
          GetClientRect(& rc);
          GLfloat dx=(GLfloat)m_mx/(GLfloat)(rc.right-rc.left);
          GLfloat dy=(GLfloat)m_my/(GLfloat)(rc.bottom-rc.top);
          //
          // If the "spacebar" is pressed then move the object away/towards
          // the camera.
          //
          if(m_bKey)
          {
            m_distance += dx*20.0f;
          }
          else
          {
            //
            // Otherwise change the model's orientation.
            //
            m_round_angle += dx * 360.0f;
            if(m_round_angle >  180.0f)m_round_angle -= 360.0f;
            if(m_round_angle < -180.0f)m_round_angle += 360.0f;
            m_up_angle += dy * 180.0f;
          }
          //
          // Draw the model to see the changes
          //
          Invalidate(FALSE);
          m_mx=point.x;
          m_my=point.y;
          m_LastPoint=point;
        }
        //
        // Call the base class
        //
        CView::OnMouseMove(nFlags, point);
    }
```

Version **GL3D_4** of the project is complete by modifying the `OnPaint(..)` handler to apply the translation and rotation transformations before the OpenGL Display List for the model is executed:

```
.
.  Modified Drawing code. Lines changed in GL3D_4 are indicated
.  by  <----
//
// Move the model into view by translating it along the
// Z-axis away from the camera. The model is pivoted so
// that an oblique view will be drawn.
//
::glPushMatrix();                      // Record any transformations.
::glLoadIdentity();                    // Build the transformation to
::glTranslatef(0.0f,                   // move the model away from camera.
               0.0f,                   // Note that this "precedes" any
               -5.0f+m_distance);      // rotational transformations. <----
//
// Rotate the model into position using the current setting of
// m_up_angle and m_round_angle. (m_round_angle is offset by
// 180 degrees so that the model faces the camera.)
//
::glRotatef(m_up_angle,1.0f,0.0f,0.0f);                          // <----
::glRotatef(m_round_angle+180.0f,0.0f,1.0f,0.0f);               // <----
//
.
.
```

The fifth stage of project development is now complete; on execution, the result is a user-adjustable view of the model: for example, that shown in Figure 10.5.

10.1.6   Viewing Several Models Simultaneously

The project (GL3D_4) is an application that uses OpenGL to display *one* view of *one* model in the applications window. Essentially we are working with a single document; i.e., each document refers to only one .3DS file. Windows has a standard, known as the Multidocument Interface (MDI), that lets one application display, modify, and view several documents of the same type simultaneously. In the context of our OpenGL application, this approach would allow us to view many 3DS models at the same time; we will use quite a bit of the OpenGL code from the project GL3D_4.

While it is possible to modify the **GL3D_4** project files to accommodate an MDI structure, it is easier to use the AppWizard to create a basic MDI application and copy the `GL3DVIEW.CPP`, `GL3DVIEW.H`, `GL3DDOC.CPP`, and `GL3DDOC.H` files from the **GL3D_4** directory. When creating the project we must take care to instruct AppWizard to use the same name for the classes as in

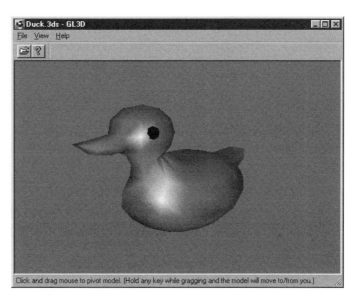

Figure 10.5. The project after completing five stages of development (project GL3D_4).

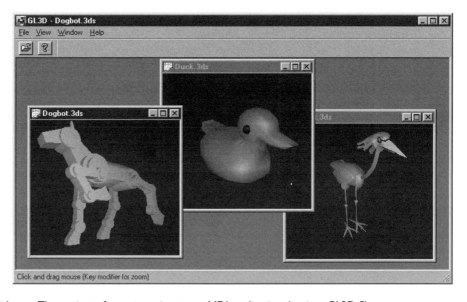

Figure 10.6. The project after conversion to an MDI application (project GL3D_5).

the Single Document Interface (SDI) projects. The MDI application has an extra class for the Child windows, CChildFrame, and in the InitInstance() function a Multidocument template object is created as follows:

```
// Register the application's document templates.  Document templates
// serve as the connection between documents, frame windows, and views.

CMultiDocTemplate* pDocTemplate;
pDocTemplate = new CMultiDocTemplate(
            IDR_GL3DTYPE,
            RUNTIME_CLASS(CGL3DDoc),
            RUNTIME_CLASS(CChildFrame), // custom MDI child frame
            RUNTIME_CLASS(CGL3DView));
AddDocTemplate(pDocTemplate);
```

Child frame windows serve as resizable parent windows for objects of the View class. In our MDI program each View object is associated with a different instance of the document object. In other words, a **View** object of class **CGL3DView** and a **Document** object of class **CGL3DDoc** are created for each child window. A new child window is created and displayed each time another 3DS document is opened.

After the basic MDI application is created, the files GL3DVIEW.CPP, GL3DVIEW.H, GL3DDOC.CPP, and GL3DDOC.H are copied from the final SDI project. Before building the MDI project (in directory GL3D_5) we must make the following changes:

1. Each MDI child window is displaying a different model; therefore, separate display lists for each model must be written and each one assigned a unique identifier. This can be done with the use of a global variable which is incremented each time a new document is created. Its current value is used to identify the next Display List to be created:

```
// In GL3DDOC.H
static GLint LatestList=1;
//


// In GL3DDOC.CPP
//
// Get a unique ID for the Display List and store it in the member variable
//
m_listID=LatestList++;
::glNewList(m_listID,GL_COMPILE);
//
```

2. An MDI application will not reuse the same child window, thus, the Display List must be deleted when the View window is destroyed. This is done in the **OnDestroy()** handler as follows:

```
void CGL3DView::OnDestroy()
{
   .
   .
   .
   // Release the Display List for this Document and View
   //
   CGL3DDoc* pDoc = GetDocument();
   ASSERT_VALID(pDoc);
   if(pDoc->listID > 0)
   {
     ::glDeleteLists(pDoc->listID,pDoc->listID);
     pDoc->listID=0;
   }
   //
   .
   .
   .
```

3. The **OnDraw()** function must execute the display list for the window being repainted, and most importantly it must **make current** the OpenGL rendering context associated with **that** child window's view. To achieve this the **CGL3DView::OnDraw(..)** function becomes:

```
void CGL3DView::OnDraw(CDC* pDC)
{
        CGL3DDoc* pDoc = GetDocument();
        ASSERT_VALID(pDoc);
   //
   // Make the GL context current for "this" view and
   // its document.  (added in GL3D_5)
   //
   ::wglMakeCurrent(m_pDC->GetSafeHdc(),m_hRC);
   //
   // clear the OpenGL window to the background color and
   // set the Z buffer to infinity.
   //
   ::glClear(GL_COLOR_BUFFER_BIT | GL_DEPTH_BUFFER_BIT);
   //
   // Set the shading mode to Gouraud shading
   //
   ::glShadeModel(GL_SMOOTH);
   //
   // Move the model into view by translating it along the
   // Z-axis away from the camera. The model is pivoted so
```

```
// that an oblique view will be drawn.
//
::glPushMatrix();                    // Record any transformations.
::glLoadIdentity();                  // Build the transformation to
::glTranslatef(0.0f,                 // move the model away from camera.
               0.0f,                 // Note that this "precedes" any
               -5.0f+m_distance);    // rotational transformations.
//
// Rotate the model into position using the current setting of
// m_up_angle and m_round_angle. (m_round_angle is offset by
// 180 degrees so that the model faces the camera.)
//
::glRotatef(m_up_angle,1.0f,0.0f,0.0f);
::glRotatef(m_round_angle+180.0f,0.0f,1.0f,0.0f);
//
// If document has a valid display list draw it after
// enabling the lighting.
if(pDoc->listID > 0){
  ::glEnable(GL_LIGHTING);
  ::glCallList(pDoc->listID);
  ::glDisable(GL_LIGHTING);
}

//::glEnable(GL_LIGHTING);
//pDoc->MakeGLlist();
//::glDisable(GL_LIGHTING);

::glPopMatrix();
//
::glFinish();
::glFlush();
//
HDC hDC = ::wglGetCurrentDC();
::SwapBuffers(hDC);
}
```

A bit of tidying up of menu, toolbar, cursors, and icons leads to the program illustrated in Figure 10.6.

10.1.7 Extending the Application

There are a very large number of ways to extend the application. For example, texture maps (or image maps as we might call them) that form part of some 3DS materials can be loaded and processed to get a more realistic interpretation of the intended appearance.

It is quite easy to use OpenGL's mapping capabilities for 3DS meshes, because 3DS applies mapping coordinates to vertices in exactly the way required for

OpenGL image mapping. Each vertex has a (u, v) mapping coordinate and these map one copy of the image for each unit of u and v. Mapping coordinates were discussed in Chapters 4 and 7. Code given in the **GL3D_6** project directories includes a data structure for image maps, the Map structure.

One instance of a Map structure is added to a list if the material found in the 3DS file has an image map associated with it. Every facet with a "mapped material" is assigned an integer index into the map list as it is read from the file. (In a 3DS file the material information precedes the vertex and facet data.)

To draw the mapped facets using OpenGL, we must modify the function that draws the model or builds a display list. Figure 10.7 presents an algorithm that summarizes the main steps in rendering a mixture of mapped and plain color facets with OpenGL. We will suppose that there are n image maps and the facets are in no particular order.

Step 1 in Figure 10.7 draws only those facets that have a simple material and skips any that use an image-mapped material. To execute Step 2a requires two actions:

1. Write functions, taking as parameter the name of a file from which the map is to be loaded. Have them return an array of pixels in 24-bit RGB format.

Step 1:
Scan the list of facets and draw any that are **not** mapped.

Step 2:
Repeat the following for each map i {
    Part a:
    Load image map i into memory and scale its size
    so that OpenGL can use it.

    Part b:
    Make this the current map.

    Part c:
    Scan the list of facets and draw any that are mapped
    with map i. As each vertex is drawn with the
    glVertex() and glNormal() function calls,
    include a call to glTexcoord() with the vertex
    mapping coordinates as a parameter.
}

Figure 10.7. Outline of an algorithm for rendering a faceted model with image maps applied.

3DS supports a number of file types (e.g., GIF, TGA, etc.) and it useful to conform to a standard interface for the file-parsing routines of each image type so that others could be added if necessary. The code of such modules could be added in external DLLs.

Calling a function to load an image might be achieved with following code template:

```
.
.


unsigned char *Image;     // Pointer to an array of RGB byte triples
                          // where the LoadMAP function will copy the
                          // image in RBG byte order across the row.
                          // The first row will be at the top of the
                          // image.
                          // The array will be of size "width*height".

long width,height;        // Returned image width and height.
.
.
.

//
// MapsFp is an array of MAP structures holding the name of the
// file holding the map. We are processing map "i".
// The function is responsible for recognizing the type of the image
// (from the filename extension), allocating memory for image, and
// composing the 24-bit data into the required byte and scanline order.
// If anything goes wrong it should return a NULL pointer and if
// (in the case of error) it has allocated any memory, this should
// be released before returning NULL.
//
Image=LoadMAP(MapsFp[i].MapName,&width,&height);
if(Image != NULL)
{
  //
  // The image data has been read and decoded successfully.
  .

  .

  . Insert the remaining code fragments here!!!
  .

  .

  //
  // release the Image memory
  //
  if(Image != NULL)free(Image);
}
.

.
```

A good source of information (and sample codes) on graphic file formats is [8].

2. OpenGL does **not** accept image maps unless their widths and heights are a power of 2 (e.g., 32×32 or 128×64) and therefore the image must be interpolated onto a pixel array of appropriate dimensions. Fortunately OpenGL provides a utility function that does just this. The input is an array in the RGB format and output can conform to several schemes. The function given below will convert an "Image" at resolution "width" by "height" to one at resolution w by h, where w and h are powers of **2**:

```
unsigned char * CGL3DDoc::InterpolateMap(
  //
  // Return pointer to scaled image or NULL if failure
  //
  unsigned char *InputImage, // Input raster
  long width, int height,    // Input raster dimensions
  long w, long h             // Desired output dimensions (power of 2)
){
 unsigned char *OutputImage;
 if((px=(unsigned char *)::malloc(w*h*3)) == NULL)
 {
   ::free(InputImage);
   return NULL;
 }
 //
 // OpenGL utility function
 //
 ::gluScaleImage(GL_RGB,width,height,GL_UNSIGNED_BYTE,InputImage,
                 w,h,GL_UNSIGNED_BYTE,OutputImage);
 ::free(InputImage);
 return OutputImage;
}
```

Part **b** of Step 2 passes the scaled map to OpenGL and the texture coordinate mode is enabled:

```
// Tell OpenGL that the image is single bytes for R G B
//
::glPixelStorei(GL_UNPACK_ALIGNMENT, 1);
//
// Put the image map into the display list; this map will be used for
// all drawing while texture coordinate mode is enabled and until
// "glTexImage" is called again with new details/
//
::glTexImage2D(GL_TEXTURE_2D,0,3,w,h,0,GL_RGB,GL_UNSIGNED_BYTE,
               (GLvoid *)Image);
```

```
//
// We could free "Image" at this time if we liked.
//
// Enable surface mapping
//
::glEnable(GL_TEXTURE_2D);
```

Step **2c** loops through all facets and, for each one that is using map i, the texture coordinates are placed in the Display List before the vertex positions:

```
.
// Add the line below before drawing the vertex.
//
// Set the texture coordinates for vertex pointed to by "v"
//
::glTexCoord2f(v->x,v->y);
//
// Continue as before ... draw the vertex, etc.
//
::glVertex3f(x,z,-y);
.
```

The final action is to disable surface texture coordinates when drawing is complete.

```
::glDisable(GL_TEXTURE_2D);
```

Making these modifications to the project in GL3D_5 will give a viewer application which simulates very well the look of the original model.

One final comment: OpenGL's lighting will not appear to affect the shading on mapped surfaces unless GL_MODULATE mode is used for the texture environment; i.e., call glTexEnvi with:

```
glTexEnvi(GL_TEXTURE_ENV, GL_TEXTURE_ENV_MODE, GL_MODULATE);
```

This chapter has dealt with a specific example of applying the OpenGL library of functions. If you want a full description of OpenGL programming for Windows, all the details can be found in the books by Walnum [9], Hill [10], or Angel [11].

References

[1] J. Neider, T. Davis and M. Woo, *OpenGL Programming Guide.* Addison-Wesley, Reading MA, 1993.

[2] N. Thompson, *3D Graphics Programming for Windows 95.* Microsoft Press, Redmond WA, 1996.

[3] *QuickDraw 3D.* Apple Computer Corp. Cupertino CA. 1996

[4] M. Andrews, *Learn Visual C++ Now.* Microsoft Press, Redmond WA, 1996

[5] V. Broquard, *Intermediate MDC.* Prentice Hall PTR Upper Saddle River NJ, 1998.

[6] OpenGL Architecture Review Board, *OpenGL Reference Manual.* Addison-Wesley, Reading MA, 1992.

[7] J. Neider, T. Davis, and M. Woo, *OpenGL Programming Guide.* Addison-Wesley, Reading MA, 1993, Chapter 4.

[8] J. D. Murray and W. vanRyper, *Encyclopedia of Graphics File Formats.* O'Reilly and Associates Inc. Sebastopol CA, 1994.

[9] C. Walnum, *3-D Graphics Programming with OpenGL.* Que Corp. Indianapolis IN, 1995.

[10] F. S. Hill, *Computer Graphics Using OpenGL.* Prentice Hall, Englewood Cliffs NJ, 2000.

[11] E. Angel, *Interactive Computer Graphics: A Top-Down Approach with OpenGL.* Addison-Wesley, Reading MA, 1999.

CHAPTER 11

3D Graphics with Direct3D

For many years it was virtually impossible to develop any sort of high-performance graphics application for the personal computer (PC). There were many reasons for this, but surprisingly the performance of the processor was **not** one of them. Other competing systems dominated in the graphics applications business, and even the introduction of a graphical user interface (GUI) in the 1980s did not lead to much enthusiasm among application developers.

At the root of the trouble was the basic architecture of the PC and the need to maintain backward compatibility (one of the main reasons for the PC's success). When the original specification for the PC was written by IBM, it was never envisaged that a display adapter would need an address space of more that 64k. Later it dawned on people that displays with resolutions greater than 640×480 and support for more than 16 colors were essential, but by then it was too late to standardize and each display device manufacturer developed their own protocol for the so-called **SVGA**.

Anyone who tried to develop a PC graphics application in those days will probably remember the nightmare of supporting innumerable display devices. You could spend all your time trying (and often failing) to solve your customer's display compatibility problems. To the graphics programmer the arrival of Windows imposed a standard but at a price, a price in performance. Unfortunately the need for more layers of software between the application and the display was the root cause. This problem and a few other bottlenecks in the system dogged Windows. Even the introduction of the 32-bit versions of the operating system, Windows NT and then Windows 95, only alleviated the problem a little. What was required was a way to bypass what is known as the *Windows Graphics Device Interface (GDI)* and allow applications to access the video display hardware directly and crucially, in a standard way. Hence the introduction of **DirectX**.

The DirectX API gives you the best of both worlds. It cuts straight through the bottlenecks posed by the standard Windows APIs, allows "direct" access to video memory (as a **flat** address space) and to the graphics acceleration provided by modern video cards. It also provides function calls to deliver high-speed drawing but still using the standard windows drawing objects: brushes, pens, bitmaps, etc. Unfortunately however, Direct3D does not offer the portability of OpenGL but with its powerful backer it does appear to be the API of choice for 3D graphics on the PC for the future.

DirectX [1] first appeared under the guise of the *Games SDK for Windows 95* in late 1995 and it has been refined and updated many times. In 2001 a number of the components required for 3D graphics have reached maturity. DirectX consists of a number of components; the most relevant for our work are:

1. DirectDraw,

2. DirectPlay,

3. Direct3D,

4. DirectSetup,

5. Autoplay,

6. DirectSound,

7. DirectInput.

For graphics applications DirectDraw is the most important component because it is the primary interface between the software and the display hardware. It achieves display performance as high as any application written to use the display adapter in a native mode.

DirectDraw was designed with computer games in mind, and so has excellent support for *Blits*(Bit block memory transfers, including transparent and 'key color' blits). Many operations are performed asynchronously, with page flipping and color fills now done in the display adapter's hardware. From a 3D point of view these very fast basic graphic capabilities are helpful. However, additional functions, specific to the stages of the rendering pipeline, will need to be added before the full advantages that DirectDraw offers can be realized in 3D applications.

Specifically, for our purposes it is the **Direct3D** *component that is of prime interest.* Direct 3D, as the name suggests, is concerned with 3D graphics applications. It can be programmed to operate in two modes:

1. Retained Mode: a library of OpenGL-like functions that make developing 3D applications relatively straightforward. We will be using Retained Mode in this chapter. It is regarded as complete in DirectX6, and in DirectX8 it moved to the DirectX Media Kit.

2. Immediate Mode: most current development in Direct3D is occuring in this area. Immediate Mode relies heavily on the display adapter to provide functionality for the main stages in the graphics pipeline. In early versions of DirectX it was very basic, but at the time of this writing (2001), DirectX8 has some really useful features, provided of course that your display hardware can accommodate them.

In the hierarchy of system software Retained Mode Direct3D sits on top of Immediate Mode Direct3D, which in turn sits on DirectDraw and then the Hardware Abstraction Layer (HAL) or Hardware Emulation Layer (HEL). We won't discuss either the HAL or HEL further in this book. Direct3D provides a standard for 3D graphics including viewing transformations, rendering of 3D primitive shapes, shading, lighting, and texturing. It is quite likely that Direct3D will become the common 3D API. For some applications it is superior to OpenGL, especially since it sits naturally along-side DirectDraw and can therefore integrate easily into the design of games and other recreational software. OpenGL has its advantages and is unlikely to disappear from PC applications, but most programs written for Windows in the future are likely to concentrate on using Direct3D.

11.1 The Component Object Model

From the programmer's point of view the API for all components of DirectX is used in a different way from the OpenGL API. OpenGL, as we have seen, operates like a conventional software library with calls to a large set of library functions. The routines silently manage any hardware acceleration and, as far as an application is concerned, only a very small number of functions take any account of whether it is executing on a PC running Windows or on a RISC workstation. On the other hand DirectX conforms to Microsoft's COM (Component Object Model) specification and all the APIs are used in that form. In order to write an application using DirectDraw/Direct3D a knowledge of the COM is essential.

The COM is orientated towards programming in **C++**; it can be used by applications written in **C** but the code is somewhat less clean. An *Object* is at the root of the COM, and in the context of DirectDraw one function call creates an instance of a COM object to represent the *Display* (either a hardware adapter or software emulation). The member functions of a COM object (its **Methods** are grouped into **Interfaces** according to their function) provide the communication between an object and the user, and all Direct3D functionality is encapsulated in the same DirectDraw object.

Thus, the first steps in using DirectDraw in an application consist of creating the DirectDraw object and then querying it to retrieve an interface to one of its supported components, for example, an interface to Direct3D. Typically this is done with the following **C++** code fragment:

```
.
.
LPDIRECTDRAW lpDD;
LPDIRECT3D   lpD3D;
ddres = DirectDrawCreate(NULL, &lpDD, NULL);
if (FAILED(ddres)) ...
.
ddres = lpDD->QueryInterface(IID_IDirect3D,  &lpD3D);
if (FAILED(ddres)) ...
.
.
```

To do the same job in **C** the following code is required:

```
.
.
LPDIRECTDRAW lpDD;
LPDIRECT3D   lpD3D;

ddres = DirectDrawCreate(NULL, &lpDD, NULL);
if (FAILED(ddres)) ...
.
/* Note the EXPLICIT use of the object as the first parameter */
/* the use of the "lpVtbl" member of the lpDD structure       */

ddres = lpDD->lpVtbl->QueryInterface(lpDD, IID_IDirect3D,  &lpD3D);
if (FAILED(ddres)) ...
.
.
```

All interface methods to COM objects are called using one of these styles; in **C++** a pointer to the originating object is always passed as an implicit parameter, the *this* parameter. A COM object is binary-compatible with C++ objects; a C++ compiler treats it like a C++ abstract class and assumes the same syntax. This results in less complex code. In **C** the *this* argument and the indirection through the *vtable* must be included explicitly.

DirectDraw and hence Direct3D offer a huge variety of possible *Surfaces* on which to draw. These range from a conventional window, which is represented in system RAM, through to a full screen display stored in the fast RAM on a display adapter. The screen can even be switched into different resolutions and color depths by the application, something Windows does not readily do unless the computer is rebooted. It is part of the initialization process of a DirectDraw application to choose the output format. This usually involves querying what modes are emulated by software or are provided by the display adapter hardware. From the result of the query a suitable mode is chosen, usually the most efficient.

DirectX is a fast moving topic; Release 8 is available at the time of writing. However the *interfaces* that we will require have been stable since Release 3. A number of texts specialize in the details of DirectX; a good quick general introduction to all aspects may be found in Dunlop [2], while Kovach [3] specializes in the Direct3D aspects of DirectX. Both these texts concentrate on the Direct3D Immediate Mode. Thompson [4] describes both the Retained Mode and Immediate Mode and develops a number of C++ classes to hide the messier aspects of the COM.

In the examples given in this chapter only the Retained Mode will be used. Retained Mode is the closest approximation in Direct 3D to the OpenGL API.

11.2 Direct3D Retained Mode

In a Retained Mode application the basic steps that need to be implemented are as follows:

1. Determine the display modes available and choose one in which to work.

2. Create an instance of a **Direct3DRM** object.

3. In order that any drawing is correctly restricted to the application's window, a **Clipper** object should be created and associated with the output window.

4. Create a Direct3DRM **device** for the appropriate display (resolution, color depth, full screen, etc.). This can be associated with the Clipper so that all output to that device is clipped correctly.

5. Create a main **Frame** object, *the scene*. All other elements: camera, lights, models, etc., will be *hierarchical descendants* of this main scene.

6. Create a **Frame** object for the camera (the viewpoint) as a first descendent of the "scene".

7. Create a **Viewport** for the Direct3DRM device and associate the camera's frame object with it.

8. Create a number of **Frame** objects, these are little frames of reference to which the lights and models are attached. The **Frame** objects are arranged in a hierarchical (parent—child) structure so that any child frames will follow their parents.

9. Build any models (using the Mesh or Meshbuilder interfaces) and attach them to a **Frame** object in the hierarchy.

10. Render the scene.

Most of the initialization steps could be executed in response to the WM_CREATE message. Direct3D requires that you take some specific action in response to the WM_PAINT, WM_SIZE, and WM_ACTIVATE messages. In a conventional Windows program, most drawing is done in response to the WM_PAINT message. In a Direct3D application, rendering can be carried out in the WM_PAINT message handler, but for high speed 3D work where the screen is continually changing the rendering code is usually placed in the main message dispatch loop. Direct 3D has *methods* to pre-program certain changes that occur every time the scene is rendered.

In the example, rendering is done in the MFC **OnDraw**() message handler. Rendering is a four stage process:

1. Move, create, or update any elements in the scene's frame hierarchy so that they are arranged as you want them at the *instant of time being rendered.*

2. Clear the viewport.

3. Render the scene to the viewport.

4. Update the device's window.

11.3   Starting the Project

To build the example using Visual C++, start with a conventional Single Document program created by the Application Wizard. Give it the base name **D3D**. Our first program will load and display Direct3D's own native model database format; Direct X files are identified with the name extension **.X**.

A **.X** file name extension may be associated with our example program by editing the *File Extension* field in the dialog which pops up when the *Advanced* button on the *Defaults* AppWizard page is pressed.

For this first version of the program all the Direct3D-specific code is placed in the project's View class named **CD3DView**. A modification to the **CD3DDoc** class is made to allow us to call through from the OnOpenDocument(..) handler (added by the Class Wizard) to our own function CD3DView::OpenNewModel(..) as follows:

```
BOOL CD3DDoc::OnOpenDocument(LPCTSTR lpszPathName)
{
  if (!CDocument::OnOpenDocument(lpszPathName))return FALSE;
  //
  // Get the Document's only view
  //
```

```
        POSITION pos = GetFirstViewPosition();
        CD3DView *v = (CD3DView *)GetNextView( pos );
        if(v == NULL)return FALSE;
        v->DeleteObject();
        v->OpenNewModel((char *)lpszPathName);
        return TRUE;
}
```

11.4   The CD3DView Class Header File

The D3DVIEW.H header should be added to the list of included files in the document class D3DDOC.CPP. This is probably a good point to mention that the library files D3DRM.LIB and DDRAW.LIB must be inserted in the list of project files so that the Visual C++ linker can resolve calls to the library functions. (These libraries are part of the DirectX SDK.)

The first modifications to make to file D3DVIEW.CPP are to add prototypes and message maps for the following handlers in the **CD3DView** class:

1. CD3DView::OnCreate(..) for the WM_CREATE message.

2. CD3DView::OnDestroy(..) for the WM_DESTROY message.

3. CD3DView::OnSize(..) for the WM_SIZE message.

4. CD3DView::OnMouseMove(..) for the WM_MOUSEMOVE message.

5. CD3DView::OnLButtonDown(..) for the WM_LBUTTONDOWN message.

6. CD3DView::OnLButtonUp(..) for the WM_LBUTTONUP message.

7. CD3DView::OnKeyDown(..) for the WM_KEYDOWN message.

8. CD3DView::OnKeyUp(..) for the WM_KEYUP message.

Direct3D requires that the CD3DView class' OnActivateView(...) handler is overridden, and naturally we would expect later to have to modify the OnDraw(..) function added by default by the AppWizard.

AppWizard defines the basic layout of the D3DView.cpp file and that includes prototypes for some of the handler functions listed above. The other handlers should be added by the Class Wizard because this creates prototypes, rudimentary function code, and message maps all in one step.

At this stage of project development all use of Direct3D is confined to the file
D3DVIEW.CPP; therefore, the DirectX system header files and useful macros can
be placed at the top of D3DVIEW.H as illustrated below:

```
//
// Include the header files for Direct3D and DirectDraw

#include <d3drmwin.h>
#include <direct.h>
//
// Basic Macros used by the standard code. Note the different procedure
// for using Interface Methods in C and C++
//
#undef RELEASE
#ifdef __cplusplus
#define RELEASE(x) if (x != NULL) {x->Release(); x = NULL;}
#else
#define RELEASE(x) if (x != NULL) {x->lpVtbl->Release(x); x = NULL;}
#endif
```

It is useful to keep pointers to the Direct3D device, viewport, and frames
of reference for scene, camera, and model. These are grouped together in an
application-defined data type AppInfo. As the example grows other items can,
if necessary, be added to the Appinfo data type:

```
typedef struct tagAppInfo
{
    LPDIRECT3DRMFRAME scene,      // Frames of reference for the
                      camera,     // scene, camera, and object.
                      object;
    LPDIRECT3DRMDEVICE dev;       // The D3D device (attached to screen)
    LPDIRECT3DRMVIEWPORT view;    // The viewport (what you see in the window)
    D3DRMCOLORMODEL model;        // Which Direct3D mechanism for using color?
    BOOL bMinimized;              // Is window minimized.
} AppInfo;
```

Frames of reference are organized hierarchically. All the Microsoft SDK examples use consistent names for the Frames and we will follow that convention as
closely as possible. The root frame is the scene, camera, and object frames
that are immediate descendants of the scene. These *child* frames are moved about
by calling interface methods such as IDirect3DRMFrame::AddRotation(...)
and/or IDirect3DRMFrame::SetPosition(...). For example, if we declare
the variable Info as a pointer to an AppInfo structure, then any model (vertices and facets) attached to the object frame of reference is moved away from
a camera located at $(0,0,0)$ by calling the SetPosition(...) method as
follows:

```
.
.  Using C++
.
Info->object->SetPosition(Info->scene,
                          D3DVAL(0.0f),D3DVAL(0.0f),D3DVAL(distance));
.
.  or for C
.
Info->object->lpVtbl->SetPosition(Info->object,Info->scene,
                          D3DVAL(0.0f),D3DVAL(0.0f),D3DVAL(distance));
.
```

Note that Direct3D uses the same coordinate system as OpenGL, i.e., a left-handed one with the z-axis lying in a horizontal plane pointing away from the vertical reference plane in which the viewport lies.

The header file also contains member variables as follows:

```
public:
//
// Member variables for the Direct3D application.
//
// A pointer to an AppInfo structure that will be created during
// window creation.
//
AppInfo            *m_Info;
//
// A pointer to the primary Interface for the Direct3DRM object.
// All other Interfaces and the Methods they contain are accessed
// through this pointer.
//
LPDIRECT3DRM       m_lpD3DRM;
//
// A pointer to a Clipper object. A Clipper is a DirectDraw object
// that we can use to clip the drawing to the current window dimensions.
// We will create our Device (the display mode) from the Clipper to
// which this points.
//
LPDIRECTDRAWCLIPPER m_lpDDClipper;
//
// The following member variables are used in exactly the same way as
// they were in the OpenGL examples.
//
BOOL  m_bTrackPan,m_bKey;        // These do the same job as in the
long  m_xs,m_ys;                 // OpenGL example for moving the
float m_round_angle,m_up_angle;  // viewpoint of the model
float m_distance;                // distance from camera
//
```

and function prototypes:

```
// Member functions added for D3D application follow.
//
// The following functions are specific to this application. They
// govern the operation of the Interfaces and Methods of Direct3D
//
void DeleteObject(void);           // Delete the old model
void OpenNewModel(char *file);     // Open a new model given a filename
BOOL CreateScene(AppInfo* info);   // Create the frames of reference,
                                   // add some lighting, set the camera
                                   // position and background.
BOOL CreateDevice(HWND, AppInfo*); // Create the device and viewport
                                   // and associate the camera with the
                                   // viewport. (So that we see what the
                                   // camera sees.)
BOOL Render();                     // Render the scene in response to the
                                   // WM_PAINT message (OnDraw handler).
//
// The following functions (helper functions) can be used in any
// Direct3D application and are only slightly modified from examples
// provided in the Direct X SDK.
//
void __cdecl Msg( LPSTR fmt, ... ); // Display Error or other message.
BOOL ResizeViewport(HWND win,      // When the window changes size the D3D
                 AppInfo* info,    // viewport most be resized
                 int width, int height);
LPGUID FindDevice(D3DCOLORMODEL cm);// Find the D3D device best suited for
                                   // the application.
DWORD bppToddbd(int bpp);          // Return a code for the number of colors
                                   // currently used by the display.
BOOL RebuildDevice(HWND win,       // Under some circumstances it may
                 AppInfo* info,    // be necessary to build the device
                 int width,        // again so that it has the same
                 int height);      // characteristics as before.
```

11.5   Setting Up Direct3D

In this section we will look at the steps that must be taken to create the Direct3D Retained Mode device, viewport, and frames of references for the scene in which a model will be placed. This is done by adding a handler for the View window's ON_CREATE message.

Before calling function CreateDevice(HWND, AppInfo *) (which builds the device scene and fills an AppInfo data structure) a Direct3D Retained Mode object and a DirectDraw Clipper object are created. The View window is attached to the Clipper (with interface pointer m_lpDDClipper), and we will tell Direct3D to use its D3DCOLOR_MONO mode for shading faces. D3DCOLOR_MONO does not mean that the result of rendering will be in shades of gray only; rather, it means that the shading calculations will be based on the blue component of a vertex color only. The same percentage shading will be applied to the other color components without further calculation. The result is faster rendering.

The code that accomplishes Direct3D initialization is given below:

```
int CD3DView::OnCreate(LPCREATESTRUCT lpCreateStruct)
{
    //
    // Call the base class Create handler
    //
        if (CView::OnCreate(lpCreateStruct) == -1)return -1;
        //
    // Create a Direct3DRM object and return a pointer to its
    // interface "m_lpD3DRM"
    //
        HRESULT  rval = Direct3DRMCreate(&m_lpD3DRM);
    //
    // Create a Clipper object and return a pointer to its interface
    //
    if(FAILED(DirectDrawCreateClipper(0,&m_lpDDClipper,NULL)))
    {
      return -1;
    }
    //
    // Associate the View's window with the Clipper object. A
    // Clipper is an Object in DirectDraw that will prevent errors
    // if an attempt is made to render outside the viewport.
    //
    if(FAILED(m_lpDDClipper->SetHWnd(0,m_hWnd))){
      RELEASE(m_lpDDClipper);
      return -1;
    }
    //
    // Allocate space for the Application Information structure
    // and initialize its members. We will start with the fastest
    // color model (D3DCOLOR_MONO); another option is D3DCOLOR_RGB.
    //
    m_Info = (AppInfo *)malloc(sizeof(AppInfo));
        memset(m_Info,0,sizeof(AppInfo));
        m_Info->model = D3DCOLOR_MONO;
    //
    // Now Create the device and everything else that follows
    // from it.
    //
    if(!CreateDevice(m_hWnd,m_Info))return -1;
    //
    // If all has gone well the handler returns 0 and the program
    // proceeds. If anything goes wrong we will have returned -1
    // and the program will terminate.
    return 0;
}
```

The function `CD3DView::CreateDevice(..)` has a number of important tasks to perform. First it must create a Direct3DRM device which uses the DirectDraw Clipper to ensure correct rendering in the View's window. The function creates the device by calling the Direct3DRM object's interface method `CreateDeviceFromClipper(..)`. The third parameter to this method is a pointer to a **GUID** which is returned by the function method `FindDevice(D3DCOLORMODEL )`. A GUID [5] is an identifier for the display mode that will be used for drawing. The mode will be different on different adapters since some will offer hardware support for Direct3D and some will not. It is envisaged that as display adapter hardware increases in power more of Direct3D's functionality will be implemented within the adapter itself.

Note that it is recommenced to use NULL as parameter value for the pointer to a GUID in Direct3D Retained Mode applications. This is because DirectX will guarantee to find a driver, hardware if possible or, if not, a software emulation mode instead. Not having to provide the code to find a suitable device would simplify our example and in the later stages of development the `FindDevice(..)` function will be removed (project D3d_4).

There are many ways to determine a device's Globally Unique Identifier (the GUID). For the moment we will consider the method suggested by an example from Microsoft's Direct Draw Software Developers Kit (SDK) and given in function `FindDevice(..)` That function tries to find the fastest device that supports the display resolution and color model needed. Hopefully the display adapter will provide this in hardware.

Once the Direct3DRM device is created, it is told that it that will be performing solid rendering (as opposed to wireframe, for example) and that any meshes will be subject to Gouraud smoothing (at the time of this writing Phong's smoothing procedure is not supported). Before the viewport is created we must put together the elements in our scene, the scene itself, a camera, and the frame of reference to which a mesh object (the model) can be attached; this is done in function `CreateScene`.

Throughout the `CreateDevice(..)` function, if any method can't perform its requested task a FALSE value is returned and the application will terminate. The `CreateDevice(..)` code is shown below:

```
BOOL CD3DView::CreateDevice(HWND win, AppInfo* info)
{
    //
    // Create the Direct3DRM device representing the display hardware if
    // possible or by emulation otherwise.
    //
    RECT r;
    int bpp;
    HDC hdc;
    //
```

```
// Default window dimensions---this will be updated in the response to a
// WM_SIZE message, which is sent when the window is sized before
//becoming visible.
//
r.right=100; r.bottom=100;
//
// The device is created with reference to the Clipper object so that
// all drawing in the window is correctly clipped to the window boundaries.
//
if (FAILED(m_lpD3DRM->CreateDeviceFromClipper(
        m_lpDDClipper,              // Clipper for window "win"
        FindDevice(info->model),    // Which device to use
        r.right, r.bottom,          // Dimensions of window
        &info->dev))){              // returned pointer to device Interface
  goto generic_error;
}
//
// Get the number of colors supported by the display,
//
hdc = ::GetDC(win);
bpp = ::GetDeviceCaps(hdc, BITSPIXEL);
::ReleaseDC(win, hdc);
//
// Set some properties of the Device and Direct3DRM object depending
// on the number of colors supported by the display mode currently
// used by Windows.
//
switch (bpp)
{
case 1:
    if (FAILED(info->dev->SetShades(4)))
        goto generic_error;
    if (FAILED(m_lpD3DRM->SetDefaultTextureShades(4)))
        goto generic_error;
    break;
case 16:
    if (FAILED(info->dev->SetShades(32)))
        goto generic_error;
    if (FAILED(m_lpD3DRM->SetDefaultTextureColors(64)))
        goto generic_error;
    if (FAILED(m_lpD3DRM->SetDefaultTextureShades(32)))
        goto generic_error;
    if (FAILED(info->dev->SetDither(FALSE)))
        goto generic_error;
    break;
case 24:
case 32:
    if (FAILED(info->dev->SetShades(256)))
        goto generic_error;
    if (FAILED(m_lpD3DRM->SetDefaultTextureColors(64)))
```

```
            goto generic_error;
      if (FAILED(m_lpD3DRM->SetDefaultTextureShades(256)))
            goto generic_error;
      if (FAILED(info->dev->SetDither(FALSE)))
            goto generic_error;
      break;
default:
      if (FAILED(info->dev->SetDither(FALSE)))
            goto generic_error;
}
//
// Tell the rendering device that we want smoothing,
//
D3DRMRENDERQUALITY quality;
quality = info->dev->GetQuality();
quality = (quality & ~D3DRMSHADE_MASK) | D3DRMSHADE_GOURAUD;
//
// and solid shading.
//
quality = (quality & ~D3DRMFILL_MASK) | D3DRMFILL_SOLID;
//
// Set it.
//
if(info->dev->SetQuality(quality) != D3DRM_OK)
{
    Msg("Setting the shading failed\n");
    return FALSE;
}
//
// Call a function to build the elements of the scene, camera, model
// lighting, etc.
//
if (!CreateScene(info))goto ret_with_error;
//
// Create the Direct3DRM object's viewport. The viewport will show its
// view on the Device created above and will show what can be seen from
// the Camera frame of reference created in function CreateScene.
//
if (FAILED(m_lpD3DRM->CreateViewport(
    info->dev,
    info->camera,
    0, 0,
    info->dev->GetWidth(),
    info->dev->GetHeight(),
    &info->view)))             // Returned pointer to viewport Interface.
    goto generic_error;
//
// Call the viewport Interface method to set position of the (back)
// clipping plane---note the positive value. (Z-coordinate is +ve away
// from the plane of the viewport.)
```

```
    //
    if (FAILED(info->view->SetBack(D3DVAL(5000.0))))
        goto generic_error;

    return TRUE;
    //
    // Error occurred.
    //
generic_error:
    Msg("An error occurred while creating the device.\n");
ret_with_error:
    return FALSE;
}
```

A *scene* represents all the elements that we usually associate with a 3D graphics application. We need a camera, here represented by the viewport through which we view the scene, some lighting, and a frame of reference to which any meshes in our model are attached. As mentioned before, Direct3D arranges the elements of a scene in a hierarchy. One frame is designated as the *root* and all others are descended from it. If the root frame is moved then all descendants are moved by the same amount.

The function `CreateScene(..)` creates the root frame by calling the Direct3DRM method CreateFrame(..) with a NULL parent. A pointer to the scene's frame interface is stored in an `AppInfo` structure; all the other important interface pointers are similarly recorded.

To illuminate the scene some lighting is required. Two lights of different types are placed in the scene: one is an ambient light which is attached to the scene's frame (of reference), and the other is a directional light attached to its own frame so that it can be moved to illuminate the scene from above and toward the right-hand side. A frame called `camera` is created and this becomes the location from which the scene is viewed when it is attached to the Viewport. (This is done after the viewport is created.) The camera frame is placed at the origin of the scene and by default it looks along the $-z$ direction.

The last frame, the *object* frame, is created later; it will be used by any meshes that are loaded from a **.X** file.

In the code for the `CreateScene(..)` function below, pointers to the interfaces for the scene, camera, and object frames are recorded in the `AppInfo` structure:

```
BOOL CD3DView::CreateScene(AppInfo* info)
{
    //
    // Create all the elements that will appear in the scene: a master
    // reference frame, the camera, a light, and frame for the model.
    //
```

```
        LPDIRECT3DRMFRAME frame = NULL;
        LPDIRECT3DRMFRAME light_frame = NULL;
        LPDIRECT3DRMLIGHT light1 = NULL;
        LPDIRECT3DRMLIGHT light2 = NULL;
        //
        // Create the master frame---"the scene" (Note that its parent is NULL)---
and
        // store the pointer to the frame in the AppInfo structure.
        //
        if (FAILED(m_lpD3DRM->CreateFrame(NULL, &info->scene)))
            goto generic_error;
        //
        // Set the background color to a dark blue.
        //
        info->scene->SetSceneBackgroundRGB(D3DVAL(0.0),D3DVAL(0.0),D3DVAL(0.4));
        //
        // Create a white directional light.
        //
        if (FAILED(m_lpD3DRM->CreateLightRGB(D3DRMLIGHT_DIRECTIONAL,
          D3DVAL(1.0), D3DVAL(1.0), D3DVAL(1.0), &light1)))
            goto generic_error;
        //
        // Create a dim ambient light.
        //
        if (FAILED(m_lpD3DRM->CreateLightRGB(D3DRMLIGHT_AMBIENT,
          D3DVAL(0.1), D3DVAL(0.1), D3DVAL(0.1), &light2)))
            goto generic_error;
        //
        // Make a frame of reference for the light. A frame of reference allows
        // us to position the light in the scene.
        //
        if (FAILED(m_lpD3DRM->CreateFrame(info->scene, &light_frame)))
            goto generic_error;
        //
        // Set the position of the light---off to the right and above the
        // model.
        //
        if (FAILED(light_frame->SetPosition(info->scene,
          D3DVAL(2.0), D3DVAL(2.0), D3DVAL(5.0))))
            goto generic_error;
        //
        // Direct the frame of reference for the light so that it points
        // down towards the model.
        //
        if (FAILED(light_frame->SetOrientation(info->scene,
          D3DVAL(-1.0), D3DVAL(-1.0), D3DVAL(1.0),
          D3DVAL(0.0), D3DVAL(1.0), D3DVAL(0.0))))
            goto generic_error;
        //
        // Add the directional light to the light's frame of reference.
```

```
        //
        if (FAILED(light_frame->AddLight(light1)))
            goto generic_error;
        //
        // We are finished with the directed light Interface, so release it.
        //
        RELEASE(light1);
        //
        // Add the ambient light to the scene
        //
        if (FAILED(info->scene->AddLight(light2)))
            goto generic_error;
        //
        // We no longer need the ambient light or the directional light's frame
        // of reference, so release them.
        //
        RELEASE(light2);
        RELEASE(light_frame);
        //
        // Create an empty frame of reference for the model and store the pointer
        // to its interface in the AppInfo structure.
        //
        if (FAILED(m_lpD3DRM->CreateFrame(info->scene, &frame)))
            goto generic_error;
        info->object=frame;
        //
        // Create a frame of reference for the camera and position it at the
        // the origin of the scene frame; by default it will look along the
        // the positive Z-axis.
        //
        if (FAILED(m_lpD3DRM->CreateFrame(info->scene, &info->camera)))
            goto generic_error;
        if (FAILED(info->camera->SetPosition(info->scene,
            D3DVAL(0.0), D3DVAL(0.0), D3DVAL(0.0))))
            goto generic_error;
        //
        // The scene is complete.
        //
        return TRUE;
generic_error:
    Msg("A failure occurred while creating the scene.\n");
    RELEASE(frame);
    RELEASE(light_frame);
    RELEASE(light1);
    RELEASE(light2);
    return FALSE;
}
```

Once `CreateScene(..)` returns it will have filled all the members of an `AppInfo` structure and the application is fully initialized; it is ready to render into the window using Direct3D retained mode.

11.6 Essential Message Handling

Direct3D requires that the window messages `WM_PAINT` and `WM_ACTIVATE` are processed in a particular way. This is in addition to any other actions that the application may wish to do in these handlers. Further, if the window changes size, then the viewport and even the device may have to be re-created.

An MFC application handles the `WM_PAINT` message in the `OnDraw(...)` function and in Direct3D, the device context handle (the **hDC**) should be passed to the `HandlePaint()` method; after that the scene can be rendered. A typical `OnDraw(..)` handler will contain the following code:

```
void CD3DView::OnDraw(CDC* pDC)
{
    CD3DDoc* pDoc = GetDocument();
    ASSERT_VALID(pDoc);
    //
    // Direct3D requires that the WM_PAINT message is handled according to
    // the following procedure.
    //
    if(m_Info != NULL){
      //
      // The device and scene have been created.
      //
      LPDIRECT3DRMWINDEVICE windev;
      //
      // Query if the D3DRM device supports the "windev" interface and
      // if it does return a pointer to it.
      //
      if(SUCCEEDED(m_Info->dev->QueryInterface(IID_IDirect3DRMWinDevice,
           (void **) &windev)))
      {
        //
        // Pass the Window's device context to the Direct3D device
        // HandlePaint method as required by the Direct 3D specification.
        //
        if(FAILED(windev->HandlePaint(pDC->m_hDC)))
            Msg("Failed to handle WM_PAINT.\n");
        windev->Release();
      }
      else
      {
        Msg("Failed to create Windows device to handle WM_PAINT");
```

```
        }
        //
        // The window still needs repainting, so render the scene.
        //
        if(!Render())Msg("Rendering failed.\n");
    }
}
```

The scene is rendered in three steps:

1. Clear the viewport.

2. Render the scene.

3. Update the Direct3D device.

These are executed by the Render(..) function as follows:

```
BOOL CD3DView::Render() // Render the scene
{
    //
    // Clear the Viewport.
    //
    if (FAILED(m_Info->view->Clear()))
        return FALSE;
    //
    // Render the scene.
    //
    if (FAILED(m_Info->view->Render(m_Info->scene)))
        return FALSE;
    //
    // Update the device so that the rendered scene is visible.
    //
    if (FAILED(m_Info->dev->Update()))
        return FALSE;
    return TRUE;
}
```

The WM_ACTIVATE message is handled in much the same way as the WM_PAINT message. The view class' OnActivateView() handler forwards the message to Direct3D's HandleActivate() method as follows:

```
void CD3DView::OnActivateView(BOOL bActivate, CView* pActivateView,
    CView* pDeactiveView)
{
    //
    // Direct3D requires that the WM_ACTIVATE message is handled according to
    // the following procedure.
    //
    //
```

```
if(m_Info != NULL){
  LPDIRECT3DRMWINDEVICE windev;
  //
  // Query if the D3DRM device supports the "windev" interface and
  // if it does return a pointer to it.
  //
  if(SUCCEEDED(m_Info->dev->QueryInterface(IID_IDirect3DRMWinDevice,
      (void **)&windev)))
  {
    //
    // Pass the Window's device context to the Direct3D device
    // HandlePaint method as required by the Direct 3D specification.
    //
    if (FAILED(windev->HandleActivate(MAKEWPARAM(bActivate,0))))
            Msg("Failed to handle WM_ACTIVATE.\n");
    windev->Release();
  }
  else
  {
    Msg("Failed to create Windows device to handle WM_ACTIVATE.\n");
  }
}
//
// Render the scene after activation in case anything has changed in
// the scene.
//
if(m_Info != NULL)
{
  if(!Render())Msg("Rendering failed.\n");
}
//
// Call the base handler.
//
    CView::OnActivateView(bActivate, pActivateView, pDeactiveView);
}
```

If the window changes size, it is possible that the viewport might adopt a different aspect ratio and thus the clipping boundaries will change. The Direct3D viewport and device will need to be recreated or updated to take account of such changes. This is done by adding a handler for the WM_SIZE message; the OnSize(..) member function of the **CD3DView** class accomplishes this as follows:

```
void CD3DView::OnSize(UINT nType, int cx, int cy)
{
  //
  // Call the base class handler
  //
```

```
       CView::OnSize(nType, cx, cy);
       if(m_Info != NULL){
         //
         // If we have a D3D device and viewport then:
         //
         int width = cx;
         int height = cy;
         if (width && height) {
           //
           // If the new window size is greater than zero then call
           // the function to change the viewport size.
           //
           ResizeViewport(m_hWnd,m_Info,width,height);
           m_Info->bMinimized = FALSE;
         }
         else{
           m_Info->bMinimized = TRUE;
         }
       }
}
```

The function `ResizeViewport()` (below) is called to change the Direct3D viewport size. `ResizeViewport()` first checks to make sure that the viewport has changed size; if it has decreased in size, the original viewport is released and created again with the new size. If it has increased in size, the Direct3D device and viewport are released and created again to adopt the size of the view window's client area:

```
BOOL CD3DView::ResizeViewport(HWND win,
                             AppInfo* info, // Our "scene etc."
                             int width,     // New dimensions for
                             int height)    // window "win"
{
    //
    // When the window changes size we must also change the size
    // of the D3D viewport, and if the window size increased then the
    // device which is associated with a clipper is also rebuilt.
    //
    int view_width  = info->view->GetWidth();
    int view_height = info->view->GetHeight();
    int dev_width   = info->dev->GetWidth();
    int dev_height  = info->dev->GetHeight();
    //
    // If nothing changes then just return.
    //
    if (view_width == width && view_height == height)
        return TRUE;
    //
    // If the width and height are reduced then the viewport is released
```

```
    // and re-created with the window's dimensions.
    //
    if (width <= dev_width && height <= dev_height)
    {
        RELEASE(info->view);
        //
        // Create the viewport again
        //
        if(FAILED(m_lpD3DRM->CreateViewport(info->dev,
            info->camera, 0, 0, width, height, &info->view)))
            goto generic_error;
        if (FAILED(info->view->SetBack(D3DVAL(400.0))))
            goto generic_error;
        return TRUE;
    }
    //
    // If the window size increases we need to rebuild the device and
    // viewport.
    //
    if(!RebuildDevice(win, info, width, height))return FALSE;
    return TRUE;
    //
generic_error:
    Msg("A failure occurred while resizing the viewport.\n");
    return FALSE;
}
```

The function `RebuildDevice(..)` uses almost exactly the same approach for the creation of the device and viewport as that given in `CreateDevice(...)`. The difference is that in rebuilding the device we must first find out which rendering method (wireframe or solid), dithering status, and shading procedure (none or Gouraud) are in effect and build the new device to the same specification:

```
    .
    .
    .
int old_dither                   = m_Info->dev->GetDither();
D3DRMRENDERQUALITY old_quality = m_Info->dev->GetQuality();
int old_shades                   = m_Info->dev->GetShades();
    .
    .
    .

m_Info->dev->SetDither(old_dither);
m_Info->dev->SetQuality(old_quality);
m_Info->dev->SetShades(old_shades);
    .
    .
```

11.6.1 Loading a Model from its X File

Like most of the 3D modeling and animation programs commercially available, Direct3D has its own native format for recording the geometric and other attributes of a model. The core data in an **X** file is a description of a mesh of vertices and faces.

Direct3D provides a *MeshBuilder* interface with a collection of methods for constructing and modifying meshes. *In the context of this chapter a mesh is a connected network of vertices and facets.* One of these methods reads and processes the **X** file to create a MeshBuilder object. The MeshBuilder is attached to a frame (a **Frame** object) to allow the object to be rendered and displayed.

In our example, this is done in the **CD3DView** class by responding to the **File Open...** command and calling function CD3DView::OpenNewModel(char *file) shown below:

```
void CD3DView::OpenNewModel(char *file)
{
 //
 // Load a model from its X file and attach it to a frame of reference
 // (the "object" frame)
 //
 LPDIRECT3DRMMATERIAL    mat;
 LPDIRECT3DRMMESHBUILDER builder;
 LPDIRECT3DRMFRAME       frame;
 HRESULT rval;
 //
 // A model consists of one or more meshes and the surface properties, the
 // facets of the mesh. In Direct3D a MeshBuilder object represents a mesh.
 // Thus the first step in loading a model description is to create a
 // MeshBuilder object and an Interface to it.
 //
 if (FAILED(m_lpD3DRM->CreateMeshBuilder(&builder)))
 {
   Msg("Failed the create a builder for the new mesh.\n");
   return;
 }
 //
 // With the MeshBuilder created we can use one of its Interface Methods
 // to load the mesh.
 rval = builder->Load(file, NULL, D3DRMLOAD_FROMFILE, NULL, NULL);
 if (rval != D3DRM_OK)
 {
   Msg("Loading %s failed.",file);
   builder->Release();
   return;
 }
 //
 // In this example we will associate a shiny surface property with the
```

```
// the mesh. This is done by creating a material (as opposed to a texture
// ---which implies an image map)and setting the mesh to that material.
// A material governs the specular reflection parameters.
//
m_lpD3DRM->CreateMaterial(D3DVAL(10.0), &mat);
//
// Apply the material to the mesh.
//
builder->SetMaterial(mat);
//
// There is no further use for the material so it can be released.
//
RELEASE(mat);
//
// Create a frame of reference (child to the main "scene") for the model
//
if(FAILED(m_lpD3DRM->CreateFrame(m_Info->scene, &frame)))
{
  Msg("Placing the mesh in the scene failed.\n");
  builder->Release();
  return;
}
//
// Attach the mesh (the model / object) to the frame we have just created.
//
if(FAILED(frame->AddVisual(builder))){
  Msg("Placing the mesh in the scene failed.\n");
  builder->Release();
  return;
}
//
// Position and orientate the model's frame of reference---this is
// exactly the same transformation that is applied in response to the
// mouse move commands.
//
frame->AddRotation(D3DRMCOMBINE_REPLACE,
        D3DVAL(1.0f),D3DVAL(0.0f),D3DVAL(0.0f),
        D3DVAL(-3.1415926f*(m_up_angle)/180.0f));
frame->AddRotation(D3DRMCOMBINE_BEFORE,
        D3DVAL(0.0f),D3DVAL(1.0f),D3DVAL(0.0f),
        D3DVAL(-3.1415926f*(m_round_angle)/180.0f));
frame->SetPosition(m_Info->scene,
        D3DVAL(0.0), D3DVAL(0.0), D3DVAL(m_distance));
//
// Store a pointer to the model's frame of reference in the AppInfo structure
//
m_Info->object=frame;
//
// The meshbuilder is no longer required, so release it.
//
```

```
builder->Release();
//
// The model is ready for viewing, so render it.
//
Invalidate(FALSE);
}
```

With the ability to load and render Direct3D meshes included in the program, all the elements for a basic Direct3D application are now in place. Figure 11.1 illustrates the use of the application to display a Direct3D retained mode mesh model using solid shading and Gouraud smoothing.

11.6.2 Viewing the Model from Any Direction and Distance

To allow inspection of the model from any viewpoint, the same approach used for the OpenGL examples can be applied here. When the left button on the mouse is pressed and the mouse is dragged, member variables m_round_angle, m_up_angle, or m_distance (of class **CD3DView**) are incremented. These variables are used to recalculate and apply transformations to the model's frame.

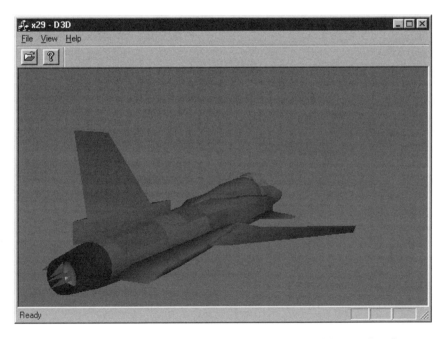

Figure 11.1.   A basic Direct3D Retained Mode application for visualizing models stored in the native (X) file format.

On rendering any meshes attached to this frame, they will take up the position and orientation dictated by any transformations acting on it.

Code to update the variables m_round_angle, etc., is inserted in the CD3DView::OnMouseMove() handler and to this are added *methods* which build transformations to rotate and move the model. This code is illustrated below:

```
void CD3DView::OnMouseMove(UINT nFlags, CPoint point)
{
.  Add the new code
.
.
     if(m_Info != NULL)
     {
       //
       // Direct3D combines transformations in much the same
       // way as is done in OpenGL, with the exception that they can be
       // arranged so that the transformation matrices are pre-multiplied
       // or post-multiplied by the current transformation.
       // The first transformation (a rotation round a horizontal axis
       // running left to right through the model---up/down pitch)
       // replaces all previous transformations of the model's
       // "m_Info->object" frame of reference.
       //
       m_Info->object->AddRotation(D3DRMCOMBINE_REPLACE,
           D3DVAL(1.0f),D3DVAL(0.0f),D3DVAL(0.0f),
           D3DVAL(-3.1415926f*(m_up_angle)/180.0f));
       //
       // After setting the pitch the other angular transformation (the
       // direction) is calculated by rotating around a vertical axis
       // (the Y-axis) and combined with the first rotation. For
       // Direct3D this means inserting this transformation matrix before
       // the first one in the matrix product chain.
       // T(final) = T(pitch) x T(direction)
       // T(final) is applied to the mesh.
       //
       m_Info->object->AddRotation(D3DRMCOMBINE_BEFORE,
           D3DVAL(0.0f),D3DVAL(1.0f),D3DVAL(0.0f),
           D3DVAL(-3.1415926f*(m_round_angle)/180.0f));
       //
       // The last transformation moves the whole frame of reference to
       // which the model is attached away from the camera.
       //
       m_Info->object->SetPosition(m_Info->scene,
           D3DVAL(0.0), D3DVAL(0.0), D3DVAL(m_distance));
     }
     Invalidate(FALSE);
.
.
.
}
```

11.7 Enhancing the Direct3D Example

Since the OpenGL example was designed to display 3DS models, we can enhance the Direct3D example by adding similar support. Our program will then display either **3DS** or **X** type files. We will also see that is very easy to create an X format file from the MeshBuilder object, achieving file format conversion!

Direct3D provides methods to load and save mesh objects, but we must provide our own functions to read from the 3DS file and create appropriate meshes. In principle the same code and data structures developed for the OpenGL examples can be used for Direct3D, but a few minor modifications are necessary.

We will add our functions to parse 3DS file to the CD3DDoc class and place the code in the D3DDOC.CPP file. Functions will be needed to read the file and use its facet and vertex data to create a series of *MeshBuilder* objects for attachment to the model's frame. A pointer to the model's frame is kept in an AppInfo structure. (*Unfortunately it is called the "object" frame; sorry about all these objects.*)

11.7.1 Adding Basic 3DS File Support

To enhance the example we must start by allowing the program to use files with either .X and .3DS filename extensions in the Open File dialog box. For MFC programs this is done by modifying the resource string "IDR_MAINFRAME" from:

```
STRINGTABLE PRELOAD DISCARDABLE
BEGIN
  IDR_MAINFRAME "D3D\n\nD3D\nD3D Files (*.x)\n.X\nD3D.Document\nD3D Document"
END
```

to:

```
STRINGTABLE PRELOAD DISCARDABLE
BEGIN
  IDR_MAINFRAME "D3D\n\nD3D\nModel Files (*.3ds *.x)\n3ds;
    .X\nD3D.Document\nD3D Document"
END
```

Thus, the text string passed to OnOpenDocument(LPSTCR) could indicate a file of either type. It is a simple matter to parse the string for the filename extension and then call the appropriate loading code:

```
BOOL CD3DDoc::OnOpenDocument(LPCTSTR lpszPathName)
{
    if (!CDocument::OnOpenDocument(lpszPathName))return FALSE;
    //
    // Identify whether we are loading an X or 3DS file
    //
```

```
int ff=IdentifyFileFormat((char *)lpszPathName);
//
POSITION pos = GetFirstViewPosition();
CD3DView *v = (CD3DView *)GetNextView( pos );
if(v == NULL)return FALSE;
//
// Clear any existing D3D model
//
v->DeleteObject();
if(ff == FI_X)
{
  //
  // For an X file call through to a function of the view
  // class to load an X file.
  v->OpenNewModel((char *)lpszPathName);
}
  .
  .
  .
```

In the Direct3D example, the 3DS files are handled slightly differently from the way they were in the OpenGL example so that image/texture mapping can be facilitated. Each group of facets in the 3DS file usually has one single *material* applied to them all. Materials are specified in a separate *chunk* in the file and each material will specify a color, specular reflection parameters, and possibly various types of texture map.

The OpenGL example did not distinguish these groups, and they all were loaded into a single list of vertices and facets. In this Direct3D example we will treat these groups individually, because it is much easier and faster to assign materials and textures to a group of facets as opposed to having to do it to every one.

To display 3DS models it will almost certainly be necessary to scale and reposition then. This is done when the location of *all* the vertices are known; therefore, we will read the 3DS file twice. The first pass reads all the vertices and determines the scaling factors. The second pass reads each chuck separately. After each chunk is read, a **MeshBuilder** object is created, the vertices and facets from the chunk are added to the MeshBuilder, material properties are assigned to it, and it in turn is placed in one of the scene's frames.

The 3DS file is read by calling Read3dsObject(...) from the second part of the CD3DDoc::OnOpenDocument(..) function:

```
  .
  .
  .
else if(ff == FI_3DS)
{
```

```
            //
            // Read all vertices and facets into one list.
            // "v" is a pointer to the View class "CD3DView"  C++ object.
            //
            Read3dsObject(v,(char *)lpszPathName,FALSE);
            //
            // Determine scaling factors.
            //
            m_scale=(float)GetScaleValue(m_c);
            //
            // Release the vertex and facet lists.
            //
            FreeObject();
            //
            // Now read again the 3DS file---this time build D3D meshes for
            // each 3DS "object chunk" in the model.
            //
            Read3dsObject(v,(char *)lpszPathName,TRUE);
            //
            // D3D holds all mesh info; free any space used by local lists.
            //
            FreeObject();
        }
        return TRUE;
}
```

The **CD3DDoc** class needs member variables, function prototypes, and data structures for vertices and facets before it can read the 3DS file. These are accommodated in the D3DDOC.H header file and are basically the same as used previously for the OpenGL examples. Thus the project's document class header file becomes:

```
// D3DDoc.h : interface of the CD3DDoc class
//
/////////////////////////////////////////////////////////////////////////////
// Add the following data structure and types---the same as OpenGL examples

#define FI_X    1
#define FI_3DS 2

// Use the Windows API memory allocation functions
#define xMalloc(s)    ::LocalAlloc(LMEM_FIXED,s)
#define xFree(p)      ::LocalFree((HLOCAL)p)
#define xRealloc(p,s) ::LocalReAlloc((HLOCAL)p,s,LMEM_MOVEABLE)

// Useful structures for 3D graphics work
typedef float vector[3];

typedef struct tagVERTEX {
```

```
  float p[3];              // position of the vertex
  float x,y;              // surface mapping coordinates
} VERTEX;

typedef struct tagFACET {
  long V[3];              // vertex identifier for triangular facet
  unsigned char color[3]; // color of facet
  unsigned char MapID;    // identify the image map
  BOOL Map;              // facet is covered by image map
  BOOL Smooth;           // facet is to have Gouraud shading applied
} FACET;

typedef struct tagMAP {
  char filename[128];     // filename for any surface map
  BOOL Map;              // TRUE if map has surface image
} MAP;

//
// The 3DS file format specifies a number of materials which
// are applied to the facets in the model. These 3DS materials
// are listed in an array of the following structures which
// are then matched up to the FACET color or, if an image map
// is involved, the image map.
//
typedef struct tagMATERIAL {
  char    N[32];          // 3DS material name
  short   Index;          // If an image map is needed this
                          // is an index to map list
  unsigned char d_colour[3];// The 3DS diffuse color or the material
} MATERIAL;


////////////////////////////////////////////////////////////////////
// The document class is modified to accommodate the loading of 3DS
// files.

class CD3DView;

class CD3DDoc : public CDocument
{
// Member variables
VERTEX   *MainVp;  // List of vertices in the model
FACET    *MainFp;  // List of facets in the model
MAP      *MapsFp;  // List of any image maps used in the model
MATERIAL *MatsFp;  // Temporary list of 3DS materials
long     Nvert,    // Number of vertices in the model
         Nface,    // Number of facets in the model
         Nmap,     // Number of image maps
         nMats,    // Number of 3DS materials
```

```
                   LastVert,   // Temporary variables used during file reading
                   LastFace;   // to keep facet indexing correct for multiple
                               // multiple meshes.

        vector   m_c;        // Center of the model
        float    m_scale;    // Scaling value for model

        // Member function prototypes

        int    IdentifyFileFormat(char *);
        void   Read3dsObject(CD3DView *, char *, BOOL);
        void   FreeObject(void);
        BOOL   get_object(long, FILE *);
        void   get_faces(FILE *);
        void   get_mapping_coords(FILE *);
        void   get_material(long, FILE *);
        long   GetMap(char *);
        void   get_vertices(FILE *);
        long   GetLong(FILE *);
        short  GetShort(FILE *);
        char   GetByte(FILE *);

        // D3D Mesh function

        void AddMeshToFrame(CD3DView *, LPDIRECT3DRMFRAME );
        float GetScaleValue(vector );
        BOOL GetNormal(vector, vector, vector, float *);
        BOOL Normalize(vector);

        // The remainder of the class definitions are those created by
        // the Visual C++ AppWizard
        .
        .
        .
        .
};
//////////////////////////////////////////////////////////////////////
```

Function `Read3dsObject(..)` is charged with the task of reading the 3DS file and it loops through all *chunks* in the 3DS file reading them one at a time. If it detects a *mesh object* chunk, then execution is passed to function `get_object(..)` and it returns TRUE (but only if any facets are present as part of that chunk—some 3DS object chunks (the camera, for example) do not contain any vertices or facets). A TRUE return value from `get_object(..)`, causes a call to `AddMeshToFrame(..)` which builds a Direct3D mesh from the vertex and facet lists created by `get_object(..)`.

The Direct3D specific code in function:

```
Read3dsObject(CD3DView *view, char *FileName, BOOL build)
```

starts by creating a *Frame* to which *MeshBuilder* objects are attached:

```
.
LPDIRECT3DRMFRAME frame;
.
if(build)view->m_lpD3DRM->CreateFrame(view->m_Info->scene,&frame);
.
```

The parameter `build` is a Boolean variable which is false when reading the file for scaling information only. Parameter `view` is a pointer to the **CD3DView** class whose members we need access to and `frame` is the pointer returned by the Direct3DRM method `CreateFrame()`; it points to the *Frame* we need.

On return from `get_object(..)`, if any vertices or facets were found in the chunk of the file, then a call is made to `AddMeshToFrame(..)` which does the work of building a mesh and applying materials and textures to it. This code fragment is given below:

```
.
.
BOOL retval=get_object(count,fi);
if(build && retval){
  //
  // A mesh of vertices and faces exists and should be added
  // to the "object" Frame
  //
  AddMeshToFrame(view,frame);
  //
  // We don't need the Vertex/Face and other information
  // in the data structures read from the 3DS file since the
  // D3D meshes have now been created.
  //
  FreeObject();
  //
}
.
.
```

Once all chunks in the file have been processed, `Read3dsObject()` performs similar actions to those used for the X file; i.e., the *Frame* is placed in the scene and its orientation is set as follows:

```
.
if(build)
{
  frame->AddRotation(D3DRMCOMBINE_REPLACE,
       D3DVAL(1.0f),D3DVAL(0.0f),D3DVAL(0.0f),
```

```
                D3DVAL(-3.1415926f*(view->m_up_angle)/180.0f));
    frame->AddRotation(D3DRMCOMBINE_BEFORE,
            D3DVAL(0.0f),D3DVAL(1.0f),D3DVAL(0.0f),
            D3DVAL(-3.1415926f*(view->m_round_angle)/180.0f));
    frame->SetPosition(view->m_Info->scene,
            D3DVAL(0.0), D3DVAL(0.0), D3DVAL(view->m_distance));
    view->m_Info->object=frame;
    view->Invalidate();
  }
  .
  .
  return;
}
```

Function `CD3DDoc::AddMeshToFrame(..)` performs the following tasks:

1. Use the list of vertices and facets to construct the vertex normals that are needed for Gouraud shading. Note: Direct3D uses a different coordinate system from that of the 3DS model; i.e., *Z* is *up* in 3DS but *y* is *up* in Direct3D.

2. Convert the data into the form needed by the Direct3D MeshBuilder object interface methods; use the methods to add vertices and faces to the MeshBuilder object.

3. Set the color of the facets.

4. Make the mesh a visible component of the reference *Frame* to which it is attached. A listing for `AddMeshToFrame(..)` follows:

```
void CD3DDoc::AddMeshToFrame(
        CD3DView *view,         // Pointer to the application's View class;
                                // we need to have access to various member
                                // variables and function of that class from
                                // within an object of the CD3DDoc class.
        LPDIRECT3DRMFRAME frame // Pointer to the "object" Frame member
                                // of the "AppInfo" structure.
                            )
{
LPDIRECT3DRMMESHBUILDER builder;
D3DVECTOR *vv,*nn;
unsigned long *ff;
float x,y,z,n[3];
FACET *fp;
VERTEX *v,*v1,*v2,*v0;
long i,j,kf;
//
// The mesh is created in pieces; each call to this function creates
// one piece (corresponding to each object chunk in a 3DS file).
```

```
// A Direct3D MeshBuilder object is needed, and when the vertices and
// faces have been added to a MeshBuilder, the mesh is made visible
// by attaching it to a Frame.
//
// We will use the Interface Method "IDirect3DRMMeshBuilder::AddFaces(..)"
// to place the mesh in the MeshBuilder, this requires that Vertices,
// Vertex Normals, and a list of indices to vertices which define faces
// are given in a specific format.
//
// The first thing we must do is compile the necessary lists.
//
if(Nface == 0)return;
//
// Allocate memory for the Vertex list (this is a set of D3DVECTORs)
//
if((vv = (D3DVECTOR *)xMalloc(Nvert*sizeof(D3DVECTOR))) == NULL)return;
//
// Allocate memory for the face list---in this example, each face is a
// triangle; therefore we need:
//   1 long integer to tell D3D that each face has 3 vertices
//   3 long integers, indexing the face's vertices in the vertex list.
//   3 long integers, indexing the surface normal list for each face vertex.
//
if((ff = (unsigned long *)xMalloc((7*Nface+1)*sizeof(unsigned long))) == NULL)
{
  xFree(vv);
  return;
}
//
// Allocate memory for the surface normal direction at each vertex.
//
if((nn = (D3DVECTOR *)xMalloc(Nvert*sizeof(D3DVECTOR))) == NULL)
{
  xFree(vv);
  xFree(ff);
  return;
}
//
// Build the vertex list of D3DVECTORS by scaling the list of vertex
// positions read from the 3DS file.
//
v=MainVp;  for(i=0;i<Nvert;i++,v++)
{
  x=(float)(v->p[0]-m_c[0])*m_scale;
  y=(float)(v->p[1]-m_c[1])*m_scale;
  z=(float)(v->p[2]-m_c[2])*m_scale;
  vv[i].x=D3DVAL(x);
  vv[i].y=D3DVAL(z);
  vv[i].z=D3DVAL(-y);
  nn[i].x = nn[i].y = nn[i].z = D3DVAL(0.0f);
```

```
      }
      //
      // Make the facet list and list of vertex normals. For vertex "i" the
      // normal is obtained by averaging the normals in all faces that are
      // attached to vertex "i".
      //
      fp=MainFp; kf=0; for(i=0;i<Nface;i++,fp++){
        long i1,i2,i3;
        i1=fp->V[0]; i2=fp->V[1]; i3=fp->V[2];
        v0=(MainVp+i1); v1=(MainVp+i2); v2=(MainVp+i3);
        GetNormal(v0->p,v1->p,v2->p,n);
        //
        // Get Normal returns a normal using a left-handed frame of reference
        // with "z" being the up direction. For D3D we must adjust to a right-
        // handed coordinate system with "y" up.
        //
        nn[i1].x += D3DVAL(n[0]);
        nn[i1].y += D3DVAL(n[2]);
        nn[i1].z += D3DVAL(-n[1]);
        nn[i2].x += D3DVAL(n[0]);
        nn[i2].y += D3DVAL(n[2]);
        nn[i2].z += D3DVAL(-n[1]);
        nn[i3].x += D3DVAL(n[0]);
        nn[i3].y += D3DVAL(n[2]);
        nn[i3].z += D3DVAL(-n[1]);
        ff[kf++]=3;
        for(j=0;j<3;j++)
        {
          ff[kf++]=fp->V[j];
          ff[kf++]=fp->V[j];
        }
      }
      for(i=0;i<Nvert;i++)
      {
        //
        // Normalize the vertex vectors.
        //
        D3DRMVectorNormalize(&nn[i]);
      }
      //
      // Place the terminating "zero" into the facet list (required by
      // the "AddFaces" method).
      //
      ff[kf++]=0;
      //
      // Create the MeshBuilder object and add the faces to it.
      //
      view->m_lpD3DRM->CreateMeshBuilder(&builder);
      builder->AddFaces(Nvert,vv,Nvert,nn,ff,NULL);
      //
```

```
// We assign a color to the faces in this mesh from the first
// color in this chunk in the 3DS file. It's not exactly correct
// because it assigns color to each triangular facet,
// but in a large number of 3DS models each object chunk will use
// a single material.
//
builder->SetColor(D3DRMCreateColorRGB(
  D3DVAL((float)(MainFp->color[0])/255.0),
  D3DVAL((float)(MainFp->color[1])/255.0),
  D3DVAL((float)(MainFp->color[2])/255.0)));
//
// Place this mesh in the "object" frame of reference.
//
frame->AddVisual(builder);
//
// We don't need the MeshBuilder, and so it may be released.
//
builder->Release();
xFree(vv);
xFree(nn);
xFree(ff);
return;
}
```

11.7.2   Creating an X File

The MeshBuilder interface provides a method,

`IDirect3DRMMeshBuilder::Save()`,

which writes all mesh information into an **X** file. To make use of this simple
feature, we need to add a menu command and appropriate code to our example, say
by inserting a `CD3DDoc::OnSaveDocument(..)` handler into the document
class. A menu item or toolbar button is readily inserted with the Visual C++
resource editor and the handler for its command message may be added by the
Class Wizard.

To use the `IDirect3DRMMeshBuilder::Save(..)` method, we need a
pointer to a MeshBuilder interface. The `AppInfo` data structure holds a pointer
to the frame on which the meshes we visualize are attached, and Direct3D provides
methods for retrieving interfaces to these meshes from that frame. Actually there
is one little complication. The Save method can only write X files for one Mesh-
Builder at a time, but the technique we used to make meshes while reading the
3DS file placed several MeshBuilders in the frame, one for each *object chunk*. Before we can save all the mesh information, we must combine all the MeshBuilders
into one; Direct3D provides methods to do this easily. All the necessary code is
encapsulated in the `CD3DDoc::OnSaveDocument(..)` function as follows:

```
BOOL CD3DDoc::OnSaveDocument(LPCTSTR lpszPathName)
{
    //
    // Start by getting a pointer to the CD3DView class object.
    //
    POSITION pos = GetFirstViewPosition();
    CD3DView *v = (CD3DView *)GetNextView( pos );
    if(v == NULL)return FALSE;
    //
    // If a mesh has been loaded from a 3DS file, it may be quite
    // useful to save this as a Direct3D native model file (an X file).
    // This is very easily done with one of the MeshBuilder methods.
    //
    LPDIRECT3DRMVISUAL visual;
    LPDIRECT3DRMVISUALARRAY visuals;
    LPDIRECT3DRMMESHBUILDER builder,composite_builder;
    //
    // We need to retrieve the MeshBuilder objects attached to
    // the "object" frame and make a composite which can be written
    // to the X file.
    //
    //
    // Start by getting a list of all visual objects attached to the
    // frame where the meshes were placed.
    //
    v->m_Info->object->GetVisuals(&visuals);
    if(visuals)
    {
        //
        // Get the number of visual objects in the list of visual objects
        //
        int n=visuals->GetSize();
        //
        // Create a MeshBuilder into which all meshbuilders will be composited.
        //
        v->m_lpD3DRM->CreateMeshBuilder(&composite_builder);
        for(int i=0;i<n;i++)
        {
            //
            // Get the next visual element
            //
            visuals->GetElement(i,&visual);
            if(visual)
            {
                if(SUCCEEDED(visual->QueryInterface(
                            IID_IDirect3DRMMeshBuilder,
                            (void **) &builder)))
                {
                    //
```

```
            // If this visual element is a MeshBuilder (it might be a
            // light or something else so we must check to see if the
            // MeshBuilder interface is supported) composite it into
            // a single meshbuilder.
            //
            composite_builder->AddMeshBuilder(builder);
            builder->Release();
          }
          visual->Release();
        }
      }
      //
      // Write the X file (Text format is the only format supported in
      // DirectX 2. All the elements (color, texture coordinates, etc.) are
      // to be recorded.
      //
      composite_builder->Save(lpszPathName,
                              D3DRMXOF_TEXT,
                              D3DRMXOFSAVE_ALL);
      composite_builder->Release();
      visuals->Release();
    }
    return TRUE;
}
```

11.7.3   Texture-Mapped Surfaces

Painting an image over the surface of a mesh is the most versatile improvement one can add to a faceted 3D model in the quest for realism. Like OpenGL, Direct3D provides a number of **IDirect3DRM** methods for mapping images onto mesh surfaces. Direct3D calls its image maps "textures," and there is an interface to a collection of methods that create textures from bitmap image files. The textures can be stored in system or video memory and applied to meshes or other DirectDraw surfaces.

Our example can be extended to make use of the textures indicated in the 3DS file. (Confusingly, 3DS calls its textures "materials"; in Direct3D "material" has a specific meaning: *specular properties*.)

To apply a texture to a mesh the vertices must be given *Texture Coordinates*. This is done by specifying a pair of numbers (v, μ) for each vertex in the mesh. 3DS files store texture coordinates in a form that can be used directly by Direct3D. Another thing we need to be careful about is that Direct3D does not support the full range of image file formats that are likely to be found embedded in a 3DS file. To keep this example as short as possible, a single small bitmap BMP-type file will be substituted for all image maps.

All the changes necessary to apply mapped textures to meshes are inserted in the `CD3DDoc::AddMeshToFrame(..)` function. Texture coordinates are added to the vertices in a mesh by inserting a call to the MeshBuilder method `SetTextureCoordinates()` as follows:

```
     .
     .
for(i=0,v=MainVp;i<Nvert;i++,v++)
{
  D3DRMVectorNormalize(&nn[i]);
  //
  // Add this line to assign the texture coordinates read from the 3DS file.
  //
  builder->SetTextureCoordinates(i,D3DVALUE(v->x),D3DVALUE(v->y));
}
     .
     .
```

To create and apply the texture to the mesh surface the following code is added in place of assigning a color to the faces in the mesh:

```
     .
     .
if(MainFp->Map)
{
  builder->SetColor(D3DRMCreateColorRGB(
    D3DVAL((float)1.0f),
    D3DVAL((float)1.0f),
    D3DVAL((float)1.0f)));

}
else
{
  builder->SetColor(D3DRMCreateColorRGB(
    D3DVAL((float)(MainFp->color[0])/255.0),
    D3DVAL((float)(MainFp->color[1])/255.0),
    D3DVAL((float)(MainFp->color[2])/255.0)));
}
//
// Make the mesh shiny by creating a specular material and applying
// it to the mesh.
//
LPDIRECT3DRMMATERIAL mat;
view->m_lpD3DRM->CreateMaterial(D3DVAL(10.0), &mat);
builder->SetMaterial(mat);
RELEASE(mat);
//
// If the faces in this mesh have a mapped texture, then create the
// the texture and set the faces in the MeshBuilder to be covered
```

```
// with the texture image.
//
if(MainFp->Map){
  //
  // Load the image for the texture. The picture file names embedded in
  // the 3DS file cannot be loaded directly because only Windows
  // Bitmap (BMP) and packed pixel (PPM) format is supported.
  // In our example we just load an arbitrary replacement.
  // Direct 3D prefers square bitmaps.
  //
  //
  if(!FAILED(view->m_lpD3DRM->LoadTexture("placeholder.bmp",&lpTx))){
    if(!(hr=builder->SetTexture(lpTx)) == D3DRM_OK){
      AfxMessageBox("Builder failed to assigned texture");
    }
    RELEASE(lpTx);
  }
  //
  // To see the actual name of the image file embedded in the 3DS
  // file uncomment the line below.
  //AfxMessageBox(MapsFp[MainFp->MapID].filename);
}
.
.
.
```

Image maps can also be used to provide a background to the Viewport. It can
be a pleasant effect to replace a plain color background in the scene. This is done
by creating a texture and replacing the call to the SetSceneBackgroundRGB(..)
method with one to the SetSceneBackgroundImage(..) method:

```
.
.
LPDIRECT3DRMTEXTURE lpTx;
lpTx = NULL;
m_lpD3DRM->LoadTexture("cloud.bmp",&lpTx);
info->scene->SetSceneBackgroundImage(lpTx);
RELEASE(lpTx);
.
.
```

A final change that we ought to make is to take account of textures specified
in an X file. This is easily done by specifying a callback function as a parameter
to the IDirect3DRMMeshBuilder::Load(..) method:

```
.
//
// With the MeshBuilder created we can use one of its Interface Methods
// to load the mesh. A callback function "MyTextureCallback" will be
// called by the MeshBuilder's Load method so that any texture images
```

```
// used by the model in the X file can be created.
//
rval = builder->Load(file,                   // Name of file
                     NULL,
                     D3DRMLOAD_FROMFILE,
                     MyTextureCallback, // Name of callback function
                     (LPVOID)this);     // Pointer to the View object
                                        // this argument is passed to
                                        // the callback function.
```

The action of the callback function is to create a texture and pass back the address of a pointer to the texture object (in argument lpTX):

```
static HRESULT MyTextureCallback(
      char *tex_name,
      void *lpArg,
      LPDIRECT3DRMTEXTURE * lpTx   // Returned
      )
{
//
// The lpArg (user's) argument points to "this" view object.
// We use it to gain access to the m_lpD3DRM member variable so that
// the method which loads textures can be called.
//
CD3DView* c=(CD3DView *)lpArg;
//
// We will use a dummy texture file, to see the name of the required
// image file uncomment the line below.
//AfxMessageBox(tex_name);
//
c->m_lpD3DRM->LoadTexture("placeholder.bmp",lpTx);
//
// return D3DRM_OK if all went well.
//
return D3DRM_OK;
}
```

Figure 11.2 illustrates the completed Direct3D viewer in action.

11.8 Animation in Direct3D

There are an infinite variety of ways one might choose to develop this application further. Since one of the main objectives in using Direct3D is real-time rendering, an obvious thing to do is to instruct a model to perform some kind of action.

Figure 11.2.   A direct 3D example showing a 3DS model with image mapped texture.

11.8.1   Basic Animation

In its current state, the example program allows its user to view a model from
any direction by pivoting it as the mouse is moved left or right, up or down. The
simplest programmable action that comes to mind is to set the model rotating about
a vertical axis through its center. This is done by starting a timer to increment the
m_round_angle variable by a few degrees each time the timer goes off.

To start or stop a timer, the command ID_FILE_ROTATE is added to the
menu with a corresponding button on the tool bar. The Visual C++ Class Wizard
will place a handler for this command in the **CD3DView** class. The handler
automatically starts a timer if one is not running. A member variable m_timer
is needed to record the timer identity ID when it is running; it holds zero when
the timer is stopped. With the Class Wizard we may also add a check mark to
the *Rotate* menu item and show the toolbar bitmap in a pressed state as required.

The following code shows how:

```
void CD3DView::OnFileRotate()
{
    if(m_timer == 0)m_timer=SetTimer(1,33,NULL);
    else
    {
        KillTimer(m_timer);
        m_timer=0;
    }
}


void CD3DView::OnUpdateFileRotate(CCmdUI* pCmdUI)
{
    if(m_timer == 1)pCmdUI->SetCheck(1);
    else            pCmdUI->SetCheck(0);
}
```

A handler for the WM_TIMER messages is added to respond to the timer. The handler increments the viewing angle, calculates new Direct3D transformations, and instructs the viewport to be rendered:

```
void CD3DView::OnTimer(UINT nIDEvent)
{
    m_round_angle += 5.0f;
    while(m_round_angle >  180.0f)m_round_angle -= 360.0f;
    //
    // Uncomment the line below if you want the model to pitch while turning
    // m_up_angle += 2.5f;
    //
    if(m_Info != NULL)
    {
      m_Info->object->AddRotation(D3DRMCOMBINE_REPLACE,
            D3DVAL(1.0f),D3DVAL(0.0f),D3DVAL(0.0f),
            D3DVAL(-3.1415926f*(m_up_angle)/180.0f));
      m_Info->object->AddRotation(D3DRMCOMBINE_BEFORE,
            D3DVAL(0.0f),D3DVAL(1.0f),D3DVAL(0.0f),
            D3DVAL(-3.1415926f*(m_round_angle)/180.0f));
      m_Info->object->SetPosition(m_Info->scene,
            D3DVAL(0.0), D3DVAL(0.0), D3DVAL(m_distance));
      Invalidate(FALSE);
    }
        CView::OnTimer(nIDEvent);
}
```

As a finishing touch to Version 4 of the **D3D** project (D3D_4), we will insert a small user interface feature so that the program remembers the position of the

Toolbar and whether it was *docked* to the frame window or not. The **CMainFrame** class provides functions to do this for us, which record in the program's `.INI` file information about where the Toolbar is positioned.

To save the information a call to `CFrameWnd::SaveBarState(...)` must be made before the application terminates. The best way to do this is to add a handler for the `WM_CLOSE` message as follows:

```
void CMainFrame::OnClose()
{
    //
    // Save the status of the toolbar and status bar and whether it
    // was docked or not.
    //
    SaveBarState("D3D:BarStatus");
        //
        CFrameWnd::OnClose();
}
```

To make use of this information, a call to `CMainFrame::LoadBarState(..)` is placed in `CMainFrame::OnCreate(..)` after the Toolbar has been created and docking enabled:

```
        .
        .
        EnableDocking(CBRS_ALIGN_ANY);
        DockControlBar(&m_wndToolBar);
    //
    // Load the last-used position of the Toolbar and whether it was
    // docked or not. Also find out whether the status and toolbars
    // are visible at startup.
    //
    LoadBarState("D3D:BarStatus");
    //
        return 0;
}
```

The text string "`D3D:BarStatus`" is the name used for a section in the `.INI` file where the application stores information about the status of the Toolbar.

11.8.2 Keyframe Animation

A very simple example of a real-time animation was discussed in the previous section. Direct3D provides a mechanism to build more sophisticated animations with mesh models, cameras and lights all taking part in the action. This support is implemented through the `IDirect3DRMAnimation` and `Idirect3DRMAnimationSet` interfaces. These interfaces implement a

Keyframe animation system for position and orientation of a mesh model. The Direct3D keyframe concept is similar to the approach discussed in Chapter 6 but with following important difference:

> *Direct3D uses a left-handed coordinate system in which the y-axis is vertical and the z-axis lies in the depth direction. Direct 3D also uses transformation matrices in a form transposed to that used throughout this book. That is, to transform the vector* **p** *to* **p**′ *the equation is written* $[p'] = [p][T]$, *whereas in Chapter 2 the transformations were expressed as* $[p'] = [T][p]$. *See the explanation in Figure 11.3.*

Not withstanding this exception, Direct3D provides the ideal functionality to implement an application for rigid-motion animation with real-time performance and most of the features described in Sections 6.1 and 6.2.

In this section we will convert the simple viewing example of project D3D_4 into one that performs keyframe animation. The project D3D_5 will be designed to present the user interface illustrated in Figure 11.4.

An `Idirect3DRMAnimation` object controls the animation by acting on one or more of Direct3D's frames of reference. Methods in the object's interface define keyframes for the position and orientation of the chosen *frame* at a specified times τ_i. After two or more keyframes have been created, an `Idirect3DRMAnimation` interface method is called to move the *frame* into the position corresponding to a given τ. The method does this by interpolation.

$$
\begin{bmatrix} p'_0 \\ p'_1 \\ p'_2 \\ 1 \end{bmatrix} = \begin{bmatrix} t_{00} & t_{01} & t_{02} & t_{03} \\ t_{10} & t_{11} & t_{12} & t_{13} \\ t_{20} & t_{21} & t_{22} & t_{23} \\ t_{30} & t_{31} & t_{32} & t_{33} \end{bmatrix} \begin{bmatrix} p_0 \\ p_1 \\ p_2 \\ 1 \end{bmatrix}
$$

Original form $[p'] = [T][p]$

$$
\begin{bmatrix} p'_0 & p'_1 & p'_2 & 1 \end{bmatrix} = \begin{bmatrix} p_0 & p_1 & p_2 & 1 \end{bmatrix} \begin{bmatrix} t_{00} & t_{10} & t_{20} & t_{30} \\ t_{01} & t_{11} & t_{21} & t_{31} \\ t_{02} & t_{12} & t_{22} & t_{32} \\ t_{03} & t_{13} & t_{23} & t_{33} \end{bmatrix}
$$

Transposed form $[p']^T = [p]^T [T]^T$

Figure 11.3. The same transformation, which takes **p** to **p**′, can be expressed in two equivalent ways. If $[T]$ is the transformation matrix, the two formulations shown are equivalent because for any two matrices $[A]$ and $[B]$, $([A][B])^T = [A]^T[B]^T$ and vector **p** can be represented as either a one-column or one-row matrix.

Figure 11.4.   The interface for a keyframe animation system derived from the simple viewer application.

On rapidly rendering images of the scene for a succession of small increments in τ, the model will move and pivot as it follows the path laid down by the keyframes. Direct3D offers a choice of interpolation methods; splines give the smoothest motion and orientation interpolation is carried out with quaternions.

To demonstrate Direct3D's animation capability we need to modify our example project to specify a time interval, establish a position in three dimensions, and set orientations (by rotation around three axes). The user interface illustrated in Figure 11.4 allows us to make settings for position and orientation in a number of keyframes by:

1. Modifying the application's toolbar to include a slider to scroll through the time allocated to the animation.

2. Using mouse movement and keyboard key modifiers to move the reference frame in three directions.

3. Using mouse movement and keyboard key modifiers to pivot the model around any one of three perpendicular axes. (In the interface two buttons on the toolbar allow the user to toggle between using the mouse for setting position or orientation.)

4. Providing a command to remove keyframes from the animation. (Keyframes will be automatically added if mouse movement occurs.)

5. Providing a command to *Play* the action so that we can view the action.

If at some point in future development several models are in use at the same time then the frame of reference of each would have an associated animation object. For this program we only need one `IDirect3DRMAnimation` object, and thus a pointer to its interface is added to the `AppInfo` data structure, which becomes:

```
typedef struct tagAppInfo
{
    LPDIRECT3DRMFRAME scene,         // Frames of reference for the
                      camera,        // scene, camera and model.
                      object;
    LPDIRECT3DRMDEVICE dev;          // The D3D device (attached to screen)
    LPDIRECT3DRMVIEWPORT view;       // The viewport (what you see in the window)
    //
    // Add a pointer to the animation object's interface. This will be
    // associated with the "object" frame of reference. The object can thus
    // be moved to different locations and adopt different orientations at
    // specific time instances (keyframe). To render into the "viewport" at
    // a time that is not a "keyframe", Direct3D will perform interpolation.
    //
    LPDIRECT3DRMANIMATION anim;

} AppInfo;
```

Some additional variables need to be added to the project's class definitions to accommodate an animation. One variable, m_time, a member of the **CD3DApp** class, defines the number of time intervals in the animation. Since a "movie" is made up from a sequence of discrete images, one image must be rendered for each time interval in the animation.

Note: *unfortunately the term "frame" in the jargon of computer animation is generally used to refer to the picture rendered at any instant of time and one talks of, for example, "a 100-frame animation". It is important not to get these "frames" confused with "frames" of reference, which Direct3D uses to position meshes, lights, etc., in the scene. Fortunately the context in which the word "frame" is used usually make its meaning clear.*

A second global variable, m_current_time (in class **CD3DView**), records which time instant is to be rendered and displayed. To *run* the animation this integer variable is incremented from one to m_time and on each increment the scene is rendered.

To build the D3D_5 project most of the code in the D3D_4 project will be reused with the exception of the OnMouseMove(..) handler which must be

replaced. Some modification to the design of the toolbar in the **CMainFrame**
class' OnCreateHandler(..) will also be necessary. The resource editor in
Visual C++ makes the addition of buttons to the toolbar straightforward. However,
we wish to add two non-button items, the "Slider" and a "Static" text control that
will show us which frame (time) is on view. To put these Windows-common
controls in a tool bar requires a little more effort, as indicated in the following
steps:

1. Use the Visual C++ resource editor to insert gaps in the toolbar between
   the buttons where the additional controls are to be placed. The size of the
   gap does not matter; it will be adjusted when the controls are created.

2. Since we must be able to process messages from the slider control as it
   is moved by the user, we need to derive a class, **CMyToolBar**, from the
   standard MFC toolbar class **CToolBar**. A handler is added to this class to
   receive and act on WM_HSCROLL messages. The derived class is used to
   create the toolbar for the application.

3. After the toolbar has been created the designated toolbar gaps (for the additional controls) are given the TBBS_SEPARATOR style and an appropriate
   size. Controls of class **CSliderCtrl** and **CStatic** are subsequently created
   and locked into these gaps.

4. Appropriate settings for text and scrolling range are made on the controls.

These changes occur mainly in the functions of class **CMainFrame**, and the
extra instances for each of these additional classes are created by adding the
following variables to the *public* section of the class definition:

```
    .
    CSliderCtrl   m_wndSlider;      // The slider control
    CStatic       m_wndMessage;     // The text control
    .
```

Calls to the Create(..) member of these classes are added to

```
    CMainFrame::OnCreate(..)
```

which becomes:

```
int CMainFrame::OnCreate(LPCREATESTRUCT lpCreateStruct)
{
    //
    // Put our own icon in the Windows Class.
    //
    ::SetClassLong(m_hWnd,GCL_HICON,
       (LONG)(AfxGetApp()->LoadIcon(IDI_ICON1)));
```

```
if (CFrameWnd::OnCreate(lpCreateStruct) == -1) return -1;
//
// Create the StatusBar.
//
if (!m_wndStatusBar.Create(this) ||
  !m_wndStatusBar.SetIndicators(indicators,
  sizeof(indicators)/sizeof(UINT)))
{
 TRACE0("Failed to create status bar\n");
 return -1;      // fail to create
}
//
// Create the ToolBar; for a change we will put this
// at bottom of the frame window.
//
if (!m_wndToolBar.Create(this,WS_CHILD | WS_VISIBLE | CBRS_BOTTOM) ||
  !m_wndToolBar.LoadToolBar(IDR_MAINFRAME))
{
  TRACE0("Failed to create toolbar\n");
  return -1;      // fail to create
}
//
// Add the "Static" text control which will be used to show which
// is the current frame.
//
// The first thing to do is open up the gap in the toolbar so that
// space is reserved for the text. (This is item "1" in the toolbar.)
//
m_wndToolBar.SetButtonInfo(1,0,TBBS_SEPARATOR,120);
//
// Adjust the size of the rectangle for the text control.
//
CRect crc;
m_wndToolBar.GetItemRect(1,crc);
crc.InflateRect(-7,-2);
crc.OffsetRect(2,1);
//
// Create the "text" control, make it a child of the ToolBar, put
// it in the gap we have created, and instruct it to use the standard
// Windows 95 font.
//
m_wndMessage.Create("Animation Frame 1",
    WS_CHILD | WS_VISIBLE,
    crc,&m_wndToolBar,101);
m_wndMessage.SendMessage(WM_SETFONT,
  (WPARAM)::GetStockObject(ANSI_VAR_FONT),MAKELPARAM(TRUE,0));
//
// Add the Slider which sets the frame in the animation. Make space
// in the toolbar and put it there. Again open up a space in the toolbar
// (150 pixels) by calling the "SetButtonInfo()" function.
```

```
//
m_wndToolBar.SetButtonInfo(3,1,TBBS_SEPARATOR,150);
//
// Reduce slightly the size of the box where the slider will go.
//
m_wndToolBar.GetItemRect(3,crc);
crc.InflateRect(-7,-2);
crc.OffsetRect(2,1);
//
// Create the slider control. It is given the identity "ID_SLIDER"
// which corresponds to the string resource supplying the ''flyby'' help
// text and ''tooltip''. Set the slider's range to cover the number
// of time instants ''frames'' (not to be confused with Direct3D's
// reference frames) in the animation.
//
m_wndSlider.Create(TBS_HORZ | TBS_NOTICKS,crc,&m_wndToolBar,ID_SLIDER);
m_wndSlider.ShowWindow(SW_SHOW);
//
// The number-of-frames variable is held in the CD3DApp class.
//
m_wndSlider.SetRange(1,((CD3DApp *)AfxGetApp())->m_time);
//
// This toolbar is set to support tooltips and flyby help but it
// cannot be un-docked or docked on the side of the frame window
// because the Slider must remain horizontal!
//
m_wndToolBar.SetBarStyle(m_wndToolBar.GetBarStyle() |
                         CBRS_TOOLTIPS | CBRS_FLYBY);
return 0;
}
```

The action of the **CMyToolBar** horizontal scrollbar handler

```
CMyToolBar::OnHScroll(..)
```

(called when the user drags the slider control) is to execute function

```
CD3DView::UpdateAnimation()},
```

which sets the current time according to the position of the slider:

```
void CMyToolBar::OnHScroll(UINT nSBCode, UINT nPos, CScrollBar* pScrollBar)
{
    //
    // In this example all the code responsible for animation occurs
    // in the CD3DView class, so we must get a pointer to the member
    // function that updates the current frame and draws the scene at
    // that time.
```

```
//
static BOOL bBusy=FALSE;
CFrameWnd *Cf = (CFrameWnd *)GetParentFrame();
if(Cf == NULL)AfxMessageBox("NULL Parent");        // Error
else{
    CD3DView *Cv=(CD3DView *)(Cf->GetActiveView());
    if(Cv == NULL)AfxMessageBox("NULL View");      // Error
    else{
        if(pScrollBar != NULL){
            switch(nSBCode){
                case TB_BOTTOM:
                case TB_TOP:
                case TB_LINEDOWN:
                case TB_LINEUP:
                case TB_PAGEDOWN:
                case TB_PAGEUP:
                case TB_THUMBTRACK:
                case TB_THUMBPOSITION:
                  if(bBusy)break;
                  bBusy=TRUE;
                  //
                  // Call the CD3DView function that updates
                  // the current frame.
                  //
                  if(Cv != NULL)Cv->UpdateAnimationFrame();
                  bBusy=FALSE;
                  break;
                case TB_ENDTRACK:
                  break;
                default: break;
            }
        }
    }
}
//
// There is no base handler to call.
//
}
```

The view class' function CD3DView::UpdateAnimationFrame() reads the slider setting, updates a text string, displays it in the text control, and renders the new scene at the current time (given by m_current_time). Here is its code:

```
void CD3DView::UpdateAnimationFrame(void){
    m_current_time=((CMainFrame *)GetParentFrame())->m_wndSlider.GetPos();
    //
    // Update the frame display.
    //
    char temp[256];
    sprintf(temp,"Animation Frame %ld",m_current_time);
```

```
((CMainFrame *)GetParentFrame())->
m_wndMessage.SendMessage(WM_SETTEXT,0,(LPARAM)temp);
//
// To display the state of the animation at the current time
// the IDirect3DRMAnimation method "SetTime" must be called
// before rendering.
//
if(m_Info->anim->SetTime(D3DVALUE(m_current_time-1)) != D3DRM_OK)
  AfxMessageBox("Bad animation set");
Invalidate(FALSE);
}
```

Version D3D_5 of our example uses a single *IDirect3DRMAnimation* object
and associates the AppInfo.object frame with it. The *IDirect3DRMAnimation*
object is created at the same time as the Direct3DRM device, viewport, etc.
We could do this in CD3DView::CreateDevice(..) or place the necessary
code immediately after the call to CreateDevice which occurs in
CD3DView::OnCreate(..). Here is one possible coding:

```
       .
       .
       .
->  if(!CreateDevice(m_hWnd,m_Info))return -1;

->  Add code for animation here
    //
    // In this project we will animate the model with the
    // use of one of Direct3D's animation objects. The first task
    // is to create the animation object, obtain a pointer to its
    // interface, and store that pointer in the "AppInfo" data
    // structure.
    //
    if (FAILED(m_lpD3DRM->CreateAnimation(&m_Info->anim)))return -1;
    //
    // The "object" frame is the one that is to be animated. Thus it
    // is attached to the animation object.
    //
    m_Info->anim->SetFrame(m_Info->object);
    //
    // Set the Animation Objects options. These options must be
    // specified if we want to animate the position and orientation
    // of the model. By choosing a "Spline" interpolation for
    // position we will get a smooth path as the model travels between
    // its location in the keyframes. The "..OPEN" setting is
    // for animations that don't loop; i.e., no interpolation is
    // made from the last keyframe back to the first.
    //
    D3DRMANIMATIONOPTIONS aa;
    aa = D3DRMANIMATION_SPLINEPOSITION |
         D3DRMANIMATION_POSITION |
```

```
                    D3DRMANIMATION_SCALEANDROTATION |
                    D3DRMANIMATION_OPEN;
              m_Info->anim->SetOptions(aa);
              //
              // To animate the model we can start by adding keyframes for the first
              // and last times in the animation.
              // Keyframes are added firstly for position.
              //
              m_Info->anim->AddPositionKey(D3DVALUE(0),                  // At start
                    D3DVALUE(0.0f),D3DVALUE(0.0f),D3DVALUE(10.0f));
              m_Info->anim->AddPositionKey(D3DVALUE(((CD3DApp *)AfxGetApp())->m_time - 1),
// At end
                    D3DVALUE(0.0f),D3DVALUE(0.0f),D3DVALUE(10.0f));
              //
              // Orientation in a keyframe is specified by a Quaternion. However
              // it is more natural to specify an orientation in terms of an angular
              // direction, pitch, and bank. To create a rotation key these values must
              // be converted to a Quaternion. Direct3D provides functions to do just this.
              //
              D3DRMQUATERNION q;
              D3DVECTOR v;
              v.x=D3DVALUE(0.0f);   // A "Vertical" vector
              v.y=D3DVALUE(1.0f);
              v.z=D3DVALUE(0.0f);
              //
              // Make a quaternion to represent a rotation of 180 degrees around a
              // vertical vector (in the Y direction).
              //
              D3DRMQuaternionFromRotation(&q,&v,3.1415826f); // No rotation
              //
              // Set this rotation in the keyframes at the beginning and end
              // of the animation.
              //
              m_Info->anim->AddRotateKey(D3DVALUE(0), &q);
              m_Info->anim->AddRotateKey(D3DVALUE(((CD3DApp *)AfxGetApp())->m_time - 1),&q);
              //
              // If all has gone well the handler returns 0 and the program
              // proceeds. If anything goes wrong we will have returned -1
              // and the program will terminate.
              //
              .
              .
```

To achieve a smooth application closure the *IDirect3DRMAnimation* interface should be released at the same time as the other Direct3D interfaces are released, this is accomplished in CD3DView::OnDestroy( ).

Apart from creating appropriate Direct3D animation objects, the most important task we need to perform is to create keyframes at user-defined times for the position and/or orientation of the model's frame of reference. We can achieve this by replacing the CD3DView::OnMouseMove(..) handler function with one which:

1. Calculates, for the currently indicated time (the current_time), the location and orientation of the model. (This will involve interpolation should the current_time variable not equal the time of any keyframe.)

2. Calculates the change of position or orientation due to mouse movement. (The flag m_move indicates whether the change is to position or orientation.)

3. Applies this change to the values determined in step 1 to give new positions and orientations at the current_time.

4. Make the current_time a keyframe for position and orientation.

These steps are implemented using the code below:

```
void CD3DView::OnMouseMove(UINT nFlags, CPoint point)
{
  //
  // If the mouse is DOWN and being moved, determine how much since
  // the last call to this function.
  //
  if(m_bTrackPan){
    RECT rc;
    float dx,dy;
    dx=(float)(point.x-m_xs); m_xs=point.x;
    dy=(float)(point.y-m_ys); m_ys=point.y;
    GetClientRect(&rc);
    dx=dx/(float)(rc.right-rc.left);
    dy=dy/(float)(rc.bottom-rc.top);
    //
    // Calculate incremental changes to the object's frame of
    // reference for the "current_time"
    //
    m_dist=m_horiz=m_vert=0.0f;
    m_round_angle=m_up_angle=m_bank_angle=0.0f;
    //
    // If any key is pressed
    //
    if(m_bKey)
    {
      //
      // If the Boolean move flag is set to ''move'' mode change the
      // movement variable.
      //
      if(m_move)m_dist = dx*50.0f;        // Z direction
      else m_bank_angle = dx*180.0f;      // angle of bank (round Z)
    }
    else{
```

```
      if(m_move){
        m_horiz = dx*5.0f;                    // side to side
        m_vert  = dy*5.0f;                    // vertical
      }
      else
      {
        m_round_angle +=dx*360.0f;            // heading
        while(m_round_angle < -180.0f)m_round_angle += 360.0f;
        while(m_round_angle >  180.0f)m_round_angle -= 360.0f;
        m_up_angle +=dy*180.0f;               // pitch
      }
    }
    //
    // If we have DirectD3
    //
    if(m_Info != NULL)
    {
      D3DVECTOR vv;
      D3DRMMATRIX4D tMatrix;
      //
      // Get the current location and orientation in the form of
      // the 4 x 4 matrix that Direct3D uses.
      //
      m_Info->object->GetTransform(tMatrix);
      //
      // Before setting the new keyframe values, delete any that
      // currently exist.
      //
      m_Info->anim->DeleteKey(D3DVALUE(m_current_time-1));
      //
      // Extract the current position from the Matrix and copy
      // it into a "translation" matrix.
      //
      vv.x=tMatrix[3][0];
      vv.y=tMatrix[3][1];
      vv.z=tMatrix[3][2];
      //
      // Create a position keyframe offset from the current position
      // by an amount proportional to the mouse movement.
      //
      if(m_Info->anim->AddPositionKey(
              D3DVALUE(m_current_time-1),
              D3DVALUE(vv.x+m_horiz),
              D3DVALUE(vv.y-m_vert),
              D3DVALUE(vv.z+m_dist)) != D3DRM_OK)
        MessageBeep(MB_OK);
      D3DRMQUATERNION qr,qp,qb,q,qq;
      //
      // Calculate a quaternion to represent the "orientation" of the
      // "object" frame.
```

```
//
QuaternionFromMatrix(tMatrix,q);
//
// Make quaternions to represent the incremental rotations
// from the incremental angles around the local axes of the
// "object" frame.
//
// A vertical axis "Y"  up/down
//
vv.x=D3DVALUE(0.0f); vv.y=D3DVALUE(1.0f); vv.z=D3DVALUE(0.0f);
D3DRMQuaternionFromRotation(&qr,&vv,m_round_angle*3.14159f/180.0f);
//
// Horizontal axis "X" left/right
//
vv.x=D3DVALUE(1.0f); vv.y=D3DVALUE(0.0f); vv.z=D3DVALUE(0.0f);
D3DRMQuaternionFromRotation(&qp,&vv,m_up_angle*3.14159f/180.0f);
//
// Horizontal axis "Z" (depth) back/front
//
vv.x=D3DVALUE(0.0f); vv.y=D3DVALUE(0.0f); vv.z=D3DVALUE(1.0f);
D3DRMQuaternionFromRotation(&qb,&vv,m_bank_angle*3.14159f/180.0f);
//
// Combine these with the existing rotational transformation.
//
if(m_local)
{
  //
  // The axis of rotation is local to the model's frame of
  // reference.
  //
  D3DRMQuaternionMultiply(&qq,&qb,&q);
  D3DRMQuaternionMultiply(&q,&qp,&qq);
  D3DRMQuaternionMultiply(&qq,&qr,&q);
}
else{
  //
  // The axis of rotation is relative to the viewport and thus
  // independent of the current orientation of the model's
  // frame of reference.
  //
  D3DRMQUATERNION q1;
  D3DRMQuaternionMultiply(&qq,&qp,&qb);
  D3DRMQuaternionMultiply(&q1,&qr,&qq);
  D3DRMQuaternionMultiply(&qq,&q,&q1);
}
//
// Apply these by adding a rotation key.
//
m_Info->anim->AddRotateKey(D3DVALUE(m_current_time-1),&qq);
//
```

```
                    // Make these changes visible.
                    //
                    m_Info->anim->SetTime(D3DVALUE(m_current_time-1));
                }
                Invalidate(FALSE);
                //
                // End of D3D-specific code.
                //
            }
            CView::OnMouseMove(nFlags, point);
    }
```

There are a few points worthy of elaboration in that last piece of code:

1. Direct3DRM has no method for determining whether a particular time corresponds to a keyframe. Thus before adding a new keyframe the `IDirect3DRMAnimation::DeleteKey()` method is called to make sure that if there had been a keyframe, it was removed.

2. All the information about the current position and orientation of the model's frame is obtained by getting the current transformation matrix, i.e., by executing the method:

   `( m_Info -> object -> GetTransform(tMatrix);).`

   This transformation will include the effect of any IDirect3DRMAnimations applied to the model's frame.

3. To set an orientation keyframe the method `AddRotateKey(D3DVALUE(time),&quaternion)` requires a quaternion description. Direct3D provides a function which, given a quaternion, calculates the equivalent rotation matrix but **not** one for calculating the equivalent quaternion from the rotational elements of a transformation matrix, so we must provide our own.

   A function which determines a quaternion from a matrix is provided in the code associated with Chapter 6, but it must be modified to conform to the structures used by Direct3D for vectors, matrices, and quaternions. The function must also code the algorithm in a suitable form for the *transposed* matrix format used by Direct3D and depicted in Figure 11.3.

4. To determine the orientation so that it includes any changes due to the movement of the mouse, a composite quaternion q_c is calculated by multiplying quaternions describing the *prior* orientation q_0 with quaternions representing the change of direction and orientation, (q_d direction, q_r roll, and q_p pitch).

   It is the order in which q_0, q_d, q_r, and q_p are multiplied that determines whether the rotation (as a result of mouse movement) appears to occur

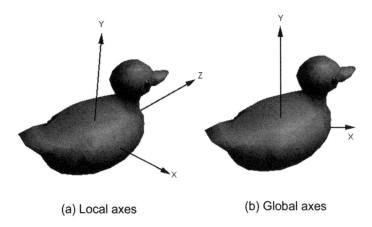

(a) Local axes   (b) Global axes

Figure 11.5.   (a) A local frame of reference; (b) A global frame of reference, the z-axis is directed into the page.

relative to the frame of reference attached to the object or to one based on the screen (the viewport). Figure 11.5 illustrates the difference.

To pivot the model around an axis system based on a frame of reference located on the model, the composite quaternion is calculated with:

$$q_c = q_d q_p q_r q_0$$

To pivot the model around the global frame of reference, the composite quaternion is determined by:

$$q_c = q_0 q_r q_b q_r$$

Once the animation has been set up it can be *played* back in realtime. To *play* the animation, a timer is started, and each time it goes off the m_current_time counter is incremented, the Idirect3DRMAnimation::SetTime(..) method is called, and the scene rendered. A suitable coding for the timer's handler is:

```
void CD3DView::OnTimer(UINT nIDEvent)
{
        UpdateInfo();
        m_Info->anim->SetTime(D3DVALUE(m_current_time-1));
        m_current_time++;
        if(m_current_time > ((CD3DApp *)AfxGetApp())->m_time)
            m_current_time=1;
        Invalidate(FALSE);
        CView::OnTimer(nIDEvent);
}
```

That completes the Direct3D animation example.

References

[1] DirectX Developer Web Site, `http://www.microsoft.com/DirectX/`

[2] R. Dunlop with D. Shepherd and M. Martin, *DirectX 7 in 24 Hours*. Sams Publishing, Indianapolis IN, 2000.

[3] P. J. Kovach, *Inside Direct3D*. Microsoft Press, Redmond WA, 2000.

[4] N. Thompson, *3D Graphics Programming for Windows 95*. Microsoft Press, Redmond WA, 1996.

[5] D. Chappell, *Understanding Active X and OLE*. Microsoft Press, Redmond WA, 1996.

CHAPTER 12

A Movie Player Using DirectDraw

In Chapter 11 Direct3D was introduced as an extension of the basic concept of DirectDraw. DirectDraw offers the application developer the ability to address directly the memory of the display adapter in a hardware-independent way and with a "*flat address space*". This is something that hasn't worked properly since the introduction of the SVGA hardware and has been quite impossible to achieve when using the standard Windows API.

Before Windows, computer animation software executing under the DOS was able to present a series of VGA resolution pictures copied from RAM at a rate of 30 or more per second. The display could be fed directly to a video recorder to make short movies. These occupied the full screen and took advantage of the PC hardware feature to switch the display from one resolution to another without having to reboot the operating system. For example, an animation program might work at a resolution of 1024×768 but show movie clips at only 320×200. The PC has a number of such low resolution modes, but up until now, there has been no way to allow a Windows application to switch easily from working in one mode to another. (The command prompt in full-screen mode switches the display adapter to a 640×480 resolution.)

In this chapter we will look at the development of an example application which takes advantage of the features of DirectDraw to change display resolution and color depth instantly and provide "flat" address access into the video memory used by display adapters. As a result, VGA resolution movies can be made to play at speeds comparable with those that used to be achieved under DOS, and in a way that occupies the full screen with no other applications or Windows decoration visible.

Before looking into the implementation of the example, a few comments regarding computer movies and how they are stored on disk should be made. Just as the Bitmap or BMP is the native format used by Windows to store picture information, the AVI (*Audio Video Interleaved*) file is the native format for movie clips, which records both pictures and sound. Before Windows, the PC was not commonly used for computer animation applications until Autodesk (as it was then known) introduced their Animator package, which set something of a standard for computer animation on the Personal Computer (PC). This package, and its later versions, is a 2D "cartoon-type" animation program that records sequences of images drawn either by hand or with the help of one of its many tools in a so-called "FLIC" file. These FLIC files utilize a *delta* compression method where only the differences between successive pictures are recorded in the file. Programs which read FLIC files and display the movies on the computer screen are able to do this particularly efficiently, and near-video speed reproduction has been possible for some time on PC processors.

The original specification for a FLIC had a limited resolution but the specification was subsequently extended to allow animations of any resolution to be recorded and replayed. A 640 × 480 display resolution is the closest PC display mode to match the requirement for TV and video; thus, FLICs made in this resolution are a good compromise between usage of disk/memory resources and acceptable viewing quality.

The AVI format is much more flexible. It allows a richer variety of data streams to be recorded than the simple FLIC. A FLIC records its images in a maximum of 256 colors with a very simple data compression algorithm, whereas AVIs can use a 24-bit mode and any one of a large selection of sophisticated *codecs* to compress the image and synchronized audio track. Today the MPEG (Motion Picture Expert Group) format, which uses compression algorithms similar to the JPEG image format, is becoming increasingly popular. MPEG is the file format used in Digital Video hardware and increasingly by PC-based video studio applications. However, in the standard desktop PC, it will be a little while yet before it is possible to display good quality 3D animated sequences in a full-screen mode at real-time frame rates.

FLICs however have the advantage that a very high display rate can be achieved during playback at high resolution and, for many animations, the quality of the images is often better than can be reproduced from an AVI. One of the features of an AVI player is its ability to skip frames, so that sound and video do not lose synchronization. Unfortunately, even FLICs played by a Windows application may suffer from unacceptable performance degradation. It is in just these situations that DirectDraw provides a solution to the performance problem, because it offers the opportunity to bypass the Windows bottleneck and, thus again, one can play video-resolution FLICs at acceptable speeds.

The sample program in this chapter not only demonstrates how to use DirectDraw for FLIC presentation but also how one might present the video information from a 640 × 480 AVI movie using the "full screen". Even for an AVI that uses a sophisticated compression codec, DirectDraw should be able to obtain a much higher display rate than is achievable when it is simply presented using the conventional Windows APIs.

The program is built by combining the code from the following three files:

1. A file containing all the DirectDraw code. The main entry point and most of the remaining Windows-specific code is included in this file.

2. A file which reads an Autodesk Animator FLIC and fills a memory buffer with the image for a given frame. (There is no specific operating system code in this file.)

3. A file with code to parse the AVI movie, find the first video stream, and fill the memory buffer with the image for a given frame.

In most scenarios the memory buffer will be in the adapter's video RAM and not in system RAM.

The FLIC and AVI image decoders are each accessed by calling two functions. To add additional decoders it would only be necessary to make a few small changes in the program, because a common parameter list is used to call both FLIC and AVI processing functions:

1. `BlitFirst(AVI/FLC)Frame(filename)` opens the file and reads the first image into a block of memory representing the screen. DirectDraw calls such an area of RAM a *surface*. Generally a *surface* is located in Video RAM on the display adapter, but it does not have to be there. DirectDraw allows surfaces to be placed anywhere; however, copying (or blitting) from one to another will be much faster if they are in display memory.

2. `BlitNext(AVI/FLC)Frame()` reads and decodes onto the screen surface the next frame's image. This function is called repeatedly until playback ceases. On the occasion when it reads the last frame the file position pointer is set back to the start.

   Note: because a FLIC stores only differences (i.e., frame i is composed from frame $i - 1$ by replacing only those pixels that have changed), an extra data chunk is appended to the end of the file and it records the differences between frames n and 1. Thus the file reads frame 1 once only and processes the other data in the sequence 1, 2, ... n, n_δ, 2 ... etc. n_δ is a list of differences that changes the last frame into the first frame.

One last general observation about the example is that since DirectDraw uses the COM and the example is written in **C**, we must call the interface methods through a **vtable**, as explained in Section 11.1.

12.1   The Main Program

The main program, in the first file, begins by introducing a few global variables needed by each file in the project and defining prototypes for the external functions linked in from the other files. The code is compatible with all DirectX versions greater than DX2.

```
//
// The following symbol must be defined so that the (G)lobal (U)nique
// (ID)entifiers used by the "QueryInterface" method are defined in only one
// of the project files which include the "windows" header.
//
#define INITGUID

#include <windows.h>
#include <commdlg.h>
#include <direct.h>
#include <ddraw.h>

#include "resource.h"

//
//  Functions defined in the second and third files of the project
//

extern BOOL BlitFirstFlxFrame(char *);
extern BOOL BlitFirstAVIFrame(char *);
extern BOOL BlitNextFlcFrame(void);
extern BOOL BlitNextFliFrame(void);
extern BOOL BlitNextAviFrame(void);

#define FLC_type 0          //  Identify the type of animation file
#define FLI_type 1          //  (found from its filename extension).
#define AVI_type 2

//
// Variables used globally
//

unsigned char   *Screen;    // A pointer to the FLAT
                            // ADDRESS space that
                            // represents the SCREEN; this
                            // is the primary display surface.

long AnimationType=FLC_type;// Default to FLC type animations.

BOOL       bInRam=FALSE;    // If TRUE then read one frame from disk and
                            // show it before reading the
                            // next, or read all the frames
```

```
                                   // into memory in their compressed
                                   // form and decompress to SCREEN;
                                   // this should be a little faster
                                   // but Windows has excellent
                                   // file caching that makes this
                                   // virtually unnecessary.

        long       pitch;          // DirectDraw tells us how many
                                   // bytes of memory span each
                                   // row on the SCREEN surface.

        unsigned char p_red[255],  // The 8-bit color palette from
                      p_green[255],// the FLIC or movie file. In this
                      p_blue[255]; // example of the use of DirectDraw,
                                   // we will exclusively use the
                                   // 8-bit paletted display mode.
```

12.1.1 The `WinMain` Function

In common with all Windows programs, the program's entry point is the `WinMain` function. The `WinMain()` function is responsible for calling `Initialize(..)` to initialize DirectDraw objects; it also provides a Windows message dispatch loop.

The specification for the example is such that there is to be an option which plays the FLIC either by using a timer or by simply rendering one frame after another as quickly as possible. To execute the latter, a call to `ReadFlicIntoSurfaces(..)` is executed inside the message dispatch loop; for the former a timer is started and `ReadFlicIntoSurfaces(..)` is called from the WM_TIMER message handler:

```
int APIENTRY WinMain(HINSTANCE hInstance,HINSTANCE hPrevInstance,
                     LPSTR lpCmdLine,int nCmdShow)
{
    MSG  msg;
    char FlicName[256];
    //
    // Get the filename of the file for the FLIC or movie we wish to
    // play; use the filename extension to determine the file type.
    //
    if(!SelectFileName(FlicName,
                "Flic files (*.FLC *.FLI *.AVI)|*.fl?;*.avi|",
                NULL,hInstance))return 0;
    if    (strstr(strupr(FlicName),".FLI") != NULL)AnimationType=FLI_type;
    else if(strstr(strupr(FlicName),".AVI") != NULL)AnimationType=AVI_type;
    else                                AnimationType=FLC_type;
    //
    // Initialize the application by creating the DirectDraw objects and
    // surfaces and then switching the display adapter into the correct mode;
```

```
        // Either 640 x 480  or  320 x 200 (both resolutions use 256 colors).
        //
        if(!Initialize(hInstance,nCmdShow))return FALSE;
        //
        // Read the first frame from the FLIC or movie into display memory.
        //
        ReadFlicIntoSurfaces(TRUE,FlicName);
        //
        // Update the display surface. (After this point the first frame should
        // be visible irrespective of whether double buffering is in use or
        // the image is being written directly into video memory.)
        //
        UpdateFrame();
        //
        // If a timer is being used to display the frames at regular times,
        // create it now.
        //
        if(bUseTimer){
          lTimer=SetTimer(hWnd,1,33,NULL);
        }
        //
        // Main message loop
        //
        while(1){
            if(PeekMessage(&msg,NULL,0,0,PM_NOREMOVE)){
                if(!GetMessage(&msg,NULL,0,0)) {
                    return msg.wParam;
                }
                TranslateMessage(&msg);
                DispatchMessage(&msg);
            }
            //
            // If not using a timer---draw the next frame.
            //
            else if(bActive && !bUseTimer){
              if(bDoubleBuffered)
                lpDD->lpVtbl->WaitForVerticalBlank(lpDD,DDWAITVB_BLOCKBEGIN,NULL);
              ReadFlicIntoSurfaces(FALSE,NULL);
              UpdateFrame();
            }
            else{
              WaitMessage();
            }
        }
        return 0;
}
```

12.1.2 Initializing DirectDraw

To make use of DirectDraw it must be initialized; this is accomplished by function `Initialize(..)`.

In the function a conventional Windows class is registered and parent Window created to provide the facility to handle messages such as `WM_KEYDOWN`, etc. The parent window is created with style `WS_POPUP` so that it does not have any titlebar or frame. It is sized to fill the whole desktop, but will never actually appear because DirectDraw is going to be given exclusive control over the display.

If the user of our example program instructs it to employ double buffering then two DirectDraw surfaces are created with a maximum size of 640×480. One surface is called the *primary* and the other the *secondary*. To use a double buffer the FLIC is composed onto the secondary surface and, when the image is ready, the second surface is "blitted" to the primary. Since both surfaces are based in video memory, DirectDraw provides a method to execute the "blit" as quickly as the display hardware permits, hopefully within the display's vertical blanking time interval.

Function `Initialize(..)` is given below:

```
static BOOL Initialize(HINSTANCE hInstance,int nCmdShow){
    WNDCLASS            wc;
    DDSURFACEDESC       ddsd;
    HRESULT             ddrval;
    DDSCAPS             ddscaps;
    //
    // Register a class for a Windows window.
    //
    wc.style=           CS_HREDRAW|CS_VREDRAW;
    wc.lpfnWndProc=     WindowProc;
    wc.cbClsExtra=      0;
    wc.cbWndExtra=      0;
    wc.hInstance=       hInstance;
    wc.hIcon=           LoadIcon(hInstance,MAKEINTRESOURCE(IDI_ICON1));
    wc.hCursor=         LoadCursor(NULL,IDC_ARROW);
    wc.hbrBackground=   NULL;
    wc.lpszMenuName=    NULL;
    wc.lpszClassName=   "DDPLAY";
    RegisterClass(&wc);
    //
    // Make a window that fills the desktop---this window will not be
    // seen because we will use DirectDraw to draw the movie so that it
    // fills the screen. The primary function of this window is to
    // process messages.
    //
    hWnd=CreateWindowEx(
        0,
        "DDPLAY",
```

```
                   "DDPLAY",
                   WS_POPUP,
                   0,
                   0,
                   GetSystemMetrics(SM_CXSCREEN),
                   GetSystemMetrics(SM_CYSCREEN),
                   NULL,
                   NULL,
                   hInstance,
                   NULL );
if(!hWnd)return FALSE;
ShowWindow(hWnd,nCmdShow);
UpdateWindow(hWnd);
//
// Create the DirectDraw object and get a pointer to its interface.
//
ddrval=DirectDrawCreate(NULL,&lpDD,NULL);
if(ddrval!=DD_OK)return StartupFailed(hWnd);
//
// We need to use the "DIRECTDRAW2" interface which provides
// additional functionality to the "DIRECTDRAW" interface. To get a pointer
// to its interface we call the "QueryInterface" method of the
// DIRECTDRAW interface. (Note the use of "lpVtbl" to get a pointer
// to the "QueryInterface" method---this is required for "C".)
//
ddrval = lpDD->lpVtbl->QueryInterface(lpDD,
                                      &IID_IDirectDraw2,  // GUID
                                      (LPVOID *)&lpDD2);
if(ddrval != DD_OK)return StartupFailed(hWnd);
//
// Tell DirectDraw we want full screen and need exclusive access
// to the video memory.
//
ddrval=lpDD->lpVtbl->SetCooperativeLevel(lpDD,hWnd,
                                         DDSCL_EXCLUSIVE|
                                         DDSCL_FULLSCREEN);
//
// If the older FLI type FLIC is to be shown then put the
// display into 320 x 200 resolution mode.
//
if(AnimationType == FLC_type || AnimationType == AVI_type){
  ddrval=lpDD2->lpVtbl->SetDisplayMode(lpDD2,640,480,8,0,0);
}
else if(AnimationType == FLI_type){
  ddrval=lpDD2->lpVtbl->SetDisplayMode(lpDD2,320,200,8,0,0);
}
if(ddrval!=DD_OK) return StartupFailed(hWnd);
//
// To draw on the screen we need a "Surface". There must be at least
// one, the PRIMARY surface. It is an area of video memory and what is
```

```
// so wonderful about DirectDraw is that this memory is provided as a "flat
// address space" which can be addressed in the same way that one used
// to use the "A000:0000" video memory area in DOS.
//
// DirectDraw allows the creation of other "surfaces" in the display
// adapter's video memory. These can be blitted onto the primary surface
// using various ROP modes and, in the context of this example such
// a second surface will allow us to implement double buffering.
//
ddsd.dwSize=sizeof(ddsd);
ddsd.dwFlags=DDSD_CAPS;
ddsd.ddsCaps.dwCaps=DDSCAPS_PRIMARYSURFACE;
ddrval=lpDD->lpVtbl->CreateSurface(lpDD,&ddsd,&lpDDSPrimary,NULL);
if(ddrval != DD_OK)return StartupFailed(hWnd);
//
// Create a second surface if double buffering is in use.
//
if(bDoubleBuffered){
  ddsd.dwSize=sizeof(ddsd);
  ddsd.dwFlags=DDSD_CAPS|DDSD_HEIGHT|DDSD_WIDTH;
  ddsd.ddsCaps.dwCaps=DDSCAPS_OFFSCREENPLAIN;
  if(AnimationType == FLC_type || AnimationType == AVI_type){
   ddsd.dwWidth=640; ddsd.dwHeight=480;
  }
  else if(AnimationType == FLI_type){
    ddsd.dwWidth=320; ddsd.dwHeight=200;
  }
  lpDD->lpVtbl->CreateSurface(lpDD,&ddsd,&lpDDSSecondary,NULL);
  if(lpDDSSecondary==NULL)return StartupFailed(hWnd);
}
bIsInitialized = TRUE;
//
// All the necessary DirectDraw objects have been created and initialized.
//
return TRUE;
}
```

12.1.3 The Window Procedure

The window procedure below handles all the messages for the application. In the case of this example, timer and keydown messages must be intercepted and acted upon. With no visible title bar or menu, key presses are the only way to communicate commands to the application.

```
static LRESULT CALLBACK WindowProc(HWND hWnd,UINT message,
                                  WPARAM wParam,LPARAM lParam){
    int speed;
    switch(message)
    {
```

```
case WM_TIMER:
 if(bActive){
   //
   // The timer has gone off, read the next image (frame)
   // into the DirectDraw surface and display it.
   //
   if(bDoubleBuffered)lpDD->lpVtbl->WaitForVerticalBlank(lpDD,
                                  DDWAITVB_BLOCKBEGIN,NULL);
   ReadFlicIntoSurfaces(FALSE,NULL);
   UpdateFrame();
 }
 break;
case WM_ACTIVATE:
   bActive = wParam;
   break;
case WM_CREATE:
   break;
case WM_SETCURSOR:
   SetCursor(NULL);
   if( bIsInitialized )
   {
       UpdateFrame();
       lpDDPal->lpVtbl->GetEntries(lpDDPal,0,0,256,pe);
   }
   break;

case WM_KEYDOWN:
   switch(wParam) {
       //
       // Use the ESCAPE or F12 key to terminate the application.
       //
       case VK_ESCAPE:
       case VK_F12:
         PostMessage(hWnd,WM_CLOSE,0,0);
         break;
       case VK_F1: speed=1;    goto SPEED;
       case VK_F2: speed=5;    goto SPEED;
       case VK_F3: speed=10;   goto SPEED;
       case VK_F4: speed=20;   goto SPEED;
       case VK_F5: speed=33;   goto SPEED;
       case VK_F6: speed=66;   goto SPEED;
       case VK_F7: speed=132;  goto SPEED;
       case VK_F8: speed=266;  goto SPEED;
         //
         // If a timer is in use these keys to
         // change the display rate.
         //
         SPEED:
         if(lTimer > 0){
           KillTimer(hWnd,lTimer);
```

```
                        lTimer=SetTimer(hWnd,1,speed,NULL);
                    }
                    break;
                }
                break;
            case WM_DESTROY:
                if(lTimer > 0)KillTimer(hWnd,lTimer);
                RemoveAll();
                PostQuitMessage(0);
                break;
        }
        return DefWindowProc(hWnd,message,wParam,lParam);
    }
```

12.1.4 Reading FLICs into Surfaces

Function `ReadFlicIntoSurfaces(..)` is responsible for decoding the image information onto the DirectDraw surface. It has to take account of whether it is processing a file for the first time or it is to acquire the next frame from the FLIC file.

Before our example can write to a display surface, the memory that surface represents must be "locked". DirectDraw insists on this and provides a method to do it. Locking a block of memory validates the pointer to the surface and informs us of the "pitch" which we must use in copying to video memory on a row-by-row basis.

By knowing the "pitch" we can calculate the address in memory of the first pixel on each row of the display; this assumes that we already have a pointer to the first memory pixel in the top left corner of the display surface. The "pitch" is an important value because, even though the display surface is represented by a contiguous range of addresses, it is not safe to assume that the last pixel on one row exists at an address one byte below the address of the first pixel on the next row.

For example, if the first pixel in row 10 of a 640×480 eight-bit display mode is at address 45000, the last pixel on that row will be at address 450639. One might expect the first pixel in row 11 to be at address 450640, but it is actually at $45000 + pitch$. This is the main significance of the "pitch", and it is likely that it will be different on display adapters from different manufacturers.

> *It is very important to remember that after the memory buffer has been used it must be unlocked.*

Another action that must be done in this function is to obtain a color palette for the eight bit display mode and instruct DirectDraw to use it. FLIC files use the same palette for all frames in an animation and therefore only one palette is needed.

Consequently it only needs to be put into effect once. In working with an AVI
or animated GIF file, there might be a different color palette for each frame. The
code below illustrates the implementation of the ReadFlicIntoSurfaces()
function:

```
static BOOL ReadFlicIntoSurfaces(BOOL first, char *FlicName){
HRESULT            ddrval;
PALETTEENTRY       pe[256];
DDSURFACEDESC      DDSDesc;
int                i;
//
// The next image is composed in this function. The main task is
// to assign a standard "BYTE" type pointer to the block of memory
// into which the image will be assembled by an appropriate function.
//
DDSDesc.dwSize=sizeof(DDSDesc);
if(bDoubleBuffered)
  ddrval=lpDDSSecondary->lpVtbl->Lock(lpDDSSecondary,NULL,&DDSDesc,0,NULL);
else
  ddrval=lpDDSPrimary->lpVtbl->Lock(lpDDSPrimary,NULL,&DDSDesc,0,NULL);
if(ddrval!=DD_OK)return FALSE;
//
// Assign values to the global variables for pitch and memory buffer.
// (These are used in the other files of the project. For an AVI movie
// the image read from the video stream is copied to "Screen").
//
pitch=DDSDesc.lPitch;
Screen=(unsigned char *)DDSDesc.lpSurface;
//
// If this is the first time this function is called, the first frame
// in the animation is displayed.
//
if(first){
  //
  // Copy the first frame into video memory.
  //
  if(AnimationType == AVI_type)BlitFirstAviFrame(FlicName);
  else                         BlitFirstFlxFrame(FlicName);
  //
  // Unlock the memory after we have written to it.
  //
  if(bDoubleBuffered)
    lpDDSSecondary->lpVtbl->Unlock(lpDDSSecondary,NULL);
  else
    lpDDSPrimary->lpVtbl->Unlock(lpDDSPrimary,NULL);
  //
  // Because the display is set to a paletted mode we must create
  // and use a color palette. FLIC files contain such a palette, and that
  // is read into global variables "p_red[]", etc., during execution of
  // BlitFirst(AVI/FLC)Frame(name);
```

```
    //
    for(i=0;i<256;i++){
      pe[i].peRed=p_red[i];
      pe[i].peGreen=p_green[i];
      pe[i].peBlue=p_blue[i];
    }
    //
    // Create the DirectDraw palette and put it to use.
    //
    ddrval=lpDD->lpVtbl->CreatePalette(lpDD,DDPCAPS_8BIT,pe,&lpDDPal,NULL);
    if(ddrval!=DD_OK)return FALSE;
    lpDDSPrimary->lpVtbl->SetPalette(lpDDSPrimary,lpDDPal);
  }
  else{
    //
    // Read the next image into video memory
    //
    if      (AnimationType == FLC_type)BlitNextFlcFrame();
    else if(AnimationType == AVI_type)BlitNextAviFrame();
    else                              BlitNextFliFrame();
    //
    // Unlock the memory buffer after we have written to it.
    //
    if(bDoubleBuffered)
      lpDDSSecondary->lpVtbl->Unlock(lpDDSSecondary,NULL);
    else
      lpDDSPrimary->lpVtbl->Unlock(lpDDSPrimary,NULL);
  }
  return TRUE;
}
```

12.1.5 Updating the Frame

When double buffering is in use, the FLIC or AVI is decoded into the secondary surface, and that must be copied to the primary surface so that it becomes visible. (The primary surface represents the screen.) Function `UpdateFrame()` uses the DirectDraw *blit* function to execute the copy operation, and normally this will be from one area of video RAM to another, thus making the operation very fast:

```
static void UpdateFrame(void){
  HRESULT         ddrval;
  RECT            rcRect;
  RECT            destRect;
  POINT           pt;
  if(!bDoubleBuffered)return;
  //
  // If double buffering is in use the secondary surface must be
  // blitted to the primary surface. The "Blt" method requires
```

```
// a source and destination rectangle and these are determined
// before executing the blit.
//
rcRect.left=0;
rcRect.top=0;
if(AnimationType == FLC_type || AnimationType == AVI_type){
  rcRect.right=640; rcRect.bottom=480;
}
else if(AnimationType == FLI_type){
  rcRect.right=320; rcRect.bottom=200;
}
GetClientRect(hWnd,&destRect);
pt.x=pt.y=0;
ClientToScreen(hWnd,&pt);
OffsetRect(&destRect,pt.x,pt.y);
while(1){
  //
  // Continue trying to execute the blit if the device is busy
  // and an error has not occurred.
  //
  ddrval=lpDDSPrimary->lpVtbl->Blt(lpDDSPrimary,
                                   &destRect,
                                   lpDDSSecondary,
                                   &rcRect,
                                   DDBLT_WAIT,NULL);
  if(ddrval==DD_OK)break;
  if(ddrval==DDERR_SURFACELOST){
    if(!RestoreAll())return;
    continue;
  }
  if(ddrval!=DDERR_WASSTILLDRAWING)return;
}
}
```

12.1.6   Restoring Surfaces

DirectDraw surfaces can become corrupt; this commonly occurs because one application (or the system) draws into the area of the screen which a second application is currently using. If this happens the surface used by the DirectDraw application is said to be '*lost*' and the application must restore its surface before it is again available for use. DirectDraw provides a method to do this. It is usually necessary for the application whose surface has been lost to redraw the "damaged" image (in addition to restoring it). However, in the movie player example, things are moving so rapidly that simply proceeding to draw the next frame will quickly re-establish the playing sequence. The code below illustrates the procedure which restores a DirectDraw surface without redrawing it:

```
static BOOL RestoreAll(void){
 //
 // It is standard practice in DirectDraw to restore the surface if
 // it should be lost (given to some other process). For our example
 // we don't need to redraw the image because this will be done
 // automatically when the next frame is shown.
 //
 BOOL bResult;
 bResult=lpDDSPrimary->lpVtbl->Restore(lpDDSPrimary) == DD_OK &&
        lpDDSSecondary->lpVtbl->Restore(lpDDSSecondary) == DD_OK;
 return(bResult);
}
```

12.1.7 Closing

When the program is terminated by the user, control must be returned to the
Windows desktop; this will probably involve a change of display resolution.

Our example will use the ESC key to cause the application to terminate. It
does this by sending a WM_DESTROY message to the window procedure. In the
WM_DESTROY message handler, all the DirectDraw objects are deleted and the
Windows desktop will be restored to whatever color depth and resolution it had
previously been working in.

```
static void RemoveAll(void){
 //
 // Release all the DirectDraw objects.
 //
 if(lpDD!=NULL) {
   //
   // Put the display back to normal windowed mode.
   //
   lpDD->lpVtbl->SetCooperativeLevel(lpDD,hWnd, DDSCL_NORMAL);
   lpDD2->lpVtbl->RestoreDisplayMode(lpDD2);
   //
   // Release the surfaces, palette, and DirectDraw object (the display).
   //
   if(lpDDSPrimary!=NULL) {
     lpDDSPrimary->lpVtbl->Release(lpDDSPrimary);
     lpDDSPrimary=NULL;
   }
   if(lpDDSSecondary!=NULL) {
     lpDDSSecondary->lpVtbl->Release(lpDDSSecondary);
     lpDDSSecondary=NULL;
   }
   if(lpDDPal!=NULL) {
     lpDDPal->lpVtbl->Release(lpDDPal);
     lpDDPal=NULL;
```

```
     }
     lpDD->lpVtbl->Release(lpDD);
     lpDD=NULL;
   }
   return;
 }
```

12.1.8 User Interface

We can provide a fairly simple user interface with a customized version of the
standard "file open" dialog when the application starts. The standard library dialog
is customized by adding check boxes, allowing the user to set flags for double
buffering, etc. The code for this is given below:

```
static unsigned CALLBACK NameHookProc(HWND hwnd,UINT msg,
                          WPARAM wparam,LPARAM lparam){
 //
 // Callback function used by the GetOpenFileName API.
 //
 switch( msg ) {
   case WM_INITDIALOG:
     if(bInRam)SendDlgItemMessage(hwnd,IDC_CHECK1,BM_SETCHECK,1,0);
     if(bDoubleBuffered)SendDlgItemMessage(hwnd,IDC_CHECK2,BM_SETCHECK,1,0);
     if(bUseTimer)SendDlgItemMessage(hwnd,IDC_CHECK2,BM_SETCHECK,1,0);
     return FALSE;
   case WM_NOTIFY:{
       LPOFNOTIFY lp=(LPOFNOTIFY)lparam;
       if(lp->hdr.code == CDN_FILEOK){
         //
         // OK is pressed get the flags
         //
         if(SendDlgItemMessage(hwnd,IDC_CHECK1,BM_GETCHECK,0,0))
             bInRam=TRUE;
         else bInRam=FALSE;
         if(SendDlgItemMessage(hwnd,IDC_CHECK2,BM_GETCHECK,0,0))
             bDoubleBuffered=TRUE;
         else bDoubleBuffered=FALSE;
         if(SendDlgItemMessage(hwnd,IDC_CHECK3,BM_GETCHECK,0,0))
             bUseTimer=TRUE;
         else bUseTimer=FALSE;
       }
     }
     break;
   default: break;
 }
 return FALSE;
}
```

```
static BOOL SelectFileName(char *szfile, char *szfilter,
                           HWND parent, HINSTANCE hInst){
//
// Get a filename or the movie or FLIC file by setting up an OPENFILENAME
// structure and calling the API "GetOpenFileName".
//
int i;
OPENFILENAME ofn;
char szFilter[80];
strcpy(szFilter,szfilter);
i=0; while(szFilter[i] != '\0'){
  if(szFilter[i] == '|')szFilter[i]='\0'; i++;
}
memset(&ofn,0,sizeof(OPENFILENAME));
ofn.lStructSize=sizeof(OPENFILENAME);
ofn.hwndOwner=parent;
ofn.lpstrFilter=szFilter;
ofn.nFilterIndex=0;
szfile[0]='\0';
ofn.lpstrFile=szfile;
ofn.nMaxFile=255;
ofn.lpstrFileTitle=NULL;
ofn.nMaxFileTitle=0;
ofn.lpstrInitialDir=NULL;
ofn.lpstrTitle="Open FLIC to Play Full Screen";
ofn.hInstance=hInst;
ofn.lpfnHook=NameHookProc;
ofn.lpTemplateName=MAKEINTRESOURCE(IDD_DIALOG1);
ofn.Flags=OFN_HIDEREADONLY|OFN_PATHMUSTEXIST|OFN_FILEMUSTEXIST|
          OFN_EXPLORER|
          OFN_ENABLEHOOK|OFN_ENABLETEMPLATE|OFN_NONETWORKBUTTON;
return GetOpenFileName(&ofn);
}
```

Figure 12.1 illustrates the appearance of the application to the user.

12.2 Reading and Decoding an AVI File

The Video For Windows (VFW) API library provides a rich set of functions that we can call on to perform most of the tasks necessary to fill a memory buffer from the video stream in an AVI file.

Most of the work is done in function `BlitFirstAviFrame(..)`. This function acquires information about the movie and stores copies of handles and pointers to memory blocks and streams that will be needed when each frame is assembled onto the DirectDraw surface. The essential handles and prototypes for

external variables are listed below; this is a fragment of code from the beginning
of file AVI.C:

```
//
// External variables declared in the main module
//
extern unsigned char p_red[],              // Palette
                     p_green[],
                     p_blue[];
extern unsigned char *Screen;              // Surface to draw in
extern long pitch;                         // Row pitch
extern long AnimationType;

static LPBITMAPINFOHEADER lpBmi = NULL; // Bitmap header to specify
                                        // the format in which we
                                        // we want the sample to be
                                        // extracted.

static LPSTR pformat        = NULL; // Text buffer for AVI stream info
static PAVIFILE pfile       = NULL; // Handle to AVI file
static PAVISTREAM ps        = NULL; // Handle to AVI data stream
static PGETFRAME  pget      = NULL; // Handle to the Video data
static long display_sample  = 0;    // Which sample should be
                                    // extracted from the file.
static long nsamples;               // The number of "samples"
                                    // in the AVI video stream
                                    // samples = frames
```

12.2.1   Opening the AVI File

BlitFirstAviFrame(..) begins by opening the AVI file and examining all
its data streams one by one until the first one, holding video information is found.
The format of the stream is determined by calling AVIStreamReadFormat(..),
which fills a BITMAPINFOHEADER structure. This structure is modified before
calling AVIStreamGetFrameOpen(..), because if we do that we will get
VFW to do the work of making sure that when a sample (what in previous chapters we have referred to as a frame) is read from the video stream, it is returned
in a one-byte-per-pixel format and with an appropriate color palette.

The first sample, sample 0, is retrieved from a video stream by calling:

```
lpBmi=(LPBITMAPINFOHEADER)AVIStreamGetFrame(....);
```

AVIStreamGetFrame(..) returns a pointer to a block of memory, where a
standard bitmap header, color palette, and image data are stored contiguously. The
file header holds details of the resolution of the movie and its palette. A little more
work will be required to map the bitmap image data into the DirectDraw surface
and we do that in function CopyScreen(). Fortunately it isn't necessary to

carry out any color quantization because the VFW library will have done that (should it have been necessary; for example, if the AVI video stream was a 24-bit one).

Function `BlitFirstAviFrame(..)` is given below:

```
void BlitFirstAviFrame(char *szFileName){
 if(szFileName != NULL){
   AVISTREAMINFO avis;
   HRESULT hr;
   RGBQUAD *pRgb;
   int i,j;
   long size;
   AVIFileInit();
   //
   // Open the AVI file.
   //
   hr = AVIFileOpen(&pfile,szFileName,OF_READ,NULL);
   if(hr == AVIERR_OK){
     for(i=0;i<10;i++){
       //
       // Get the first video stream.
       //
       if(AVIFileGetStream(pfile,&ps,0,i) == AVIERR_OK){
         AVIStreamInfo(ps,&avis,sizeof(avis));
         if(avis.fccType == streamtypeVIDEO){
           //
           // This is a video stream.
           //
           AVIStreamFormatSize(ps,0,&size);
           if((pformat = (LPSTR)malloc(size)) != NULL){
             //
             // Get the format of the stream---most importantly
             // the number of frames in the animation.
             //
             if(AVIStreamReadFormat(ps,0,pformat,&size) == AVIERR_OK){
               lpBmi=(LPBITMAPINFOHEADER)pformat;
               nsamples=AVIStreamEnd(ps);     // number of frames in stream
               //
               // Before reading the image data specify the format
               // in which the image data should be returned. In this
               // program we need an eight bit paletted image
               // (Not an RGB one!).
               //
               lpBmi->biCompression=BI_RGB;  // read it back as 8 bit
               lpBmi->biBitCount=8;          // paletted image
               lpBmi->biClrUsed=256;         //
               lpBmi->biSizeImage=((((UINT)lpBmi->biBitCount*lpBmi->biWidth
                           +31)&~31)/8)*lpBmi->biHeight;
               //
               // Open the video stream using the format needed.
```

```
                              //
                              if((pget=AVIStreamGetFrameOpen(ps,lpBmi)) != NULL){
                                //
                                // Retrieve the image.
                                //
                                lpBmi=(LPBITMAPINFOHEADER)AVIStreamGetFrame(pget,0);
                                if(lpBmi != NULL){
                                  //
                                  // Extract the palette information.
                                  //
                                  pRgb=(RGBQUAD *)((LPSTR)lpBmi + lpBmi->biSize);
                                  for(j=0;j<256;j++){
                                    p_red[j]   = pRgb[j].rgbRed;
                                    p_green[j] = pRgb[j].rgbGreen;
                                    p_blue[j]  = pRgb[j].rgbBlue;
                                  }
                                  //
                                  // Copy the image data from temporary DIB to
                                  // DirectDraw surface.
                                  //
                                  CopyToScreen();
                                  //
                                  // Keep the stream open and memory reserved for
                                  // DIB.
                                  //
                                  return;
                                }
                              }
                            }
                          }
                        }
                      }
                    }
                  }
                else pfile=NULL;
              }
            return;
            }
```

12.2.2 Copying to the DirectDraw Surface

Since the VFW function `AVIStreamGetFrame(...,ff)`; returns a pointer
to a contiguous bitmap header, color palette, and image data for frame (or sample)
`ff`, our function must copy this data to the DirectDraw display surface.

It is fortunate that VFW can be instructed to return a paletted image irrespective
of whether the video stream was paletted or not. However, we must still take care
to copy it one row at a time and index the destination pointer by "`pitch`" bytes
each time. It should also be remembered that the image in a bitmap is *upside down*;

therefore, row 0 is at the bottom of the image, and on DirectDraw's surface row 0 is at the top.

This work is done in function `CopyScreen()` as shown below:

```
static void CopyToScreen(void){
 LPSTR lpB,s;
 long j,x,y;
 lpB =  (LPSTR)(lpBmi);
 lpB += (lpBmi->biSize+256*sizeof(RGBQUAD));  // points to Image
 x=(long)lpBmi->biWidth;
 y=(long)lpBmi->biHeight;
 //
 // Copy each display line from DIB to screen. A DIB is upside down
 // in relation to the screen, in which the rows start at the top.
 // DirectDraw specifies that each raster line is separated by "pitch"
 // bytes (number of bytes). This might or might NOT be the same as
 // the horizontal resolution of the display. For this reason it is
 // important to copy one row at a time and increment the "Screen"
 // pointer by "pitch" for each row.
 //
 for(j=0;j<y;j++){
   s=(LPSTR)Screen+(y-j-1)*pitch;     // s -> start of raster row "j"
   memcpy(s,lpB,x);
   lpB += x;                          // lpB -> next DIB row
 }
 return;
}
```

12.2.3 Reading Subsequent Frames

So long as the video stream remains open, a call to `AVIStreamGetFrame(..);` as follows will fill a bitmap data structure with the next image in the animated sequence:

```
void BlitNextAviFrame(void){
 //
 // Read the next frame (called the "sample"). Remember that the
 // video stream and file remain open.
 //
 lpBmi=(LPBITMAPINFOHEADER)AVIStreamGetFrame(pget,display_sample);
 if(lpBmi != NULL)CopyToScreen();
 //
 // If we are about to go beyond the end of the video stream, reset
 // the frame count so that the first frame is loaded next time.
 //
 if(++display_sample >= nsamples)display_sample=0;
}
```

Note that any memory allocated by the last call will be reused or freed by `AVIStreamGetFrame(...)`, so we don't have to worry about that.

12.3   Reading FLIC Files

FLIC files have two formats which are identified by their filename extension: .FLI, the original format, is restricted to a resolution of 320×200; .FLC is the enhanced format in which FLICs can take any resolution. Information on these formats can be found in the Encyclopedia of Graphics File Formats [1]. Basically the files are structured into a number of chunks which contain information like:

1. The palette.

2. A run-length encoded compression of the first frame.

3. Delta compression of subsequent frames.

4. Uncompressed frames (used when run-length or delta compression produces a chunk that exceeds the uncompressed size).

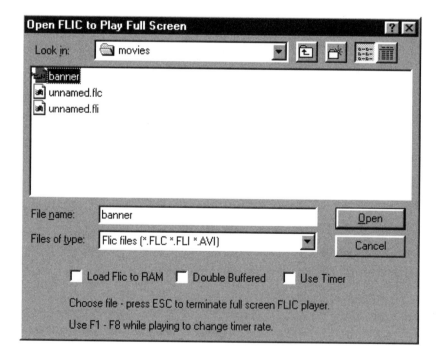

Figure 12.1.   The DDPLAY application user interface is nothing more that a standard File Open dialog with some custom controls added.

For this chapter's example, the file `FLX.C` contains code for functions to read and decode the FLIs and FLCs. The code is organized so that the decompression functions can work from a file or from a memory buffer in those cases where the whole FLIC has been read into system memory during initialization (this code accompanies the book).

References

[1] J. D. Murray and W. vanRyper, *Encyclopedia of Graphics File Formats.* O'Reilly and Associates Inc. Sebastopol, CA, 1994.

APPENDIX

Additional Mathematical Results

In this appendix we consider some useful mathematical results that are relevant to 3D computer graphics but were not considered in Chapter 2.

A.1 The Intersection of a Line with Non-Planar Primitive Shapes

In this section we consider the calculation of the point of intersection between a line and some non-planar shapes that often occur in 3D computer graphics work.

A.1.1 Intersection of a Line with a Sphere

A sphere is specified by two parameters: a position vector $\mathbf{P}_c$, giving the center of the sphere, and a scalar r, its radius. A line $\mathbf{p} = \mathbf{P}_l + \mu\mathbf{d}$ intersects the sphere once, twice, or not at all.

Figure A.1 shows two paths from the origin O to the point $\mathbf{p}$ on the surface of the sphere where the line pierces it.

Equating the two vector paths to the point $\mathbf{p}$ gives:

$$\mathbf{P}_c + \mathbf{q} = \mathbf{P}_l + \alpha\mathbf{d} \qquad (A.1)$$

α is the length along the line from $\mathbf{P}_l$ to the point of intersection between line and sphere. Since $\mathbf{q}$ is a vector that extends from the center to the surface of the sphere, its length is r, and thus $\mathbf{q} \cdot \mathbf{q} = r^2$. Writing Equation A.1 as:

$$\alpha\mathbf{d} + (\mathbf{P}_l - \mathbf{P}_c) = \mathbf{q}$$

and taking the dot product of each side with itself gives:

$$(\mathbf{d} \cdot \mathbf{d})\alpha^2 + 2\mathbf{d} \cdot (\mathbf{P}_l - \mathbf{P}_c)\alpha + (\mathbf{P}_l - \mathbf{P}_c) \cdot (\mathbf{P}_l - \mathbf{P}_c) = \mathbf{q} \cdot \mathbf{q} = r^2 \qquad (A.2)$$

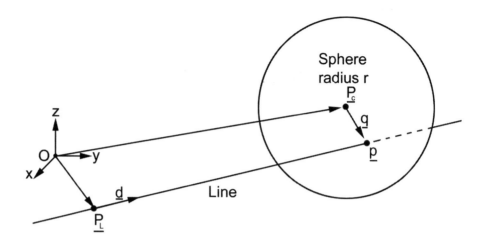

Figure A.1.   Geometry of the intersection between line and sphere.

Eliminating $\mathbf{q}$ reveals a quadratic equation of the form $(a\alpha^2 + b\alpha + c = 0)$ in α. In this equation the coefficients are given by:

$$
\begin{aligned}
a &= \mathbf{d} \cdot \mathbf{d} \\
b &= 2\mathbf{d} \cdot (\mathbf{P}_l - \mathbf{P}_c) \\
c &= (\mathbf{P}_l - \mathbf{P}_c) \cdot (\mathbf{P}_l - \mathbf{P}_c) - r^2
\end{aligned}
$$

Once α has been determined we can locate $\mathbf{p}$ from the equation of the line $\mathbf{p} = \mathbf{P}_l + \alpha\mathbf{d}$. The procedure is illustrated in the form of the algorithm given in Figure A.2.

A.1.2 Intersection of a Line and a Cylinder

A similar argument to that used to calculate the points(s) of intersection between a line and sphere will produce an algorithm that:

- determines whether there are one, two, or no points of intersection; one point of intersection is quite rare.

- determines whether the intersection is on the side (curved part) or at the end (flat disks) of the cylinder.

- determines the position vector of the intersection point(s), when they exist.

$$\mathbf{P}_{lc} = (\mathbf{P}_l - \mathbf{P}_c)$$
$$a = \mathbf{d} \cdot \mathbf{d}$$
$$b = 2\mathbf{d} \cdot \mathbf{P}_{lc}$$
$$c = \mathbf{P}_{lc} \cdot \mathbf{P}_{lc} - r^2$$
$$b_4 = b^2 - 4ac$$

if $b_4 < 0$ then no intersection
else {
    if $b_4 < \epsilon$ {
$$\alpha_1 = \alpha_2 = \frac{-b}{2a}$$
    }
    else {
$$b_4 = \sqrt{b_4}$$
$$\alpha_1 = \frac{(-b + b_4)}{2a}$$
$$\alpha_2 = \frac{(-b - b_4)}{2a}$$
    }
$$\mathbf{p}_1 = \mathbf{p}_l + \alpha_1 \mathbf{d}$$
$$\mathbf{p}_2 = \mathbf{p}_l + \alpha_2 \mathbf{d}$$
}

Figure A.2.   Algorithm for determining the intersection of a line and sphere.

The geometry of the problem is shown in Figure A.3. The cylinder is specified by position vectors $\mathbf{P}_1$ and $\mathbf{P}_2$, which define points lying at each end of the axis of a finite cylinder. The cylinder has radius r and the vector $\mathbf{s} = (\mathbf{P}_2 - \mathbf{P}_1)$ determines the axis of the cylinder. As before we will use the following equation for the line: $\mathbf{p} = \mathbf{P}_l + \mu \mathbf{d}$.

To develop an algorithm to solve this problem we proceed in the following steps:

1. Find the intersection point(s) between an **infinitely long cylinder** of radius r and central axis passing through $\mathbf{P}_1$ and $\mathbf{P}_2$.

As before, we find two alternate paths leading from the origin to the point of intersection. They give rise to the equation:

$$\mathbf{P}_l + \mu \mathbf{d} = \mathbf{P}_1 + \lambda \mathbf{s} + \mathbf{q} \qquad \text{(A.3)}$$

where λ is the proportion of $\mathbf{s}$ that leads from $\mathbf{P}_1$ to a point on the cylinder's axis where the vector $\mathbf{q}$ originates. (The argument now proceeds to obtain a quadratic in μ and also to eliminate λ.)

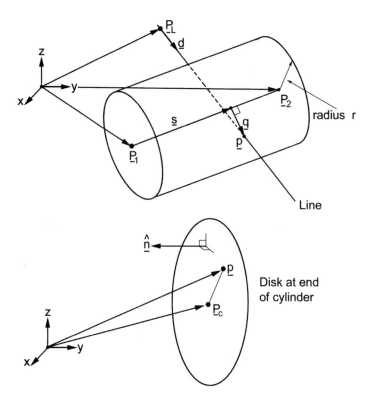

Figure A.3.   Geometry of an intersection between a line and a cylinder.

The vectors s and **q** are perpendicular; therefore:

$$\mathbf{s} \cdot \mathbf{q} = 0 \tag{A.4}$$

Since **q** runs from the cylinder's axis to its surface:

$$|\mathbf{q}| = r \tag{A.5}$$

Eliminating **q** and λ from Equation A.3 results in a quadratic in μ from which the point(s) of intersection can be determined.

Taking the dot product of both sides of Equation A.3 with s and using Equation A.4 gives:

$$(\mathbf{P}_l - \mathbf{P}_1) \cdot \mathbf{s} + \mu \mathbf{d} \cdot \mathbf{s} = \lambda \mathbf{s} \cdot \mathbf{s}$$

which may be rearranged to give:

$$\lambda = \frac{(\mathbf{P}_l - \mathbf{P}_1) \cdot \mathbf{s} + \mu \mathbf{d} \cdot \mathbf{s}}{\mathbf{s} \cdot \mathbf{s}} \qquad (A.6)$$

Substituting Equation A.6 into Equation A.3 gives:

$$(\mathbf{P}_l - \mathbf{P}_1) + \mu \mathbf{d} - \left(\frac{(\mathbf{P}_l - \mathbf{P}_1) \cdot \mathbf{s} + \mu \mathbf{d} \cdot \mathbf{s}}{\mathbf{s} \cdot \mathbf{s}}\right) \mathbf{s} = \mathbf{q} \qquad (A.7)$$

Taking the dot product of both sides of Equation A.7 with themselves and using Equation A.5 to eliminate $\mathbf{q}$, a quadratic equation in μ is obtained which may be written as:

$$a\mu^2 + 2b\mu + c = 0$$

where (with $\mathbf{t} = (\mathbf{P}_l - \mathbf{P}_1)$, for clarity):

$$a = \left(\mathbf{d} - \left(\frac{\mathbf{d} \cdot \mathbf{s}}{\mathbf{s} \cdot \mathbf{s}}\right)\mathbf{s}\right) \cdot \left(\mathbf{d} - \left(\frac{\mathbf{d} \cdot \mathbf{s}}{\mathbf{s} \cdot \mathbf{s}}\right)\mathbf{s}\right)$$

$$b = \left(\mathbf{d} - \left(\frac{\mathbf{d} \cdot \mathbf{s}}{\mathbf{s} \cdot \mathbf{s}}\right)\mathbf{s}\right) \cdot \left(\mathbf{t} - \left(\frac{\mathbf{t} \cdot \mathbf{s}}{\mathbf{s} \cdot \mathbf{s}}\right)\mathbf{s}\right)$$

$$c = \left(\mathbf{t} - \left(\frac{\mathbf{t} \cdot \mathbf{s}}{\mathbf{s} \cdot \mathbf{s}}\right)\mathbf{s}\right) \cdot \left(\mathbf{t} - \left(\frac{\mathbf{t} \cdot \mathbf{s}}{\mathbf{s} \cdot \mathbf{s}}\right)\mathbf{s}\right) - r^2$$

No real roots to this quadratic implies that the line does not intersect the infinitely long cylinder and we need proceed no further.

2. If there is at least one real root we must investigate further to determine if the intersection occurs between the points $\mathbf{P}_1$ and $\mathbf{P}_2$. For this we need values for λ corresponding to the root(s) of the quadratic in μ. Starting with the smaller root ($\mu = \mu_1$), a λ is calculated and if $0 \le \lambda \le 1$ there is an intersection on the outside surface of the cylinder at the point given by $\mathbf{P}_l + \mu_1 \mathbf{d}$. If this is not the case, a λ corresponding to the larger root($\mu = \mu_2$) is determined and, if $0 \le \lambda \le 1$, there is an intersection on the inside surface.

3. If the point of intersection is on the inside surface of the cylinder, it will be necessary to check the intersection with a pair of disks with radius r and surface normal in the direction $\mathbf{P}_2 - \mathbf{P}_1$. One of the disks contains the point $\mathbf{P}_2$ and the other the point $\mathbf{P}_1$.

To obtain the point of intersection $\mathbf{P}_i$ with the disks, use the algorithm of Section 2.5; if the intersection is within the disk, $(\mathbf{P}_i - \mathbf{P}_c) \cdot (\mathbf{P}_i - \mathbf{P}_c) < r^2$.

A complete algorithm for the intersection of a line and a cylinder is given in two steps, shown in Figures A.4 and A.5

Step 1: Calculate the intersection point or points

$$\mathbf{s} = (\mathbf{P}_2 - \mathbf{P}_1)$$
$$\mathbf{P}_{l1} = (\mathbf{P}_l - \mathbf{P}_1)$$
$$\mathbf{A} = \mathbf{d} - \left(\frac{\mathbf{d} \cdot \mathbf{s}}{\mathbf{s} \cdot \mathbf{s}}\right) \mathbf{s}$$
$$\mathbf{B} = \mathbf{P}_{l1} - \left(\frac{\mathbf{P}_{l1} \cdot \mathbf{s}}{\mathbf{s} \cdot \mathbf{s}}\right) \mathbf{s}$$
$$a = \mathbf{A} \cdot \mathbf{A}$$
$$b = 2\mathbf{A} \cdot \mathbf{B}$$
$$c = \mathbf{B} \cdot \mathbf{B} - r^2$$
$$b_4 = b^2 - 4ac$$

if $b_4 < 0$ no intersection points
else {
    if $b_4 < \epsilon$ {
        thus one intersection point, so set
$$\mu_1 = \mu_2 = \frac{-b}{2a}$$
    }
    else {
        two intersection points determined by
$$b_4 = \sqrt{b_4}$$
$$\mu_1 = \frac{(-b + b_4)}{2a}$$
$$\mu_2 = \frac{(-b - b_4)}{2a}$$
    }
$$\mathbf{P}_1 = \mathbf{p}_l + \mu_1 \mathbf{d}$$
$$\mathbf{P}_2 = \mathbf{p}_l + \mu_2 \mathbf{d}$$
}

Figure A.4.   Step I in determining the intersection between a line and a cylinder; the geometry of the problem is shown in Figure A.3.

A.1.3   Intersection between a Line and a Regular Cone

The argument used in determining the intersection of a line and a cylinder may be developed further to enable the points of intersection between a line and cone to be obtained. As in the case of a sphere and a cylinder, there may be either none, one, or two intersection points. Figure A.6 illustrates the location of the point of intersection $\mathbf{P}_i$ between a line specified by:

$$\mathbf{p} = \mathbf{P}_0 + \mu \hat{\mathbf{d}}$$

Step 2: Consider the values μ_1 and μ_2 in turn

$\mu = \max(\mu_1, \mu_2)$

$\lambda = \dfrac{\mathbf{P}_{l1} \cdot \mathbf{s} + \mu \mathbf{d} \cdot \mathbf{s}}{\mathbf{s} \cdot \mathbf{s}}$

if $0 \le \lambda \le 1$ {

    return intersection on front face

}

$\mu = \min(\mu_1, \mu_2)$

$\lambda = \dfrac{\mathbf{P}_{l1} \cdot \mathbf{s} + \mu \mathbf{d} \cdot \mathbf{s}}{\mathbf{s} \cdot \mathbf{s}}$

if $0 \le \lambda \le 1$ {

    intersection on back face

    check disks at ends of cylinders

}

Figure A.5.   Step 2 in determining the intersection between a line and a cylinder.

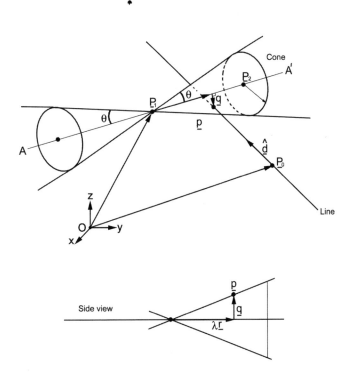

Figure A.6.   Geometry for determining the intersection between a line and a cone.

and a cone that is defined by the points $\mathbf{P}_1$, the apex of the cone, $\mathbf{P}_2$ at the base of the cone, and the half angle θ of the cone.

To determine the point of intersection $\mathbf{P}_i$, a four-step algorithm follows:

1. For the infinite double cone, with axis AA', determine any points of intersection with the line $\mathbf{P}_0 + \mu\hat{\mathbf{d}}$ and their location.

2. For points of intersection determine which, if any, intersect the half cone between $\mathbf{P}_1$ and $\mathbf{P}_2$; reject any other intersections.

3. Determine whether and where the line intersects a disk centered on $\mathbf{P}_2$ and perpendicular to $\mathbf{P}_2 - \mathbf{P}_1$.

4. Depth sort the intersections of cone and disk to make the final choice for $\mathbf{P}_i$

Note:

An important application of this calculation occurs when rendering atmospheric effects associated with spotlights; for example, dust scattering, volume shadowing, and volumetric fog.

One point worth making in connection with these scenarios is that the line might originate inside the cone and this will necessitate some other special tests to determine whether the line is passing from outside to inside or inside to outside at $\mathbf{P}_i$.

For completeness the algebra of the first step is now discussed. Consider the intersection of a line with the double cone as illustrated in Figure A.6. The cone extends to infinity in both directions. The key step in the procedure is to equate two different paths from the coordinate origin O to $\mathbf{P}_i$.

First obtain the unit vector $\hat{\mathbf{r}}$:

$$\hat{\mathbf{r}} = \frac{\mathbf{P}_2 - \mathbf{P}_1}{|\mathbf{P}_2 - \mathbf{P}_1|}$$

Using two alternate paths $\mathbf{P}_i$ may be expressed as:

$$\begin{aligned} \mathbf{P}_i &= \mathbf{P}_0 + \mu\hat{\mathbf{d}} \text{ or} \\ \mathbf{P}_i &= \mathbf{P}_1 + \lambda\hat{\mathbf{r}} + \mathbf{q} \end{aligned}$$

for appropriate λ and μ. These can be equated:

$$\mathbf{P}_0 + \mu\hat{\mathbf{d}} = \mathbf{P}_1 + \lambda\hat{\mathbf{r}} + \mathbf{q} \qquad (A.8)$$

The vector $\mathbf{q}$ is directed radially from the axis of the cone; thus $\mathbf{q} \cdot \hat{\mathbf{r}} = 0$. The vector $\lambda\hat{\mathbf{r}}$ joins $\mathbf{P}_1$ to the base of $\mathbf{q}$. The length of $\mathbf{q}$ is $l = \lambda\tan\theta$ and, since $l = |\mathbf{q}|$, we can write: $\mathbf{q} \cdot \mathbf{q} = (\lambda\tan\theta)^2$

To determine λ from Equation A.8, take the dot product of both sides with $\hat{\mathbf{r}}$:

$$\lambda = \mu(\hat{\mathbf{d}} \cdot \hat{\mathbf{r}}) + (\mathbf{P}_0 - \mathbf{P}_1) \cdot \hat{\mathbf{r}} \qquad (A.9)$$

Substituting Equation A.9 in Equation A.8 eliminates λ and therefore:

$$\mu\hat{\mathbf{d}} + (\mathbf{P}_0 - \mathbf{P}_1) - (\mu(\hat{\mathbf{d}} \cdot \hat{\mathbf{r}}) + (\mathbf{P}_0 - \mathbf{P}_1) \cdot \hat{\mathbf{r}})\hat{\mathbf{r}} = \mathbf{q} \qquad (A.10)$$

Writing Equation A.10 as a polynomial in μ:

$$\mathbf{A}\mu + \mathbf{B} = \mathbf{q} \qquad (A.11)$$

with:

$$
\begin{aligned}
\mathbf{A} &= \hat{\mathbf{d}} - (\hat{\mathbf{d}} \cdot \hat{\mathbf{r}})\hat{\mathbf{r}} \\
\mathbf{B} &= (\mathbf{P}_0 - \mathbf{P}_1) - ((\mathbf{P}_0 - \mathbf{P}_1) \cdot \hat{\mathbf{r}})\hat{\mathbf{r}}
\end{aligned}
$$

Taking the dot product of each side of Equation A.11 with itself gives a quadratic equation in μ:

$$(\mathbf{A} \cdot \mathbf{A})\mu^2 + 2(\mathbf{A} \cdot \mathbf{B})\mu + (\mathbf{B} \cdot \mathbf{B}) = \mathbf{q} \cdot \mathbf{q} = (\lambda \tan \theta)^2 \qquad (A.12)$$

Substituting λ from Equation A.9 and rearranging gives a quadratic with μ as the only unknown:

$$a\mu^2 + 2b\mu + c = 0 \qquad (A.13)$$

where:

$$
\begin{aligned}
a &= (\mathbf{A} \cdot \mathbf{A}) - (\hat{\mathbf{d}} \cdot \hat{\mathbf{r}})^2 \tan^2 \theta \\
b &= (\mathbf{A} \cdot \mathbf{B}) - (\hat{\mathbf{d}} \cdot \hat{\mathbf{r}})((\mathbf{P}_0 - \mathbf{P}_1) \cdot \hat{\mathbf{r}}) \tan^2 \theta \\
c &= (\mathbf{B} \cdot \mathbf{B}) - ((\mathbf{P}_0 - \mathbf{P}_1) \cdot \hat{\mathbf{r}})^2 \tan^2 \theta
\end{aligned}
$$

Once the values of μ satisfying Equation A.13 are known, a similar argument to that outlined in Step 2 of Section A.1.2 may be used to complete the determination of the intersection points $\mathbf{P}_i$.

A.2 Some Other Useful Non-Geometric Mathematical Results

Chapter 2 dealt primarily with geometrical results necessary for developing algorithms used in 3D computer graphics. There are a few other mathematical topics that have utility when developing these algorithms, and they are dealt with in this section.

A.2.1   Random Number Generation

Computer languages, particularly **C** and **C++**, normally have quite poor random number generation. They are limited to returning pseudo-random integers in the range $0 - 32767$. Some computers now offer the `drand48()` function, which is good but, for systems that don't offer it, the short function below which is based on [1] generates a pseudo-random double in the interval $[0, 1]$.

```
long IX=9123,IY=8844,IZ=20846; /* initial state */

void dSeedRandom(long i){
  /* use internal integer random number generator to seed the algorithm */
  srand(i); IX=rand(); IY=rand(); IZ=rand();
}

double dRandom(void){
  IX=imod(171*IX,30269);
  IY=imod(172*IY,20207);
  IZ=imod(170*IZ,30323);
  return (double)fmod((double)IX/30269.0+
                      (double)IY/30307.0+
                      (double)IZ/30323.0,1.0);
}
```

A.2.2   Solving a Set of n Simultaneous Equations

A mathematical task that occurs quite often in computer graphics is finding the solution to a set of n linear simultaneous equations. Gauss elimination and a host of other techniques have been developed to perform this task efficiently. Many excellent algorithms have been published on this subject, some of which are described in [2]. In general the problem can be stated in matrix form as $[A][x] = [y]$; the matrix $[A]$ is of dimension $n \times n$ and the matrices $[x]$ and $[y]$ are of size $n \times 1$. The matrix $[x]$ is the unknown. One method of solution is to obtain the inverse of $[A]$ and write $[x] = [A]^{-1}[y]$. This approach is very inefficient. However, sometimes the equations show a particular structure when shortcuts may be taken.

For example, the problem of finding the parameters for the cubic spline curves (Section 2.15) gives rise to a set of linear equations where many elements of the $[A]$ matrix are zero. In fact all the non-zero elements lie on the three central diagonals of $[A]$. Matrices with this special property are solved very rapidly and the algorithm for their solution is presented here.

Given the known matrix A of dimension $n \times n$, the known vector y of dimension $n \times 1$ and the unknown vector of dimension $n \times 1$ satisfying $[A][x] = [y]$, the problem may be expressed as:

$$
\begin{bmatrix}
b_0 & c_0 & 0 & 0 & .. & 0 \\
a_1 & b_1 & c_1 & 0 & .. & 0 \\
0 & a_2 & b_2 & c_2 & & \\
.. & .. & .. & .. & .. & .. \\
0 & .. & 0 & a_{n-2} & b_{n-2} & c_{n-2} \\
0 & .. & 0 & 0 & a_{n-1} & b_{n-1}
\end{bmatrix}
\begin{bmatrix}
x_0 \\
x_1 \\
x_2 \\
.. \\
.. \\
x_{n-1}
\end{bmatrix}
=
\begin{bmatrix}
y_0 \\
y_1 \\
y_2 \\
.. \\
.. \\
y_{n-1}
\end{bmatrix}
$$

where a_i, b_i, and c_i are the non-zero entries of $[A]$. To solve for the x_i, the following efficient two-step algorithm is used:

1. Work through all the i from 1 to $n-1$, replacing the b_i with:

$$
b_i - \frac{a_i}{b_{i-1}} c_{i-1}
$$

At the same time replace the y_i with:

$$
y_i - \frac{a_i}{b_{i-1}} y_{i-1}
$$

2. Obtain the results; first set:

$$
x_{n-1} = \frac{y_{n-1}}{b_{n-1}}
$$

Then work through all the i from $n-2$ back to 0 to calculate the remaining x_i:

$$
x_i = \frac{y_i - c_i y_{i+1}}{b_i}
$$

The execution time of this algorithm is near linear with respect to n.

References

[1] B. A. Wichman and I. D. Hill, *An Efficient and Portable Pseudo-Random Number Generator.* Applied Statistics, Vol. 32, No. 2, 188-190, 1992.

[2] T. R. McCalla, *Introduction to Numerical Methods and FORTRAN Programming.* John Wiley and Sons, NY, 1967.

Index